CW01467815

Mediterranean Spain

Strait of Gibraltar to the French border

Mediterranean Spain

Strait of Gibraltar to the French border

Steve Pickard

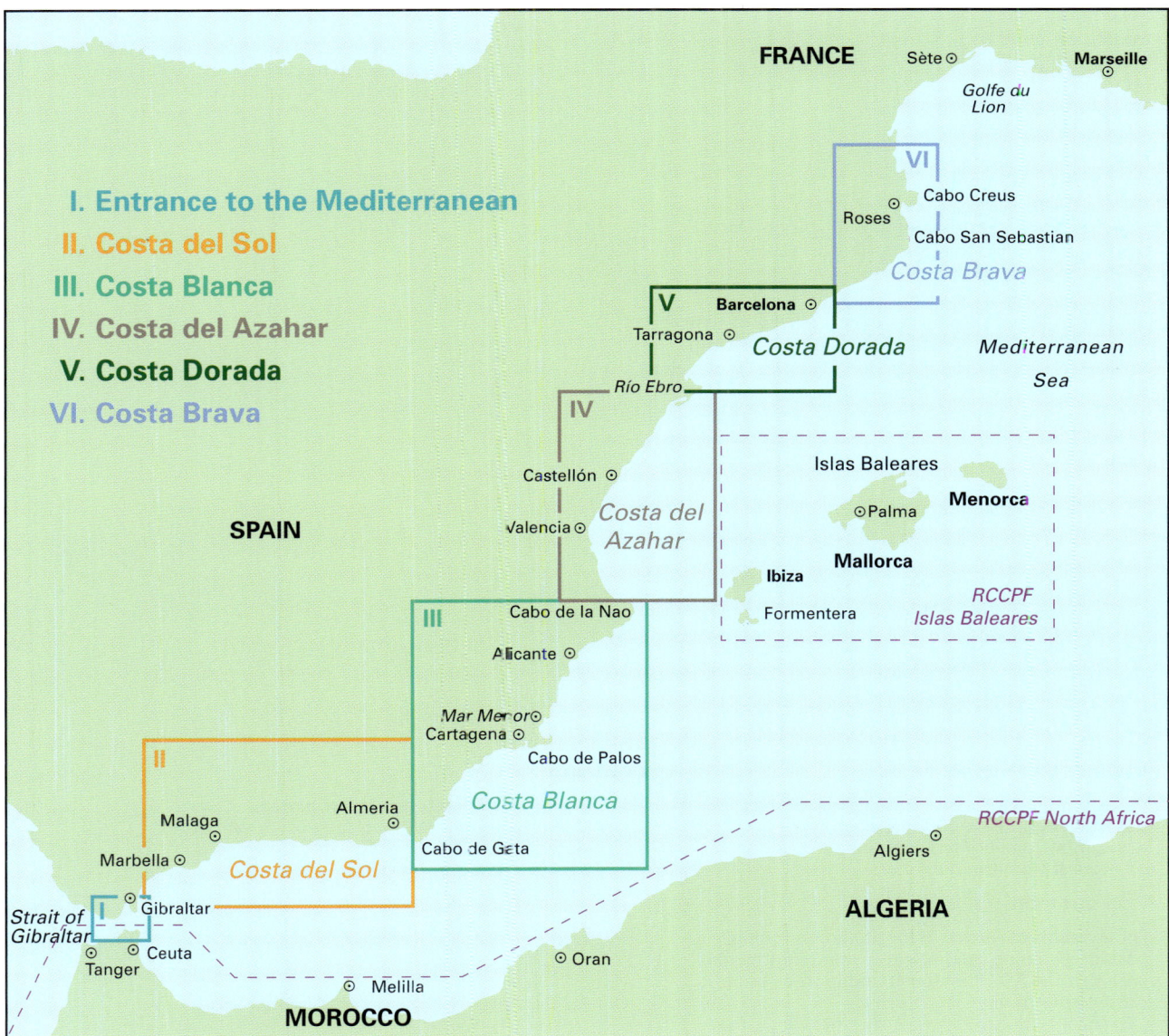

I. Entrance to the Mediterranean
II. Costa del Sol
III. Costa Blanca
IV. Costa del Azahar
V. Costa Dorada
VI. Costa Brava

Imray Laurie Norie & Wilson

Published by
Imray Laurie Norie & Wilson Ltd
Wych House St Ives Huntingdon
Cambridgeshire PE27 5BT, England 2002
✆ +44 (0)1480 462114 *Fax* +44 (0)1480 496109
Email ilnw@imray.com
www.imray.com
2017

1st edition 1989
2nd edition 1995
3rd edition 1999
4th edition 2002
5th edition 2008
6th edition 2012
Combined 1st edition 2017

ISBN 978 184623 650 1

British Library Cataloguing in Publication Data.
A catalogue record for this book is available from the British Library.

This work, based on surveys over a period of many years, has been corrected to December 2016 from land-based visits to the ports and harbours of the coast, from contributions by visiting yachtsmen and from official notices. The air photographs were taken by Anne Hammick in September 1997, and Patrick Roach in 2004.

Printed in Croatia by Zrinski

CAUTION

Whilst the RCC Pilotage Foundation, the author and the publishers have used reasonable endeavours to ensure the accuracy of the content of this book, it contains selected information and thus is not definitive. It does not contain all known information on the subject in hand and should not be relied on alone for navigational use: it should only be used in conjunction with official hydrographical data. This is particularly relevant to the plans, which should not be used for navigation. The RCC Pilotage Foundation, the authors and the publishers believe that the information which they have included is a useful aid to prudent navigation, but the safety of a vessel depends ultimately on the judgment of the skipper, who should assess all information, published or unpublished. The information provided in this pilot book may be out of date and may be changed or updated without notice. The RCC Pilotage Foundation cannot accept any liability for any error, omission or failure to update such information. To the extent permitted by law, the RCC Pilotage Foundation, the author and the publishers do not accept liability for any loss and/or damage howsoever caused that may arise from reliance on information contained in these pages.

Positions and Waypoints

All positions and waypoints are to datum WGS 84. They are included to help in locating places, features and transits. Do not rely on them alone for safe navigation.

Bearings and Lights

Any bearings are given as °T and from seaward. The characteristics of lights may be changed during the lifetime of this book. They should be checked against the latest edition of the UK Admiralty *List of Lights*.

Updates and Supplements

Corrections, updates and annual supplements for this title are published as free downloads at www.imray.com. Printed copies are also available on request from the publishers.

Find out more

For a wealth of further information, including passage planning guides and cruising logs for this area visit the RCC Pilotage Foundation website at www.rccpf.org.uk

Feedback

The RCC Pilotage Foundation is a voluntary, charitable organisation. We welcome all feedback for updates and new information. If you notice any errors or omissions, please let us know at www.rccpf.org.uk

Contents

RCC PILOTAGE FOUNDATION

The RCC Pilotage Foundation was formed as an independent charity in 1976 supported by a gift and permanent endowment made to the Royal Cruising Club by Dr Fred Ellis. The Foundation's charitable objective is 'to advance the education of the public in the science and practice of navigation'.

The Foundation is privileged to have been given the copyrights to books written by a number of distinguished authors and yachtsmen. These are kept as up to date as possible. New publications are also produced by the Foundation to cover a range of cruising areas. This is only made possible through the dedicated work of our authors and editors, all of whom are experienced sailors, who depend on a valuable supply of information from generous-minded yachtsmen and women from around the world.

Most of the management of the Foundation is done on a voluntary basis. In line with its charitable status, the Foundation distributes no profits. Any surpluses are used to finance new publications and to subsidise publications which cover some of the more remote areas of the world.

The Foundation works in close collaboration with three publishers – Imray Laurie Norie & Wilson, Bloomsbury (Adlard Coles Nautical) and On Board Publications. The Foundation also itself publishes guides and pilots, including web downloads, for areas where limited demand does not justify large print runs. Several books have been translated into French, Spanish, Italian and German and some books are now available in e-versions.

For further details about the RCC Pilotage Foundation and its publications visit **www.rccpf.org.uk**

PUBLICATIONS OF THE RCC PILOTAGE FOUNDATION

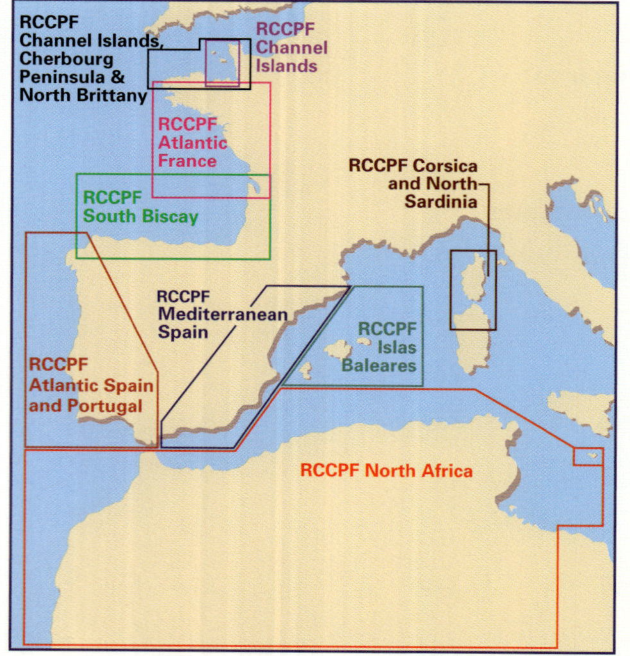

Imray
Arctic and Northern Waters
Atlantic France
Atlantic Islands
Atlantic Spain & Portugal
Black Sea
Cape Horn and Antarctic Waters
Channel Islands, Cherbourg Peninsula and North Brittany
Chile
Corsica and North Sardinia
Islas Baleares
Isles of Scilly
North Africa
Norway
South Biscay
The Baltic Sea and approaches

Adlard Coles Nautical
Atlantic Crossing Guide
Pacific Crossing Guide

On Board Publications
South Atlantic Circuit
Havens and Anchorages for the South American Coast

RCC Pilotage Foundation
Supplement to Falkland Island Shores
Guide to West Africa
Argentina

RCCPF website www.rccpf.org.uk
Supplements
Support files for books
Passage Planning Guides
ePilots - from the Arctic to the Antarctic Peninsula

FOREWORD

This combined edition of *Mediterranean Spain* is the first in which the RCC Pilotage Foundation has covered the whole of the coast between Gibraltar and the French border, however its origins go back more than forty years to the 1975 first edition of the *East Spain Pilot*. This new work brings together all of the information from the previous editions of *Mediterranean Spain Costas del Sol and Blanca* and *Mediterranean Spain Costas del Azahar, Dorada and Brava*.

The RCC Pilotage Foundation is extremely grateful to Steve Pickard who, already established author of RCC Pilotage Foundation *South Biscay*, agreed to step into the shoes of Graham Hutt and the late, much missed, John Marchment. In his research for this edition, Steve has sailed the full length of this varied coastline and explored a multitude of havens along the way in his Westerly Corsair, *Hobo*. The Foundation is also very grateful to the whole team at Imray who have done such a good job in bringing everything together into this new volume.

The RCC Pilotage Foundation continues to depend on all of the yachtsmen and women who cruise Mediterranean Spain to help to keep this book up to date by contributing information based on their own experience of the region. If you have some information or photographs for us we would love to hear from you at info@rccpf.org.uk. Any feedback will be published on our website at www.rccpf.org.uk and annual correctional supplements to the book will be available via the Imray website at www.imray.com.

Jane Russell
Editor in Chief

PREFACE TO THE FIRST COMBINED EDITION

The Mediterranean coast of Spain runs from the Rock of Gibraltar to the mighty Cap Bear, final outpost of the Pyrenees which forms the border with France. If coasts could speak what a tale this 600 mile stretch of rock and sand could tell!

Almost from the beginning of civilization boats have sailed there and been wrecked there. Invading armies have landed there and been driven back into the sea, or, conquered the resident population and effected vast cultural changes. The seabed is littered with the bones of ships, bones of men and cargoes seen only by fish since their distant demise. Ashore, the remnants of these civilizations are visible to all and, because so much depended on access by sea, the cruising yachtsman is in a very good position to sample this historical pot pourri.

I first came to this region in the winter of 1978 on a delivery trip from the Hamble to Greece. In Gibraltar we took over a Nicolson 39 that had spent Christmas hove to off NW Spain. Almost certainly as a result of these excesses the rudder dropped off on our first night out from Gib and I was amazed to find out how warm the winter sea was! As Almeria drew close I was treated to my first sight of Moorish Spain with the town's imposing castle dominating the very welcome port. I have cruised this coast many times since and always too quickly for I have found that the slower the progress, the greater the rewards.

Steve Pickard

The author and his son *Steve Pickard*

Cape Palos, Costa Blanca, one of many capes to pass *Steve Pickard*

ACKNOWLEDGEMENTS

We all stand on the shoulders of those that came before us and nowhere is this more true than when a new pilot comes out. Even those brave souls who have created a pilot where there was none before such as Judy Lomax and her magnificent mariners guide to Norway have, to some extent, used the notes, logs and observations of those that have cruised there before. In my case thanks are due to Robin Brandon who first surveyed this coast 40 years ago, John Marchment and Graham Hutt. For some of the proof reading I am indebted to Charles Lloyd for burning the midnight oil in search of errors. Special thanks are due to Jane Russell, whose searchlight gaze and attention to detail removed so many mistakes.

Many thanks are also due to those who cruise this coast and take the trouble to correct such errors that have crept into this pilot and those who, having noted changes, or formed an impression of a place, use the feedback option on the home page of the rccpf website www.rccpf.org.uk or simply drop a line to info@rccpf.org.uk.

The author's yacht, *Hobo* *Steve Pickard*

Key to symbols used on plans

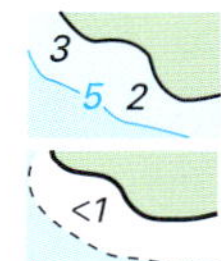
depths in METRES

shallow water with a depth of 1m or less

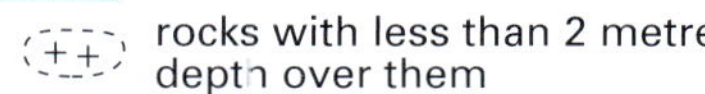
rocks with less than 2 metres depth over them

rock just below or on the surface

a shoal or reef with the least depth shown

wreck partially above water

wreck

dangerous wreck with depth over it

eddies

rock ballasting on a mole or breakwater

above-water rocks

cliffs

church

mosque

windmill

wind turbine

chimney

pine

trees other than pine

castle

ruins

houses / buildings

waypoint

fish farm

anchorage

prohibited anchorage

harbour with yacht berths

yacht harbour / marina

visitors' berths

port of entry

customs

port police

water

electricity

shower

waste pump-out

fuel

travel-hoist

chandlers

tourist information

crane

post office

tourist information

airport

yacht berth

local boats (usually shallow or reserved)

beacon

port hand buoy

starboard hand buoy

mooring buoy

Characteristics

light

lighthouse

F. fixed

Fl. flash

Fl(2) group flash

Oc. occulting

R red

G green

W white

M miles

s sand

m mud

w weed

r rock

P.A. Position approximate

Cartagena looking S towards the entrance *Jane Russell*

INTRODUCTION

OVERVIEW OF THE REGION

From the rock of Gibraltar to the French border, Gibraltar and the five Mediterranean costas of Spain form the subject matter of this pilot. It links to the RCCPF *Islas Baleares* for those heading east or to the Islands from Denia. With Morocco just 12 miles from Gibraltar, another link is made to the RCCPF *North Africa pilot* which covers all the ports in North Africa on the Mediterranean coast and the West African Moroccan coast as far down as Mauritania. West of Gibraltar coverage is provided by the RCCPF *Atlantic Spain and Portugal*.

The cultural heritage left by the Moors, who occupied Spain for 800 years, and the early Christians, is mentioned in the text along with interesting places to visit – often using local transport.

Millions of tourists are drawn regularly to the area and the effect is clear to see amd hear – high rise and densely packed resorts, strip development along the coast line, packed beaches and the noise of bars, restaurants and discos. However, there are still areas that the developers have yet to reach and much more to this coast of Spain than this popular image. The yachtsman has plenty to choose from – both afloat and ashore. The area offers a clear climate, good food, great scenery, modern marinas and many anchorages as well as the cultural heritage of the Moors and Christians.

Chapter 1 includes the Straits, Algeciras Bay and Gibraltar.

Chapter II covers the Costa del Sol. This aptly named coast stretches east from Gibraltar to the Cabo de Gata. To the west lie the sherry bodegas of Jerez. North is the dramatic ravine town of Rhonda and the white rural villages of Andalucia. Further east is Grenada and the wonders of the Alhambra Palace – and easy access to the skiing mountains of the Sierra Nevada. Coastal villages offer the chance to anchor for a swim or a paella lunch ashore.

Chapter III details the Costa Blanca. The white coast provides anchorages to the north of Cabo de Gata before giving way to the sports grounds of La Manga and the tourist resorts stretching up to Cabo de la Nao.

Chapter IV deals with the Costa Azahar. The high cliffs in the south rapidly give way to long sandy beaches running up to the Ebro Delta. Azahar means blossom and reflects the huge groves of orange and lemon trees. The America's Cup of 2007 has led to much recent development around Valencia.

Chapter V describes the Costa del Dorada. This area runs between the rivers Ebro and Tordera. The major ports of Tarragona and Barcelona break the run of golden beaches which give this coast its name.

Chapter VI winds up with the Costa Brava. The rocky savage coast, with few marinas but many deep calas, heads towards the Pyrenees and the border with France.

In the Mediterranean, yachts are usually in commission from May to October, the north European holiday season. However, whilst there is little chance of a gale in summer, there are few days when there is a good sailing breeze. In contrast during the winter, whilst it is true that off-shore the Mediterranean can be horrid, there are many days along this coast with a good sailing breeze and the weather is warmer and sunnier than the usual summer in the English Channel. Storms and heavy rain do occur but it is feasible to dodge bad weather and slip along shore from harbour to harbour as they are not far apart (see page 16 Weather forecasts). In general the climate is mild and, particularly from January to March, very pleasant. A great advantage is that there are no crowds and the local shops and services are freer to serve the winter visitor. Many Clubs Náutico, which have to turn people away in summer, welcome winter visitors. Local inhabitants can be met, places of interest enjoyed and the empty beaches and coves used in privacy.

History

There are many traces of prehistoric inhabitants but recorded history starts with a group of unknown origin, the Ligurians, who came from N Africa and established themselves in southern Spain in about the 6th century BC. The Carthaginians based themselves at Málaga and the Phoenicians, who had been trading in the area since the 12th century BC, lived in various small colonies dotted along the coast.

In 242BC a force of Carthaginians under Hamilcar Barca, who had previously been driven from Sicily by the Romans, captured and held the south of Spain until 219BC when the Romans took over. This occupation lasted until the Barbarian invasion in the 5th century AD. This period prior to this invasion was one of development and construction when many of the towns were first established. The Barbarians – the Suevi, Vandals and Alans – were, in turn, overrun by the Visigoths who held the area from the 5th to the 8th century AD.

In 711AD a huge force of Moors and Berbers under Tarik-ibn-Zeyab crossed the Strait of Gibraltar and captured the whole of Spain except for a small enclave in the N. The Moors took over the S and the Berbers the N. By the 10th century AD huge strides had been made in education and development and Cordoba, which had become independent, was renowned throughout Europe as a seat of learning.

By the 13th century, the Moors and Berbers had been driven out of the country by a long series of wars undertaken by numerous Spanish forces who were supported by the armies of the nobles of France. Granada alone remained under the Moors until 1491 when they were finally driven out by Isabella of Castile and Ferdinand of Aragon who united Spain under one crown.

Then followed a period of world-wide expansion and when the crown went to the house of Hapsburg in the 16th century then began a period of interference in the affairs of Europe which continued when the house of Bourbon took over in the 18th century.

Over the years the country has been in constant turmoil. Wars and rebellions, victories and defeats, sieges and conquests were common occurrences but none were quite as terrible as the Civil War which started in 1936 and lasted for two-and-a-half years, leaving nearly a million dead. Since then the country has moved away from a dictatorship into the different turmoils of democracy and the European Union, but the Civil War has not been forgotten. Though the country is governed centrally from Madrid, provinces have considerable local autonomy.

Local economy

Tourism has been the most obvious and significant factor in the Spanish economy along the Costas for many years. Some areas are overdeveloped, but inland little has changed, with small 'white' (painted) villages not much changed over hundreds of years.

In the south, the hydroponic farming with thousands of square kilometres of plastic sheeting force-growing farm produce is very evident from Motril to beyond Cabo de Gata. This does much to help the economy which, with the low price of oil and the ECB monetary policies, has lifted the spanish GDP. Unemployment is still high amongst Spaniards – especially the young workers – and the government is doing everything it can to increase tax revenue.

This downturn, coupled with a particular tax imposed on yachts – matriculation tax – has led to marinas being far less full and offering better prices than they have for years. A much better situation than when they hiked them up every year.

Matriculation tax

Nothing has damaged the Spanish yacht tourism industry more than the application of matriculation tax. An estimate by the Baleares Islands Tourist office calculates that Spain has lost tens of thousands of yachts since its implementation. Most left for Portugal, Italy, Sardinia, Malta, the UK and North Africa. Representations have been made to the government by those most affected – the marina and tourist operators in the Baleares Islands and marinas along the Costa del Sol and Blanca.

The tax itself is nothing new, but its application and interpretation is so wide and varied in different areas of Spain, that it has simply scared many of those who are perfectly entitled to have their yachts in Spain without having to pay the 12% tax based on the yachts valuation by a customs official, plus all the legal fees involved and change of flag at a later stage.

In brief, if you do not own or rent property in Spain and do not spend more than 183 days in any year here, then there is no liability. If the above applies, then the tax is required. This should be followed by re-registration of the yacht to a Spanish flag and changing your yacht qualifications for Spanish paperwork. A similar procedure as is required for road vehicles. However, these latter two items are not as yet being enforced in some provinces. In 2015, exemption from matriculation tax was made available to all charter yachts regardless of size. There are many articles on this tax online if more information is required.

Currency

The unit of currency in Spain is the Euro. Major credit cards are widely accepted, as are Euro cheques. Bank hours are normally 0830 to 1400, Monday to Friday, with a few also open 0830 to 1300 on Saturday. Most banks have automatic telling machines (ATM).

Gibraltar uses the Sterling Pound but also prints its own Pound currency, which carries the same value as Sterling – but ONLY in Gibraltar.

Language

There are many differences in the Spanish language between regions. Along the Costa del Sol, you will usually hear Andalusian. Castilian is, however, considered the 'proper' Spanish and is usually taught in language classes. Further East, there is a mixture of French, Italian and Spanish in the Catalan language, which is used from Valencia to the French border. The Islas Baleares has its own brand of Catalan with differing words and accents even on islands only a few miles apart.

Communication, however, is rarely a problem. This is partly due to the fact that there are many guest workers from all over the EU, most of whom – unlike most Spanish – speak English along with their native languages. They work in bars, restaurants, offices etc and are more often encountered in some places than Spanish nationals.

Place names used in this book are, where possible, Castilian, which is also used on British Admiralty charts.

Time zone

Spain keeps Standard European Time (UT+1), advanced one hour in summer to UT+2 hours. Changeover dates are now standardised with the rest of the EU as the last weekends in March and October respectively.

Unless stated otherwise, times quoted are UT.

National holidays and fiestas

There are numerous official and local holidays, the latter often celebrating the local saint's day or some historical event. They usually comprise a religious procession, sometimes by boat, followed by a fiesta in the evening. The Fiesta del Virgen de la Carmen is celebrated in many harbours during mid-July. Official holidays include:

1 January	*Año Nuevo* (New Year's Day)
6 January	*Reyes Magos* (Epiphany)
19 March	*San José* (St Joseph's Day)
	Viernes Santo (Good Friday)
	Easter Monday
1 May	*Día del Trabajo* (Labour Day)
early/mid-June	Corpus Christi
24 June	*Día de San Juan* (St John's Day, the King's name-day)
29 June	*San Pedro y San Pablo* (Sts Peter and Paul)
25 July	*Día de Santiago* (St James' Day)
15 August	*Día del Asunción* (Feast of the Assumption)
11 September	Catalan National Day
12 October	*Día de la Hispanidad* (Day of the Spanish Nation)
1 November	*Todos los Santos* (All Saints)
6 December	*Día de la Constitución* (Constitution Day)
8 December	*Inmaculada Concepción* (Immaculate Conception)
25 December	*Navidad* (Christmas Day)

When a national holiday falls on a Sunday it may be celebrated the following day.

Dolphins off the Balearics *Steve Pickard*

PRACTICALITIES

Formalities and documentation

All yachts calling at any Spanish port are required to report to the marina administration office – usually located close to the arrival or waiting berth. A form is then completed which asks for yacht information, crew nationalities, insurance details and passport information. This form is in Spanish and English. Though insurance information is required, third party insurance is sufficient. If there are foreign (non EU) personnel on board, or if the yacht is non EU flagged, border agencies police or customs officials may visit, but this is rare. If the stay is for no longer than 24 hours, payment is usually made to the duty *marinero* if the office is closed. Credit / debit card facilities are available in most marinas. The same routine is applicable in Gibraltar, where forms are filled out in the marina offices or in advance online – see note on page 30.

Certificates of competence are rarely asked for and are only mandatory for skippers whose countries issue and demand them.

Spain is a member of the European Union. Other EU nationals may visit the country for up to 90 days with a passport but no visa, as may US citizens. EU citizens wishing to remain in Spain may apply for a *permiso de residencia* once in the country; non-EU nationals can apply for a single 90-day extension, or otherwise obtain a long-term visa from a Spanish embassy or consulate before leaving home.

In practice the requirement to apply for a *permiso de residencia* does not appear to be enforced in the case of cruising yachtsmen, living aboard rather than ashore and frequently on the move. Many yachtsmen have cruised Spanish waters for extended periods with no documentation beyond that normally carried in the UK. If in doubt, check with the authorities before departure.

Under EU regulations, EU registered boats are not required to fly the Q flag on first arrival unless they have non-EU nationals or dutiable goods aboard.

At the time of writing it remains to be seen whether Brexit will result in different requirements on UK vessels and crews.

Official addresses

See Appendix VIII

Useful websites

Spanish Tourist Office www.tourspain.co.uk
British Airways www.britishairways.com
Iberia Airlines www.iberia.com
Andalucía www.andalucia.org
Murcia www.murciaturistica.es
Valencia www.comunidadvalenciana.com
Easyjet www.easyjet.com
Ryanair www.ryanair.com

Weather websites on page 17.

Port websites at each port.

Temporary import and laying up

A VAT paid or exempt yacht should apply for a *permiso aduanero* on arrival in Spanish waters if intending to stay for an extended period. This is valid for twelve months and renewable annually, allowing for an almost indefinite stay. Possession of a *permiso aduanero* establishes the status of a vessel and is helpful when importing equipment and spares from other EU countries.

A boat registered outside the EU fiscal area on which VAT has not been paid may be temporarily imported into the EU for a period not exceeding six months in any twelve before VAT is payable. This period may sometimes be extended by prior agreement with the local customs authorities (for instance, some do not count time laid up as part of the six months). While in EU waters the vessel may only be used by its owner, and may not be chartered or even lent to another person, on pain of paying VAT (*see Appendix VIII for further details*). If kept in the EU longer than six months the vessel normally becomes liable for VAT. There are marked differences in the way the rules are applied from one harbour to the next, let alone in different countries – check the local situation on arrival.

Chartering

There is a blanket restriction on foreign-owned and/or skippered vessels based in Spain engaging in charter work. See Appendix VII for details.

Light dues

A charge known as *Tarifa G5* is supposedly levied on all vessels. Locally-based pleasure craft (the status of a charter yacht is not clear) pay at the rate of €5 per square metre per year, area being calculated as LOA x beam. Visiting pleasure craft pay at one tenth of that sum and are not charged again for ten days. Boats of less than 7m LOA and with engines of less than 25hp make a single payment of €30 per year. In practice this levy appears to be added to the marina or mooring charges on a daily basis. It may be included in marina fees without note.

Charts

See Appendix II for a detailed list of Imray charts. Current British Admiralty information is largely obtained from Spanish sources. The Spanish Hydrographic Office re-issues and corrects its charts periodically and issues weekly *Notices to Mariners*. Corrections are repeated by the British Admiralty, generally some months later.

Many yachtsmen are turning to electronic charts. Apps developed by Imray and Navionics, amongst others, cover the Mediterranean. These have the advantage of frequent updates and are generally accurate.

Pilot books

Details of principal harbours and some interesting background information appear in the British Admiralty Hydrographic Office's *Mediterranean Pilot Vol 1 (NP 45). NP 291, Maritime Communications* will be found useful.

For French speakers, *Votre Livre de Bord – Méditerranée* (Bloc Marine) may be helpful.

Positions and waypoints

All positions in this pilot are to WGS 84 and have been derived from C-Map electronic charts. If plotting onto paper charts then the navigator is reminded that some source charts of this area remain at European 1950 datum (ED50) and appropriate use of offsets may be necessary. This pilot includes waypoints: note the caution on page ii. The list is given in Appendix I.

Magnetic variation

Magnetic variation is noted in the introduction to the coastal sections. It is however nowhere much greater than 1° east or west.

Traffic zones

There are traffic separation zones in the Strait of Gibraltar, off Cabo de Gata, Cabo de Palos and Cabo de la Nao.

NAVIGATION AIDS

Lights

It should be noted that, whilst every effort has been taken to check that the lights agree with *Notices to Mariners* and the annual *List of Lights and Fog Signals*, the responsibility for maintaining the lights appears to rest with the local *capitanía* and, depending on their efficiency, this can mean some lights may be defective or different from the stated characteristics at times.

Buoyage

Buoys follow the IALA A system, based on the direction of the main flood tide. Yellow topped black or red rusty buoys 500m offshore mark raw sewage outlets. Many minor harbours, however, maintain their own buoys to their own systems. Generally, yellow buoys in line mark the seaward side of areas reserved for swimming. Narrow lanes for water-skiing and sail boarding lead out from the shore and are also buoyed.

HAZARDS

Restricted areas

Restricted areas are outlined in the coastal sections.

Night approaches

Approaches in darkness are often made difficult by the plethora of background lights – fixed, flashing, occulting, interrupted – of all colours. Though there may be exceptions, this applies to nearly all harbours backed by a town of any size. Powerful shore lights make weaker navigation lights difficult to identify and mask unlit features such as exposed rocks or the line of a jetty. Do be aware that unlit and unmarked nets are often stretched across the entrance of harbours after dark. Look out for flashing lights of a torch and listen out for any shouting as you enter. Lights are rarely used to mark the nets and the boats, fishing illegally, often have no lights displayed. If at all possible, avoid closing an unknown harbour in darkness.

Skylines

Individual buildings on the coast – particularly prominent hotel blocks – are built, demolished, duplicated, change colour, change shape, all with amazing rapidity. They are not nearly as reliable as landmarks as might be thought. If a particular building on a chart or in a photograph can be positively identified on the ground, well and good. If not, take care.

Tunny nets and fish farms

During summer and autumn these nets, anchored to the sea bed and up to six miles long, are normally laid inshore across the current in depths of 15–40m but may be placed as far as 10 miles offshore. They may be laid in parallel lines. The outer end of a line should be marked by a float or a boat carrying a white flag with an 'A' (in black) by day, and two red or red and white lights by night. There should also be markers along the line of the net.

These nets are capable of stopping a small freighter but should you by accident, and successfully, sail over one, look out for a second within a few hundred metres. If seen, the best action may be to sail parallel to the nets until one end is reached.

Many *calas* and bays have fish farms proliferating. These are often lit with flashing yellow lights but great care should be taken when entering small *calas* at night.

The positions of some fish farms are indicated on the latest charts but be aware these farms change position frequently. Fish farming is developing along this coast and navigators must be prepared to encounter ones not shown on plans and charts. Where there are no buoys marking these farms, vessels can transit through or close, but stopping, anchoring or fishing is prohibited.

Commercial fishing boats

Commercial fishing boats should be given a wide berth. They may be:

- Trawling singly or in pairs with a net between the boats.
- Laying a long net, the top of which is supported by floats.
- Picking up or laying pots either singly or in groups or lines.
- Trolling with one or more lines out astern.
- Drifting, trailing nets to windward.

Do not assume they know, or will observe, the law of the sea – keep well clear on principle.

Small fishing boats

Small fishing boats, including the traditional double-ended *llauds*, either use nets or troll with lines astern and should be avoided as far as possible. At night many *lámparas* put to sea and, using powerful electric or gas lights, attract fish to the surface. When seen from a distance these lights appear to flash as the boat moves up and down in the waves and can at first be mistaken for a lighthouse.

Speed boats etc

Para-gliding, water-skiing, speedboats and jet-skis are all popular, and are sometimes operated by unskilled and thoughtless drivers with small regard to collision risks. In theory they are not allowed to exceed five knots within 100m of the coast or within 250m of bathing beaches. Water-skiing is restricted to buoyed areas.

Scuba divers and swimmers

A good watch should be kept for scuba divers and swimmers, with or without snorkel equipment, particularly around harbour entrances. If accompanied by a boat, the presence of divers may be indicated on the parent boat either by International Code Flag A or by a square red flag with a single yellow diagonal, as commonly seen in north America and the Caribbean. The divers often tow a small, red float.

In summer, swimmers are protected by lines of (usually yellow) buoys parallel to the shore. It is illegal to anchor or sail within these buoys. The coast is patrolled and fines are high.

PREPARATION

The crew

Clothing

Summer sunburn is an even more serious hazard at sea, where light is reflected, than on land. Lightweight, patterned cotton clothing is handy in this context – it washes and dries easily and the pattern camouflages the creases! Non-absorbent, heat retaining synthetic materials are best avoided. When swimming wear a T-shirt against the sun and shoes if there are sea-urchins around.

Some kind of headgear, preferably with a wide brim, is essential. A genuine Panama Hat, a *Montecristi*, can be rolled up, shoved in a pocket and doesn't mind getting wet (they come from Ecuador, not Panama, which has hijacked the name). A retaining string for the hat, tied either to clothing or around the neck, is a wise precaution whilst on the water.

Footwear at sea is a contentious subject. Many experienced cruisers habitually sail barefoot but while this may be acceptable on a familiar vessel, it would be courting injury on a less intimately known deck and around mid-day bare soles may get burnt. Proper sailing shoes should always be worn for harbour work and anchor handling. Ashore, if wearing sandals the upper part of the foot is the first area to get sunburn.

At the other end of the year, winter weather may be wet and cold. Foul weather gear as well as warm sweaters, etc. will be needed.

Shore going clothes should be on a par with what one might wear in the UK – beachwear is not often acceptable in restaurants and certainly not on more formal occasions in yacht clubs.

Medical

No inoculations are required. Minor ailments may best be treated by consulting a *farmacia* (often able to dispense drugs which in most other countries would be on prescription), or by contact with an English-speaking doctor (recommended by the *farmacia*, marina staff, a tourist office, the police or possibly a hotel). Specifically prescribed or branded drugs should be acquired before setting out in sufficient quantity to cover the duration of the cruise. Medicines are expensive in Spain and often have different brand names from those used abroad.

Apart from precautions against the well recognised hazards of sunburn (high factor sun cream is recommended) and stomach upsets, heat exhaustion (or heat stroke) is most likely to affect newly joined crew not yet acclimatised to Mediterranean temperatures. Carry something such as *Dioralyte* to counteract dehydration. Insect repellents, including mosquito coils, can be obtained locally.

UK citizens should carry a European Health Insurance Card (EHIC) application for which can be obtained at a Post Office or online at www.ehic.org.uk. This usually provides for free medical treatment under a reciprocal agreement with the National Health Service. Brexit, of course, could change all of this. Private medical treatment is likely to be expensive and it may be worth taking out medical insurance (which should also provide for an attended flight home should the need arise).

The yacht

A yacht properly equipped for cruising in northern waters should need little extra gear, but the following items are worth considering if not already on board.

Radio equipment

In order to receive weather forecasts and navigational warnings from Coast Radio Stations, a radio capable of receiving short and medium wave Single Sideband (SSB) transmissions will be needed. Do not make the mistake of buying a radio capable only of receiving the AM transmissions broadcast by national radio stations, or assume that SSB is only applicable to transmitting radios (transceivers).

Most SSB receivers are capable of receiving either Upper Side Band (USB) or Lower Side Band (LSB) at the flick of a switch. The UK Maritime Mobile Net covering the Eastern Atlantic and Mediterranean uses USB, and again it is not necessary to have either a transceiver or a transmitting licence to listen in, just a receiver. All Coast Radio Stations broadcast on SSB – whether on USB or LSB should be easy to determine by trial and error.

Digital tuning is very desirable, and the radio should be capable of tuning to a minimum of 1kHz and preferably to 0·1kHz.

Ventilation

Modern yachts are, as a rule, better ventilated than their older sisters though seldom better insulated. Consider adding an opening hatch in the main cabin, if not already fitted, and ideally another over the galley. Wind scoops over hatches can be a major benefit.

Awnings

An awning covering at least the cockpit is essential and provides much relief for the crew, while an even better combination is a bimini which can be kept rigged whilst sailing, plus a larger ‘harbour’ awning, preferably at boom height or above and extending forward to the mast.

Fans

Harbours can be hot and windless. The use of 12V fans for all cabins can have a dramatic effect on comfort but better still is a 220v fan running from the shore supply.

Cockpit tables

It is pleasant to eat civilised meals in the cockpit, particularly while at anchor. If nothing else can be arranged, a small folding table might do.

Refrigerator/ice-box/freezer

If a refrigerator or freezer is not fitted it may be possible to build in an ice-box (a plastic picnic cool box is a poor substitute), but this will be useless without adequate insulation. An ice-box designed for northern climes will almost certainly benefit from extra insulation, if this can be fitted – 100mm (4in) is a desirable minimum, 150mm (6in) even better. A drain is also essential.

If a refrigerator/freezer is fitted but electricity precious, placing ice inside will help minimise battery drain.

Hose

Carry at least 25 metres. Standpipes tend to have bayonet couplings of a type unavailable in the UK – purchase them on arrival. Plenty of five or 10 litre plastic carriers will also be useful.

Deck shower

If no shower is fitted below, a black-backed plastic bag plus rose heats very quickly when hung in the rigging or laid on the deck. (At least one proprietary model is available widely).

Mosquitoes

Not a great problem unless berthed up a river. Some advocate fitting screens to all openings leading below. Others find this inconvenient, relying instead on mosquito coils and other insecticides and repellents. Again 220v devices work best, don’t make your eyes water and can be used in the place most likely to have a mosquito problem, marinas. For some reason mosquitoes generally seem to bother new arrivals more than old hands. Anchorages rarely have a problem, an onshore breeze makes the yacht inaccessible.

Snorkel, mask and wetsuit

Much inconvenience can be avoided by the inclusion on board of the above.

HARBOURS, MARINAS AND ANCHORAGES

In spite of the growth in both the number and size of marinas and yacht harbours there is still a chronic shortage of berths in summer. A recent expansion of many marinas has eased the situation. One must check in advance whether a berth is available and note that mobile phones are replacing VHF for this function.

Harbour organisation

It is not difficult to become thoroughly confused regarding marina nomenclature throughout Spain. The port authority is basically concerned with the harbour itself and the safe navigation within, under the direction of the *Capitan de Puerto*. His office is the *Capitania*. Within the port, however, may be several yacht facilities, which are all autonomous but under his overall supervision.

Most harbours host a *club náutico* or Real Club Náutico if smarter. Also in this group is the club des regattes. These are private yacht marinas for club members and are often (though there are many exceptions) not at all welcoming to visitors. This is indicated in the text. Then there are the commercial *puerto deportivos* and marinas.

Some marinas are handled by the *Junta de Andalucîa*. These are run by the local authority or leased by them and almost always ask a much lower rate than the clubs.

Adding to the confusion, many of the clubs above also have their own *capitania* and *capitan de puerto*!

Many ports have three facilities – a *club náutico*, a *club de regatta* and a marina or *puerto deportivo*.

Calling up on the VHF Ch 9 using just the harbour name can bring in several responses, so try to ascertain exactly the right designation from the book before calling.

For the best rates try heading to '*la marina*' or '*puerto deportivo*.' It is also helpful to note that in Spanish, the use of the word port, marina or harbour on a local chart does not necessarily refer to anything grander than a cove, a natural feature, or, sometimes, even a stretch of beach where it is possible to anchor!

Harbour charges

All harbours and marinas charge on a scale depending on the month of the season. May to September are usually considered the 'high' season and increases in cost every year have been usual for years. Usually, VAT (at 21%) is not included in the price lists. Often water and electricity are also added either on a flat rate or metered – plus VAT. The difference between summer and winter rates are often double.

In the current state of uncertainty, along with the matriculation tax, however, many marinas are trying to attract yachtsmen by offering cheaper rates, especially if you are prepared to pay six months or a year in advance.

Although some indications are given in the text, actual pricing is best found on the internet for the marina concerned as prices change so frequently – and not always upwards these days! As a rough guide, for a 12m boat €20 is low, €30 medium and €60 high.

Berthing

Due to the vast numbers of yachts and limited space available, berthing stern-to the quays and pontoons is normal.

For greater privacy berth bows-to. This has the added advantages of keeping the rudder away from possible underwater obstructions near the quay and making the approach a much easier manoeuvre. An anchor may occasionally be needed, but more often a bow (or stern) line will be provided, usually via a lazyline to the pontoon though sometimes buoyed. This line may be both heavy and dirty and gloves and a bucket of water will be useful. Either way, have plenty of fenders out and lines ready.

Most cruising skippers will have acquired some expertise at this manoeuvre but if taking over a chartered or otherwise unfamiliar yacht it would be wise both to check handling characteristics and talk the sequence through with the crew before attempting to enter a narrow berth.

Detailed instructions regarding Mediterranean mooring techniques will be found in *Mediterranean Cruising Handbook* by Rod Heikell.

Mooring lines – surge in harbours is common and mooring lines must be both long and strong. It is useful to have an eye made up at the shore end with a loop of chain plus shackles to slip over bollards or through rings. Carry plenty of mooring lines, especially if the boat is to be left unattended for any length of time. Steel springs or rubber shock absorbers in the lines help enormously.

Gangplanks – if a gangplank is not already part of the boat's equipment, a builder's scaffolding plank, with holes drilled at either end to take lines, serves well. As it is cheap and easily replaced it can also be used outside fenders to deal with an awkward lie or ward off an oily quay.

Moorings

Virtually all moorings are privately owned and if one is used it will have to be vacated should the owner return. There are generally no markings to give any indication as to the weight and strength of moorings so they should be used with caution, especially in calas where the bottom block may be no bigger than a paving slab linked by ropes to other paving slabs. Lobster pot toggles have been mistaken for moorings.

Laying up

Laying up either afloat or ashore is possible at most marinas, though a few have no hard standing. Facilities and services provided vary considerably, as does the cost, and it is worth seeking local advice as to the quality of the services and the security of the berth or hard standing concerned.

In the north of the area, the northwesterly *tramontana* (*mistral*) can be frequent and severe in winter and early spring, and this should be borne in mind when selecting the area and site to lay up. Yachts with wooden decks and varnished bright work will benefit with protection from the winter sun.

Yacht clubs

Most harbours of any size support at least one *club náutico*. However the grander ones in particular are basically social clubs – often with tennis courts, swimming pools and other facilities – and may not welcome the crews of visiting yachts. Often there is both a marina and a club, and unless there are special circumstances the normal first option for a visitor is the marina. That said, many *club náuticos* have pleasant bars and excellent restaurants which appear to be open to all, while a few are notably helpful and friendly to visitors. The standard of dress and behaviour often appears to be somewhat more formal than that expected in a similar club in Britain.

GENERAL REGULATIONS

Harbour restrictions

All harbours have a speed limit, usually three knots. There is a five knot speed limit within 100m of coast, extending to 250m off bathing beaches.

In most harbours anchoring is forbidden except in emergency or for a short period while sorting out a berth.

Harbour traffic signals

Traffic signals are rare, and in any case are designed for commercial traffic and seldom apply to yachts.

Storm signals

The signal stations at major ports and harbours may show storm signals, but equally they may not. With minor exceptions they are similar to the International System of Visual Storm Warnings.

Flag etiquette

A yacht in commission in foreign waters is legally required to fly her national maritime flag; for a British registered yacht, this is commonly the Red Ensign. If a special club ensign is worn it must be accompanied by the correct burgee. The courtesy flag of the country visited, which normally is the national maritime flag, should be flown from the starboard signal halliard. The maritime flag for Spain is similar to the Spanish national flag but without the crest in the centre.

Insurance

Many marinas require evidence of insurance cover, though third party only may be sufficient. Many UK companies are willing to extend home waters cover for the Mediterranean, excluding certain areas.

Rubbish

It is an international offence to dump rubbish at sea and, while the arrangements of local authorities may not be perfect, rubbish on land should be dumped in the proper containers. Marinas require the use of their onshore toilet facilities or holding tanks.

Large yachts

Many harbours are too small, or too shallow, for a large yacht, which must anchor outside whilst its crew visit the harbour by tender. It is essential that the skipper of such a yacht wishing to enter a small harbour telephones or radios the harbour authorities well in advance to reserve a berth (if available) and receive necessary instructions.

Scuba diving

Inshore scuba diving is strictly controlled and a licence is required from the *Militar de Marina*. This involves a certificate of competence, a medical certificate, two passport photographs, the passport itself (for inspection), knowledge of the relevant laws and a declaration that they will be obeyed. The simplest approach is to enquire through marina staff. Any attempt to remove archaeological material from the seabed will result in serious trouble.

Spear fishing

Spear fishing while scuba diving or using a snorkel is controlled and, in some places, prohibited.

Water-skiing

There has been a big increase in the use of high powered outboards for water-skiing over the past decade, accompanied by a significant increase in accidents. In most of the main ports and at some beaches it is now controlled and enquiries should be made before skiing. It is essential to have third party insurance and, if possible, a bail bond. If bathing and water-skiing areas are buoyed, yachts are excluded.

Security

Crime afloat is not a major problem in most areas and regrettably much of the theft which does occur can be laid at the door of other yachtsmen. Take sensible precautions – lock up before leaving the yacht, padlock the outboard to the dinghy, and secure the dinghy (particularly if an inflatable) with chain or wire rather than line. Folding bicycles are particularly vulnerable to theft, and should be chained up if left on deck.

Ashore, the situation in the big towns is no worse than in the UK and providing common sense is applied to such matters as how handbags are carried, where not to go after the bars close etc., there should be no problem.

The officials most likely to be seen are the *guardia civil*, who wear olive green uniforms and deal with immigration as well as more ordinary police work, the *Aduana* (customs) in navy blue uniforms, and the *Policía*, also in blue uniforms, who deal with traffic rather than criminal matters.

It is not uncommon to be stopped by the *guardia civil* at sea. They are courteous and wear sailing footwear, not boots. It is their duty to prevent smuggling of drugs and human trafficking.

ANCHORAGES

There are a large number of attractive anchorages in *calas* and off beaches, even though many have massive buildings in the background and crowds in the foreground. Where known, particular hazards are mentioned but an absence of comment in the text or on the sketch charts does not mean there are no hazards. There are always hazards approaching and anchoring off the shoreline. The plans are derived from limited observation and not from a professional survey; depths, shapes, distances etc. are approximate. Any approach must be made with due care. Skippers are advised that in season anchorages near hotels and towns may be cordoned off with small floating buoys, to protect swimmers and therefore not be available. It cannot be assumed that anchorages listed in this book are always useable for use by cruising yachtsmen.

The weather can change and deteriorate at short notice. During the day the sea breeze can be strong, especially if there is a valley at the head of an anchorage. Similarly a strong land breeze can flow down a valley in the early hours of the morning. If anchored near the head of a *cala* backed by a river valley, should there be a thunderstorm or heavy downpour in the hills above take precautions against the flood of water and debris which will descend into the *cala*.

Many *cala* anchorages suffer from swell even when not open to its off-shore direction. Swell tends to curl round all but the most prominent headlands. Wash from boats entering and leaving, as well as from larger vessels passing outside, may add to the discomfort. If considering a second anchor or a line ashore in order to hold the yacht into the swell, take into account the swinging room required by yachts on single anchors should the wind change.

In a high-sided *cala* winds are often fluky and a sudden blow, even from the land, may make departure difficult. This type of anchorage should only be used in settled calm weather and left in good time if swell or wind rise.

Whatever the type of *cala*, have ready a plan for clearing out quickly, possibly in darkness. It is unwise to leave an anchored yacht unattended for any length of time.

Note Some formerly free anchorages have been overrun with buoys in an attempt to gain income locally. Sometimes the buoys are removed during the winter months, along with the swimming exclusion zone marker buoys. Other *calas* may become military zones with little or no notice. It is impossible to keep on top of what is going on, so a degree of circumspection and preparedness to weigh is needed wherever one anchors. In some ports the local authorities will insist that anchoring is prohibited in order to have another customer in the marina. We try to keep abreast of the situation as regards the anchoring facilities and post regular updates on the website www.imray.com.

Choice of anchor

Many popular anchorages are thoroughly ploughed up each year by the hundreds of anchors dropped and weighed. At others the bottom is weed-covered compacted sand. Not without good reason is the four-pronged grab the favourite anchor of local fishermen, though difficult to stow. A conventional fisherman-type anchor is easier to stow and a useful ally. If using a patent anchor – Danforth, CQR, Bruce, Fortress etc. – an anchor weight (or chum) is a worthwhile investment and will encourage the pull to remain horizontal.

Anchoring

Once in a suitable depth of water, if clarity permits look for a weed-free patch to drop the anchor. In rocky or otherwise suspect areas – including those likely to contain wrecks, old chains etc. – use a sinking trip line with a float (an inviting buoy may be picked up by another yacht). Chain scope should be at least four times the maximum depth of water and nylon scope double that. It is always worth setting the anchor by reversing slowly until it holds, but on a hard or compacted bottom this must be done very gently in order to give the anchor a chance to bite – over enthusiasm with the throttle will cause it to skip without digging in.

SUPPLIES AND SERVICES

Fresh water

Good drinking water (*agua potable*) is available almost everywhere. Price is usually included, as with electricity, as part of the mooring fee for yachts of 12m and under, but often metered for larger yachts. Known exceptions to this are Gibraltar, where a charge is made per litre in both marinas. Marina del Este and Denia's Club Náutico also meter all usage.

Quality is usually good, though sometimes over chlorinated. It Is worthwhile asking other long stay yachties for their opinion. Bottled water is always available from supermarkets.

Ice

Block ice for an ice-box is widely obtainable – use the largest blocks that will fit; chemical ice is sometimes available in blocks measuring 100 x 20 x 20cms. The latter must not be used in drinks, the former only after inquiring of those who have tried the product. Cube or 'small' ice is obtainable and generally of drinks quality, particularly if bought in a sealed bag.

Fuel

Diesel (*gasoleo, gasoil* or simply *diesel*) is sold in two forms throughout Spain, *Gasoleo B* which attracts a lower tax and is only available to fishing craft, and *Gasoleo A* which is available to yachts. Not all harbours sell *Gasoleo A*, particularly the smaller fishing harbours. A more limited number also have a pump for petrol (*gasolina*). *Petróleo* is paraffin (kerosene). Credit cards are widely, but not universally, accepted – if in doubt, check first.

Bottled gas

Camping Gaz is widely available from marinas, supermarkets or *ferreterias* (ironmongers), in the 1·9kg bottles identical to those in the UK.

REPSOL/CAMPSOL depots will no longer fill any UK (or any other countries') Calor Gas bottles even with a current test certificate. It is therefore essential to carry the appropriate regulator and fittings to permit the use of Camping Gaz bottles. Yachts fitted with propane systems should consult the Calor Gas Customer service agent (✆ 0800 626 626).

Almost all gas bottles can be filled just over the water in Marina Smir, Morocco – if you happen to be going that way. The blue 'camping gas' bottles are less than €5 to fill/ exchange. (See Mohammed in the boatyard.)

Electricity

Marina standard electrical supply is 220v at 50Hz. This is fed via a blue 3-pin socket which comes in three amperages, depending roughly on berth size. The most common are the same as those used for caravans mains cables and may be cheaper from hardware suppliers than chandlers. Most marinas keep suitable connecting plug/sockets which they lend for a deposit for the duration of your stay. Larger yachts using berths of 20m and over often use 380v which is also catered for.

Food and drink

There are many well stocked stores, supermarkets and hypermarkets in the larger towns and cities and it may be worth doing the occasional major stock-up by taxi. As a rule, availability and choice varies with the size of the town. Most older settlements (though not all tourist resorts) have a market with local produce at reasonable prices. Alcohol is cheap by UK standards with, unsurprisingly, good value Spanish wines. Spanish gin and vodka are also good value; Scotch whisky can only come from Scotland but the genuine article is often lower in price than in the UK Shop prices generally are noticeably lower away from tourist resorts.

Excellent yet cheap seafood along the Costas *Graham Hutt*

Most shops, other than the largest supermarkets, close for *siesta* between 1400 and 1700 and remain closed on Sunday though some smaller food shops do open on Sunday mornings. In larger towns the produce market may operate from 0800 to 1400, Monday to Saturday; in smaller towns it is more often a weekly affair. An excellent way to sample unfamiliar delicacies in small portions is in the form of bar snacks, *tapas* or the larger *raciónes*. Tapas once came on the house but are now almost invariably charged – sometimes heavily.

Repairs and chandlery

There are many marinas equipped to handle all aspects of yacht maintenance from laying up to changing a washer. Nearly all have travel-hoists and the larger have specialist facilities – GRP work, electronics, sail making, stainless welding and so forth. Charges may differ – widely so – if practicable, shop around.

The best equipped chandleries will be found near the larger marinas. Smaller harbours or marinas are often without a chandlery, though something may be found in the associated town. Basic items can sometimes be found in *ferreterias* (ironmongers).

Telephones and fax

A mobile phone is undoubtedly the device for telecommunications and with roaming charges decreasing annually the cruising yachtsman need look no further. Should this device be lost however, the following notes may be useful.

Telephone kiosks are common, both local and *teléfono internacional*, and most carry instructions in English. Both coins and phone cards, available from tobacconists (*estancos*), are used. If no kiosk is available marina offices have telephones and many have faxes. Most bars and hotels have metered telephones and the latter usually have faxes, though these are seldom metered. WiFi is widely available.

- When calling from within Spain, dial the whole code (beginning with the figure 9) whether or not the number you are calling from has the same code. In some areas the number of digits to be dialled is nine, in others eight. To make an international call, dial 00 followed by the relevant country code (44 for the UK). If calling the UK do not dial the first figure of the number if it is 0.
- To reach the international operator dial 025. A telephone number beginning with the figure 6 indicates a mobile telephone which will have no area code and its own code for calling its international operator. The main emergency number throughout Spain is 112. Sea Rescue services are on 900 202202.
- To call Spain from abroad, dial the international access code (00 in the UK) followed by the code for Spain (34), then the area code (which begins with 9 except for mobile phones) followed by the individual number.

Warning Apart from a major re-organisation of area codes, individual numbers in Spain change surprisingly often.

Mail

Letters, if not sent by email, may be sent poste restante to any post office (*oficina de corréos*). They should be addressed with the surname (only) of the recipient followed by *Lista de Corréos* and the town. Do not enter the addressee's initials or title: that is likely to cause misfiling. Collection is a fairly cumbersome procedure and a passport is likely to be needed. Alternatively, most marinas and some *club náuticos* will hold mail for yachts, but it is always wise to check in advance if possible. Uncollected letters are seldom returned.

Mail to and from the UK should be marked 'air mail' (*por avión*) but even so may take up to ten days, so if speed is important communicate by fax or email. Post boxes are yellow; stamps are available from tobacconists (*estancos*), not from post offices though the latter will accept and frank mail. Almost every town has a Post Office; ask – *donde esta el Correo*?

Tourist offices

There is at least one tourist office in every major town or resort. Their locations vary from year to year and often do not correspond with the signs posted for their location – ask at the port or marina office.

Transport and travel

Every community has some form of public transport, if only one *autobús* a day and many of the coastal towns are served by rail as well.

Taxis are easily found in the tourist resorts though less common outside them, but can always be ordered by telephone. Car hire is simple, but either a full national or international driving licence must be shown and many companies will not lease a car to a driver over 70 years old.

Air – Alicante, Barcelona and Valencia have year round international flights and seasonal charter flights; Gibraltar has year round connections with the UK. Other airports, Málaga, Murcia, Alicante and Tarragona, have international scheduled and charter flights in summer and year round connections within Spain.

WESTERN MEDITERRANEAN WEATHER

The weather pattern in the basin of the western Mediterranean is affected by many different systems. It is largely unpredictable, quick to change and often very different at places only a short distance apart. See Appendix III for Spanish meteorological terms.

Winds

Winds most frequently blow from the west, northwest, north and east but are considerably altered by the effects of local topography. The Mediterranean is an area of calms and gales and the old saying that in summer there are nine days of light winds followed by a gale is very close to reality.

Levante cloud over Gibraltar creates gloomy conditions in the town *Graham Hutt*

'Flying Saucer' clouds: indication of strong E winds to come in 2–3 days *Graham Hutt*

Close to the coast, normal sea and land breezes are experienced on calm days. Along the Costa Brava, northwest, north and northeast winds are most common, especially in winter, though winds from other directions frequently occur. This area is particularly influenced by the weather in the Golfo de León and is in the direct path of the northwesterly *tramontana* (see below), making it particularly important to listen to regular weather forecasts. Further W on the Costas del Sol and Blanca, these winds translate to an E or W airstream, following the coast near Gibraltar.

The winds in the Mediterranean have been given special names dependent on their direction and characteristics. Those that affect this coast are detailed below.

Northwest *tramontana*

This wind, also known as the *maestral* near Río Ebro and the *mistral* in France, is a strong, dry wind, cold in winter, which can be dangerous. It is caused by a secondary depression forming in the Golfo de León or the Golfo de Génova on the cold front of a major depression crossing France. The northwesterly airflow generated is compressed between the Alps and the Pyrenees and flows into the Mediterranean basin. In Spain it chiefly affects the coast to the north of Barcelona, the Islas Baleares, and is strongest at the northern end of the Costa Brava.

The *tramontana* can be dangerous in that it can arrive and reach gale force in as little as 15 minutes on a calm sunny day with virtually no warning.

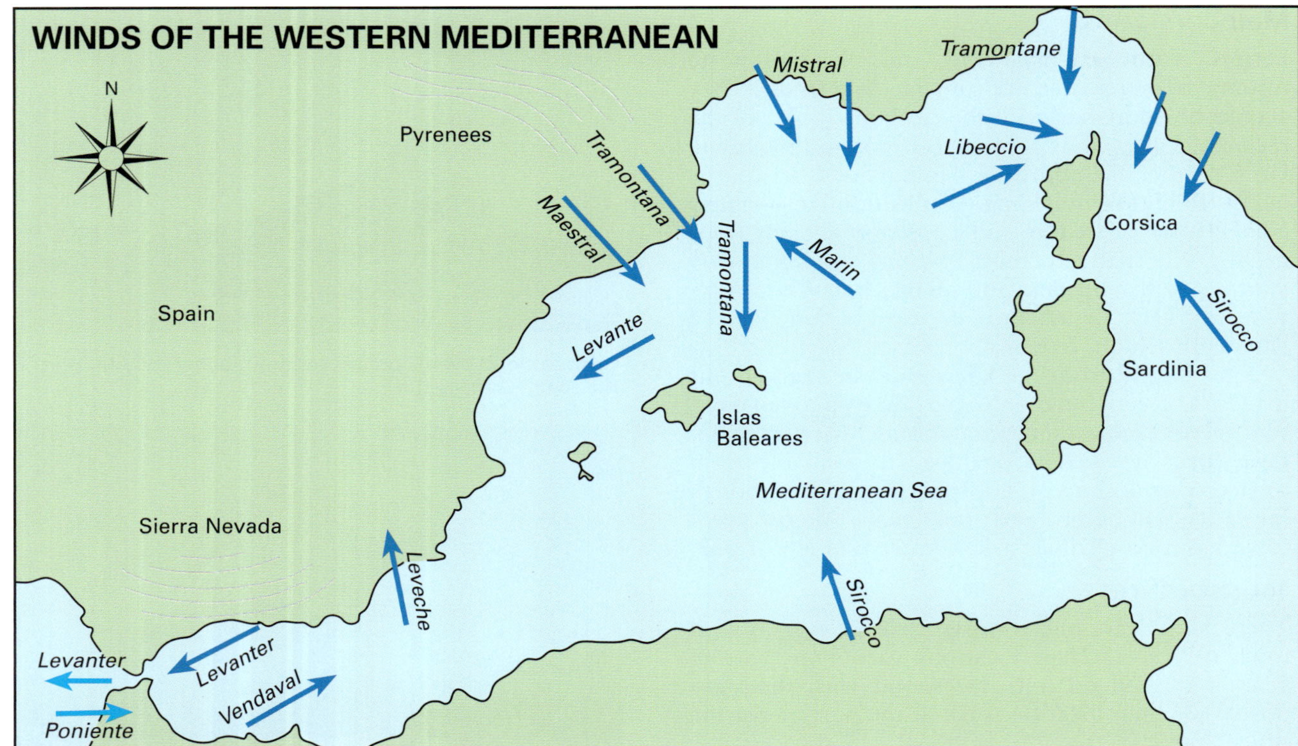

Signs to watch for are brilliant visibility, clear sky – sometimes with cigar-shaped clouds – very dry air and a steady or slightly rising barometer. On rare occasions the sky may be cloudy when the wind first arrives although it clears later. Sometimes the barometer will plunge in normal fashion, rising quickly after the gale has passed. If at sea and some way from land, a line of white on the horizon and a developing swell give a few minutes' warning. Warnings are given by radio from Marseille and Monaco, but these can also be seen on the internet and are increasingly accurate in their predictions. See pages 16–17 for transmission details.

The *tramontana* normally blows for at least three days but may last for a week or longer. It is frequent in the winter months, blowing for a third of the time and can reach Force 10 (50 knots) or more. In summer it is neither as strong nor as frequent.

West *vendaval*

A depression crossing Spain or southern France creates a strong southwest to west wind, the *vendaval* or *poniente*, which funnels through the Strait of Gibraltar and along the south coast of Spain. Though normally confined to the south and southeast coasts, it occasionally blows in the northeast of the area. It is usually short-lived and at its strongest from late autumn to early spring.

East *levante*

Encountered from Gibraltar to Valencia and beyond, the *levante*, sometimes called the *llevantade* when it blows at gale force, is caused by a depression located between the Islas Baleares and the North African coast. It is preceded by a heavy swell (*las tascas*), cold damp air, poor visibility and low cloud which forms first around the higher hills. Heavy and prolonged rainfall is more likely in spring and autumn than summer. A *levante* may last for three or four days.

South *sirocco*

The hot wind from the south is created by a depression moving east along or just south of the North African coast. By the time this dry wind reaches Spain it can be very humid, with haze and cloud. If strong it carries dust, and should it rain when the cold front comes through, the water may be red or brown and the dust will set like cement. This wind is sometimes called the *leveche* in southeast Spain. It occurs most frequently in summer, seldom lasting more than one or two days.

Clouds

Cloud cover of between 4/8 and 5/8 in the winter months is about double the summer average of 2/8. The cloud is normally cumulus and high level. In strong winds with a southerly component, complete cloud cover can be expected.

Precipitation

Annual rainfall is moderate and decreases towards the north from about 760mm at Gibraltar to 560mm at Barcelona. The rainy season is predominantly in autumn and winter and in most areas the summer months are virtually dry. The Costa Brava, however, usually manages about 25mm of rain during each summer month, as does the Costa del Sol. Most of the rain falls in very heavy showers of 1–2 hours.

Thunderstorms

Thunderstorms are most frequent in the autumn at up to four or five each month, and can be accompanied by hail.

Water spouts

Water spouts occur in the Strait of Gibraltar in winter and spring, usually associated with thunderstorms.

Snow

Snow at sea level is very rare but it falls and remains on the higher mountain ranges inland. Snow on the Sierra Nevada is particularly noticeable from the sea. This can cause strong catabatic winds along parts of the Costa del Sol in winter and early in the season.

Visibility

Fog occurs about four days a month in summer along the Costa de Sol but elsewhere is very rare. Occasionally, when the wind is a very light easterly and humidity high, a very thick fog can descend around 0900 and may not lift before around 1400. This is particularly a problem between Gibraltar and Estepona. Sometimes dust carried by the southerly *sirocco* reduces visibility and industrial areas such as Valencia and Barcelona produce haze.

Temperature

Winter temperatures at Gibraltar average 10–15°C, rising steadily after March to average 20–29°C in July and August. Afternoon (maximum) temperatures may reach 30–33°C in these months. At Barcelona, summer temperatures are much the same as at Gibraltar but winter temperatures are lower, 6–13°C, as they are further west along the Costa del Sol.

Humidity

The relative humidity is moderate at around 60% to 80%. With winds from the west, northwest or north, low humidity can be expected; with winds off the sea, high humidity is normal. The relative humidity increases throughout the night and falls by day.

Local variations

Towards the E end of the Costa del Sol, the common winds blow between northwest and northeast. Gales may be experienced for 10% of the time during the winter, dropping to 2% in July and August, sometimes arriving with little warning and rapidly building to gale force.

THE SEA

Currents

There is a constant E-going surface current of one to two knots, passing in to the Mediterranean through the Strait of Gibraltar between the Costa del Sol and the African coast to replace water lost by evaporation. Northeast of Cabo de Gata up to the border with France, a significant inshore counter-eddy runs roughly SSW at one to 1½ knots. The shape of the coast produces variations in both direction and strength, especially around promontories.

It should be noted that prolonged west winds increase the E-going current, whilst E – *levante* – winds will reverse the surface current – often creating steep seas.

Tides

Tides should be taken into account at the west end of the Costa del Sol and are noted in the introduction to that section. From Alicante to the border with France, the tide is hardly appreciable.

Swell

Strong winds – sometimes in a different part of the Mediterranean basin and from a different direction to local winds, can set up a large confused swell.

Swell has a nasty capability of going round corners and getting into *calas*.

Internet forecasts are now helpful in predicting swell height and direction as well as information on wind patterns (see page 17).

Scouring and silting

Many harbours and anchorages are located in sandy areas where depths can change dramatically in the course of a storm or a season. Dredging is a common feature but there is no certainty that depths will be maintained. Charts and drawings give no sure guide. When approaching or entering such areas, it is of great importance to sound carefully and to act on the information received.

Sea temperature

Sea temperatures in February are around 14°C on the Costa del Sol and 12°C on the Costa Brava. In summer, along the Costa Blanca it can rise to 20°C. Winds from the south and east tend to raise the temperature and those from the west and north to lower them.

RADIO AND WEATHER FORECASTS

Details of coast radio stations, weather forecasts, weatherfax (radio facsimile) Navtex and Inmarsat-C coverage follow. See individual harbour details for port and marina radio information. All times quoted are in UT (universal time) unless otherwise specified. France Inter on LW, 163kHz, France Info on MW and Monaco 3AC on 4363kHz all use local time. Details of frequencies, channel and times are to be found in ALRS Vol 3 (1), RYA Booklet G5 and on the internet.

Coast radio stations

VHF/MF

Coast radio stations are controlled from Málaga or Valencia – see diagram below. Full details will be found in the Admiralty *List of Radio Signals Vol 1 Part 1 (NP281/1)*.

On receipt of traffic, Spanish coast radio stations will call vessels once on Ch 16; after that the vessel's call sign will be included in scheduled MF traffic lists.

Weather forecasts

Marine VHF and MF

Inshore waters and sea area forecasts are broadcast in Spanish and English on marine VHF all round Mediterranean Spain and the Balearic Islands. There are also broadcasts of inshore waters forecasts and actual weather in Spanish only. For local area FM broadcast near Gibraltar see page 29 for details of BFBS and Gibraltar BC.

Sea area forecasts can also be heard in English and Spanish on MF radio.

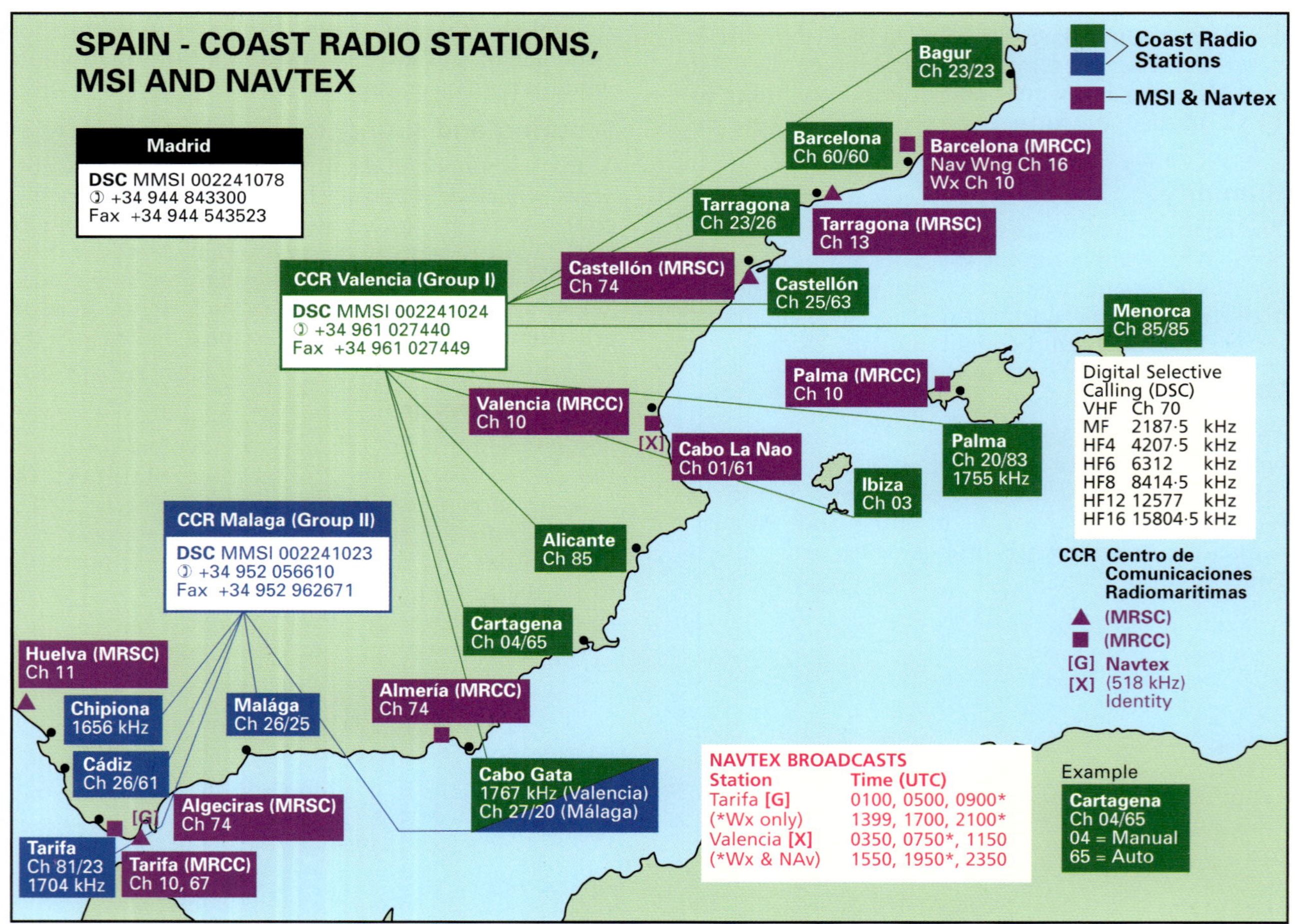

Sea area and inshore waters forecasts are broadcast in Spanish as follows

MRCC Málaga	*VHF Ch*	*Times UT*
Cádiz	26	
Tarifa	81	0833, 2003
Málaga	26	
Cabo Gata	27	
MRCC Valencia	*VHF Ch*	*Times UT*
Cartagena	4	
Alicante	85	
Cabo La Nao	1	
Castellón	26	
Tarragona	23	0910, 2110
Barcelona	60	
Bagur	23	
Menorca	85	
Palma	20	
Ibiza	3	

Inshore waters forecasts and reports of actual weather are broadcast in English and Spanish as follows

MRCC	*VHF Ch*	*Time UT*
CZCS Tarifa	10, 67	H2+15
CLCS Algeciras	74	0315, 0515, 0715, 1115, 1515, 1915, 2315
CRCS Almería	74	H1+15
CRCS Barcelona	10	0700, 1100, 1600, 2100
CRCS Valencia	10, 67	H2+15
MRSC Castellón	74	0900, 1400, 1900
CLCS Tarragona	13	0630, 1030, 1630, 2130
CRCS Palma	10	0635, 0935, 1435, 2035

(+1hr in winter) H1 = odd hours. H2 = even hours

Sea area forecasts are broadcast in English and Spanish as follows

Station	*kHz*	*Time UT*
Chipiona	1656kHz	0733, 1233, 1933
Tarifa	1704kHz	0733, 1233, 1933
Cabo de Gata	1767kHz	0750, 1303, 1950
Palma	1755kHz	0750, 1303, 1950

Non-radio weather forecasts

A recorded marine forecast in Spanish is available by ✆ +34 906 36 53 71. The 'High Seas' bulletin includes the Islas Baleares.

Spanish television shows a useful synoptic chart with its land weather forecast every evening after the news at approximately 2120 weekdays, 1520 Saturday and 2020 Sunday. Most national and local newspapers also carry some form of forecast.

Nearly all marinas and yacht harbours display a synoptic chart and forecast, generally updated daily (though often posted rather too late to be of use).

Internet forecasts

There is now an enormous wealth of weather information available via the internet. Internet forecasts are, in layman's terms, either purely computer modelled, or they are interpreted by specialists who include local factors within the predictions. It is not always easy to know which forecasts are which, so it is a good idea to monitor several weather websites. During stable weather patterns the various sites will tend to give similar predictions. In less stable conditions the sites may vary widely in what they predict. This alone can be a very useful indicator. Crucially important to comfortable cruising, websites also provide expected swell and wave heights and directions.

GRIB coded forecasts

This service enables arrow diagram forecasts for up to five days ahead, and other information to be obtained in email form (or by marine HF and HAM radio). The data is highly compressed so that a great deal of information can be acquired quickly, even using a mobile phone connected to a laptop. See websites below. There is no charge for this service.

GRIB files do not incorporate any interpretation for coastal areas, but up to seven days of weather charts for your selected region are quick and easy to access using free downloads from www.grib.us

Other useful websites

Spanish websites are more likely to incorporate local knowledge within their weather predictions and may be more accurate for coastal sailing:

www.aemet.es/en/eltiempo/prediccion/maritima or
www.eltiempo.es/

French sites are also a very useful reference:
http://marine.meteofrance.com/ or
http://marine.meteoconsult.fr/

Other useful sites may include:
www.passageweather.com/

Internet access

Increasingly ubiquitous smartphones and other mobile devices are making internet access on board quicker and easier than ever before. Data roaming charges can be excessive, depending on your contract. However, these charges are due to be abolished by 2018. The use of a local SIM card for both data and voice may be a more affordable option. If you don't have a smartphone or tablet it is possible to use a laptop linked to a 'dongle', sometimes with an extension lead to allow the dongle to be suspended under the boom to gain better reception. Many marinas, harbours and anchorages now have WiFi available. A booster may improve WiFi reception on board. Internet access is also possible, with the appropriate modem, via Marine SSB or HF radio.

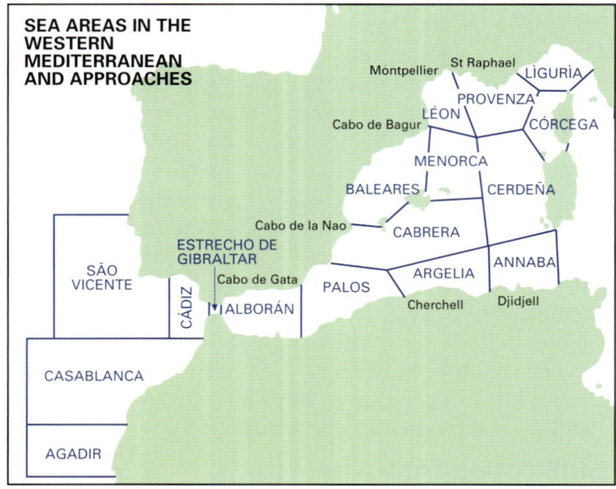

The Spanish and French use a common set of sea areas and use the same names although spelling and pronunciation differ at times.

The French names for the Mediterranean Sea areas are Alboran, Palos, Alger, Cabrera, Baléares, Minorque, Lion, Provence, Ligure, Corse, Sardaigne, and Annaba.

In the approaches to the Mediterranean the French names are identical to the Spanish.

Rescue and emergency services

In addition to VHF Ch 16 (MAYDAY or PAN PAN as appropriate) the marine emergency services can be contacted by telephone at all times on ✆ 900 202 202.

The National Centre for Sea Rescue is based in Madrid but has a string of communications towers. On the spot responsibility for co-ordinating rescues lies with the Capitanías Marítimas with support from the Spanish Navy, customs, guardia civil etc. Lifeboats are stationed at some of the larger harbours but the majority do not appear to be all-weather boats.

The other emergency services can be contacted by dialling 112 for the operator and asking for policía (police), bomberos (fire service) or Cruz Roja (Red Cross). Alternatively the police can be contacted direct on 092 or *Guardia Civil* on 062.

Radio fax and teleprinter

Northwood (RN) broadcasts a full set of UK Met Office charts out to five days ahead on 2618·5, 4610, 8040 and 11086·5kHz. (Schedule at 0236, surface analysis at three hourly intervals from 0300 to 2100 and 2300.) Deutscher Wetterdienst (DWD) broadcasts German weather charts on 3855, 7880 and 13882·5kHz. (Schedule at 1111, surface analysis at 0430, 1050, 1600, 2200.)

DWD broadcasts forecasts using RTTY on 4583, 7646 and 10001.8kHz (in English at 0415 and 1610), 11039 and 14467·3kHz (in German at 0535). Note that the 4583 and 14467·3kHz may not be useable in the Mediterranean. The most useful products are forecasts up to five days ahead at 12 hourly intervals and up to two days ahead at six hour intervals. Alternatively, a dedicated receiver 'Weatherman' will record automatically: see www.nasamarine.com.

UK Marine Mobile Net

The Net covering the Eastern Atlantic and the Mediterranean, can be heard daily on 14303kHz USB at 0800 and 1800 UT. On Saturday morning the broadcast sometimes contains a longer period outlook. Forecasts will be a rehash of what the Net leader has gleaned from various sources. No licence is required if a receive-only HF radio is used.

Monaco 3AC

Monaco 3AC broadcasts on 8728 and 8806kHz USB at 0715 and 1830 in French and English. The texts are those broadcast by INMARSAT-C for the western part of METAREA III. Monaco also broadcasts on 4363kHz at 0903 and 1915 LT in French and English and at 1403 in French only. Texts are as the latest Toulon NAVTEX broadcast.

NAVTEX and INMARSAT-C

NAVTEX and INMARSAT-C are the primary GMDSS modes for transmission of all Marine Safety Information. Broadcast times for weather are as follows:

Transmitter	Times (UTC)
Tarifa – G (518kHz)	0900 and 2100
Cabo la Nao – X (Valencia) (518kHz)	0750 and 1950
La Garde – W (Toulon) (518kHz)	1140 and 2340
La Garde – S (Toulon) (490kHz)	0700 and 1900
INMARSAT-C METAREA III	1000 and 2200

I. ENTRANCE TO THE MEDITERRANEAN

STRAIT OF GIBRALTAR

Ports

Introduction

Around Gibraltar, weather usually conforms to the local area forecast, (unlike further E where local forecasting is notoriously difficult). There is almost always some wind in the Strait and can be expected to be either E (*levante*) or W (*poniente*). The E winds bring a large cloud which hangs over the W side of the rock, often for several days, producing high humidity and miserable conditions. On rare occasions, as low pressure and associated fronts move N from the Canaries in winter, strong SW

Alcaidesa Marina: a mile N of Gibraltar *Marina Alcaidesa*

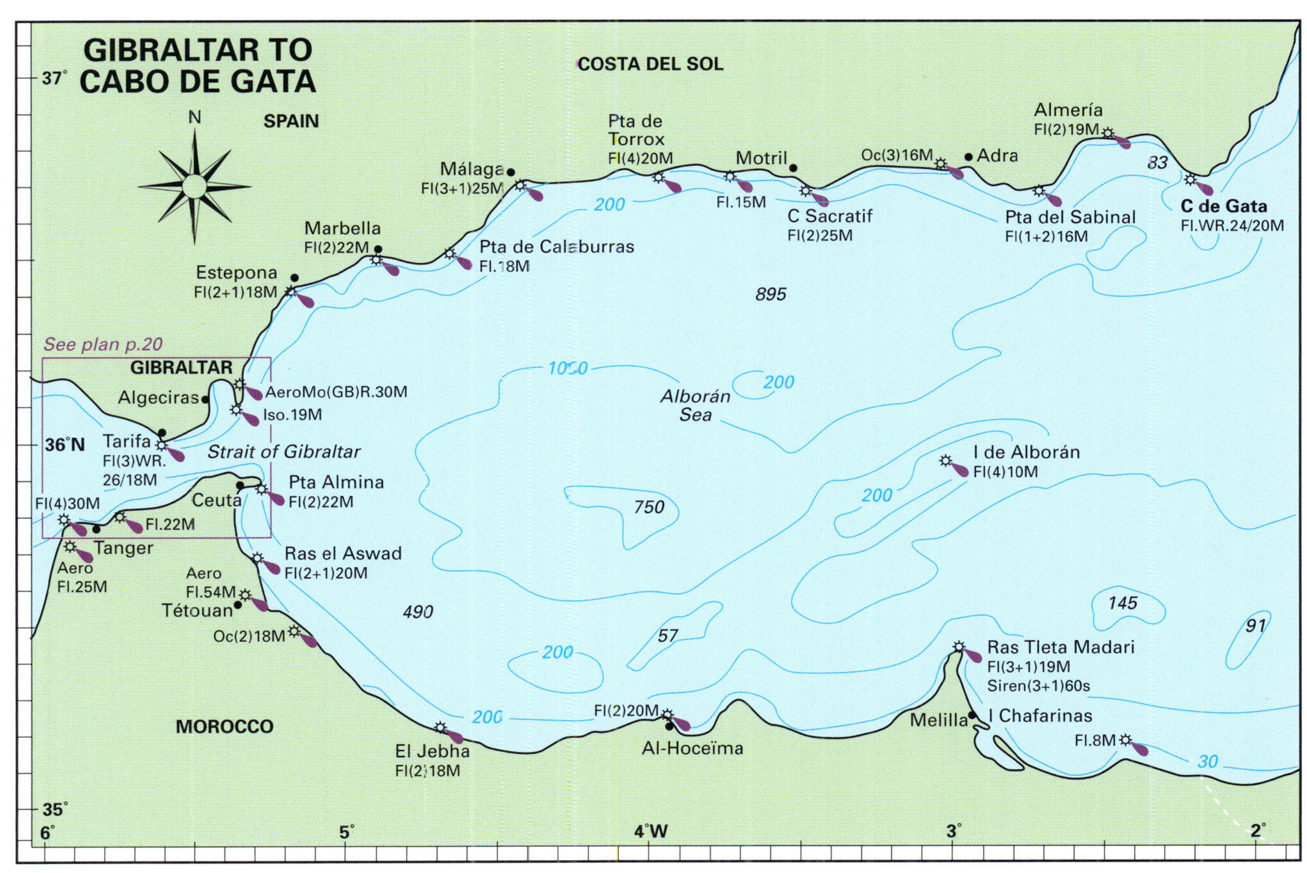

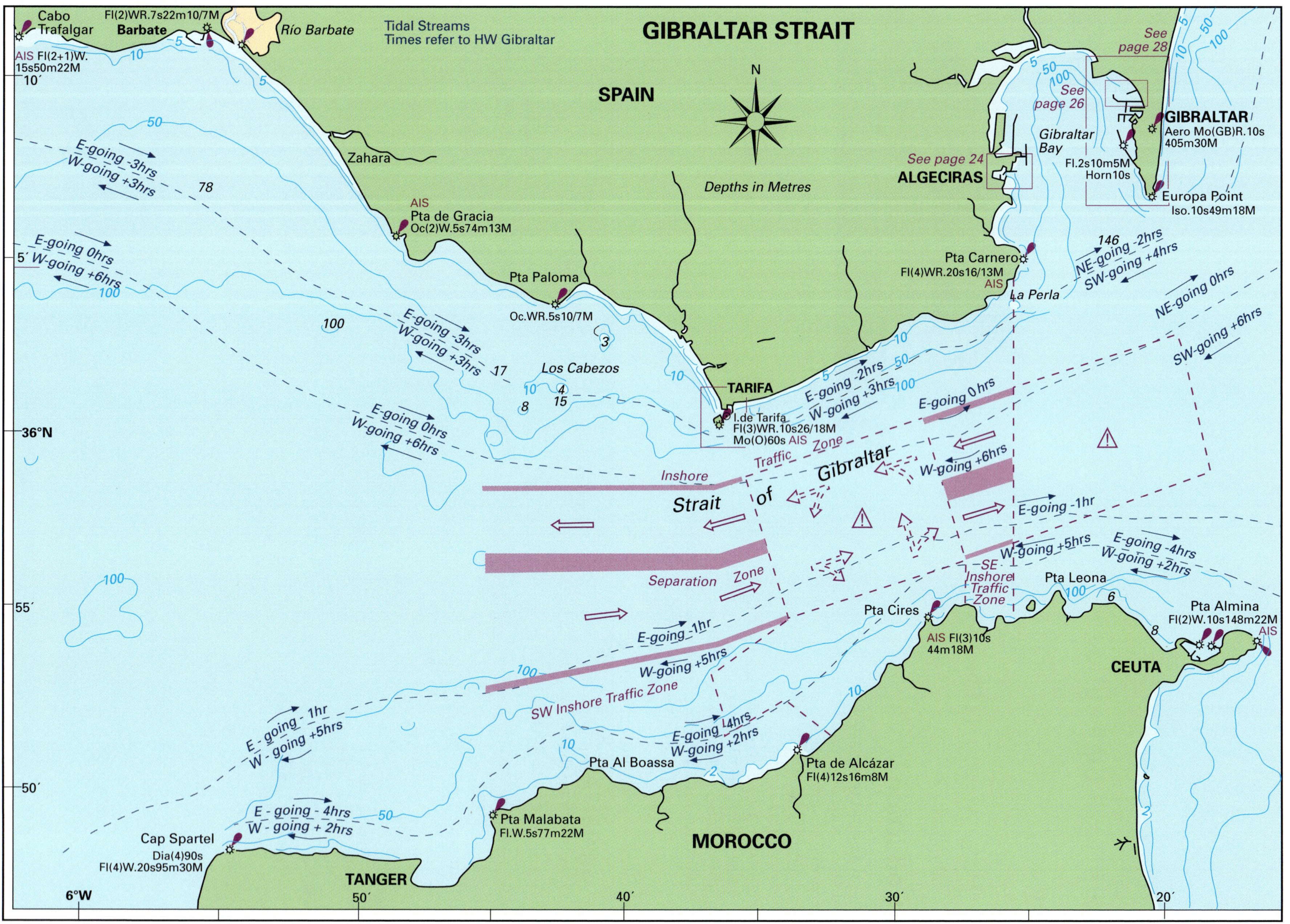
GIBRALTAR STRAIT
SPAIN
MOROCCO
Depths in Metres
Tidal Streams
Times refer to HW Gibraltar
GIBRALTAR
Aero Mo(GB)R.10s
405m30M
Europa Point
Iso.10s49m18M
Fl.2s10m5M
Horn10s
See page 28
See page 26
Gibraltar Bay
See page 24
ALGECIRAS
Pta Carnero
Fl(4)WR.20s16/13M
AIS
La Perla
TARIFA
I.de Tarifa
Fl(3)WR.10s26/18M
Mo(O)60s AIS
Pta Paloma
Oc.WR.5s10/7M
Los Cabezos
AIS
Pta de Gracia
Oc(2)W.5s74m13M
Zahara
Río Barbate
Barbate
Fl(2)WR.7s22m10/7M
Cabo Trafalgar
AIS Fl(2+1)W.
15s50m22M
Inshore Traffic Zone
Strait of Gibraltar
Separation Zone
SE Inshore Traffic Zone
SW Inshore Traffic Zone
Pta Almina
Fl(2)W.10s148m22M
AIS
CEUTA
Pta Leona
Pta Cires
AIS Fl(3)10s
44m18M
Pta de Alcázar
Fl(4)12s16m8M
Pta Al Boassa
Pta Malabata
Fl.W.5s77m22M
TANGER
Cap Spartel
Dia(4)90s
Fl(4)W.20s95m30M
E-going -3hrs
W-going +3hrs
E-going 0hrs
W-going +6hrs
NE-going 0hrs
SW-going +6hrs
NE-going -2hrs
SW-going +4hrs
E-going -2hrs
W-going +3hrs
E-going -1hr
W-going +5hrs
E-going -4hrs
W-going +2hrs
36°N
6°W
55´
50´
5´
10´
20´
30´
40´

Principal lights

Europe
Cabo Trafalgar Fl(2+1)15s49m22M
White conical tower and building 34m
Punta de Gracia (Punta Camarinal)
Oc(2)5s75m13M Masonry tower 20m
Punta Paloma Oc.WR.5s44m10/7M
010°-W-340°-R-010° (over Bajo de Los Cabezos)
White 4-sided tower 5m
Tarifa Fl(3)WR.10s41m26/18M
089°-R-113°-W-089° (over Bajo de Los Cabezos)
Racon Mo 'C'(–···)20M White tower 33m
Masonry structure 10m
Punta Carnero Fl(4)WR.20s42m16/13M
018°-W-325°-R-018° (Red sector covers La Perla and Las Bajas shoals) Round masonry tower and white building 19m
Europa Point, Gibraltar
Iso.10s49m19M 197°-vis-042°, 067°-vis-125°
Oc.R.10s19M and F.R.15M 042°-vis-067°
(Red sector covers La Perla and Las Bajas shoals)
Horn 20s White tower, red band 19m

Africa
Cabo Espartel Fl(4)20s95m30M
Yellow square stone tower 24m
Pta Malabata Fl.5s76m22M
White square tower on white dwelling 18m
Ksar es Srhir Fl(4)12s16m8M
Column on metal framework tower 11m
Pta Cires Fl(3)10s44m18M Brown truncated conical tower 3m
Pta Almina Fl(2)10s148m22M
White tower and building 16m

winds bring rain and squally conditions. These winds often mean the airport is closed. The general summer wind pattern is light overnight, rising to Force 3 or 4 during the afternoon and going down at sunset.

Traffic Separation Zone

There is a Traffic Separation Zone in the Strait of Gibraltar between 5°25'·5W and 5°45'W – see plan on page 20. The Inshore Traffic Zone to the north is nowhere less than 1·7M wide (off the Isla de Tarifa) and generally more than 2M. Tarifa Traffic monitors VHF Ch 16 and 10 and vessels are advised to maintain a listening watch whilst in the area. Weather and visibility information for an area including the Traffic Separation Zone is broadcast on VHF Ch 10 and 67.

Transiting the Strait of Gibraltar

Many yachts use Gibraltar as their departure point for trips to the east, west or south. Many elements combine to produce a complex system of tides and current in the Strait, an appreciation of which will greatly help yachtsman, especially when heading west as it is possible to spend many fruitless hours trying to make a passage through the Strait. The paragraphs below are included to assist the yachtsman transiting the Strait.

Eight miles separate Europe from Africa at its narrowest point in the Strait. The water at the western end of the 30 mile stretch is some 2–3m higher than at the eastern end, thus causing a constant surface flow into the Mediterranean. This is partially due to evaporation in the Mediterranean, which is three times faster than the rate at which the combined waters from rivers flow into it; and the fact that the Atlantic is tidal with a predominantly westerly swell, whereas the land-locked Mediterranean, is virtually non tidal. This produces a standing E-going surface current of between one and two knots.

Differences in salinity between the Atlantic and the Mediterranean force the heavier water down, causing a sub surface current in the opposite direction.

Wind also creates a surface current, depending whether it is E (*levante*) or W (*poniente*), which confuses the equation still further. Easterlies rarely reach more than F8, but often blow for several days. The weather systems crossing the Atlantic from the west can be stronger, but only usually last a day or so, as the system rolls from the Canaries up the Moroccan coast and through the Straits. Very strong winds have been noticeably scarce over the past few years, with gale centres usually passing well to the north of Iberia and over the French coast. This shift apparently due to the position of the jet stream.

Then there are the tides, which are well documented in Admiralty tide tables. At the eastern end of the Strait the range is only half a metre and negligible once a few miles into the Mediterranean, whereas at Tanger, Morocco, the spring range is 3m. Barometric pressure differences also affect the height of water.

On the N side of the Western Strait is Tarifa. Winds in excess of 30 knots are said to blow there for 300 days of the year, whereas at the same time, winds at the eastern end may be negligible, resulting in conditions at one end of the Strait being very different from those at the other.

Currents also vary in different parts of the Strait, and even run in opposite directions at the same time, as shown on the tidal charts. From these conflicting and confusing parameters some guidelines can be extracted.

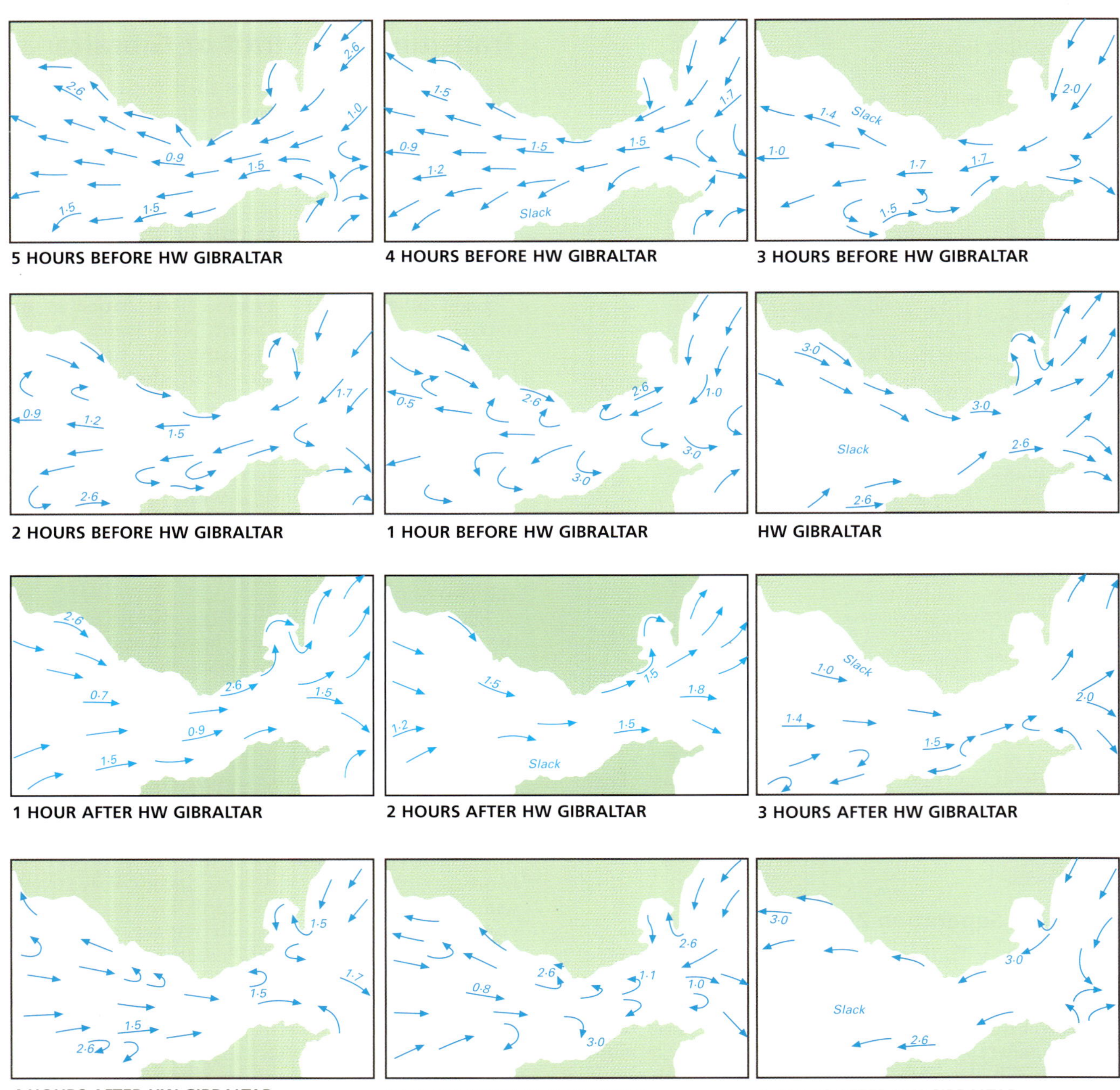

Eastbound vessels

For yachts entering the straits from the W there is no real problem going eastwards, unless there is a strong easterly wind, in which case the passage will be rough, especially around Tarifa, where winds often reach 40 knots. If strong winds are forecast, stay in Tanger or Barbate until it drops, or anchor in the lee of Tarifa if strong E winds are encountered once on passage.

During periods of light easterly winds, sea mist or fog may be persistent in the Strait, especially during the morning.

The best time to depart for the trip east is soon after LW. From Tanger, keeping close inshore, the light and increasing E-going current off Punta Malabata will be useful. If going to Gibraltar, most vessels cross to Tarifa from Punta Malabata, or from Punta Ciris, 12 miles further E.

Westbound vessels

In strong westerlies it is almost impossible to make headway W, due to the combined E-going current that can, with unfavourable tide, reach six knots or more, with heavy steep swell and overfalls off Ceuta Point, Tarifa and Punta Malabata.

In good conditions, to make use of the favourable current, set off from Gibraltar two hours after HW. Keeping close inshore, a foul current of around a knot will be experienced off Punta Carnero.

A favourable W-going current four hours after HW will assist passage during springs, although this is weak and E-going at neaps.

Crossing from Tarifa to Tanger it is usually wise to use the engine to make a fast passage, to combat the increasing E-going current, or anchor in the sheltered W side of Tarifa and wait for the next favourable tide, around LW, to make the crossing. It is possible, using the engine, to make a fast passage from Gibraltar without encountering heavy adverse currents.

From Ceuta, the timing is similar: set off two hours after HW, keeping close inshore to make use of the counter current.

Gibraltar to Ceuta

Crossing from N to S and vice versa can normally be undertaken at any state of tide, since winds through the Strait are predominantly E or W, although it is important to leave enough sea room to counter the tide and currents.

Remember, in general, a combined current of 1–2 knots is usually E-going, in addition to tidal effects. Beware of rough over-falls and stronger currents around Europa Point and Ceuta Point. Entering Ceuta harbour, this is particularly noticeable one mile NE, off the entrance.

The currents in the Strait are still full of surprises and for sailing purists who do not want a motor-assisted transit, this can be very challenging.

1. ALGECIRAS

36°07'·05N 5°25'·64W

Tides
Standard port Gibraltar

Mean time differences
HW –0010; LW –0010

Heights in metres

MHWS	MHWN	MLWN	MLWS
1·1	0·9	0·4	0·2

Or refer to EasyTide at www.ukho.gov.uk

Charts	Approach	Harbour
UKHO	91, 773, 142, 3578, 1448	1455
Imray	C19, C50	
Spanish	44C, 45A, 105, 445, 445A	4451

Lights

Commercial Harbour

NE breakwater Fl.R.5s11m7M Red round tower 6m
Work is still going on re-filling SE of Isla Verde and there are now two breakwaters that have nearly joined just N of the yacht basin. There are lights at the ends of the breakwaters but yachts should keep well clear of the on-going work.

Dársena del Saladillo (Marina Inner Jetty)

South breakwater Fl(4)R.11s4m1M
Red ■ on red round post 2m

Night entry
Not advised, since all three marinas in the Dársena del Saladillo are private and anchoring is forbidden.

Coast radio station
Algeciras Digital Selective Calling
MMSI 002241001 VHF Ch 16, 74
Weather bulletins and navigational warnings
Weather bulletins in Spanish and English VHF Ch 74 at 0315, 0515, 0715, 1115, 1515, 1915, 2315 UT
Navigational warnings in Spanish and English: on request

Port communications
Port Authority VHF Ch 08, 13, 16, 68, 74 (call *Algeciras Tráfico*) ✆ +34 956 585400/585431
comercial@apba.es www.apba.es
Real Club Náutico de Algeciras VHF Ch 09, 16

The Dársena del Saladillo at Algeciras, seen from east-southeast.
Although the Real Club Náutico de Algeciras, the Club Náutico Saladillo and the Club Deportivo El Pargo all have pontoons in the harbour, none currently accept visitors

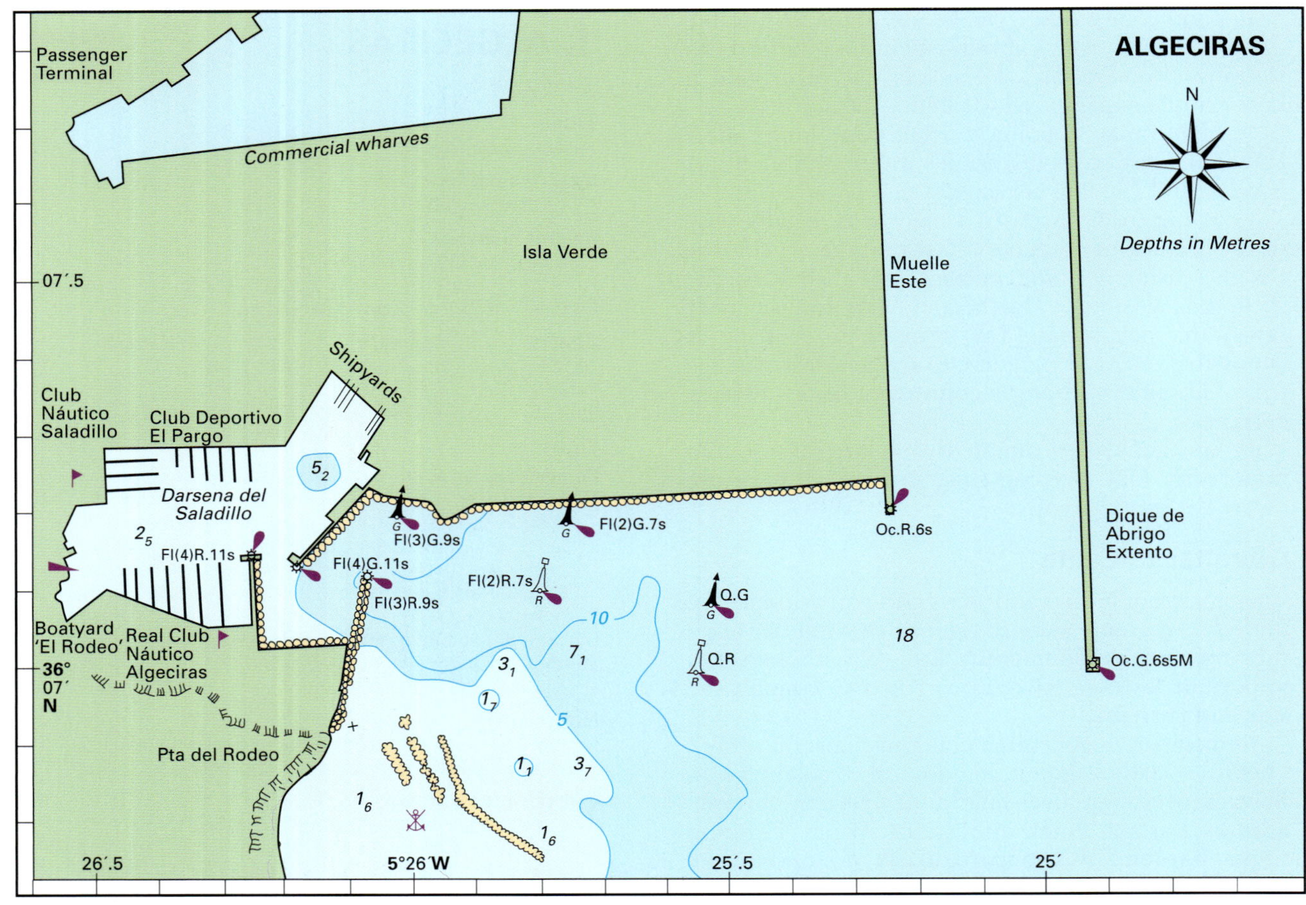

Major commercial harbour, with three private marinas in a separate basin

Algeciras is primarily an industrial and ferry port, through which pass many of the guest-workers returning to Africa with roof racks bending under their loads.

Yachts have their own basin – the Dársena del Saladillo – south of the main harbour, where three separate clubs run three separate marinas. Sadly none welcome visiting yachts (See *Berthing*). The following approach and entrance instructions are given for the Dársena del Saladillo in the hope that this situation may one day change.

Approach

The approaches to Algeciras are extremely busy with commercial traffic of all sizes. In particular, a sharp watch needs to be kept for the many high-speed ferries, including hydrofoils, which run between Algeciras and Morocco. These are notorious for maintaining their course and speed at all times.

Coming from the west, there are dangers up to 1M offshore between Punta de Cala Arenas and Punta Carnero. On rounding this headland the city and harbour will be seen some 3M to the north behind a mile-long breakwater terminating with a light. Various ledges run out from the headlands between Punta Carnero and the entrance to the Dársena del Saladillo (also lit).

If approaching from Gibraltar or other points east, the entrance to the Dársena del Saladillo should be easily seen south of the oil tanks on the commercial quay and it can be approached directly.

If approaching from the south, possibly from Ceuta or elsewhere in Morocco, head for a point 1M E of La Perla, then follow a course of 346° for 3·4M leading to the approaches to the Dársena del Saladillo, passing close to a spherical yellow ODAS buoy off Punta Calero en route.

Yachts can safely cut inside the east cardinal buoy placed nearly a mile offshore, though an offing of at least 0·5M should be maintained. Further ledges lie both north and south of the entrance, and the three buoys marking the approach should under no circumstances be ignored. Major infilling work is taking place to the north of the Saladillo entrance, outside of which a new breakwater is under construction, marked by additional east cardinal light buoys. Keep well clear.

Entrance

The dogleg entrance to the Dársena del Saladillo has been very well designed, such that when visited in a 30 knot easterly wind no swell at all found its way inside the entrance. As noted above, three buoys mark the final approach, after which the entrance itself is straightforward.

Berthing

As stated above none of the three marinas in the Dársena del Saladillo accept visitors. Taken clockwise on entry these are the Real Club Náutico de Algeciras, which previously had premises in the main harbour, the Club Náutico Saladillo and the Club Deportivo El Pargo. The first (southern) marina is also the largest by a considerable margin, and would undoubtedly be the best one to try in an emergency. It is also the club where some English is most likely to be spoken, and visitors are welcome to dine in the Real Club Náutico's restaurant.

Facilities

Fuel at the Real Club Náutico marina. End of the breakwater which forms its eastern limit.

Repairs - Astilleros y Varaderos 'El Rodeo'. On the west side of the basin. ✆ +34 956 600511

Chandelry - Náutica Iberia.

Charts - Spanish charts may be obtained either from SUISCA SL ✆ +34 902 220007, admiraltycharts@suiscasl.com or in the Centro Blas Infante; or from Valnáutica SL, Avenida 28 de Febrero 33 ✆ +34 956 570677 at .

Shops, banks, restaurants in the city, but at some distance.

Trains and buses in the town.

2. MARINA ALCAIDESA (LA LÍNEA)

36°09'N 5°22'W

Charts

UKHO	1455
Imray	C19, C50
Spanish	4451

Lights

Dique de Abrigo head Fl.G.5s8m5M
Green ▲ on green post concrete base 3m

Puerto Chico Jetty Muelle de San Felipe south head
Fl.R.5s Red ■ on red round column 3m

Puerto Deportivo de La Alcaidesa N Pier N head
Fl(2+1)R.14·5s5m1M
Red round column with green band 3m
S head Fl(2)R.7s5m1M Red tower 3m

Central Pier head Fl(3)G.9s5m1M
Green tower 2m

Dique de Capitania, Head Fl(2)G.7s5m3M Green post 3m

Note Three starboard hand buoys form an approach channel for the RoRo ferries.

Port communications

Puerto Deportivo Alcaidesa ✆ +34 956 021 660, rcorrales@alcaidesa.com
www.puertodeportivoalcaidesa.es

Club Maritimo Linense ✆ +34 956 176 506,

Alcaidesa Group ✆ +34 956 791 000
www.alcaidesa.com

Harbour charges Low

Vast and spacious marina in Gibraltar Bay

Marina Alcaidesa, in the NE corner of the Bay of Gibraltar, close to the Gibraltar airport runway has 625 moorings for vessels 8–50m. The Club Náutico

Marina Alcaidesa looking S *Marina Alcaidesa*

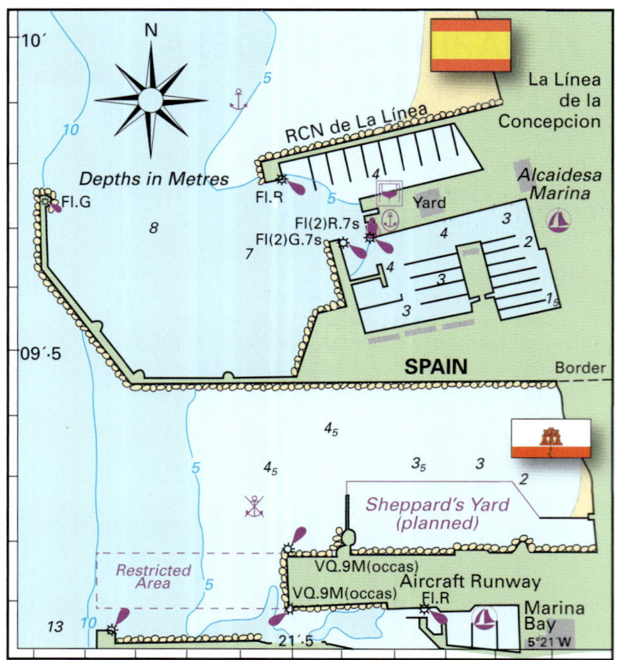

which has 11 pontoons at the N end of the marina, has no room for visitors. The club house and restaurant, however, are open to all (but expensive).

Prices for moorings and boatyard facilities are low in comparison with the local competition and offer excellent facilities including a 75-ton travel hoist. Wintering afloat is good here, and dry-stack facilities for boats up to 8m are available.

Access to Gibraltar is almost instantaneous by foot or bicycle but still a nightmare by car.

Hard standing to E of entrance *Steve Pickard*

Facilities

Water and 220v AC supply for all berths.

WiFi internet service as well as TV and telephone services.

Shipyard equipped with a crane, 75-ton travel-lift system, pressure jet cleaning, dry marina and showers.

Dry dock storage for boats from 6–8m on a rental basis for winter usage.

Repairs - 17,000m^2 hard standing.

Chandlers - Almost 8,000m2 of shops and services.

1,000 parking bays.

Closed circuit television system and security surveillance and control.

Toilets, showers and laundry.

Fuel immediately opposite entrance.

A large supermarket and an excellent produce market in the town.

Gibraltar is well within walking distance but note it is necessary to show one's passport to cross the border.

Anchorage in the approach

Anchoring seems possible in the area to the N of the Muelle de San Felipe.

Looking N to a potential anchorage *Steve Pickard*

3. GIBRALTAR

Tides

Gibraltar is a standard port.

Heights in metres

MHWS	*MHWN*	*MLWN*	*MLWS*
1·0	0·7	0·3	0·1

Charts	**Approach**	**Harbour**
UKHO	91, 142	145
	773, 3578	144
Spanish	445, 445A	4452
SHOM	7042	702
Imray	M11, C19	M11
	C50	C50

Lights

Approach

Tarifa 36°00'·1N 05°36'·6W Fl(3)WR.10s41m26/18M
White tower 33m 113°-W-089°-R-113°

Punta Carnero 36°04'·6N 05°25'·6W
Fl(4)WR.20s42m16/13M 018°-W-325°-R-018°
Round tower and white building 19m

Gibraltar Aeromarine 36°08'·6N 05°20'·6W
AeroMo(GB)R.l0s405m30M
Obscured on westerly bearings within 2M

Europa Point 36°06'·6N 05°20'·7W Iso.10s49m18M
White round tower, red band 19m

Harbour

South breakwater, north end (A head)
Fl.2s10m5M Horn 10s White tower 7m

Detached breakwater, south end (B head)
Q.R.9m5M Metal structure on concrete building 11m

Detached breakwater, north end (C head)
Q.G.10m5M Metal structure on concrete building 11m

North breakwater, southwest arm (D head)
Q.R.18m5M Black 8-sided tower 17m

Port communications

Gibraltar Port Control VHF Ch 16, 6, 12, 13, 14 (24 hours)

Lloyds radio VHF Ch 8, 12, 14, 16 (24 hours)

Queens Harbourmaster VHF Ch 8 (0800–1600 Monday to Friday)
All marinas VHF Ch 71 (0830–2030, later in summer)

GIBRALTAR MARINAS USE VHF 71 CALLING WORKING VHF 68 or 69

Port Captain ☏ +350 200 77254

Port Operations Room ☏ +350 200 78134/ 200 77004

Queensway Quay ☏ +350 200 44700, qqmarina@gbnet.gi

Marina Bay Office ☏ +350 200 73300, pieroffice@marinabay.gi
www.marinabay.gi

Ocean Village ☏ +350 200 40048 info@oceanvillage.gi
www.oceanvillage.gi

Sheppards Marina Repair facilities
☏ +350 200 76895
Chandlery ☏ +350 200 77183

Introduction

Gateway to the Mediterranean

Gibraltar: a tiny self-ruled British Colony and Sovereign territory of 30,000 nationals with its own government. Gibraltar has a substantial port with dry docking facilities and two marinas.

Its location at the tip of the Iberian peninsula and its predominantly English speaking population, make it invaluable to British yachtsmen. It has an airport with daily flights to different destinations in the UK, duty free fuel and extensive repair facilities. Since Sheppards relocated, there is no longer a travel hoist available, but a 75-ton hoist is located in the nearby Alcaidesa Marina less than a mile from Gibraltar.

There are several large supermarkets, including Morrisons, Coviran and Eroski making it an ideal stop for supplies.

Gibraltar: Rounding Europa point. Note the mosque behind the light
Graham Hutt

LA LINEA DE LA CONCEPCION
SPAIN
Shipyard
Q(3)G.9s3M
Q.G.3M
Q.G.3M
Fl(5)Y.20s
ODAS
See plan p.26
Fl.R
Fl.G
Marina Alcaidesa
Dique de Abrigo
Border
(80)
(R Lts)
Sheppards Yard (planned)
Runway
Airport
Entry Restricted
VQ
Aero Q.Y
F.R.5M
North Mole
Ferry Waterport Wharf
Marina Bay
(R Lts)
Ocean Village
Western Arm
Varyl Begg Estate
D. Head Q.R.5M
C. Head Q.G.5M
Aero Mo(GB)R.10s
405m30M
East Side Marina (planned)
Mid Harbour Marina
Numerous Masts
Detached Mole
2F.G(vert)
Cormorant Camber
Coal Is
2F.R(vert)
GIBRALTAR
Queensway Quay Marina
B. Head Q.R.5M
A. Head Fl.2s18M Horn 10s
Ordance Wharf
Hotel
Casino
South Mole
Gibraltar Bay
Catalan Bay
Mediterranean Sea
Rosia
Rosia Bay
Fl.R. 6s3M
Fl.G.8s5M
Aero Q.Y
Pasage Pt
Minaret PA
Europa Point
Europa Pt Iso.10s49m18M
Mackerel Bank
Q(3)10s
BYB
Q(9)15s
YBY
Q(6)+LFl.15s
YBY
Q(6)+LFl.15s
YB
Depths in Metres
N
0
0·5
1
Nautical Mile
36° 09′ N
10′
08′
07′
06′
5°23′W
22′
21′
20′

GIBRALTAR

Two yacht chandleries are operating: the main one being Sheppards – close to Ocean Village. Another operates from the Hire-U-Shop at Watergardens, nearby. If an item is not in stock, it can easily be ordered and, if the yacht is in transit, there is no duty to be paid.

Truly a major commercial port with good facilities. There are two marinas, both on the W side of the Rock, with others planned for the future.

There are other harbours apart from the commercial facilities. Cormorant Camber on Coaling Island is a marina for local vessels, as is Mid Harbour Marina, and a military base lies S of Queensway Quay. These are not accessible to visiting vessels. There is also a permanent barrier stretched across the military and S harbour area (between Queensway Quay and the S mole), which is only opened to allow vessels accessing the dockyard and military facilities adjoining Queensway Quay.

Sheppards has light haul out and engineering facilities on Coaling Island.

Approach

By day Gibraltar Rock, rising to 426m, is clearly visible except in fog, which is rare, though more frequent in summer. It is safe to enter the Bay of Gibraltar (Algeciras Bay) in almost any conditions but beware of squalls near the Rock once in the bay, particularly during strong easterlies, when strong downdraughts occur off the Rock. From the south and east, Europa Point is prominent, with its lighthouse at the end. A short distance further up the point, the minaret of a new mosque will be observed. Strong currents and overfalls occur around the tip of the point when wind is against tide. From the west, Pta Carnero light lies at the southwest entrance to the bay near an old whaling station. The coast is fringed with wrecks from all eras, many popular as dive sites – any vessel flying International Code Flag A (white with a blue swallowtail) should be given a generous clearance. Yachts must also give way to naval and commercial vessels at all times.

By night The west side of the Rock is well illuminated by the town; and to the east by the bright red lights marking the radio antennas on the north face; which is itself illuminated by spotlights. This can be confusing even in good visibility and makes lights difficult to identify. The most conspicuous are likely to be those on the south mole's A head and north mole's D head. To the south is the lighthouse on Europa point, easily seen from north-northeast clockwise to north-northwest, with a small red sector indicating the dangerous rocky shoreline to the west between Pta del Acebuche and Pta Carnero, which must be given a wide berth. If approaching in poor visibility beware the amount of traffic in the vicinity. Also if approaching from the east, Spanish fishermen occasionally lay nets at night from the detached mole to the S mole of Gibraltar harbour. Keep well clear if you see flashing lights and police activity as this is a disputed area.

Gibraltar weather forecasts

Radio Gibraltar (GBC) and British Forces Radio (BFBS) broadcast local weather forecasts (see table below).
The marinas post weather faxes on their notice boards daily.
See also www.bbc.co.uk/weather/coast/pressure/ and http://meteonet.nl/aktueel/brackall.htm for five day forecasts.
www.sto-p.com/atol and www.accuweather.com give complete hour-by-hour predictions over 16 hours and general forecasts up to 15 days.

Tarifa Radio broadcasts area weather on Channel 16 at regular intervals, in Spanish and English.

Gibraltar weather forecasts

LT	BFBS 1			BFBS2	Gibraltar BC		
	Mon-Fri	Sat	Sun	Mon-Fri	Mon-Fri	Sat	Sun
0530					X	X	
0630					X	X	X
0730					X	X	X
0745	X						
0845	X	X	X				
0945		X	X				
1005	X						
1030					X		
1200				X			
1202		X	X				
1230					X	X	X
1602			X				
1605	X						

Also storm warnings on receipt — 1438AM
93·5FM 89·4FM — 91·3FM
97·8FM 99·5FM — 92·6FM
Includes high and low water times — 100·5FM

Entry formalities

Whereas in the past all yachts calling at Gibraltar first proceeded to the customs and immigration offices opposite Marina Bay, this no longer applies. Proceed to any marina where paper formalities are part of the check-in process carried out by marina staff. See note below.

Gibraltar, like the UK, is not party to the Shengen agreement, which has different visa requirements to Spain. Check for latest information from the Gibraltar government website www.gibraltar.gov.gi or

Gibraltar: a monkey keeps watch over the detached mole and Queensway Quay *Graham Hutt*

One of Gibraltar's important assets is the colony of Barbary Macaques seen here at their base half way up the west side of the Rock. In the background is Jebel Moussa in Morocco, on the other side of the Strait where similar colonies of monkeys live *Graham Hutt*

contact the immigration department ✆ +350 200 46411, rgpimm@gibynex.gi.

Crew intending to remain ashore, or obtain work in Gibraltar should inform Immigration Authorities of their intention and supply an address.

Note The Gibraltar authorities request all vessels to notify them in advance of arrival and to fill out the online entry form. This saves time and paperwork on arrival and gives advance notice if non EU nationals requiring a passport stamp are on board. This can be done before departing for Gibraltar from last port of call.
www.hmcustoms.gov.gi/index.jsf
Go to 'vessel pre-arrival notifications' under electronic pre-declarations.

Anchoring in the Bay

Once a very convenient and safe anchorage for vessels accessing both Spain and Gibraltar, anchoring in the N end of the Bay is now prohibited.

The area to the N of the runway is a Gibraltar airport security zone, whilst vessels attempting to anchor in the area along the Alcaidesa Marina *dique* and to the west, will be moved on by the Spanish authorities.

Queensway Quay Marina

Location 36°08'·1N 05°21'·3W
Harbour dues Low

New, well equipped but bland

Closest to Europa Point, Queensway Quay has the advantage of being furthest from the airport with its noise and dust. Over the past few years the marina has undergone several major changes to overcome problems with the original design of 2005. The entrance is now at the NW end of the marina and many steps have been implemented to overcome the surging which formally damaged many yachts during storms. This has now been overcome and it is a safe and comfortable marina in all conditions experienced to date.

This is a small pleasant marina, very well run. It is surrounded by luxury apartments and there are several good restaurants and bars on the quay. Morrisons supermarket is within walking distance and is also served by bus routes 1 and 3. *Marineros* are on hand to assist with mooring. This marina should not be confused with the small boat marina in the Cormorant Camber, the new 400 berth small boat Mid Harbour Marina, almost complete, just behind it.

Entry formalities

Both marina and entry formalitles are now completed at the marina office.

Approach

The marina is approached through the main harbour via either of the two entrances, continuing towards the gap between Coaling Island and the new island which forms the W side of Queensway Quay. On passing through this gap the entrance lies immediately to starboard. The buildings overlooking the marina are floodlit.

Berthing

Visitors' berths are few and it is imperative that you call on VHF 71 in advance of entry. Moorings are stern or bows-to on long floating pontoons with

Queensway entrance looking west *Steve Pickard*

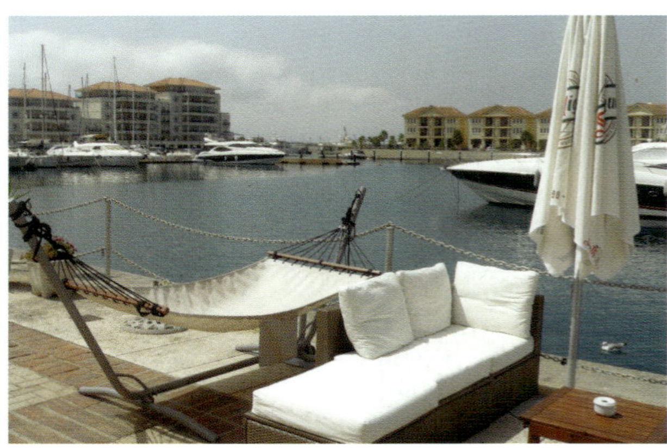

Queensway shoreside facilities *Steve Pickard*

Queensway Quay (centre) with Coaling Island (right) and the military base (left) *Graham Hutt*

lines tailed. A limited number of deep moorings in 3–7m are available on the S wall of the marina. Pontoons are very low.

Note 1 A boom is drawn across the marina entrance at night from 2000 in summer and 2100 in winter. Reopening at 0830. This is to prevent oil from the bay entering as well as acting as a security device. The marina office is located at the NW end of the jetty overlooking the seaward entrance.

Note 2 During strong *levante* conditions (E winds), very strong katabatic gusts blow from the Rock down into the marina and the S mole area. These often reach over 40 knots, but only last a few minutes.

Facilities

Water and 220v AC (metered) on pontoons.
TV, WiFi and phone lines available for a monthly fee.
Pontoon access via a locked gate with coded key pad. Security is excellent.
Parking within the marina complex.
Toilets and showers sited near the marina entrance and car park. These are closed at night, but a smaller facility is available out of hours using the same lock code as the pontoons.
Laundry (plus self service) and dry-cleaners are available in the marina near the car park.
Several excellent restaurants located along the main quay.
Repairs - none in the marina.

Ocean Village / Marina Bay

Location 36°08'·9N 05°21'·4W

Harbour dues Low

Sheppards old marina

Ocean Village and Marina Bay are under the same administration and management and are situated on either side of the main jetty running West to the marina office. Ocean Village took over the space vacated by Sheppards Marina on the S side of Marina Bay and is linked to the casino and recreational centre. It offers floating pontoons rather than lines tailed to the quay, and is closer to the shore facilities – bars and restaurants. There are around 300 berths available with a small number of

From the west, Marina Bay (left) and Ocean Village. The arrival of a large luxury cruise ship (*The Sunborn*), not pictured but now permanently berthed on the north side of the casino, reduces the number of yacht moorings available

Gibraltar: Ocean Village Marina. The arrival of the 150m *Sunborn* floating luxury hotel in February 2014, casting its long shadow in Marina Bay and Ocean Village Marina, has created some waves in Gibraltar and is a permanent fixture. Moored alongside the main jetty, it has reduced the number of yacht berths available and dwarfs the casino and luxury apartments behind *Graham Hutt*

places for super-yachts and mega yachts up to 150m. Despite all this turbulence Marina Bay, largely becausee of its iconic marina office, still retains that ocean crossroad ambience.

Plans for the marina have changed several times over the past five years and another change took place in February 2014 when the 150m floating hotel *Sunborn* arrived. With 200 luxury cabins, the ship is now permanently grounded alongside the main jetty. It will be used as a permanent luxury accommodation vessel, conference and events centre, with a second casino. There are also plans to re-orientate the floating pontoons to facilitate easier mooring with the prevailing winds on the Ocean Village side.

Marina Bay (Sheppards) marina office, a familiar crossroads *Steve Pickard*

Approach

The marina is 0·5M E of the N mole and is approached by rounding the N Mole's E head. At night a row of red lights at the end of the airport runway mark the N side of the channel. Note that yachts **may not move in the vicinity** while the runway lights are flashing, There is also a height restriction of 23m.

Berthing

Call the marina office on Ch 71 for berth allocation. Note: Depths in the marina are around 2·5m but some areas are less. Make sure the berthing master knows your draft to ensure the correct location in the marina. If staff are not around, berth alongside the office, towards the outer end of the main pier or find an empty mooring. Office open 24 hours. Berthing is Mediterranean-style – bow or stern-to with a buoy and lazy-line provided to the pontoon. Note Marina Bay/Ocean Village has a similar barrier to the Queensway marina but it is only deployed in the event of an oil spill.

Facilities at Ocean Village / Marina Bay

Water and 220v AC (metered) on pontoons.

WiFi, sat TV, and phone lines Available in Ocean Village.

Pontoon access is open.

Car and bike parking available close to the marina complex.

Toilets and showers sited near the marina office. Open 24 hours.

Laundry and dry-cleaners in the marina near the car park.

Several excellent restaurants located along the main quay of Marina Bay.

Shops/Provisioning Many shops nearby.

Repairs Marine Maintenance Ltd (Perkins & Yanmar agent) ☏ +350 200 78954, marine@MMgib.com www.MMgib.com

General facilities

Gas Available from New Harbours ☏ +350 200 7026 and the Shell office at the fuel berth and most filling stations.

Fuel Diesel (and water) is obtainable at the Shell or BP stations opposite Marina Bay. Shell ☏ +350 200 48232, BP ☏ +350 200 72261.

Provisions Morrisons supermarket is a short walk from Queensway Quay and not far from Marina Bay. It is on the No. 4 bus route.

Duty-free stores Albor Ltd ☏ +350 200 73283, at Marina Bay – which doubles as a newsagent, bookshop and cybercafé – where almost anything in almost any quantity for a yacht in transit can be purchased.

Charts Gibraltar Chart Agency Irish Town ☏ +350 200 78954, charts@mmgib.com

Chandlery Sheppards have the best range of chandlery currently and will order anything required. The shop is on the Ocean Village side a short walk from Marina Bay. ☏ +350 200 77183, www.sheppard.gi

Repair facilities Marine Maintenance Ltd. (Perkins and Yanmar agent) ☏ +350 200 78954,

marine@MMgib.com, www.MMgib.com
Sheppards (engineering) agents for Volvo and Mercury ✆ +350 200 76895 Including: at Coaling Island: light engineering, a small 5-ton lift-out facility. 30 ton facility at North Mole. Welding, mechanical services and electronic repairs. (Raymarine agents).
Medmarine Ltd ✆ +350 200 48889 (Yamaha agents)
Electro-Med (Queensway Quay) ✆ +350 200 77077, www.electro-med.com
Tempco Marine Engineering ✆ +350 200 74657 (refrigeration and radio repairs)

Engineers Sheppard's can handle light engineering, welding, engine servicing and repairs to most makes and are Volvo Penta agents. Also-Marine Maintenance Ltd ✆ +350 200 78954, fred@gibnet.gi (Perkins and Yanmar) at Manna Bay, and Medmarine Ltd ✆ +350 200 48888 (Yamaha) at Queensway Quay, Tempco Marine Engineering ✆ +350 200 74657, specialise in refrigeration and radio repairs Sheppard's workshops (as above) or ElectroMed ✆ +350 200 77077, mail@electro-med.com www.eletro-med.com at Queensway Quay, who can supply and repair equipment from most major manufacturers.

Sailmaker/sail repairs Sail makers, ✆ +350 200 41469 in South Pavilion Road, who also handle general canvaswork and upholstery. Alternatively Magnusson Sails ✆ +34 952 791241, about 35 miles away in Estepona, who may be willing to deliver/collect. Canvas work and sprayhood (but not true sailmaking) is also undertaken by ME Balloqui & Sons ✆ +350 200 78105, at 3941 City Mill Lane.

Rigging Sheppard's workshops, as above.

Liferaft servicing (and compass adjusters) GV Undery & Son ✆ +350 200 73107, compass@gibtelecom.net

Money The British pound sterling is legal tender, along with the Gibraltar pound and of equal value, but only in Gibraltar. Euros can also be used in most shops but not in the Post Office where only sterling is accepted. There are several Bureaux de Change agencies in Main Street. Visa, Switch, American Express, Mastercard etc, are accepted almost everywhere, though not the post office and some government offices. ATMs at Barclays Bank in Main Street and Morrisons supermarket.

Banks Gibraltar has well established banking services for both offshore and local customers with a full range of international banks, including several UK institutions, Banking hours are generally between 0900–1530 Monday to Friday.

Yacht brokerage & yacht registration Boat Shed Gibraltar, John and Lynda Alcantara. Excellent agency and service ✆ 00350 200 78885, *Mobile* 00350 5800999 / 0034 667 666753 boats@boatshedgibraltar.com

International travel Gibraltar airport is located close to the frontier for daily flights to the UK and onward connections ✆ +350 200 12345. Málaga airport is a little an over an hour's drive up the coast (A7 or AP7 *peaje* toll road) for more destinations. Taxis are expensive – about €100 or £75.
There is a very reasonably priced airport carpark opposite the airport, near the border which charges about 50p an hour short term and £4 for 24 hour parking.
La Línea bus station is just across the border.

Fuel berths to the N of Marina Bay office *Steve Pickard*

Locally

Gibraltar may be a tiny enclave, but it has many interesting sites to visit. The upper rock is home to monkeys – actually barbary macaques – made famous by the remark of Churchill that Gibraltar would cease to be British if the monkeys disappeared, this is unlikely as they now forage down as far as Main Street. Also at the upper rock is a spectacular cave network – St Michael's cave. Bones have been found here and in other close locations indicating civilisation has existed on the rock for many thousands of years. Views from the road running around the upper rock are really spectacular, taking in Morocco, Ceuta, Spain and on a good day, down to Tanger. A cable car is located near the Queens Hotel, close to the end of Main Street to transport visitors to the St Michael's cave area. Organised tours are available as well as taking a long walk to the different caves and artefacts. These are well preserved and presented. Information is available at the tourist office at the frontier with Spain and in Casemates Square. If you wish to do your own tour, just follow the signs to the 'Upper Rock.'

There are reputed to be over 40 miles of tunnels inside the Rock of Gibraltar which have facilitated some great acts of military skill and determination over hundreds of years. Much of the tunnel and cave system is open to the public and well worth visiting. Tunnels which are usually closed can also be visited by arrangement with the Gibraltar Heritage Trust (John Mackintosh Square).

The 18th century was a key time in the history of Gibraltar, which finally saw a treaty between Spain and Great Britain, giving the Rock to the British for as long as the people wanted to be British. Spain wishes to abandon the 300 year old treaty (of Utrecht) with claims that Gibraltar should revert back to Spanish rule. Very long queues to enter and exit the frontier with Spain are the consequences of the dispute although this only applies to cars. Pedestrians and bicycles pass freely.

Main Street is worth a visit with its bustling shops and bazaars and very English pubs. Although Gibraltar is VAT free, there are other taxes which make local purchases similar to prices in Spain – apart from tobacco and alcohol.

II. COSTA DEL SOL

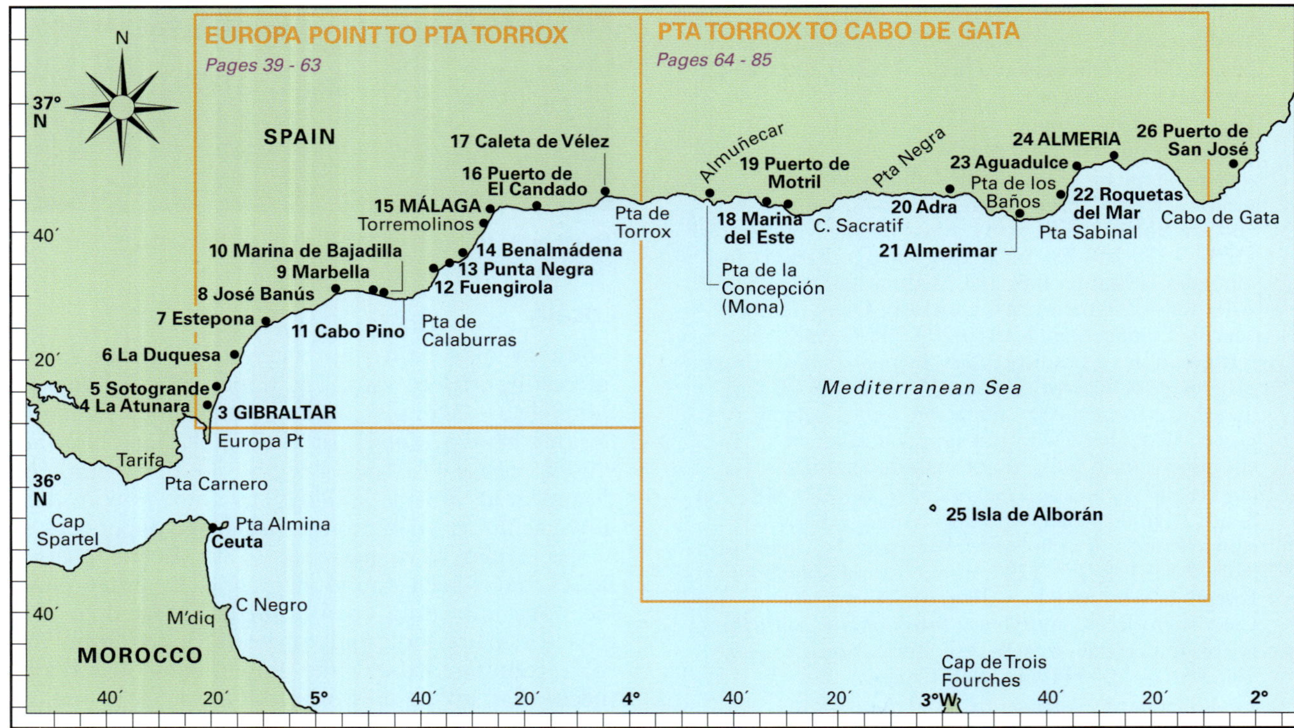

Costa del Sol planning guide and distances (See Appendix for waypoint list)

Miles		Harbours, anchorages & headlands
8M	3.	**Gibraltar** *(page 27)*
		Europa Point
	4.	**La Atunara** *(page 40)*
7M	⚓	*Río Guadiaro*
	5.	**Puerto Sotogrande** *(page 41)*
5M	⚓	*Cala Sardina*
		Punta de la Chullera
		Punta de la Salo de la Mora
	6.	**Puerto de la Duquesa** *(page 43)*
5M	⚓	*Fondeadero de la Sabinilla*
	7.	**Puerto de Estepona** *(page 45)*
11M	8.	**Puerto José Banús** *(page 47)*
4M	9.	**Puerto de Marbella** *(page 49)*
1M	10.	**Marina de Bajadilla** *(page 52)*
7M		Punta Calaburras
	11.	**Puerto Cabo Pino** *(page 53)*
9M	12.	**Puerto de Fuengirola** *(page 54)*
4M	13.	**Puerto de Punta Negra** *(page 56)*
12M	14.	**Puerto de Benalmádena** *(page 57)*
9M	15.	**Puerto de Málaga** *(page 59)*
4M	16.	**Puerto de El Candado** *(page 61)*
14M	⚓	*Fondeadero de Vélez-Málaga*
	17.	**Puerto Caleta de Vélez** *(page 62)*
17M		Punta de Torrox
	⚓	*Fondadero de Nerja*
	⚓	*Cala de la Miel*
	⚓	*Cala de los Cañuelos*
	⚓	*Ensenada de la Herradura*
	18.	**Marina del Este** *(page 66)*

Miles		Harbours, anchorages & headlands
10M	18.	**Marina del Este** *(page 66)*
		Punta de la Concepción
	⚓	*Ensenada de los Berengueles*
	⚓	*Punta San Cristóbal and Almuñecar*
	⚓	*Fondeadero de Almuñecar*
	⚓	*Ensenada de Belilla*
	⚓	*Ensenada de Robaina*
	⚓	*Surgidero de Salobreña*
	19.	**Puerto de Motril** *(page 68)*
26M	⚓	*Anchorage east of Cabo Sacratif*
		Cabo Sacratif
	⚓	*Cala Honda*
	⚓	*Anchorages to Castell de Ferro*
	⚓	*Fondeadero de Castell de Ferro*
	⚓	*Anchorages in La Rábita*
		Punta Negra
	20.	**Puerto de Adra** *(page 71)*
12M	⚓	*Balerma*
	⚓	*Punta de los Baños*
		Punta de los Baños
	⚓	*Ensenada de las Entinas*
	21.	**Puerto de Almerimar** *(page 75)*
14M	22.	**Puerto de Roquetas del Mar** *(page 77)*
4M	23.	**Puerto de Aguadulce** *(page 79)*
4M	24.	**Puerto de Almería** *(page 81)*
60M	⚓	*Cabo de Gata anchorages*
		Punta del Río
		Cabo de Gata
	25.	**Isla de Alborán** *(page 84)*

Introduction

The coastline between Gibraltar and 155M East to Cabo de Gata, is known as the Costa del Sol – The Sun Coast. An apt name in view of the average 300 days of sunshine per year. Not that it is hot all year round: although temperatures can occasionally reach over 40°C in August, ice can be found frequently on car windows in winter, even at sea level. The nearby Sierra Nevada mountain range is famous as a skiing resort in winter.

The three primary ports of the Costa del Sol are Gibraltar, Málaga and Almeria. A further 17 smaller harbours are covered.

Looking like an island from the sea, the Rock of Gibraltar, standing vertical at its N end at a height of 426m (1,400ft), is unmistakable from any direction. Impressive and visible from a great distance, Gibraltar is connected to the Spanish town of La Línea by a low lying sand spit – on which the airport has been built – linking the Atlantic to the Costa del Sol. Towards Marbella and inland is a spectacular mountainous region. Behind Málaga and towards the NE lies the Sierra Nevada mountain range, with tops covered in snow for much of the year; even into late summer.

From the port of Motril, can be seen an increasing number of huge polythene sheets covering fruit and vegetables farmed by (mostly) temporary workers and illegal immigrants from Morocco. These terraced mountainsides with plastic sheeting extend towards Capo de Gata and beyond.

Vacation and residential tourism has been a mainstay of Spanish income for many years. Currently, however, despite the upturn in the Spanish economy, many properties on the coastline are up for sale.

Some major tax reforms have adversely affected foreigners who are retreating home in droves. One tax that has been a particular problem for yachtsmen is the matriculation tax levied on all vehicles and yachts belonging to residents – which includes those considered 'fiscally resident' by virtue of their being in Spain for more than 183 days in any year. It is understandable, but has been a bone of contention for many who have lived here for years without having to worry about taxes.

Strait of Gibraltar 10M north of Europa point looking south from Point Carbonera and the golf course at Alcaidesa village *Graham Hutt*

Jimena de la Frontera, a typical country village nestling in the hills of Andalucia on the Costa del Sol *Graham Hutt*

Although Spain was one of the first countries to promote budget price package holidays for those seeking the sun on the cheap, contrary to what we often hear, the 'Costa' is far from spoiled. Some towns – like Torremolinos and Benidorm – cater primarily for foreign package tourists and are noisy and cheap. However, nestling amongst the nearby hills and mountains all along the coast inland are beautiful peaceful ancient villages offering hospitality. For those wishing to tour inland, excellent publications are available from the Spanish tourist information offices located in all towns. The larger towns of Seville, Granada and Cordoba are full of historic buildings left over from the Moors who ruled Spain for 800 years, from the 7th to 15th century, bringing culture, science and spectacular buildings and innovative architecture to the country. A network of inter-city coaches provide a cheap and reliable service around the country and trains are available in Málaga heading W to Fuengirola and N to Madrid, as well as to Valencia and Barcelona.

Sailing East from the Strait of Gibraltar into the Mediterranean, the turbulent seas soon give way to calmer and almost tideless waters. The Spanish coast can be approached to within 100m in most places.

Gales – harbours of refuge

In the event of onshore gales and heavy seas, Gibraltar, Málaga and Almería are the safest to enter. No attempt should be made to enter small harbours until the seas have subsided.

Formalities

As covered more fully in the introduction: all yachts on arrival are now required to complete a form giving information about the yacht, insurance and crew. The marina staff take care of all that is necessary from this form, which is in Spanish and English. All customs formalities are followed up if necessary. Usually nothing more is required, although, if you have a non-EU national aboard needing a visa, or if this is your port of entry from outside the EU, you may get a visit from the authorities.

Visits inland

Cordoba The cathedral was formerly the second largest mosque in the world before it was partially demolished and converted into a cathedral, following the re-conquering by Spanish forces in 1492. The cordwainers city of old, most people agree that it was one of the most spectacular cities in the world a millennium past. Its glory was largely destroyed when Queen Isabella had the mosque turned into a cathedral. Seeing its breathtaking beauty and grandeur today leaves one aghast at what must have been destroyed in the name of religion. The site of the oldest synagogue in Spain is also in Cordoba *Graham Hutt*

Granada Famous as far away as Japan and China, the Alhambra draws millions of visitors annually from all over the world. The Alhambra palace is another spectacular site built by the Arabs during their 800 year occupation. The water gardens are a feature used throughout the Arab ancient world bringing tranquility and life to the gardens. The peace of this place is not even broken by the hoards of visitors hurriedly rushing through, cameras in hand.
Be sure to book well in advance (available online).
Graham Hutt

The green countryside of Andalucia where semi-wild horses roam *Graham Hutt*

Seville, capital of Andalucia The city is full of ancient buildings and treasures dating from the Moorish 800 year occupation. Many have been restored to their former glory. Narrow streets keep the sun at bay in summer, when temperatures can reach 50°C. A three day visit will take in most of the sights, museums and evening shows and memories will remain with you for a lifetime *Graham Hutt*

Arcos town One of the many mountain top fortified towns built with palaces by the Moors *Graham Hutt*

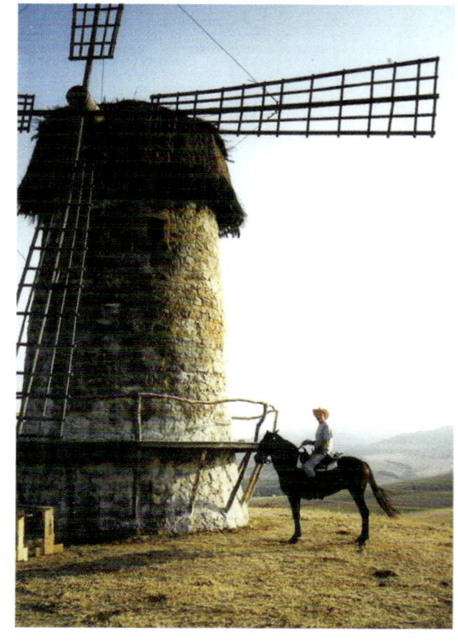

One of the famous windmills of Andalucia recalling the story of Don Quixote and Sancho Pancha *Graham Hutt*

Pilotage and navigation

Tides

The standard port is Gibraltar; secondary ports are Málaga and Almería. From Alicante to the northeast the tide is hardly appreciable. The figures are:

		Heights		*Mean*		
		MHWS	*MHWN*	*MLWS*	*MLWN*	*Level*
Gibraltar		1·0	0·7	0·3	0·1	0·50
Differences						
HW	LW					
Málaga						
+0005	–0005	–0·3	–0·1	0·0	+0·1	0·45
Almería						
+0010	–0010	–0·5	–0·3	0·0	+0·2	0·40

Currents

There is usually a standing E going current – around 2kns at La Línea (Mediterranean side) – decreasing to a knot or less towards Estepona. It is especially noticeable around headlands and is accounted for by evaporation of the Mediterranean sea. It is also very much influenced by the wind direction. Strong E winds, which sometimes blow for many days, will cancel and even reverse the surface current, often creating steep seas, whilst W winds will increase the flow E.

Soundings

In most harbours sand builds up at or near the entrance, particularly after a blow, and is periodically dredged. Reported depths are not necessarily accurate and care should be taken to sound whilst approaching and entering harbour.

Magnetic variation

Costa del Sol (Málaga) 01°24′W (2017) decreasing 11′ annually.

Restricted areas

Anchoring is not permitted in the following areas which should be avoided if possible:

- W and E of the Rock of Gibraltar
- The prolongation of the airstrip at Gibraltar
- An area 2M to E of Estepona
- An area 2M to SW of Málaga
- An area 1M to S of Málaga where passage is also forbidden.

Tunny nets

During the summer months, tunny nets may be set between February and October in the following localities:

- Off La Línea (Mediterranean side)
- Off the coast N of Fuerte de Santa Barbara
- Near Marbella
- Near Adra
- Off Punta del Sabinal
- To W of Cabo de Gata.

Fish havens

There are many fish havens along the coast. Most are simply areas where fishing is prohibited.

Fish farms, however can take many forms and can be either totally submerged with exclusion zone extremities marked by cardinal buoys, or are floating rafts easily spotted. Fish havens can generally be sailed over, whereas fish farms usually present surface obstacles and need to be given clearance.

Landings

Beaches are regularly patrolled by Guardia Civil officers who keep a good look out for drug smugglers and people-traffickers.

Note that many beaches along the coast have buoys stretched parallel to the shoreline in summer to protect bathers. It is illegal to anchor or sail inside these buoys with any vessel, including jet-skis. The buoys are spaced evenly and usually coloured yellow, extending around 50m from the beach, but further out if waters are shallow. Gaps in the buoyage enable jet-skiers and dinghies to transit in and out of the restricted zones.

Plastic sheets

Gales can rip off and blow the polyculture sheeting into the sea. These sheets can be up to 100m long, easily become entangled in the prop and stop an engine. This is a potential problem especially around Motril and the Bay of Almeria.

Plastic sheets and tunnels cover vegetables and fruit over many miles of coastline. Some of these are over 100m long
Graham Hutt

Across the Strait of Gibraltar to North Africa and the Spanish Enclaves

VISITS ACROSS THE STRAIT OF GIBRALTAR

Other possibilities for local visits outside of the area are across the Strait of Gibraltar and the Costa del Sol to Northern Morocco and the Spanish enclaves of Ceuta and Melilla.

For those wanting to explore further afield from a base on the Costa or from Gibraltar, most ports along the N coast of Morocco can be reached within 24 hours sailing time. Many motor vessels from the Costa are seen visiting Saidia and Marina Smir, where formalities are easy and fast. Ferries also run from some ports on the Costa to Melilla and, in summer, to Al Hoceima.

The Spanish enclave of Ceuta lies a short distance across the Strait of Gibraltar, just 12 miles from Europa Point, giving access to Morocco and taking less than half an hour to cross the land frontier. The local towns are M'Diq and World Heritage city of Tetouan. Marina Smir is a popular destination from Gibraltar, Sotogrande and Estepona or Marbella, just 10 miles from Ceuta. Marina Smir is owned by Marina Marbella. Extensive repair, haul-out and wintering facilities are available in Marina Smir with excellent prices. Many RYA school yachts visit from Gibraltar on a weekly basis.

Further to the E from Ceuta are Al Hoceima port and another Spanish enclave: Melilla. A new marina has just opened on the inland lake, Mar Chica, a few miles SE of Melilla and to the W of the huge new marina at Saidia.

Full details of the North Africa and Spanish enclave facilities are covered in the RCCPF *North Africa* pilot.

Melilla The ancient city, overlooking the lighthouse *Graham Hutt*

Cala Cangrejo near Jebha, north Morocco, a short distance from Costa del Sol *Terry Vadrouille*

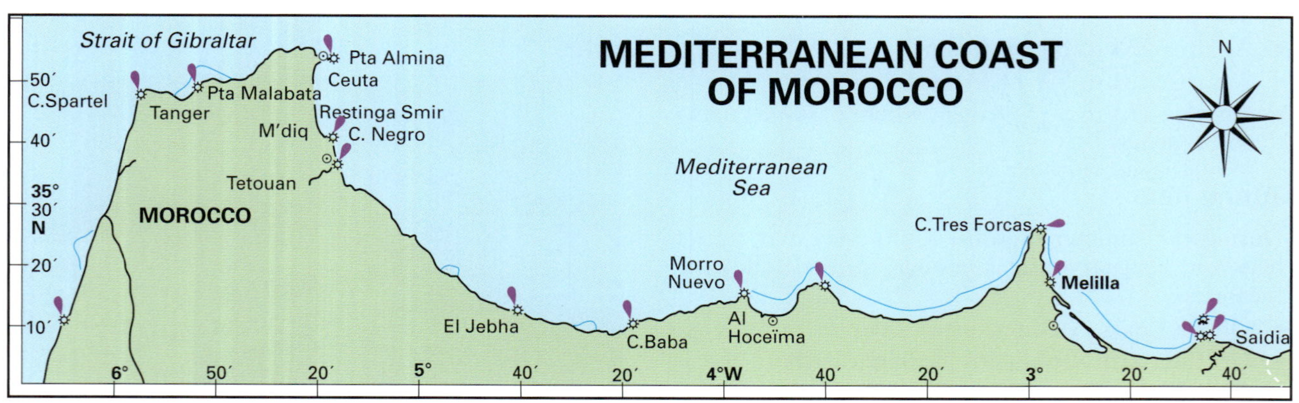

EUROPA POINT TO PTA DEL TORROX

Ports

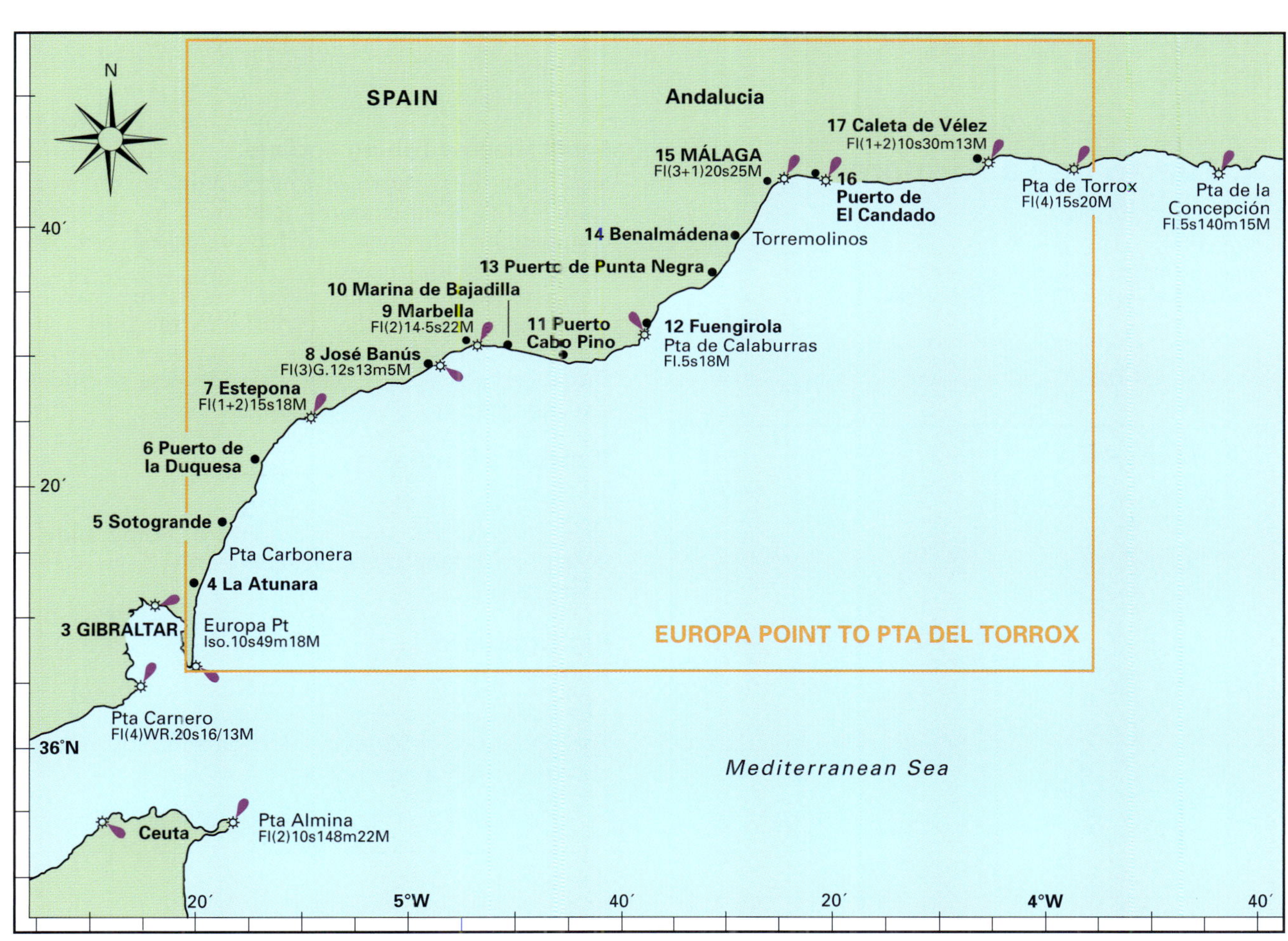

N
SPAIN
Andalucia
17 Caleta de Vélez
Fl(1+2)10s30m13M
15 MÁLAGA
Fl(3+1)20s25M
16
Puerto de
El Candado
Pta de Torrox
Fl(4)15s20M
Pta de la
Concepción
Fl.5s140m15M
14 Benalmádena
Torremolinos
13 Puerto de Punta Negra
10 Marina de Bajadilla
9 Marbella
Fl(2)14·5s22M
11 Puerto
Cabo Pino
12 Fuengirola
Pta de Calaburras
Fl.5s18M
8 José Banús
Fl(3)G.12s13m5M
7 Estepona
Fl(1+2)15s18M
6 Puerto de
la Duquesa
5 Sotogrande
Pta Carbonera
4 La Atunara
3 GIBRALTAR
Europa Pt
Iso.10s49m18M
EUROPA POINT TO PTA DEL TORROX
Pta Carnero
Fl(4)WR.20s16/13M
36°N
40´
20´
Mediterranean Sea
Ceuta
Pta Almina
Fl(2)10s148m22M
20´
5°W
40´
20´
4°W
40´

Vast but unusable – La Atunara harbour looking SW *Steve Pickard*

The dogleg entrance to La Atunara looking SE *Steve Pickard*

4. Puerto de La Atunara

36°10'·7N 05°19'·9W

Lights

Dique de Abrigo head Fl(3)G.11m5M Green post 5m
Contadique head F(3)R.9s8m1M Red tower 4m

www.eppa.es/en/fishing-harbour-la-atunara

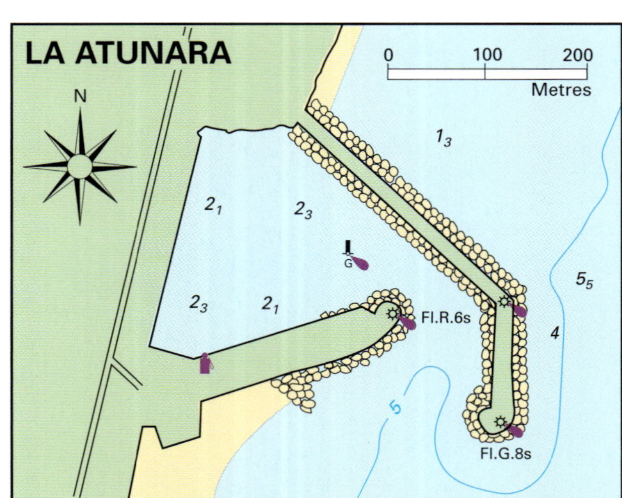

Small shallow fishing enclave

Some five miles north of Europa Point is the small fishing port of La Atunara. It is solely for the use of commercial fishermen and has a locked gate and fences all round.

Apart from a fuelling point (for fishing trawlers only) there are no other facilities at the port apart from the normal café. It is a long way from any shops and the port is only included here to inform passing craft of a possible refuge.

Punta Carbonera

36°16'·9N 5°17'·9W

This insignificant point just south of Sotogrande is now lit with light 0012 Oc.4s39m14M from a 14m white tower.

Río Guadiaro

36°16'·9N 5°16'·6W

The river is permanently silted up and should not be approached as a sandbar extends some distance E and towards Sotogrande marina entrance.

5. Puerto Sotogrande

36°17'N 05°16'W

Charts
UKHO *3578, 773* Imray *M11*
SHOM *7658* Spanish *453*

Lights
Dique Levante S head Fl(2)G.10s8m5M
Green 6-sided tower 3m
Dique Levante N head Q(3)10s8m4M E card
(with ♦ topmark)
Embarcadero Capitania Fl(3)G.10s3m1M
Contradique head Fl(3)R.15s4m1M Red post 2m
External espigón Fl(2)R.8s2m3M Red round pillar

Port communications
Port ✆ +34 956 79 00 00 VHF Ch 9.
informacion@puertosotogrande.com
www.puertosotogrande.com

Harbour charges High

Vast, intricate and smart

A 1380 berth marina complex easy to enter except in high winds and swell from the E. Surging problems within the marina have been resolved in recent years by the extension to the dique de Levante. The interior waterways are a replica of Port Grimaud in France.

The marina has an excellent, though expensive, boatyard. This is one of the safest marinas on the coast, quiet and peaceful for most of the year. Like all other marinas, July and August are busy months with lots of sailing activities organised by the local yacht club. New facilities have now been built to house the yacht club and sailing school.

Approach

From the south Having rounded Europa Point follow the coast at 500m in a general NNE direction. Torre Nueva and Torre de Punta Carbonera may be identified. The mass of buildings at Puerto Sotogrande can be seen from afar.

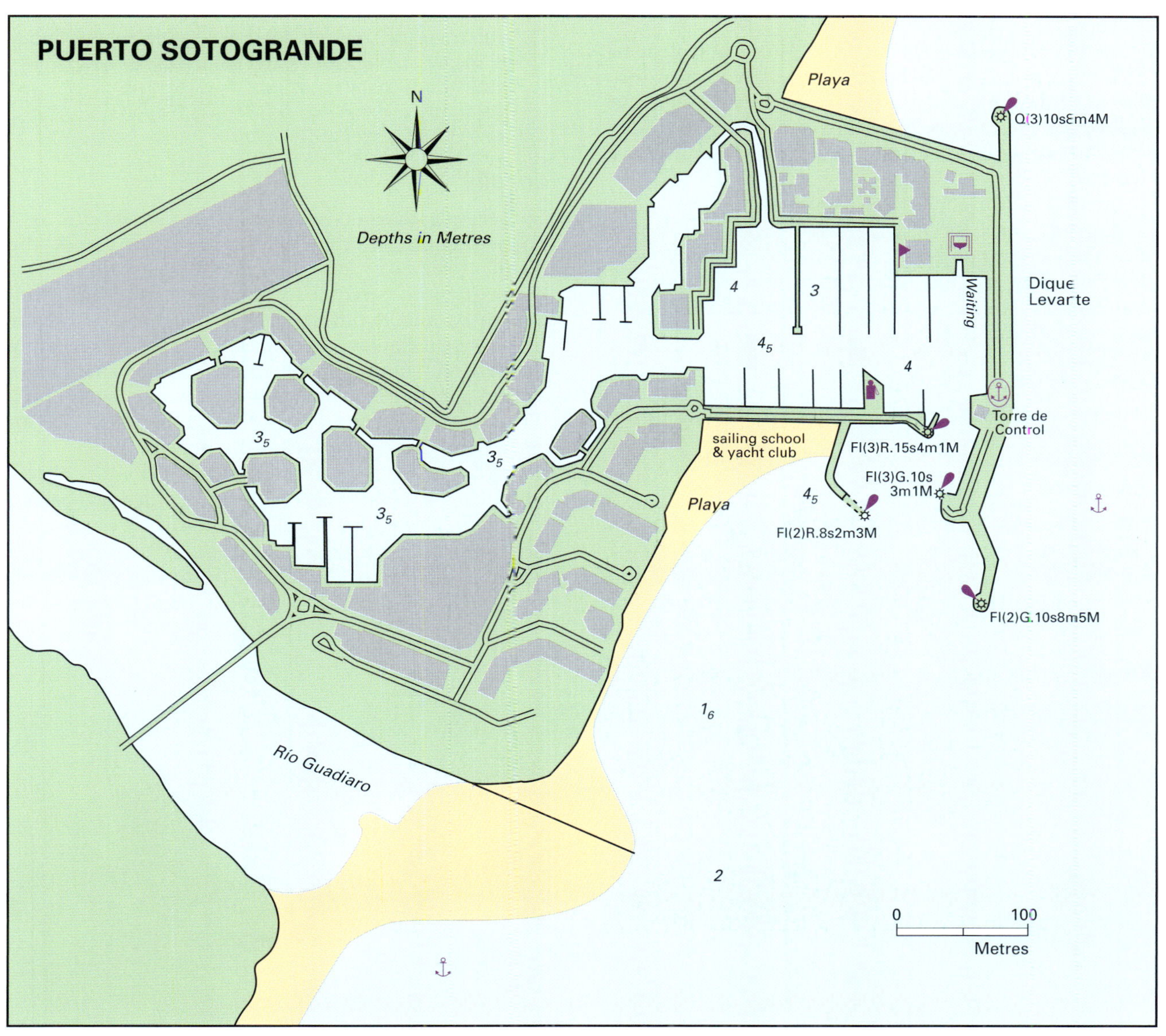

Puerto Sotogrande. A huge, well run and pleasant marina
Pública de Puertos de Andalucía

From the NE Follow the coast at 500m in a general SSW direction. The harbour and breakwaters of José Banús, Estepona and La Duquesa may be seen but caution is needed as there are a number of rocky sand-retaining breakwaters which can be mistaken for harbours.

A mile N of the port are two high blocks of flats – the only ones around. Between these blocks and Puerto Sotogrande is the bay and anchorage: Cala Sardina. The marina office *(torre de control)* is a handsome, square, castellated stone tower with cupola and flag-staff.

Anchorage in the approach

Anchor in 3m sand 300m offshore to N or S of the harbour.

Entrance

The harbour is easily entered by day: approach the S head of the dique with around 30m clearance. At night it is hard to see the entry lights until around 100m off due to the background lights. Strong S to E sector winds create quite a swell in the entrance requiring a fast approach rounding close to the S dique to maintain steerage and avoid the tow beachward. Entry is dangerous in very strong E winds when seas break over the dique de Levante.

Berths

Secure beneath the *torre de control* and ask there for a berth which will be on one of the yacht harbour pontoons. Two bow lines may be needed.

Formalities

If entering from abroad (e.g. Gibraltar) the office in the *torre* will arrange for customs clearance, should that be required.

Facilities

Max length overall 70m, with alongside facility for up to 100m.
Water and 220v AC at every berth
Shower and toilet facilities with access key
Gymnasium
Chandlery
200 ton travel lift and full dockyard and storage facilities
Cover maker, manufacturer and trimmer (sail covers, spray hoods, biminis, etc).
Aqu Covers ✆ +34 637 47 33 22
Gasoleo A and petrol at the control tower.

Locally

Sotogrande marina is currently rather empty as a consequence of the recent recession and the application of the matriculation tax. It is consequently spacious. Yacht berths are well separated and maintained. The marina is attractive and safe but lacks some basic amenities for visiting yachtsmen – like a supermarket or even a small store within the marina: all have closed in recent years. The nearest general store is a short walk to Torreguadiaro to the NE of the puerto.

Although there is no supermarket there is a post office (open 1000–1200 Monday–Saturday), banks, excellent though generally expensive restaurants, boutiques, a gift shop and gym. All are grouped around attractive squares with orange trees and fountains. Good access to the beach. Staff are

Sotogrande invites you in – looking N *Steve Pickard*

The inner elements of Sotogrande *Steve Pickard*

helpful and pleasant and most speak English. Poste Restante at the *torre de control*.

For more extensive shopping the well stocked Mercadona and Supercor supermercados are about 2km away opposite Pueblo Nuevo.

There is a bus stop on the main road near the marina for buses to Estepona, La Línea and Algeciras although these are infrequent, only every two hours. (Approximate times given in the local *El Periodico de Sotogrande* newspaper – along with other local information.) Taxi ☎ +34 956 78 01 01 / 607 548550 (English spoken).

Sandy beaches extend either side of the port and are well used in summer and clean. Beach restaurants (*chironghitos*) are set up in July and August providing locally caught fresh fish.

Sotogrande is a safe marina in which to leave a yacht for any length of time. Gibraltar is close, and it is worth hiring a vehicle for local trips, or use the extensive and cheap inter-city coach service to explore the cities of Cadiz and Sevilla. These depart from the main town bus stations in Algeciras and La Línea connecting via the service mentioned under 'Communications'. Sevilla is a microcosm of all that is beautiful in Andalucia. Splendid countryside with miles and miles of olive groves and citrus orchards as well as other fruits and sunflowers. In the city are some of the most spectacular buildings in the world with the Moorish, Berber and Arab architecture, many of which are as fine today as in the 9th to 12th century when they were built.

Closer to home are the mountain top villages of Castellar and Jimena de la Frontera and Ronda, just a few miles inland. On the way is the ancient villa of the Moorish Mayor, Almoirama, which today has the original timber Mosque tower and is now a splendid hotel and conference centre. Local game is a speciality of the restaurant – partridge, pheasant, wild boar, etc.

⚓ Cala Sardina
36°18'·5N 5°15'·3W

A pleasant anchorage 1·5M N of Sotogrande. Punta de la Chullera is a low sloping point with a conspicuous tower and a few houses amongst the trees. On the other side of the bay a square fort-like building, Casa Cuartel, is easily seen. Anchor in 3m sand and pebbles about 75m off. There is foul ground 100m off Punta de la Chullera which is sometimes called Punta Europa. The main coast road is behind the beach.

6. Puerto de la Duquesa

36°21'·3N 05°13'·7W

Charts
UKHO *3578, 773* Imray *M11*
SHOM *7658* Spanish *453*

Lights
Dique de Levante S head Fl.G.5s8m5M
Green truncated conical tower 3m
Dique de Levante N head Q(3)10s7m5M
♦ black post, yellow band 3m
Contradique head Fl.R.5s6m3M
Red truncated conical tower 4m
External espigón head Fl.R.5s7m3M
Round post 5m

Port communications
Port ☎ +34 952 89 01 00 VHF Ch 9.
duquesa@marinasmediterraneo.com
www.marinasmediterraneo.com/duquesa.htm

Village feel
A marina surrounded by blocks of apartments and with good facilities. Approach and entrance are easy and good shelter is available inside. It is a useful first port of call after Gibraltar which is less than 20M away. Good beaches on either side of the harbour. With many restaurants in the marina, this used to be

Duquesa looking SE *Pública de Puertos de Andalucía*

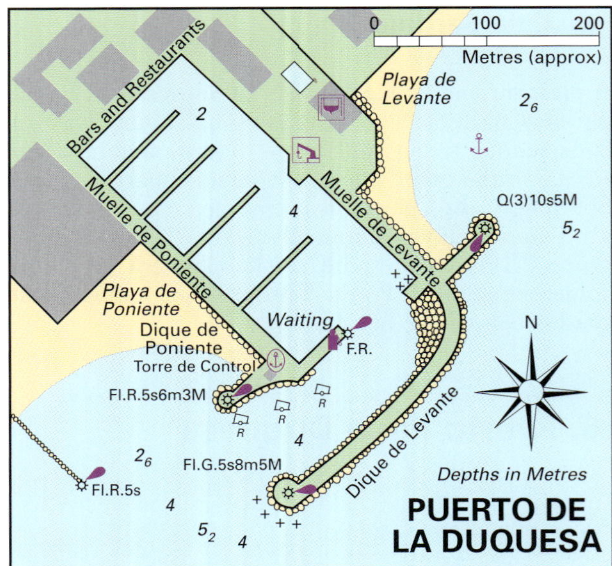

Duquesa's charming interior looking S *Steve Pickard*

a good stop for lunch on the way to or from Gibraltar, but a charge is now made even for lunch stops.

This is a safe marina for long or short stays although subject to some surging with a W wind. The marina has a pleasant 'lived in' community feel to it.

Approach

From the south Punta de la Chullera, with a tower, has rocks extending up to 100m offshore. Castillo de la Duquesa just SSW of the harbour is conspicuous.

From the north Punta de Salto de la Mora with its old watch tower can be seen. Foul ground extends 200m off this point. The new buildings around the harbour and its breakwater are visible during the closer approach.

Anchorage

Good anchorage is available to the NE of the harbour, about 150m offshore in 5m sand.

Entrance

Approach the head of the Dique de Levante on a NW course, round it and enter on a NE course. Give the breakwaters a 25m berth; underwater obstructions are marked by small buoys.

Berths

Secure alongside fuelling berth on the port hand side of the entrance and ask at the *torre de control* or call on Ch 9.

Formalities

If entering Spain, the *capitán de puerto* and *aduana's* offices are in the *torre de control*.

Facilities

Berthing for 328 vessels up to 20m

Left Duquesa entrance looking N *Steve Pickard*
Below Puerto de la Duquesa

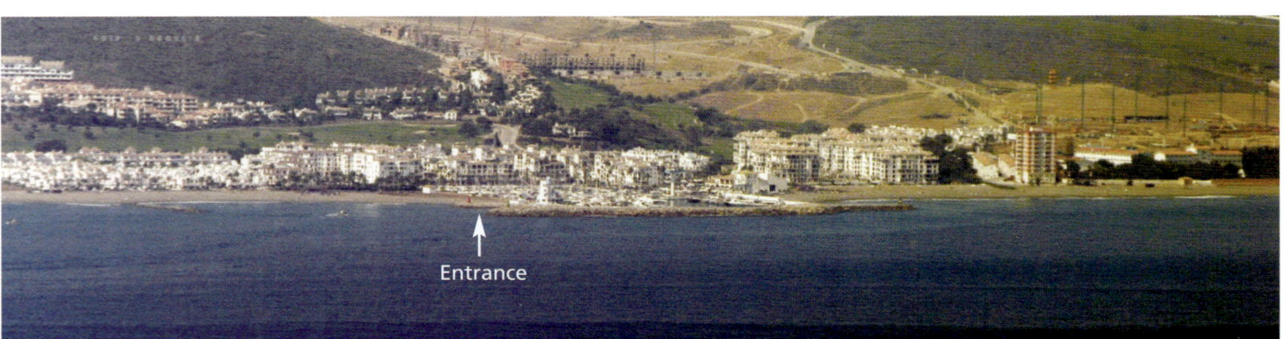

Limited workshops on E side of harbour.
75-tonne crane on NE side of harbour.
Showers at torre de control.
Water and 220v AC on all quays and pontoons.
Ice on fuel quay.
Gasoleo A and petrol.
Clubhouse with pool.
Local supermarket. Other shops in Manilva village 1½M away and Las Sabinillas ½M away.
Washing machine in *torre de control*.

Communications

Bus service. Airfield at Gibraltar. ✆ Area code 952. Taxi ✆ +34 952 80 29 00.

7. Puerto de Estepona

36°24'·8N 5°09'·4W

Charts

UKHO *3578*	Imray *M11*
SHOM *7658*	Spanish *453*

Lights

Approach

Punta de la Doncella LtHo Fl(1+2)15s32m18M
Dark 8-sided tower, grey lantern, white house 25m

Harbour

Dique de Abrigo spike Q(6)+LFl.15s9m5M
Black ⧗ on yellow tower, black base 6m

Dique de Abrigo head 36°24'.8N 5°09'.4W Fl.G.5s9m5M
Green pole 7m

Dique de Poniente Fl(2)R.7s9m3M
White truncated tower, red top 6m

Buoy 36°25'.2N 5°08'.4W Q(6)+LFl.15s6m2M
⧗ card S

Port communications

Capitanía de Marina ✆ +34 952 80 18 00 VHF Ch 9
estepona@eppa.es
Club Náutico de Estepona ✆ +34 952 80 09 54
cnestepona@teleline.es
www.marinasmediterraneo.com/workspaces/estepona

Harbour charges Medium to high

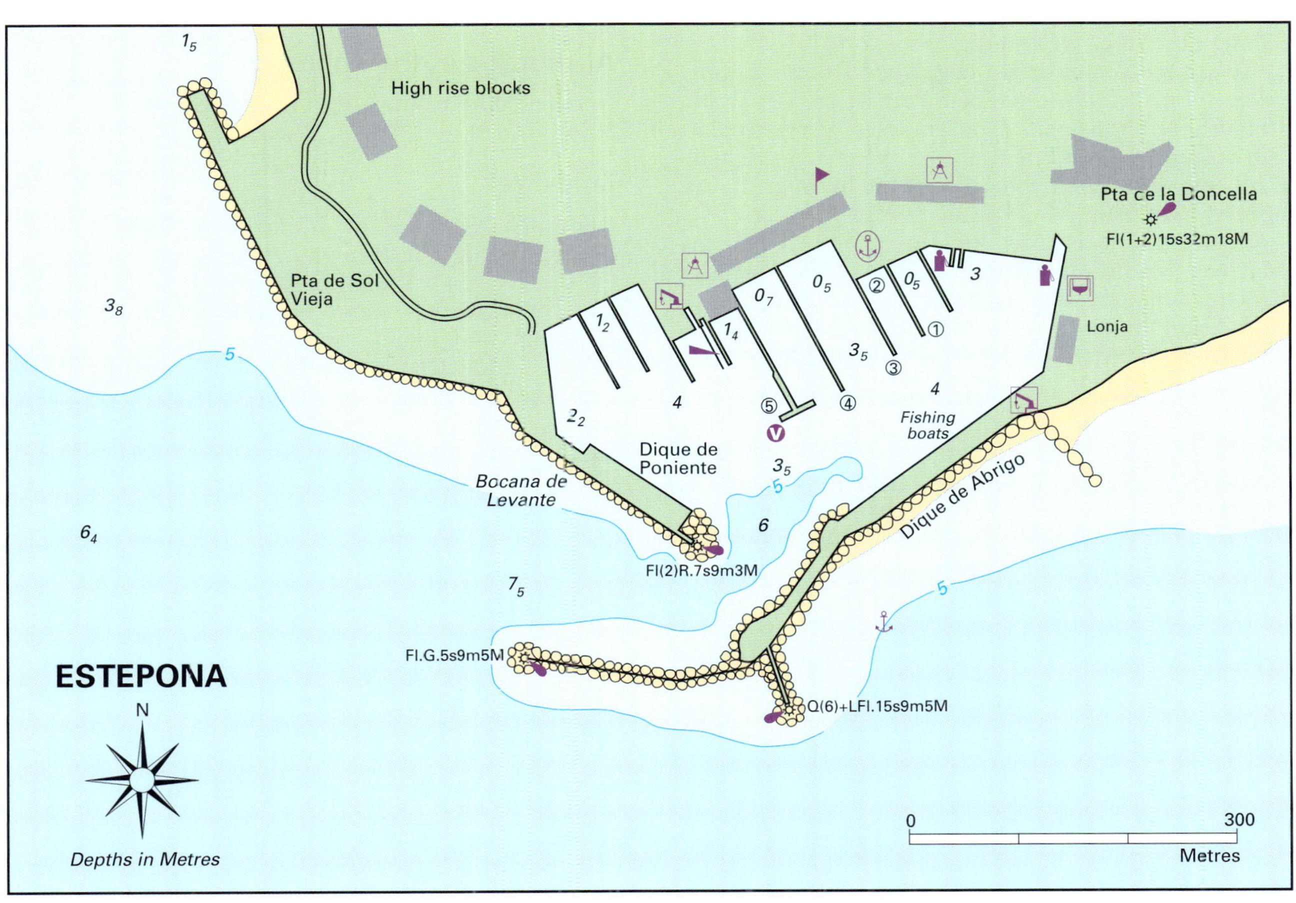

II. COSTA DEL SOL

Estepona from the south *Pública de Puertos de Andalucía*

Harbour and tourist resort

One of the oldest Spanish marinas and an ancient fishing port. very welcoming to visitors.

Town of Roman origin developed from a fishing village into a close-packed tourist resort with restaurants, shops and a supermarket. Very popular fish retaurant at end of fish port. Very noisy! There is an early morning fishmarket at the harbour. Local holidays are from 24–29 June.

This marina is part of the group 'Groupas Marinas Mediterraneo' which also own Duqesa, Benelmadena and Marina del Este.

A small number of berths are operated by the local Club Náutico. These are usually occupied.

Approach

The harbour is backed by four tower blocks of flats. The dark octagonal lighthouse 31m high capped by a grey lantern is to the NE of the harbour entrance. The outer breakwater (Dique de Abrigo) has been extended westwards leaving the old entrance tower in its original position.

Estepona entrance looking W *Steve Pickard*

Anchorage in the approach

Anchor 200m to the NE of head Dique de Abrigo in 5·5m sand.

Entrance

Approach the head of Dique de Abrigo on a N course, round it at 20m and enter on a NE course.

In a SW gale the entrance could be dangerous. The breakwaters have underwater projections. Dredgers may be in operation as this harbour's mouth frequently silts up. Most harbours along this coast have reported severe reduction in entrance depths in spring due to winter storms. Beware fishing boats manoevering to starboad as you enter.

Berths

Secure to the Muelle de Espera, which is at the end of Pantalan 5, and ask at the *capitanía* which is in a blue building, like a towered wedding cake with white icing, on the north side of the harbour. The *pantalanes* have lockable gates at their shore ends.

Facilities

Maximum length overall 30m, 447 moorings.

Repairs (most services) at a shipyard to NE of the harbour.

Sailmaker under the club náutico is Magnusson Sails (Antonio Rodriguez Carrasco) ✆+34 952 79 12 41 (the only sailmaker on the west of Costa del Sol. Excellent work has been reported and English is spoken).

80-tonne travel-lift and 3·5-tonne mobile crane.

Estepona visitors' waiting berth to port on entry *Steve Pickard*

Yachts up to 25-tonnes may be hauled out on the slipway immediately SW of the *club náutico*.
Hardstanding.
Chandlery in harbour.
Life-raft servicing.
Water taps on quays and pontoons.
Butane: the Marina can arrange refills for 10lb Calor bottles.
220v AC on the Dique de Poniente and pontoons, 380v on berths 20–35m.
Ice from the fish auction building or waiting quay.
Gasoleo A and petrol not available.
Club Náutico de Estepona has showers, a restaurant and bar and is usually open to non-members.
Provisions from shops in the town about 1M away and from supermarket on N side of the harbour and one nearby, across the main road.
Laundry in port, launderettes in the town.
To the N of the marina Estepona has a huge 'Poligono Industrial' within which are units capable of undertaking almost any type of mechanical, carpentry or electrical repairs or manufacturing.

Communications

Bus services. ✆ Area code 952.
Taxi ✆ +34 952 80 29 00.

⚓ Fondeadero de Estepona

An anchorage to the NE of the harbour off the town of Estepona, 500m from the shore in 5m sand. To E of the harbour where five breakwaters were built is a submerged breakwater parallel to the coast and about 400m offshore marked by a S card buoy. The anchorage is somewhat protected by Punta de los Marmoles, a small cliffed headland with a tower surrounded by trees.

Note Further East, anchoring is forbidden between Torre del Padrón and Punta de Guadalmaza because of submarine cables.

8. Puerto José Banús

36°29'N 04°57'·2W

Charts
UKHO *3578, 773* Imray *M11*
SHOM *7658* Spanish *454*

Lights
Dique de Benabolá W head Fl(3)R.10s7m3M
Truncated masonry tower red lantern 4m
E Head Q(4)R.10s1M Red post
Dique de Levante W head 36°29'.1N 04°57'.2W
Fl(3)G.12s13m5M
Truncated masonry tower green lantern 9m
E head Q(6)+LFl.15s10m3M ⯆ on black post 6m

Port communications
VHF Ch 9. *Capitanía* ✆ +34 952 90 98 00
torrecontrol@puertobanus.com
www.puertojosebanus.es
Club de Mar José Banús
✆ +34 952 81 77 50
info@puertojosebanus.es
www.puertojosebanus.es/club/ing/presentacion.htm

Harbour charges High

Upmarket marina

Pleasant in a large kind of way this upmarket marina handles large and very large yachts, motor and sail, and corresponding high prices. The mature waterfront also contains apartments, shops boutiques, restaurants, night clubs, casinos and so forth, patrolled by armed security guards and protected from the outside world by automated barriers allowing the passage of selected vehicles. It has good repair facilities.

There is a hotel beach and swimming pool to W of the harbour which is available to yachting visitors. Entrance tickets from third floor office of the tower. It is worth escaping to Ronda by taxi.

Approach

The lone rocky-peaked mountain Pico de la Concha in the Sierra Blanca, called Sierra de Marbella on

Puerto José Banús as seen from the SE corner *Steve Pickard*

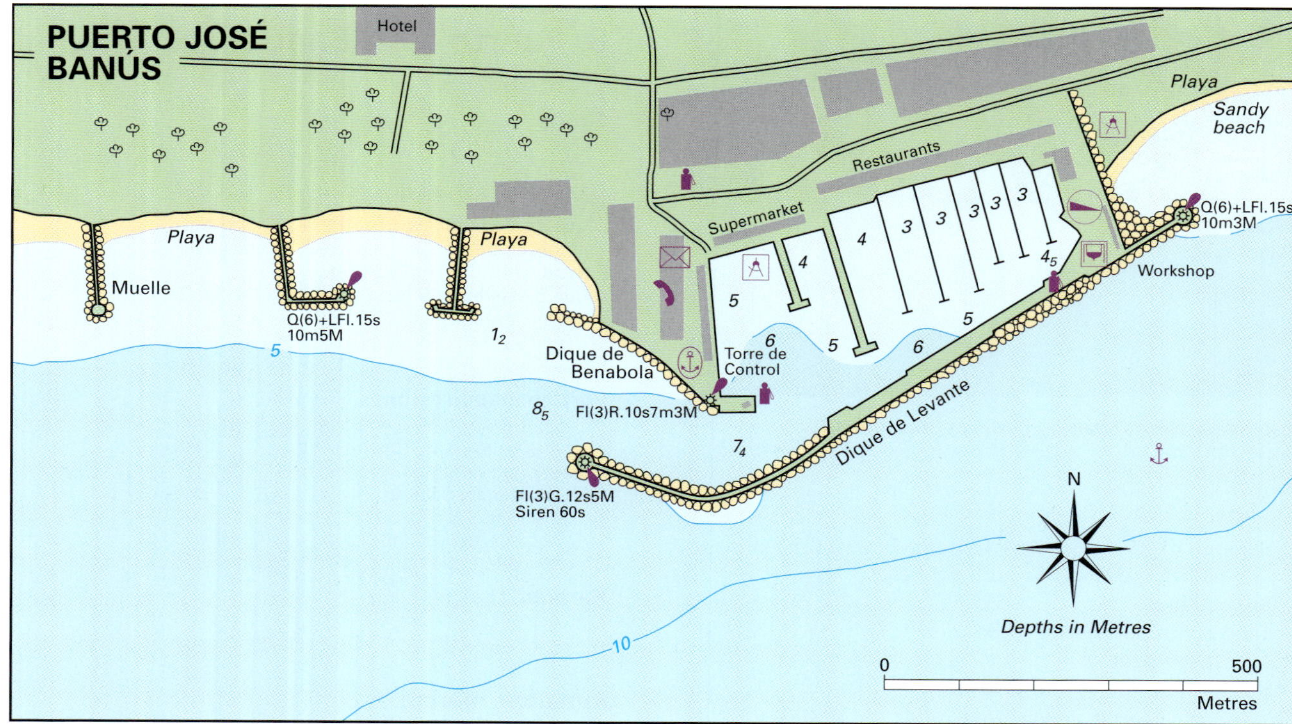

British charts, can be seen from afar. Closer in, some yellow tower blocks 2M to W and the very large Hotel Nueva Andalucía, the bull ring close E and a white flag-poled terrace are conspicuous. The old stone tower with a number of windows at the entrance and the mass of buildings around the harbour are also conspicuous.

Anchorage in the approach

500m E of S head of Dique de Levante in 8m sand.

Entrance

Approach the S head of Dique de Levante on a N course, leave it 50m to starboard and enter on an E course.

In a SW gale, the entrance could be difficult except for powerful vessels as it involves turning sharply across the waves in a restricted area of disturbed water.

Berths

Secure alongside E side of Dique de Benabolá near the fuel station for the allocation of a berth from the control tower.

Facilities

Maximum length overall: 80m.
Two travel-lifts, 50 and 25 tonnes and a 5-tonne mobile crane.
Launching slipway at E of the harbour.
Most shipwright and electronic work possible.
Sailmaker on N side of harbour.
Two chandlers beside the harbour.
Water points on quays and pontoons.
Showers by the tower.
220v AC to berths and 380v AC to berths over 15m.
Petrol.
Ice from fuelling point or slipway.
Yacht Club: Club Náutico Internacional Nueva Andalucia.
Supermarket at the harbour but fresh food has to be obtained from Marbella, 15 minutes away by bus or taxi, or from San Pedro.
Laundry in port and launderette behind the house on Dique de Riberea.

Puerto José Banús fueling berth with entrance beyond – looking W
Steve Pickard

Puerto José Banús *Pública de Puertos de Andalucía*

Locally

This is an excellent night spot with bars, clubs and restaurants as well as a nearby supermarket.

As with Marbella, this is a good place from which to visit Ronda; a mountain village built by the Moors in the 10th century. It has one of the most spectacular bridges in Spain, connecting two sides of a ravine. The scenery on the journey is spectacular. A train also goes daily to Ronda from Algeciras, stopping also at the nearby Estacion San Roque. Worth the trip even just for the scenery en route.

Communications

Bus service. ✆ Area code 952.
Taxi ✆ +34 952 78 38 39.

9. Puerto de Marbella (Marbella Yacht Harbour)

36°30′·3N 04°53′·4W

Charts

UKHO 3578, 773 Imray M11
SHOM 7658 Spanish 454

Lights

Approach
Marbella LtHo Fl(2)14·5s35m22M
White round tower 29m

Marina
Dique de Levante Fl(2)G.7m4M
White tower, green top 4m
Dique de Poniente Fl.R.4s6m2M
Red pyramidal tower 4m
Note There may be several fish farms off this harbour which normally have four buoys, Fl.Y.5s marking their extent

Port communications

Capatania VHF Ch 9 +34 952 77 55 24
puertodeportivo@marbella.es
www.marbella.es/puertodeportivo

Small older marina

Opened 35 years ago, Marbella Yacht Harbour with its 377 berths to 20m is another older facility. Approach and entry are easy although a swell builds in the entrance with SW winds, making entry dangerous in strong winds. Depths are not more than 3m in the marina.

Visitors are berthed on the N side of the dique after checking in at the fuel jetty / small boatyard.

The entrance is prone to silting and regularly dredged.

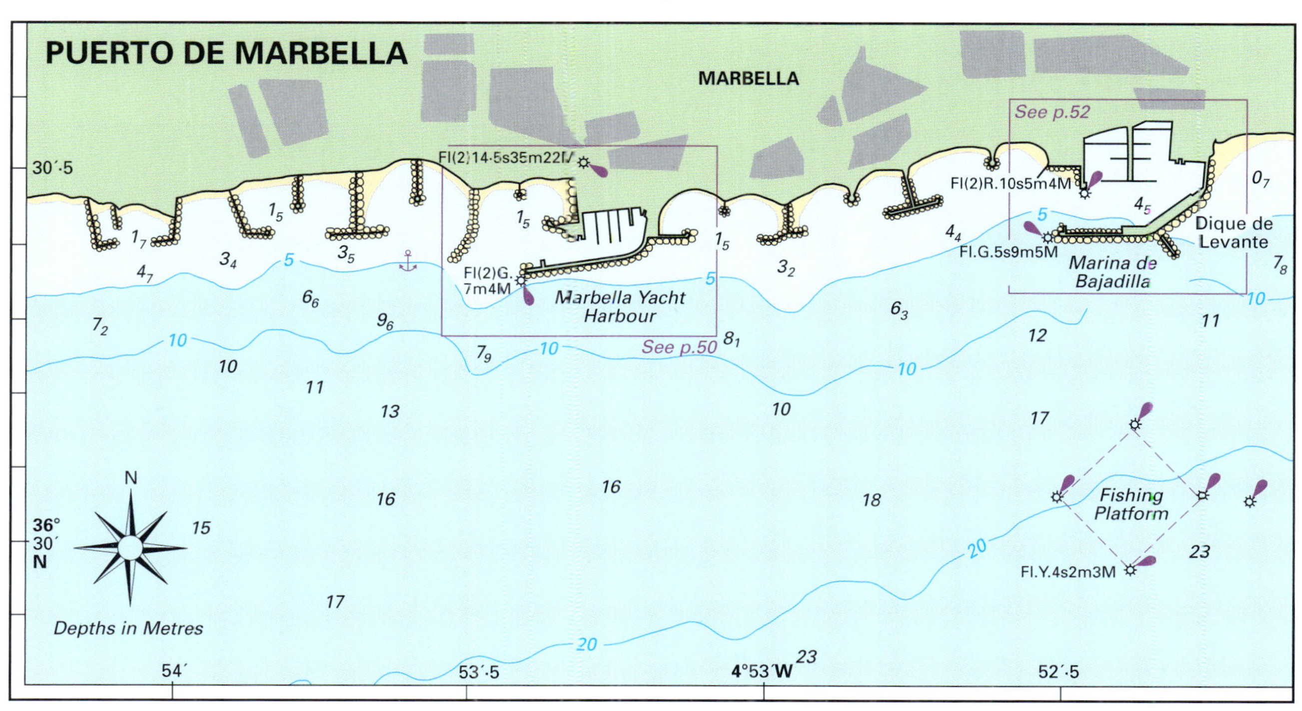

Marbella Yacht Harbour *Pública de Puertos de Andalucía*

The harbour is noisy at night during the high season and during the day the long sandy beaches on either side of the harbour are often crowded.

The local holidays are 10–18 June, Ferias de San Bernabé. 18–24 August, Semana del Sol. 18 October, San Pedro de Alcantara.

Approach

The mass of skyscraper apartments and hotels along the seafront and the high Sierra Blanca mountain range behind make the whereabouts of the marina easy to locate. The marina itself is immediately S of Marbella light; in day time the lighthouse is difficult to spot as it is the middle of a group of high-rise buildings. Do not be confused by a number of rocky jetties between the marina and the fishing harbour, built as breakwaters to retain sand for bathing beaches, and look out for a fishing platform at 36°30′·0N 04°52′·4W, about half a mile off the fishing harbour. The marina breakwater has been heightened to give extra protection within.

Anchorage in the approach

Anchor in 5m sand anywhere 200m to W of the entrance to the yacht harbour.

Entrance

Give the jetty heads a good berth as they are not vertical at the foot. Line of small red can buoys on the north side of the entrance and a wreck on the south side, leave to port and starboard respectively.

Berths

Secure to the fuelling station on the port side of the entrance and ask at the *capitanía*, behind the fuel station.

Facilities

Maximum length overall: 15–20m.

A fork-lift type hoist on a tractor, rated at 16 tonnes.

A small slipway in NE corner of the harbour and a slipway on the W side of the harbour.

Small hardstanding.

Chandlery shop in the town.

Water from club marítimo and on pontoons and quays.

125v, 220v AC on quayside and pontoons and 380v on berths of 20m.

Gasoleo A and petrol.

Ice from factory 100m NE of the club marítimo.

Club Marítimo de Marbella is really a high quality hotel and restaurant with showers and other services in the basement.

There is a market about 1M to N of the club marítimo. Buy food from shops in back streets, they have better quality provisions and are cheaper.

Several launderettes in town.

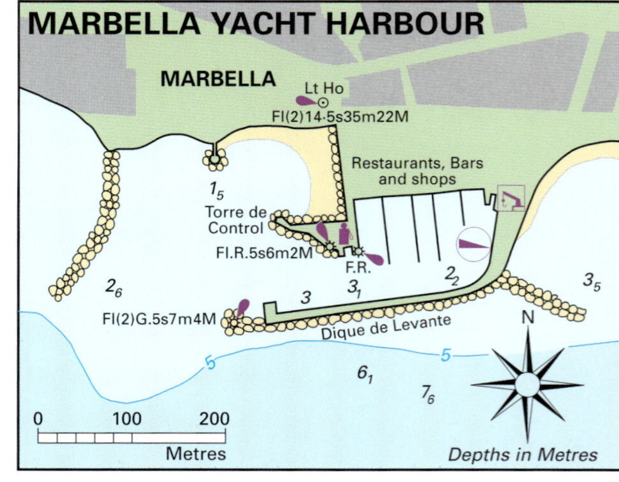

Marbella entrance. Note the lighthouse far left *Graham Hutt*

General

Despite the recent recession the town, which extends to the marina, is busy and bustling, frequented by celebrities from across the world. In summer, sounds of the marina surroundings – bars, restaurants and street entertainers – fill the air. It gives a good atmosphere for those loving the nightlife. The marina is one of the best and busiest on the *costa*, fun at night and inexpensive.

Fuel berth immediately to port on entrance *Steve Pickard*

Communications

Bus service along the coast. ✆ Area code 952. Taxi ✆ +34 952 77 44 88.

Marbella lighthouse: insignificant among the taller buildings and many lights at night *Graham Hutt*

Marbella entrance looking W – note hazardous low rocky breakwater *Steve Pickard*

10. Marina de Bajadilla

36°30'·4N 04°52'·5W

Lights

Dique de Levante head 36°30'·4N 04°52'·5W Fl.G.5s9m5M
White tower, green top 4m

Dique de Poniente head Fl(2)R.10s5m4M
Grey tower, red top 3m

Port Communications

Capitanía +34 952 867266 VHF Ch 9.
marbellad@eppa.es
www.eppa.es/en/marina-la-bajadilla

Marina de Bajadilla. Note the tinted blue building behind marina *Pública de Puertos de Andalucía*

Fishing and yachting harbour

Formerly a busy fishing harbour, this is now, mostly, a quiet and friendly marina with 250 moorings up to 15m. The entrance is quite straightforward but the harbour is subjected to swell from W and SW.

Approach

Marbella with its line of high-rise buildings can be seen from afar but the tall (35m) Marbella lighthouse is difficult to spot amongst them. Close the coast aiming at the east end of the high-rise buildings until the breakwater and/or the lighthouse can be identified. The marina is just over half a mile east of the lighthouse. 50m E of the marina is a large blue glass tinted building which is more easily seen than the Marbella lighthouse.

Note Fishing nets and hundreds of buoys are in place just outside and running parallel to the S dique at a distance of around 80m running almost the full length of the dique. Entry from the E can be between the dique and the nets, though depths are unknown. The nets are clear of the entry at the W end of the marina.

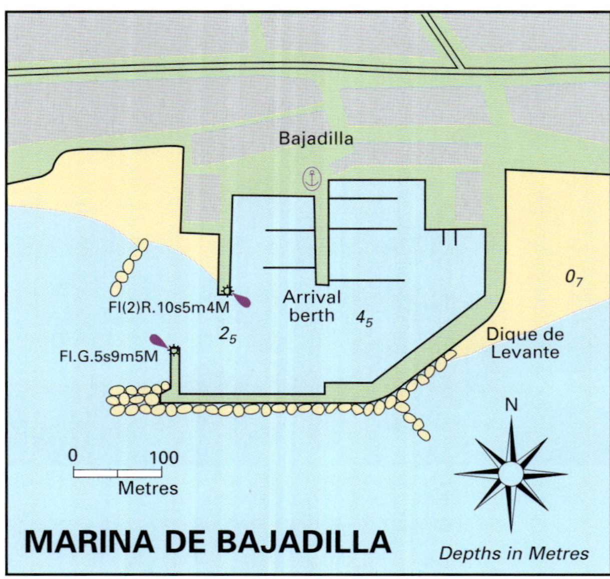

Berths

Moor to the end of the main pontoon, where a sign reads 'Muelle de espera' (waiting quay), not at the fuel berth. If you have called in on VHF Ch 9, a marinero will be waiting. The capitania is at the end of the quay in the NW corner of the harbour.

Facilities

Maximum LOA 15m.
Crane, travel-lift, hardstanding, etc.
Water and 220v AC on pontoons.
Showers etc at base of main pier.
Restaurant in marina.
Shops in town.

Bajadilla's dogleg entrance as seen looking N from the southern breakwater *Steve Pickard*

11. Puerto Cabo Pino

36°29'N 04°44'·4W

Charts

UKHO *3578, 773* Imray *M11*
SHOM *7658* Spanish *454*

Lights

Note 3F.R vertical means port closed.

To the east

Punta de Calaburras Fl.5s46m18M
Truncated conical tower 25m

Port communications

Port manager ✆ +34 952 83 19 75 VHF Ch 9.
marinacabopino@terra.es

Harbour charges High

Small very shallow private harbour

An attractive small private harbour with houses built in the local style; it is one of the less oppressive in terms of not being surrounded by high rise buildings and boutiques. The approach and entrance may be problematic – see below – but there is good protection once inside. Facilities are good and there are beaches on either side of the harbour.

Approach and entrance

Cabo Pino lies 8M to the E of Marbella and 4M to WSW of Punta Calaburras lighthouse, both of which are easily recognised. The high white apartment blocks and harbour breakwater can be seen from afar. The partly ruined square, Torre de Cala Honda, located just to W of the harbour will be seen closer in.

The approach and entrance silt. Enter on the flood, sounding, and pass the Dique de Levante at about one third the distance between it and the Espigón Antiarena; sand builds up off the head of the Dique de Levante. Care is particularly necessary in strong SW–W winds or swell which may effectively reduce depths. If in doubt, call the marina and inquire about depths.

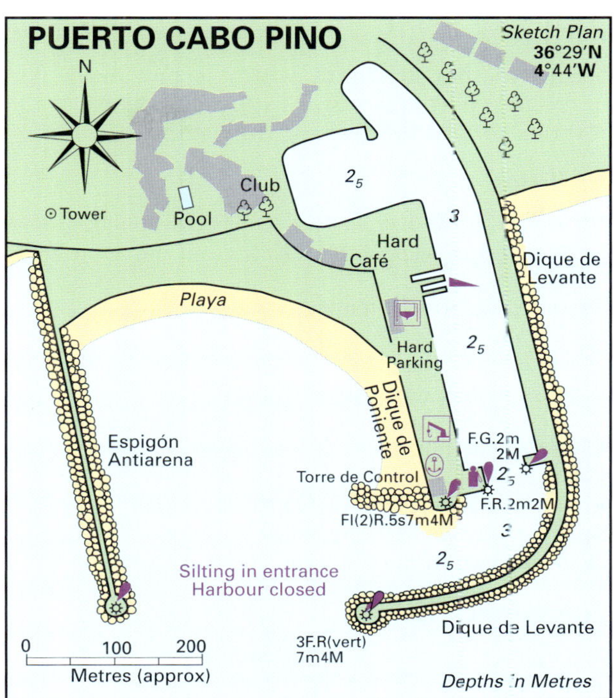

Anchorages

The sea floor near the harbour is mainly stony with poor holding, particularly on the E side, though some sandy patches may be found.

In the approach

Cala Moral 36°29'·8N 04°40'·7W 2M to ENE has a sandy bottom. Anchor between Torre Pesetas on Punta de la Torre Nueva and Torre de Cala Moral 200m from the shore in 3m sand.

Cabo Pino entrance looking W with outer harbour beyond *Steve Pickard*

Shoreside facilities on the Dique de Poniente *Steve Pickard*

II. COSTA DEL SOL

Berths

Secure to the fuel berth which is just inside the harbour to port and near the F.R light and ask at the *torre de control* for berthing instructions.

Facilities

Maximum length overall: 16m (Four berths only).
2 x Small yards which can pressure clean and apply anti foul.
8-tonne crane and 26-tonne travel-lift.
Slipway on W side of the harbour.
Engine mechanics.
Showers at torre de control.
Water and 220v AC points on all quays. Some at 380v by the larger berths.
Gasoleo A and petrol.
Ice from the bars or from fuel quay.
Supermarket behind the harbour.
Launderettes near harbour.

Communications

Bus along the coast. ✆ Area code 952.
Taxi ✆ +34 952 77 44 88.

12. Puerto de Fuengirola

36°32′·5N 04°36′·9W

Charts
UKHO *3578, 773* Imray *M11*
SHOM *7658* Spanish *455, 454*

Lights
Dique de Abrigo 36°32′·6N 04°36′·8W Fl(3)R.10m5M
Red metal pyramidal tower 4m
Contradique Fl.G.6m3M
Green truncated pyramidal tower 4m
Espigón S head 36°32′·8N 04°36′·7W Fl(3)G.5m3M
Green tower 4m (on submerged groyne to the north of entrance)
To the west
Punta de Calaburras 36°30′·5N 04°38′·3W Fl.5s46m18M
Truncated conical tower 25m

Port communications
Port ✆ +34 952 46 80 00 VHF Ch 9
puertofuengirola@gmail.com
www.marinasdeandalucia.com

Fishing and yacht harbour with good shelter and facilities

A small friendly harbour with close access to shops, bars and restaurants, with 226 moorings up to 20m.

Planned as a harbour in two parts, only the western side has been built. It has good shelter and facilities. All necessary provisions may be bought from large modern tourist town nearby. Usually the approach and entrance are easy but could be difficult with strong NE–E winds and/or swell. In these conditions parts of the harbour are uncomfortable.

The town is very busy and noisy in the season. There are good beaches each side of the port but they are crowded in summer. Local holidays: three days in August and 7–10 October for their Patron Saint.

Fuengirola's spacious entrance looking NE from the contradique *Steve Pickard*

Fuengirola *Pública de Puertos de Andalucía*

Approach

From the SW The low headland of Punta Calaburras with its conspicuous lighthouse and a mast 6·2M to N, is about 2M SW of Fuengirola. An old castle on a small hill lies halfway between this point and the harbour. The town of Fuengirola with its high-rise hotels and apartments is easily seen.

From the NE The massive high-rise tourist development around Torremolinos continues with minor interruptions along the coast as far as Fuengirola after which it peters out.

The four minarets in the marina are no longer conspicuous, having lost the tinted roof cappings. Only the framework remains.

With strong E and NE winds it is advisable to enter close to HW, rounding the dique with speed enough to maintain steerage to counter the surging currents towards the beach near the entrance. Once inside, there are no problems. The extra half metre of depth at HW seems to make quite a difference in this marina when entering in adverse conditions.

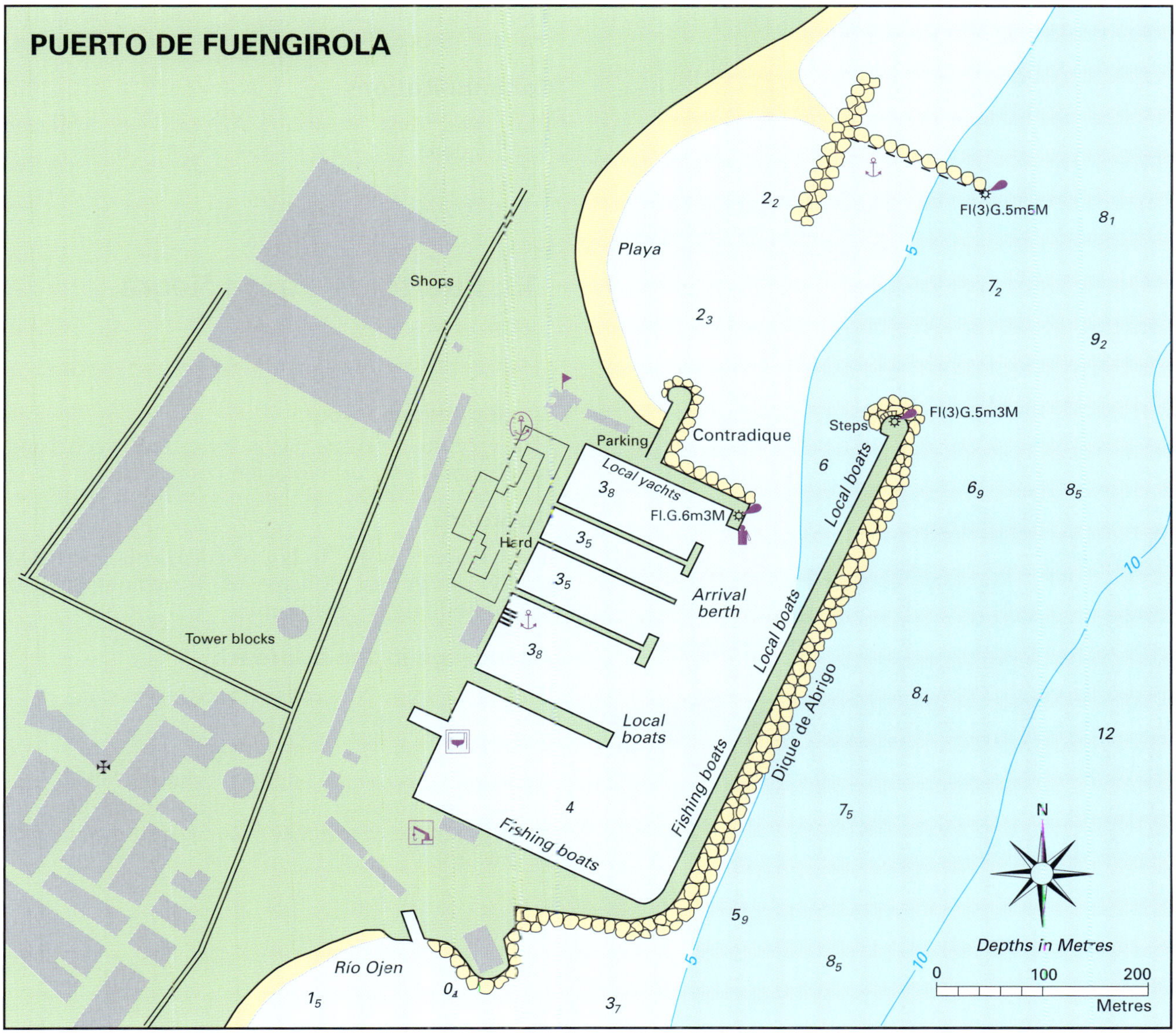

PUERTO DE FUENGIROLA

Playa
Shops
Tower blocks
Parking
Contradique
Local yachts
Fl.G.6m3M
Hard
Arrival berth
Local boats
Fishing boats
Steps
Fl(3)G.5m3M
Fl(3)G.5m5M
Dique de Abrigo
Río Ojen
N
Depths in Metres
0 100 200
Metres

The town as seen from the contradique *Steve Pickard*

Anchorage in the approach

Anchor 200m to N of the head of the breakwater in 3m sand. An alternative deeper anchorage lies 500m to SE of the harbour in 15m sand.

Entrance

Approach the head of the Dique de Abrigo on a NW course and round it. A shallow area has developed on the starboard side of the entrance; keep in mid-channel.

Berths

Pick up a mooring line and go bows- or stern-to one of the new concrete pontoons and check with the office near SW corner of the port.

Considerable shoreside facilities in Fuengirola *Steve Pickard*

Facilities

Maximum length overall: 20m.
Repairs – limited; there is a small yard to the SW of the harbour.
35-tonne travel-lift and 6-tonne crane.
Chandlery.
Water and 220v AC on pontoons and quays.
Gasoleo A and petrol.
Ice at the SW end of the harbour.
Club Náutico – inquire about using its facilities.
Shop in the town for provisions.
A market near the centre of town and an open market on Tuesdays.
Launderettes in the town.

Locally

Fuengirola has many cheap touristy restaurants. Finer ones are around, but harder to find. It is a busy town and marina with many bars and restaurants within the harbour. The marina is close to Benalmádena and Torremolinos and not far from Málaga airport. There is only Benalmádena marina between Fuengirola and Málaga, so it is a good place from which to visit Málaga or Ronda. A local rail and bus service ply from the town centre to Málaga.

Communications

Rail and bus service. Airport at Málaga. ✆ Area code 952. Taxi ✆ +34 952 47 10 00.

13. Puerto de Punta Negra

36°34'·7N 04°32'·43W

Small private harbour

This very small private harbour for small yachts and runabouts is part of the casino complex.

Approach

The harbour lies 4M to NE of Fuengirola and 0·5M to SW of Puerto Principe at Torremolinos. The casino building is conspicuous.

Anchorage in the approach

Anchor 200m to S of the entrance in 7m sand.

Entrance

Approach the casino building heading NNW and identify the entrance in the centre of the harbour breakwater. Go in to either basin. Depths believed to be 2m or less

14. Puerto de Benalmádena

36°35'·7N 04°30'·7W

Charts

UKHO *773* Imray *M11*
SHOM *7658* Spanish *455, 455A*

Lights

Laja de Bermeja Q(3)10s7m5M
♦ E card post 7m
Dique Sur SW head Fl(2)G.5s9m5M
Conical masonry tower with green band 5m
Dique Sur NE corner Q(3)10s9m3M
♦ Truncated conical masonry tower 5m
Dique Sur inner head Fl(3)G.9s4m4M
Conical tower, green band 3m
Dique del Oeste head Fl(2)R.5s4m3M
Truncated conical masonry, red band 3m

Port communications

Capitanía ☎ +34 952 57 70 22 VHF Ch 9
puertodeportivo@benalmadena.com
www.puertobenalmadena.es
Club Náutico Maritimo ☎ +34 952 44 42 34
info@cnmbenalmadena.com
www.cnmbenalmadena.com

Approach

The approach requires care to avoid the shoal, Laja de Bermeja (see plan) which breaks in heavy weather. The entrance is easy and good protection is offered once inside though there is some swell in outer harbour with W gale.

From the west The prominent walls of Benalmádena can be seen when passing the large casino building and small harbour of Punta Negra. Keep over ½M off the coast to pass south of the Laja de Bermeja and make for a position where the S end of the harbour is due W.

From the east Passage is forbidden through the area of an oil terminal located 1M to S of Puerto de Málaga. This area is about ½M square and lies ¾M off the coast. From Puerto de Málaga keep ½M off coast and pass inside prohibited area. Pay attention to an exposed wreck in the area. The mass of high rise blocks of flats at Torremolinos ends shortly before Benalmádena. Keep well to the east of Laja de Bermeja.

Huge yacht harbour

One of the largest marinas along the coast with a very safe – if noisy – inner complex. Over 1,100 berths available up to 30m.

This is a huge artificial yacht harbour enclosing 150,000 square metres of water located at the SW end of Torremolinos. The area near the harbour is a mass of soulless high-rise buildings but as it is very difficult to find a berth in Málaga, Benalmádena is a good alternative. Good beaches on each side of the harbour and a considerable range of tourist bars and restaurants. As in most harbours, there is also a *Club Náutico*. This is a private members club and more expensive than the main *Puerto Deportivo*. Plans are at an advanced stage to increase the size and capacity of this marina.

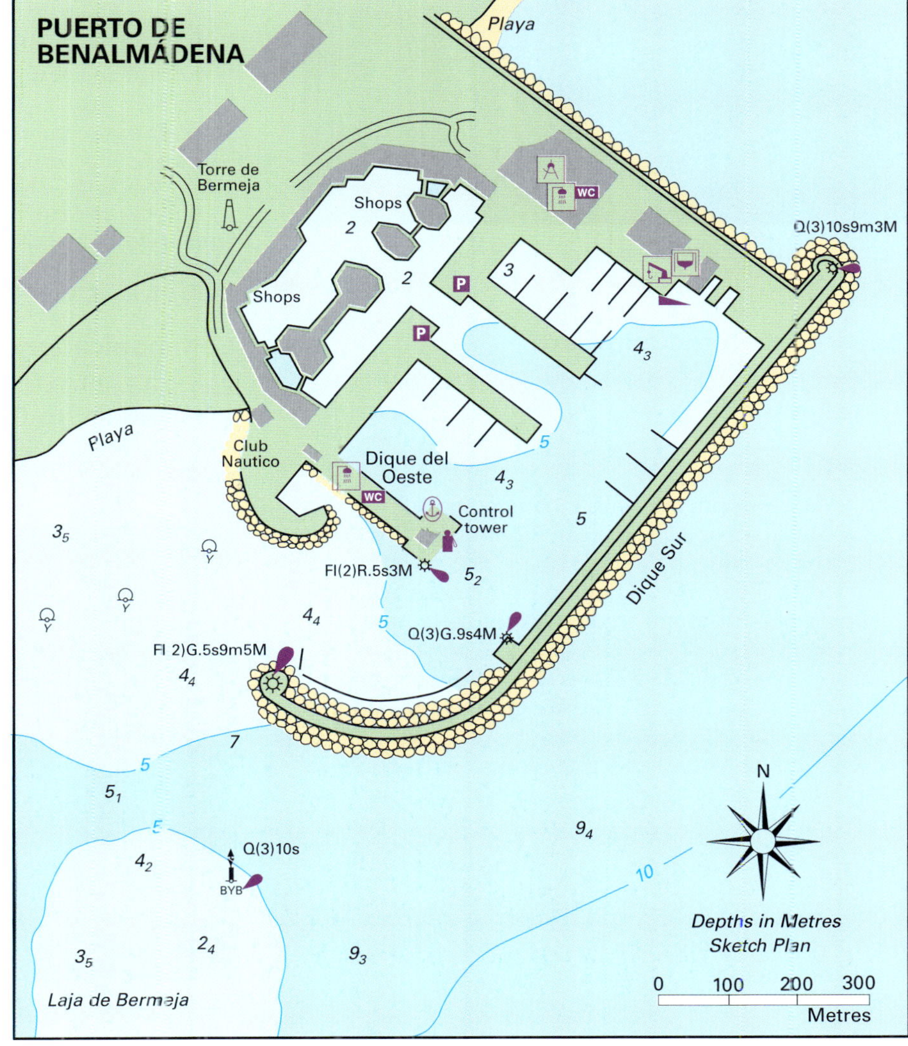

Benalmádena entrance looking W from the Dique Sur *Steve Pickard*

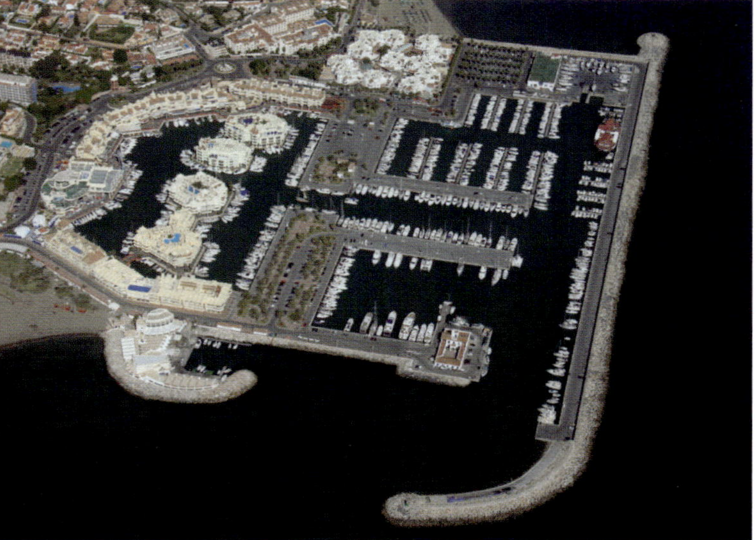

Benalmádena *Pública de Puertos de Andalucía*

Anchorage in the approach

Anchor 200m to the NE of the E end of the Dique Sur in 5m sand.

Entrance

The Laja de Bermeja (2·5m), lying some 250m S of Dique Sur head light, is the easterly outlier of a large rock strewn and shallow area to the west of the actual rock. The E cardinal post marks this large shallow area (although to the west of the actual Laja de Bermeja!)

From a position ½M out and where the S end of the harbour is due W, approach on this course leaving the Laja de Bermeja post well to port. Follow the Dique Sur to its head then round it, keeping at least 30m clear and enter on an east-northeasterly course.

Berths

Go to the fuelling point and ask at the control tower for a berth. It seems to be usual practice here always to be told there is no space available, and then to be offered a berth very much longer than your vessel – at a correspondingly higher price. Avoid the breakwater berths as they are subject to a considerable swell during or after winds of F5 or more.

Facilities

Maximum length overall: 30m.
Most yacht maintenance services including sailmaker.
Slipway in the E corner of the harbour.
50-tonne travel-hoist and 5-tonne crane.
Chandleries inside and outside the port.
Showers.
Water and 220v AC on all pontoons and 380v AC on berths between 18–30m.
Gasoleo A and petrol pumps by the control tower.
Ice on fuel quay.
Supermarket in port.
Shops and supermarkets in Benalmádena Costa and Torremolinos, 1M away. Good shops and market (Friday) at Arroya del Miel 1½M inland.
Laundry collected within the port and launderettes in the town.
Diving school.

Communications

Bus and rail services to most parts of Spain, bus stop on main road near the marina. Airport at Málaga. ☎ Area code 952.
Taxi ☎ +34 952 44 15 45.

Benalmádena waiting and fuel berth to port on entry
Steve Pickard

15. Puerto de Málaga

36°43'N 04°25'W

Tides

Time differences based on Gibraltar		*Height difference*				*Mean level*
HW	LW	MHWS	MHWN	MLWS	MLWN	
+0005	–0005	–0·3	–0·1	0·0	+0·1	0·45

Currents

Offshore these are normally E-going but a counter-current sometimes runs off the entrance. The tidal streams up to 0 5 knots run NE and SW in the entrance.

Charts

UKHO *1850, 1851* Imray *M11*
SHOM *7658, 7294* Spanish *455, 455A, 4551*

Lights

Approach
Málaga LtHo Fl(3+1)20s38m25M 243°-vis-047° White truncated conical tower on white two-storey building 37m
Harbour
Dique del Este head Fl(2)G.7s13m3M 000°-vis-20C° Conical masonry tower 4m
New Dique de Levante NE head QR.1s12m3M Red round tower 2m
New Dique de Levante S head Fl.G.5s7m5M Green tower 4m
Submerged breakwater head Q(6)+LFl.15s3M ⯆ cardinal post 4m
Contradique E head Fl.R.5s5M Red pyramid 5m.
Dique del Oeste head Fl(2)R.7s13m4M 374°-vis-231° Conical masonry tower 8m
Puerto Pesquero Espigón Sur Q.R.4m2M Conical stone tower 3m
Puerto Pesquero Espigón Norte Q.G.5m2M Conical stone tower 4m
Dique Transversal del Este head Fl(2)G.7s2M Green post
Muelle Transversal del Oeste head Fl(2+1)R.12s7m2M Tower with red top 4m
Muelle de Romero Robledo Fl(4)R.11s7m2M Tower with red top 5m
Muelle Canovas del Castillo head Fl(2+1)G.12s6m2M Tower with green top 4m

Port communications

Port VHF Ch 9, 11, 12, 13, 14, 16 ✆ +34 952 22 85 28 ✆ +34 952 125000
www.puertomalaga.com
sac@puertomalaga.com
Real Club Mediterraneo VHF Ch 9 ✆ +34 952 226300
cbotes@realclubmediterraneo.com
www.realclubmediterraneo.com

Storm signals

Storm signals may be displayed at the signal station.

Harbour charges Very high

Málaga Port

The major commercial, passenger and fishing port of the Costa del Sol. There is a small yacht club, the Real Club Mediterráneo de Málaga, but it is reputed to not welcome visitors. Yachts have been turned away from Málaga by the harbour authorities and sent to Benalmádena. It has been reported that this applies even in difficult conditions so this is a port to be avoided unless prior arrangements have been made for a berth.

Approach by day

From the west The line of high-rise apartments and hotels at Torremolinos and Puerto de Benalmádena are conspicuous, as are the round storage tanks and the power station with two very tall chimneys 1·5M to SW of the port. Keep within ½M of the shore or more than 1½M off-shore to avoid the Passage Prohibited Area. Pay attention to the exposed wreck in the area.

From the east A grey cement factory about four miles to E of the port is identifiable and the wide flat valley between high ranges of mountains where the port and city are located can be seen from afar. Avoid the prohibited area.

Prohibited area

There are a number of mooring buoys and yellow lit buoys 1½M S of the port, opposite the oil terminal, about 1M offshore and surrounding an oil pipeline terminal. Passage is forbidden through these buoys. Pass inside within ½M of the shore or more than 1½M offshore.

Anchorage in the approach

Anchor to E of port with lighthouse about 300m to NW in 6m sand. Open to the S and W with swell due to large ships entering.

Entrance

For the yacht club berths keep to the E of the Dique del Este. For the harbour proper, enter on a NE course between breakwater heads. Then on a N course between the inner two quays, the port hand quay being very low.

Berths

The Real Club Mediterráneo de Málaga is on the E side of the Dique del Este.

Larger yachts are sometimes allowed alongside the N side of the Dique Transversal del Oeste while on other occasions yachts have been directed to the NE corner of the Dársena del Guadiaro where the quay wall is high.

Formalities

Check with the harbour authorities on VHF Ch 9.

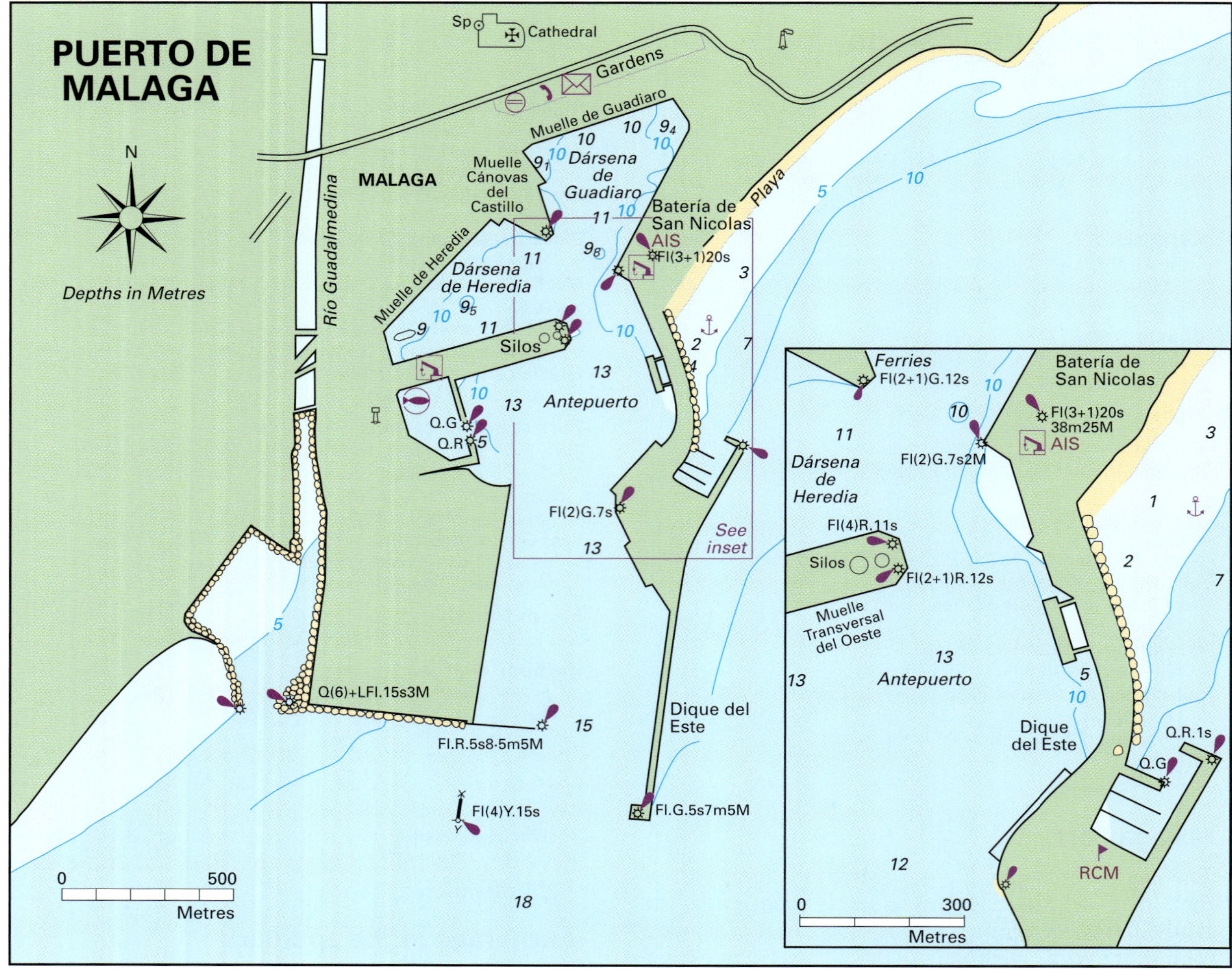

Facilities

Geared towards large commercial vessels. There are points for 220v AC and water. Cranes (no travel hoist), a slipway, ice etc. all something of a hassle to organise.

Chandleries, shops, supermarkets in town but the harbour is enclosed and only the main gate (which has to be negotiated) is open at night.

Spanish chart agency at the Comandancia de Marina near the lighthouse.

Communications

Málaga airport is halfway between Málaga and Benalmádena and has year-round international services. Ship ferry service to Tanger, Barcelona, Canary Islands, Genoa and Marseille. Rail and bus services. Railway. ✆ Area code 952.

British Consulate Málaga
Edificio Eurocom, Calle Mauricio Moro Pareto, 2-2°, 29006 Málaga ✆+34 952 35 23 00.

The coast between Málaga and Candado

There are several bathing beaches along this stretch of the coast which are protected by breakwaters. From the sea they may appear to be harbours. They are not.

16. Puerto de El Candado

36°42'·8N 04°20'·8W

Charts
UKHO *773* Imray *M11*
SHOM *7658, 7294, 6569* Spanish *455*

Lights
Dique de Levante head LFl.G.8s7m3M

Port communications
Club Náutico VHF Ch 9 ✆ +34 952 296097
administracion@clubelcandado.com
www.clubelcandado.com

Harbour charges Low

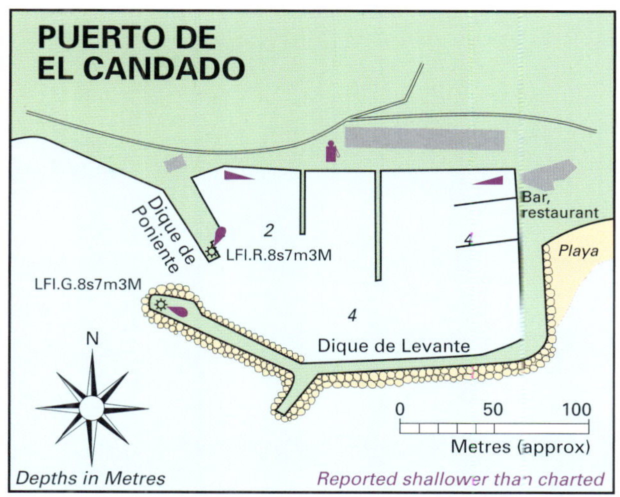

Small shallow harbour

A very small harbour, 280 berths up to 15m. Long silted up, 3·5M E of Málaga. All berths are privately owned and used by small motor boats only. Two fixed vertical lights by night and shapes by day indicate the harbour is closed.

The club appears to be thriving, however, and there are port and starboard buoys laid to lead the locals into the harbour. The depth in the entrance was stated to be 1·5m with a lot of hand-waving so it is probably less than that! This is another marina to bypass.

El Candado entrance looking S *Steve Pickard*

Puerto de El Candado *Pública de Puertos de Andalucía*

Approach

There is a large, grey cement factory just to the E of the harbour.

Anchorage in the approach

Anchor 200m to SW of entrance in 10m sand.

Entrance

Approach a point 200m to NW of the entrance of the harbour, sounding continuously. Leave three small red buoys to port and four small green buoys to starboard. Leave the head of the Dique de Levante 10m to starboard.

Berths

Berth stern-to the quay or pontoon with anchor or mooring buoy from the bow.

Facilities

Maximum length overall: 10m.
A hard in the corner of the harbour.
Water and 220v AC on the pontoons and quays.
Chandlery to N of harbour.
Club Náutico with bar, showers.

Communications

Bus service. ✆ Area code 952.

⚓ Fondeadero de Vélez-Málaga

36°44'·2N 4°05'·5W

An open anchorage off the town of Torre del Mar. Anchor in 6m sand 100m offshore, E of the lighthouse (Fl(1+2)10s30m13M white tower 28m) or further NE. Everyday supplies from the town which has a *club náutico*. The new Puerto Caleta de Vélez lies 1½M to NE.

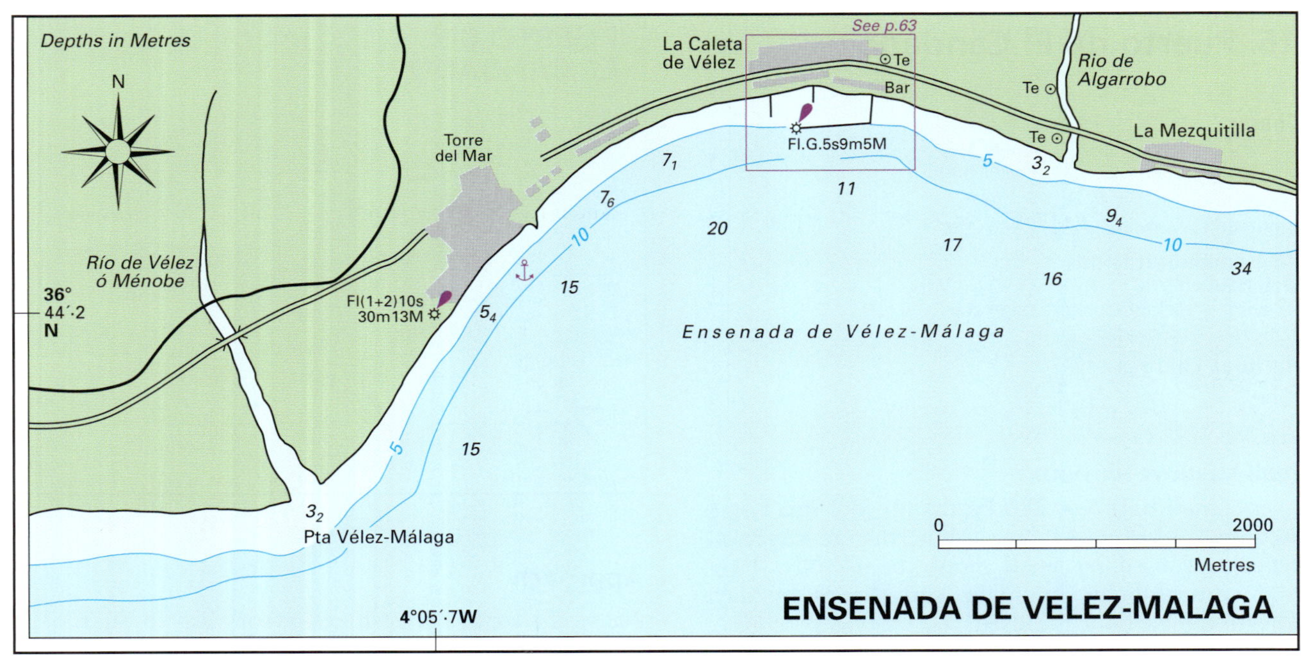

17. Puerto Caleta de Vélez

36°44'·8N 04°04'W

Charts
UKHO *773* Imray *M11*
SHOM *6569* Spanish *455*

Lights
To the west
Torre del Mar (Torre de Vélez) Fl(1+2)10s30m13M
White round tower 28m
Harbour
Dique de Abrigo head Fl.G.5s9m5M
White and green truncated conical tower 4m
Breakwater Head Fl.R.4s8m3M
Contradique Fl(2)R.7s4m3M
White post, red band 2m
To the east
Punta de Torrox Fl(4)15s29m20M
White tower and building 23m

Port communications
Capitanía VHF Ch 9. ✆ +34 951 509476 / +34 600 149214
caleta@eppa.es www.eppa.es
www.puertosdeandalucia.es/es/puerto-de-caleta-de-velez

Harbour charges Medium

Small quiet fishing harbour

This small, fishing harbour with 274 berths to 20m lies at the head of the Ensenada de Vélez Málaga. The absence of tourists make it a quiet place though this may be due to the lack of shoreside facilities. It is one of eleven yacht harbours run by the *Junta de Andalucía*. It is easy to approach and enter though care is necessary with heavy onshore wind and/or swell. Facilities for yachts are limited but it is a useful place to spend a day or two on passage between Málaga and Motril. Sand and pebble beaches either side of the harbour.

Approach

From the west The sandy coast from Málaga eastward is relatively featureless, lined with small housing estates. Punta de Vélez Málaga, which is the delta of a river, is not prominent. Only after rounding it, will Torre del Mar light become plain among the houses and flats of the town. A factory chimney to its NE is conspicuous.

From the east Punta de Torrox is on a low, flat sandy delta which itself is not prominent. The lighthouse is conspicuous. The large block of flats at La Mezquitilla, 1M to the E of the harbour, and the road bridge over the Río del Algarrobo will also be seen. In the closer approach the harbour walls are conspicuous.

Vélez entrance looking W from the Dique de Abrigo – note low lying outer breakwater *Steve Pickard*

Puerto Caleta de Vélez *Pública de Puertos de Andalucía*

Anchorage in the approach

Anchor 200m offshore in 5m sand either side of the harbour.

Entrance

Approach the W end of the Dique de Abrigo on a northerly course and round the *dique* noting the low lying espigon projecting some 20 metres N. Fishing boats exit the port at high speed and are obscured due to the high *dique*.

Berths

Secure stern to the quay or pontoon at the E end of the harbour. There are mooring buoys but they are private.

Facilities

Maximum length overall: 20m.
45-tonnes hoist. The whole E side of the harbour is hard.
220v AC and water on the quay.
Gasoleo A, petrol 0900–1230, 1600–2000hrs.
Supermarket 100m from the port, more in Torre del Mar and a hypermarket about 3km from the port towards Torre del Mar.

Locally

Vélez Málaga is an excellent place from which to visit Nerja and its nearby caves. The recently discovered cave complex with its huge towering stalactites and stalagmites rising several stories high became famous with evidence of occupation dating beyond neolithic times. Well worth a visit.

Communications

Bus service along the coast. ✆ Area code 951.

Vélez fuel berth to port on entrance *Steve Pickard*

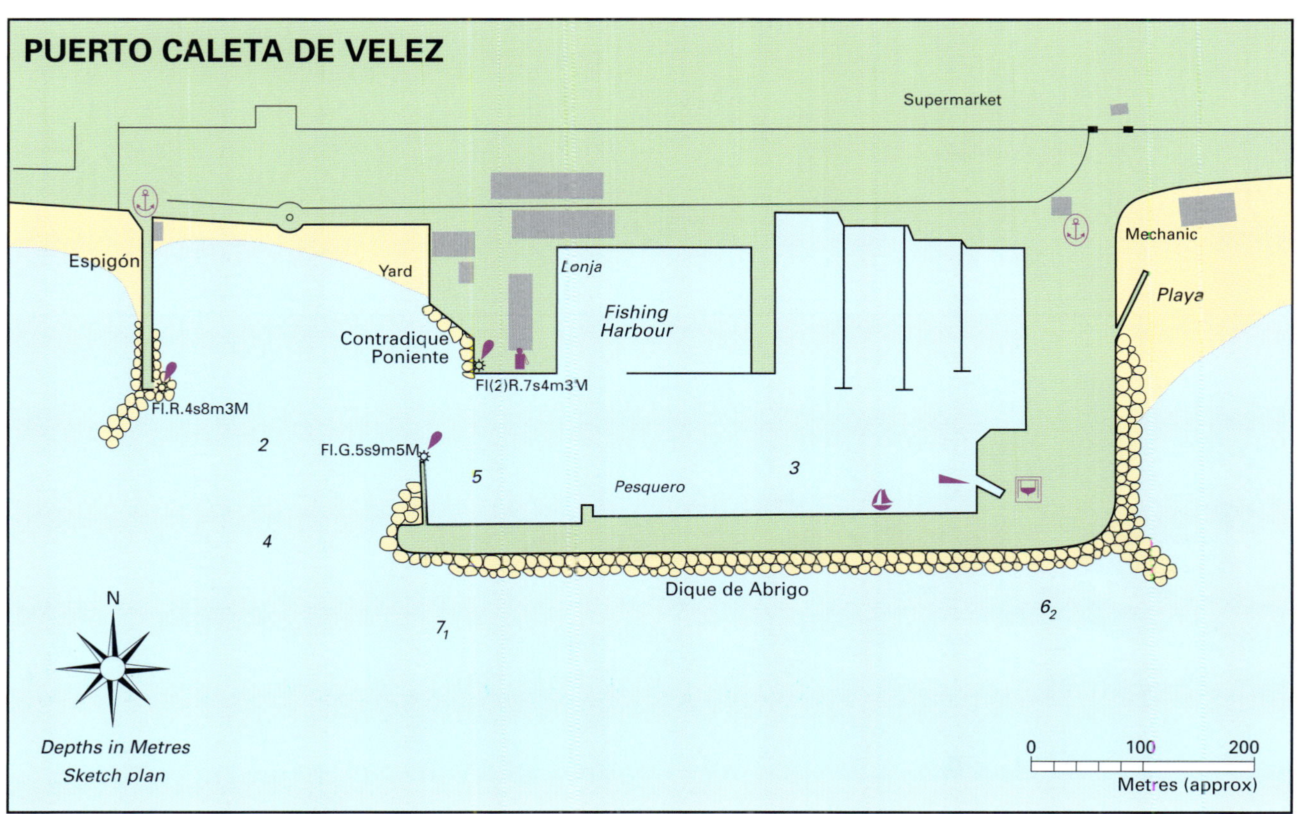

PTA DEL TORROX TO CABO DE GATA AND ISLA DEL ALBORÁN

Ports

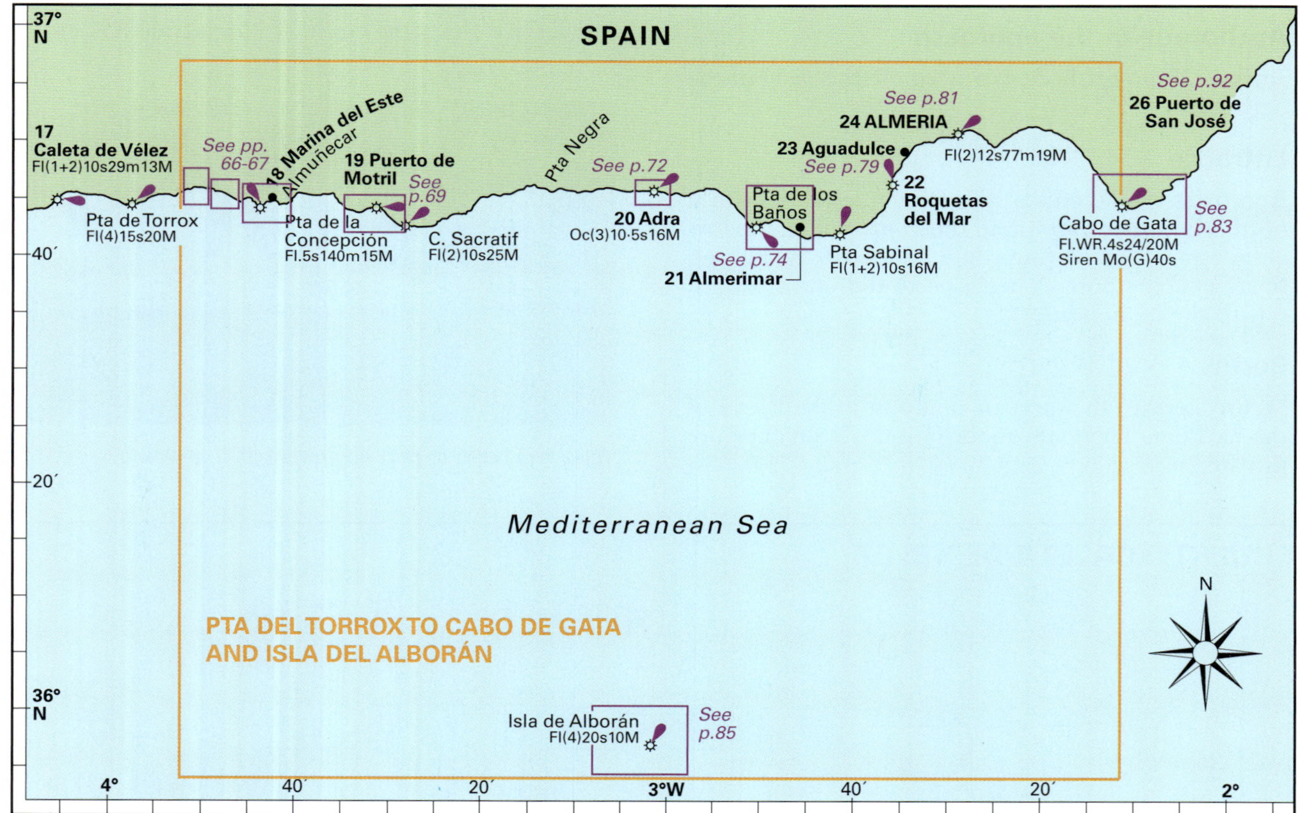

Punta del Torrox

Anchorages between Pta del Torrox and Motril

⚓ Fondeadero de Nerja

35°45'N 3°51'·8W

A pleasant anchorage just E of Nerja where everyday supplies are available. Anchor 100m from the Playa de Barranja in 5m, sand, or 400m off in 18m, stones.

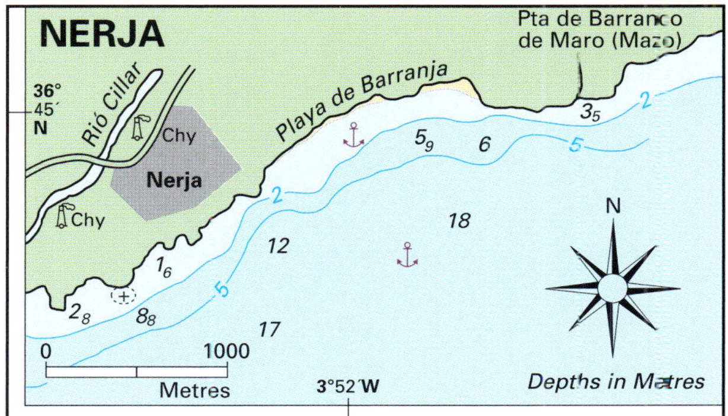

⚓ Cala de la Miel

36°45'·1N 3°49'·5W

An interesting and attractive open anchorage with a stony beach and a track to the main road on the cliffs behind. Anchor in 5m sand and pebbles. Conspicuous ruined tower on cliff to W of bay with three small disused houses. There is a freshwater spring.

⚓ Cala de los Cañuelos

36°44'·6N 3°47'·5W

Anchor in 5m sand and pebble off the centre of the shingle beach which has isolated rocks at either end of the beach. The track leads to the main road.

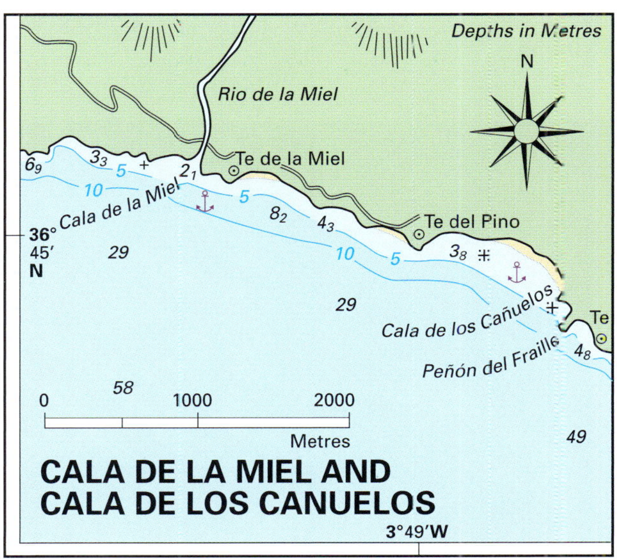

Cañuelos

⚓ Ensenada de la Herradura

36°44'N 3°44'·8W

A bay a mile wide between Puntas Cerro Gordo and de la Mona. Anchor in 5m sand 100m from the beach or 200m out in 11m mud. Additonal shelter at either end but beware rocks. Everyday supplies from the town.

Ensenada de la Herradura west

Ensenada de la Herradura east and *below* Herradura

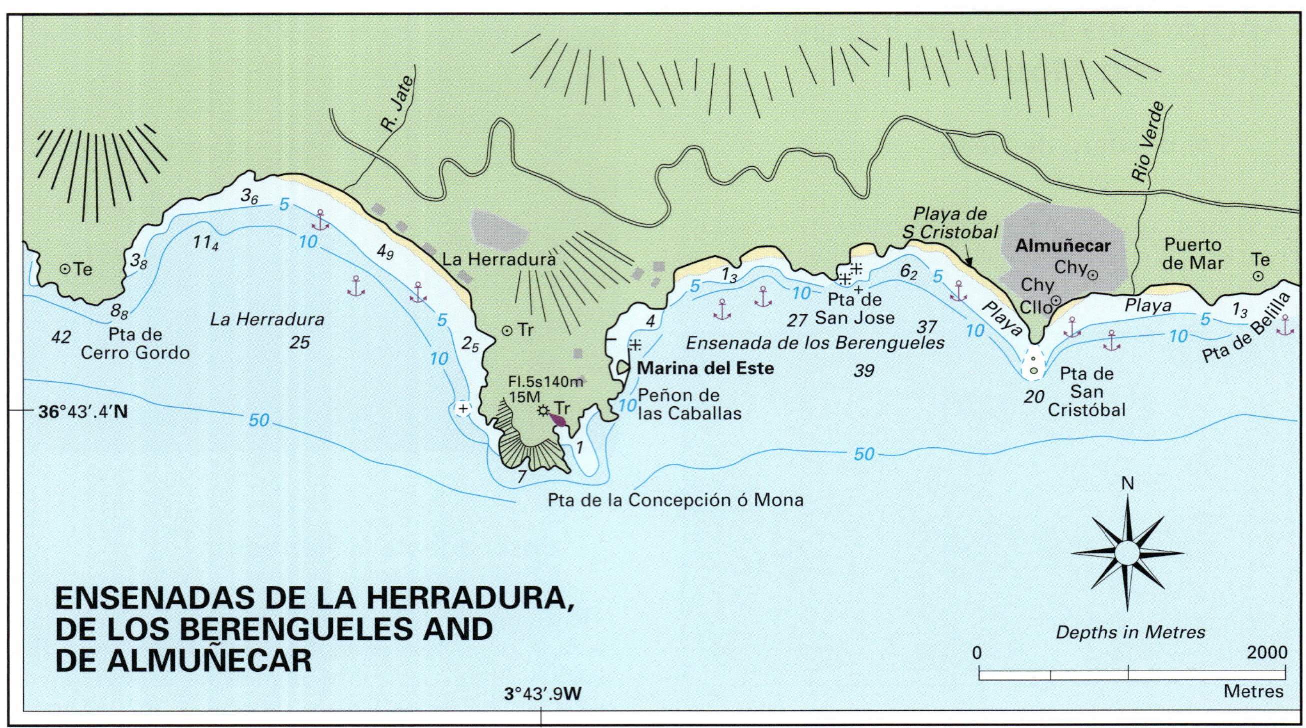

18. Marina del Este (Puerto de la Mona)

36°43′·7N 03°43′·5W

Charts

UKHO *773*	Imray *M11*
SHOM *6569*	Spanish *456*

Lights

To the south

Punta de la Mona Fl.5s140m15M Masonry tower 14m

Harbour

Dique de Abrigo Fl(2)R.5s13m4M Red tower 5m

Contradique Fl(2)G.6s5m3M Green tower 3m

To the east

Cabo Sacratif Fl(2)10s98m25M
White tower and building 17m

Port communications

Capitania VHF Ch 9. ✆ +34 958 640 801
marinaeste@marinasmediterraneo.com
www.marinasmediterraneo.com

Harbour charges Low in low season (1 November to 1 March). Medium in summer.

Small harbour in beautiful area

A small artificial yacht harbour with 227 berths up to 30m which forms part of a huge housing development in a beautiful area. Approach and entry are easy with generally good protection from the W sector. However, strong winds from the E and NE bring a very unpleasant swell and surging into the marina and make entry dangerous. It is particularly difficult for sailing yachts that often have to moor up against large motor vessels with high fixed protruding guardrails. Basic facilities and restaurants are provided. This harbour, together with the Puerto Caleta de Vélez (Torre del Mar), form useful stopping places between Málaga and Motril, but prices are high. A small beach near the harbour, pool at yacht club.

Approach

From the west Nerja and the Punta de Cerro Gordo are easily recognised. The high prominent Punta de Concepción (Mona) is unmistakable; the harbour lies round the corner.

From the east After passing the delta of Río Guadalfeo the coast becomes hilly. Almuñecar with an old fort above it is conspicuous at the beginning of the Ensenada de los Berengueles. The harbour lies on the W side of this Ensenada, about half-way along the ridge leading to Punta de Concepción (Mona).

Marina del Este *Pública de Puertos de Andalucía*

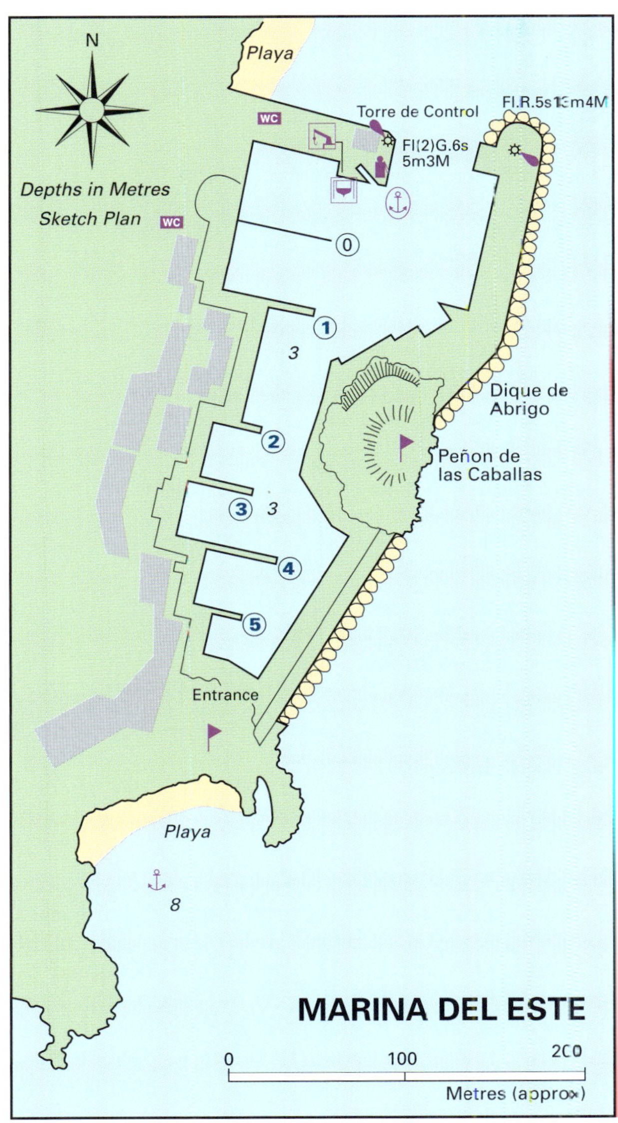

Marina entrance looking W from Dique de Abrigo – note the small boat moorings *Steve Pickard*

Anchorage in the approach

Anchor 100m off the beach in 5m sand in the NW corner of the Ensenada de Berengueles, or off the beach S of the marina.

Entrance

Approach the W side of the Ensenada de los Berengueles keeping 400m from the coast, due to off-lying rocks, until the N end of the harbour bears W then approach and round the head of the breakwater leaving it 25m to port and enter on a S course.

Berths

Secure to fuel berth on the starboard side on entering and ask at control tower.

Facilities

Maximum length overall: 30m.
30-tonnes travel-lift and a 3·3-tonne crane.
A large hard for laid-up yachts.
Limited repair facilities. The marine engineer and chandler can find specialists.
Showers at yacht club.
Water and 220v AC points on the quays and pontoons, 380v on large berths.
Gasoleo A and petrol.
Ice near the fuel quay.
Small supermarket and laundry in the marina. Other shops in Herradura 2M over the hill.

Locally

The prehistoric caves at Nerja, the old villages in the hills and the famous city of Granada can all be visited easily from here. The mountains of Sierra Nevada lying inland are very beautiful.

The nearby town of Almuñecar and the castle of San Miguel have some of the greatest historic treasures of Spain. The Alhambra palace of Granada is one of the most visited historical sites in the world and a World Heritage site.

Communications

Bus service on the main road 1M away – a long, steep climb. ✆ Area code 958.
Taxi ✆ +34 958 63 00 17.

Marina del Este entrance looking NE - beware rocks off head of Dique de Abrigo *Steve Pickard*

⚓ Ensenada de los Berengueles

36°43'·9N 3°43'W (See plan on page 66)

Another large anchorage on the E side of Punta de la Mona in attractive surroundings. There are several places where anchorage is possible – 100m off the Playa de San Cristóbal that lies to the W of Almuñecar in 5m sand or off the two beaches in the NW corner of the bay. All normal facilities from the town of Almuñecar and some repairs possible. Almuñecar fort is conspicuous.

⚓ Punta de San Cristóbal and Fondeadero de Almuñecar

36°43'N 3°42'·2W (See plan on page 66)

Anchor 200m off the beach in 5m sand or 400m out in 20m stones. Punta de San Cristóbal gives protection from the west. Almuñecar has a conspicuous fort. Everyday supplies in the town.

⚓ Ensenada de Belilla

36°43'·7N 3°41'·1W (See plan on page 66)

An anchorage 150m off the Playa de Belilla in 5m clay and sand, or further out in 30m stones. Modern holiday development along the coast where everyday supplies may be found.

⚓ Ensenada de Robaina

36°44'·5N 03°39'·4W

A pleasant small anchorage 3M E of Almuñecar. Anchor 50m off a pair of small sand and pebble beaches in 5m sand. A conspicuous small fort is located on Punta de Jesus o del Tesorillo and a large block of flats behind the W beach.

⚓ Surgidero de Salobreña

36°44'·1N 03°35'·7W

Peñón and Surgidero de Salobreña, 3M W of Motril: anchor either side of the conspicuous *peñon* (rock), 100m off the coast in 5m, sand and pebbles, or 400m out in 25m, mud. The Moorish castle above the town of Salobreña is easily seen.

Salobreña with conspicuous peñon at the left hand end of the shoreline

19. Puerto de Motril

36°43'·4N 3°30'·7W

Charts
UKHO *773, 774, 1854* Imray *M11*
SHOM *6569* Spanish *4571, 457*

Lights
To the west
Punta de la Mona Fl.5s140m15M
Masonry tower 14m
Harbour
Dique de Poniente head Fl(2)R.6s11m10M
Red truncated conical tower 5m
Dique del Este Fl(2)G.7s9m5M Metal post 4m
Dique de Levante head Fl(2+1)G.12s6m5M
Green tower, red band 5m
Espigón head Fl.R.5s6m2M
Red truncated conical tower 5m
Nuevo Dique de Levante elbow Fl(3)G.12s6m5M
Green truncated conical tower 4m
Nuevo Dique de Levante head Fl.G.5s6m2M
Green truncated conical tower 5m
To the east
Cabo Sacratif Fl(2)10s98m25M
White tower and building 17m

Port communications
Port VHF Ch 12 (Tugs), 13. Marina Ch 9. ✆ +34 958 60 00 37
info@nauticomotril.com
www.realclubnauticomotril.com

Harbour charges Low.

Primarily a commercial harbour

A large commercial harbour that started life as a small fishing port. A small Club Náutico lies at the NW end with 193 berths – all usually occupied by club members. The harbour has recently been doubled in size. It has an easy approach and entrance but rather poor facilities for yachtsmen. The harbour is uncomfortable in strong easterly winds but some shelter can now be found behind the huge new *contradique*. The little village near the harbour can provide basic needs but there are many more shops in Motril itself, two miles away. Local holidays occur on 15 August and 15 October.

Reclamation work is continuing on the NE side of the harbour creating a major shipping terminal.

Approach

From the west The flat open plain of the delta of the Río Guadalfeo and the cranes, buildings and tall silos just to the W of Cabo Sacratif show the location of this harbour. Several large blocks of flats line the coast just to the W of this harbour. The town of Motril 2M inland shows in the closer approach.

From the east Cabo Sacratif, a distinctive headland with an isolated conspicuous lighthouse at its summit can easily be recognised from afar. There are two white radar domes on the mountain Sierra do Pelaos 4M to NE of this cape.

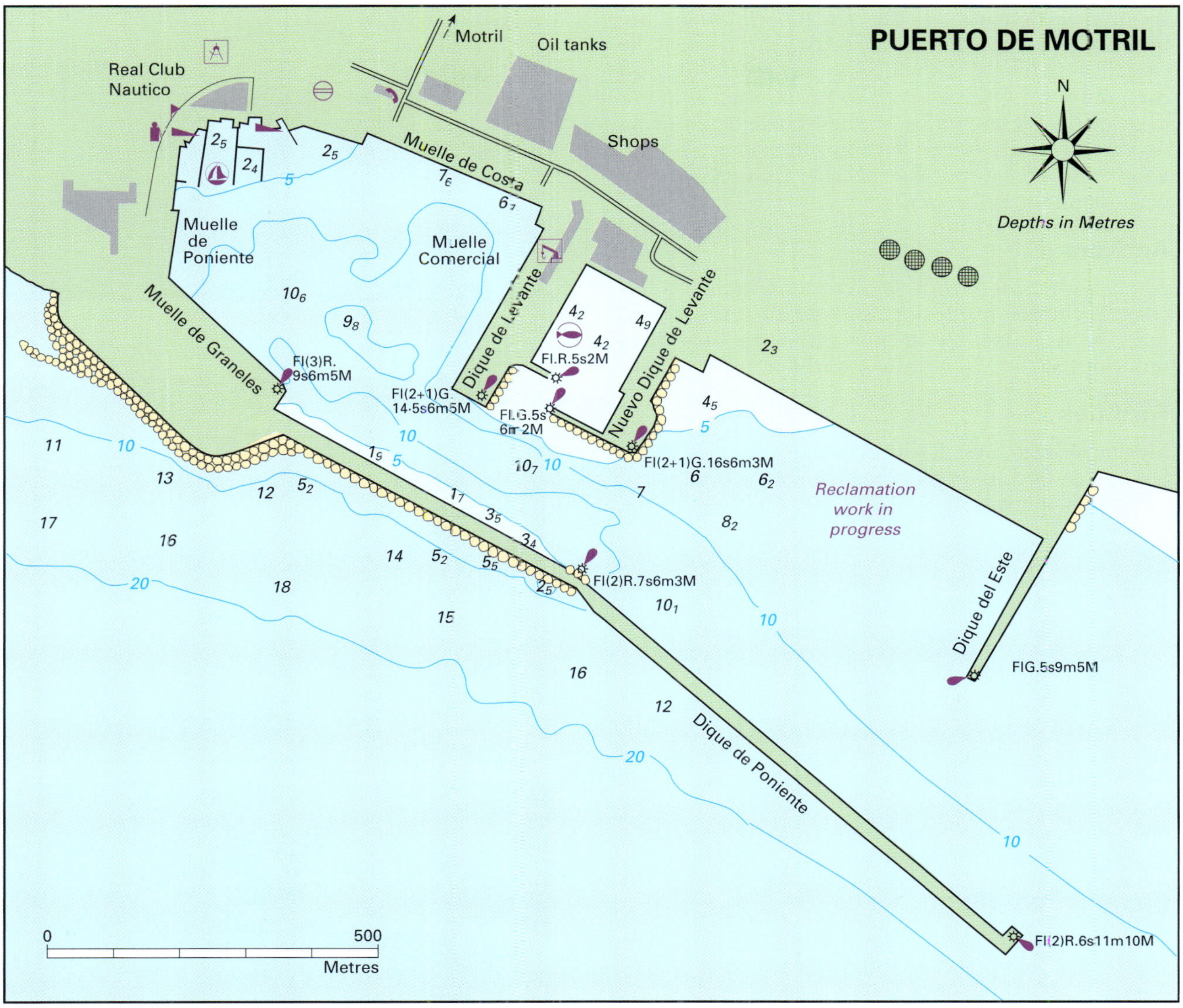

Puerto de Motril Club Náutico
Pública de Puertos de Andalucía

Entrance

Approach the new head of the Dique de Poniente on a N course. Round it and enter between the heads, and steer parallel to the *dique* up the harbour on a WNW course.

Berths

The Real Club Náutico, located at the NW end of the port rarely has any space but is accommodating if it has a berth. Sometimes there is space on the hammerhead end of the W pontoon. It may be worth trying, particularly if the afternoon winds are impeding passage along the coast, as is often the case. Alternatively if there is space, go stern-to on the pontoons. Otherwise go stern-to either side but clear of the diesel pumps on the Muelle de Poniente on the west side of the harbour. In strong SE or E winds, lie alongside the Muelle Comercial with permission of the *capitanía*.

Anchorage

Along with most of the commercial harbours on this coast anchoring in the port is expressly forbidden. It may be possible to anchor close to the yacht moorings at the W end of the harbour.

Facilities

Maximum length overall (club náutico): 20m.
Slipways at the yard in the NW corner of the main harbour and in the Puerto Pesquero can handle up to 100 tonnes.
Cranes up to 2·5 tonnes.
Engine and mechanical workshops outside the harbour.
A small chandlery shop in the village.
Water and 220v AC on quays and pontoons. For water hose, contact a harbour official if using water from quays.
Gasoleo A on west side of harbour.
Ice from the ice factory in the village or from restaurant.
Club Náutico de Motril has bars, lounge, terrace and restaurants, also showers and a pool. Visiting yachtsmen are welcomed.
Supermarket just outside harbour area. Market and many more shops in Motril.

Communications

Frequent bus service to Motril. Buses to Granada and back (a long day's outing). ✆ Area code 958. Taxi ✆ +34 958 60 18 54.

⚓ Anchorage E of Cabo Sacratif

36°41'·5N 03°28'W

An open coastal anchorage tucked under the E end of the rocky cliffed Cabo Sacratif. Anchor 100m offshore in 5m sand and pebbles. The main road runs a little way inland.

⚓ CalaHonda

36°42'·1N 03°24'·7W (see plan)

There are now yellow beach buoys all along the beach and the available area for anchoring is in 20+ metres of water. The village, which has a church tower like a lighthouse, has everyday supplies.

⚓ Anchorages between CalaHonda and Castell de Ferro (see plan)

This 3M stretch of high, rocky cliffed coast is broken into several deep bays. It is possible for experienced navigators to anchor at the heads of these bays in good conditions providing the water is clear enough to see the odd isolated rock. The busy coast road runs along the top of the cliff.

Calahonda

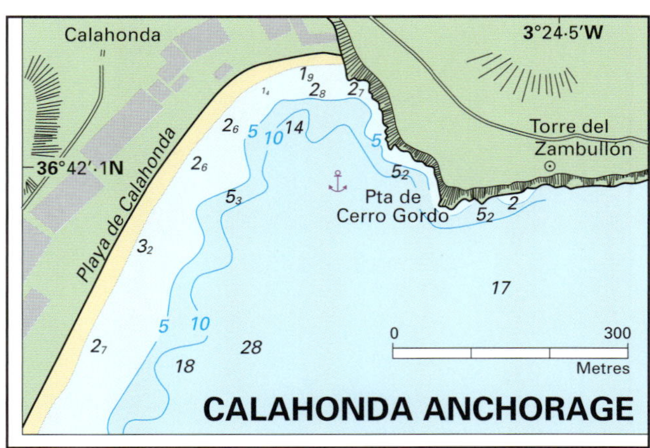

Fondeadero de Castell de Ferro

⚓ Fondeadero de Castell de Ferro

36°43'·1N 03°21'·6W (see plan)

Anchor in the corner of the bay near Punta del Tajo Justos (at the left of the photograph), 100m from the shingle beach, 5m sand and mud or further out in 10m, mud. Good protection from the west. Everyday supplies in the village.

⚓ Anchorages in La Rábita

36°44'·7N 03°10'·5W

A useful coastal anchorage at the W end of a gravel beach. Anchor 100m offshore in 5m sand and stones. The small village is readily recognised by the small blocks of flats 'hung' on a cliff face behind the village with a tower nearby. There is a small fort to the E of the tower. Everyday supplies from the village. Another possible anchorage is small bay to E of Punta Negra.

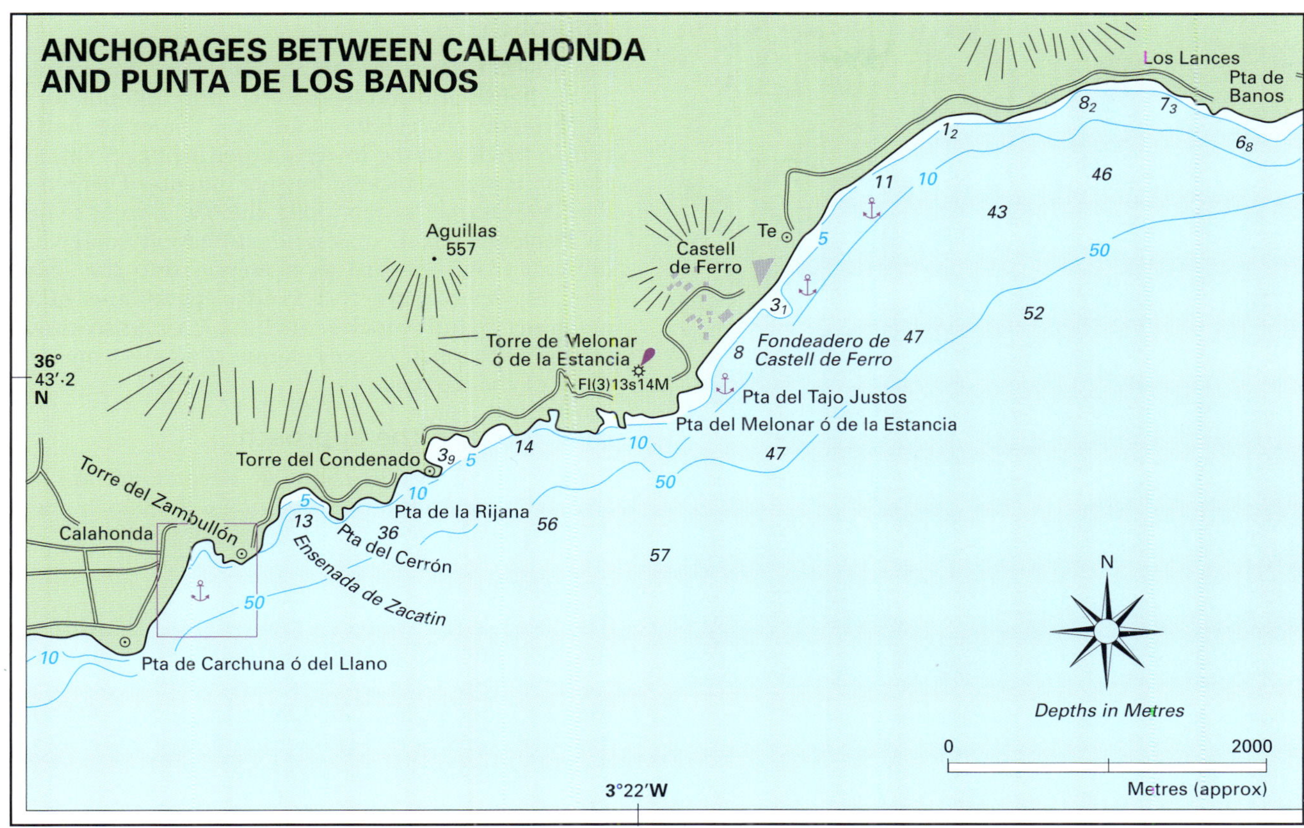

20. Puerto de Adra

36°44′·7N 03°01′·2W

Charts

UKHO *773, 774, 1854* Imray *M11*
SHOM *6569* Spanish *457, 458*

Lights

To the west
Castell de Ferro Fl(3)13s237m14M White tower 12m
Adra lighthouse 36°44′·9N 03°01′·8W Oc(3)10·5s49m16M White tower, red bands 26m
Harbour
Dique de Poniente head N end 36°44′·6N 03°01′·1W Fl(2)R.6s8m3M Red masonry tower 6m
Inner breakwater head Fl(3)R.10s5m2M Red post 3m
Dique de Levante head Fl(2)G.10s8m3M Green masonry tower 5m
Inner breakwater head Fl(3)G.9s5m2M Green post 3m
To the east
Punta de los Baños Fl(4)11s22m11M Rectangular white tower 21m
Punta Sabinal Fl(1–2)10s34m16M Tower above white houses 32m

Port communications

Capitanía ✆ +34 950 805061 / 600 149118
www.eppa.es/en/marina-adra
Real Club Náutico de Adra ✆ +34 950 403487
rcna@realclubnauticodeadra.es
www.realclubnauticodeadra.es

Harbour charges High in commercial harbour but no effective pricing in new marina (2016).

A working harbour

A rather desolate commercial and fishing harbour established by the Phoenicians who called it Abdera. In use ever since it has accommodation for small motor boats but is less suitable for keeled yachts. The new marina is much more civilised and has 267 berths with electricity and water. The approach and entrance is easy in normal conditions but in strong winds, especially those from the E, the entrance can be dangerous and the commercial harbour is very uncomfortable, the constant movement of fishing boats does not help. There are sandy beaches on either side of the harbour. The town is small and without much tourist development. Local holidays September 6–10 in honour of Our Lady of the Sea and St Nicholas of Tolentino.

Adra working harbour looking N from the inner southern breakwater *Steve Pickard*

Puerto de Adra *Pública de Puertos de Andalucía*

Approach

From either direction the harbour can be identified by the lighthouse and by the very large and tall Torre de Perdigones which has windows. The upper half is brown brick and the lower painted white. A smaller similar tower is located further inland. There is a deep grey sandy beach along the SW side of Dique de Poniente which makes identification somewhat difficult from seaward as it merges into the shore line. However there is a sand elevator and other machinery and blocks of flats. A conspicuous factory with a pair of grey chimneys stands some 2M to W of the harbour.

Anchorage in the approach

Anchor 200m to E of Dique de Levante in 5m sand and pebbles. Alternative anchorage in deep water S of the harbour.

Entrance

The head of the Dique de Poniente is T-shaped and the NE spur extends about 30m in that direction from the light. Give it a good berth and pass between the two inner moles. The depths in the entrance and harbour frequently change and are sometimes dredged; depths are approximate.

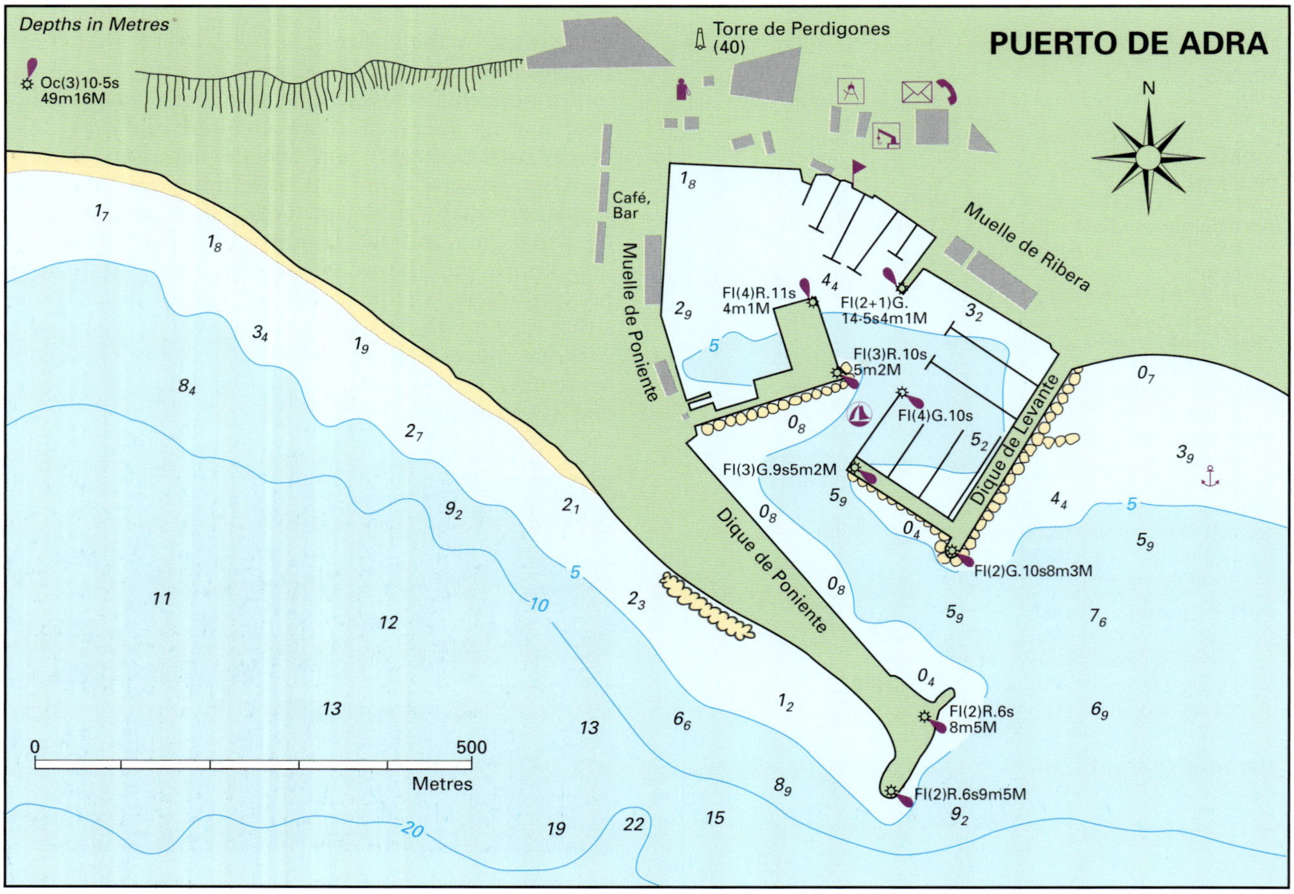

PUERTO DE ADRA

Depths in Metres

Oc(3)10·5s 49m16M

Torre de Perdigones (40)

Café, Bar

Muelle de Poniente

Muelle de Ribera

Dique de Levante

Dique de Poniente

Fl(4)R.11s 4m1M

Fl(2+1)G. 14·5s4m1M

Fl(3)R.10s 5m2M

Fl(4)G.10s

Fl(3)G.9s5m2M

Fl(2)G.10s8m3M

Fl(2)R.6s 8m5M

Fl(2)R.6s9m5M

0 500 Metres

Puerto de Adra's new marina *Steve Pickard*

Berths - marina

Officially not open (2016). The absence of any management does not prevent its use but lack of pontoons makes mooring alongside difficult if not impossible. Some buoyage on second pontoon may enable stern-to mooring.

Berths - commercial harbour

Alongside or stern-to the off-shore end of the Muelle de Poniente. The Real Club Náutico marina is crowded with small boats. It has four visitors berths but check to see if you will fit.

Anchorage

Anchor in 3m mud near centre of harbour using an anchor with a trip line. Anchor light and shape are necessary.

Facilities

Maximum length overall: 20m for berthing.
Shipyards geared towards fishing boats.
150-tonnes travel hoist and hardstanding in fishing harbour.
5-tonnes crane.
Several slipways which will take the largest yachts.
Chandlers shop in town.
Water, 124v 220v AC from points on quay or from old club náutico.
Water and 220v AC on the new pontoons.
Ice factory on NE side of the harbour.
Club náutico with a bar and restaurant.
Supermarket and shops in the village.

Communications

Bus service along the coast. ✆ Area code 950.

⚓ Balerma

36°43'·6N 02°53'·7W

An open coastal anchorage some 100m off the beach in 5m sand and pebbles, opposite the low Torre de Balerma which has a few buildings around and a factory to NE. A somewhat unattractive flat coast with plastic-covered greenhouses stretching for miles.

⚓ Punta de los Baños

36°41'·6N 02°51'·2W

An extraordinary and rather exposed anchorage between the double spurs of a point. Anchor about 50m from the coast in 3m sand and stones. The very conspicuous Castillo de Guardias Viejas stands on a small hill just within the double point and Punta de Los Baños light is on the eastern side. There are a few buildings and shacks in the area but the nearest small village is about 2M away.

Balerma: miles of plastic sheeting covering valuable crops for the markets of Europe. Strong winds can rip sheets off and carry them into the sea

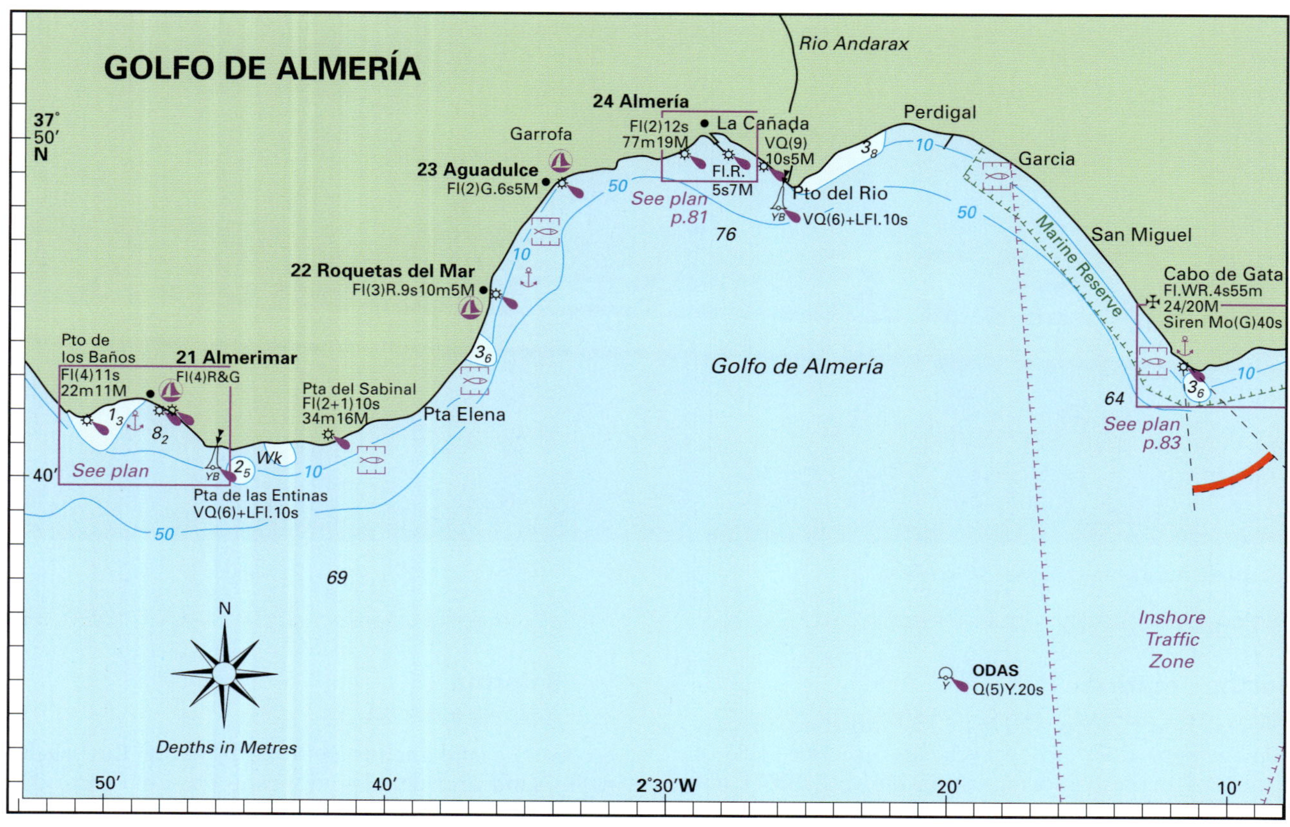

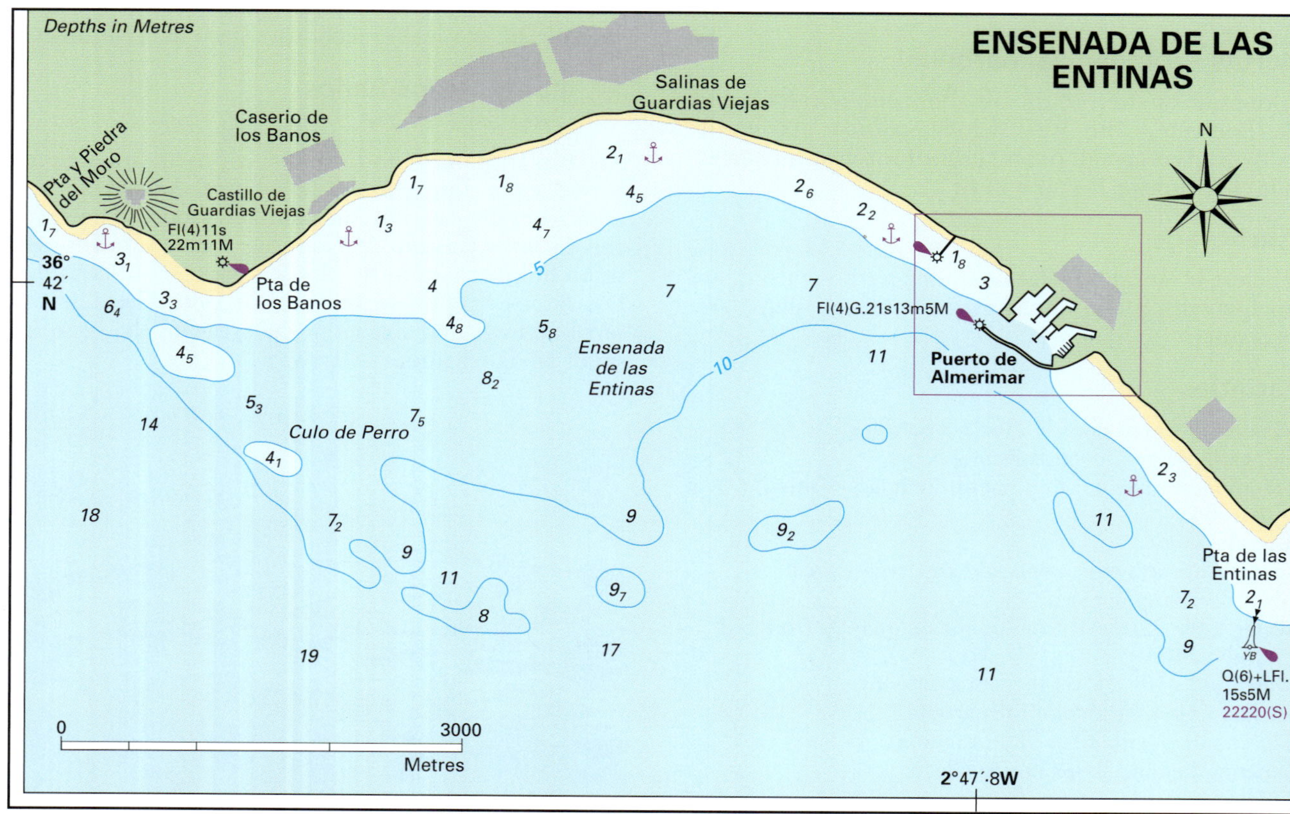

⚓ Ensenada de las Entinas

36°41′·8N 02°49′·0W

Spanish chart *3550*. A wide bay where anchorage is possible anywhere along the coast in three to 5m and 50 to 100m offshore. The shore is flat and the whole area covered with plastic greenhouses. The Castillo de Guardias Viejas on Punta de los Baños and the high-rise flats and buildings around the Puerto de Almerimar near Punta Entinas are both very conspicuous. Supplies from the Puerto de Almerimar.

21. Puerto de Almerimar

36°41'·7N 02°47'·6W

Charts

UKHO *774, 1589* Imray *M11, M12*
SHOM *6569* Spanish *458*

Lights

To the west
Punta de los Baños Fl(4)11s22m11M
Rectangular white tower 21m
Harbour
Red port hand buoy Fl.R.7.5s2M
Espigón Fl(4)R.11s5m3M Post on red turret 3m
Dique Sur head Fl(4)G.21s13m5M Green tower 8m
Dique Sur Middle LFl.G.9.5s4m2M Green turret 1m
Contradique head Fl(2)R.9.5s2m2M Red tower 1m
Ldg Lts *Front* Iso.10s3m2M
White tower, winged top 2m
Rear Oc.10s4m2M White tower, winged top 3m
To the east
Bajo Punta de las Entinas Q(6)+LFl.15s5M ⯯ card buoy
Punta Sabinal Fl(1+2)10s34m16M
Tower on white buildings 32m

Buoys

There may be five or six small yellow buoys marking the starboard and port hand of the entrance channel as the leading lines are sometimes difficult to make out.

Port communications

Port Control VHF Ch 9. ✆ +34 950 60 77 55 / 49 73 50
infomarina@almerimarpuerto.com
www.almerimarpuerto.com

Harbour charges Medium

Welcoming good yacht harbour

This artificial yacht harbour is one of the best marinas along the coast. Cheap and safe in all conditions with a helpful staff, good facilities and berthing for almost 1,000 yachts up to 60m. Much of the hinterland is a sheet of plastic under which a major proportion of north Europe's winter vegetables are grown. Approach and entrance are easy except in strong SW winds which can build big seas at the entrance and sometimes send a swell into the harbour. Very secure with good shelter from easterly gales. Rates, which are on the low side, can be examined on the website.

Winter live aboard community.

Approach

From the west The coast from Adra is low and flat, Puerto de Adra and the Castillo de Guardias Viejas which is on a small hill near Punta de los Baños are easily recognised while the high blocks of flats to the E of Puerto Almerimar can be seen from afar.

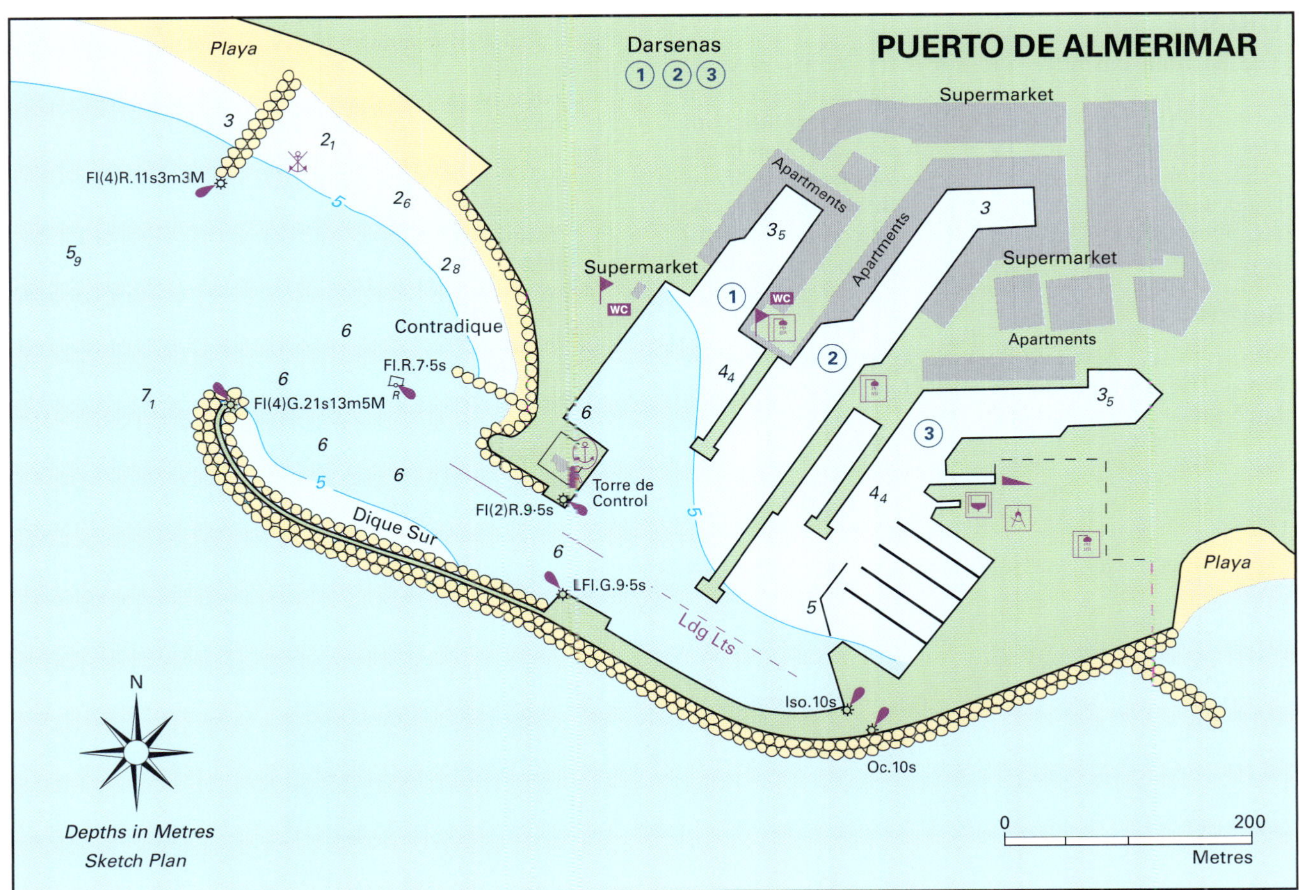

Puerto de Almerimar *Pública de Puertos de Andalucía*

From the east The conspicuous lighthouse on the low flat Punta del Sabinal will be seen and also the blocks of flats mentioned above.

Anchorage in the approach

It is possible to anchor either side of the harbour about 100–150m from the coast in 5m sand.

Entrance

The harbour entrance silts but is frequently dredged to 6m. In spite of frequent dredging it has been reported that there is a shallow patch running out along the breakwater. Exercise care and watch the echo-sounder on entry, giving the hooked end of the breakwater a reasonable berth (50m or so). Leave the red buoy to port and enter between two lines of small yellow buoys or pick up the leading lines at night.

Berths

Secure to fuel berth and ask at the control tower.
Note The four pontoons shown at the east of the harbour are for small craft only.

The Torre de Control, immediately to port on entry
Steve Pickard

Facilities

Maximum length overall: 60m.
Most repair and maintenance facilities.
Volvo dealer and servicing.
110 and 60-tonne travel-lift.
5-tonne crane.
Slipways on the E side of the harbour.
Large hardstanding.
Two chandlers in the port plus other useful shops.
Water points on all quays and pontoons – potable but taste before filling tanks.
Showers in the service block and in the port.
220v AC points on all quays and pontoons. 380v AC on the larger berths.
Gasoleo A and petrol.
Ice available from control tower and bars.
Club náutico.
A small supermarket at the west end of the harbour and a well-stocked one near the boatyard.
Launderettes.
An active Live-Aboard Club has a small club room near the boatyard.
A hypermarket is on the bus route to the town of El Ejido.
Yachtsmen are not allowed to work on their own vessels while in the yard.
Almerimar Marine Services has an excellent well stocked chandlery in the port and can undertake just about any marine repairs. Including rigging, electrical and electronic repairs and installation, refrigeration, marine engineering, etc. ✆ +34 619 99 25 20, info@almerimarmarine.com www.almerimarmarine.com

The working quays on the Dique Sur looking SE, as seen from the Torre de Control
Steve Pickard

Note: Several 220v AC installations around the port are broken and in need of replacement. They use a non-standard connection socket and often need attention by the marineros before they work.

Locally

Almería and the Alcazaba are worth a visit. There are beaches on either side of the harbour. Fishing, wind surfing, diving, golf, tennis and horse-riding.

Communications

Regular bus service to El Ejido whence further buses. Airport at Almería, year round services to Barcelona, Madrid and Melilla, summer charter flights from other European countries. ✆ Area code 950.
Taxi ✆ +34 950 57 06 11 / 48 00 63.

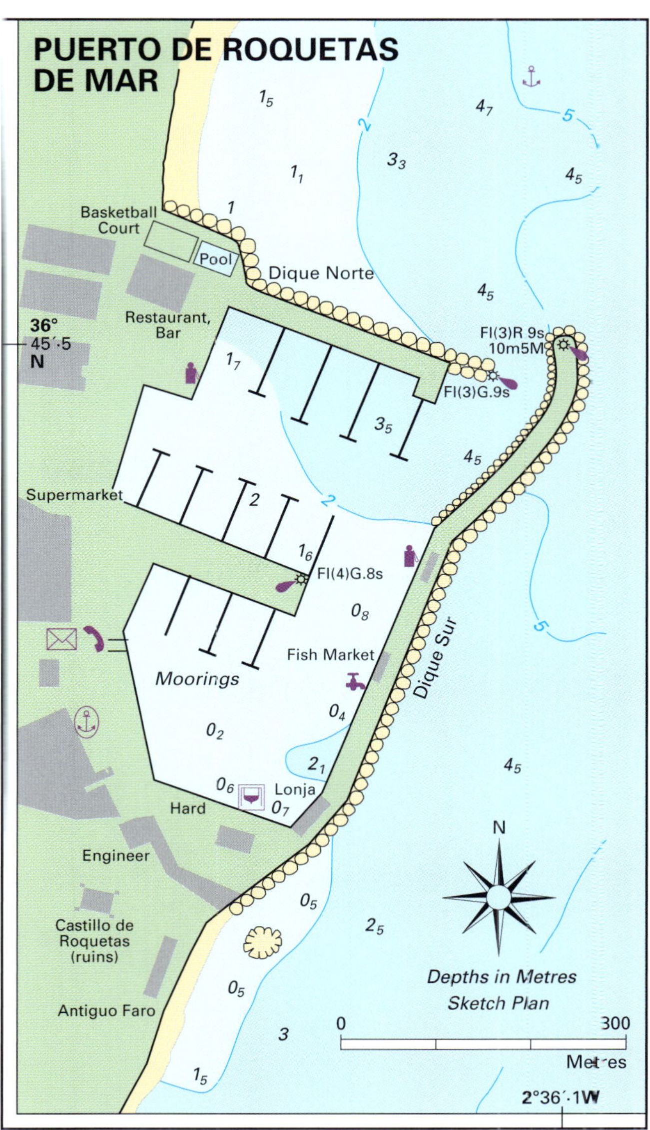

22. Puerto de Roquetas de Mar

36°45'·4N 02°36'·3W

Charts
UKHO *774* Imray *M11, M12*
SHOM *6569* Spanish *459*

Lights
To the west
Punta Sabinal Fl(1+2)10s34m16M
Tower on white buildings 32m
Harbour
Dique Sur head Fl(3)R.9s10m5M
Red round concrete tower 4m
Dique Norte head Fl(3)G.9s5m3M
Green round tower on square base 3m
To the east
Cabo de Gata Fl.WR.4s55m24/20M 356°-W-316°-R-356°
Siren Mo(G)40s White tower, grey lantern on yellow dwelling 19m

Port communications
Capitanía VHF Ch 9 ✆ +34 950 10 04 87 / 600 14 91 22
roquetas@eppa.es
www.eppa.es/en/marina-roquetas-de-mar
Club náutico ✆ +34 950 32 07 89
info@realclubnauticoroquetas.es
www.realclubnauticoroquetas.es

Harbour charges Low

Primarily for fishing boats

A small, mostly shallow harbour for sardine fishing boats and a few yachts. Easy to approach and enter but would be uncomfortable in heavy weather between SE and NE. Attractive in a simple way but tourist development is taking place around this area. There are a few facilities, some basic shops near the harbour and other, better shops in the village about two miles away.

The fuel point on the Dique Sur is for fishing vessels only. The yachts' fuel point is on the NW corner quay but it is very shallow there and fuel Is best obtained with jerrycans.

Fine beaches each side of the harbour. Local holidays 7 and 8 October in honour of the Virgen del Rosario.

Approach

From the SW The low flat-topped headland of Punta Sabinal which has an isolated lighthouse and tower with radomes. A large tourist complex of high-rise buildings is located between this headland and the port. The old disused yellow lighthouse and small castle just S of the harbour are recognisable.

From the NE From Almería the cliffs reach within 4M of Roquetas which is at the edge of a plain covered with plastic greenhouses. There are buildings and blocks of flats behind the harbour.

Entrance

Straight-forward between *dique* heads which have small stone towers. Give Dique Sur head a reasonable berth in case sand has built up off the end. The entrance is dredged and depths vary.

Roquetas de Mar from NE *Pública de Puertos de Andalucía*

Berths

Bow or stern to pontoons on the north side of the entrance but make up wherever possible in the outer harbour and ask at the *club náutico*. Due to the shallow harbour, keel yachts should only attempt to berth at the easternmost pontoon. The harbour becomes crowded when the fishing fleet returns.

Anchorage

The area N of the harbour entrance is popular for local boats. In westerly winds the swell finds its way in. Tuck in as close to the N dique as possible outside of the beach buoys.

Facilities

Maximum length overall: 15m.
50-tonnes travel hoist and 8-tonnes crane.
Water and 220v and 380v AC points on quays.
Club náutico with restaurant and bar.
Several small shops and a supermarket in the village. A market and some other shops 2M away.

Communications

Bus service to Almería. ✆ Area code 950.

Entrance looking N *Steve Pickard*

Fishing harbour looking SW from the Dique Sur *Steve Pickard*

23. Puerto de Aguadulce

36°48'·9N 02°33'·7W

Charts

UKHO *774* Imray *M11, M12*
SHOM *6569* Spanish *459*

Lights

To the west

Punta Sabinal Fl(1+2)10s34m16M
Tower on white buildings 32m

Harbour

0092.6 **Dique head** Fl(2)G.6s5m5M
Green pyramid 4m

Contradique head Fl(2)R.7s6m3M
Red concrete tower 4m

To the east

San Telmo LtHo Fl(2)12s77m19M
White square tower oblong black stripes 7m

Cabo de Gata Fl.WR.4s55m24/20M 356°-W-316°-R-356°
Siren Mo(G)40s White tower, grey lantern
yellow building 19m

Port communications

Capitanía/club náutico VHF Ch 9 ✆ +34 950 34 15 02
contacto@puertodeportivoaguadulce.es
www.puertodeportivoaguadulce.es

Harbour charges Low

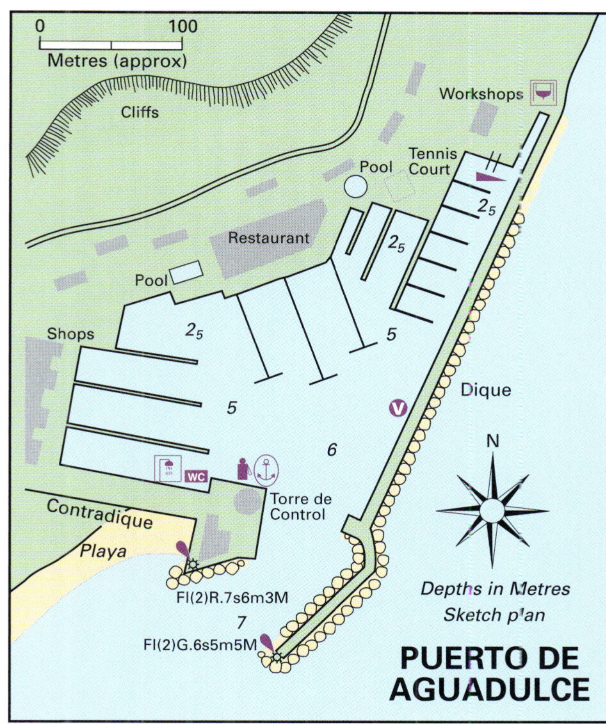

Popular harbour

Aguadulce, only 4 miles from Almeriá provides a useful alternative to Puerto de Almería. Its harbour is easy to enter and provides good shelter except in strong ESE winds when some swell enters making it uncomfortable. Facilities are good. The Alcazaba at Almería should be visited. Long sandy beaches to SW. Popular for winter live aboards.

For visitors, who are usually berthed on the W site of the main Dique de Levante, it is a very long walk around the 764 berth marina (max length 25m) to the town. The marina is somewhat run down with seemingly little maintenance over the years.

Local holidays: The 10 days before the last Sunday in August and the first two weeks in January.

Approach

From the SW Round the low headland of Punta del Sabinal with its conspicuous white, round lighthouse tower. Follow the low featureless coast dotted with various housing estates in a NE direction until

Aguadulce looking S from the cliffs *Steve Pickard*

Puerto de Aguadulce *Pública de Puertos de Andalucía*

Puerto de Roquetas del Mar which has a disused lighthouse, a small square fort and a breakwater, has been passed. Puerto de Aguadulce is located just beyond the point where a range of rocky hills reaches down to the coast. The rocky breakwaters, *torre de control* and low blocks of flats will be seen in the close approach.

From the east Round the unmistakable Cabo de Gata and cross the Golfo de Almería on a WNW course. The mass of buildings of Almería surmounted by the Alcazaba castle and fronted by the harbour breakwater are all conspicuous. The S cardinal light buoy, Q(6)+LFl, off Punta del Río may also be seen. This harbour is located near where the rocky range of coastal hills drops back and the low flat coast commences.

Entrance

Approach the head of the *dique* on a course between SW and N, round it and then the head of the *contradique* to port.

Berths

Secure to the quay by the *torre de control* and report to the office for allocation of a berth.

Facilities

Maximum length overall: 25m.
Workshops at N end of harbour for mechanical, electrical and hull repairs; maintenance, painting etc. Work on own boat permitted.
50-tonnes travel-lift.
Slipway at N end of the harbour.
Hardstanding at N end of the harbour; additional space for 100 yachts under cover.
Sailmaking.
Showers.
Water and 220v AC on quays and pontoons.
Gasoleo A and petrol.
Ice at fuel quay.
Club náutico with good facilities.
Many shops and a large market at Almería about 5M away.
Swimming pool beside the harbour.

Locally

Almeria is well worth a visit, and especially the ancient Alcazaba. A local bus service runs frequently to the town.

Communications

Bus to Almería on road behind the harbour.
Airport (11 miles) and rail (five miles) at Almería.
✆ Area code 950. Taxi ✆ +34 950 34 05 46.

24. Puerto de Almería

36°49'·8N 02°27'·9W

Tides

Time differences based on HW Gibraltar		*Height difference*				*Mean level*
HW	LW	MHWS	MHWN	MLWS	MLWN	
+0010	–0010	0·5	0·4	0·3	+0·3	0·40

Current

Constant E-going current across the mouth of the bay.

Charts

UKHO	*774, 1589*	Imray	*M11, M12*
SHOM	*7504, 6569*	Spanish	*4591, 459*

Lights

To the west

San Telmo LtHo Fl(2)12s77m19M
White square tower black band 7m

Puerto Pesquero

Dique del Oeste head Fl(2)R.6s10m3M
Red tower 5m

Dique Sur head Fl(2)G.6s10m1M
Green tower 5m

Interior mole head Fl(3)R.8s5m1M
Red tower 3m

Main harbour

Dique de Poniente head Fl.R.5s19m7M
White 8-sided tower, red top and base 12m

Cargadero No. 2 head Fl.G.5s8m4M
Green metal structure 3m

Cargadero No. 1 head Fl(3)R.9s5m1M

Corner Fl.Y.5s5m1M Yellow concrete tower 3m

Club de Mar del Almería Dique de Abrigo Fl(2)G.10s4m1M
Green inclined concrete tower 3m

Club de Mar del Almería Contradique Fl(4)R.12s4m1M
Red 3-sided column 3m

Muelle de Poniente o Comercial E corner Fl(2)R.7s5m1M
Red 3-sided column 3m

Dique de Levante head Fl(2+1)G.14·5s4m2M
Green structure, red band 1m

Power station wharf head VQ(9)10s11m5M ⧗ on yellow metal framework tower, black band 9m F.R on building 360m E

To the east

Cabo de Gata Fl.WR.4s55m24/20M 356°-W-316°-R-356° Siren Mo(G)40s White tower, grey lantern on yellow dwelling 19m

Buoys

Black and yellow S card lightbuoy Q(6)+LFl
⧗ topmark off Punta del Río de Almería

Port communications

Port VHF Ch 12, 14 and 16. Club de Mar VHF Ch 9
☎ +34 950 23 60 33
almeria@apalmeria.com
www.apalmeria.com

Harbour charges High

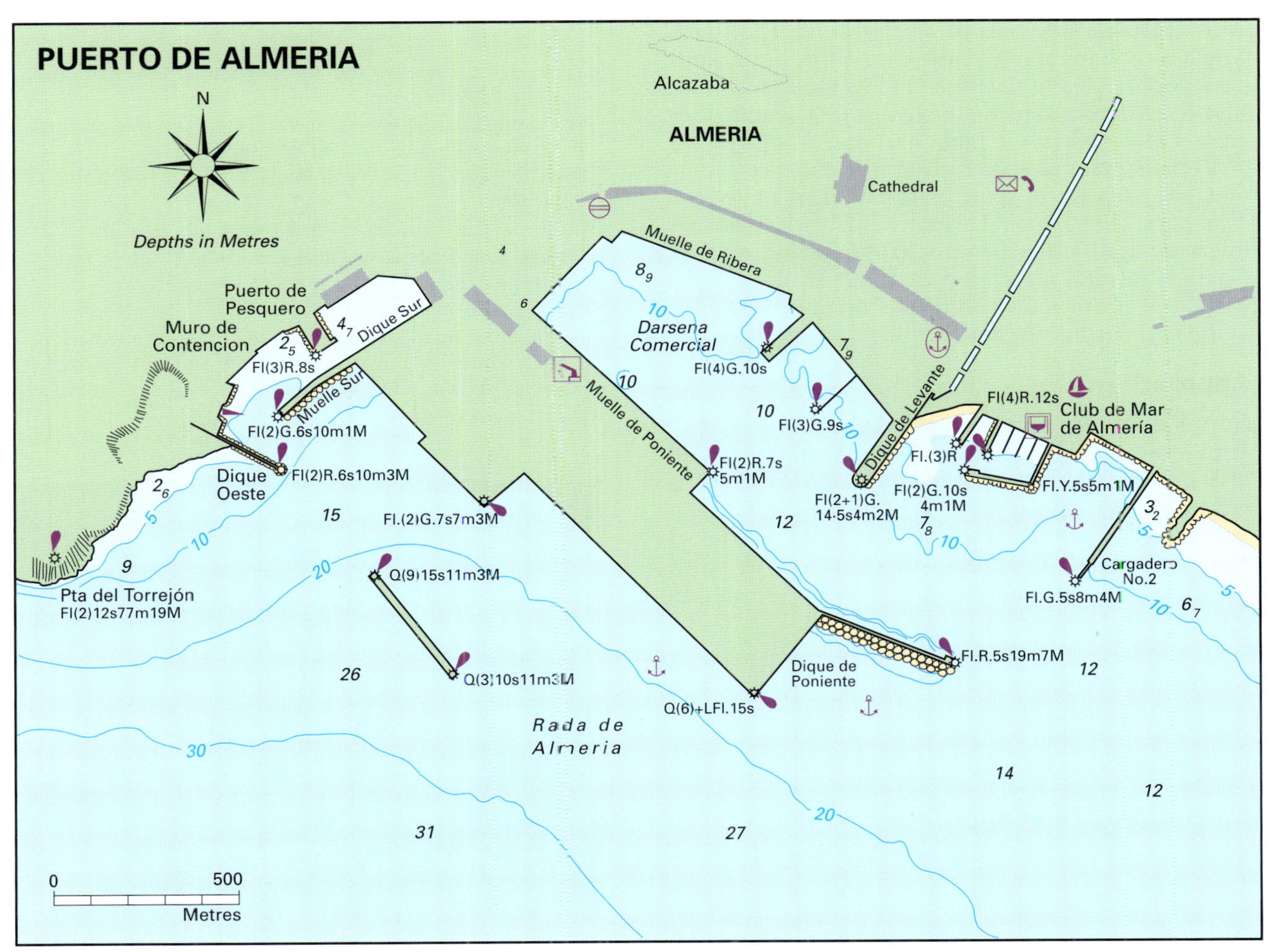

Almería Club de Mar, looking ENE
Pública de Puertos de Andalucía

Useful commercial harbour

A commercial and fishing port with an old and interesting town and castle nearby. Approach and entrance can be made in almost any conditions and good shelter obtained but winds from the E cause an uncomfortable swell inside the harbour. The town, which is the capital of the province of the same name has good shops and markets. Yachts use the Club de Mar del Almería, outside the Dique de Levante; they are not welcome in the main harbour.

Reclamation and construction work has been going on in the harbour for some years making it a busy and dirty port. The yacht club with its 277 berths is always full and visitors are directed to Aguadulce, 4M W. Another private yacht club at the NW end of the harbour is for members only. Anchoring is prohibited in the harbour but see note below.

Approach

From the SW Almería lies at the head of a wide bay at the foot of the mountains. The low flat headland of Punta del Sabinal with its isolated lighthouse is recognisable 10M to SW. The Alcazaba (castle) on a hill near the town is conspicuous at a distance but is dwarfed by tower blocks of flats to E. The town buildings and the long Dique de Poniente are seen in the closer approach.

From the east After Cabo de Gata, a rugged high promontory, the coast is low and flat. The town and harbour are visible from afar; there is a very tall port authority building on the end of the Dique de Levante which is prominent.

Anchorage in the approach

Anchor close to SW side of Dique de Poniente. It is deep at 10–15m. Swell builds here in the afternoon breeze making it untenable in any S sector winds.

Anchoring within the inner harbour is prohibited.

Entrance

Straightforward but keep a lookout for commercial and fishing vessels leaving, sometimes at speed. Inside the harbour there are a number of unlit mooring buoys.

Berths

Visiting yachts are now sent four miles west to Puerto de Aguadulce. The Club de Mar moorings are reserved for members' yachts although occasionally, and with a great deal of persuasion space can be found for a visitor.

Anchorage

Anchor in 6m sand and mud 150m S or E of Club de Mar, clear of moorings. Depths vary 7–10m. Show anchor light and shape.

Facilities

The Club de Mar del Almería is a tennis and yachting club with a bar, restaurant, showers and terrace. Visitors should first contact the secretary for permission to use the facilities.

Maximum length overall: 15m in the Club de Mar.

Shipyards geared to fishing boats beside the slipway and also at the W end of Puerto Pesquero.

Slipways in both the main of the harbour and the Puerto Pesquero.

Cranes 4–12 tonnes in the harbour and a 4-tonne crane at the Club de Mar.

Several engineering workshops in town and one on the quay on Muelle Sur.

Chandlers and Engineers in the NW corner of the main harbour.

Water and 220v AC on all berths at Club de Mar.

Gasoleo A and petrol at Club de Mar.

Ice from ice factory between Puerto Pesquero and Dársena Comercial.

A number of small shops and a small market near the port. Many large and varied shops and a large market about 1M away in the town.

Several launderettes in the town.

Club de Mar del Almería

Locally

The Moorish castle (Alcazaba) is very attractive and worth a visit. Several museums and ancient churches make a trip to the town worthwhile.

Local holidays are the 10 days before the last Sunday in August, and the first two weeks of January.

During the Summer festivities the locals re-enact the defeat of the Moors in their colourful costumes.

Communications

Airport with summer charter flights from Europe and year-round services to Madrid or Barcelona. Railway. Occasional service by boat to Marseille, Algeria, Canary Isles and South America. ✆ Area code 950. Taxis ✆ +34 950 25 11 11.

⚓ Cabo de Gata anchorages

Anchor off the village of San Miguel de Cabo de Gata to the NW of the Cabo and its conspicuous tower in 5m of sand some 200m off the coast. One can also anchor 100m off Playa de los Corrales further to the SE in sand, well sheltered from N and E and 150m NW of Cabo de Gata light in 5m sand and stone. There is a small settlement and conspicuous church by the saltworks on the road to San Miguel de Gata. Tunny nets are sometimes laid in this area.

Cabo de Gata: The distinctive white patch on the SW cliff face is a welcome sight when coming from the west
Jane Russell

Notes on rounding Cabo de Gata

1. Stay close inshore or 1·0M offshore to avoid Laja de Cabo de Gata shoal (3m) which breaks in heavy weather
2. Winds tend to increase around this cape
3. Current is normally east-going and can be very strong.

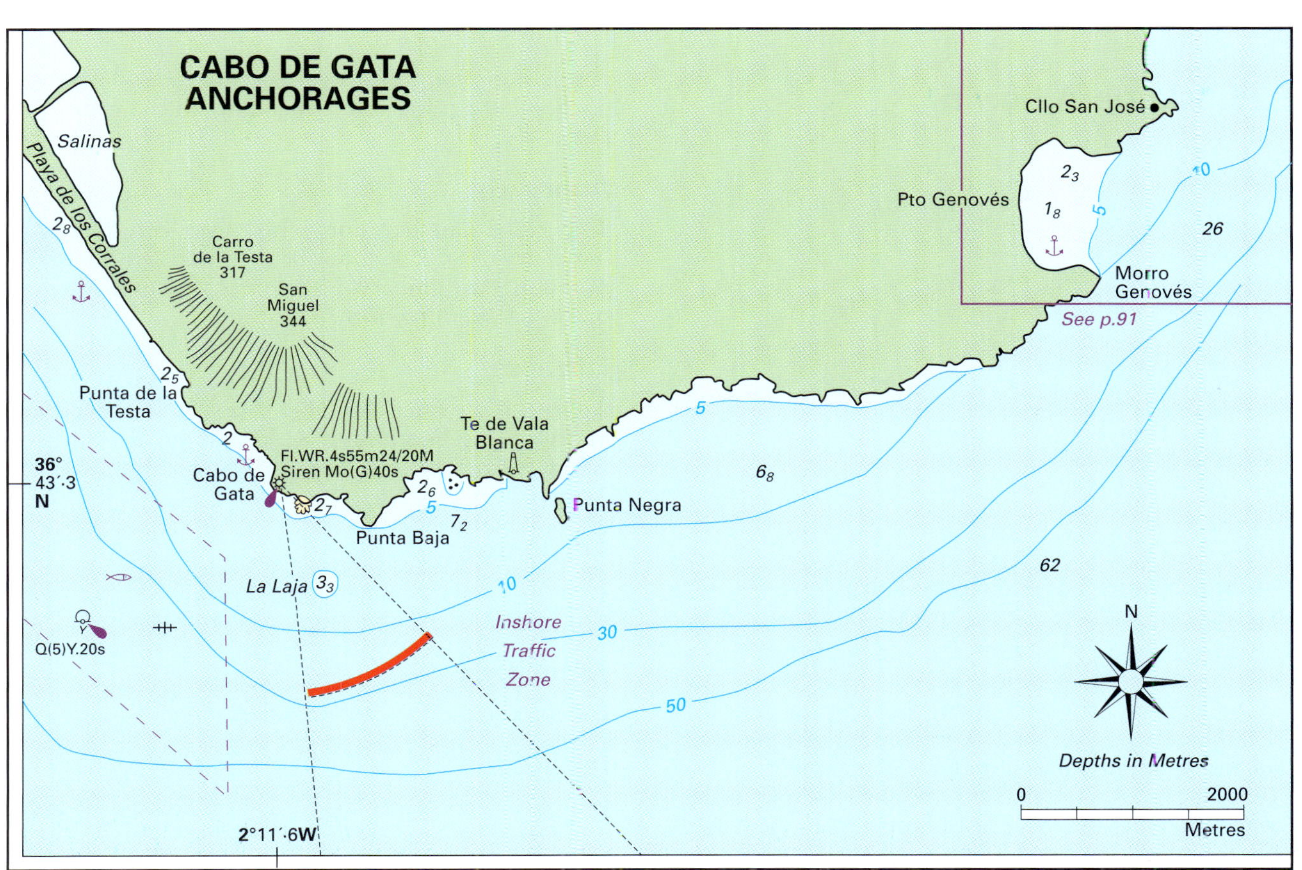

II. COSTA DEL SOL

Cabo de Gata from the east

25. Isla de Alborán

35°56'·3N 03°02'·1W

Current

A permanent current of up to three knots runs past the island on an E and SE-going direction.

Charts

UKHO *774*
Imray *M11*
SHOM *5864, 6569, 7672*
Spanish *4351, 435*

Lights

Alborán lighthouse Fl(4)20s40m10M
Grey conical tower and house 20m
Puerto refugio E wharf head Fl.R.3s4m3M
Red post 3m
Dique de Abrigo head Fl.G.2s9m3M
Green square column 3m

Isolated island S of Puerto de Adra

This small island lies some 49M to S of Puerto de Adra and about 30M from the African coast. It is a bare, low, reddish-cliffed island 700m long and 300m wide with two small landing jetties and several anchorages. The sole inhabitants are the staff for the lighthouse and a military detachment.

Facilities are non-existent and, officially, in order to visit, permission must be obtained from the Naval Commander in Almería. If you arrive without permission you may or may not be allowed to anchor for a short visit depending on the officer on duty.

Approach

The island can be approached from any direction but as it is low, it will not be seen until within 10M. There are a number of sunken rocks extending in places to 200m from the coast.

Entrance

Approach the E jetty on a W course with the jetty in line with the lighthouse. Keep a sharp lookout for submerged rocks during the last 200m of the approach.

Anchorages

There are several anchorages to suit the prevalent wind direction in about 6m sand and stone.

Formalities

Call on the military commander.

Facilities

In an emergency, water and food might be obtained from the garrison.

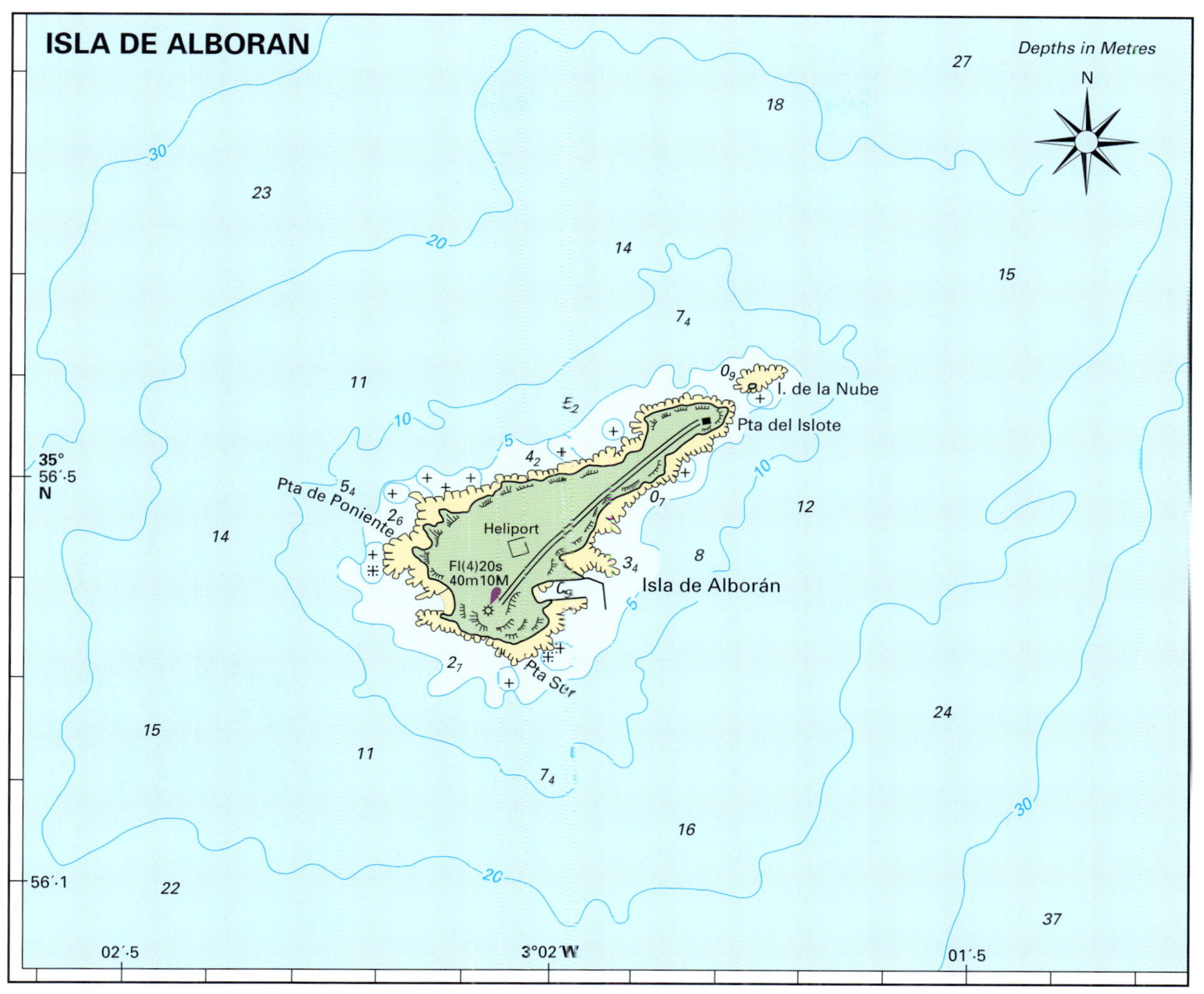
ISLA DE ALBORAN
Depths in Metres
N
I. de la Nube
Pta del Islote
Pta de Poniente
Heliport
Fl(4)20s
40m10M
Isla de Alborán
Pta Sur
35°
56'.5
N
56'.1
02'.5
3°02'W
01'.5

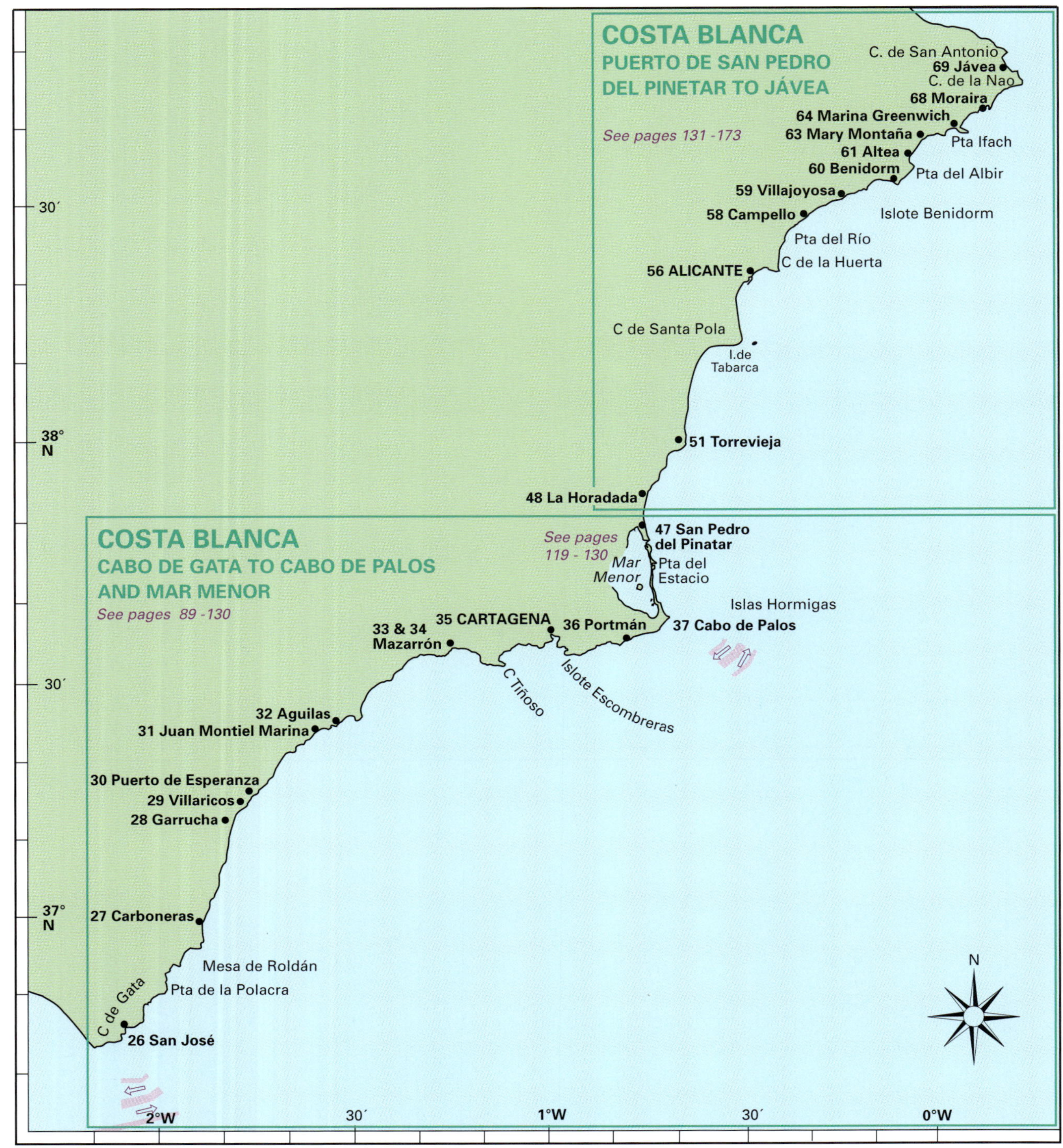
COSTA BLANCA
PUERTO DE SAN PEDRO DEL PINETAR TO JÁVEA
See pages 131 -173
C. de San Antonio
69 Jávea
C. de la Nao
68 Moraira
64 Marina Greenwich
63 Mary Montaña
Pta Ifach
61 Altea
60 Benidorm
Pta del Albir
59 Villajoyosa
58 Campello
Islote Benidorm
Pta del Río
C de la Huerta
56 ALICANTE
C de Santa Pola
I.de Tabarca
51 Torrevieja
48 La Horadada
COSTA BLANCA
CABO DE GATA TO CABO DE PALOS AND MAR MENOR
See pages 89 -130
See pages 119 - 130
47 San Pedro del Pinatar
Mar Menor
Pta del Estacio
Islas Hormigas
33 & 34 Mazarrón
35 CARTAGENA
36 Portmán
37 Cabo de Palos
C Tiñoso
Islote Escombreras
32 Aguilas
31 Juan Montiel Marina
30 Puerto de Esperanza
29 Villaricos
28 Garrucha
27 Carboneras
Mesa de Roldán
Pta de la Polacra
C de Gata
26 San José
30′
38° N
30′
37° N
2°W
30′
1°W
30′
0°W
N

III. COSTA BLANCA

Costa Blanca planning guide and distances (See Appendix for waypoint list)

⚓ Anchorage

Miles		*Harbours, Anchorages and Headlands*
21M	⚓	*Puerto Genovés*
		Cabo de Gata
	⚓	*Ensenada de San José/Cala Higuera*
	26.	**Puerto de San José** *(page 92)*
18M	⚓	*Ensenada de los Escullos*
	⚓	*Ensenada de Rodalquilar*
	⚓	*Las Negras*
		Punta de la Polacra
	⚓	*Cala de San Pedro*
	⚓	*Ensenada de Agua Amarga*
	27.	**Puerto de Carboneras** *(page 95)*
14M	⚓	*2 commercial harbours – emergency only*
	⚓	*Marina de las Torres*
	⚓	*Punta de la Media Naranja*
	28.	**Puerto de Garrucha** *(page 97)*
5M	⚓	*Palomares y Villaricos*
		Río de Aguas
	29.	**Puerto de Villaricos** *(page 99)*
0·3M		Río Almanzora
	30.	**Puerto de Esperanza** *(page 100)*
14M	⚓	*Anchorages 2M to N of Río Almanzora*
	⚓	*Ensenada de Terreros*
	⚓	*Punta Parda*
	31.	**Puerto Juan Montiel de Aguilas** *(page 102)*
	32.	**Puerto de Aguilas and El Hornillo** *(page 103)*
19M		Punta Parda
	⚓	*Cala Bardina*
	⚓	*Ensenada de la Fuente*
	33.	**Club Regatas, Mazarrón** *(page 107)*
3M		Punta Negra
	34.	**Puerto Deportivo de Mazarrón** *(page 108)*
15M	⚓	*Ensenada de Mazarrón*
	⚓	*Cala Cerrada*
	⚓	*Rincón de la Salitrona*
	⚓	*El Portús*
		Cabo Tiñoso
	35.	**Puerto de Cartagena** *(page 110)*
8M	⚓	*Cala del Gorguel*
	36.	**Puerto de Portmán** *(page 115)*
9M		Cabo del Agua
	37.	**Puerto de Cabo de Palos** *(page 117)*
8M	⚓	*Cabo de Palos*
	⚓	*Playa de Palos*
	⚓	*Isla Grosa*
	38.	**Puerto de Tomás Maestre entrance to Mar Menor** *(page 121)*
5M	**39.**	**Puerto de Dos Mares** *(page 124)*
	40.	**Puerto de la Manga** *(page 124)*
	41.	**Puerto de Mar de Cristal** *(page 124)*
	42.	**Puerto de las Islas Menores** *(page 126)*
	43.	**Puerto de los Nietos** *(page 127)*
	44.	**Puerto de los Urrutias** *(page 128)*
	45.	**Puerto de los Alcázares** *(page 129)*
	⚓	*Puerto Santiago de Ribera*
	46.	**Puerto de Lo Pagan** *(page 130)*
	⚓	*Ensenada del Esparto*
	47.	**Puerto de San Pedro del Pinatar** *(page 132)*

	47.	**Puerto de San Pedro del Pinatar** *(page 132)*
3M	**48.**	**Puerto de la Horadada** *(page 133)*
3M	**49.**	**Puerto de Campoamor** *(page 135)*
2M	**50.**	**Puerto de Cabo Roig** *(page 136)*
5M	**51.**	**Puerto de Torrevieja** *(page 137)*
9M	**52.**	**Marina de la Dunas (Puerto de Guardamar)** *(page 140)*
6M		Cabo Cervera
	⚓	*Bahía de Santa Pola*
	53.	**Puerto de Santa Pola** *(page 142)*
2M	**54.**	**Puerto de Espato** *(page 143)*
4M	**55.**	**Puerto de Isla de Tabarca** *(page 144)*
11M	**56.**	**Puerto de Alicante** *(page 146)*
3M	⚓	*Ensenada de la Albufereta*
	57.	**Puerto de San Juan** *(page 150)*
7M	⚓	*Playa de la Huerta*
	58.	**Puerto de Campello** *(page 151)*
9M		Cabo de las Huertas
	59.	**Puerto de Villajoyosa (Alcoco)** *(page 152)*
6M	**60.**	**Puerto de Benidorm** *(page 154)*
7M	⚓	*Ensenada de Benidorm*
	⚓	*Cabezo del Tosal*
	⚓	*Anchorage E of Punta de Canfali*
	⚓	*Anchorage W of Punta de la Cueva del Barbero*
		Punta de la Esalata
	⚓	*Anchorages NW of Punta del Albir*
		Punta del Albir
	61.	**Puerto de Altea** *(page 157)*
2M	**62.**	**Puerto de la Olla de Altea** *(page 158)*
1M	**63.**	**Puerto de Mary Montaña** *(page 160)*
1M	**64.**	**Marina Greenwich (Mascarat)** *(page 161)*
2M	⚓	*Punta Mascarat*
	65.	**Puerto Blanco** *(page 163)*
2M		Cabo Toix
	⚓	*Ensenada de Calpe*
	66.	**Puerto de Calpe** *(page 164)*
3M	⚓	*Cala la Fosa*
		Punta Ifach
	67.	**Puerto de las Basetas** *(page 166)*
3M	⚓	*Cala Canaret*
	⚓	*Cala Blanco*
	⚓	*Cabo Blanco*
	⚓	*Cala del Dragon*
		Cabo Blanco
	68.	**Puerto de Moraira** *(page 168)*
11M	⚓	*El Rinconet*
	⚓	*Anchorages between Cabo Moraira and Jávea*
	⚓	*La Grandadilla*
	⚓	*Isla del Descubridor*
	⚓	*Punta Negra*
	⚓	*Isla del Portichol*
		Cabo de la Nao
	⚓	*Cabo de San Martin*
	⚓	*Cala Calce*
	⚓	*Cala de la Fonta na*
	69.	**Puerto de Jávea** *(page 172)*
		Cabo de San Antonio

III COSTA BLANCA

Introduction

Currents

Along this coast the current is reasonably consistent and is not discussed under each port. Off Cabo de Gata the current is normally E-going and can be strong. It changes its direction to NE-going and becomes weaker along the coast, although it is stronger off Cabo de Palos. In the summer and autumn months this NE and ENE-going current is felt as far as Cabo de San Antonio but in the other months it is usually SW-going between Cabo de Palos and Cabo de San Antonio.

Tides

Maximum spring range is less than 1m and its effects are small.

Gales – harbours of refuge

In the event of gales and heavy seas, Cartagena, Torrevieja and Alicante are the safest to enter. Shelter may sometimes be found where a small harbour is located behind a promontory which protects the entrance from the wind and swell.

General description

This 195M stretch of coast between Cabo de Gata to just beyond Cabo de San Antonio is called Costa Blanca (the White Coast). Much of the coastal rock is a light grey which appears white in the bright sunlight. There has been much development in the past two decades. Communications and services have been much improved, many harbours have been built and old harbours adapted for yachts but the discovery of the Costa Blanca by the developers has resulted in many of the once deserted *calas* becoming surrounded by holiday homes and, in some cases, high-rise buildings for package tourists.

However, some sections remain comparatively deserted and with isolated anchorages. By no means all anchorages are noted here and the cruising yacht should be able to find unlisted spots where there is peace and quiet.

The section begins with the impressive promontory of Cabo de Gata which has several white patches of rock on its W side. The high coastal cliffs are broken by many valleys and small coves with good anchorages. The major promontories are high with steep cliffs; Punta de la Media Naranja (half an orange!), Cabo Cope and Cabo Tiñoso are examples. Beyond Cartagena, which is one of the few natural harbours, lies the long, low sand bar that separates the Mar Menor from the sea, now looking more like a high-rise breakwater. From here to Alicante and beyond, the coast is made up of low rolling hills coming down to broken cliffs with long sandy beaches. Inland ranges of higher hills can be seen and these mountainous features reach the sea in places such as Cabo de La Huerta, Sierra Helada, Cabo de la Nao and Cabo de San Antonio.

Outlying dangers are the small islands: Isla de los Terreros near Aguilas, Isla Grosa and some smaller islets off the Mar Menor, Isla de Tabarca off Cabo de Santa Pola, Islote de Benidorm off Benidorm and the Isla de Portichol. In general, deep water can be carried quite close to the coast with the exception of some areas bordering the Mar Menor.

Visits inland

Apart from places mentioned in the text, there are many interesting places to visit and things to see further inland which may be reached by taxi, bus or, in some cases, by rail. The narrow gauge FEVE runs from the north station of Alicante to Dénia and puts on the 'Lemon Express' for tourists during summer – an expedition which includes a bottle of 'champagne'. Suggestions for other expeditions can be obtained from the various information offices but the following are worth considering: Lorca, a very picturesque old town; Murcia, the capital city of the province of the same name, which has interesting churches, museums and art galleries; Orihuela, with an old church and valuable paintings; Jijona, where the nougat-like sweet turrón is made and with a ruined Moorish castle; and Alcoy, an old Visigoth town with many ancient remains.

Pilotage and navigation

Tunny nets

In spring, summer and autumn tunny nets may be laid at the places listed below (see the Introduction, page 6).

- Off San José
- Near Punta del Esparto
- Off Punta de la Polacra
- In Cala de San Pedro
- 2M to SW of Punta de la Media Naranja
- 1½M to N of Villaricos
- 3M to SW of Isla de los Terreros
- ½M to N of Isla de los Terreros
- 2M and 1M to SW and 1M to E of Aguilas
- In Cala Bardina
- S of Cabo Cope
- 1M to NE of Punta de Calnegre
- 5M, 3M and 1M to W of Punta Negra
- Off Punta de la Azohía
- Centre and E end of Ensenada de Mazarrón
- N of Cabo Tiñoso
- Off Puerto de Portmán
- Off Cap de Palos
- N of Cabo de las Huertas
- In the Ensenada de Benidorm
- W of the Peñón de Ifach
- Ensenada de Moraira

Fish havens

There are extensive fish havens along this coast.

Restricted areas

In Cartagena there are areas reserved for the Spanish navy which may not be entered by yachts. Submarines exercise in areas from Cabo de Gata to Cabo San Sebastian and there is a firing area S of Cartagena. Anchoring is prohibited in an area to the S of Puerto de Jávea where there are underwater cables.

Magnetic variation

Costa Blanca (Cartagena) 0°00'E (2017) decreasing 11 annually.

CABO DE GATA TO CABO DE PALOS AND MAR MENOR

Ports

The ports of Mar Menor

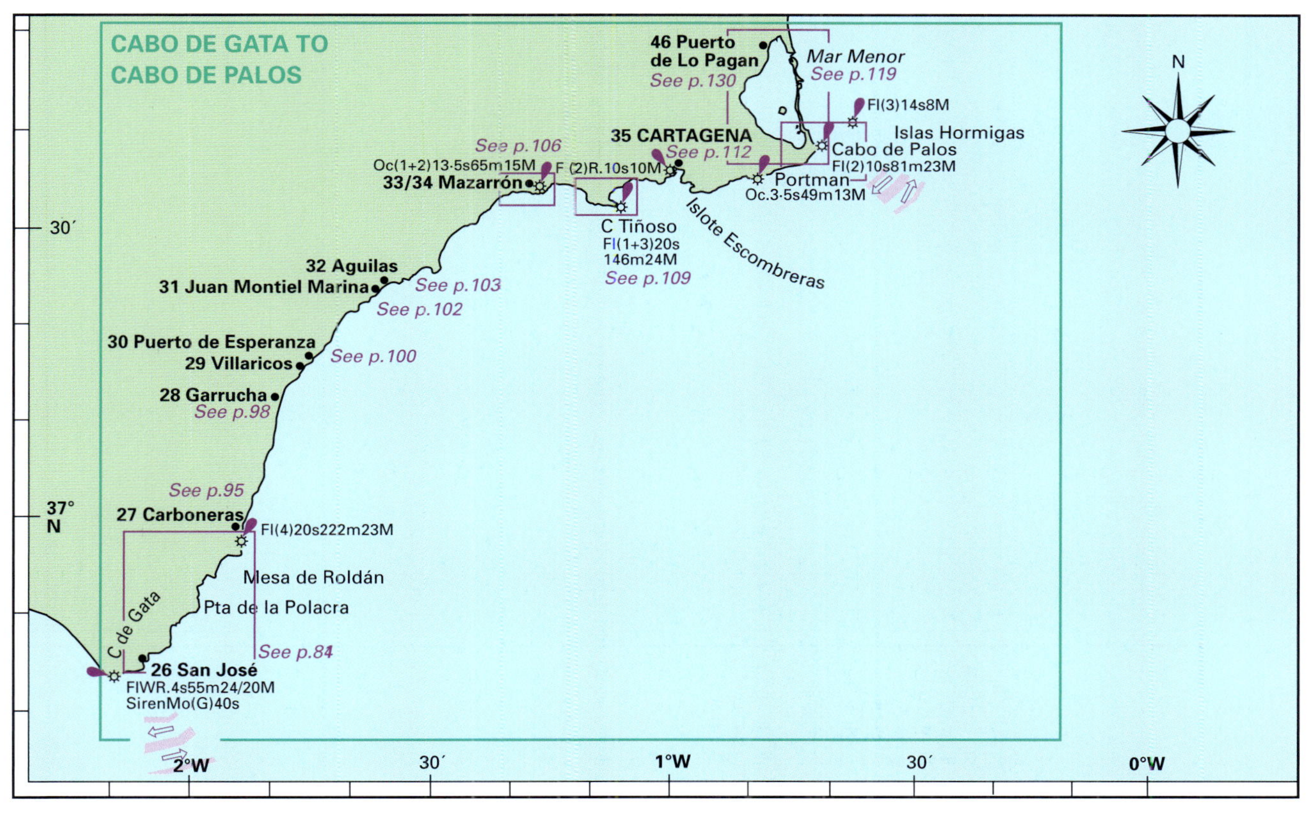

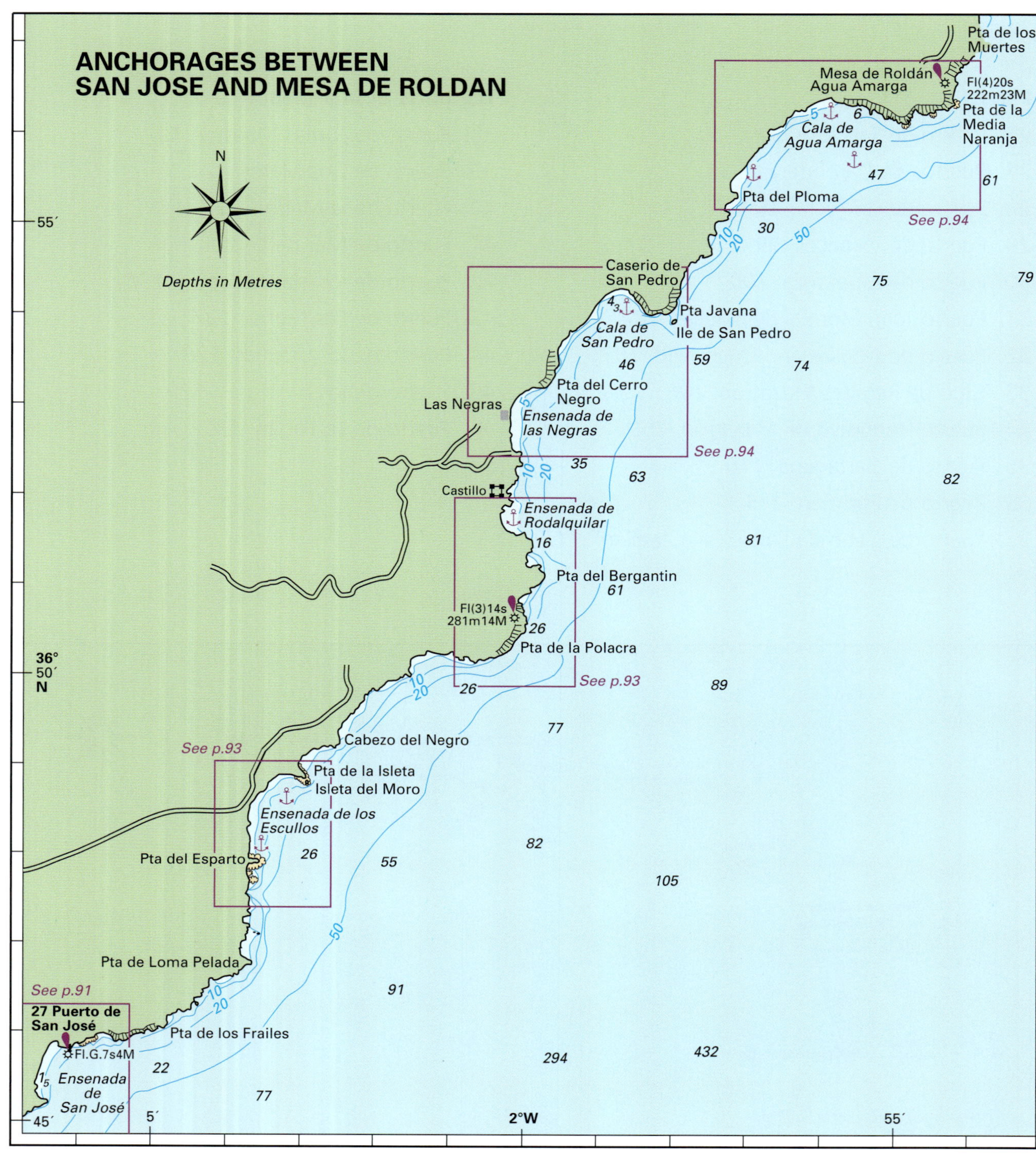

During calm weather, there are many really beautiful bays to visit. Several Roman mine workings are clearly visible.

Note

All the anchorages along this stretch of coast are susceptible to swell. With an E or NE wind, a surprisingly high and confused sea can develop due to the NE-going counter-current. Likewise with a W or SW wind, combined with the current going NE following the coast, the headlands concentrate the effect of a short sea, creating an unpleasant swell in the bays and, for those heading W, a slow passage.

⚓ Puerto Genovés

36°44′·6N 2°07′W

A bay on the E side of Cabo de Gata with a gently sloping sandy bottom. Open between NE and SE with good protection from other winds especially close inshore at N and S sides of bay. Anchor to suit wind in 5m, sand and mud.

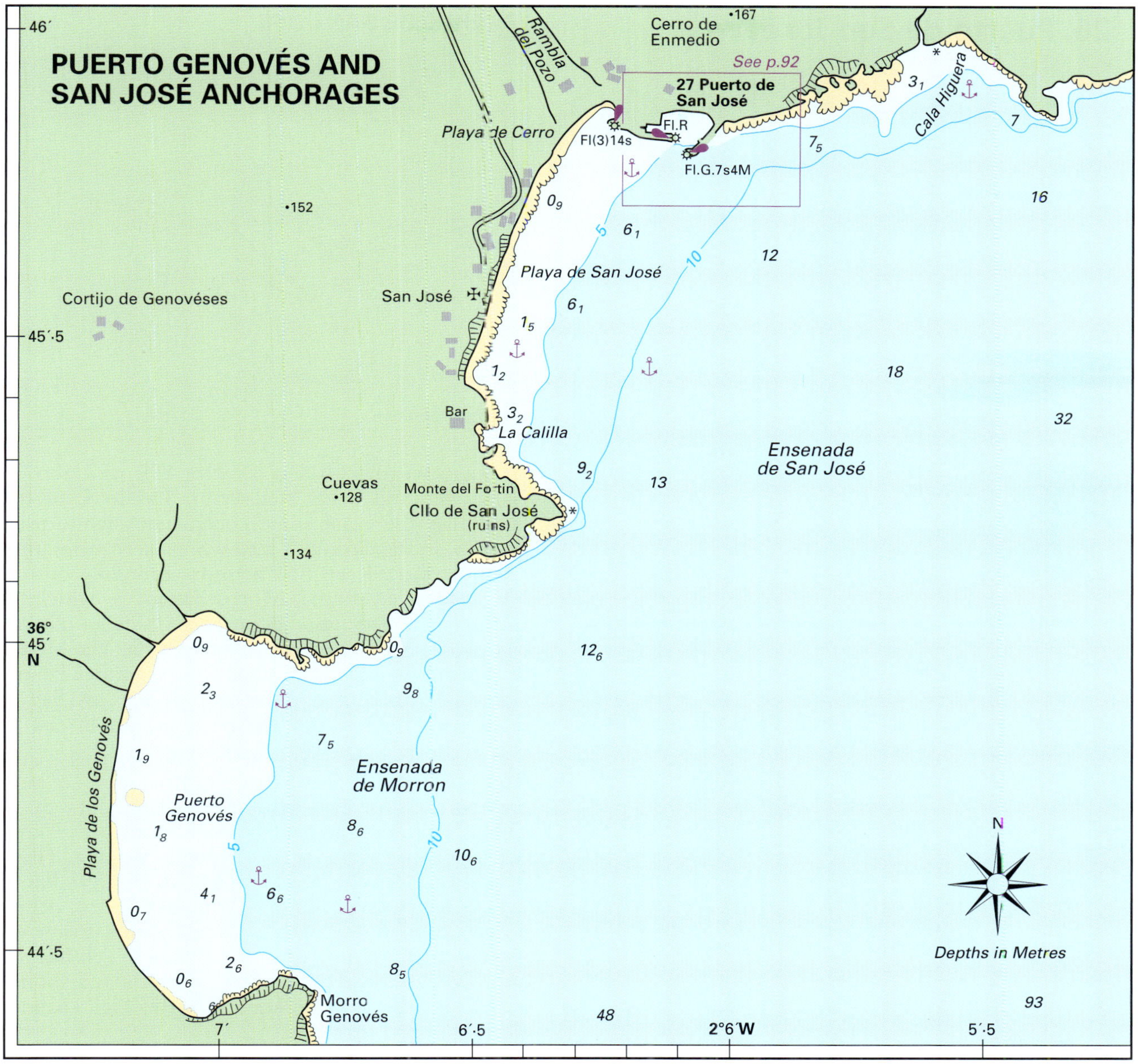

PUERTO GENOVÉS AND SAN JOSÉ ANCHORAGES

27 Puerto de San José
See p.92
Cerro de Enmedio •167
Rambla del Pozo
Playa de Cerro
Fl(3)14s
Fl.R
Fl.G.7s4M
Cala Higuera
Playa de San José
San José
Cortijo de Genovéses
•152
Bar
La Calilla
Cuevas •128
Monte del Fortin
Cllo de San José (ruins)
•134
Ensenada de San José
Ensenada de Morron
Puerto Genovés
Playa de los Genovés
Morro Genovés
46′
45′·5
36° 45′ N
44′·5
7′
6′·5
2°6′W
5′·5
Depths in Metres

Note that there are rocks to the SE of Morro Genovese so do not pass too close to the cliffs on entering bay from the south.

⚓ Ensenada de San José/Cala Higuera

36°45′·6N 2°06′·3W

Similar open bay to Puerto Genovés but with sandy and rocky beach with developments. A small village now exists with a road to Almería. Protection from N–NE winds at NE end of bay under cliffs.

In strong S to SW winds the swell curls round the headland into this *ensenada* but Porto Genovés is quieter and should be used in these conditions.

Puerto Genovés. The word 'puerto' covers both an enclosed harbour and a bay with some shelter

26. Puerto de San José

36°46'N 02°06'W

Charts
UKHO *774* Imray *M11, M12*
SHOM *7671* Spanish *461*

Lights
To the southwest
Cabo de Gata Fl.WR.4s55m24/20M 356°-W-316°-R-356°
Siren Mo(G)40s White tower, grey lantern on yellow dwelling 19m
Harbour
Dique Este head Fl.(3)G.12s8m5M
Green ▲ on truncated tower 3m
Dique Sur E head Fl.(3)R.10s7m3M
Red ■ on truncated tower 3m
To the northeast
Mesa de Roldán Fl(4)20s222m23M
White octagonal tower 18m
Punta de la Polacra 36°50'·6N 02°00'·1W Fl(3)14s281m14M
Tower 14m

Port communications
Capitanía VHF Ch 9. ✆ +34 950 38 00 41
correo@clubnauticodesanjose.com
www.clubnauticodesanjose.com

Harbour charges High

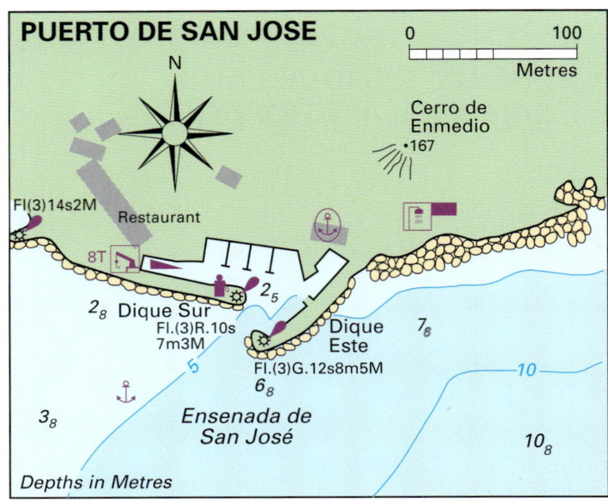

Attractive small harbour

A small shallow yacht harbour in attractive surroundings which is a useful break in the 50M stretch of coast between Almería and Garrucha. The 244 berth harbour is subject to swell from E–SE but is otherwise well protected. A small village nearby can supply basic requirements. There are walks in empty country, fine views from the hills, caves near top of Monte del Fortin and excellent sandy beaches. Unfortunately, there is rarely room for visitors and although the *capitan* and *marineros* are enthusiastic and welcoming, they have to turn visitors away – at least in summer. Not recommended for yachts over 12m.

Approach

From the south Round the prominent Cabo de Gata (344m), either close inshore or 1M offshore to avoid the Laja de Cabo de Gata shoal (3.3m) which breaks in heavy weather. It lies 1,300m SSE of Cabo de Gata light and in its red sector. 1M to E of the lighthouse there are some conspicuous white rock patches on the dark cliff face which, seen from afar, resemble sails. Keep ½M offshore rounding onto a NE course after the Morro Genovés which is conically shaped and lies at the S side of Puerto Genovés, a deep bay with a sandy beach. The Monte del Fortin, which has a ruined fort, separates Puerto Genovés from Ensenada de San José. This bay is lined with houses and the harbour lies in the N corner under a small white rock patch.

From the north The Mesa de Roldán is a high plateau (221m). The lighthouse is on Punta de la Media Naranja and can be seen from afar. Agua Amarga is just to the west of Media Naranja. These features can easily be identified. To the SW Punta Javana has a small island, Isla de San Pedro, off its point. Punta de la Polacra (263m) with a tower on its summit and Punta de Loma Pelada which has the high Cerro de los Frailes (489–444m) inland should be recognised. San José lies SW of this high ground. Keep over ¼M offshore.

San José *Pública de Puertos de Andalucía*

Anchorage in the approach

The whole of the Ensenada de San José is suitable for anchorage – 200m to SW of the harbour entrance in 5m sand is recommended. If wind is strong from N an alternative is in a small bay off Playa de Cala Higuera, just under ½M E of the harbour.

Entrance

Approach the harbour heading N and give the head of Dique Sur 10m clearance.

Berths

Secure to starboard-hand quay or fuel berth to port and ask at the *capitanía* for a berth.

Facilities

Maximum length overall: 14m.
Slipway.
8-tonne crane.

Water and 220v AC on pontoons but water may be salty.
Gasoleo A and petrol.
Shops in village.

Communications

Bus service to Almería. ✆ Area code 950.

⚓ Ensenada de los Escullos

36°48'·2N 02°03'·2W

An open bay anchorage with sloping sandy bottom, some sandy beaches. Coast road, some development. The ruined castle, *guardia civil* barracks and a point with a white, skull-shaped rock, lie near the centre of the bay. The bay is wide open to E but some protection from NE in N corner of the bay is possible under Punta de la Isleta.

Los Escullos

Punta de la Isleta

⚓ Ensenada de Rodalquilar

36°51'·6N 02°00'W

The holding is reportedly poor in places. Open between NE and SE.

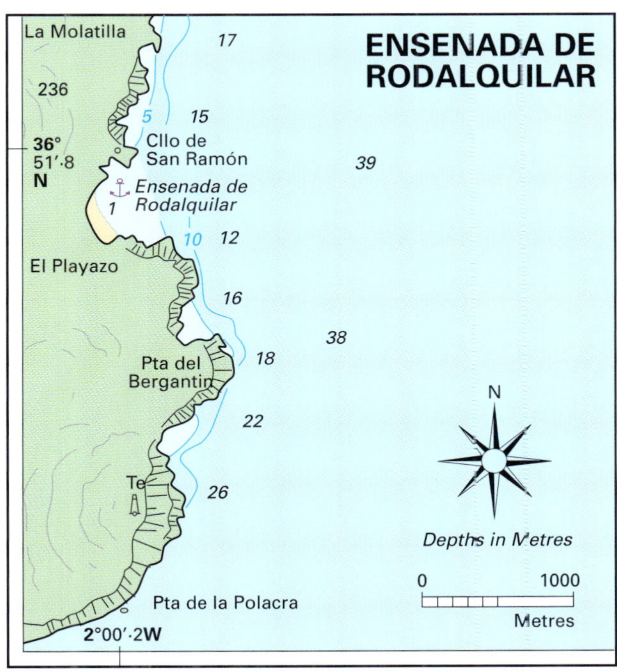

Rodalquilar

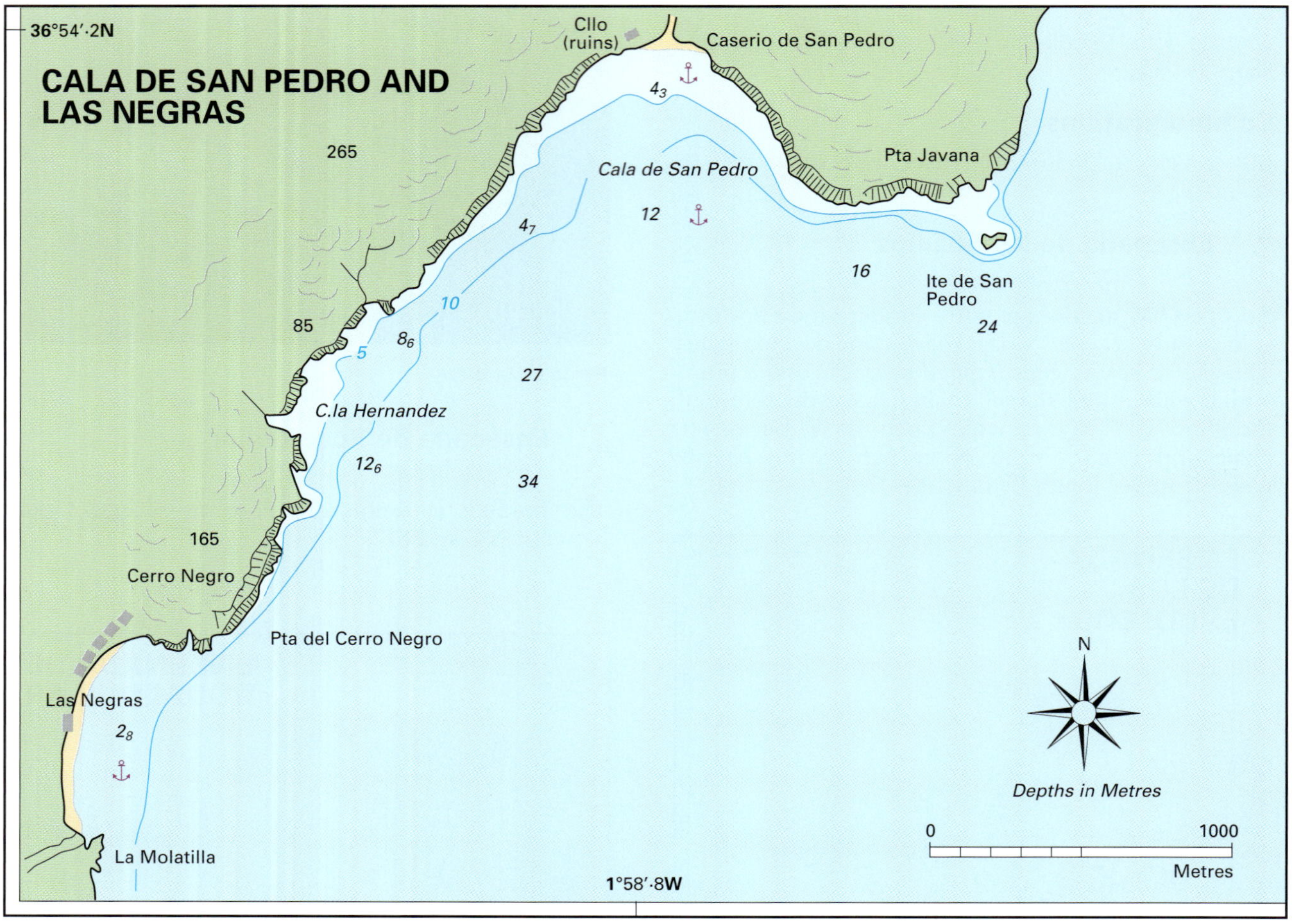

36°54′·2N
CALA DE SAN PEDRO AND LAS NEGRAS
Cllo (ruins)
Caserio de San Pedro
265
Cala de San Pedro
Pta Javana
12
16
Ite de San Pedro
24
10
85
5
C.la Hernandez
27
34
165
Cerro Negro
Pta del Cerro Negro
Las Negras
La Molatilla
N
Depths in Metres
0
1000
Metres
1°58′·8W

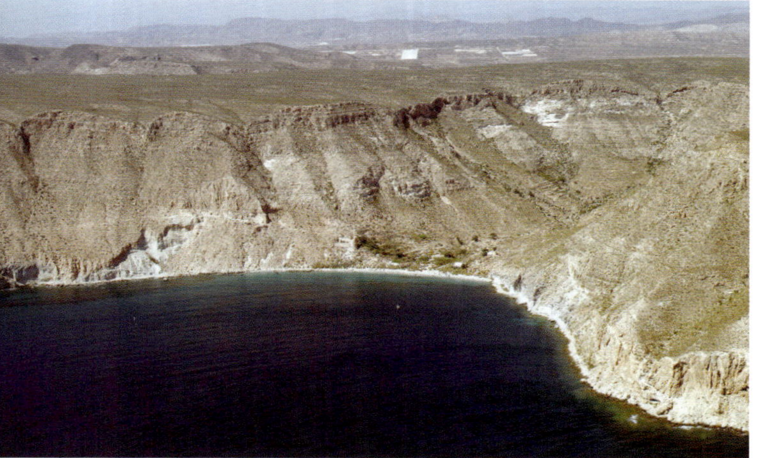

San Pedro

⚓ Las Negras 36°52′·6N 01°59′·9W

Anchor in 3m sand and weed off the village. Open between NE and SE. The beach is sand and rock. The village has some shops.

⚓ Cala de San Pedro 36°53′·9N 01°58′·7W

An imposing anchorage where fluky and strong gusts may be expected. Anchor to suit draught in sand and weed.

⚓ Ensenada de Agua Amarga (Bitter Water Bay)

36°56′·0N 01°56′·0W

Anchor outside the small boat moorings in 6–8m of water. Excellent shelter from the NE winds but open between E and S. Alternative anchorages lie off the hamlet of El Ploma 2M to SW or off a small cove 1M to SW of Agua Amarga. Use these with care.

Depths in Metres
N
36° 56′·5 N
Agua Amarga
Fl(4)20s222m23M
Mesa de Roldán
Tr
5
10
24
6
13
Pta de la Media Naranja
Ensenada de Agua Amarga
33
ENSENADA DE AGUA AMARGA
El Plomo
Pta del Plomo
45
30
0
1000
Metres
1°54′·4W

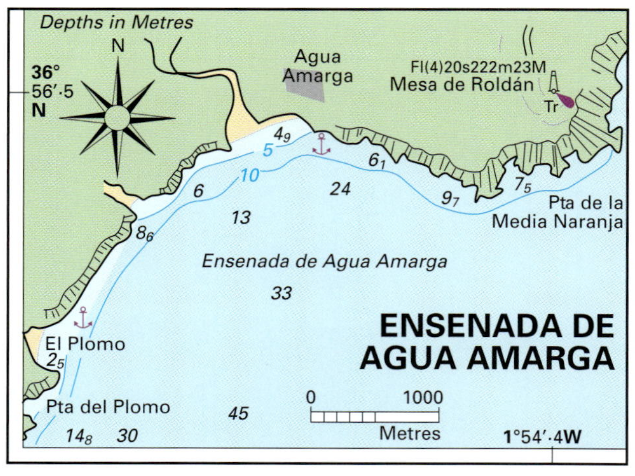

27. Puertos de Carboneras

36°59'·3N 01°53'·8W

Charts

UKHO *1515, 774* Imray *M12*
SHOM *7671* Spanish *4621, 462*

Lights

South Harbour (Puerto de Hornos Ibéricos SA)
Dique Este head Fl(2)G.10s12m5M
Green round tower 3m
Dique Este elbow Q(3)10s12m3M
♦ card BYB tower 3m
Dique Oeste head Fl(2)R.10s7m3M
Red round tower 3m
Middle harbour (PUCARSA – Puerto de Generar Electricidad)
Dique de Abrigo 36°58'.5N 01°53'.6W Fl.G.10s14m5M
Green metal post 4m
North harbour (Puerto Pescaro de Carboneras)
Dique Este Fl(3)G.12s10m5M
Green hexagonal tower 4m
Contradique Fl(4)R.12s8m3M
Red hexagonal tower 6m

Port communications

Puerto de Hornos Ibéricos VHF Ch 9, 12.
Puerto Departivo (northern harbour) ✆ +34 950 13 07 39
Caroneras@eppa.es
www.eppa.es/en/fishing-harbour-carboneras

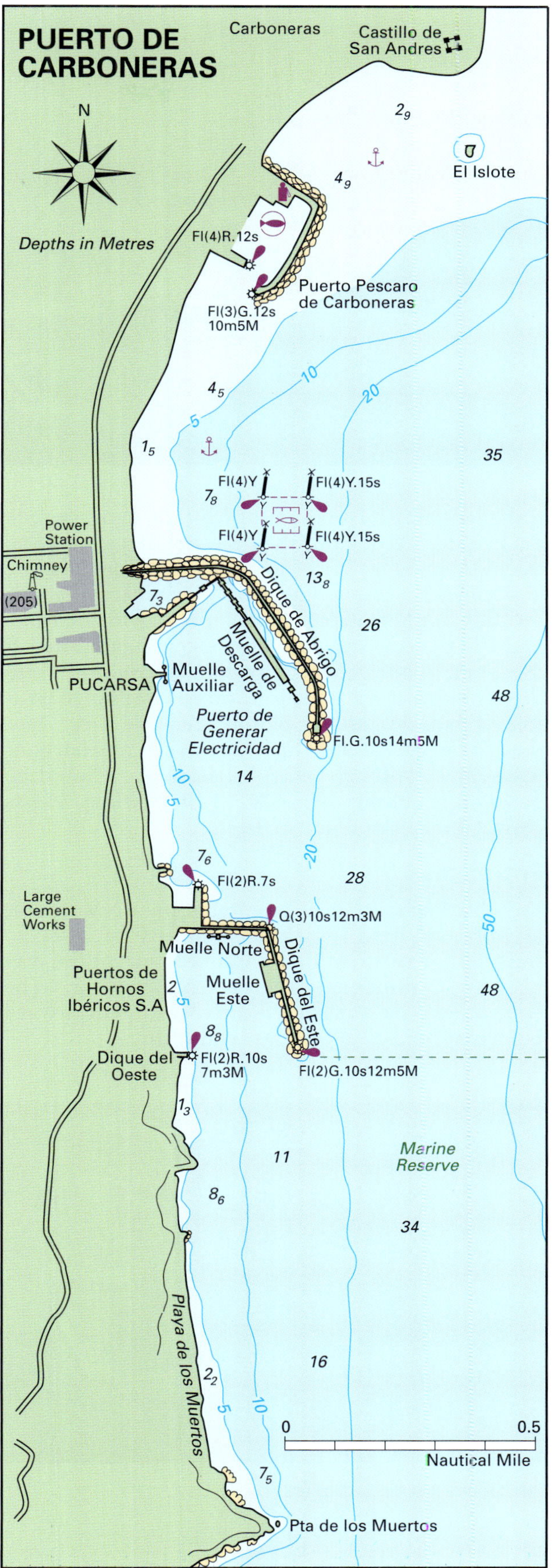

Commercial and fishing harbours

Three harbours, two commercial, large and forbidding, the Puerto de Hornos Ibéricos SA and the Puerto Generar del Electricidad and the third a working fishing harbour. However the first two offer good refuge from winds from all directions except SE though they should only be used in an emergency. Local facilities are about zero but provisions can be found in Carboneras village. The immediate area is dominated by the huge cement plant and electric generating station but the hinterland is wild and attractive. The fishing harbour is busy and has no special facilities for yachts. In poor weather it is likely to be crowded and a yacht would have to take its chance alongside a fishing boat.

Approach

From the south After Cabo de Gata the coast is broken by headlands enclosing sandy bays. Puerto Genovés is a wide sandy bay and the Ensenada de San José, which has a small harbour and village, can be identified. Further N, El Fraile (489m) is conspicuous as are the Isleta del Moro and Punta de la Polacra (263m) which has a tower. Cala de San Pedro which has a few houses and Agua Amarga may also be seen. The white lighthouse of Mesa de Roldán (221m) can be seen from afar. Once the points of La Media Naranja and Los Muertos have been rounded the large breakwaters and the industrial buildings belching smoke will be seen.

From the north From Puerto de Garrucha, backed by the town of the same name, the coast is flat, sandy and unbroken, with high ranges of hills inland and

The two commercial harbours at Carboneras with Puerto Pescaro at top right

some low cliffs. The town of Mojacar may be seen on its hill, ¼M inland, then the buildings stop and the mountains begin, which last until shortly before Carboneras. The village of Carboneras stands behind a rather inconspicuous point with El Islote and Isla de San Andreas (14m) extending 600m off the point. Foul ground stretches nearly ½M from this point in a SE direction, otherwise the coast is free of dangers and can be followed at 400m. Once the Isla de San Andreas has been passed, the harbour walls and buildings may be seen. A 3·5m deep passage, running NE–SW, 150m wide, exists between this island and El Islote.

Entrances

Both big harbours may be entered on a NW course leaving the head of either Dique Este 50m to starboard. Pay attention to and keep out of the way of any commercial vessel manoeuvring. The entrance to the Puerto Pescaro is straightforward but shoals and may be alive with traffic.

Puerto Pescaro de Carboneras

Berths

The two main commercial harbours are to be avoided and only used in an emergency. There are usually large commercial vessels in port, so even in an emergency it would not be easy to berth. There is a plan to extend the fishing port and a new breakwater is being constructed between the Puerto Pescaro and the dique protecting the north commercial harbour – NW of the fish farm.

Anchorages

Between Puerto de Carboneras and Puerto Pescaro there is a good anchorage inside the fish farm, off the beach, outside the swim buoys. This anchorage is well protected in strong W winds.

A temporary anchorage may be available in 5m sand and stone on the E side of the south and middle harbours, close inshore and clear of commercial works.

Outside, there are two possibilities: between Puerto de Carboneras and Puerto Pescaro and between Puerto Pescaro and El Islote. Both are open to the SE but the latter has better shelter from the NE. Sand, stone and weed.

Formalities

In the commercial harbours, contact the shore by radio for permission to stay. In the fishing harbour, inquire ashore.

⚓ Marina de las Torres

37°09'·7N 01°49'W

An open coastal anchorage off the mouth of Río de Aguas in 5m sand, stone and weed. Exposed between NE and SE. The towns of Mojacar and Garrucha lie 2M and 1M away. There is a small landing jetty nearby. A road runs behind the beach and there is a conspicuous old factory chimney.

28. Puerto de Garrucha

37°11'N 01°49'·1W

Charts
UKHO *1515, 774* Imray *M12*
SHOM *7671* Spanish *462*

Lights
Garrucha LtHo Oc(4)13s19m13M
White tower house 10m
Dique (unattached) Q(3)10s4m3M ♦ card BYB 3m
Dique de Levante head head Fl(3)G.9s13m5M
Green tower 11m
Dique de Poniente head Fl(3)R.6m3M
Red tower 3m

Port communications
Old marina ✆ +34 950 13 24 10
www.eppa.es/en/marina-garrucha
New marina Call Ch 9 ✆ +34 950 80 80 90 / 600 14 91 15

Busy commercial harbour with a small fishing fleet and new marina

A small town with an active fishing fleet, Garrucha is known for its seafood: *mariscos*.

The old marina with 250 berths up to 12m and fuel pump has always been accommodating, but overstretched, with little room for visitors. This is a convenient and inexpensive stopping place for yachts heading to Cabo de Gata and beyond, or to Cartagena and the Baleares. A well stocked supermarket is on the main road heading NE about 100m from the old marina.

In 2012 the port was extended to accommodate a new marina at the N end of the harbour. This is a substantial facility with over 300 berths up to 18m. The harbour is open to the S and SE, which causes some surging in strong E winds.

Garrucha harbour with its north extension and the addition of its new marina in 2012 *Pública de Puertos de Andalucía*

Garrucha's spacious entrance looking S from the Dique de Poniente *Steve Pickard*

Approach

From the south The Sierra Cabrera, whose foothills are easily identified, lead to Garrucha; one of these hills is covered with tourist housing development. An isolated obelisk-like chimney on a small hill behind the town is conspicuous. The lighthouse shows at close range.

From the north The low plain and dry river mouths SSW of Sierra Almagrera lead to Garrucha which has an isolated chimney and cranes on the Dique de Levante.

Note Fish farms are sometimes indicated on charts. One such farm, which was located 5M NE of Garrucha (centred 37°13'·4N 1°44'·9W), has disappeared but may return.

Anchorage in the approach

Anchor 200m S of elbow of Dique de Poniente in 5m sand.

Entrance

Straightforward, but commercial vessels have right of way. There is often a conspicuous large freighter moored on the inside S end of the Dique de Levante loading and unloading a cargo of gypsum. The ship is far more conspicuous than the dique, which can cause confusion until close.

Berths

The old Puerto Deportivo marina is still operating, along with the fuelling berth, though usually full with local vessels. It may be convenient to moor on the end of the T pontoon fuelling point if arriving at night, where there is room for two 12m yachts.

In 2016 nothing seems to have changed in the new marina since it opened in 2012. The marina is partially operational with a few yachts berthed alongside the pontoons rather than fore and aft which must be the intention. This is not a good arrangement as the pontoons are on piles and tidal range could wreak havoc.

The Puerto Deportivo fueling berth to port on entry
Steve Pickard

Facilities

Maximum length overall: 18m in new marina
Simple wood hull repairs by yard on slipway or in workshop in terrace to W of port.
12-tonne crane on Dique de Levante.
Slipways.
Water on quays.
Showers in the office block (key from harbourmaster).
125v and 220v AC supply point on Dique de Poniente and on pontoons.
Gasoleo A and petrol.
Ice from factory on front near capitán de puerto's office.
Club Cultural y Marítimo de Garrucha.

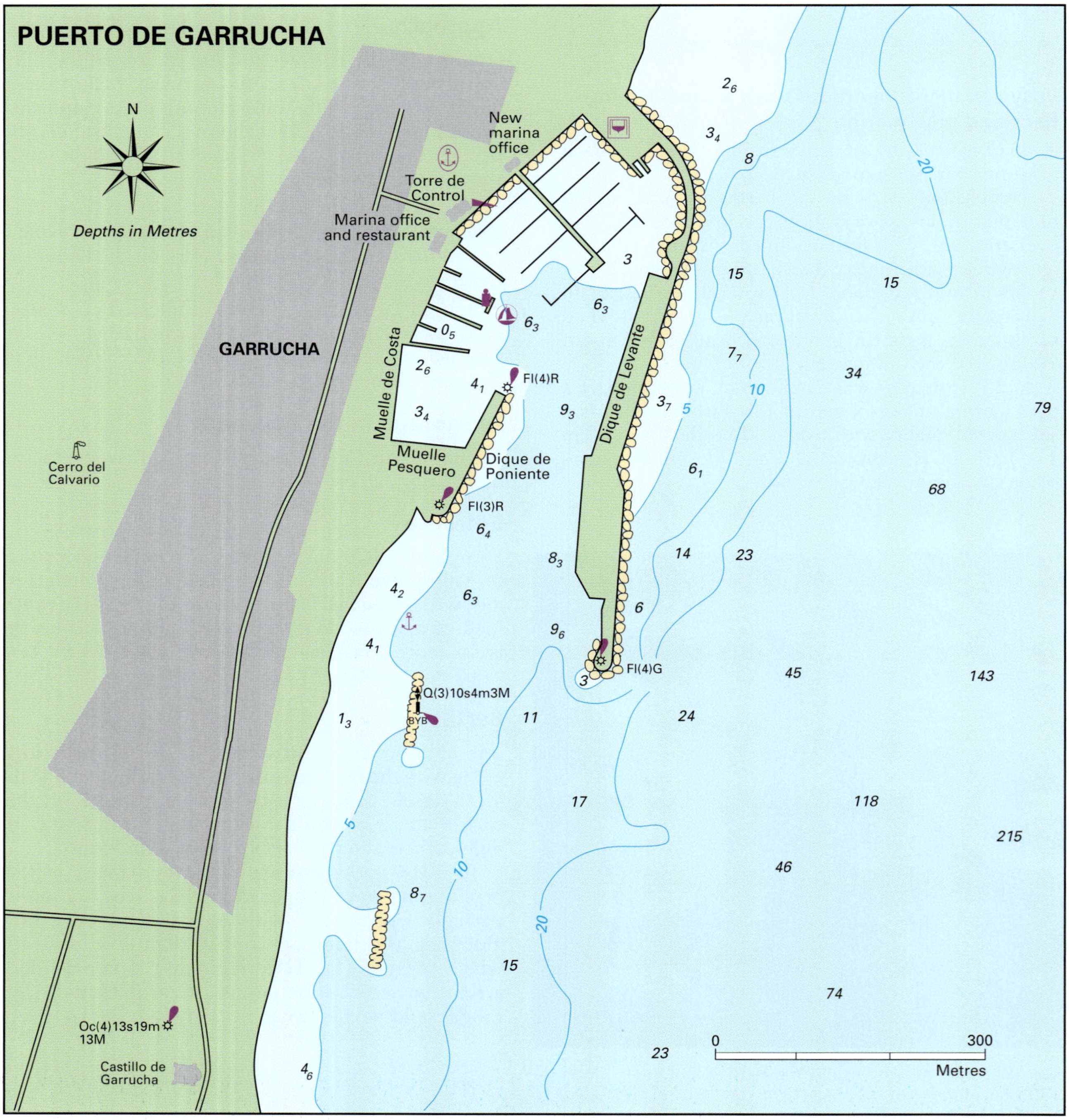

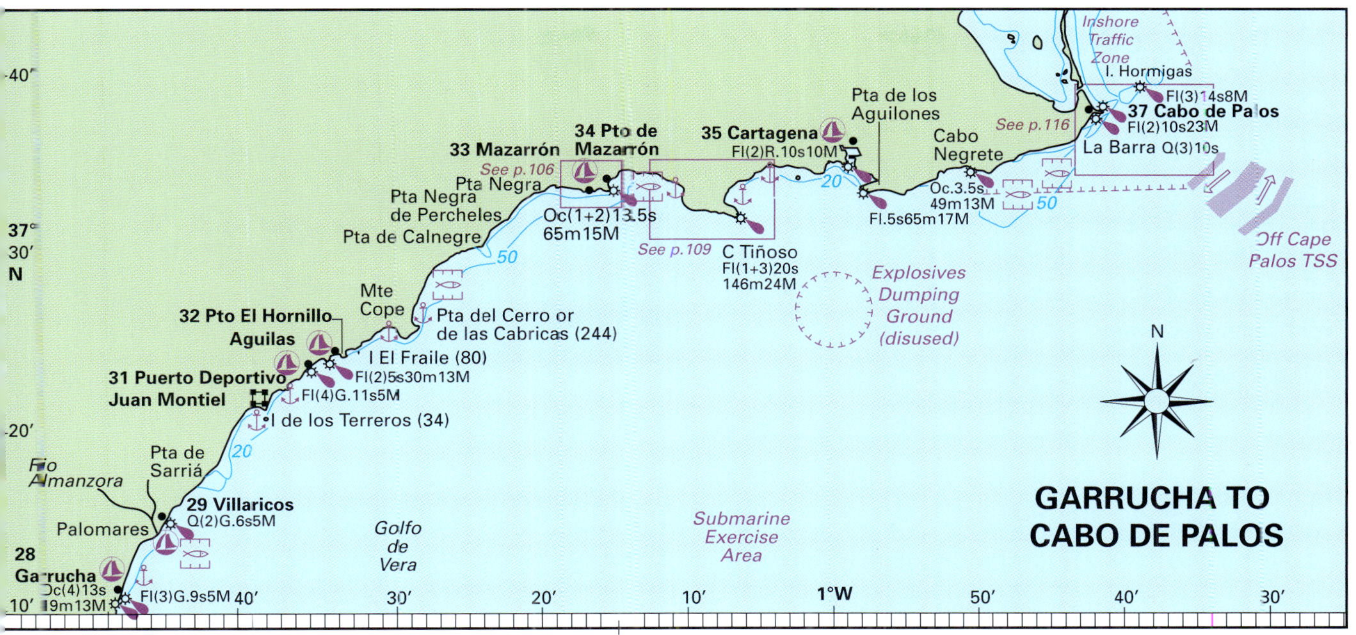

A number of shops and a small market in the village SW of the harbour.

Litter bins around the harbour.

Locally

This is an amazingly industrious area rich in minerals, including gypsum which is transported to the harbour daily and loaded onto freighters, creating a lot of dust. Many mines have been operating in the area since Roman times.

A few km NE of the harbour lies a huge holiday complex on the beach, mostly used by German and Scandinavian vacationers who come all year round. There are beaches either side of the port and many coves and isolated beaches all along the coast.

Communications

Bus service to Vera. ✆ Area code 950.

29. Puerto de Villaricos

37°14′·8N 01°46′W

Charts

UKHO *774*	Imray *M12*
SHOM *7671*	Spanish *462, 46*

Lights

Villaricos. Balsa breakwater head 37°14′.8N 01°46′.1W
Fl(2)G.6s8m5M
Green truncated tower 3m

Outer breakwater head Fl(2)R.10s4m3M
Red truncated tower 3m

Port communications

www.eppa.es/en/puerto-villaricos-la-balsa

No room for visitors

A pleasant but very small 50 berth artificial harbour built for the town's pleasure craft (at last sighting there were only small motor boats). There is little or no room for visitors, no harbour facilities. Max length 5·6m.

⚓ Palomares y Villaricos

Open anchorages either side of the mouth of the Río Almanzora. Note the shoals of the delta.

The village of Villaricos is right of centre in the photograph below.

Puerto de Villaricos with Esperanza at the right of the photo

30. Puerto de Esperanza

37°15'N 01°46'W

Charts

UKHO *774* Imray *M12*
SHOM *7671* Spanish *46, 462*

Lights

Dique de Abrigo head Fl.G.4s8m5M Green tower 3m
Contradique (centre) Fl(2)R.10s3m3M Red post 1m
Espigón Fl(2)G.6s3m3M Green square column 2m
Contradique head Fl(2)R.6s4m1M Red tower 3m

Port communications

Capitania VHF Ch 9 ✆ +34 950 46 71 37
villaricos@eppa.es
www.eppa.es/en/marina-villaricos-la-esperanza

Tiny Puerto de Esperanza looking SW towards the entrance *Steve Pickard*

Tiny fishing harbour

Esperanza's tiny 80 berth fishing harbour is only suitable for small (<8m) craft for a short stay. It is an attractive setting but even one visiting craft may be too many. Depths are reported to be 2m in the approach and port but caution and careful sounding is advised during any approach.

Approach

From the south The coast north of Garrucha is flat and sandy with few features and can be followed at about 200m offshore except off the delta of the River Almanzora when 400m should be maintained. The village of Palomares may be seen south of the river mouth with the village of Villaricos north of the river.

From the north From the easily identified Ensenada de Terreros with its off-lying island (24m) and small village, the coast is cliffed with small sand and stone beaches in breaks of the cliffs. Inland the hills rise to 350m. The coast is steep-to; two off-lying shallows (6m) – Piedra del Celor and Losa del Payo – break in heavy seas.

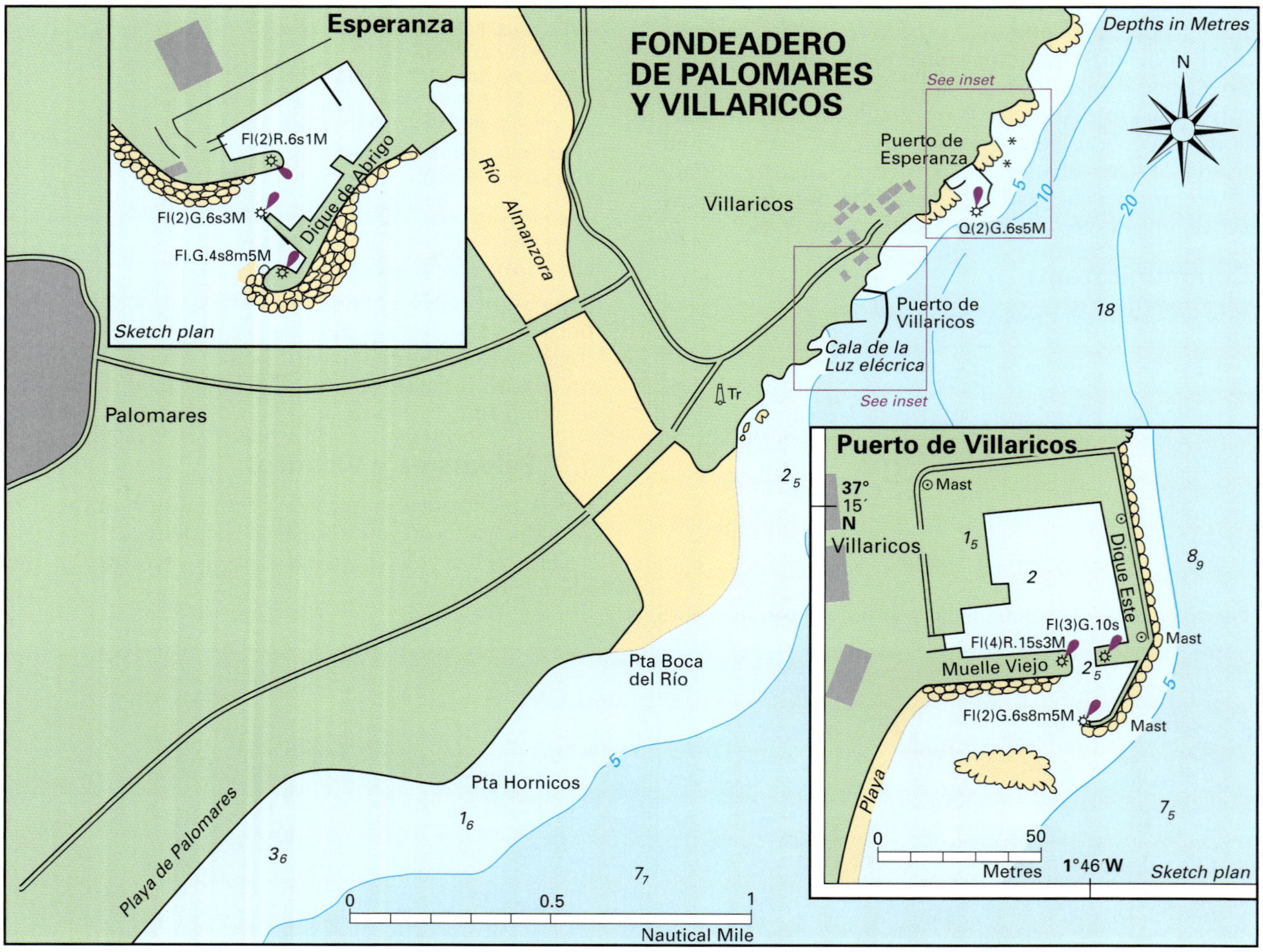

Entrance

Approach the head of the Dique de Abrigo on a W to NW course, round it at 10m and pass fairly close to the quay extension with its small green tower.

Facilities

Slipway in SW corner.
Shops in village 200m to SW.

⚓ Anchorages 2M to N of Río Almanzora

At least 10 small anchorages in *calas*, some with piers and quays – use with care.

Anchorages to the SW of Aguilas

⚓ Ensenada de Terreros

37°21'N 01°39'·7W

A well-protected anchorage but open to SE and subject to swell in all except N sector winds. The 600m passage between the Punta el Cañon and Isla de los Terreros (34m) is 6m deep. Anchor off San Juan de los Terreros in N part of bay. A few shops and the main road.

⚓ Punta Parda

37°22'·5N 01°37'·5W

At the N end of Ensenada de los Tarais, which is open between E and S, there are two anchorages on the west side of Punta Parda, off Cala Reona and Cala Cerrada, and one on the east, Cama de los Novios (beware of the small island in the entrance to this bay). Anchor according to draught, sand and weed. Whether the name, Cama de los Novios, the bed of the newly-married, reflects turbulent or peaceful nights is anyone's guess.

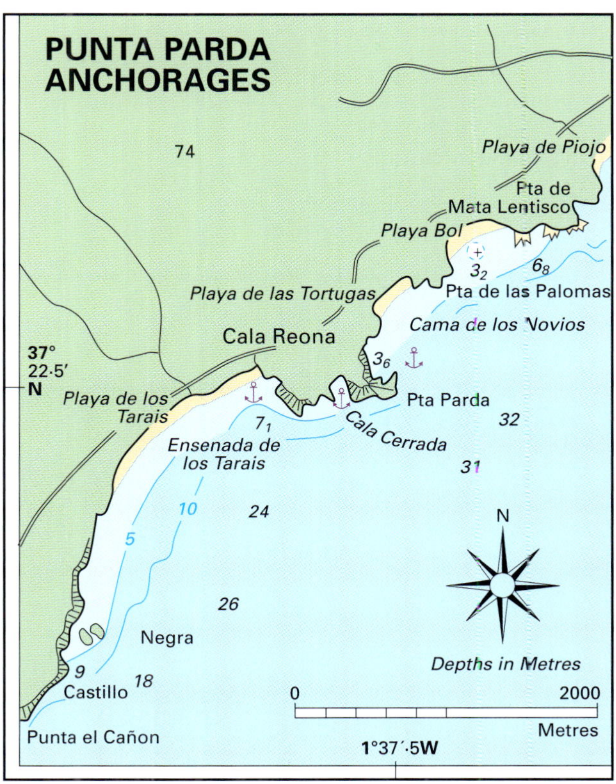

Looking N into Cala Cerrada with Punta Parda at right foreground; Cama de los Novios is just showing behind the point

III. COSTA BLANCA

31. Puerto Deportivo Juan Montiel de Aguilas

37°23'·69N 01°35'·93W

Charts

UKHO *1515, 774*	Imray *M12*
SHOM *7671*	Spanish *463*

Lights

Juan Montiel (Casica Verde). Breakwater Head 37°23'·63N 1°35'·97W Fl(4)G.11s5M Green truncated pyramidal tower
Jetty Head 37°23'·70N 1°36'·40W Fl(4)R.11s3M Red round column 3m
Corner 37°23'·70N 1°36'·00W Fl.R.3s1M Red round column 5m
Head 37°23'·67N 1°35'·97W Fl(2)R.7s1M Red post 2m
Marina. S Breakwater. Head 37°24'·39N 1°34'·40W Fl(2)G.7s6m3M White truncated tower, green top 5m
W Breakwater 37°24'·42N 1°34'·41W Fl(2)R.7s5m1M White truncated conical tower, red top 4m

Port communications

✆ +34 968 41 49 68
info@puertodeportivojuanmontiel.com
www.puertodeportivojuanmontiel.es

Montiel entrance looking W - note the buoyed channel
Steve Pickard

Welcoming marina

Opened in 2012 this 355 berth private marina is owned by a hotel and holiday complex. Room for visitors alongside the Dique de Levante. Max length 30m. Very little ashore except apartement blocks.

Approach

A high chimney is conspicuous behind the marina.

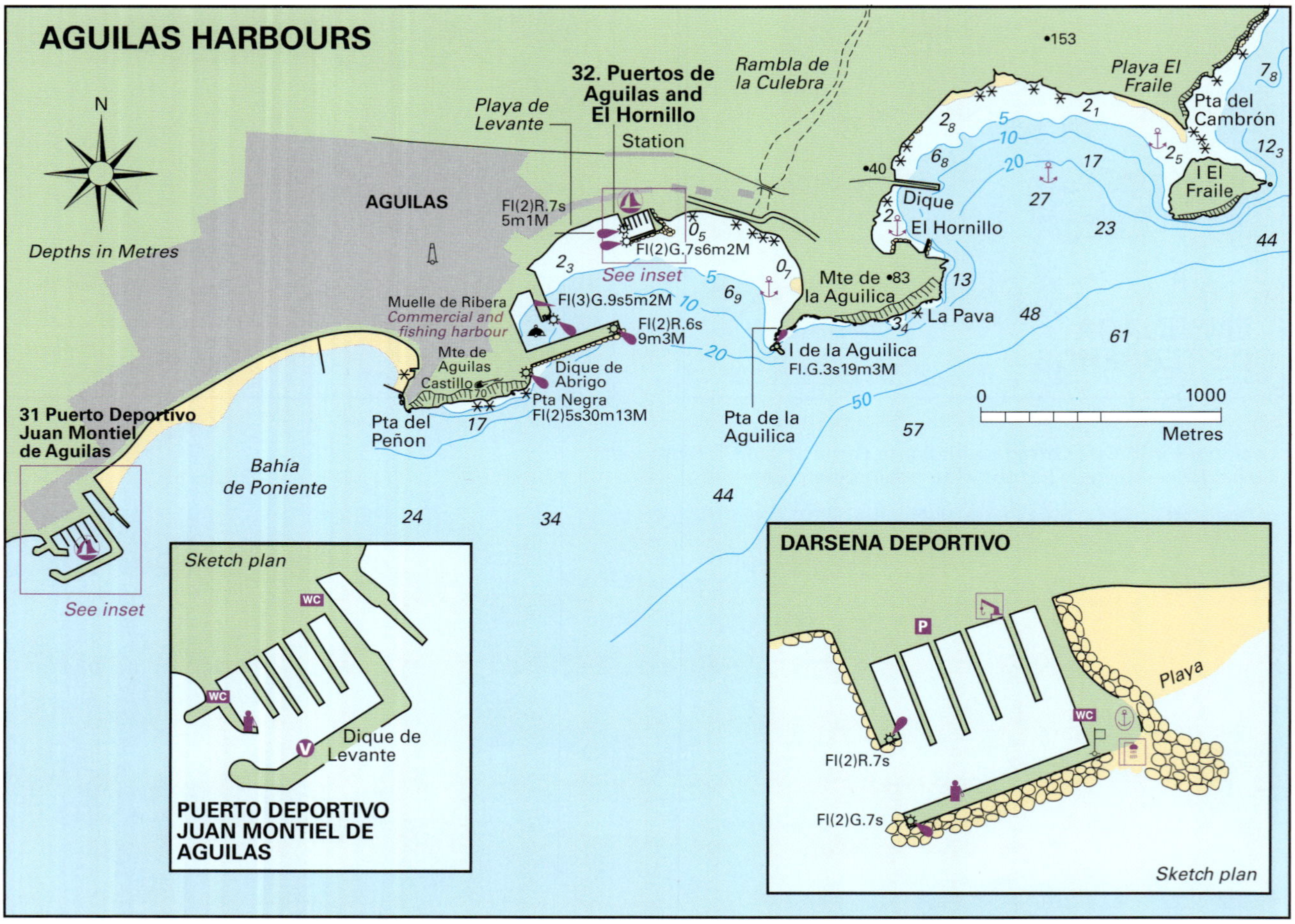

AGUILAS HARBOURS

Depths in Metres

AGUILAS

32. Puertos de Aguilas and El Hornillo

31 Puerto Deportivo Juan Montiel de Aguilas

Bahía de Poniente

Sketch plan

PUERTO DEPORTIVO JUAN MONTIEL DE AGUILAS

DARSENA DEPORTIVO

Sketch plan

Montiel shoreward from the Dique de Levante *Steve Pickard*

Berths

Berth initially at reporting / fuelling berth port side of marina on entry. The office is just behind. Calling on Ch 9 will ensure a *marinero* is present to assist with lines. Visitors are berthed opposite side of the marina, alongside.

32. Puertos de Aguilas and El Hornillo

37°24'·4N 01°34'·4W

Currents

Currents inside these two bays tend to set in the direction of recent winds.

Charts

UKHO *1515, 774* Imray *M12*
SHOM *7671* Spanish *463*

Lights

Approach
Punta Negra Fl(2)5s30m13M
Black and white bands 23m
Islote de la Aguilica Fl.G.3s19m3M
Square white building
Commercial Harbour
Mole head Fl(3)R.9s9m3M
Red post 5m
Contradique head Fl(3)G.9s5m2M
Grey Post 3m
Yacht Harbour (Darsena Deportiva)
Dique Sur head Fl(2)G.7s6m3M
White truncated tower, green top 5m
Dique Oeste Fl(2)R.7s5m1M
White truncated tower, red top 4m

Port communications

Port VHF Ch 9 ✆ +34 968 41 02 28
Club Náutico de Aguilas VHF Ch 9 ✆ +34 968 41 19 51
Marina Mobile 670445725
admon@cnaguilas.com
www.cnaguilas.com

Darsena Deportivo entrance looking SE.
Note the beach buoys *Steve Pickard*

Useful anchorage bays

Two bays separated by a headland, Monte de la Aguilica. The western bay, Puerto de Aguilas, has a small fishing port on its west shore and, as part of it, a small crowded yacht harbour on its N shore with room for 150 vessels of 10m max, collectively known as Aguilas Fishing Harbour. In the NE corner of the bay lies a small club Náutico (Darsena Deportivo) with 182 berths up to 12m.

To the east, on the other side of the headland, is El Hornillo, an old anchorage with a project for a marina. Both bays are open to the S and E sector and uncomfortable in a wind or swell from this direction but have attractive surroundings.

Aguilas was an important Roman port which fell into disuse after repeated invasions by the Berbers. In 1765 the village and harbour were rebuilt and the

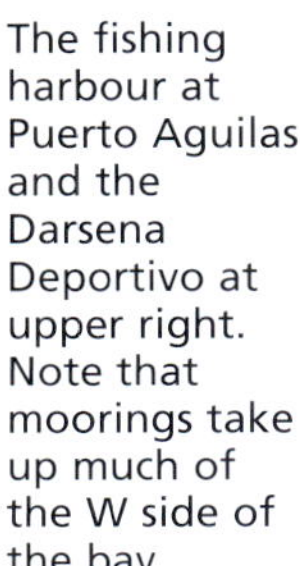

The fishing harbour at Puerto Aguilas and the Darsena Deportivo at upper right. Note that moorings take up much of the W side of the bay

III. COSTA BLANCA

Aguilas Fishing Harbour *Steve Pickard*

castle restored by Count Aranda, a minister of Charles III. A climb to the castle of San Juan (18th century) on Montaña de Aguilas above the harbour is worthwhile for the view. Good beaches on either side of the harbour.

Note that there are two headlands with lights named Punta Negra in this area: Punta Negra de Aguilas, normally listed under Punta Negra and Punta Negra de Mazarrón, normally listed under Mazarrón.

Approach

From the SW Follow the coast, passing the conspicuous Isla de los Terreros. In the distance four high, steep-sided headlands will be seen (Mt de Aguilas, Mt de la Aguilica, Isla el Fraile and Mt Cope). Aguilas lies behind the first headland, which has a small castle on its summit. A tall lone chimney stands in the bay to the W of the first headland.

From the NE Having rounded the large promontory of Mt Cope, see plan on page 105, a group of tree high, steep-sided rocky headlands will be seen, the first actually on an island. The harbour lies between the second and third headland.

Entrance

In Aguilas bay, give the head of mole a 50m berth; a buoyed channel leads to the Darsena Deportivo. Fishing nets are sometimes laid near the entrance to both bays. In heavy weather the entrance to both harbours might be dangerous.

Berths

In Aguilas fishing harbour secure to any vacant berth in the yacht harbour or as directed by harbour staff. In the fishing port a possibility is to go alongside at the root of the mole, clear of commercial craft; alternatively secure stern-to a fishing quay with a bow anchor using an anchor trip-line. Before arriving, check with the harbourmaster that there is room (VHF Ch 09).

Anchorages

It is possible to anchor almost anywhere clear of quays and swim buoys. There may not be much protected space in Aguilas outside the moorings if a S/SW swell is running. In these conditions there may be more shelter at El Hornillo.

Note Suggested anchorages are shown on the plan on page 105.

Facilities

Aguilas Fishing Harbour
50-tonne travel-lift and hardstanding.
12-tonne crane.
Slipway at the SW corner.
Engine repair mechanics in the town.
Small repairs to woodwork and hulls can be carried out at workshop by slipway.
Chandlers shop near the fish quay, another near the yacht harbour.
Water on the commercial mole. Supply also available at lonja de pescadores.
Ice from a factory to W of the town or at the harbourmaster's office.
Darsena Deportiva -
Maximum length overall: 12m.
Water and 220v AC on the quays.
Gasoleo A and petrol.
Club Náutico de Aguilas at yacht harbour.
A good selection of shops in the town and a small market.

Communications

Bus and rail services. ✆ Area code 968.

Anchorages between Aguilas and Mazarrón

(See plans opposite)

⚓ Cala Bardina

37°25'·6N 01°30'·5W

The first 50m offshore is cordoned off for swimmers and small boats. A channel for these boats is marked with a red and a green buoy – watch out for a submerged rock some 20m south of the green buoy! There is still plenty of room to anchor in six to eight metres outside the buoys. Well protected from the N and E by Mt Cope (244m) but open between SE and SW and with swell from E winds.

⚓ Ensenada de la Fuente

37°26'·1N 01°28'·7W

An anchorage open to NE but well protected by Mt Cope from other directions. Anchor in SW corner of the bay in 3m sand.

⚓ Other anchorages west of Puerto de Mazarrón

A large number of small coastal anchorages exist on this stretch of coast, see plans. Use with care. Most are off small, sandy beaches and any obstructions can be seen in the clear water. Some anchorages have a stony bottom but most are sand or shingle.

CALA BARDINA AND ENSENADA DE LA FUENTE
N
Depths in Metres
Pta del Ciscar
Playa de los Hierros
Playa Larga
Cala Blanca
Pta de la Galera
Chapa de la Galera
Playa Abejorro
Playa Elena
Playa Rafal
Pta del Charco
Pta del Sombrerico
Aguilas
Te Cope
Ensenada de la Fuente
Cala Bardina
Mt Cope 210
Pta del Cerro de la Cruz o de las Cabricas
Pta del Peñón de S. Maria
Pta del Caballo
37° 25′·6 N
01°27′·4W
0 1000 2000 3000
Metres

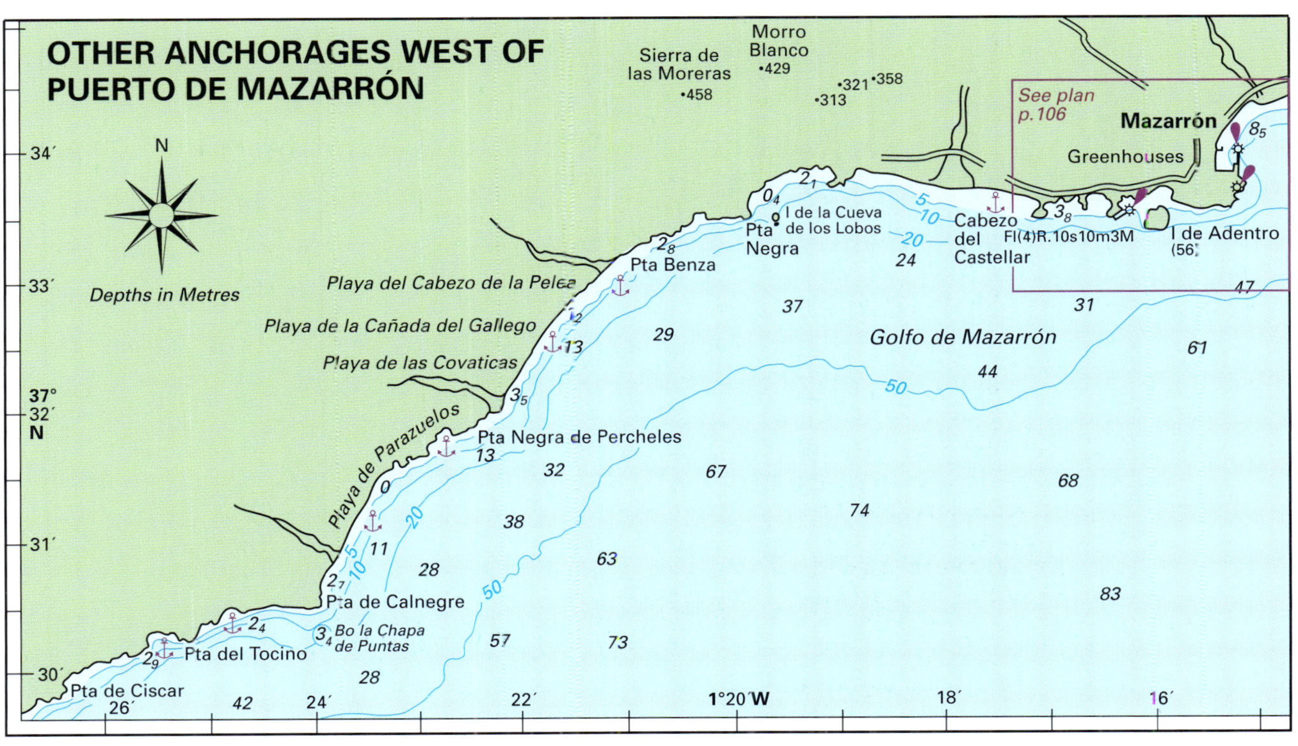
OTHER ANCHORAGES WEST OF PUERTO DE MAZARRÓN
N
Depths in Metres
Sierra de las Moreras
Morro Blanco
See plan p.106
Mazarrón
Greenhouses
I de la Cueva de los Lobos
Pta Negra
Cabezo del Castellar
Fl(4)R.10s10m3M
I de Adentro
Pta Benza
Playa del Cabezo de la Pelea
Playa de la Cañada del Gallego
Playa de las Covaticas
Golfo de Mazarrón
Playa de Parazuelos
Pta Negra de Percheles
Pta de Calnegre
Bo la Chapa de Puntas
Pta del Tocino
Pta de Ciscar
37° 32′ N
1°20′W

III. COSTA BLANCA

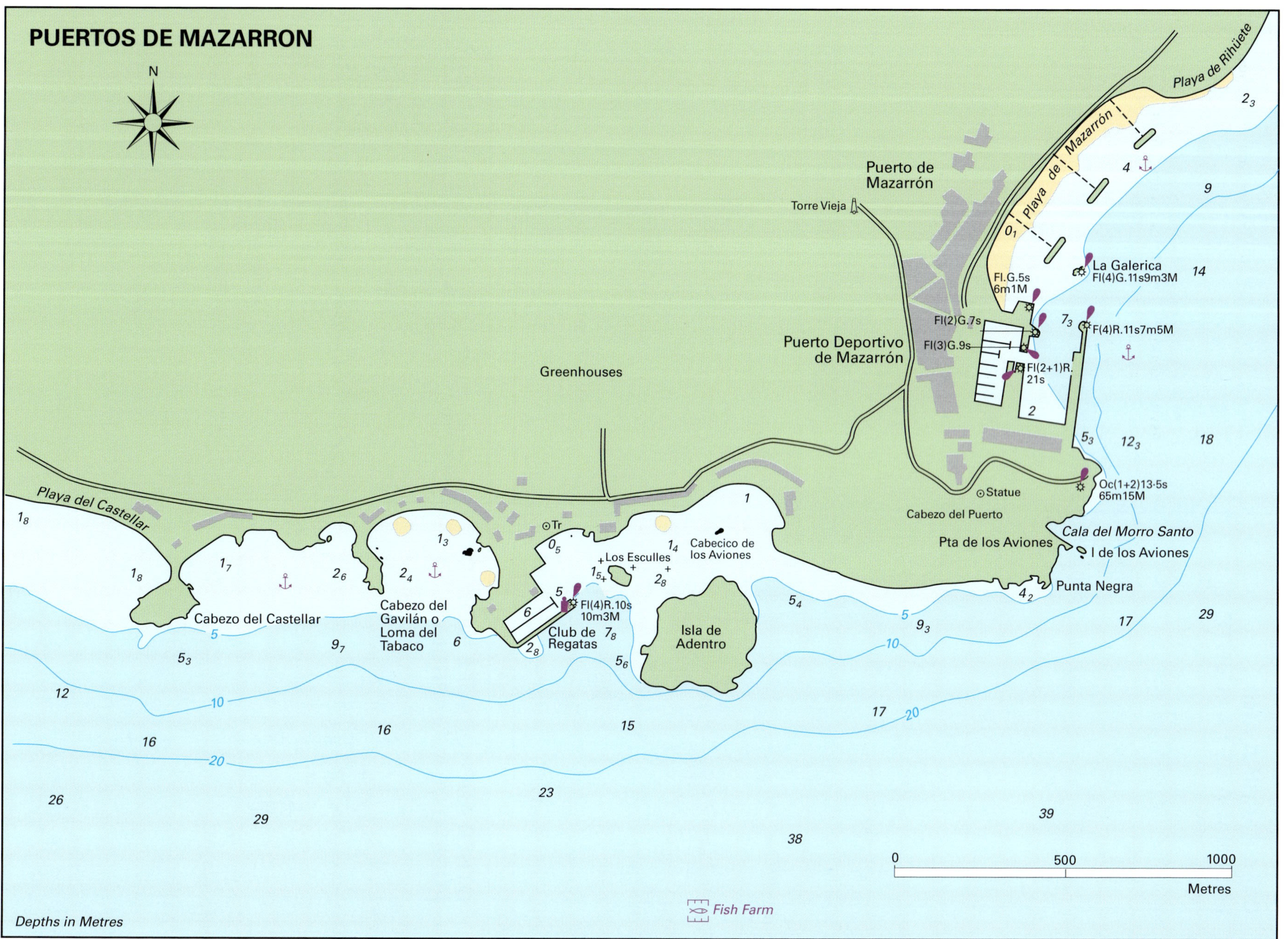
PUERTOS DE MAZARRON
N
Playa de Rihüete
Playa de Mazarrón
Puerto de Mazarrón
Torre Vieja
La Galerica
Fl(4)G.11s9m3M
Fl.G.5s 6m1M
Fl(2)G.7s
Fl(3)G.9s
F(4)R.11s7m5M
Fl(2+1)R.21s
Puerto Deportivo de Mazarrón
Greenhouses
Oc(1+2)13·5s 65m15M
Statue
Cabezo del Puerto
Cala del Morro Santo
Pta de los Aviones
I de los Aviones
Punta Negra
Playa del Castellar
Tr
Los Esculles
Cabecico de los Aviones
Fl(4)R.10s 10m3M
Club de Regatas
Isla de Adentro
Cabezo del Castellar
Cabezo del Gavilán o Loma del Tabaco
Metres
Fish Farm
Depths in Metres

33. Club de Regatas, Mazarrón

37°33'·4N 01°16'·3W

Charts
UKHO *774* Imray *M12*
SHOM *7671* Spanish *4632, 463*

Lights
Yacht club jetty head Fl(4)R.10s10m3M
Red metal tower, white band 4m
To the east
Mazarrón LtHo Oc(1+2)13·5s65m15M
White tower 11m

Port communications
Yacht club VHF Ch 9 ✆ +34 968 59 40 11
info@crmazarron.com
www.crmazarron.com

Pleasant harbour good shelter

The westerly of two marinas in Mazarrón and situated round the corner and about a mile west of the old fishing harbour and other marina in Mazarrón. This 200 berth marina offers very good shelter from all directions but sadly does not welcome visitors. There are pleasant beaches beside the harbour.

Note that there are two headlands with lights named Punta Negra in this area: Punta Negra de Mazarrón, normally listed under Mazarrón, and Punta Negra de Aguilas, normally listed under Punta Negra.

Approach

Tunny nets are sometimes laid off this section of coast and there are presently fish farms 1M SE of Pta del Calnegre and 1M S of Isla de Adentro. Submarines exercise in the south of this area.

From the SW The Sierra de las Moreras, with two peaks (458 and 429m), and the Isla de Adentro (56m) are recognisable. Punta Negra de Mazarrón with its lighthouse and large statue of Jesus is unmistakable. The harbour lies to W of Isla de Adentro.

From the NE The 4M-wide Ensenada de Mazarrón is easy to identify as is Punta Negra, described above, which has the appearance of an island from this direction. When Punta Negra has been closed Isla de Adentro will be seen; the harbour lies to W of this island.

Club de Regatas, Mazarrón from the SW

Anchorage in the approach

Depths to the NE of the harbour are shallow and the bottom is rocky so anchoring is not recommended but there are two very attractive sandy coves just west of the harbour with 3m in their centres.

Entrance

From the SW Approach Isla de Adentro on a NE course and, when 200m from it, turn onto a N course towards the harbour breakwater. Leave it 10m to port. Beware the rocky islet, Los Esculles, lying just to the north of the line between the north side of Isla de Adentro and the marina entrance.

From the NE Having identified the statue and Isla de Adentro round the Isla leaving it 200m to starboard (do not attempt to pass to the north of the Isla as the water is shallow with rocky outcrops) and proceed on a NNW course to close the breakwater end. Note the warning about Los Esculles in previous paragraph.

Berths

Secure to quay on port-hand side of entrance near fuel pumps and ask at the Club de Regatas office for a berth. Visitors berths are limited to three at the end of the 'T' pontoon. Visitors may be put elsewhere if there is room.

Facilities

Maximum length overall: 25m (four yachts only; more at lesser length).
Marine Engineer (Volvo agency).
Slipway at N side of harbour and for dinghies at E side.
8-tonne crane.
Hardstandings.
Water and 220v AC points on pontoons and quays.
Gasoleo A and petrol.
Ice at entrance.
Club de Regatas de Mazarrón has a bar, restaurant, showers etc.
Provisions from village of Mazarrón.

Communications

✆ Area code 968. Taxi ✆ +34 968 59 51 22.

III. COSTA BLANCA

34. Puerto Deportivo de Mazarrón

37°33'·9N 01°15'·W

Charts
UKHO *774* Imray *M12*
Spanish *4632, 463*

Lights
Dique de Abrigo head Fl.R.3s7m3M Red post 3m
Dique de Abrigo corner Fl(4)R.11s7m5M Red post 3m
Contradique N head Fl.G.5s6m1M Green post 3m
Contradique Elbow Fl(2)G.7s5m1M Green post 3m
Darsena N entrance Fl(3)G.9s4m1M Green post 5m
Darsena S entrance Fl(2+1)R.21s4m1M
Red post, green band 3m

Port communications
Marina office VHF Ch 9. ✆ +34 609 36 02 60 /
+34 968 15 40 65
boltursa@yahoo.es

Puerto Deportivo de Mazarrón

Fishing and commercial harbour with a Puerto Deportivo for yachts

A new marina with almost all 250 berths sold out to individuals. Visitors welcome, though space is limited. Several restaurants (some excellent) and bars on the quayside make it a busy and noisy place in summer. This fishing and commercial harbour at the W end of the Ensenada de Mazarrón is easy to enter and offers good protection from all directions except NE. Over the past five years there has been a vast injection of money and the rocky jetties of the 90s have been replaced with new quays and promenades with first class buildings and pontoons. The town of Mazarrón, about 3M inland, has good shops and may be reached by taxi or bus. A climb to the lighthouse is worthwhile for the view. Good beaches in the bay.

Approach

Tunny nets are sometimes laid off this section of coast and there is a fish farm 1M south of Isla de Adentro. Submarines exercise in the south of the area.

From the SW The Sierra de las Moreras and a few islands close to the coast are recognisable. Punta Negra with its lighthouse and a large statue of Jesus is especially conspicuous.

From the NE Punta Negra resembles an island and, with its lighthouse and statue, is conspicuous across the wide Rada de Mazarrón.

Entrance

Approach the head of the breakwater on a westerly course, keeping well clear of Isla de la Galerica and round the head at 25m.

Berths

This new marina is safe but with surging reported during NE and E winds. Most of the pontoon berths have been sold privately, leaving little room for visitors, who are berthed alongside the inner marina wall close to the bars and the office.

Anchorages

Anchor to E or N of the harbour entrance. Keep clear of La Galerica rock.

Miscellaneous

The beacons on Punta de la Azohía mark a measured distance of 1857·47m on the N side of the bay, near the centre, on an axis of 104°.

Entrance to Puerto Deportivo Mazarrón looking N, with La Galerica as the starboard entrance marker *Steve Pickard*

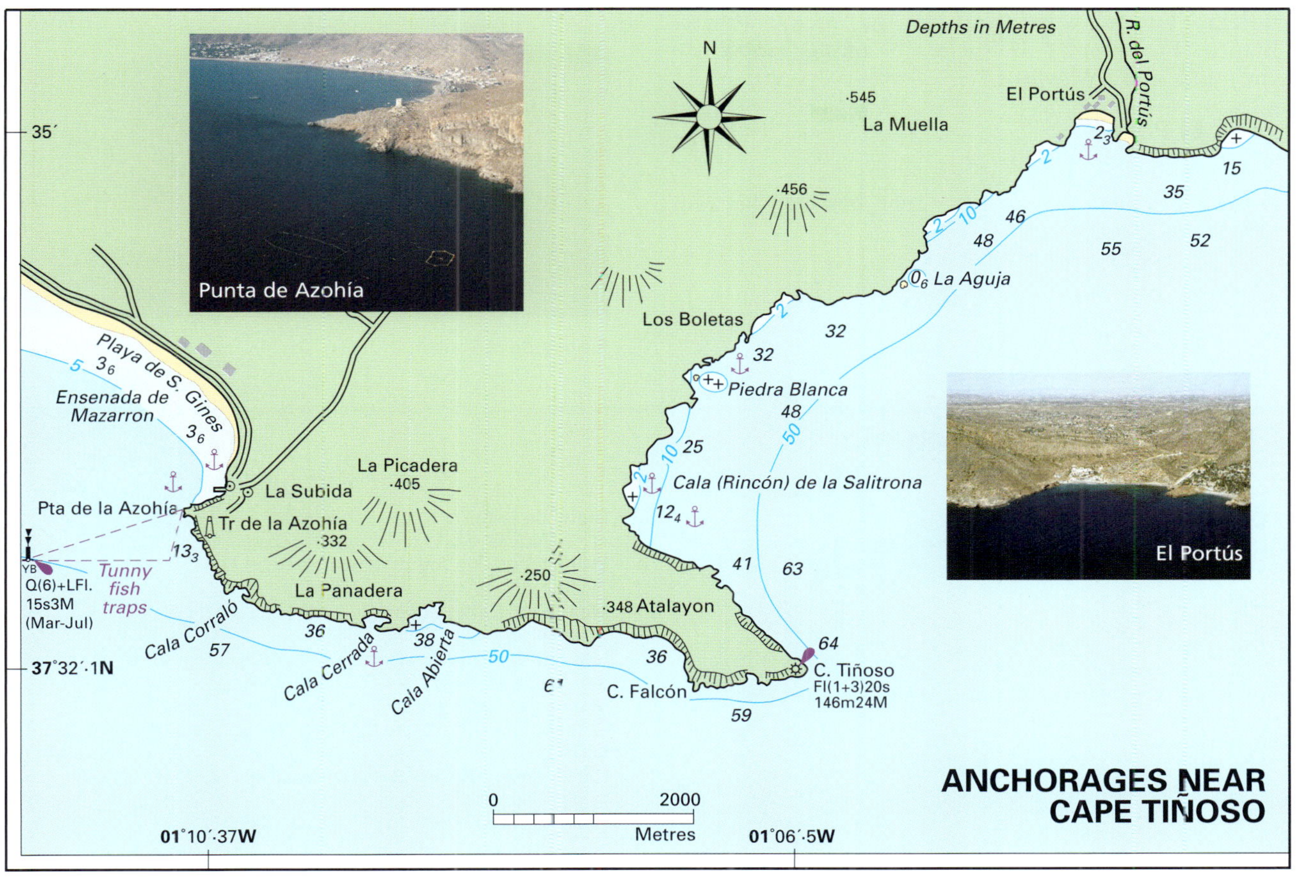

Facilities

Water and 220v AC points on pontoons and quays.
Two hards ashore with large travel-lift on centre quay.
Water from fish quay.
Ice from a small factory.
Shops and a supermarket and market in the village.
Many more in the town itself some 3M inland.

Communications

Bus to Mazarrón town. ✆ Area code 968.

⚓ Ensenada de Mazarrón

37°33′·4N 01°10′·6W (See plans above and page 106)

It is possible to anchor almost anywhere around this bay in 5M sand and weed. The recommended places are to the sides of the three *ramblas* (dry river beds) or just NE of Punta de la Azohía off the small hamlet of La Subida, both open to S. Watch out for fishing boat moorings. A pair of beacons are situated NE and SW of the hamlet. A small supermarket is located in a housing estate ½M along the road to Mazarrón. In the centre of the bay a small private harbour has been developed alongside and behind the Isla Plana.

There is a fish farm off Punta de la Azohía, but one can go between the farm and the point.

Cala Cerrada

⚓ Cala Cerrada

37°32′·4N 01°09′·25W

Use with caution. Open to S. Anchor in the NE corner, in eight to 10 metres. The whole *cala* is very deep and is 8m even 20m from the beach.

⚓ Rincón de la Salitrona

37°33′·2N 01°07′·5W

Anchor off the north beach, in 5m sand and weed, or the south beach which is more sheltered but deeper at eight to 10m. An alternative is off Los

Boletas but pay attention to the rocks, Piedra Blanca. Freighters gain shelter N of C. Tiñoso in strong W and SW winds.

⚓ El Portús

37°34'·8N 01°04'·4W (see plan page 109)

Anchor off the sandy beach. Open between SE and SW. Small shops.

Rincón de la Salitrona

35. Puerto de Cartagena

37°35'·98N 00°59'·1W

Charts

UKHO *774, 1700, 1189, 1194* Imray *M12*
SHOM *7642, 7671* Spanish *4642, 464A, 464*

Lights

To the west
Cabo Tiñoso Fl(1+3)20s146m24M
White tower and building 10m.
A magnetic anomaly 3M to S of Cabo Tiñoso has been reported.
Approaches
Plan below
Western Approach
Dique, Algameca Grande Fl(4)R.11s10m7M
White and yellow tower 5m
The Point, Algameca Grande Fl(3)G.9s8m3M
White and yellow tower 5m
Entrance
Dique de Navidad Fl(2)R.10s15m10M
White tower red top 11m
Bajo de Santa Ana Fl(2)G.7s5M
Green conical 5m
Eastern Approach
Bajo Las Losas VQ(6)+LFl.10s5m5M ⧗ card 5m
Escombreras
Dique Muelle Bastarreche head Fl(2)G.7s10m5M
White tower 7m
Dique de Abrigo head Fl.G.3s10m10M
Green and white tower 7m
Islote Escombreras Fl.5s65m17M
Tower with aluminium cupola on white building 8m
Harbour Plan page 112
Dique de Navidad Fl(2)R.10s15m10M
White tower red top 11m
Dique de la Curra Fl(3)G.14s14m5M
Cylindrical white tower green cupola 11m
Espalmador floating breakwater, Head Q.R.1s4M
Red column 4m
Muelle del Carbón head Fl(2+1)R.14.5s8m3M
Red post, green band 5m
Marina outer breakwater Q.G.1s5m1M Green tower 4m
Muelle de Sta Lucia Fl(4)G.12s5m1M Green post 3m
Muelle Santiago head Fl(4)R.11s5m1M Red post 3m
Dolphin Fl(2+1)G.16s5m1M Green column, red band 3m
Yacht basin
Darsena de Yates breakwater head 37°35'.7N 00°58'.8W
Fl(3)R.9s5m1M Red support 1m
Outer harbour elbow SW Fl(2+1)G.12s3m1M
Green column, red band 1m
Club de Regatas mole SW corner Q.G.3s5m1M
Green post 5m

Port communications

Port VHF Ch 11, 12, 14
Real Club de Regatas Cartagena VHF Ch 9
☎ +34 968 50 15 07 ☎ +34 968 50 15 09
contacto@clubregatascartagena.es
www.clubregatascartagena.es
Yacht Port Cartagena VHF Ch 9 ☎ +34 968 12 12 13
Mobile +34 618 332101
marina@yachtportcartagena.com
www.yachtportcartagena.com

Storm signals

Flown from the signal station in Castillo de Galeras.

Harbour charges Low

Major naval harbour with good facilities

One of the safest and most interesting ports in the Mediterranean with facilities for over 1,000 yachts in two marinas. Good safe wintering stop and popular with the international cruising fraternity. A large naval, commercial and fishing port of great antiquity which is easy to approach and enter under almost any conditions. Cartagena is an attractive city with good shops, many restaurants and several museums.

There are two yacht clubs: RCRC – Real Club de Regatas Cartagena – and to its east the YPC – Yacht Port Cartagena. The RCRC is pleasant and welcomes visitors if a berth is available but is primarily for members. It has a splendid club house and restaurant, which visitors in either marina are welcome to use. The YPC is more geared for visitors with staff speaking English and responding quickly to VHF from land and RIB to greet new arrivals. The marina was originally designated for super-yachts, but the failure to attract any resulted in a change of ownership and a re-organisation of the marina to accept any vessel from 6–25m but with a few places for 60m vessels near the office.

There are also a small number of moorings to the W of RCRC, along the old town quay belonging to the port authorities (Puerto Deportivo). These are reported to have always been occupied by tourist boats.

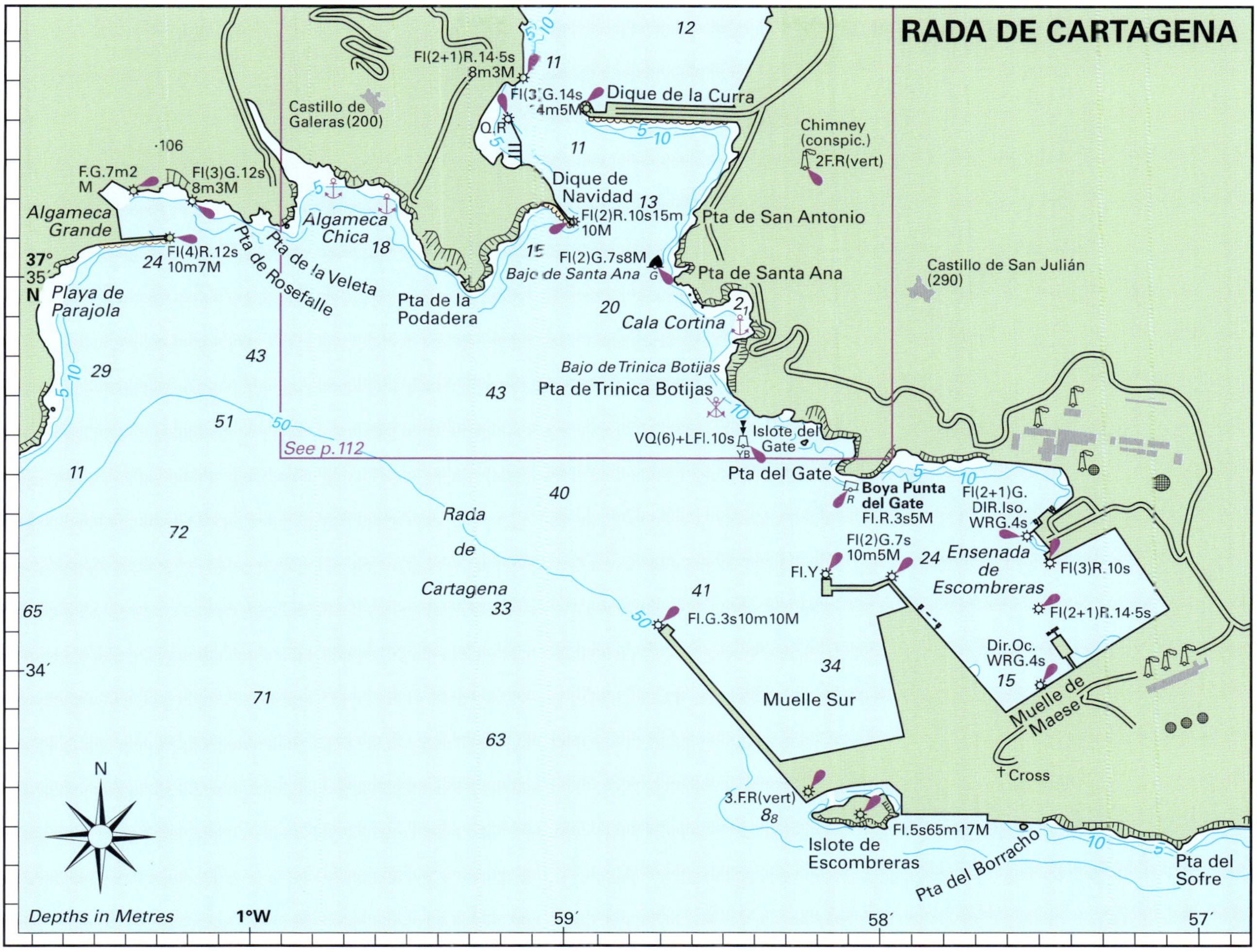

RADA DE CARTAGENA

Castillo de Galeras (200)
Fl(2+1)R.14·5s 8m3M
11
12
Fl(3)G.14s 4m5M
Dique de la Curra
Q.R
11
Chimney (conspic.)
2F.R(vert)
·106
F.G.7m2M
Fl(3)G.12s 8m3M
Dique de Navidad
13
Fl(2)R.10s15m 10M
Pta de San Antonio
Algameca Grande
Algameca Chica
18
Pta de Rosefalle
Pta de la Veleta
37°35′N
Fl(4)R.12s 10m7M
24
15
Fl(2)G.7s8M
Bajo de Santa Ana
Pta de Santa Ana
Castillo de San Julián (290)
Playa de Parajola
Pta de la Podadera
20
Cala Cortina
2
29
43
Bajo de Trinica Botijas
Pta de Trinica Botijas
43
51
See p.112
VQ(6)+LFl.10s
Islote del Gate
Pta del Gate
11
40
Boya Punta del Gate
Fl.R.3s5M
Fl(2+1)G. DIR.Iso. WRG.4s
72
Rada de Cartagena
33
Fl(2)G.7s 10m5M
Fl.Y
24
Ensenada de Escombreras
Fl(3)R.10s
65
41
Fl.G.3s10m10M
Fl(2+1)R.14·5s
34′
34
Dir.Oc. WRG.4s
15
71
Muelle Sur
Muelle de Maese
63
Cross
N
3.F.R(vert)
8
Fl.5s65m17M
Islote de Escombreras
Pta del Borracho
Pta del Sofre
Depths in Metres
1°W
59′
58′
57′

The YPC looking W *Yacht Port Cartagena*

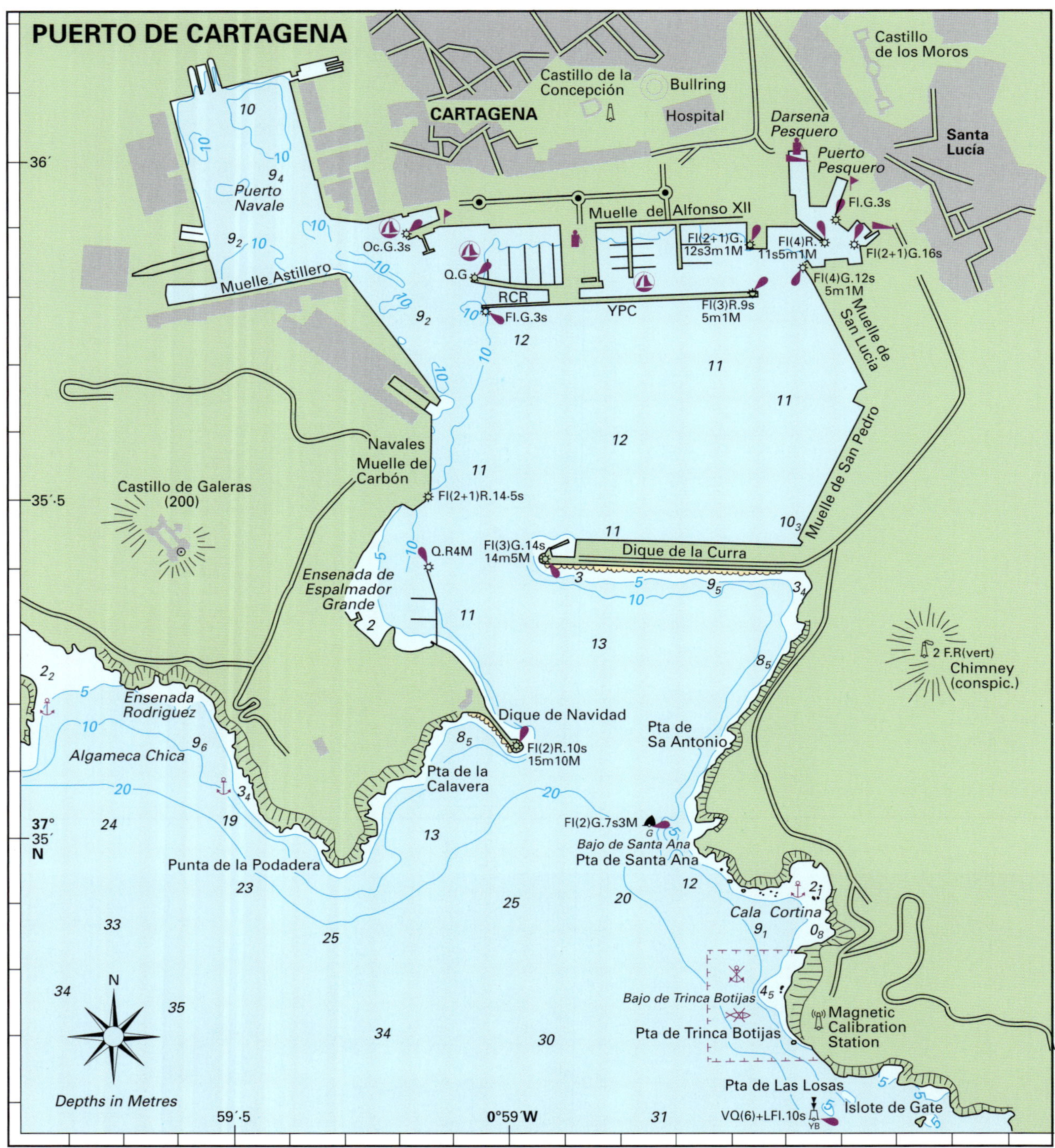

Approach

From all directions the entrance to Rada de Cartagena is made obvious by the high steep reddish cliffs of Cabo Tiñoso to the W and Islote de Escombrera to the E. The large oil refinery near this island is visible from afar. A large chimney, with black top and white band is conspicuous between Castillo de San Juan and Punta de San Antonio. There is vast construction work going on to enlarge the port of Escombreras. The passage between the Islote and Punta del Borracho has been closed while an 800 metre breakwater now runs NW from the west point of the Islote.

From the west The course goes past Puerto de Algameca Grande, a naval port on the W side of the Rada de Cartagena which is prohibited to yachts. Large unlit mooring buoys are located opposite Algameca Grande and Chico. A firing range exists to the S of this port and submarines exercise in the area.

From the east From Cabo de Palos follow the land keeping a good watch out for fish farms, which proliferate in this area especially off Portman and Cala de Gorguel. Pass south of Cabo del Agua and Islote de Escombreras and steer parallel to the new breakwater until the entrance to Cartagena proper opens up. It is recommended to keep well clear of all

The distant entrance to Cartagena, looking S *Steve Pickard*

the ongoing construction work at the port of Escombreras. Although this port may be still used in dire emergency, one will normally be sent away to the marina in Cartagena.

Verify which marina you have made contact with on VHF Ch 9. This can be confusing as it is not always clear which one is responding.

Cartagena offers agreeable surroundings for a longer stay *Steve Pickard*

Cartagena looking SSE. YPC: a spacious marina liable to some surging on the E side *YPC*

Entrance

Straightforward but check that there are no large vessels entering or leaving port. Seas build up in the entrance during strong onshore winds.

Anchorages

Anchoring is forbidden in the harbour or its immediate approaches although a berth off the Ensenada de Espalmador Grande has been known. Anchoring is possible 4M to W of the harbour (see plan page 109) in Rincón de la Salitrona behind and to N of Cabo Tiñoso, El Portús, Algameca Chica and Cala Cortina (pay attention to rock on N side). The latter two lie to the W and E, respectively, of the harbour entrance. Algameca Chica is smelly and may have fishing nets. Cala Cortina has a rocky bottom. Expect to be moved if you finish up in a defence or commercial area. In summer the entire bay can be closed off with swim buoys

Berths

Calling on VHF will elicit a response with directions (for YPC) to pass Dique de la Curra and head on a course of 040° to the entrance, where a berth will be allocated over VHF. There is often a large orange ocean going lifeboat moored on the dique.

For RCRC, head on a course of 350° from Dique de la Curra. The harbour and quays are sometimes oily and with a SE wind, smoke and fumes from the refinery at Escombreras can be unpleasant. Muelle de Alfonso Xll is often used by YPC for short stay visitors and can be unpleasant with a lot of rubbish being brought in on S sector winds. Ask for a different berth if this is the case. Staff are always helpful.

The YPC office (looking temporary, housed in two portacabins) and a small boatyard are on the E end of the Muelle de Alfonso XII, and quite a walk. There are as yet no club facilities at YPC, though there is a very contemporary building housing a museum and restaurant and bar just outside the marina fence.

III. COSTA BLANCA

An amphitheatre right in the centre of town and beautifully restored in its original setting *Maria Kanayama*

A lovely clean elegant town, with so much to see! *Maria Kanayama*

Facilities

Maximum length overall: 25m.
All types of repairs, mostly by the naval workshops; contact the marina for advice.
Cranes up to 20 tonnes; contact capitán de puerto.
Marine radio shop next to the Scandinavian Consul's office in the Muralla del Mar.
Several chandlers, two near Dársena Pesquera.
Charts from Esqui Náuticas, Campos.
Water and 230/380v AC on marina pontoons.
Gasoleo A and petrol at the marina.
New shower and toilet facilities
Hypermarket 'Continente' about a kilometre away – ask for directions or take a taxi. Many varied provision shops and two markets in the town, none near.
Launderette in Plaza de San Francisco.

History of the port

A port well used by Phoenicians, it was developed by Hasdrubal about 243BC and became the centre of Carthaginian influence in Europe, helped by slaves working the gold and silver mines of the region. Hasdrubal's brother, Hannibal, used it as a base for his expedition across the Alps and it became the primary target of Scipio the elder ('Africanus' – Cathargo delenda est). The Romans duly destroyed Carthaginian influence. St James the Great is said to have landed here in AD 36 bringing Christianity to Spain from Palestine (a sea passage which according to legend took four days). It subsequently passed into the hands of the Barbarians and then the Moors. Philip II fortified the surrounding hills in the 16th century, Drake stole its guns in 1585 and took them to Jamaica, Charles III established the arsenal and naval base in the 18th century and the Republicans held out for months against Madrid during the Civil War in 1936. But the chief remnants of its troubled history lie in the minds of its inhabitants, not its artefacts.

Locally

There is a good view of the harbour from the Castillo de la Concepción and the old churches are worth visiting. A 10-day local holiday starts the Sunday before Trinity Sunday.

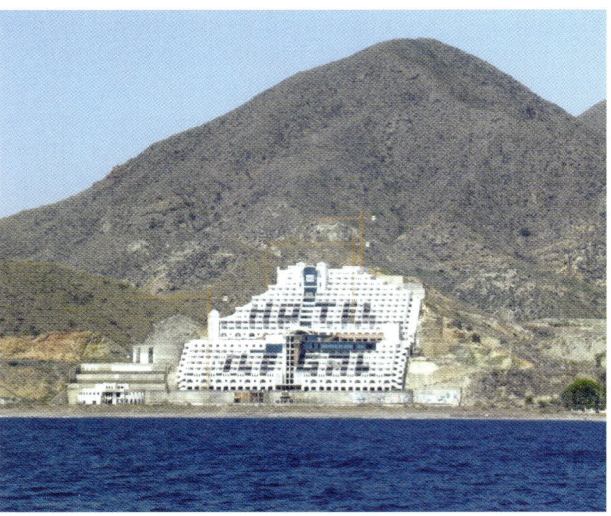

'Hotel Illegal'. Standing idle and never opened, this is one of thousands of properties along the Costa del Sol built in the past 20 years with illegally issued (or no) licences and now to be demolished after years of legal proceedings *Graham Hutt*

Do visit the tourist office close to the marinas and purchase the multi-museum ticket which covers all the museums and archaeological sites. It takes you on an amazing circuit of layers of the ancient city's beautifully preserved and inter-connected past, with amazing architecture. The modern town is hardly noticeable once you enter the labyrinth underground. A lift in the old castle wall ascends to the higher levels of the castle: again well worth a visit.

Communications

Murcia Airport 30 minutes by taxi, international flights. Railway to Murcia from FEVE and Los Nietos from RENFE station and bus services. An occasional service by sea to the Canary Isles.
✆ Area code 968. Taxi rank at marina.

36. Puerto de Portmán

Lights
Punta de la Chapa Oc.3.5s49m13M
White tower on white building 8m
Breakwater head Fl(2)R.6s6m2M Red post 4m
Bajo de la Bola Q(6)+LFl.10s5M card buoy 4m

Silted up port with fish farms

Called Portus Magnus by the Romans, Portmán has been completely silted up by effluent from the lead and zinc mines inland. The scars in the hillside and the new wind farm on the top of the hill inland make recognition of Portmán relatively easy. There is a huge fish farm to the west of the bay which leaves little space to anchor. The small dinghy harbour, on the east side, has a breakwater running out from the beach with a red column at its end. The harbour is totally sheltered but only has about 0·5m depth at the entrance and is only for dinghies and RIBS. There is a *club náutico* on the west side of the beach but there are no facilities at all in the small village. Anchor between the two buoys in the bay in about 4m and land on the beach by dinghy – open between SE and SW.

Puerto de Portmán

Cala de Gorguel

⚓ Cala del Gorguel

37°34′·4N 0°52′·5W

An unlit fish farm virtually blocks the entrance to this *cala*, approach with care from the east. The *cala* is full of floating gear and boats for the farm. Anchor (if there is room) in small rocky cove in 5m mud off the beach. There are off-lying rocks on W side of beach. Open between SE and S. There are also fish farms, mostly unlit, off-shore between La Manceba and Cabo Negrete.

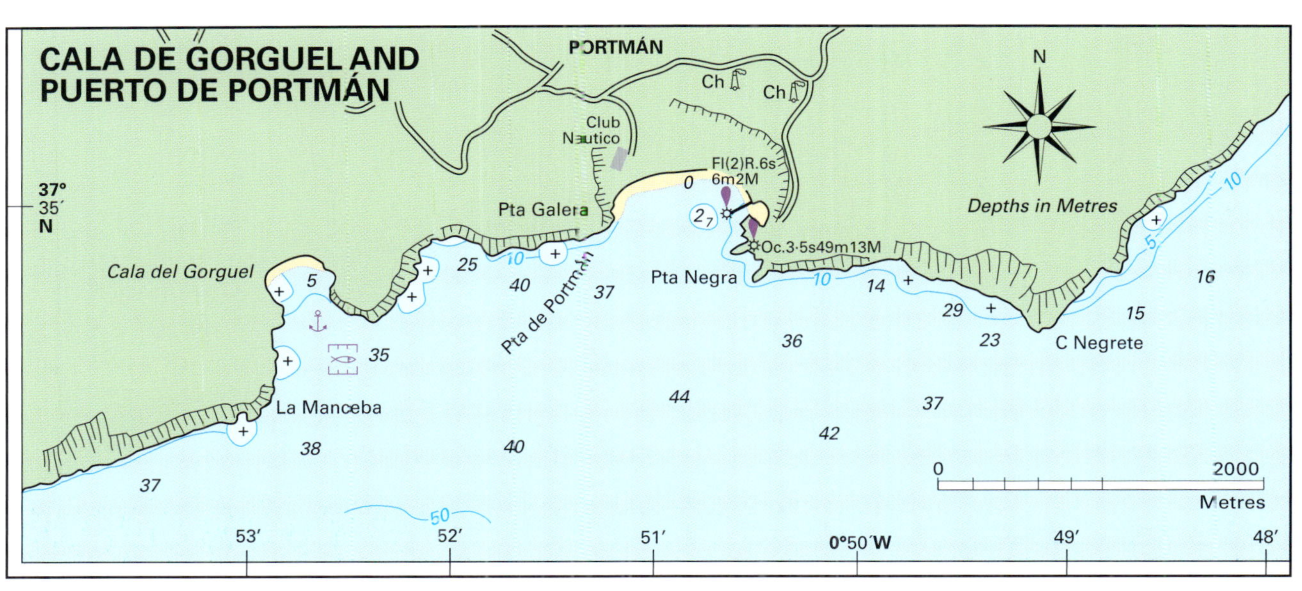

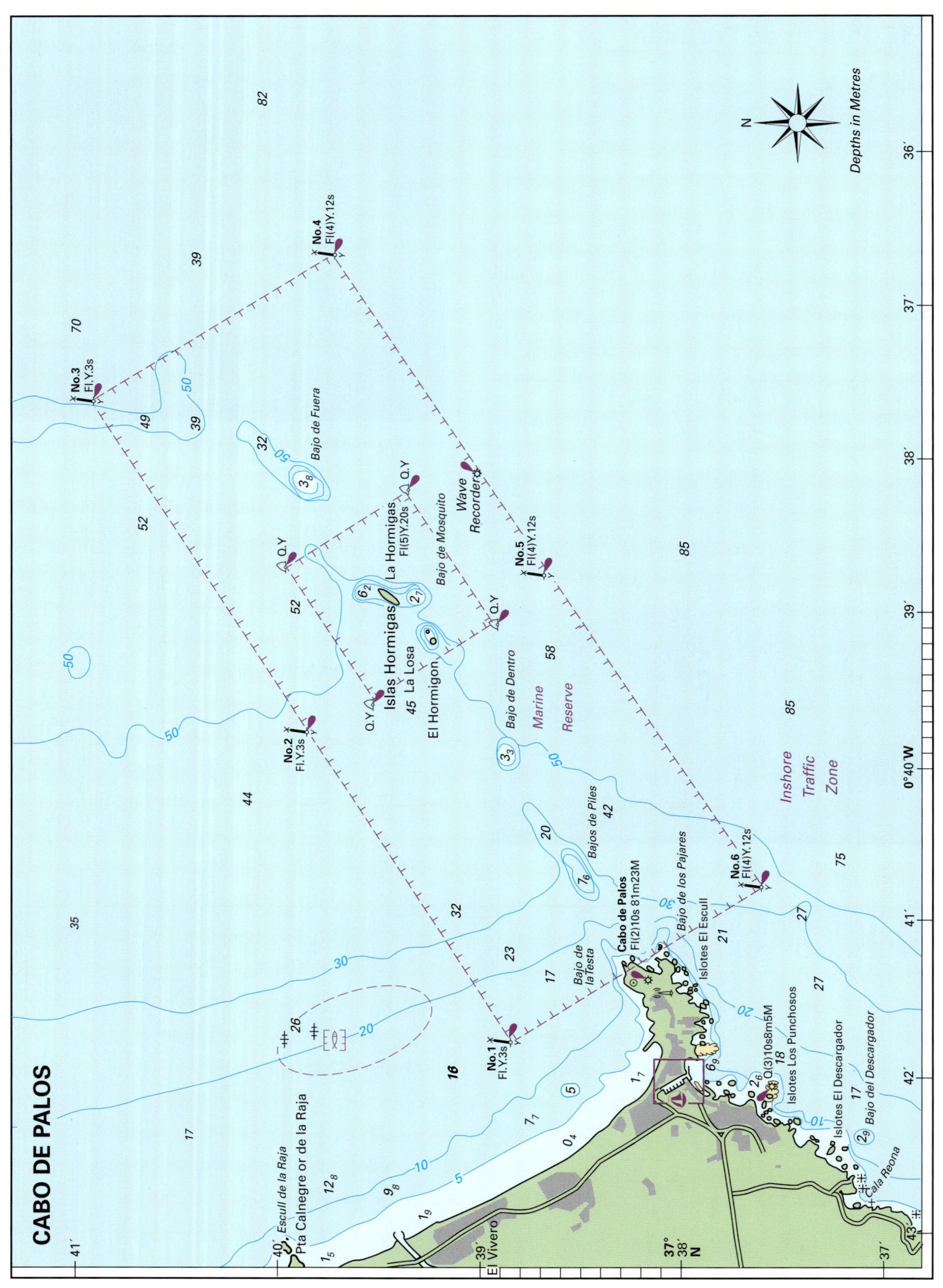
CABO DE PALOS
Depths in Metres
N
No.1
Fl.Y.3s
No.2
Fl.Y.3s
No.3
Fl.Y.3s
No.4
Fl(4)Y.12s
No.5
Fl(4)Y.12s
No.6
Fl(4)Y.12s
Q.Y
La Hormigas
Fl(5)Y.20s
Islas Hormigas
La Losa
El Hormigon
Bajo de Fuera
Bajo de Mosquito
Wave
Recorder
Bajo de Dentro
Marine
Reserve
Inshore
Traffic
Zone
Bajos de Piles
Cabo de Palos
Fl(2)10s 81m23M
Bajo de los Pajares
Islotes El Escull
Bajo de la Testa
Q(3)10s8m5M
Islotes Los Punchosos
Islotes El Descargador
Bajo del Descargador
Cala Reona
Escull de la Raja
Pta Calnegre or de la Raja
El Vivero
0°40'W
37° 38' N

37. Puerto de Cabo de Palos (Cala Avellán)

37°37'·8N 00°42'·8W

Charts

UKHO *774, 1700*	Imray *M12*
SHOM *7670, 7671*	Spanish *464, 471*

Lights

Espigón de la Sal Fl(2)G.7s6m5M
Green post 3m
Beacon Fl(2)R.7s5m3M
Red round post 3m
Escollo Las Melvas VQ(6)+LFl.10s5m5M
⯆ card post YB 3m

To the northeast
Cabo de Palos Fl(2)10s81m23M Round tower 51m

To the southwest
Los Punchosos Q(3)10s8m5M Grey pole 5m

Port communications

VHF Ch 9. ✆ +34 968 56 35 15

Small yacht and fishing harbour

In a very dramatic setting, this 175 berth yacht and fishing harbour is prone to silting and has a tight 'dogleg' entry. Located at the western edge of a prodigious tourist development running along the edge of the Mar Menor it and its surroundings are crowded. A pleasant short walk out to the lighthouse. Excellent sandy beaches to N.

The zig-zag entrance requires care and is not really suitable for yachts over 12m.

Approach

From the south From Cartagena to Cabo de Palos the coast has steep rocky cliffs with a few sandy bays lying between points. The hinterland is rugged and hilly. There are no dangers more than 200m off-shore and the coast is steep-to. Portmán may be recognised by the vast hillside of open-cast mining behind it with a wind farm with 8 turbines on top of the hill. The large lighthouse at Cabo de Palos (81m) is easily identified. The harbour lies ½M to the W of it. Pay attention to off-lying rocks in the approach to the harbour.

From the north Isla Grosa (95m) is unmistakable. The coast as far as the prominent Cabo de Palos, is low, flat, sandy and lined with high-rise buildings. No dangers lie more than 600m off-shore. Round Cabo de Palos at 200m paying attention to isolated rocks and islets in the western part of the bay inside this distance, in particular, the rock just under water southeast of Espigón de la Sal, which is now marked by a S cardinal beacon, Las Melvas.

Puerto de Cabo de Palos – note underwater rock in the lower right-hand corner (now marked by beacon), looking N to Mar Menor on left and Isla Grosa on right

The entrance channel looking S. Note rock marking port marker *Steve Pickard*

Anchorage in the approach

The bottom to the S of Cabo de Palos peninsula is rocky out to the 20m contour. It is better to anchor in 5m sand to the N of this peninsula.

Entrance

Approach the harbour keeping the church, which has an unusual open-work, tripod tower with a bell on a cross bar and a cross on top, approximately NNW (between 325° and 345°), keeping the awash rock, Las Melvas, with its S cardinal pole, well to starboard. Turn to starboard around the end of the Espigón de la Sal (with its green post) keeping close to the quay, leaving the white pole on the 2m diameter red beacon well to port. Then turn to port round the end of the Dique de Abrigo and go alongside the quay parallel to the *dique*.

Berths

Although there are pontoons inside the harbour these are for locals only and visitor berths are alongside the quay in the outer harbour.

Facilities

Maximum length overall: 10m.
A slipway at N end of the harbour and a small slipway in outer harbour to W of entrance to inner harbour.
Chandlery and diesel in the village.
Water taps and 220v AC on quays.
A few local shops.

Cabo de Palos lighthouse *Graham Hutt*

Looking N into Puerto de Palos from the Dique de Abrigo *Steve Pickard*

Communications

Bus services to Cartagena, Murcia and La Manga where there is a large supermarket. ☽ Area code 968.

⚓ Cabo de Palos

37°38'·1N 0°41'·55W

Anchorage in bay to NW of Cabo de Palos open to NE in 5m sand and stones. Shops in nearby Playa Honda and at La Barra. Note there is now a traffic separation scheme (TSS) some nine miles ESE of the lighthouse which should not seriously affect pleasure craft as they are generally closer to the point but one should be aware of its position.

Marine Reserve Cabo de Palos

This low sandy point with its 51m-high grey lighthouse has a large marine reserve some 2M by 4M extending to the ENE. It is marked by six buoys, the three northern ones are Fl.Y.3s while the three southern ones are Fl(4)Y.12s. There is an inner reserve, around Islas Hormigas, marked with four buoys Q.Y some of which may be missing at times. There is also a yellow, spherical wave recorder buoy at 37°39'·3N 00°38'·2W with a light Q(5)Y.20s.

⚓ Playa de Palos

37°39'N 0°42'·7W

Coastal anchorage along a 6M stretch of sandy beach in 5m sand and weed. Wide open E and facing wall to wall high-rise buildings – access to the coast road is through private properties. A shallow patch, Banco El Tabal (1·7m), is near the centre of the beach.

⚓ Isla Grosa

37°43'·5N 0°42'·6W

Anchorage in the W quarter of the island to suit draught in clay with weed. The island, 95m high, offers some protection from sea and wind. There are houses on the W side and a landing place. This area is occupied by the military and approach within 300m is discouraged.

MAR MENOR
47 Puerto de San Pedro del Pinatar
Fl(4)G.12s13m5M
46 Lo Pagán
Ciudad del Aire
San Javier
Santiago de la Ribera
Naval Pto de San Javier
Aero Fl.6s
Fl(4)G.11s1M
Fl(4)R.11s1M
Aeropuerto de San Javier
Pta de Casablanca
Playa de Pals
Los Punchosos
Pta de Algas
Escolletes de Fuera
Pta del Pudrimel
See p.122
Los Narejos
Pta Galera
Fl.R.5s7m3M
Fl.G.5s7m3M
38 Puerto de Tomás Maestre
Pta del Estacio
Fl(4)20s32m14M
VQ(3)5s7m3M
la Laja
El Farallón
Isla Grosa
(95)
Fl.3s97m5M
Los Alcázares
45 Puerto de los Alcázares
Fl.G.5s5m5M
Mar Menor
Pta Seca
Ite de la Galera
Entrance to Mar Menor
Airfield
Isla Perdiguera
Pta del Fraile
Isla Mayor (or del Barón)
Pta del Galán
44 Los Urrutias
See p.125
Isla del Sujeto
Isla Redondo
39 Pto de dos Mares
Escull de la Raja
Pta Calnegre o de la Raia
Isla del Ciervo
43 Puerto de los Nietos
42 Pto de las Islas Menores
41 Puerto de Mar de Cristal
40 Puerto de la Manga
Urmenor
Bajo del Piles
Cabo de Palos
Fl(2)10s81m 23M
37 Cabo de Palos
Q(3)10s8m5M
Islotes Los Punchoses
Islotes del Descargador
Bajo del Descargador
Los Belones
Pta de la Espada
Depths in Metres
N
49′
37° 45′ N
40′
50′
0°45′W
40′

Mar Menor – an inland sea

An extraordinary inland sea some 12M long and 6M wide separated from the Mediterranean by a narrow band of sand, La Manga, from which a line of mini sky-scrapers rise. In addition to the intensive encouragement of tourists on land, yacht harbours are being built around the shores of the inland sea. The towns themselves are generally dull and the ports small and shallow but in terms of pottering around, anchoring off, small boating and so forth the Mar has its attractions.

Of the three entrances, one is deep and two very shallow. The major entrance is through Puerto de Tomás Maestre, which is the largest harbour of the Mar Menor and is supposedly dredged to 4m though 3m may be nearer the mark. Details of the approach and entrance are given later; the other two entrances are not described. The second largest harbour, San Javier in the NW, is a naval air force harbour and part of the air academy. It is not open to visitors. Seven small harbours are built around the Mar. A number of moorings have been laid but they are generally private.

The five islands are Isla Mayor or del Barón (102m), Perdiguera (45m), del Ciervo (46m) which is actually joined to La Manga by a causeway, Rondella or Redonda and del Sujeto. The first two are large and steep-to. The passage between Isla Mayor and La Manga has uncertain depths, generally less than 1m, and the passage between Isla del Sujeto and La Manga has even less water.

There are depths of 5–6m over the greater part of Mar Menor with gently shallowing sides and the bottom is sand or mud with weed. This makes anchoring possible almost anywhere, according to draught, but a strong wind can quickly kick up a nasty sea with marked currents. The north part is shallower than the south and though the Mar Menor is not tidal, the water level can vary by as much as 50cm or more over a period of weeks, driven by winds or changed by rain. In general terms, do not get on the shoreward side of any harbour entrance.

Beware floating nets; They may be set in a circle about 100m in diameter around a central buoy and supported by small floats which are difficult to see.

The seawater temperature is considerably higher than outside. Unfortunately there are lots of very large and small jellyfish, mostly *Rhizostoma pulmo*, and although not recognized as a vicious stinger, there are enough to put many off swimming amongst them.

Facilities

The better shops of the area are along La Manga and at Los Belones. Shopping elsewhere is basic. There are banks on La Manga (see Puerto de la Manga) Los Nietos and at La Union.

Communications

San Javier airfield, besides holding the Air Force Academy, handles charter flights during the summer. A light railway runs between Los Nietos, La Union and Cartagena (where the station is fairly close to the Continente hypermarket).

THE PORTS OF MAR MENOR

Ports

38. Puerto de Tomás Maestre

Entrance into Mar Menor from the Mediterranean 37°44'·3N 00°43'·4W (between beacons of Los Escolletes).

Entrance from the Mar Menor 37°44'·5N 00°43'·8W

Charts

UKHO *1700* Imray *M12*
SHOM *7670* Spanish *4710, 471*

Lights

Entrance from seawards
To the south
Cabo de Palos Fl(2)10s81m23M Round tower 51m
Isla Grosa Fl.3s97m5M White round tower 2m
Islote La Hormiga Fl(3)14s24m8M White tower 12m
Punta del Estacio Fl(4)20s32m14M White tower, black bands 29m
Los Escolletes VQ(3)5s7m3M ♦ on black column, yellow band 5m

Canal del Estacio
Buoy No.1 Fl.G.5s5M Green spar
Buoy No.1 Fl.R.5s5M Red spar
Buoy No.2 Fl(2)G.7s3M Green spar
Buoy No.2 Fl(2)R.7s3M Red spar
Buoy No.3 Fl(3)G.9s1M Green spar
Buoy No.3 Fl(3)R.9s1M Red spar
Buoy No.4 Fl(4)G.11s1M Green spar
Buoy No.4 Fl(4)R.11s1M Red spar
Buoy No.5 Fl.R.5s1M Red cylinder
Buoy No.6 Fl(2)R.7s1M Red cylinder

Mar Menor entrance
Dique N Fl.R.5s7m3M Red tower 4m
Dique S Fl.G.5s7m3M Green mast 3m.

Note that the entrance channel may be marked with small buoys in high season

Port communications

Capitanía VHF Ch 9 ☎ +34 968 14 08 16
puertomaestre@puertomaestre.com
www.puertomaestre.com

Harbour charges High in summer, low in winter

Tomás Maestre – canal, harbour, marinas

The Puerto de Tomás Maestre consists of an outer harbour under development, a canal and a modern marina with plenty of room for visitors built into the western end of the 1½M long canal which connects the sea with the Mar Menor. In normal conditions approach and entrance are easy but because the area is shallow, entry should not be attempted in strong E or SE winds which kick up heavy seas. Facilities are good except that provision shops are limited. It forms a useful base for the exploration of the Mar Menor and as a staging point between the port of Cartagena and the harbours further N. Golf course and swimming pool nearby.

The entrance is now marked with pillar buoys and the entrance to the Mar Menor may be marked from June to October with red and green light buoys joined with floating ropes.

Tomás Maestre marina from south

Approach from seaward

From the south Round the prominent and conspicuous Cabo de Palos at 200m off and follow the low-lying coast in a NNW direction at 1½M. The narrow sand spit has wall-to-wall high-rise buildings along it with a small gap just before the approach to Tomás Maestre. The canal approach is 1M to NW of the off-shore Isla Grosa (95m).

From the north Cabo Roig is prominent and reddish in colour. It has a tower and some buildings above a small yacht harbour which lies on the S side of the cape. Two other small yacht harbours, which may be recognised, lie 1½M and 3M further S. Puerto de San Pedro del Pinatar is easily recognised by its high breakwater.

Follow the coast, which sprouts high rise buildings as Punta de Estacio is approached, in a SSE direction and at least ¼M offshore. Isla Grosa (95m) which is peaked should be easily recognised. Pass about half way between the island and Los Escolletes and then head N/NW for the entrance beacons. NE of Isla Grosa is the rock El Farallón and further out, a shoal of 1·3m – see charts. A shallow rocky spit sticks out a short distance south of Los Escolletes.

Anchorages in the approach

From the south Anchor to the west of Isla Grosa (see page 119).
From the north Anchor off Playa del Pudrimel (see page 119).
Outer harbour Anchorage (see note on plan page 122).

Canal entrance

From seawards Having passed about halfway between Los Escolletes and Isla Grosa (coming from the north) or keeping Isla Grosa well to starboard (coming from the south) identify the two port and starboard buoys marking the entrance to the canal.

III. COSTA BLANCA

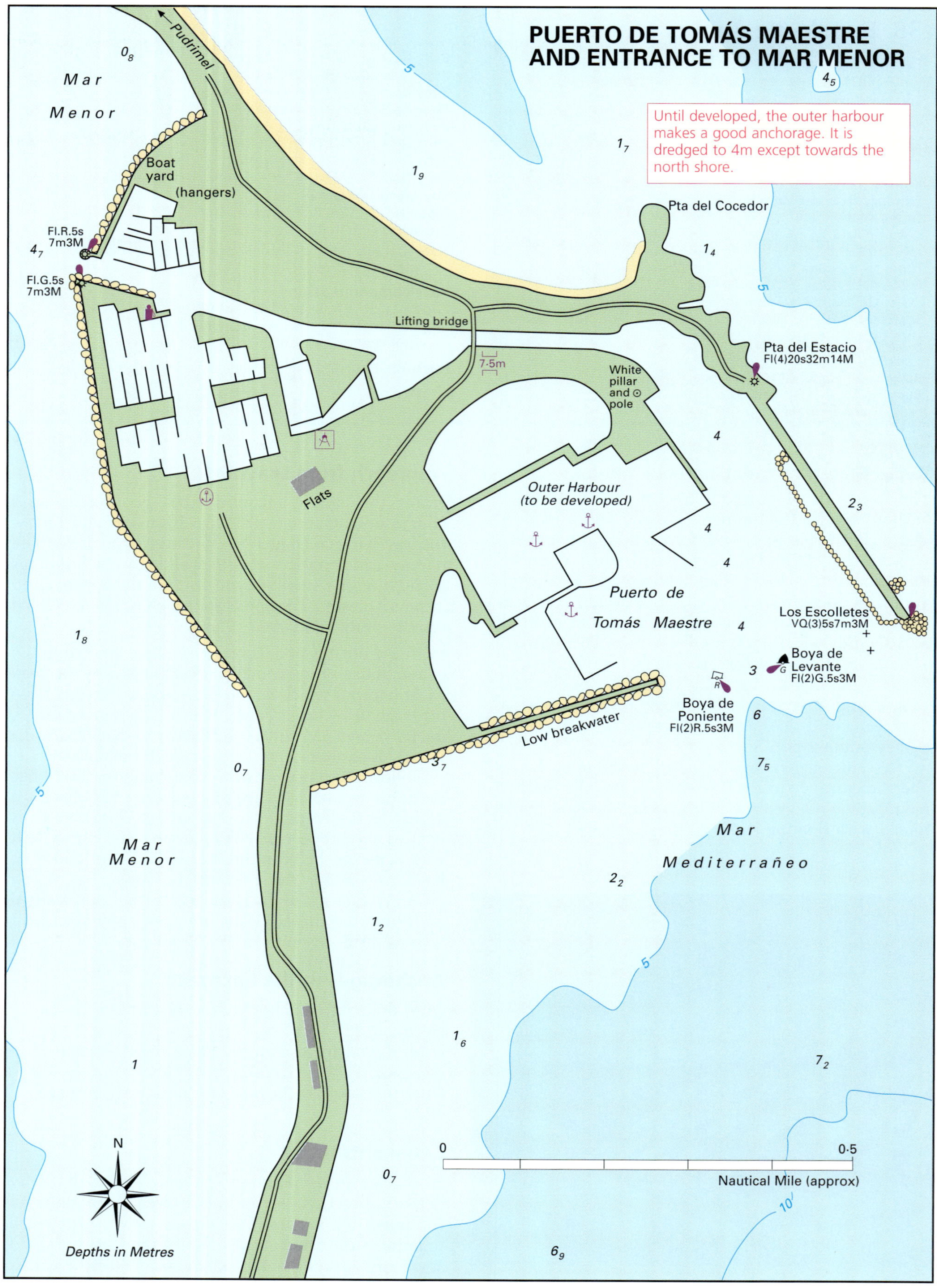
PUERTO DE TOMÁS MAESTRE
AND ENTRANCE TO MAR MENOR
Until developed, the outer harbour makes a good anchorage. It is dredged to 4m except towards the north shore.
Pudrimel
Mar Menor
Boat yard
(hangers)
Fl.R.5s
7m3M
Fl.G.5s
7m3M
Lifting bridge
7·5m
Pta del Cocedor
Pta del Estacio
Fl(4)20s32m14M
White pillar and ⊙ pole
Flats
Outer Harbour
(to be developed)
Puerto de Tomás Maestre
Los Escolletes
VQ(3)5s7m3M
Boya de Levante
Fl(2)G.5s3M
Boya de Poniente
Fl(2)R.5s3M
Low breakwater
Mar Menor
Mar Mediterraneo
0
0·5
Nautical Mile (approx)
N
Depths in Metres

Tomás Maestre from the east

Proceed on a west of north course to pass between the buoys and on through the outer harbour passing between a series of posts marking the narrow canal entrance. Passing the posts the channel bends round to a west-northwesterly course towards the swing bridge. Note that a falling barometer or an E sector winds can cause a two knot or more inflowing current; a rising barometer with W sector winds an outflowing current. The new lift bridge opens Monday to Friday at 1100 and 1700 and at 1100, 1400 and 1700 at weekends. The headroom is 7·5m when closed. Clients of the marina may call VHF Ch 9 or ✆ 968 14 07 25 at any time to have it opened. The canal continues for a further ½ mile past Tomás Maestre marina into the Mar Menor itself. In high season the channel into and out of the Mar Menor itself may be marked with two green and two red lightbuoys joined by floating ropes with small white floats attached.

Watch for stalled road traffic on either side of the bridge, to gauge when it is about to open.

Note Several yachts have reported depths no greater than 2·3m in the buoyed (posts) channel approaching either side of the lifting bridge.

From Mar Menor Straightforward between the pier heads but beware traffic.

Marina entrance

The yacht harbour is on the south side of the canal, opposite the workshop area which has conspicuous working hangars.

Berths

Normal stern-to berths are available. Usually someone is around to tell you where to go. Otherwise, make up where you can and if nobody moves you, go to the *capitanía* under the entrance archway (a long way from most of the marina) to confirm your location.

Facilities

Maximum length overall: 22m.
Facilities for most types of repairs (the boatyard is expensive).
100-tonnes slipway.
50 and 15-tonne travel-hoists.
5-tonnes crane.
Chandlers (also provide gas and one which repairs sails).
Shower block on pontoon.
Water and 220v and 380v AC on pontoons and quays.
Ice on fuel quay or from office.
Gasoleo A and petrol (the fuelling jetty is at the entrance and may be an awkward lie if there is a current running in the canal).

Communications

✆ Area code 968. Taxis ✆ +34 968 56 30 39. There may be an hourly bus to La Manga for shopping.

SHALLOW HARBOURS IN MAR MENOR

The following describes a number of mostly small, shallow, private harbours in Mar Menor, most with little room for visiting yachts, especially those over 12m with deep keels. These are built essentially for local motor vessels. Several have depths of less than 2m, which can be considerably reduced with high barometric pressure and with sustained strong offshore winds. Dredging takes place in most of these harbours as required, but there is no reliable information on when this was last done and marinas often carry out minimal work due to the cost. See plan on page 119.

Puerto de la Manga

39. Puerto de Dos Mares Club Náutico

37°40'N 00°44'·5W

Port communications
Club VHF Ch 9 ☏ +34 968 14 01 17
www.clubnauticodosmares.com

Shopping stop off

A small private shallow harbour with 230 berths only suitable for small yachts but useful for shopping along La Manga. Limiting factors are a depth of about 1·9m and maximum length overall length of about 12m. It may pay to investigate by dinghy before entering.

Approach

There is no channel between Isla Sujeto and La Manga. Enter between the red and green buoys on the north side of the entrance, with 1·9m in the channel.

Berth

Bows to floating pontoons.

40. Puerto de la Manga

37°38'·8N 00°43'·6W

Lights
Breakwater head Fl(3)R.9s5m1M Red mast
Right bank Fl(3)G.9s1M Green mast

Port communications
Club Náutico la Isleta VHF Ch 9 ☏ +34 968 14 53 39
admin@nauticolaisleta.net
www.clubnauticolaisleta.es

A private club

Another small shallow harbour only suitable for 180 smaller craft up to 9m. Visitors are made welcome though not particularly encouraged. If in doubt about depths, a visit by dinghy would pay off.

The south and east sides of the harbour are beaches used for bathing.

Approach

The passage east of Isla Mayor should only be taken with local knowledge and there is no passage east of Isla del Sujeto. It is best to keep west of those two and of Redonda as well.

Entrance

Said to be 1·8m. Come in from the west. The harbour wall is marked 'Club Náutico La Isleta' and the entrance is at the southern end. Keep between the line of buoys, if placed (they are all likely to be small, red and spherical).

Berth

Bows-to piers.

Facilities

Maximum length overall: 12m.
Water and 220v AC at the berths.
The shops of La Manga: Bop's hypermarket, shops, banks at Plazas Cavanah and Bohemia.
Club Náutico La Isleta has a bar, showers and a part-time restaurant.
Do not pump ship in harbour.

41. Puerto de Mar de Cristal

37°38'·7N 00°45'·7W

Lights
Breakwater head F.R.3s5m5M
Red round tower 3m
Contradique F.G.3s4m5M
White tower, green bands 3m

Port communications
VHF Ch 9 ☏ +34 968 13 34 28
mardecristal@convasa.com

Small shallow harbour

A private harbour with 160 berths up to 12m built as a part of a housing development and located on the SE corner of the Mar Menor. Easy to approach and enter. The facilities are limited and there is little room for visitors. The name sums up the nature of the seas in this area: 'The sea of glass.'

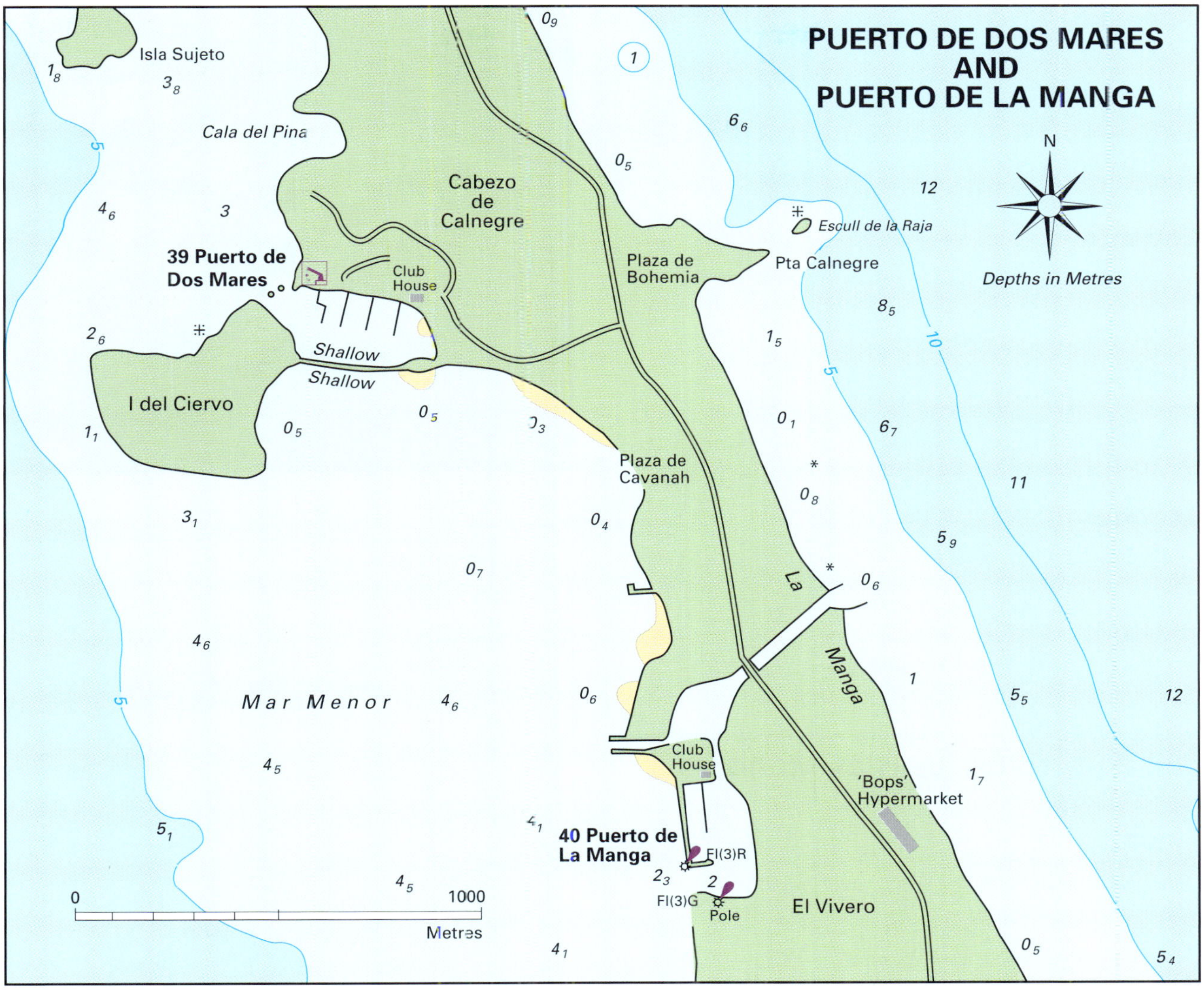

PUERTO DE DOS MARES
AND
PUERTO DE LA MANGA
N
Depths in Metres
Isla Sujeto
Cala del Pina
Cabezo
de
Calnegre
39 Puerto de
Dos Mares
Club
House
Shallow
Shallow
I del Ciervo
Plaza de
Bohemia
Pta Calnegre
Escull de la Raja
Plaza de
Cavanah
La
Manga
Mar Menor
Club
House
40 Puerto de
La Manga
Fl(3)R
Fl(3)G
Pole
'Bops'
Hypermarket
El Vivero
0
1000
Metres

Puerto de Mar de Cristal

PUERTO DE
MAR DE CRISTAL
F.R.5M
Dique Norte
F.G.3M
Contradique
Restaurant
bar, shops
Playa
Playa
N
0
100
Metres (approx)
Depths in Metres

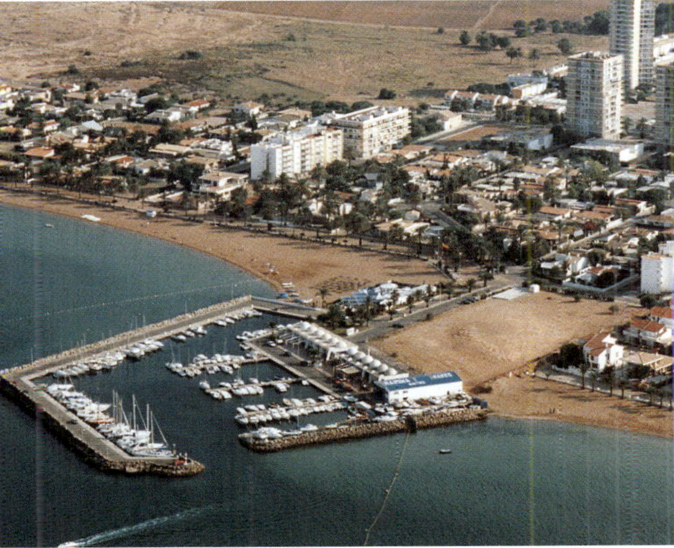

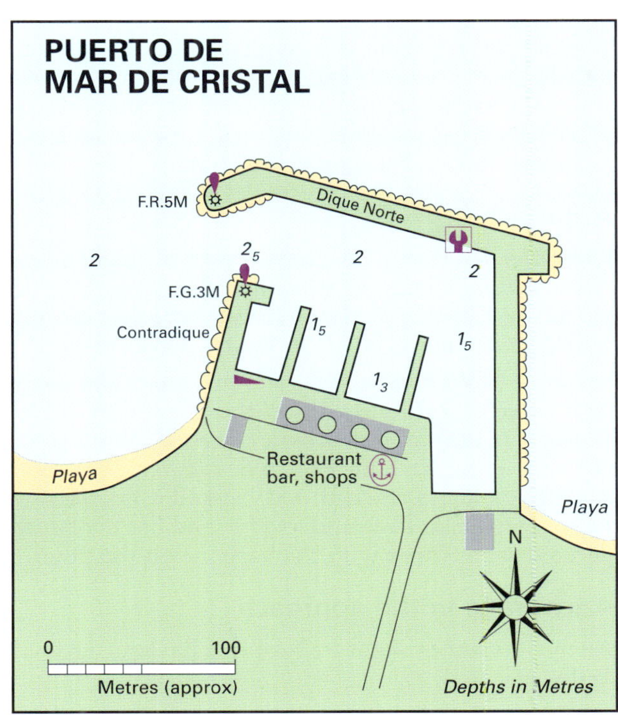

Approach

In the NW, from the hill El Carmoli (112m) and the tower of Los Urrutias the coast is almost straight, low and flat, and most is under cultivation. The village of Los Nietos, the harbours of Los Nietos and Islas Menores may be seen. In the SE, Punta de Plomo is low and has a lone house on it.

Entrance

When entering keep as far off-shore as is consistant with entering as the water shoals sharply near the shore.

Berths

The arrivals berth is alongside the North Wall, immediately to port on entering. If no room there, go alongside another boat and ask ashore.

Facilities

Maximum length overall: 10m.
Slipway in SW corner of the harbour.
Water and 220v AC on quays and pontoons.
Club Náutico de Mar de Cristal.
Some shops in housing development.

42. Puerto de las Islas Menores

37°38'·9N 00°46'·1W

Lights
Outer breakwater Fl(4)G.11s3M Green round column
Breakwater head Fl(4)R.11s3M Red round column

Port communications
Puerto VHF Ch 9 ✆ +34 968 13 33 44
info@clubnauticoislasmenores.com

Small, shallow, private harbour

A small private yacht club with 100 berths suitable for dinghies, runabouts and small yachts but no room for visiting cruising yachts. Easy to approach and enter. It has a palatial yacht club with associated facilities, but other facilities are limited.

Approach

From the SE Punta de Plomo with a single large house can be identified as can the Puerto de Mar de Cristal ¾M further E. The harbour projects into the Mar Menor and its large clubhouse is conspicuous.

From the NW The low, flat and almost straight coast is relatively featureless with the exception of El Carmoli (112m) and the town of Los Urrutias, until the large yacht harbour Puerto de Los Nietos, which is conspicuous, is reached. ¾M beyond it lies the low Punta Lengua de Vaca and ½M beyond lies the Punta de Los Barrancones with the harbour on the point.

Anchorage in the approach

Anchor to suit draught to N of this harbour in sand and weed.

Puerto de las Islas Menores

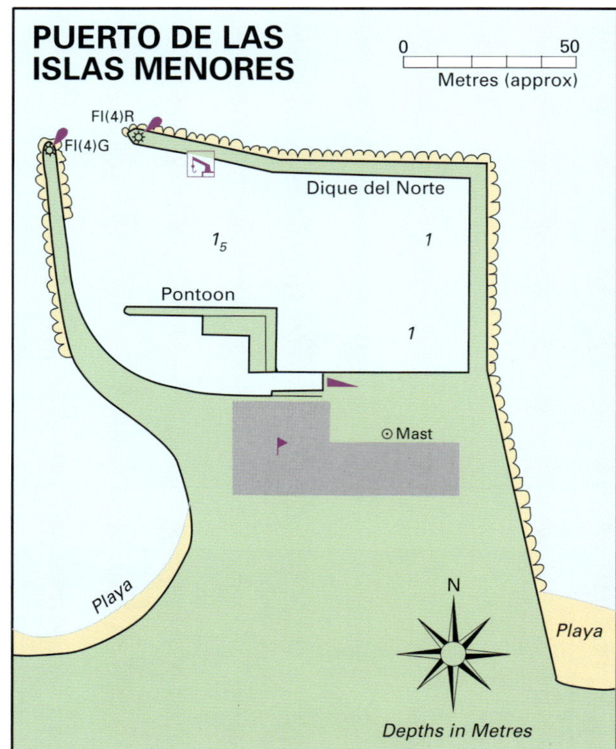

Entrance

Straightforward but harbour shoals to 1m.

Berths

Secure to the inside of Dique del Norte and ask at yacht club for allocation of a berth.

Facilities

Maximum length overall: 8m.
Slipway at yacht club.
Small davit-type crane at head of Dique del Norte.
Water from yacht club.
Small shops near harbour.
The Club Náutico des Islas Menores has bar, restaurant and showers.

43. Puerto de los Nietos

37°39'·2N 00°47'W

Lights

Muelle Norte NW head Fl(3)R.9s3M
Red round column 3m

Muelle Norte E corner VQ0·5s1M
‡ on black post yellow base 4m

Contradique head Fl(3)G.9s5m1M Green tower 3m

Port communications

Capitanía VHF Ch 4 or 9. ✆ +34 968 56 07 37
Club Náutico de Los Nietos ✆ +34 968 13 33 00
puerto@cnlosnietos.com / administracion@cnlosnietos.com
www.cnlosnietos.com

Harbour charges Low

Large yacht harbour

A large artificial yacht harbour with 440 berths constructed out from the shore on a spit across the shallows and connected to the shore by a causeway. Good wintering facilities. Most of the marina is less than 1·5m deep Yachts can winter ashore or afloat.

Approach

Pass between Islas Perdiguera and Mayor and head south. El Carmoli hill to the west will identify Los Urrutias. To the south, there is a small, dark wood, just east of the Rambla del Beal. Los Nietos is just east of the wood. The breakwater and masts will be seen as the coast is approached.

Anchorage in the approach

Anchorage is possible in sand and weed anywhere to N of this harbour to suit draught.

Entrance

Approach the head of the Muelle Norte on a S heading. There may be a line of multi-coloured buoys to leave to starboard. Do not go inshore of the harbour entrance as the water shoals quickly.

Berths

Secure alongside the Muelle de Espera, immediately to port on entry (go alongside another if necessary) and ask at the office. Alternatively, call on Ch 9 or 4 before entering.

Facilities

Maximum length overall: 12m.
Slipway at the NE side of yacht club.
An 8-tonne crane at NE corner of the harbour.
A 28-tonne mobile crane.
Hardstanding for winter lay-ups.
Water (but strange taste) and 220v AC points on quays and pontoons.
Club Náutico de Los Nietos, ✆+34 968 13 33 00, restaurant open at weekends, bar, showers and washing machine.
Supermarkets, ferretarías with gas, Post Office, butcher, baker, bank etc. at Los Belones, 2½km SE.
Bank without a cash point.

Communications

Light railway to Cartagena (where the station is close to the hypermarket Continente). ✆ Area code 968.

Puerto de los Nietos

44. Puerto de los Urrutias

37°40'·6N 00°49'·3W

Lights

Dique de Levante head Fl(2)G.7s7m3M
Breakwater head Fl(2)R.7s7m3M

Port communications

Club de Regatas Mar Menor VHF Ch 9 ✆ +34 968 13 44 38
informacion@clubregatasmarmenor.com

Harbour communications High

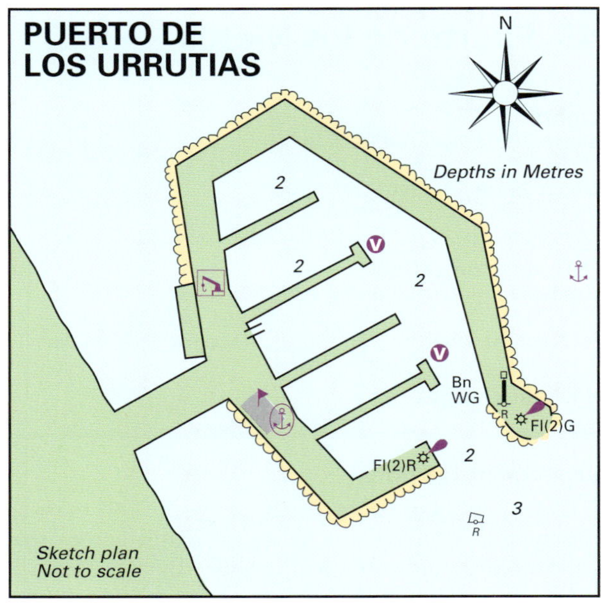

Another shallow harbour

This harbour which, like Los Nietos, is connected by a spit across the shallows to the shore. Mostly for local small craft up to 12m, with 250 berths the harbour lies at the SE end of the village of Urrutias which is underneath the odd-shaped El Carmoli hill. Easy to approach and enter. Spanish holiday village with a good beach to the N of the harbour. This marina is owned by the local authority but the concession for running it is with Club de Regatas Mar Menor.

Approach

From the north Past the airport and Los Alcázares. There is a conspicuous hangar-type building before the village and the yacht club is the last major building.

From the south Urrutias lies 2·5M NW of Puerto de los Nietos.

Anchorage

N or S of entrance to suit draught in sand and weed.

Berths

Secure to east wall and ask at the club secretary's office.

Facilities

Maximum length overall: 12m.
Slipway by crane.
10-tonne crane.
Water and 220v AC on pontoons and quays.
A few shops in the village, street-market every Thursday.
Club de Regatas Mar Menor has a restaurant, bar, showers and washroom.
Dinghy sailing school.

Communications

✆ Area code 968.

⚓ Isla Perdiguera

Anchor to the SW in 4m sand and mud. Beach bars ashore at weekends. (See plan page 119.)

Puerto de los Urrutias

45. Puerto de los Alcázares

37°44'N 00°50'·9W

Lights

Dique Este head Fl.G.5s5m5M Green tower
Dique Oeste Fl.R.5s5m3M Red top tower

Port communications

Club Náutico los Alcazares VHF Ch 9 ✆ +34 968 57 51 29
cnautico@cnmarmenor.es www.cnmarmenor.es

Shallow harbour

A shallow (2m or less), 280 berths up to 12m artificial yacht harbour alongside an attractive old Victorian-type seaside resort, least touched by mass tourism. Easy to approach and enter. The coast is lined with many piers and shelters of various sizes to enable the inhabitants to fish and bathe. The nearby Aeropuerto de San Javier, its associated harbour and a large amount of land around are part of the Spanish Naval Air Academy and should not be entered. Not much room for visitors or cruising yachts.

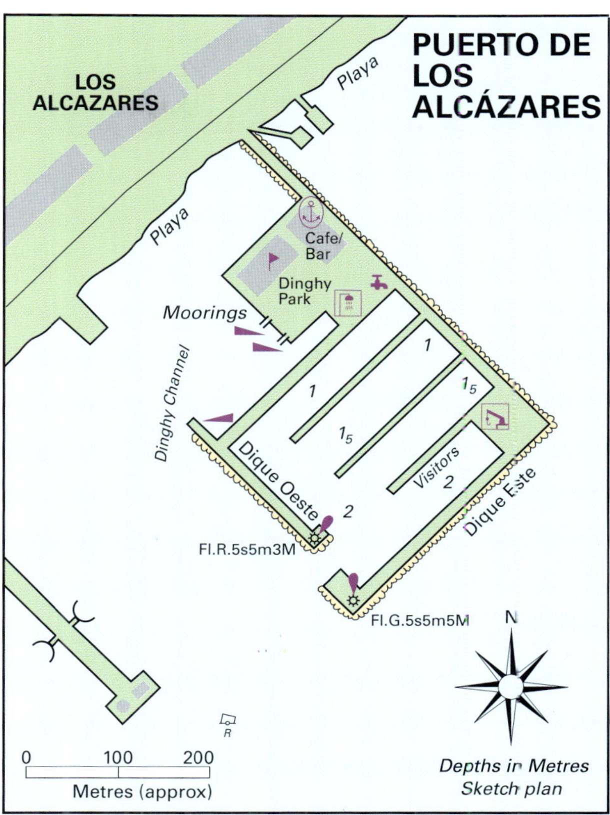

Approach

From the SE Follow the low flat coast in a NE–N direction. The town of Los Urrutias and El Carmoli (112m), a conical hill, will be recognised. Further E a light aircraft field and a camp site may be seen. Just S of this harbour is a long pier and some large old hangars. The houses of the town of Los Alcázares will be seen from afar.

From the NE The large town of Santiago de la Ribera and the Aeropuerto de San Javier, which has a large shallow harbour alongside (entrance forbidden), will be easily recognised. Punta Galera and Punta de las Olas are not easily identified. The town of Los Alcázares can be seen from afar.

Anchorage in the approach

Anchor off the harbour in suitable depth to suit draught in sand and weed.

Puerto de los Alcázares

III. COSTA BLANCA

Entrance

Approach the head of Dique Este on a course between W and NNW. A line of white buoys parallel to the military *espigón* marks the boundary of the no-go area; leave them to port.

Berths

Go alongside the pier immediately opposite the entrance and ask at the office.

Facilities

Maximum length overall: 12m.
Simple repairs possible.
Two slipways and a crane at E corner of the harbour.
Water and 220v AC points on quays and pontoons.
Many shops in the town including supermarket and a large market.
The Club Náutico de Mar Menor at N corner of harbour has little but they include open-air showers and a bar.

Communications

Excellent and regular buses to Alicante, Cartagena. Coaches to Bilbao, Madrid, Barcelona.
✆ Area code 968.

⚓ Puerto Santiago de La Ribera

An open anchorage off a large town serving the air base and the air port and with tourist interests. The *club náutico* has a pier for small boats. (See plan page 119.)

46. Puerto de Lo Pagan

37°49'N 00°47'W

Lights
Entrance buoy Fl(2)G.7s Lateral starboard
Entrance buoy Fl(2)R.7s Lateral port
Dique head Fl(3)G.9s3m1M Green mast
Contradique head Fl(3)9s3m1M Red post

Port Communications
Club náutico VHF Ch 9 ✆ +34 968 18 69 69
info@clubnauticolopagan.es
www.clubnauticolopagan.es

New marina but shallow

A new marina has been developed over the last few years off Lo Pagan at the north end of the Mar Menor. It has berths for about 350 craft up to 14m and has reasonable shore side facilities of fuel, cranage and a slip. The water is very shallow at the north end of the Mar Menor and there are buoys to indicate the 'deep' entrance channel which is understood to be 1·8 metres, but great care should be exercised in the approach with constant attention paid to the echo-sounder. Once again, only a small number of visitors berths are available.

Berths

It is essential to call ahead to enquire whether there is a berth available for your vessel, as there are only 20 berths allocated for visitors and these are mostly taken in the high season.

Facilities

All facilities are available for the yachtsman and there is reasonable shopping in the nearby town of Lo Pagan. Close by is the Parque Regional de las Salinas which is an important wetlands area which is of great interest to birdwatchers. Note however, that if one does not wish to enter the Mar Menor, Puerto de San Pedro del Pinatar (see page 132) is but three kilometres to the east and is also close to this park.

Club Náutico Lo Pagan

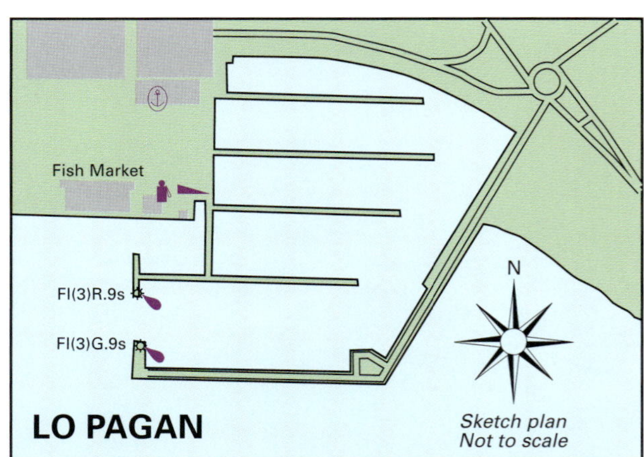

PUERTO DE SAN PEDRO DEL PINATAR TO JÁVEA

Ports

C. de San Antonio
70 Dénia
See p.170
Fl(4)20s175m26M
69 Jávea
Cabo de la Nao
Fl.5s122m23M
See p.162
68 Moraira
67 Puerto de las Basetas
See p.156
66 Calpe
Fl(4)R.10s8m3M
64 Marina Greenwich
Pta Ifach
65 Puerto Blanco
61 Altea
63 Mary Montaña
See p.155
Pta del Albir
Fl(3)27s112m15M
60 Puerto de Benidorm
59 Villajoyosa
Islote Benidorm
Fl.5s60m6M
30′
58 Campello
Pta del Río
Fl.G.3s8m5M
57 Pto de San Juan
C de la Huerta
56 ALICANTE
Fl(5)19s38m14M
See p.147
C de Santa Pola
Fl(2+1)20s
152m16M
54 Pto Espato
53 Santa Pola
55 Isla de Tabarca
Q(3)10s
BYB
LFl.8s29m15M
See p.144
52 Pto de Guardamar
(105)
Oc.R.1·5s443m15M
Radio mast
& 7F.R(vert)
38° N
51 Torrevieja
C. Cervera
Fl.G.4s15m7M
50 Pto de Cabo Roig
49 Campoamor
48 La Horadada
47 San Pedro del Pinatár
See p.119
Fl(4)G.12s13m5M
Mar Menor
Pta del Estacio
Fl(4)20s32m14M
FL(3)14s24m8M
Islas Hormigas
Fl(5)Y.20s
40′
20′
0°W
N
PUERTO DE SAN PEDRO DEL PINATAR TO JAVEA

47. Puerto de San Pedro del Pinatar

37°49'·2N 00°45'·3W

Charts

UKHO *1700* Imray *M12*
SHOM *7670* Spanish *471, 4710*

Lights

Dique Norte Fl(4)G.12s13m5M Green post 3m
Dique Sur Fl(4)R.12s6m3M Red post 3m
C.N. San Pedro Dique head Fl(2)G.7s3m1M Green post 3m
C.N. San Pedro contradique Fl(2+1)R.14s3m1M Red post 3m

Port communications

Club Náutico villa de San Pedro ✆ +34 630 42 21 26 / 968 18 28 80
Marina de las Salinas VHF Ch 9 ✆ +34 619 27 49 32 / +34 676 38 87 90
administracion@marinadelassalinas.es
www.marinadelassalinas.es

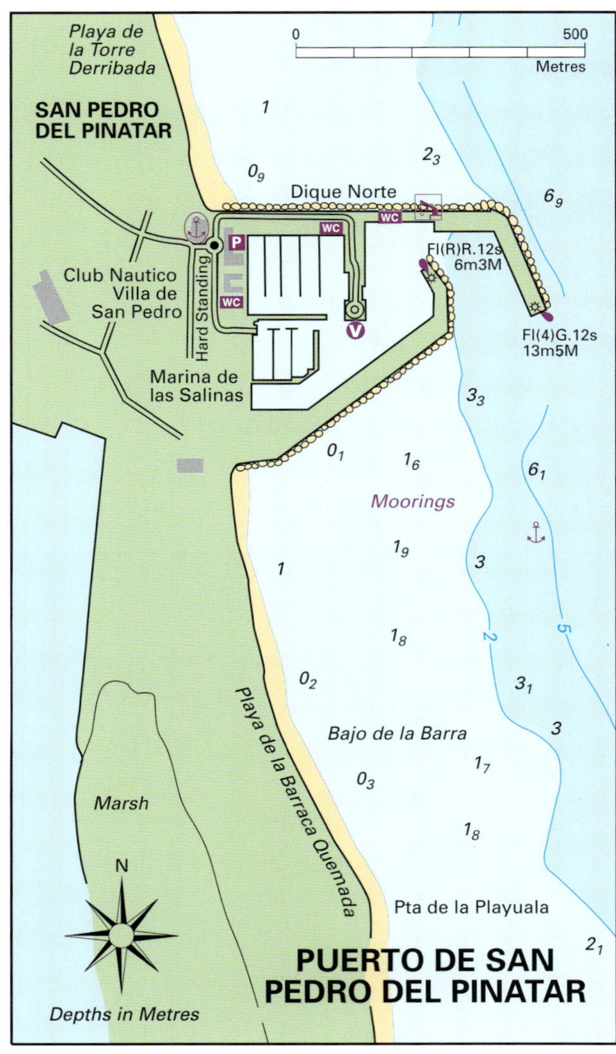

Two modern marinas behind fishing port

Two marinas built just to the N of the ever popular Mar Menor (see plan on page 119) with 600 berths between them up to 30m. but with depth limited to 2m or less. Room for visitors, but miles from civilization.

At the NW of the harbour is Club NauticoVilla de San Pedro, with 400 berths up to 15m.

The S marina is relatively new: Marina de las Salinas, with 200 berths up to 30m, with most berths sold off to private yacht owners; a trend throughout Spain, as marinas are trying not to sink after the recession. There is a yacht club and stores around the port, but not all open in winter. Ashore there is nothing. Depths are not more than 2m and often around 1·5m.

San Pedro del Pinatar looking W and note there is a new marina constructed in the SW darsena - Marina de las Salinas

Approach

The high breakwater of Puerto de San Pedro del Pinatar can be seen from afar (and is a useful coastal mark).

From the south Follow the coast up from Punta del Estacio. (See plan on page 119.) Development along the sand strip bordering the Mar Menor dies away before the harbour is reached.

From the north Pass Punta de la Torre de la Horadada which has a tower on the point with buildings at its base and yacht harbour on its S side. There is a rocky reef off this head; keep at least 200m off. From there on, keep half a mile off-shore to avoid small rocky islets.

Entrance

Approach the end of the Dique Norte on a westerly heading rounding the head at 30m, keeping a close watch for fishing vessels leaving the harbour. Steer west of north and round the head of the Dique Sur keeping reasonably close to the Dique Norte. Steer south through the outer harbour, turning to starboard at the end of the internal quay.

Pinatar outer harbour looking N *Steve Pickard*

Hard standing Pinatar *Steve Pickard*

Berths

Having entered the harbour moor to the end of the internal quay and enquire at the fuel berth or at the *capitanía* in the NW corner of the marina for berth availability.

Facilities

Maximum length 15m.
30-ton travel-hoist and crane.
220v AC and water at all berths.
Fuel.
Showers, WC and rubbish bins.
Club náutico.
Bar and small shops for essentials.

48. Puerto de la Horadada

37°52'N 00°45'·5W

Charts

UKHO *1700* Imray *M12*
SHOM *7670* Spanish *471*

Lights

Dique de Levante head Q(3)10s8m3M
♦ on black tower yellow band 6m
Inner spur head Fl(3)G.10s9m5M
Green and white column 6m
Contradique head Fl(2)R.7s9m4M
Red and white column 6m
Channel outer buoy Fl.G.2s1M
Green conical buoy
Channel outer buoy Fl.R.2s1M
Red cylindrical buoy

Port communications

Club Náutico Torre Horadada ✆ +34 966 76 90 87
info@cnth.es
www.cnth.es

Harbour communications Low

Shallow approaches to yacht harbour

A large yacht harbour characterised by its big blue walls. Established in an old fishing anchorage to S of Punta de la Horadada this marina has 500 berths up to 12m but with shallows in the approaches and a restriction to 12m. It is well-protected from all directions except S. Swell between W and S can make the approach dangerous as the water is shallow but otherwise it is easy to approach and enter. Facilities are limited in the port but a pleasant village can be found ashore.

Approach

The approach to this harbour is shallow and strangers should sound their way in.

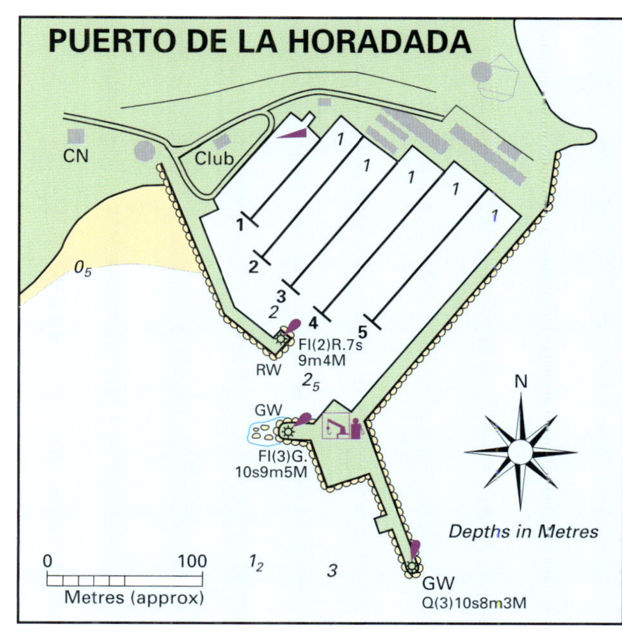

III. COSTA BLANCA

Puerto de la Horadada

Horadada entrance looking S. Note unlit beach buoys
Steve Pickard

From the south The long, low 10M-long sand strip that separates the Mar Menor from the sea is unmistakable as is Isla Grosa (95m) and the breakwater of the harbour of San Pedro del Pinatar. Between Pinatar and Horadada, 3M north, give the coast a ½M berth to avoid rocky islets. The Torre de la Horadada, on a low promontory, has buildings at its foot and is conspicuous. It has a rocky reef with exposed heads extending 150m off it. In the approach, the harbour walls will be seen.

From the north Between the large harbour of Torrevieja and Punta de la Horadada the coast is only moderately high with rocky cliffs in places. The small promontory of Punta Primo (or Delgada) lies between Torrevieja and Cabo Roig. Cabo Roig is of reddish sandstone and is prominent with a white tower and buildings on its summit. A small yacht harbour lies on the S side of Cabo Roig and another lies to the S of Punta El Cuervo which is to S of Cabo Roig. There are a number of small rocks and islets offshore along this section of coast and a berth of ½M is advised. The Torre de la Horadada is conspicuous from the north and has a reef extending some 150m to the NNE.

Entrance

From a position 200m to S of the harbour entrance, approach sounding continuously. Red and green channel buoys to the SW of the entrance now define the beginning of the entrance channel. About 50m from the entrance change to a NW course. Give the inner spur head at least 25m berth as rocks extend 10m west of it. Note the entrance frequently silts up, especially after SW winds and the depth is often less than the 2.5m shown on the plan.

Berths

Secure to the first pontoon and ask at the *capitanía*.

Facilities

Maximum length overall: 12m.
Small slipway in the NW corner of the harbour with 1m off it.
5-tonne crane to starboard side of the entrance and a large mobile crane.
Engine mechanics – Volvo agency.
Showers and WC.
Water and 220v AC points on quays and pontoons.
Some shops in the village.
Gasoleo A and petrol.

Communications

Coastal bus service on main road. ☎ Area code 966.

49. Puerto de Campoamor (Dehesa de Campoamor)

37°53'·9N 00°45'·9W

Charts

UKHO *1700*	Imray *M12*
SHOM *7670*	Spanish *471*

Lights

Espigón Este FL(2)G.5s8m5M
Green metal mast, white bands 6m

Contradique head FL(2)R.5s8m3M
Red metal mast, white bands 6m

Buoys

Two small green conical buoys mark submerged rocks 200m off the root of the *contradique*

Port communications

Club Náutico de Campoamor VHF Ch 9
✆ +34 965 32 03 86
cncampoamor@cncampoamor.com
www.cncampoamor.com

Harbour mainly for motor boats

A private 350 berth yacht harbour with a maximum depth of 2m. Built primarily for motor boaters on the site of an old anchorage. It is organised as a residential club; there are a few berths for transit yachts but visitors who stay for any length of time may be expected to join the club, if found acceptable. Approach and entrance are not difficult but care must be taken as it is shallow. Facilities in the harbour and village cater for normal requests. Swell from S–SW tends to enter the harbour. Fine sandy beaches.

Approach

From the south The high breakwater of Puerto de San Pedro del Pinatar is conspicuous. The low coast, which should be given a berth of ½M or more to avoid isolated patches of rocks and rocky islets, stretches as far as the Punta de la Horadada which has a *torre* with a building at its foot. The coast further N has low cliffs. Punta El Cuervo, which has a shoal 50m off its eastern edge, is inconspicuous unlike the high-rise apartment blocks behind Puerto de Campoamor.

Campoamor

From the north The large Puerto de Torrevieja is easily recognised. The coast to the S should be given a ½M berth due to off-lying dangers; this coastline has low rocky sandstone cliffs. Cabo Roig which is of a reddish colour has a tower on its summit and a small yacht harbour lies on its S side. Puerto de Campoamor lies just under 2M to S. There is a shallow river valley just to N of the harbour.

Entrance

Keep well away from the harbour walls until the heads of the two *diques* are in line on approximately 320° and then approach, sounding. There is a shoal patch (0·3m) 500m SSE of the harbour, on an approach of approximately 337°. When 50m off the entrance, divert to port and then round the head of Dique de Levante.

Berths

Secure to the outer pontoon and ask at the control office in a hut on the centre pontoon or at the yacht club if no one is in the office.

Facilities

Maximum length overall: 14m.
Small hardstanding.
Slipway in the W corner of the harbour.
3-tonne crane also in the W corner of the harbour.
Water and 220v AC points on quays and pontoons.
Gasoleo A and petrol.
Supermarket in the village.
Club Náutico de Campoamor on the W side of the harbour has a bar, showers etc.

Communications

Bus service on the main road. ✆ Area code 965.

III. COSTA BLANCA

50. Puerto de Cabo Roig

37°54'N 00°43'W

Charts
UKHO *1700* Imray *M12*
SHOM *7670* Spanish *471*

Lights
Dique de Levante head Fl.G.3s9m5M
Green and white pole 6m
Contradique head Fl.R.3s4m4M
Red and white pole
Inland to the North
Guardamar del Segura 38°04'·4N 00°39'·7W, Aero, Oc.R.1.5s443m15M and 7F.R(vert).

Port communications
Capitanía VHF Ch 9 ✆ +34 966 76 01 76
info@marinacaboroig.com www.marinacaboroig.com

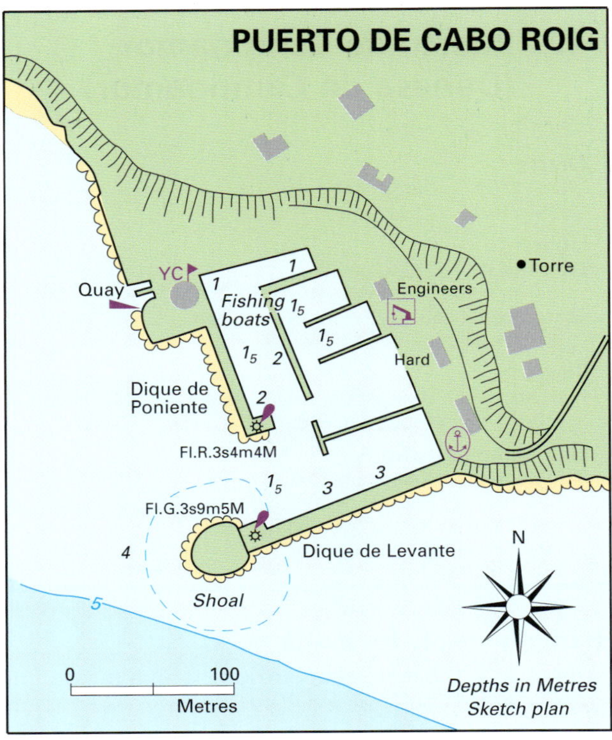

Pleasant small yacht harbour

A small, attractive 200 berth yacht harbour set in lovely suroundings but prone to silting in the entrance. Located at a well-established anchorage, only open to the SW. It is tucked away on the W side of Cabo Roig which is entirely given over to low-rise, detached buildings and gardens. The beach to the N is buoyed-off for swimmers. Inshore there is a small village at some distance which has everyday supplies. There is a castle nearby, pleasant cliff walks and and pebble beaches either side of the harbour and a golf course at Villamartin, 5M.

Approach

From the south From Puerto de San Pedro del Pinatar the coast northwards should be given a ½M berth as there are islets and submerged rocks. Puerto de Torre de la Horadada can be recognised by the tower and buildings on the top of the point of the same name. From here low rocky cliffs stretch 2M to Punta El Cuervo where there is another yacht harbour, Puerto de Campoamor, backed by a group of high-rise apartment buildings. 1½M further along the coast to N is the reddish sandstone Cabo Roig with a large white tower surrounded by trees and villas. The harbour is to SW of the point below the tower.

From the north The Bahía de Santa Pola is 14M wide. The coast is low in the N half and has low rocky cliffs in the S. Sierra de Callosa (547m), 11½M to WNW of Guardarmar, a town on the coast 5M to N of Cabo Cervera, is a good landmark as is the radio mast at Guardamar del Segura. The breakwaters of Puerto de Torrevieja and the town of the same name are conspicuous. 2M to S of this

Puerto de Cabo Roig as seen from the *torre*
Steve Pickard

harbour is Punta Prima (or Delgada) which has rocky cliffs and 2M further on is the prominent Cabo Roig which has a white tower on its summit. The harbour lies SW of the tower.

Entrance

Sand often builds up off the head of the Dique de Levante and it is wise to give it a good 30m berth. There may be a small green buoy near the end of the dique, which signals the extent of the accumulated sand. Care must be exercised on entry with constant sounding recommended.

Berths

Secure to a pontoon T-piece and ask at the *capitanía* or the *club náutico*.

Anchorage in the approach

Anchorage possible off the harbour in suitable depth to suit draught in sand and weed.

Facilities

Maximum length overall: 12m.
Slipway on NE side of the harbour – 1·5m of water off it.
1-tonne crane beside the slipway.
Water and 220v AC points on quays and pontoons.
Supermarket in village.
Club Náutico de Cabo Roig has all normal facilities.

Communications

Bus service on main road 1M inland to Torrevieja.
✆ Area code 966.

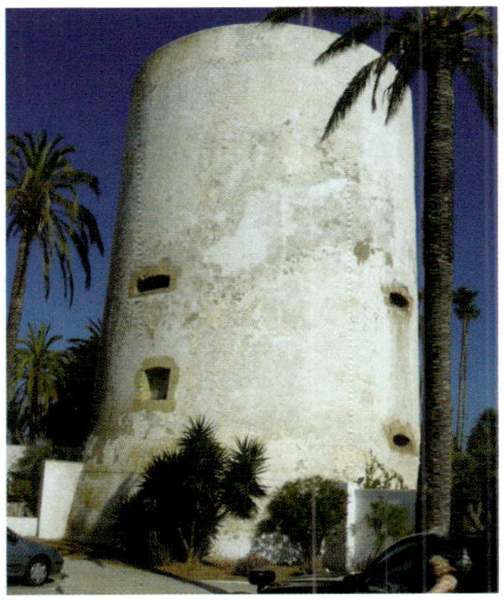

The old *torre* of Torrevieja
Steve Pickard

51. Puerto de Torrevieja

37°58'·3N 00°41'·2W

Charts

UKHO *1700* Imray *M12*
SHOM *7670* Spanish *4710*

Lights

Dique de Levante head Fl.G.4s15m7M
Octagonal tower 10m
Muelle de la Sal Fl(3)R.11·5s11m3M
Metal framework tower 6m
Pontoon head F.R
Dársena Pesquera breakwater NW head Fl(2)G.7s4m2M
Green structure 3m
Club Náutico jetty E head Fl(4)R.11s4m2M
Red column 3m
To the north
Isla de Tabarca LFl.8s29m15M
White tower 14m
Inland to the north
Guardamar del Segura, Oc.R.1·5s 443m15M and 7F.R(vert)
37°58'·3N 0°41'·4W Buoy Fl.R.6s Red
(This buoy signals the work to construct a new jetty for the fishing fleet)

Port communications

VHF Ch 06, 09, 11, 14.
Real Club Náutico de Torrevieja
✆ +34 965 71 01 12 /
+34 679 183104 (night number)
info@rcnt.com
www.rcnt.com
Marina Internacional de Torrevieja (Puerto Deportivo)
✆ +34 965 71 36 50
info@puertodeportivomarinainternacional.es
www.pertodeportivomarinainternacional.com
Marina Salinas ✆ +34 965 709 701
info@marinasalinas.com
www.marinasalinas.com

Useful major harbour

A nice clean harbour with three marinas and over 2,000 berths. Also a good yacht club and an excellent anchorage west of the marina (rare along the coast), but where yachts have sometimes been banned by the harbourmaster. This has been challenged by the local yachtsmen but it seems to be a general feature all along this stretch of coast which comes under the jurisdiction of Valencia. The yacht harbour, Marina Internacional de Torrevieja SA is on the northwest side of the harbour. The commercial quay, Muelle de la Sal, handles large quantities of salt. The approach and entrance are simple and there is good shelter from winds except those from S to SW which make parts of the harbour

Torrevieja entrance looking S. Note anchored yacht to left of picture
Steve Pickard

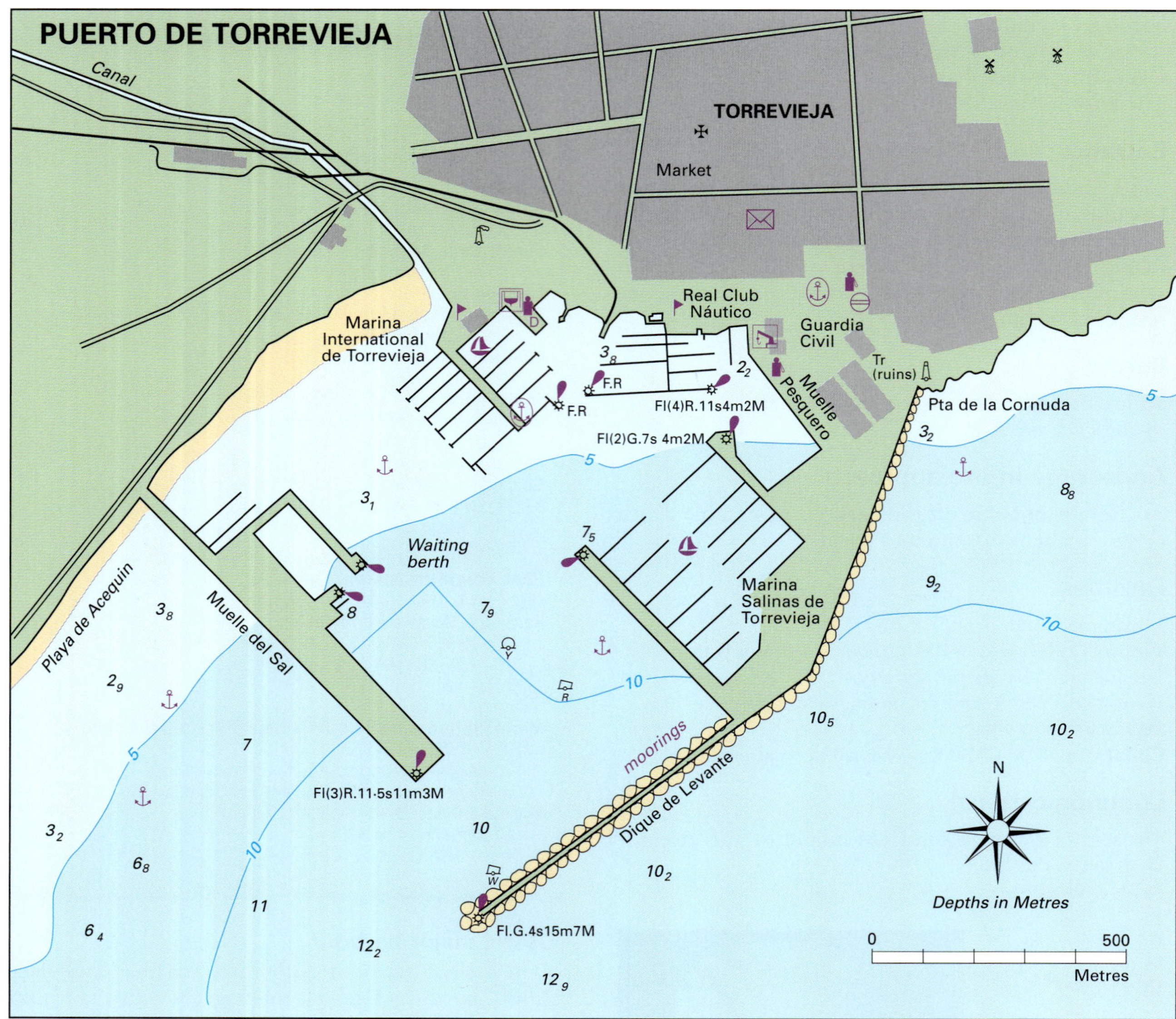

uncomfortable. There is now a new marina, Marina Salinas, in the SE corner of the harbour. It has 700-odd berths and should be a great benefit to yachtsmen on this crowded coast.

The town is of no great interest but it has several restaurants and there are shops quite close to the harbour. A visit to the saltworks, the 'Salt Cellar of the World', is of interest. Good beaches on either side of the harbour.

Approach

From the south Isla Grosa (95m), off the breakwater of Puerto de Tomás Maestre and near the centre of the 10M building strip separating Mar Menor from the sea, is unmistakable as is the high breakwater of Puerto San Pedro del Pinatar. The following three promontories all have yacht harbours on their S sides: Punta de la Torre de la Horadada with a tower on the point and buildings around its base; Punta El Cuervo which has a group of high-rise buildings; and the reddish-coloured Cabo Roig which has a white tower. Keep at least ½M off the coast. From Punta Prima (or Delgada) the rocky cliffs fall away to a low, flat coast near Torrevieja. The breakwaters and town of Torrevieja are visible from afar though quite well inset from Cabo Cervera.

From the north Cross the wide Bahía de Santa Pola which has cliffs in its S part. The Sierra de Callosa (547m) 11½M to WNW of the town of Guardamar and the radio mast at Guardamar del Segura are useful marks. Cabo Cervera is prominent but low; to S of it are several smaller rocky points with coves between. The harbour breakwaters appear when these points have been rounded.

Anchorage in the approach

Anchor just west of the Muelle Sal to suit draught but keeping out of the way of the harbour entrance.

Club Náutico (on right of photo) and Marina Torrevieja moorings

Entrance

Straightforward but fishing boats move at speed and, at night, often without lights. Their wash can make the outer berths at the marina uncomfortable.

Note Ships manoeuvring off the salt quay take hawsers out to a yellow buoy in the centre of the harbour. Beware of these cables, being just submerged. If in doubt, leave the buoy to port on entering the harbour.

Berths

There are several possibilities within the harbour. The original marina was the Real Club Nautíco. This welcomes visitors but is primarily for local members and long term cruising yachts. It has a superb club house, bar and restaurant which can be used by anyone. In the late '80s, what is now called Marina International de Torrevieja, was constructed in the NW of the harbour. This has served visiting and wintering vessels and crews for years and continues to do so. More recently Marina Salinas has opened due to a need for more moorings. All welcome visiting yachts for long and short stays. Pontoons in the extreme W of the harbour are without facilities, very shallow and for dinghies or small local motor vessels only.

The new Marina Salinas usually berths visitors on the pontoons at the W end of the marina: a very long walk to the office and town. It is worth asking for a berth more conveniently located if you intend to stay more than a day or two.

Note that the larger berths for both Marina International de Torrevieja and Real Club Náutico are on the outer S and SE jetties, which are rather exposed and experience surging with strong S and SW sector winds

Anchoring

Excellent anchorages are to be found within the huge harbour SW of Marina Salinas and to the SW of Marina International de Torrevieja. Buoys have been laid in both areas (September 2016) and anchoring was prohibited as long ago as 2007. However, as elsewhere, this led to contention between local yachtsmen who demand to use these areas, and the port authorities. The situation seems to be that officially, anchoring is prohibited anywhere in the harbour, but is usually overlooked! Just outside of the harbour, good anchorages are to be found on the 5m contours NE of Dique de Levante and SW of Muelle del Sal, near Playa Acequin in 5m.

Do keep well clear of Muelle de Sal, where freighters moor and load salt on either side of the muelle and take a wide turning circle.

Facilities

Maximum length overall: Club Náutico vessels up to (and over) over 50m
Marina internacional up to 30m
Marina Salinas up to 35m.

Moorings behind the Dique de Levante *Steve Pickard*

III. COSTA BLANCA

The RCN pontoons in the middle distance looking S
Steve Pickard

Repairs and technical service area, contact yacht club for advice.
Slipway alongside the yacht club and a large one near root of Dique de Levante.
80-tonne travel-lift.
Cranes up to 12 tonnes.
Chandlery – Network Yacht & Rigging Services (run by an English couple) have a well stocked shop between the International Marina and the Club Náutico Marina. There is another chandler in the town and also one outside of town on the road to Cartagena.
Water and 220v AC points on quays and pontoons.
Gasoleo A and petrol.
Ice from factory near customs office or from club.
The Réal Club Náutico de Torrevieja has good facilities including bar, restaurants, lounges, terraces and showers. Visitors are made welcome.
Good shops and small market in the town.
Supermarket in street behind the garage on the N side of the main road in town.
Launderette in the marina or two streets back from the club náutico.

Locally

Torrevieja is a large tourist town with many Scandinavian, British and German visitors, thanks to budget price flights from Northern Europe. Within the harbour complex is a maritime museum which includes a Delfin class submarine.

The tourist office is now located next to the main entrance of Club Náutico: a good starting point for any trip into town in summer as they have great air conditioning and a helpful friendly staff.

Communications

Rail and bus services. ✆ Area code 965.
Taxi ✆ +34 965 71 22 77.

52. Marina de las Dunas (Puerto Guardamar)

38°06'·5N 00°38'·6W

Charts

UKHO *1700* Imray *M12*
SHOM *7670* Spanish *472, 4721*

Lights

Guardamar del Segura Oc.R.1·5s443m15M and 7F.R(vert). Antenna white and red bands 440m (light is 2·5M S and 0·5M inland of marina)
S Breakwater head Fl(3)R.9s8m5M Red tower 5m
Interior elbow Fl(4)R.11s4m1M Red column 3m
N Breakwater head Fl(3)G.9s5m3M Green tower 5m
Middle breakwater head Fl(4)G.11s5m1M Green tower on white base 3m
Centre Fl.G.3s4m1M Green column 3m
W of Fish Wharf QG.4m1M Green column 3m
Fish Wharf W head QG.4m1M Green column 3m
Starboard hand entrance Fl(2+1)G.15s6m1M Green tower, red band, white base 3m
Port hand entrance Fl.R.3s6m1M Red tower on white base 3m

Buoys

A number of small yellow and white buoys mark the 3m channel into the marina.

Port communications

Capitanía VHF Ch 9 ✆ +34 966 72 65 49 24 hour
Mobile +34 639 68 71 57
administracion.madusa@telefonica.net
www.marinadunas.es

Harbour charges Medium

Quiet sheltered marina

The mouth of the Río Segura has been widened and a channel dug to the south of the old river mouth to give access to a 500-berth marina of which 116 are for use by visitors The land approach is to the NW corner where a new road leads to the town of Guardamar – about 1km away.

The marina is fully operational with a café and some small shops.

Approach

From the south The large harbour and town of Torrevieja is easily recognised. To N of this harbour are a series of points with small *calas* between, the coast being rocky cliffs. The coast from Cabo Cervera to N is low and sandy. The town of Guardamar, which has a ruined castle, lies 1M to S of the mouth of the Río Segura which has rocky breakwaters. The radio mast Guardamar del Segura is 4½M to NNW of Cabo Cervera.

From the north Cross the Bahía de Santa Pola from Cabo de Santa Pola on a SW course leaving Isla de Tabarca to port and Puerto de Santa Pola to starboard, both of which are easily identified. 2½M to N of Río Segura is the Torre del Pinet off which at 2M ESE lies a fish farm. The coast is low and sandy.

Río Segura and Marina de las Dunas

Entrance

Although the entrance has been dredged to 6m between the breakwaters it is liable to silting. Approach the mouth of the river, half way between the green and red towers at the ends of the breakwaters on a SW course, sounding carefully.

MARINA DE LAS DUNAS

Fl(4)G.11s 5m1M

Río Segura

Fl(2+1)G

Fl.R.3s

Fishing pontoon

Marina Seca

Capitania

Waiting

N

Depths in Metres

0 200 Metres

Once inside the mouth keep between the lines of yellow buoys until abeam of the marina entrance, turn to port and enter the marina itself. The waiting berth is immediately to starboard on entering, in front of the *capitanía*.

Facilities

Maximum length 15m.
Café and small shops in high season.
220v AC and water on pontoons.
Repair yard with crane and travel-hoist.
Hardstanding with covered hangers.
Fuel berth.
Showers and toilets.
Parking.
24-hour security.

⚓ Bahía de Santa Pola

38°11'.3N 0°34'.9W

Anchor to suit draught along the coast from Cabo Cervera to Santa Pola in sand, mud and stones with weed. Sandy beach with low cliffs, road inland and some development. Flamingos use the nearby *salinas*.

53. Puerto de Santa Pola

38°11'·2N 00°33'·8W

Charts

UKHO *473, 1700* Imray *M12*
SHOM *7670* Spanish *4721, 472*

Lights

To the south
Guardamar del Segura Oc.R.1·5s 443m15M and 7F.R(vert)
Harbour
Dique de Levante head Fl.G.5s9m5M
Green and white tower 8m
Contradique head Q(2)R.5.3s8m3M
Red and white octagonal tower 5m
Espigón head 38°11'.3N 00°33'.6W Fl(2)G.7s4m1M
Green post 3m
To the east
Wave buoy 38°15'.1N 00°24'.9W Q(5)Y.20s
Yellow spherical
To the northeast
Cabo Santa Pola Fl(2+1)20s152m16M Square white tower with metal superstructure 15m vis over 270° arc

Port communications

Club náutico VHF Ch 9. ✆ +34 965 41 24 03
admin@cnauticosantapola.com
www.cnauticosantapola.com
Marina Miramar VHF Ch 9, ✆ +34 650 56 98 69 (24 hours)
info@marinamiramar.com www.marinamiramar.com

Spacious entrance to Santa Pola, looking SW *Steve Pickard*

Busy fishing port with friendly club and new marina

An old Roman port and settlement, now a busy, small fishing port with a good harbour for visiting yachts and an unattractive tourist town. There are repair yards, adequate shops and a good market. In high season, the disco may be very noisy.

Approach

From the south The town of Guardamar and nearby Guardamar del Segura are easily identified, as is Cabo de Santa Pola which lies to NE of this harbour.

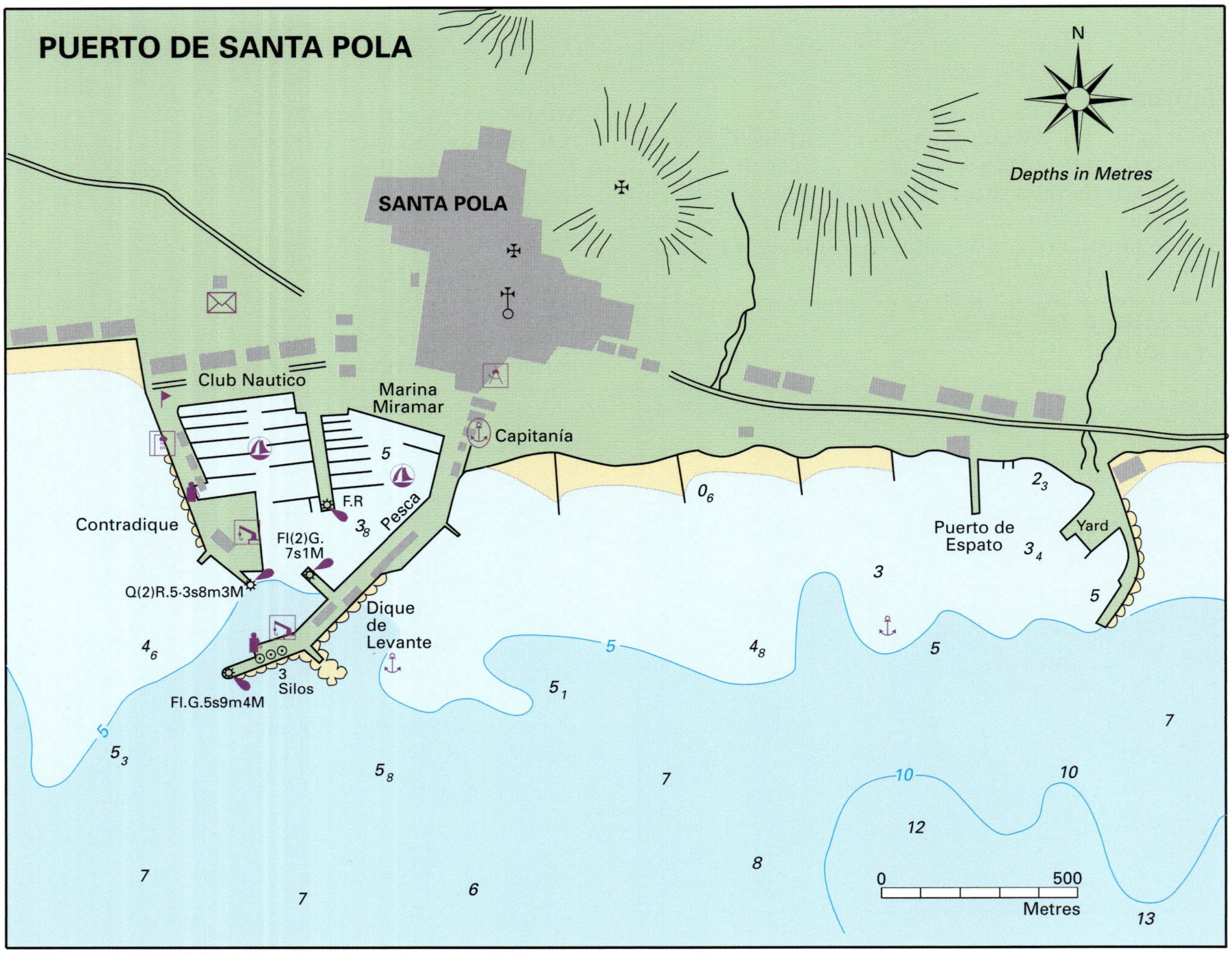

PUERTO DE SANTA POLA

There is a large yellow crane and building at the end of the Dique de Levante and a large blue boat shed at the end of the *contradique*.

From the north Cabo de Santa Pola and the Isla de Tabarca are easily recognised. There is a large yellow crane and building at the end of the Dique de Levante and a large blue boat shed at the end of the *contradique*.

Anchorage in the approach

Anchor 200m to E of the Dique de Levante in four to five metres on mud and weed.

Entrance

Approach on a NE course and round head of Dique de Levante at 20m to starboard. Keep a watch for fishing boats leaving at speed.

Berths

There are two areas to berth, to the east the public pontoons have been removed and there is now a new marina, Marina Miramar, in their position. To the west are the yacht club pontoons. Normal 10m+ craft in the approach should call the YC or the new marina on VHF Ch 9 (or, preferably, phone) for berth availability – there are no actual visitor berths but the club and/or marina will do their best to find a berth for you but berths are very limited and virtually non-existent in high season.

Facilities

Maximum length overall: 60m.
Two major fishing boat repair and building yards located to the E of the harbour will undertake yacht repairs.
Hard at the shipyard and at N of harbour.
Two large slipways on the coast to E of the harbour.
Cranes at the shipyards and two on Dique de Levante. A special crane for yachts to S of pontoons.
Two small chandlers in the town near quays.
Water from taps on the quays and pontoons.
220v/380v AC in shipyard.

Yacht Club Santa Pola *Steve Pickard*

Fuel berth to port on entry at Santa Pola *Steve Pickard*

WiFi available in Marina Miramar.
Gasoleo A.
Ice available in the town and on fuel quay.
Club Náutico de Santa Pola with bar, restaurant and swimming pool.
A number of fairly good shops in town and a good market.

Locally

There is a 16th-century castle and for the energetic, excellent views of the coast from Cabo de Santa Pola. The *salinas* west of the town has flamingos, stilts, avocets and other birds in winter and spring. Beaches on both sides of the harbour.

Communications

Bus service on the main road. ✆ Area code 965. Taxi +34 965 41 35 36.

54. Puerto de Espato

38°11'·2N 00°38'W (see photo on next page)

Service station

This is more of a service station than a port, immediately to the north of Punta Espato. It has large slipways, hardstandings and a travel-lift.

Anchorage in the approach

A good anchorage in 5m sand and weed lies 500m to SW of Puerto de Espato. This is a useful anchorage for yachts on passage up or down the coast and to and from the Balearics.

Facilities

Some heavy engineering.
50-tonne travel-lift.
Hardstanding.

Puerto de Espato
(See harbour description on previous page.)

55. Puerto de Isla de Tabarca (Isla Plana)

38°10'N 00°28'W

Charts

UKHO *473, 1700* Imray *M12*
SHOM *7670* Spanish *472A, 472*

Lights

Isla Tabarca LFl.8s29m15M
White round tower 14m

Harbour

Dique-escolera Fl(2)R.6s9m3M Metallic tower 4m
Bajo de la Nao Q(3)10s5M ♦ card E buoy 4m

Port communications

Asociación de Empresarios de Turismo de Tabarca
VHF Ch 9 ✆ +34 *965 96 12 72*
Información Turística VHF Ch 9 ✆ +34 *902 10 09 10*

Island and marine reserve

Small harbour, but with space for 25 yachts up to 10m along the S side of the Dique Escolera. A large area around this island is a reserve where fishing, diving and anchoring is forbidden (see chart below). The reserve is marked by six buoys, the northern three are Fl(4)Y.12s, while the southern three are Fl(5)15s, all with cross topmarks.

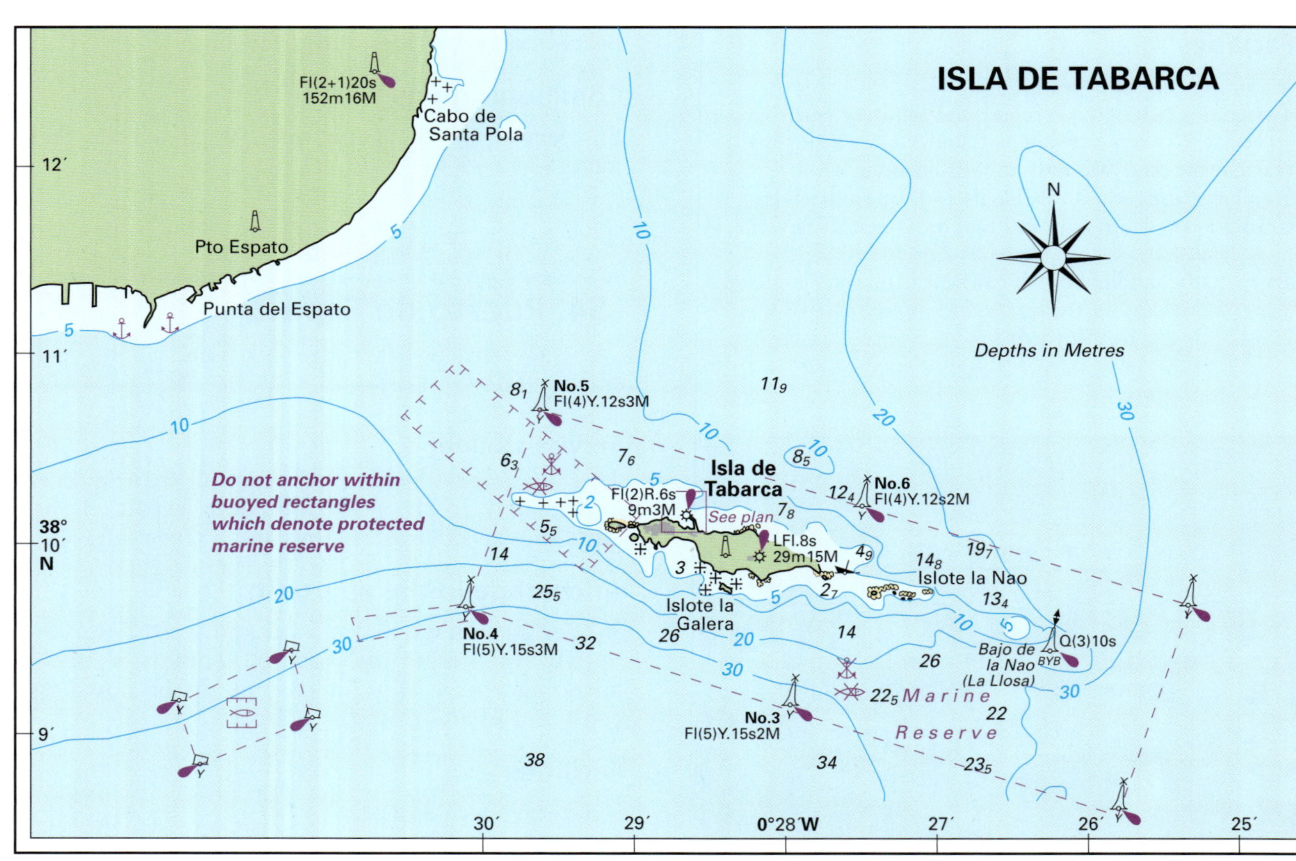

Isla de Tabarca

Approach

From the SW Make for the prominent Cabo de Santa Pola, passing about halfway between the extreme W of the island and the mainland. When the N coast of the island has opened up and the lighthouse bears 300°, approach with the lighthouse lined up with the head of the *dique*.

From the NE Aim at the centre of the island. In the closer approach the *dique* will be seen. Head for it on a southeasterly course.

Entrance

Go for the *dique* head between 300° and 315° and leave it 30m to port.

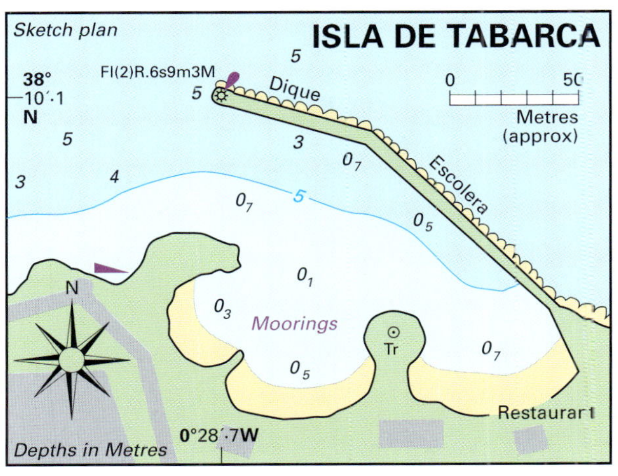

Berths

Secure to quay. In any swell, use an anchor to hold off. Leave space for ferries to the mainland and fishing boats near the head of the *dique*.

Anchorage

An area around the island is marked with buoys to define a 'protected' nature reserve. Anchoring and fishing is technically prohibited, but a strangely calm berth can be found in rock and sand ¼M to the west of the town's harbour.

Facilities

Water from the village if you must – it is in short supply, stored in a cistern and issued each evening.

A few small shops in the village.

Locally

The island was once an old pirate base. They were eventually driven out and a small fortified village built to hold the island against further occupation and garrisoned by Spaniards who were exchanged prisoners of war. The inhabitants have, for generations, lived a very frugal, isolated life based on a small fishing fleet. There is an old fort from the reign of Charles III which is falling into disrepair and small beaches on the S and E side of the island.

56. Puerto de Alicante

38°20'·3N 00°28'·9W

Charts

UKHO *469, 473, 1700* Imray *M12*
SHOM *7670* Spanish *4722, 472A, 472*

Lights

To the south

Cabo Santa Pola Fl(2+1)20s152m16M Square white tower with metal superstructure 15m vis over 270° arc

Isla Tabarca LFl.8s29m15M White round tower 14m

New Darsena Sur

Dique de Abrigo head Fl(2+1)R.21s18m5M Red tower, green band 10m

Interior Jetty head Fl(2)G.7s10m5M Green tower 4m

Dique de Abrigo centre Fl.R.5s12m7M Red tower 4m

Contradique head Fl(2)R.7s8m3M Red tower 5m

New Fishing Harbour

East breakwater head Fl(3)G.9s10m5M Green tower 8m

West breakwater head Fl(3)R.9s7m3M Red tower on white base 6m

Interior jetty head Fl(2+1)R.21s3m1M Metal post 2m

Old Harbour

Dique de Abrigo de Levante head Fl.G.5s14m10M Green truncated tower 9m

Terminal granelles sólidos NE end Fl(2)R.7s9m3M Red tower on white base 6m

Muelle 11 S corner Fl(2+1)R.14·5s8m3M Red tower, green band 6m

Muelle 11 N corner Fl(4)R.11s8m3M Red tower on white base 6m

Muelle A SW corner Fl(2+1)R.14·5s8m3M Red metal column, green band 6m

Muelle de Poniente head Fl.R.3s8m3M Red and white post 6m

Real Club jetty S head Fl(2+1)R.21s4m1M Red post green band 3m

Bifurcation Buoy (just SE off new Dique Sur) Fl(2+1)R.21s3M Red, green, red tower

To the east

Cabo de las Huertas 38°21'·2N 00°24'·3W Fl(5)19s38m14M White tower 9m

Port communications

Port VHF Ch 14, 20 ✆ +34 965 13 00 95

Marina VHF Ch 9 ✆ +34 965 21 36 00 recepcion@marinaalicante.com www.marinaalicante.com

Real Club de Regatas VHF Ch 9 ✆ +34 965 92 12 50 info@rcra.es www.rcra.es

Harbour charges High

A large city with centrally located marina

One of the largest ports in Spain which can be entered in any conditions. Two private marinas with 1,300 berths but space for visitors is limited in high season. Easy to enter and obtain shelter in almost any conditions.

The new fishing harbour has now been completed to the SW of the port with a conspicuous new breakwater with sheds behind it. This is not a harbour for yachts so do not approach it. However infilling and dredging is still going on between the new breakwater and the Terminal Granelles Sólidos but the main quays and lights are now completed. There is a new bifurcation buoy just off the southern

Alicante

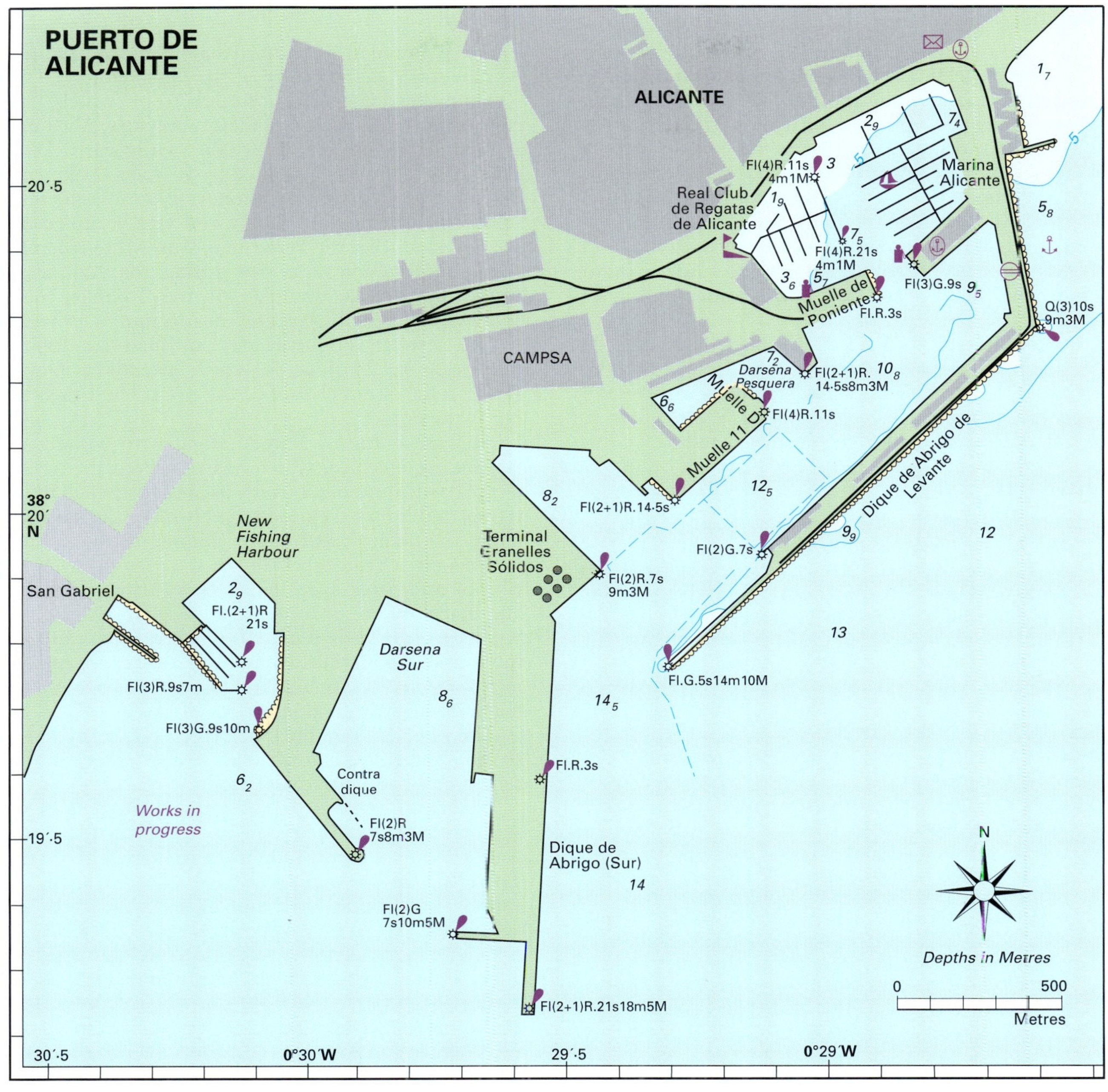

end of the Dique de Abrigo and all pleasure craft must leave this to port and proceed north to the old harbour.

Approach

From the south Round Cabo de Santa Pola, pass inside Isla de Tabarca and the hills behind the port topped by a castle will appear and be easily identified.

From the north Cabo de la Huerta is prominent with a whitish hill behind. Beyond it, three steep hills of a light yellow colour are noticeable.

Entrance

Infilling work is going on to extend the Terminal Granelles Sólidos to the SW and to construct a new container harbour. A new *dique* has been constructed and there may be several buoys indicating the extent of the work. Keep well clear of this construction work. After rounding the Abrigo de Levante, follow it at 100m ignoring the first two entrances to port. The entrance to the inner harbour is the third gap. Keep clear of ships entering and leaving.

Anchorage in the approach

Possible anchorage E of the Dique de Abrigo de Levante.

Berths

There are two marinas in the NE basin. Call Marina Alicante on VHF Ch 9 (or phone) and moor at the waiting berth just to the NE of the fuel berth, immediately to starboard on entering the marina. Take your documents to the office and arrange a berth. Spaces are limited but the marina does its best to accommodate visitors using privately owned berths. All berths have finger pontoons. Although busy and often full in summer, space is usually found in Marina Alicante, though it may be a longer berth than your yacht – and at a correspondingly higher price.

Alternatively, call Real Club de Regatas de Alicante and request a berth in their facilities on the W side of the marina basin. This is a private club and not particularly welcoming to visitors, but a good alternative if Marina Alicante is full.

Facilities

Maximum length overall: Marina Alicante up to 60m Real Club de Regatas up to 40m.

Repairs of a limited nature can be undertaken. Contact Alicante Marine Services. The shipyard is prepared to slip, clean and paint yachts.

Two slipways in W corner of the inner harbour with capacity of up to 500 tonnes.

A number of cranes in the port with capacity of up to 30 tonnes.

Several chandlery shops in the town.

Water and 220v AC points on quays and pontoons.

Gasoleo A and petrol.

Ice from door No. 2 of the ice factory in Dársena Pesquera or from club.

The Real Club de Regatas de Alicante has good facilities. It is both a social and a yacht club and an introduction may be required. Contact the secretary before using the club.

Many shops of all kinds and qualities but inconveniently placed for the marina. There is a good market about 1M into the city; use a No. 6, 7 or 8 bus.

Several launderettes some distance into the city.

TV satellite connections available for larger craft.

The Real Club de Regatas has moved to a new building over the slipway in the west corner of the inner harbour. Tripper boats now ply from the old position of the YC at the centre of the NW side of the inner harbour.

Locally

The city, founded by the Carthaginians and named Akraheuta, was the centre of the Punic empire. The Romans renamed it Lucentum from which the Moors derived Lekant and their successors, Alicante. It became of interest to Britain in the early 18th century when it was assaulted by Sir John Leake and defended by General O'Mahoney; it became the seat of a British mercantile colony and was occupied by the British during the Peninsular War. More recently it was a Republican centre during the civil war; Primo de Rivera, founder of the Falange, was somewhat hurriedly executed in Alicante in 1936.

The festival, Foqueres de San Juan (St John's bonfires), on 24 June is worth attending. Good sandy beaches either side of the port. The beach to NE is the nearest.

Alicante is full of history along with wonderful elegant architecture, which has preserved it. Access to the castle on the hill overlooking the town is via a tunnel and lift sited close to the N end of the marina, along the main road running parallel to the beach. Well worth a visit, especially in the evening when it is cool and gives spectacular views over the town and marinas.

There are literally hundreds of street restaurants in town near the marinas with cheap local tapas or full menu on offer. Top quality restaurants can be found to the W of the town and in the marina itself.

The town is 'humming' at night, with many bars, street magicians, musicians, street artists stalls selling just about anything, etc.

The main street becomes active around 9pm in summer when stalls are set up all along the wide pedestrian walkway running parallel to the sea. There is a lull around 10pm and nightlife begins in earnest at around midnight when thousands of people hit the bars. A very gregarious town and a popular nightspot for Spanish and foreign tourists alike. Unlike nightlife in Benedorm and Ibiza, these nights out are very much for the whole family. One of the most exciting and interesting places in Spain with something for everyone and far enough away from the marina to get a peaceful sleep aboard after a night on the town.

Alicante viewed from the castle N of the harbour
Graham Hutt

Replica 18th-century naval galleon *Santísima Trinidad*. The most heavily armed ship of her day *Maria Kanayama*

A local publication *What's on in Alicante* can be obtained from the tourist office along with piles of information on the location of museums the fortress, art galleries, churches, concerts, etc.

Communications

Major international airport – good for crew change. Rail service to Madrid. One terminal of the narrow gauge coast railway which runs a tourist excursion train as far as Dénia. Bus service along the coast. International airport (with connections to British provincial airports). Ferries to the Islas Baleares, Marseille and other ports. ☏ Area code 965. Taxi ☏ +34 965 25 25 11.

British Consulate Plaza Calvo Sotelo 1/2
Post: Apartado 564 ☏ +34 965 21 61 90, 21 60 22

L'Albufereta

38°21'N 00°28'W

Small, shallow dinghy harbour

A small artificial dinghy harbour with depths of less than a metre, little shelter and no facilities apart from a dinghy ramp and hardstanding. Real Club des Regates and some sailing schools use this harbour extensively.

⚓ Ensenada de Albufereta

38°21'.2N 0°26'.8W

Anchorage in 3m sand in the middle of the Bahía de Alicante open E. Coast road with many houses and flats. Shops nearby.

L'Albufereta

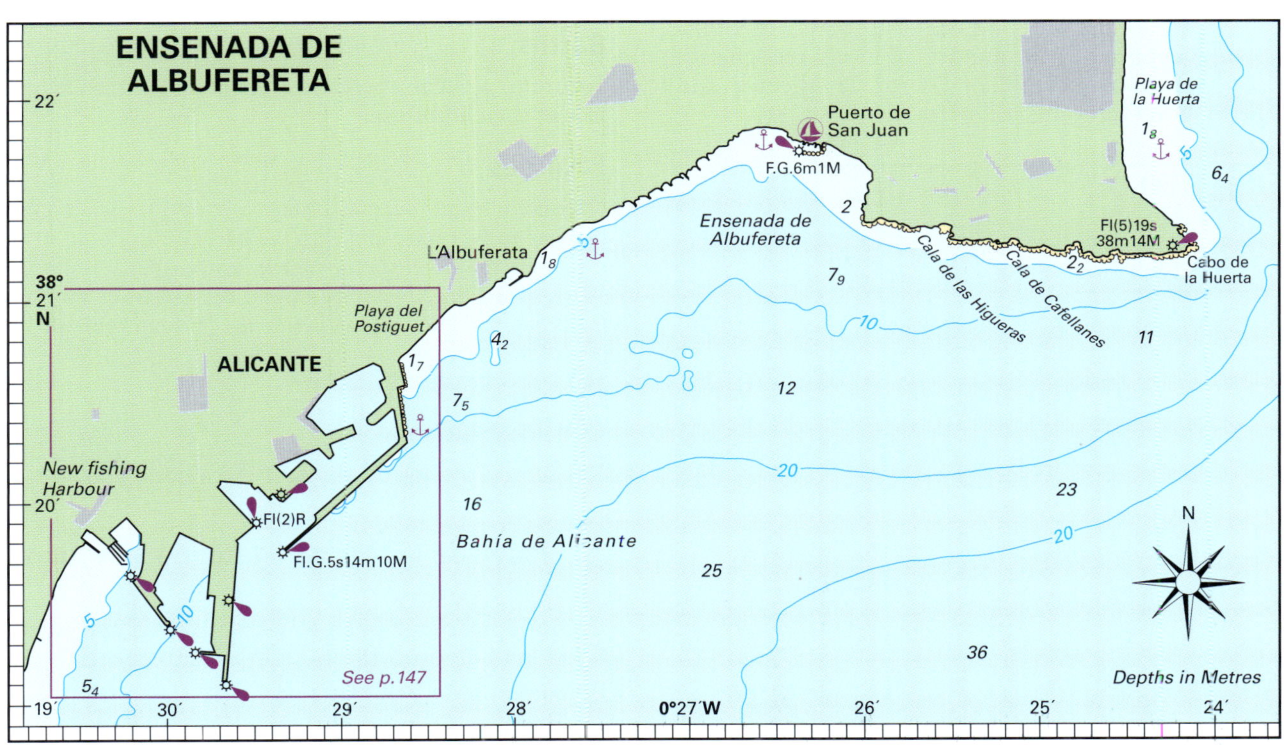

57. Puerto de San Juan (Club Náutico Costa Blanca)

38°21'·7N 00°26'·3W

Charts
UKHO *469, 1700* Imray *M12*
SHOM *7670* Spanish *472A, 472*

Lights
Dique head F.G.5s6m3M Green and white column 3m
Contradique head F.R.5m1M
Red and white column 4m

To the east
Cabo de la Huerta Fl(5)19s38m14M White tower 9m
Buoy 38°21'·3N 00°26'·2W Q(6)+LFl.15s4M ⧫ cardinal some 50m W of a submerged quay (under construction) off Puertoamor

Port communications
Club Náutico Costa Blanca VHF Ch 9 ✆ +34 965 15 44 91
info@cnacb.es
www.cnacb.es

Friendly but limited

A small private yacht club suitable for 230 yachts of 12m or less. Popular yacht harbour with a very friendly *club náutico* but as it is very crowded, especially in summer, one must ring ahead to ascertain whether a berth is available. Although well sheltered by Cabo de la Huerta and normally with an easy approach via the shallow entrance, a heavy swell from the SSW could make the final stage difficult. Facilities for yachts are limited. Sandy beaches either side of the harbour.

Approach

From the south – see Alicante. The prominent Cabo de Santa Pola the off-lying Isla de Tabarca, the hills, town and port of Alicante are all easily recognised. The harbour is 3M NE of Puerto de Alicante and 2M to W of Cabo de la Huerta.

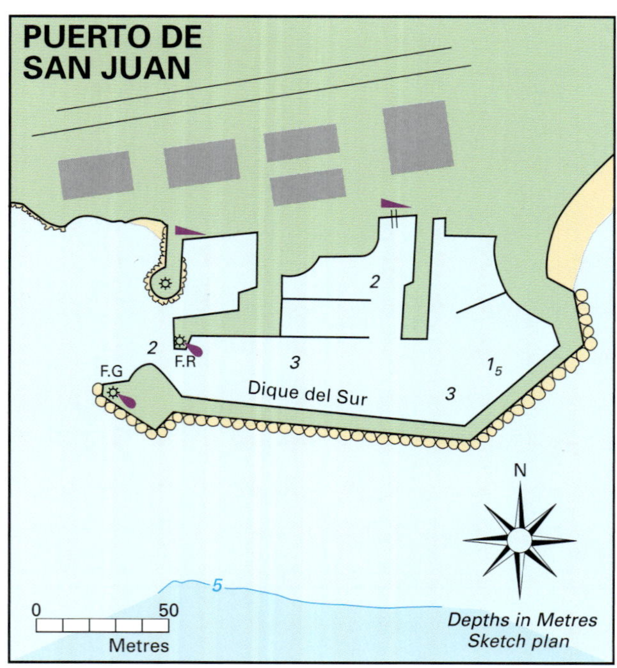

San Juan

From the north After Villajoyosa the coast is low and sandy with many small seaside villages. A small range of coastal hills 8M to SW of Villajoyosa and a small peninsula, La Illeta, which has a harbour on its S side may be recognised. The low 'Punta del Río' has a number of high-rise buildings; Cabo de las Huertas is a low promontory with the Monte de las Matas (181m) just inland. Give it a ¼M berth as there is a submerged reef off it, then round Punta de la Cala and the harbour will open up 1½M to W.

Anchorage in the approach

Anchor to the E or W of the harbour in 5m sand.

Entrance

Straightforward but look out for small craft.

Berths

Secure to a vacant berth just inside the entrance and ask at the clubhouse.

Facilities

Maximum length overall: 10m.
Slipway in N, centre and E of the harbour.
2-tonne semi-mobile crane on the central spur.
Water and 220v AC points around the harbour.
Club Náutico de San Juan beside the harbour with all normal facilities.
Several supermarkets nearby.

Communications

Bus service along the coast. ✆ Area code 965.

⚓ Playa de la Huerta (Platja de San Juan)

38°21'·7N 0°24'·5W

Coastal anchorage open to E in 5m sand and weed. Road and houses along shore, sandy beach. (See plan page 149.)

58. Puerto de Campello

38°25'·8N 00°23'·1W

Charts
UKHO *1700* Imray *M12*
SHOM *7670* Spanish *473*

Lights
To the south
Cabo de las Huertas Fl(5)19s38m14M
White tower 9m
Harbour
Dique de Levante Fl.G.3s8m5M
Green rhombic (with hole) tower 5m
Contradique head Fl(2)R.8s7m3M
Red round concrete tower 4m

Port communications
Club Náutico de El Campello VHF Ch 9
✆ +34 965 63 34 00 info@cncampello.com
www.cncampello.com

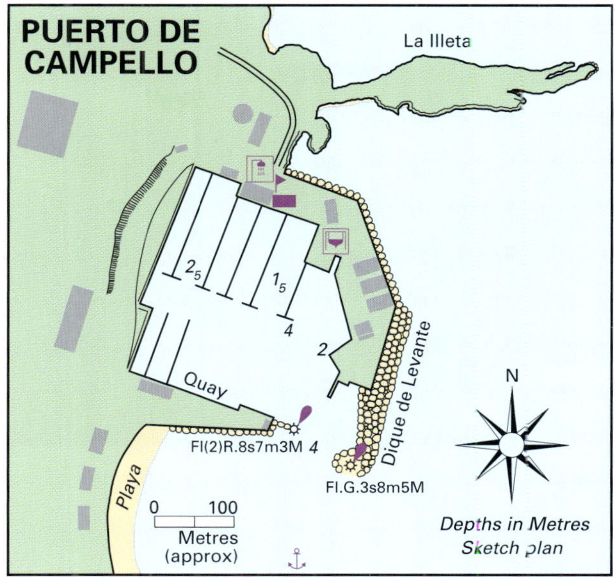

Small modern marina

Formerly a small fishing village and anchorage, now submerged in holiday homes and apartments. The private marina with 474 berths is easy to approach and enter. It has better facilities than several locally. Good shelter inside but swell enters with strong winds between SE and W. The caves, Cuevas de Canalobre, 10M inland, are of interest. Very good sandy beaches either side of the harbour. A pleasant town.

Campello entrance looking W from the Dique de Levante
Steve Pickard

Approach

From the south The low promontory of Cabo de la Huerta, backed by Monte de las Matas (190m), is conspicuous. Give the headland ¼M berth as an underwater reef runs out SE-ly from it. The coast northwards is low, flat and dull with a long, sandy beach and seaside villages backed by high-rise buildings.

The (usually dry) mouth of the Río Montenegre (or de Castellá) is just S of Punta del Río which is low and flat but has a group of high-rise buildings. The harbour can be recognised by a grey/black tower block with red sun blinds on its SW side and an old tower with two creamy coloured high rise buildings to its NW.

Puerto de Campello

From the north The harbour and town of Villajoyosa are easily recognised. The coast to S is of broken cliffs with small coves and small hills inland. La Illeta is quite low and inconspicuous but the harbour can be recognised by the two creamy-coloured high-rise buildings to the NW of the old tower and harbour.

Anchorage in the approach

Anchorage in 5m sand 100m to S of the entrance.

Entrance

Approach the harbour entrance on a NW heading and enter leaving the head of Dique de Levante at least 25m to starboard, or even more at night, as the *dique* sticks out a long way past the beacon, especially to the west.

III. COSTA BLANCA

The distinctive tower and fuel berth towards the end of the Dique de Levante *Steve Pickard*

Berths

Call office on Ch 9 or secure to a vacant berth and ask at the yacht club.

Facilities

Maximum length overall: 15m.
Electricians, radio, radar and engine mechanics, shipwright.
Slipway in NE corner of the harbour.
45-tonne travel-lift and covered dry storage (including a 'filing cabinet' for 200 motor boats).
Water and 220v AC points on quays and pontoons.
Gasoleo A and petrol.
The Club Náutico de Campello has showers, a restaurant, and launderette.
A few local shops with a supermarket a few hundred metres to the south.

Communications

Bus service along the coast and rail to Alicante and along the coast to Dénia in the N. ✆ Area code 965. Taxi ✆ +34 965 63 02 11.

The view S over Campello harbour *Steve Pickard*

59. Puerto de Villajoyosa (Alcocó)

38°30'·4N 00°13'·1W

Charts

UKHO *1700* Imray *M12*
SHOM *7670* Spanish *473, 4731*

Lights

To the southwest
Cabo de la Huerta Fl(5)19s38m14M White tower 9m

Harbour
Dique de Levante head Fl.G.3s14m5M Green tower, white base 7m
Dique de Poniente head Fl(2)R.6s7m1M Red octagonal tower, white base 6m
Espigón head Fl(2)R.6s8m3M Red octagonal tower, white base 7m

To the east
Islote de Benidorm Fl.5s60m6M White truncated pyramid 4m

Port communications

VHF Ch 9 ✆ +34 965 89 36 06 / +34 965 89 07 19
administracion@cnlavila.org/ deportes@cnlavila.org
www.cnlavila.org

Useful but sometimes uncomfortable

A fishing harbour now largely given over to yachts with a small yacht club with 330 berths up to 20m. Approach and entrance are easy but shelter is not very good, and with SE and S winds it can be uncomfortable. The harbour is sometimes oily and depths change with silting and dredging.

Approach

From the SW Cabo de la Huerta which has a conspicuous lighthouse is easily recognised as are the many high-rise buildings at Villajoyosa. A very large white tower block of flats, Cinco Torres (60m), lies just inland of this harbour.

From the NE Having rounded the long high rocky feature of Sierra Helada, the mass of high-rise buildings of Benidorm with its outlying Isla Benidorm are easily identified, together with the large white tower block of flats, Cinco Torres (60m), inland of this harbour.

Anchorage in the approach

Anchor 100m to NW of the head of Dique de Levante in 5m mud and weed.

Entrance

Approach the entrance on a N course and round the head of Dique de Levante at 20m, passing between it and the artificial island with a light at the end of the submerged Espigón Antiarena on the north side of the entrance. The harbour tends to silt up and is periodically dredged and depths shown may not be correct. Keep clear of ferry berth near head of Dique de Poniente.

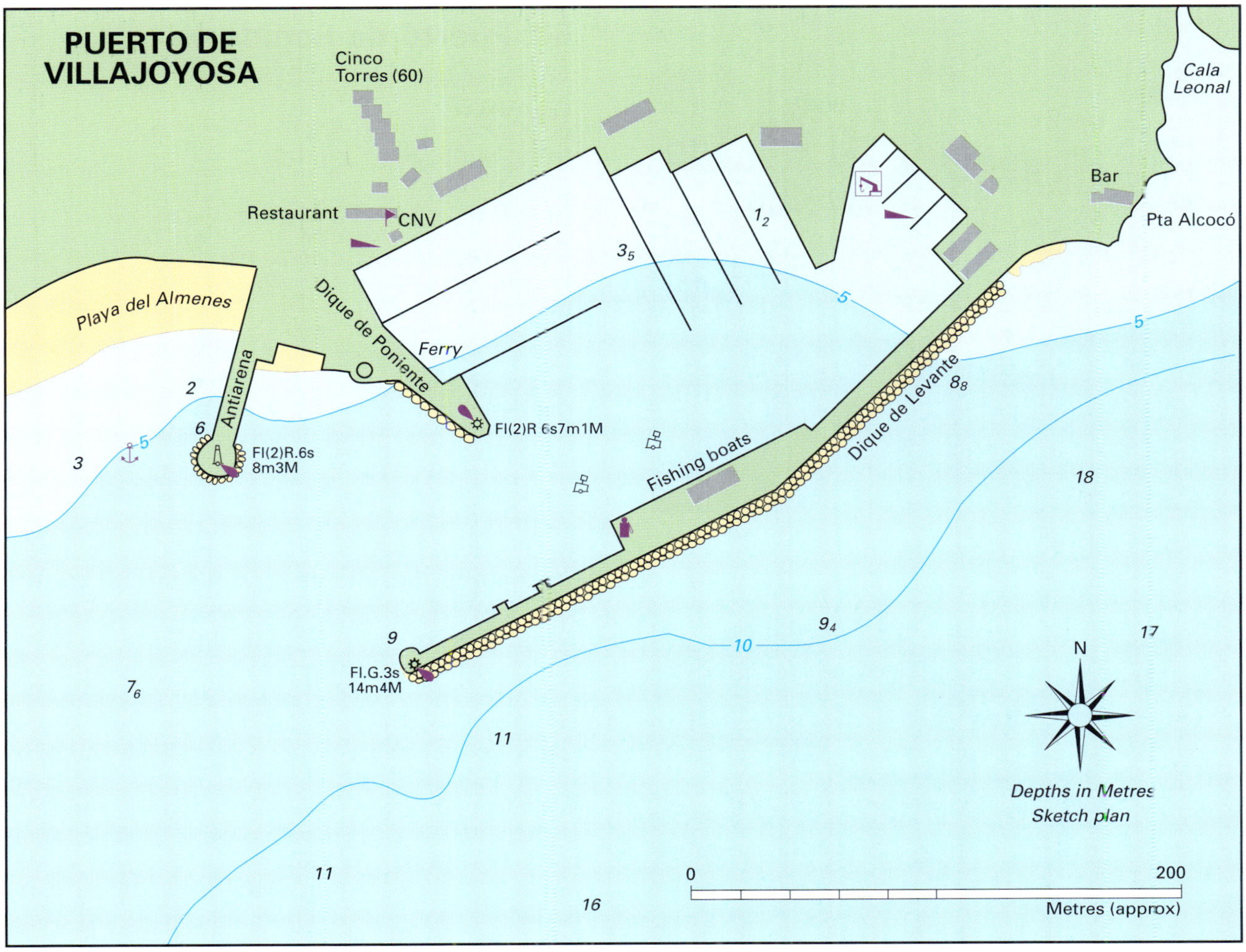

PUERTO DE VILLAJOYOSA

Cinco Torres (60)
Restaurant
CNV
Playa del Almenes
Antiarena
Dique de Poniente
Ferry
Fl(2)R.6s 8m3M
Fl(2)R 6s7m1M
Fishing boats
Dique de Levante
Fl.G.3s 14m4M
Cala Leonal
Bar
Pta Alcocó
N
Depths in Metres
Sketch plan
0 200
Metres (approx)

Villajoyosa looking N from the Dique de Levante *Steve Pickard*

Berths

Secure to the pontoon just inside the Dique de Poniente and inquire at the yacht club for a more sheltered berth within.

Facilities

Maximum length overall: 20m.

Major repairs and engine work by the shipyard at the NE end of the harbour.

Slipway at the NE corner of the harbour, 100 tonnes and 3m.

35-tonne travel-hoist.

5- and 10-tonne cranes at the slipway.

Water taps on the Dique de Levante and pontoons.

220v AC points on pontoons.

Gasoleo A and petrol.

Club Náutico Alcocó-Villajoyosa.

A few small local shops but there are many in the town about 1M away.

Launderettes in town.

Villajoyosa looking N

Villajoyosa's limited haul-out facilities *Steve Pickard*

Locally

The old wall, ruined castle and fortified church in the town are interesting as is the Amadorio dam, some miles inland. About 24 to 31 July, there is a Christian feast in honour of the patron saint Sta Marta. Good beaches on either side of the harbour.

Communications

Buses and railway. ✆ Area code 965.
Taxi ✆ +34 965 89 00 24.

60. Puerto de Benidorm

38°32'N 00°08'W

Charts

UKHO *1700*   Imray *M12*
SHOM *7670*   Spanish *473, 4731*

Lights

Dique de Abrigo head Fl.G.3s8m5M
White hut, green tower 3m
Interior Jetty head Fl(3)G.7s5m1M Post 3m
Submerged jetty head Fl.R.3s5m3M Post 3m
To the south
Islote de Benidorm Fl.5s60m6M
White truncated pyramid 4m

Port communications

Club Náutico de Benidorm VHF Ch 9 ✆ +34 965 85 30 67
info@cnbenidorm.com
www.cnbenidorm.com

Tiny harbour unsuitable for any cruising yacht

For such a huge developed town with so many foreign tourists, it is amazing that there is not a major marina at Benidorm. The small, old fishing harbour, consisting of one pier, one jetty and two pontoons, is now overwhelmed by one of the biggest tourist developments on the coast. It has minimal shelter. Approach and entrance are easy except in winds from S to SW, when it is impossible and the harbour untenable. Anchoring off is feasible. Long sandy beaches can be found on either side of the harbour. There have been talks of building a large marina here for many years and it seems more likely now as this highly touristic area has grown into a huge township.

Approach

From the SW Follow the flat and rather monotonous coast from Villajoyosa towards the high massive rocky feature of Sierra Helada, which is seen from afar and stands beyond Benidorm. Islote Benidorm, a pyramid-shaped island, lies off the harbour. The small, white, rocky-cliffed Punta de Canfáli with houses and a blue-domed church on it lies just beyond the *dique*.

From the NE Round the massive bulk of Sierra Helada and the harbour will be found just beyond it, near the white, rocky-cliffed Punta de Canfáli and among a mass of high-rise buildings. A water-ski area with overhead tow lines on metal posts is laid out in the bay to E of Punta de Canfali.

Entrance

Approach the head of the dique on a N course; round it at 50m. Beware underwater debris closer to the *dique*.

Benidorm harbour from SE

Berths

A temporary berth may be found alongside the NW face of the *dique* but it is frequently used by ferries and fishing boats.

Anchorage

Anchor 150m to S of the head of the *dique* in 6m sand.

Facilities

Engine mechanics in town, mainly with experience in cars.
Hardstanding by the yacht club.
Chandler's shop in the town.
Water from tap near the root of the *dique*.
Many shops in the town and a market.
Club Náutico de Benidorm has a bar, lounge, restaurant, terrace and showers.
Several launderettes in town.

Communications

Bus, rail, taxis, car hire. ✆ Area code 96.

⚓ Ensenada de Benidorm

The three anchorages that follow are along sandy beaches stretching between Cabezo del Tosal and Punta de la Escalata. Backed by massive high-rise buildings for package holidaymakers and open to S, anchor in suitable depth offshore; sandy bottom.

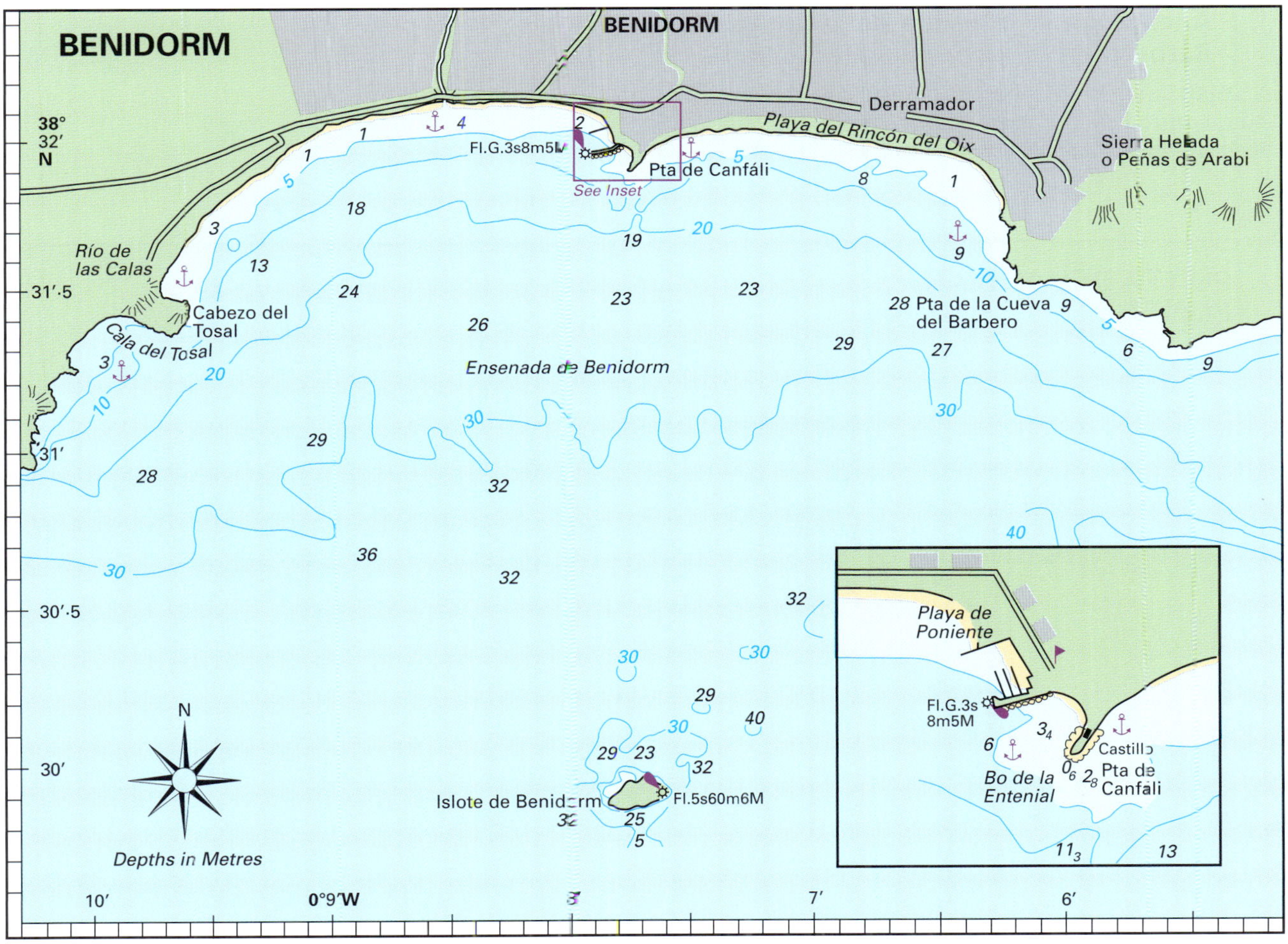

BENIDORM
BENIDORM
Derramador
Playa del Rincón del Oix
Sierra Helada o Peñas de Arabi
Fl.G.3s8m5M
Pta de Canfáli
See Inset
Río de las Calas
Cabezo del Tosal
Cala del Tosal
Ensenada de Benidorm
Pta de la Cueva del Barbero
Islote de Benidorm
Fl.5s60m6M
Depths in Metres
Playa de Poniente
Fl.G.3s 8m5M
Bo de la Entenial
Castillo
Pta de Canfali

Cabezo de Tosal, south anchorage from SW

⚓ Cabezo del Tosal

38°31′·6N 0°09′·5W (see plan page 155)

There are anchorages N and S of this promontory, both open to the East. Anchor in 3m, sand.

⚓ Anchorage E of Punta de Canfali

38°32′N 0°07′·7W (see plan page 155)

Anchor in 3m sand open to S. Considerable holiday development ashore with skyscrapers. A water-ski circuit is established in this anchorage. Not recommended in summer for this reason.

⚓ Anchorage W of Punta de la Cueva del Barbero

38°31′·9N 0°06′·6W (see plan page 155)

A small anchorage open to S and swell from W. Road and development ashore, sand and shingle beach, bottom has rocky patches.

Punta del Albir lighthouse from SE and first anchorage to NW

⚓ Anchorages to NW of Punta del Albir

38°34′N 00°03′·1W

Three anchorages in three bays spread over a distance of 1M to the NW of Punta del Albir. Well protected except from N–NE by the Sierra Helada (438m). Sandy bottom with rocky patches. Down draughts from S–SW winds may be experienced.

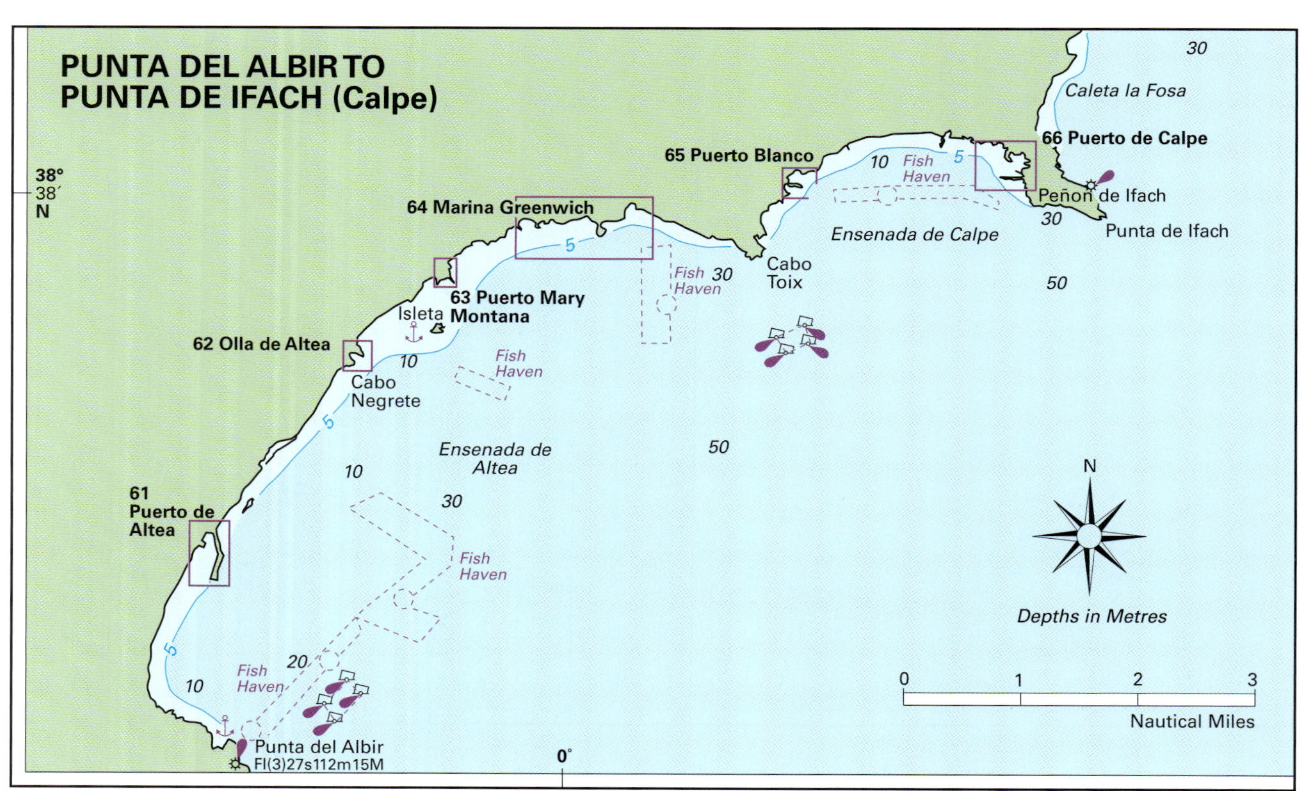

61. Puerto de Altea

38°35'·3N 00°03'·2W

Charts

UKHO *1700* Imray *M12*
SHOM *7670* Spanish *473, 4732*

Lights

To the south

Punta del Albir Fl(3)27s112m15M
White tower on house 8m

Harbour

Dique de Levante head Fl(3)G.9s12m5M
Green octagonal stone tower 6m

Dique de Poniente head Fl(2)R.6s9m3M
Red octagonal tower 6m

Port communications

Puerto de Altea ✆ +34 966 88 01 05
Club Náutico de Altea VHF Ch 9 ✆ +34 965 84 15 91
cnaltea@cnaltea.com
www.cnaltea.com

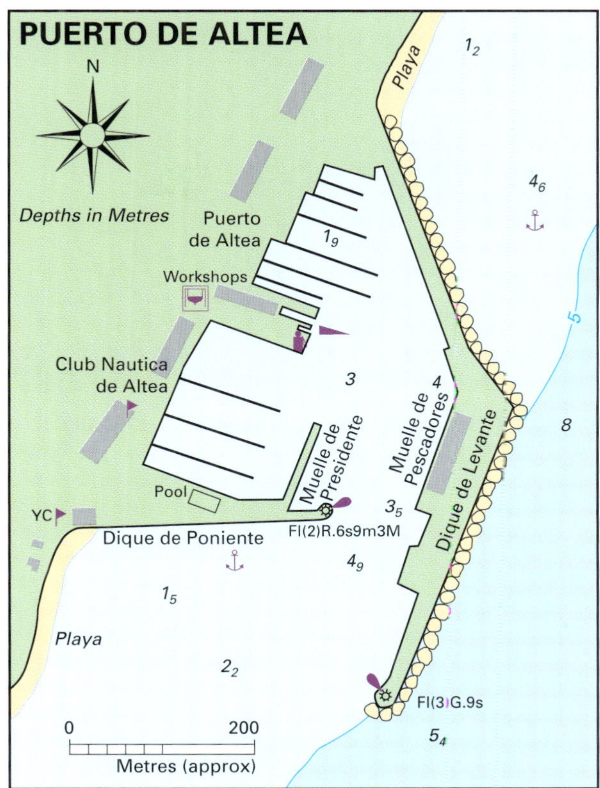

Excellent fishing and yachting harbour

A large and very safe marina with over 500 berths in the Club Náutico, and for a small number of vessels under 8m in Puerto Altea. Welcoming to visitors but prone to silting in the approaches, though frequently dredged. Built near the place where Scipio landed and sacked the Greek colony of Honosca, Altea is a busy artificial fishing harbour with an excellent yacht facility and an easy approach. The area is surrounded by high mountains which make it attractive. The old town on the top of the hill and its church are worth a visit. Locally shops can be found. The village and castle at Guadalest some 9M inland is worth a visit. There are good sandy beaches on either side of this harbour.

Approach

From the SW Round the high-cliffed feature of Sierra Helada which has a conspicuous lighthouse on its NE end, Punta del Albir. From here the harbour walls will be seen and, beyond them, the church of Altea which stands on top of a small hill. The church has conspicuous blue domes.

From the NE The unique high, steep-sided peninsula of Ifach and the lower Cabo Toix are easily recognised. When rounded, the blue-domed church on the hilltop at Altea will be seen. The harbour walls will not be seen until much closer in.

Puerto de Altea

Anchorage in the approach

If draught allows, anchor immediately S of the Dique de Poniente where a considerable amount of shelter can be gained from the Dique de Levante. Keep out of the way of speeding fishing boats using the harbour entrance. Alternatively, but not so good, to the NE of the Dique de Levante in 5m sand.

Entrance

Approach on a NW course and round the head of Dique de Levante at 20m. Enter the yacht harbour behind the Muelle Presidente. The harbour silts up and is frequently dredged which may change the depths. Watch for commercial traffic.

Berths

Secure to Muelle Presidente and ask at the yacht club on the SW corner of Dique Poniente for a berth.

Puerto de Altea entrance looking S toward the Punta del Albir *Steve Pickard*

Facilities

Maximum length overall: 23m.
Two shipyards for yacht repairs.
Engine mechanics.
A 100-tonne slipway; other slipways on the NW side of the harbour near head of the spur and root of Muelle Presidente.
30-tonne travel-hoist.
A chandlery on the seafront and others in the town.
Water and 220v AC points on quays and pontoons.
Gasoleo A and petrol.
Ice is available near the yacht club.
Club Náutico de Altea, located on W side of yacht harbour, has a bar, restaurant, patio, showers and launderette.
Most of the shops and the local market are on or near the main road to the E of the church at the foot of the hill. There are a few small shops near the harbour.
Launderettes in town.
Swimming pool on Dique de Poniente.

Communications

Bus and rail services. ✆ Area code 965.
Taxi ✆ +34 965 84 02 36.

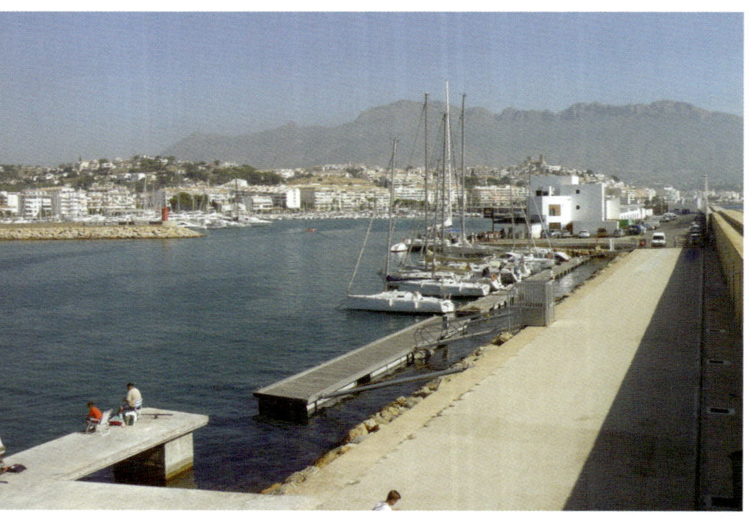
Altea looking N from the end of the Dique de Levante *Steve Pickard*

62. Puerto de la Olla de Altea (El Portet)

38°36'·8N 00°01'·9W

Charts

UKHO *1700*	Imray *M12*
SHOM *7670*	Spanish *473, 4732*

Lights

Dique de Levante Fl(4)G.11s7m1M Green round tower white base 4m
Dique de Poniente Fl(4)R.11s7m3M Red round tower white base 4m

Port communications

✆ +34 965 84 06 97

Minute harbour

This minute harbour with only 36 berths for vessels under 9m is only suitable for day boats, dinghies and small yachts which can be hauled ashore in the event of bad weather. Approach and entrance present no problems in good weather but would be dangerous in heavy seas from E. Facilities ashore are limited and in the summer months it is very crowded. Small pebble beaches either side of the harbour. Large beach to S of Cabo Negrete.

Approach

From the south After the large high rocky mass of the Sierra Helada (Peñas de Arabi) (438m) pass outside Isla Mediana (Mitjana). Having cleared Punta del Albir, the town of Altea will be seen. It has a conspicuous church with two blue domes on top of a hill and its harbour lies to the S. Northwards of Altea harbour the coast should be given a 300m berth for ½M when Cabo Negrete will be identified by its rocky point and a large, white house in dark trees. There are rocks off the point. Olla del Altea lies 250m to N of this point and can be identified by a large private house behind the harbour.

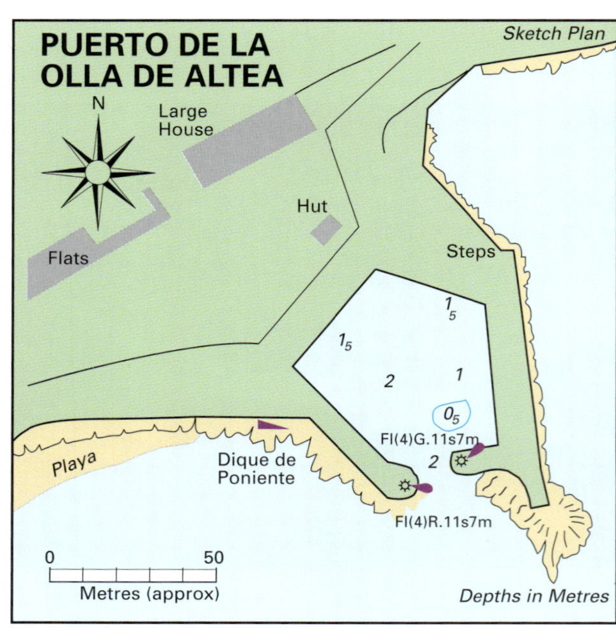

Tiny Olla de Altea looking N from the Dique de Poniente
Steve Pickard

From the north Round the prominent and steep-to Cabo Toix. Pass Puerto de Mascarat, which will be identified by its breakwaters and the smaller private harbour of Puerto de Marymontaña. Pass outside Islote and Isleta, two offshore islands, the latter with a shallow patch 0·2m inshore and having passed Isleta, go W towards the harbour. The large private house also shows up from this direction.

Olla de Altea

Anchorage in the approach

Anchor E of the harbour, as draught allows, on mud and stones.

Entrance

Approach the harbour on a W to NW heading and keep a watch on soundings. Enter on a NNW heading at slow speed; note shallow patch to starboard just inside the harbour.

Berths

Secure to quays to starboard, ground on slipways if a bilge keeler or haul out ashore.

Facilities

Slipways on W and N side of the harbour for day boats and dinghies.
Simple everyday requirements from local shops.

Communications

Rail and bus services. ✆ Area code 965.

63. Puerto de Mary Montaña

38°37'·5N 00°01'·1W

Charts

UKHO *1700, 1701* Imray *M12*
SHOM *7670* Spanish *473, 4732*

Lights

Dique de Levante head Fl(3)G.9s9m3M
Green column on white hut 8m
Dique de Poniente head Fl(3)R.9s9m1M
Red column on white hut 7m

Puerto de Mary Montaña

Private harbour

An attractive private harbour, suitable for small and medium-sized yachts, belonging to a large estate and for use only as a harbour of refuge; it should not be entered without good reason. Facilities are limited to water and electricity. The main coast road lies 500m to NW from the harbour up a hill.

Approach

The approach is shallow. A shallow, rocky area lies to E of the harbour culminating in Islote, a small islet 350m to E–NE of the entrance. A larger rocky island, Isleta, lies 700m to S of the entrance with a reef stretching NW to the coast.

From the south From Altea which can be recognised by its harbour and the town on a hill, which is crowned by a church with two blue domes, the sandy coast runs in a N–NE direction and is backed by a range of hills. Cabo Negrete and the Puerto de la Olla de Altea will only be recognised if close to the shore. In the approach from this direction it is advisable to pass outside Isleta which lies 550m off the shore and then turn on to a N course and approach the harbour, sounding carefully with a lookout posted forward. From Isleta the harbour should be seen, backed by the rocky Montaña Bernia (1,129m) which is a pyramid shape. In the closer approach, the triple-arched gateway may be seen behind the harbour wall.

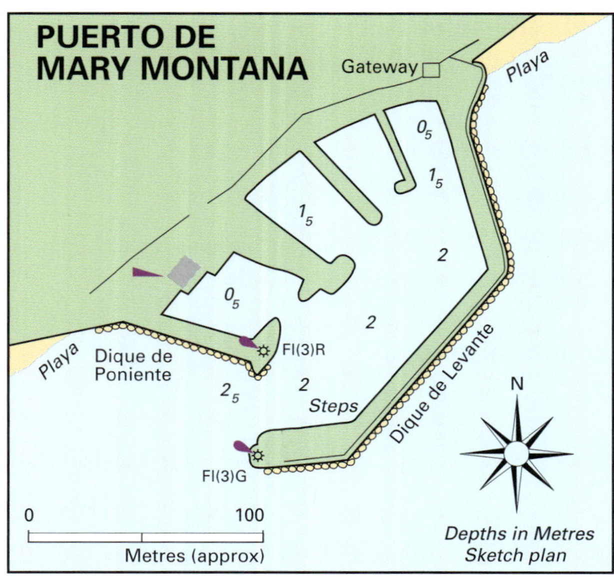

From the north Cabo Toix which is steep-to and the large harbour of Puerto Mascarat are easily recognised. Keep outside the 10m depth contour which lies some 400m from the shore until 100m NE of Isleta. The harbour lies in a N direction and a direct approach can be made from here towards the entrance, sounding carefully and with a lookout forward.

Anchorage in the approach

The area near the harbour is of rock and the nearest suitable anchorage is in 5m sand 300m W of Isleta. (See plan page 156.)

Entrance

Approach the entrance on a N course and enter on a NE heading.

Berths

Secure to the inner side of the Dique de Levante and report to the harbour official at the *caseta* by the gateway. If no one is to be found there to allocate a berth, proceed some 200/300m up the hill to a large house and report there.

Facilities

Water taps on all quays.
220v AC points on all quays.

Communications

Bus service along the main road and the coastal railway station at Olla de Altea.

64. Marina Greenwich (Mascarat)

38°37'·7N 00°00'·3W

Charts
UKHO *1700, 1701* Imray *M12*
SHOM *7670* Spanish *473, 4732*

Lights
Dique Sur W head Fl(2)G.7s8m5M
Green round tower white base 6m
Dique Sur E head Q(6)+LFl.15s10m3M
Black and yellow round tower 6m
Contradique head Fl(2)R.7s8m1M
Red round tower, white base 6m

Port communications
Port Office VHF Ch 9. ✆ +34 965 84 22 00
marina@marinagreenwich.com
www.marinagreenwich.com

Convenient and pleasant marina

The harbour with 540 berths up to 30m lies on the Greenwich meridian and is surrounded by high rocky hills with an attractive hinterland well worth visiting by car. It should be noted that the marina Is bigger than the nine shoreside apartment blocks that constitute the village. There are plans for the marina to be extended to accommodate additional berths but this appears to be still way in the future. The harbour itself has good facilities. It becomes crowded in summer and it is prudent to book ahead. A small shingle beach to W of the harbour and a golf course nearby.

Marina Greenwich (Mascarat)

Approach

From the south Give the coast a 500m berth NE from Altea to Cabo Negrete. From thence to Isleta, which should be left to port, as will the small rocky islet of Islote. Approach the harbour entrance on N course.

From the north Round the unmistakable Punta Ifach and cross the Ensenada de Calpe. Cabo Toix, which is steep-to, is prominent and has high cliffs which slope up the higher ground inland. On rounding this point, part of the harbour breakwater will be seen. Punta Mascarat obscures the rest of the harbour when seen from this area. The harbour entrance is at the west end of the breakwater.

Anchorage in the approach

Anchor in 5m sand between Punta de Mascarat and the E side of the harbour to suit prevalent wind.

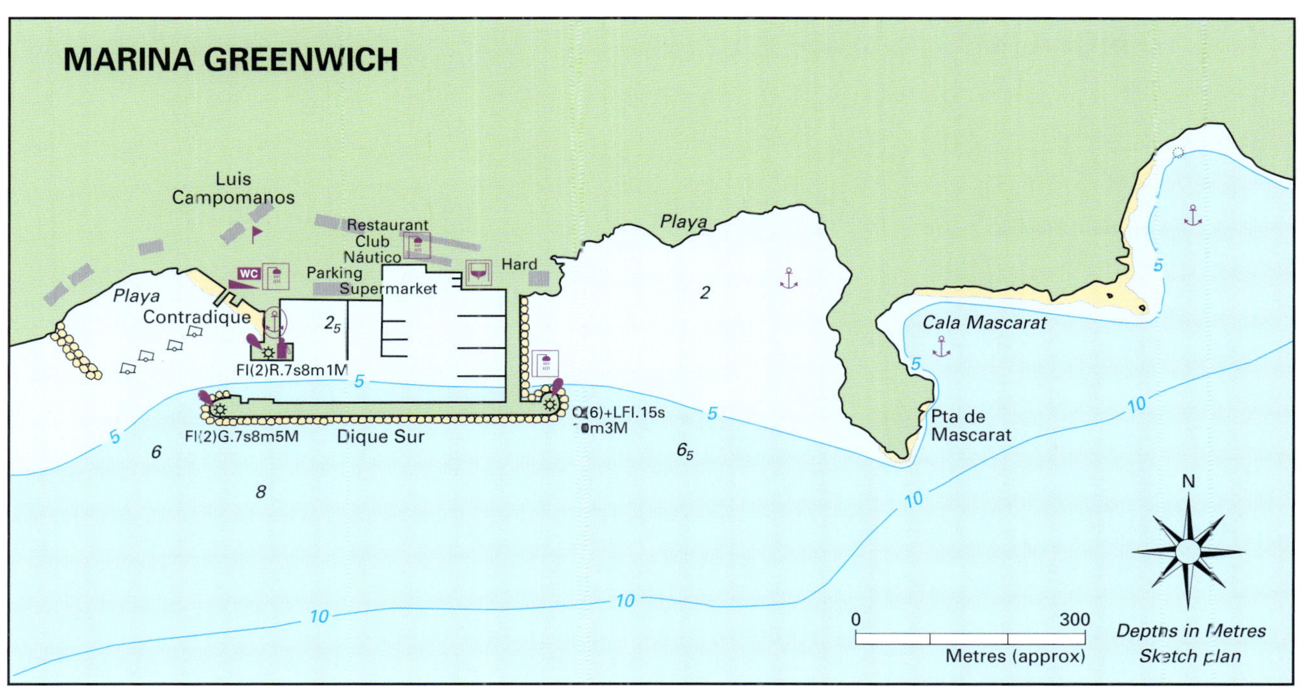

Marina Greenwich looking E. Beware beach buoys at night *Steve Pickard*

Entrance

Approach the Dique Sur western end from the south quadrant, round it to starboard at 20m and steer east for the fuel quay, immediately to port on entering.

Berth

Secure to fuel quay and ask at the port control office.

Facilities

Maximum length overall: 30m.
Engine mechanics and general repairs.
Crane.
50-tonne travel-hoist.
Chandlery behind the harbour.
Showers.
Water and 220v/380v AC points on quays and pontoons.
Gasoleo A and petrol.
Ice on fuel quay.
Shops for everyday requirements and a supermarket behind the harbour.

Communications

Buses on main road above the harbour. Railway at Olla de Altea. ☏ Area code 965. Taxi ☏ +34 965 84 02 36.

⚓ Punta Mascarat

38°37'·7N 0°00'·4E (see plan page 161)

Three anchorages in 5m sand and stone. As mentioned in Marina Greenwich *Approach*, one to W of Punta Mascarat, one to E and the third off the mouth of Barranco del Collada. By choosing the anchorage, the high cliffs can give protection except from S winds and there may be swell from SE or SW. The main road is at top of the cliffs.

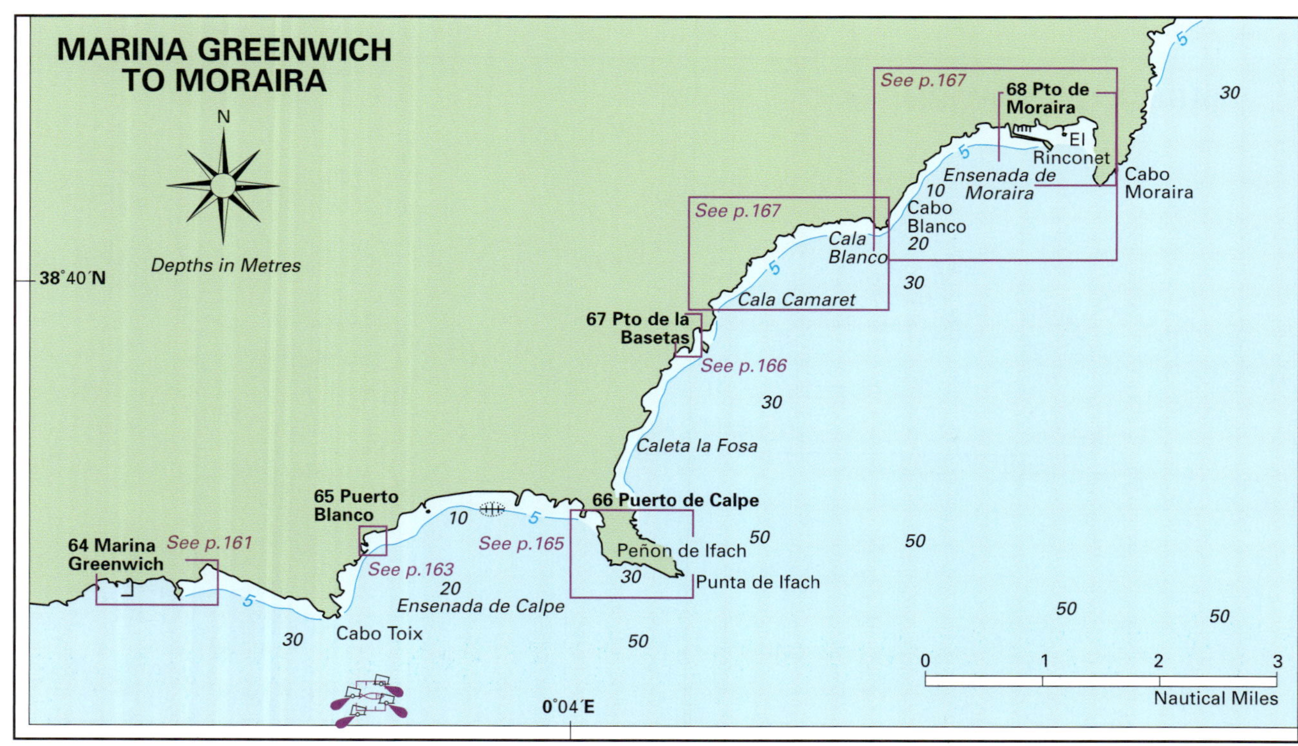

65. Puerto Blanco

38°38'·1N 00°02'·1E

Charts
UKHO *1700, 1701* Imray *M12*
SHOM *7670* Spanish *473, 4732*

Lights
E breakwater head Fl.R.5s7m3M
Red castellated tower 6m

Port communications
Try Ch 9. ✆ +34 965 83 18 60
administracion@puertoblanco.es
www.puertoblanco.es

Harbour charges Medium

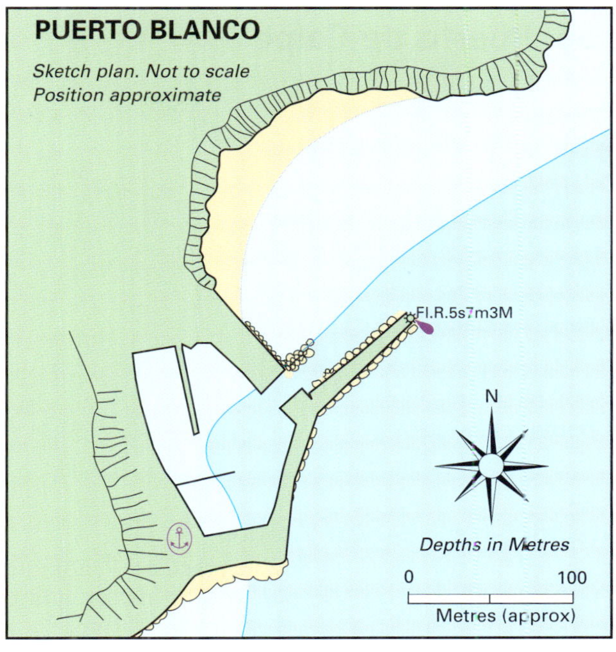

Small boat harbour

A small-boat harbour with 112 berths up to 13m lying NNE of Cabo Toix and 800m W of Puerto de Calpe. It may be a useful alternative when Calpe is full but it may also be full itself. It has good shelter except in an easterly when there will be swell in the harbour. Facilities are limited. Some housing estates in the area.

Approach

From the SW From the conspicuous promontory of Punta de Albir (112m) the equally conspicuous Cabo Toix and Punta Ifach will be seen. The harbour lies on the E side of Cabo Toix which is steep-to.

From the NE From Cabo Moraira set course to round the conspicuous Punta Ifach, then on to a W course towards Puerto Blanco which will be seen in the closer approach just to the N of Cabo Toix.

Entrance

Usually straightforward but may not be possible in a strong easterly.

Berths

Secure to a vacant berth and ask at the *capitanía*.

Facilities

Engineer and workshop available.
Water taps on quay.
Supermarket ½ a mile away.

⚓ Ensenada de Calpe

38°38'·4N 0°03'·2E

The Ensenada de Calpe lies between Puerto Blanco and Calpe. Anchorage off sandy beach in 3–5m sand open E. Pay attention to unmarked wrecks off Playa del Bou and Playa del Almadrat. Road ashore with some apartment buildings.

Puerto Blanco Looking NW

66. Puerto de Calpe

38°38'·2N 00°04'·2E

Charts
UKHO *1700, 1701* Imray *M12*
SHOM *7670* Spanish *473, 4732*

Lights
Contradique head Fl(4)R.10s8m3M
Truncated masonry tower, red top 4m
Dique head Fl.G.4s13m5M
Masonry tower, green top 6m

Port communications
VHF Ch 9. ✆ +34 965 83 18 09
info@rcnc.es
www.rcnc.es

Harbour charges High

Harbour in spectacular location

Located at the base of the spectacular Peñón de Ifach, the old fishing harbour, with a history going back to the Phoenicians, has been transformed into a very welcoming harbour with 264 berths and room for visitors. It is a busy harbour which can be approached and entered with ease. The shelter is good though a SW wind can bring swell into the harbour. It is worth visiting to admire the Peñón de Ifach; a climb from its NW side through a tunnel and along a perilous pathway to the top results in a spectacular view of the coast and a demonstration of the uncontrolled nature of high-rise and other commercial building. Good beaches either side of the harbour. Golf Club de Ifach nearby.

Approach

A dangerous wreck lies ½M to W of the harbour.

From SW having rounded the massive Sierra Helada, the Peñón de Ifach will be seen in the distance appearing as an island. Cabo Toix, another massive cape en route, is easy to identify.

From NE round Cabo de la Nao, high and prominent with a conspicuous lighthouse on top. Cabo Moraira, another prominent cape with a new yacht harbour to its W is also easy to recognise. The Peñón de Ifach can be seen from afar but appears as an island.

Anchorage in the approaches

Anchor 100m to W of the head of the *contradique* in 5m sand or on the other side of Ifach in Cala de la Fosa, 5m sand and stone.

Entrance

Straightforward, but it is a bit tight inside and there may be some ship movements. With N winds, there can be strong gusts in the harbour from the Peñón de Ifach.

Berths

Call on Ch 9 and the marina office will respond with a *marinero* who will direct you to a berth. Visitors are usually berthed at the E side of the marina either side of the Club Náutico N/S pontoons. The marineros are on call during the night and always assist with berthing. There is surging with SW winds, which are frequent in the afternoons in summer. Visitors with vessels 12m or less are berthed close to the sailing and diving school at the extreme E of the harbour on the inside of the N/S jetty.

Facilities

Maximum length overall: 30m.
The shipyard can carry out most repairs to hull and engines.
Other engine mechanics in the town.
Two slipways at the shipyard.
10-tonne crane.
Chandlery shop in the town and at the shipyard.
Water taps on pontoons but test it before filling tanks.
220v AC on pontoons.

Calpe and the Peñón de Ifach with Cala de la Fosa anchorage beyond the narrow isthmus. Cabo Moraira in the distance

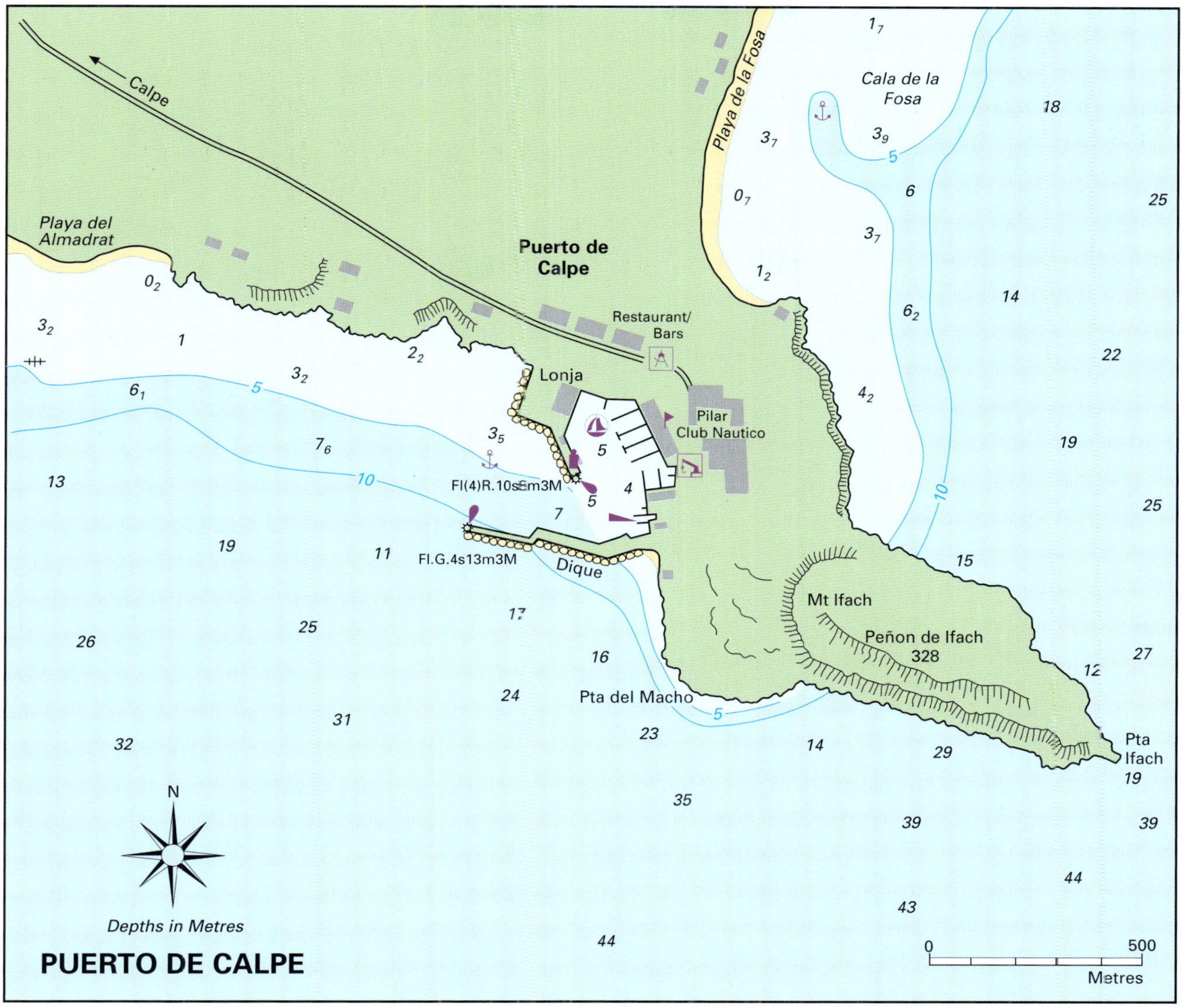

Depths in Metres

PUERTO DE CALPE

Gasoleo A.
Ice on quay.
Club Náutico de Calpe with the usual facilities.

Puerto de Calpe, looking SE over a possible anchorage between beach buoys and the entrance channel
Steve Pickard

There are two supermarkets beyond the steps leading over the ridge behind the marina. More shops in Calpe about 1M away.
Launderette at the club house.

Locally

There are two excellent restaurants in the marina, one run by the Royal Club Náutico de Calpe, serving excellent fare, at a reasonable price.

Communications

Bus and rail services. ✆ Area code 965.

⚓ Cala de la Fosa (N of Peñon de Ifach)

38°38′·6N 0°04′·5E

Anchor off middle of Playa de la Fosa in 5m sand. Road and high-rise apartment buildings ashore. Open to E.

67. Puerto de les Basetes

38°39'·6N 00°05'·2E

Charts

UKHO *1700, 1701* Imray *M12*
SHOM *7669* Spanish *474*

Lights

Dique de Levante head Fl(3)R.9s6m3M Red tower 3m
Contradique head Fl(3)G.9s6m1M Green tower 3m

Port communications

Port Office VHF Ch 9. ✆ +34 965 83 12 13
info@cnlesbasetes.com
www.cnlesbasetes.com

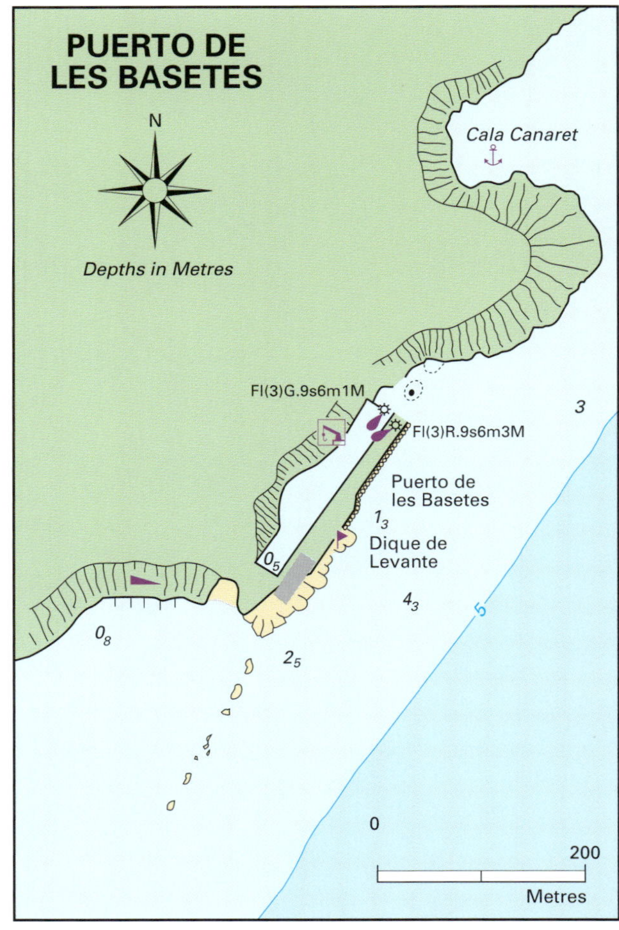

Small boat harbour

An attractive little harbour but for small yachts and dinghies only. The entrance is narrow and space inside is limited. The sea wall is based on a line of rocks lying parallel to the shore within which quays have been built. La Cala 400m to S has a shingle beach.

Approach

From the south Round the unmistakable Peñón de Ifach(328m) which is steep-to. The harbour lies 2M N. A large tower on Cabo Blanco to NE is very conspicuous. The harbour is difficult to see until close in, when the harbour wall, with a small white house on it, will be identified.

From the north Round Cabo Moraira which is steep-to. Cross the Ensenada de Moraira in a SW direction closing the coast after 3M. Pass the large yacht harbour at Moraira and Cabo Blanco, which is steep-to but not very prominent; it has a sloping silhouette and a cliffed face on the E side. In the close approach, the harbour wall and a small white building on it will be seen.

Puerto de les Basetes

Entrance

Approach the entrance at the N end of the harbour on a NW-ly course, sounding and with a forward lookout posted. Go S of the small exposed rock and round the head of the Dique de Levante taking care of isolated rocky heads.

Berths

Secure to quay to port in a suitable gap and consult the *capitanía*.

Facilities

Slipways at the S end of the harbour.
Small hardstanding.
3-tonne crane.
Water from a yacht club tap.
220v AC in the Club.
Small yacht club.
Scuba school.

Communications

Bus service to Calpe on coast road behind harbour.
✆ Area code 965.

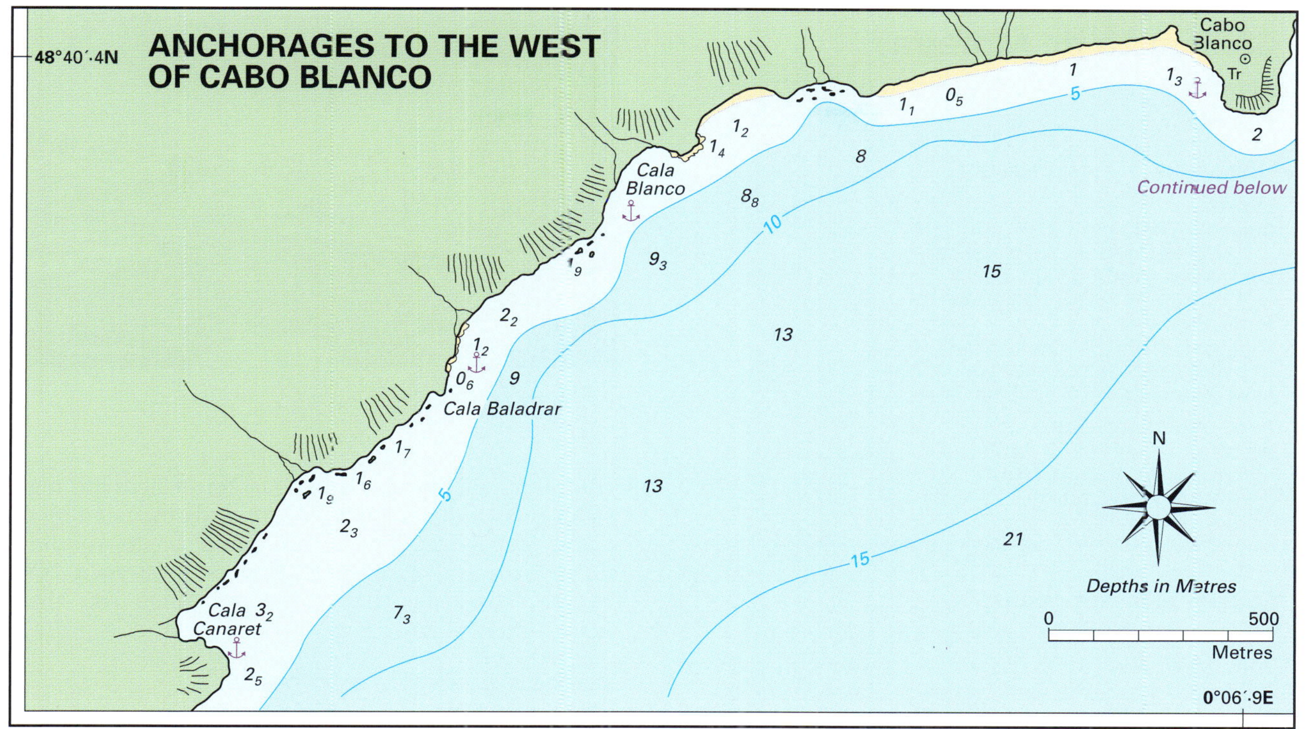

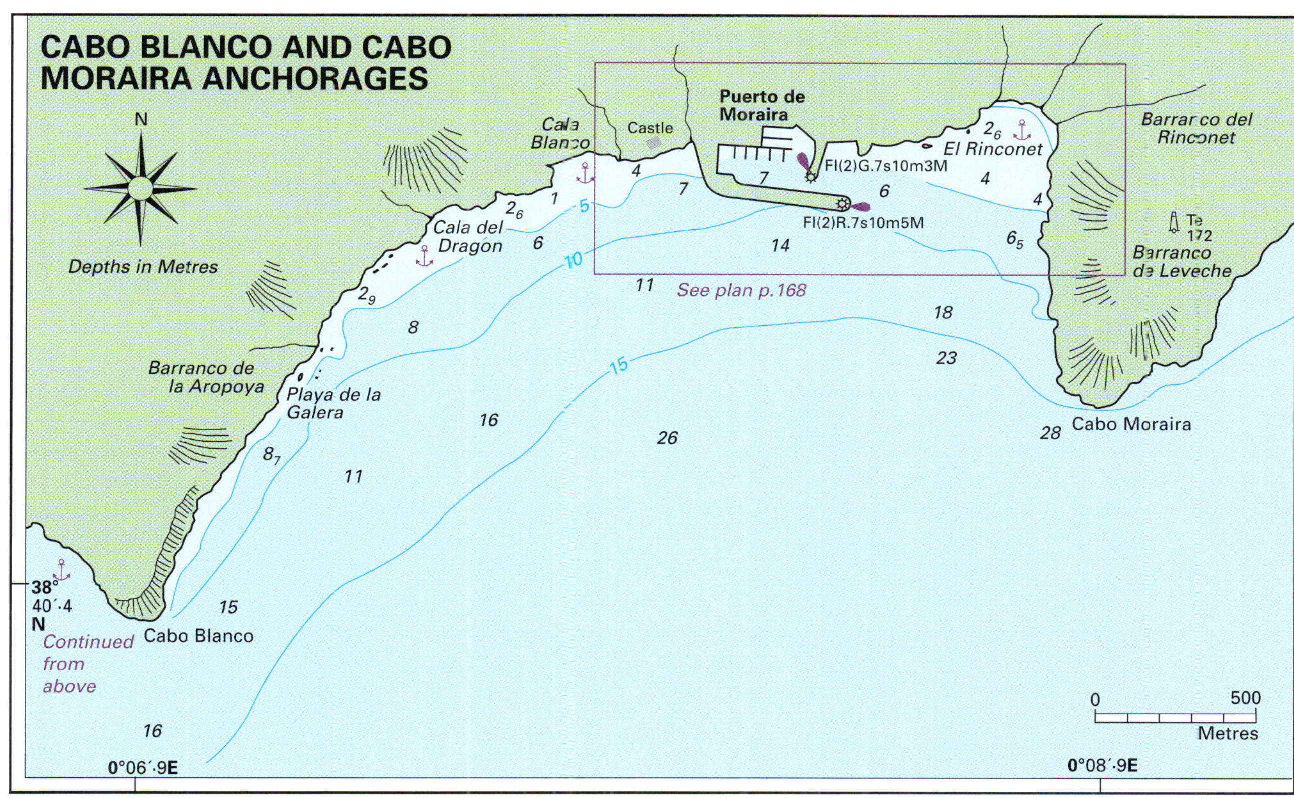

⚓ Cala Canaret, Cala Baladrar, Cala Blanco (W of Cabo Blanco) and Cabo Blanco

These anchorages should be used with care. There are submerged rocks which can usually be seen in the clear water. Rocks make poor holding in some areas. All wide open to the SE.

⚓ Cala del Dragon and Cala Banco (E of Cabo Blanco)

38°40′·9N 0°07′·3E

Anchorage off small sandy bay in 2·5m sand. Wide open to the SE. Road inland. (May be buoyed off in summer.) Cala Blanco is E of Cala del Dragon.

68. Puerto de Moraira

38°41'·1N 00°08'·3E

Charts
UKHO *1700, 1701* Imray *M12*
SHOM *7669* Spanish *474*

Lights
Dique de Abrigo head Fl(2)R.7s10m5M
White round tower, red bands 6m
Contradique head Fl(2)G.7s10m3M
White round tower, green bands 6m
To the northeast
Cabo de la Nao Fl.5s122m23M 049°-vis–190°
White octagonal tower and house 20m
Inner jetty head Fl(3)G.9s5m3M

Port communications
VHF Ch 9. ✆ +34 965 74 43 19
recepcion@cnmoraira.com
www.cnmoraira.com

Modern pleasant resort

A large modern yacht harbour with 620 berths up to 25m. Set in an attractive setting it is one of the easier harbours to enter in bad weather and well sheltered from wind and waves once inside. The new harbour takes up some of the old anchorage of the bay but the most sheltered part, which is more suitable for yachts, is still available.

Moraira is a useful point of departure for San Antonio-Abad in Ibiza, 55M. A climb to the Torre de Moraira is rewarded with a fantastic view of the coast. Sandy beach at El Rinconet. Golf Club de Ifach 4M.

Approach

There may be tuna nets in the bay.

From the south After Peñón de Ifach go NE-ly towards the prominent Cabo Moraira which is high, with steep cliffs and a tower on its summit (172m). The peak of Montaña Isabela (La Liorenza) (442m) lies behind. In the closer approach the houses of Moraira village and tower blocks will appear. The harbour lies just E of the semi-circular fort located near the village.

Puerto de Moraira *Steve Pickard*

From the north From Cabo de la Nao which has high steep cliffs, the course is SW towards the prominent Cabo Moraira, 172m with a tower on its summit. Cabo Moraira is steep-to. Round it on to a NW course towards the harbour which is then immediately visible.

Anchorage in the approach

Anchor in the Ensenada del Rinconet (see below) or to the W in Cala Blanco.

Berths

Make up on the fuel quay to starboard on the inner side of the *contradique* and ask at the *capitanía.* Note that all berths are privately owned so one should be prepared to be shifted around if staying for a few days. Some quays have rocky feet extending some distance. In summer, when it is very crowded, boats double-up alongside the *contradique.*

Harbour charges

High. Note that the *club náutico* only permits a cumulative total of seven days berthing in the season for a visiting yacht after which temporary membership of the club has to be paid at the current weekly rate, in addition to the berthing charges.

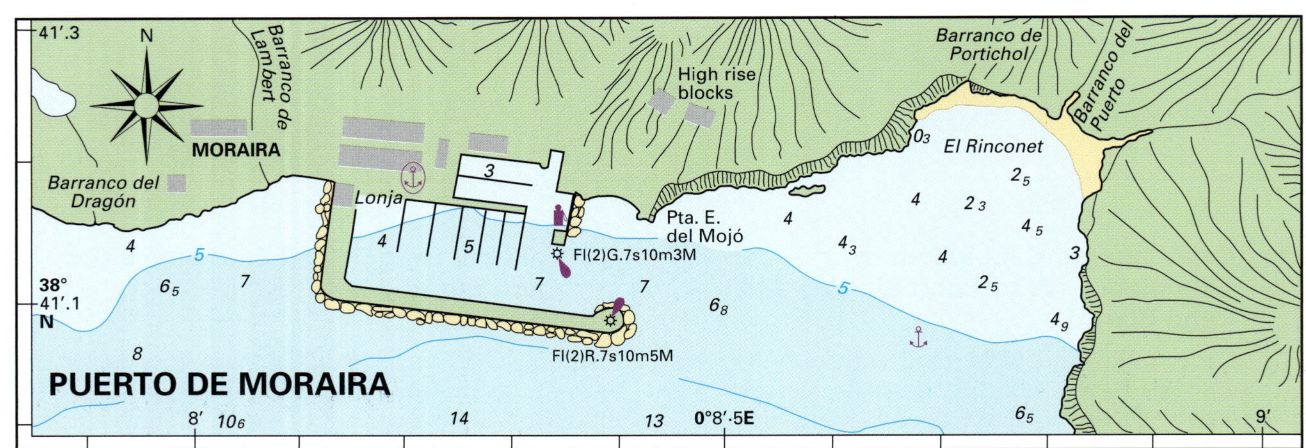

Moraira

Moraira entrance looking E *Steve Pickard*

Facilities

Maximum length overall: 30m.
Workshops.
Slipway in NE corner.
50-tonne travel-hoist.
10-tonne crane.
Chandlery shop beside the harbour and another in the village.
220v/380v AC on pontoons.
Water taps on quays and pontoons but drinking water only on the two western pontoons and head of the *contradique*.
Showers.
Gasoleo A.
Butane Gasolinera de Benissa Monday–Friday 1200–1300.
Ice on fuel quay.
Club Náutico de Moraira.
Supermarket close by outside.
Shop at the N side of harbour and several in the village.

Communications

Buses to Jávea and Calpe on coast road. Railway at Benisa. ✆ Area code 965.
Taxi ✆ +34 965 83 17 16 / 74 42 81.

⚓ El Rinconet

38°41′·1N 0°08′·7E

Anchor according to depth, in sand up to 150m from the shore; sand, rock and weed beyond that. Open between S and SE. See plans on page 168 and 170.

El Rinconet, note the bathing buoys

III. COSTA BLANCA

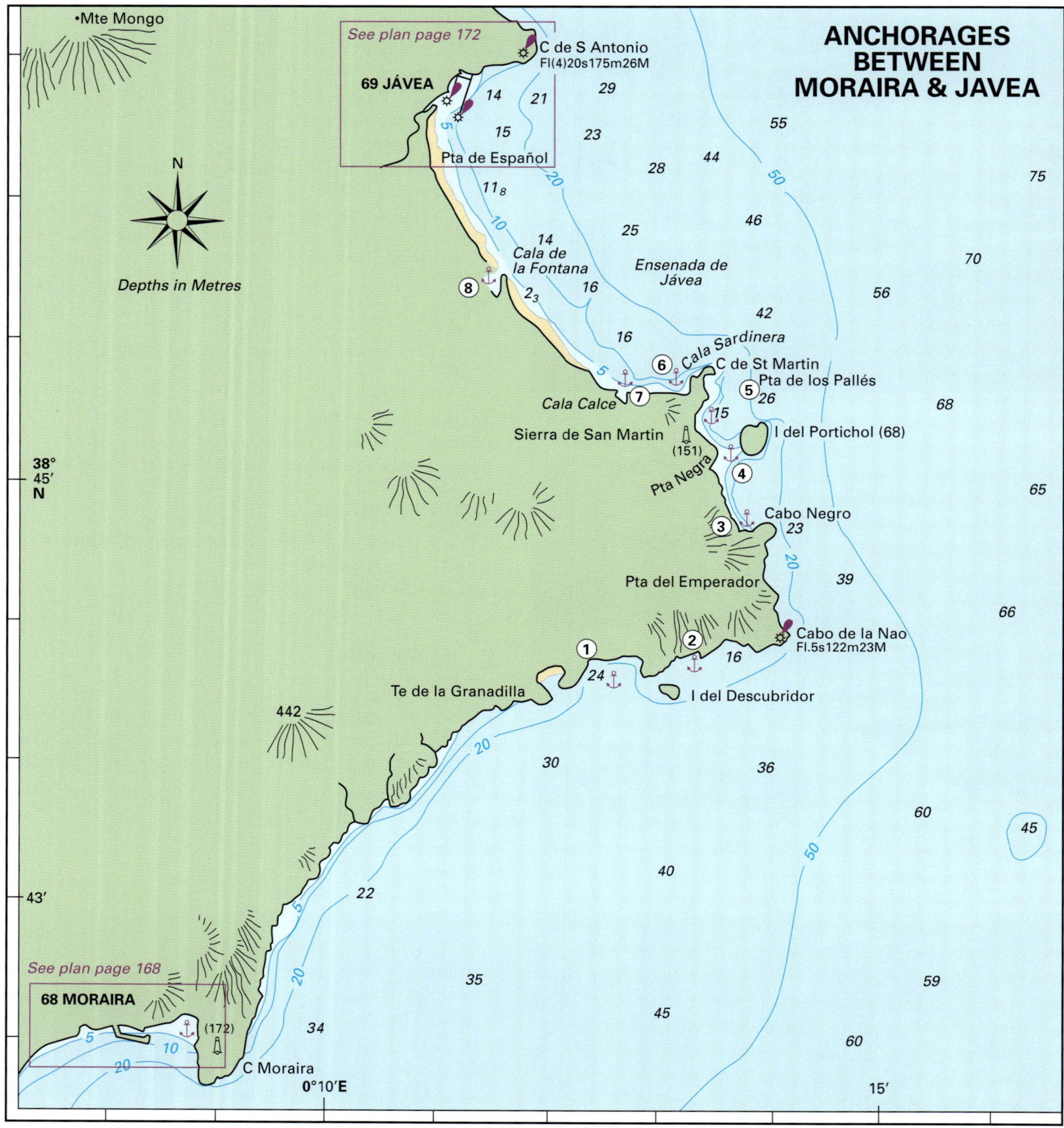

Anchorages between Cabo Moraira and Jávea

There are several interesting anchorages between Moraira and Jávea. Granadilla and Descubridor lie south west of Cabo de la Nao. The others to its north west. They all need to be treated with caution in terms of wind and swell conditions and because of submerged rocks inshore. Note that there is a traffic separation scheme (TSS) some nine miles ESE of Cabo de la Nao which should not seriously affect pleasure craft as they are generally closer to the point but be aware of its presence. In bad weather vessels using the TSS may be directed further inshore – skippers should be aware.

1. ⚓ La Granadilla

38°43′·6N 00°12′E

Anchoring may be restricted by yellow buoys marking the swimming area. Beware submerged rocks near both sides of the entrance.

2. ⚓ Isla del Descubridor

38°43′·5N 00°13′·1E

The island appears as a point. There are many submerged rocks.

La Granadilla

Isla del Descubridor

3. ⚓ Cabo Negro

38°45'·2N 00°13'·6E

The anchorage is to the south of Punta Negra off Playa de Portichol's southern end.

4. ⚓ Isla del Portichol

38°45'·4N 00°13'·9E

Behind the Island but tending to it to stay clear of the foul ground off Punta Negra.

5. ⚓ Cabo de San Martin

38°45'·8N 00°13'·5E

Anchor in the middle of the bay after sounding in to suitable depth. Open between W and NE.

6. ⚓ Cala Sardinera

38°45'·7N 00°13'E

Anchor according to draught as close in as possible.

7. ⚓ Cala Calce

38°46'N 00°12'·5E

A very small cove offering anchorage for small craft in stone 1·5m. Open between N and NE.

8. ⚓ Cala de la Fontana

38°46'·4N 00°11'·5W

A suburb of Jávea. Open between NE and E. The bay is silting up.

Cabo de la Nao *Martin Walker*

Cabo de San Antonio to the E of Jávea – from the S

69. Puerto de Jávea

38°48'·9N 00°11'·2E

Charts
UKHO *1700, 1701* Imray *M12*
SHOM *7669, 7661* Spanish *474, 4741*

Lights

To the southeast
Cabo de la Nao Fl.5s122m23M
White octagonal tower and house 20m 049°-vis-190°
Harbour
Dique head Fl.G.3s11m5M
Green octagonal tower 6m
Inner jetty head Fl(3)G.9s5m3M
Contradique head Fl(2)R.6s9m3M Red tower 6m
To the northeast
Cabo de San Antonio Fl(4)20s175m26M White tower and building 17m

Port communications
Club Náutico de Javea VHF Ch9 ☏ +34 965 79 10 25
info@cnjavea.net
www.cnjavea.net

Harbour charges High

Warning
A traffic Control Zone lies 5M off Cabo de la Nao to the S and is relevant to yachts heading to/from the Baleares.

Shabby chic marina

A large private busy marina with 380 berths up to 22m. From being one of the most pleasant friendly marinas on the coast in recent years, Javea is now crowded and reported as turning yachts away by rudely shouting *marineros*, even in severe weather when there are seemingly many berths vacant.

Approach

From the SE Round Cabo de San Martin which has several off-lying islets and, sometimes, tunny nets. The wide Ensenada de Jávea then opens up. The town stretches south and harbour is in the NW corner under the steep-sided mountain with abandoned windmills on the skyline.

From the NW Round Cabo de San Antonio which is a high, steep-sided, flat-topped promontory with a conspicuous lighthouse and signal station; follow round onto a SW course and the harbour wall will be seen in the closer approach.

From all directions the high pyramid-shaped Montaña Mongo, which stands to the W of the harbour, is very conspicuous.

Anchorage in the approach

Anchoring is prohibited S of the harbour; *see plan*.

Entrance

The breakwaters have stone feet and should be given a good 10m berth.

Berths

Berth stern-to the yacht club quay on the N side of harbour with anchor and trip-line from the bow or

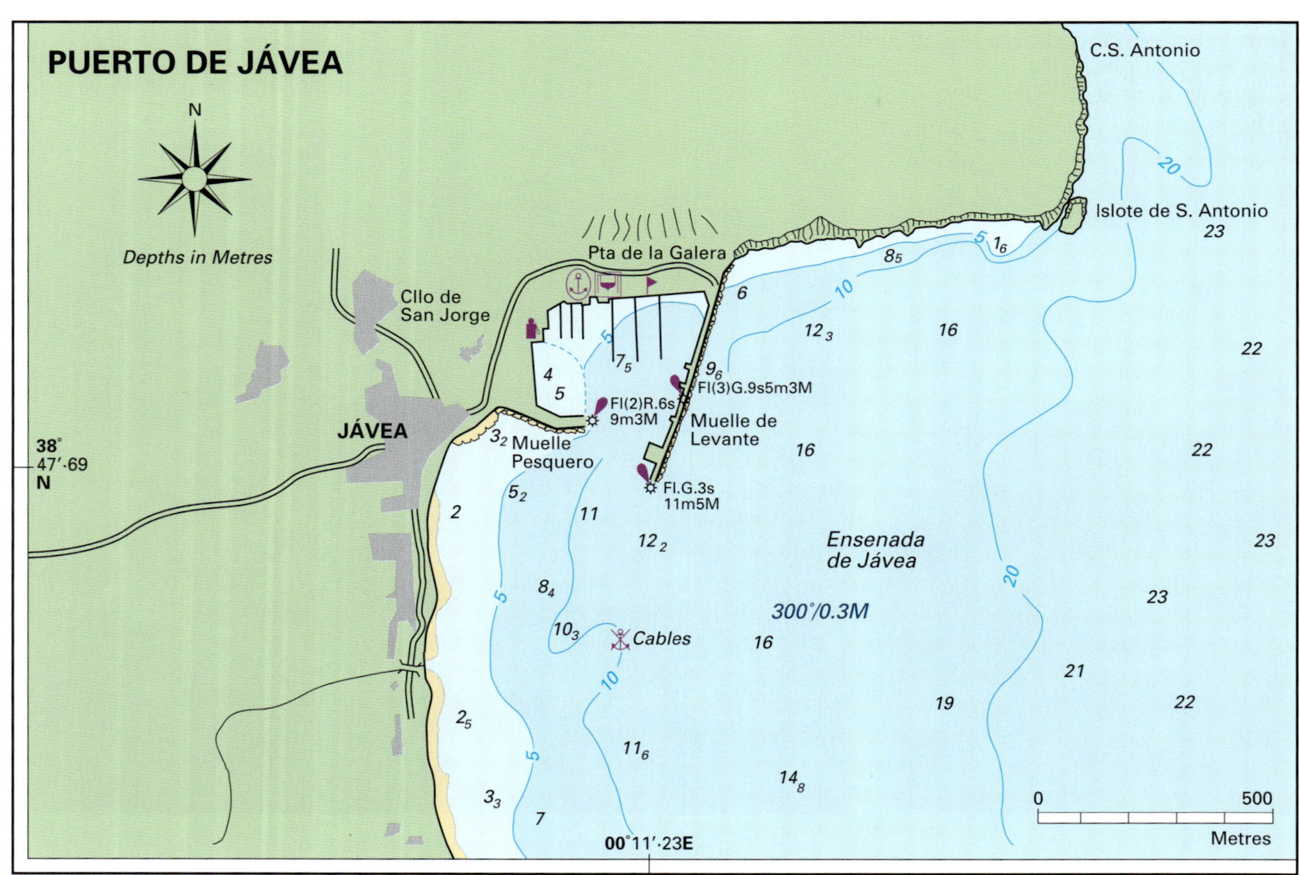

Puerto de Jávea

Yacht Club pontoons from the Muella de Levante
Steve Pickard

in a similar manner to a pontoon using the pick-up buoys. An alternative berth is sometimes available on the inner side of the *dique*, secured stern-to. There are underwater projecting rocky foundations to the *dique*: the three short spurs are in constant use.

Facilities

Maximum length overall: 22m.
Limited hull and engine repairs.
Slipway to the W side of the yacht club.
65-tonne travel-lift and 6-tonne crane.
Water from a hose at the yacht club.
220v AC points at the yacht club.
Ice from the yacht club.
Gasoleo B only.
Club Náutico de Jávea with bar, restaurant, cabins, showers, swimming pool, etc.
Small shops and supermarket near the harbour, large supermarket, most shops, launderette and the market itself are in the town, about a mile away.

Locally

There are many caves in the area, some of which can only be visited by boat. The Gothic church at Jávea and the modern boat-shaped church near the harbour are both worth visiting. The view from the top of Cabo de San Antonio is good. There is a fine sandy beach about a mile south of the marina and a small pebbly one at the root of the Muelle de Levante.

Communications

Buses and railway in town. ✆ Area code 965.
Taxis ✆ +34 965 79 32 24.

Puerto de Jávea entrance looking E *Steve Pickard*

COSTA DEL AZAHAR
N
Depths in Metres
Amposta
Río Ebro
Cabo Tortosa
Fl.WR.6s18m 14-10M
Fl.Y.3s
Fl.Y
Oil wells
92 Sant Carles de la Rápita
Oc(4)R.10s10m11M
91 Puerto de Alcanar
90 Las Cases d'Alcanar
Puerto de los Alfacs
Pta de la Baña
Fl(2)12s27m12M
Costa Dorada
See p.222
89 Vinaròs
Fl.G.5s14m8M
88 Benicarló
87 Peñiscola
Fl(2+1)15s56m23M
CASTELLON DE LA PLANA TO VINARÒS
See p.207
86 Las Fuentes
85 Puerto de Copfre
C. de Oropesa
Fl(3)15s24m21M
84 Castellón de la Plana
Oc(1+2)10s32m14M
83 Islotes Columbretes
Columbrete Grande
Fl(3+1)22s85m21M
I La Ferrera
82 Burriana
Placer de la Barra Alta
Nules
Oc(2)11s38m14M
C Canet
Fl(2)10s33m23M
80 Sagunto
Aero RC
81 Puerto de Siles
79 Pobla Marina
Aero
AlFl.WG
4s65m15M
CABO DE SAN ANTONIO TO ISLOTES COLUMBRETES
See p.176
78 Puerto Saplaya
76 & 77 Puertos de Valencia
Fl.10s35m24M
Golfo de Valencia
75 El Perellónet
74
El Perelló
Cabo Cullera
Fl(3)20s28m19M
73 Cullera
72 Gandía
Fl.G.5s15m7M
71 Puerto de Oliva
70 Denia
C de San Antonio
Fl(4)20s175m26M
69 Jávea
C de la Nao
Fl.5s122m23M
Calpe
Pta Ifach
Fl(4)R.10s8m3M
Costa Blanca
See p.131
SEE RCC ISLAS BALEARES
Islas Baleares
Pta Moscarte
Fl.5s93m18M
I Conejera
Fl(4)20s85m18M
I Bleda Plana
Fl(3)15s28m10M
San Antonio Abad
Isla de Ibiza
Ibiza
Fl.5s11M
Isla Formentera
40′
20′
40°
N
39°
W0°E
1°E

IV. COSTA DEL AZAHAR

Introduction

This 115M section of coast, which stretches from a point just to the N of Cabo de San Antonio to a few miles to the S of the Río Ebro, is called the Costa del Azahar (Orange Blossom Coast) because of the huge areas of orange groves which stretched along the coast of Valencia. Sections of this coast have since been industrialised and both sea and air pollution are such that it might easily be called the Costa Negra (Black Coast) in places! Where industry does not exist the coast is pleasant and to a large extent unspoilt even by tourist development though construction of large apartment blocks continues apace.

From the high cliffs and mountains immediately to the N of Cabo San Antonio, of which Montaña Mongó is a conspicuous feature, the coast becomes low and flat. This whole section of coast has, in general, straight sandy beaches, sometimes with low cliffs or sand dunes behind them and with mountain ranges some distance inland. The only exceptions are near Cabos Cullera, Oropesa and Irta where there are mountainous features on the coast. A number of rivers flow into the sea, most of which do not dry out in summer. The Arabs brought prosperity to the area by building and organising the irrigation system and introducing the orange and lemon trees which they planted in huge orchards but it is perhaps due to the lack of natural harbours the larger towns are of comparatively recent origin.

Visits

Details of interesting places to visit are given in the section dealing with the harbour concerned. There are large numbers of caves, some of which were occupied by prehistoric man, located in the hills which lie inland of the S section of this coast.

The old town of Sagunto is an exceptional place and it should be visited even if not going to the harbour itself; it can easily be reached from Valencia. Onda, where the famous blue *azulejas* tiles are made, also has a ruined castle which can be visited. It lies inland from Castellón de la Plana. For those who like walking, the Monasterio del Desierto de las Palmas which lies behind Benicasim should be visited. Inland from Vinaroz lies the exceptional town of Morella which has remains of Iberian, Celtic, Greek, Carthaginian, Roman and Arab civilisations.

Many other places of interest lie further inland and can be visited by taxi, bus and some by train. Details are best obtained from the local tourist office.

Gales – harbours of refuge

Gales are rare and hardly ever occur in summer. The *levante* from the E, preceded by heavy swell and rain, is possibly the worst. In the event of onshore winds and heavy seas, Valencia, Sagunto and Castellón de la Plana are the safest to enter.

Magnetic Variation

0°31′E (2017) decreasing 11′ annually.

Costa del Azahar planning guide and distances

(See Appendix for waypoint list)

Miles		Harbours, anchorages and headlands
		I. CABO DE SAN ANTONIO TO ISLOTES COLUMBRETES *(page 176)*
		Cabo de San Antonio
	70.	**Puerto de Denia** *(page 177)*
11M	⚓	*Cala Almadraba*
	71.	**Puerto de Oliva** *(page 180)*
5M	**72.**	**Puerto de Gandía** *(page 181)*
10M	⚓	*El Broquil*
		Rio Jucar
	73	**Puerto de Cullera** *(page 184)*
8M	⚓	*S of Cabo Cullera*
	⚓	*Cabo Cullera*
		Cabo Cullera
	⚓	*N of Cabo Cullera*
	74.	**Puerto El Perelló** *(page 188)*
2M	**75.**	**Puerto de Perellónet** *(page 189)*
11M		**Valencia** *(page 190)*
	76.	**Real Club Náutico Valencia** *(page 192)*
4M	**77.**	**Marina Real Juan Carlos I** *(page 193)*
	78.	**Puerto Saplaya** *(page 194)*
5M	**79.**	**Pobla Marina** *(page 197)*
6M	**80.**	**Puerto de Sagunto** *(page 199)*
1·5M		Cabo Canet
	81.	**Puerto de Siles** *(page 200)*
13M	**82.**	**Puerto de Burriana** *(page 202)*
8M	**83.**	**Islotes Columbretes** *(page 205)*
		II. CASTELLON DE LA PLANA TO VINAROS *(page 207)*
9M	**84.**	**Puerto de Castellón de la Plana** *(page 208)*
	⚓	*Olla de Benicasim*
	⚓	*S of Cabo Oropesa*
	85.	**Oropesa de Mar** *(page 210)*
11M		Cabo Oropesa
	86.	**Puerto de las Fuentes** *(page 212)*
8M	**87.**	**Puerto de Peñíscola** *(page 214)*
	⚓	*N of Peninsula de Peñíscola*
4M	**88.**	**Puerto de Benicarló** *(page 216)*
4M	**89.**	**Puerto de Vinarós** *(page 218)*

CABO DE SAN ANTONIO TO ISLOTES COLUMBRETES

Ports

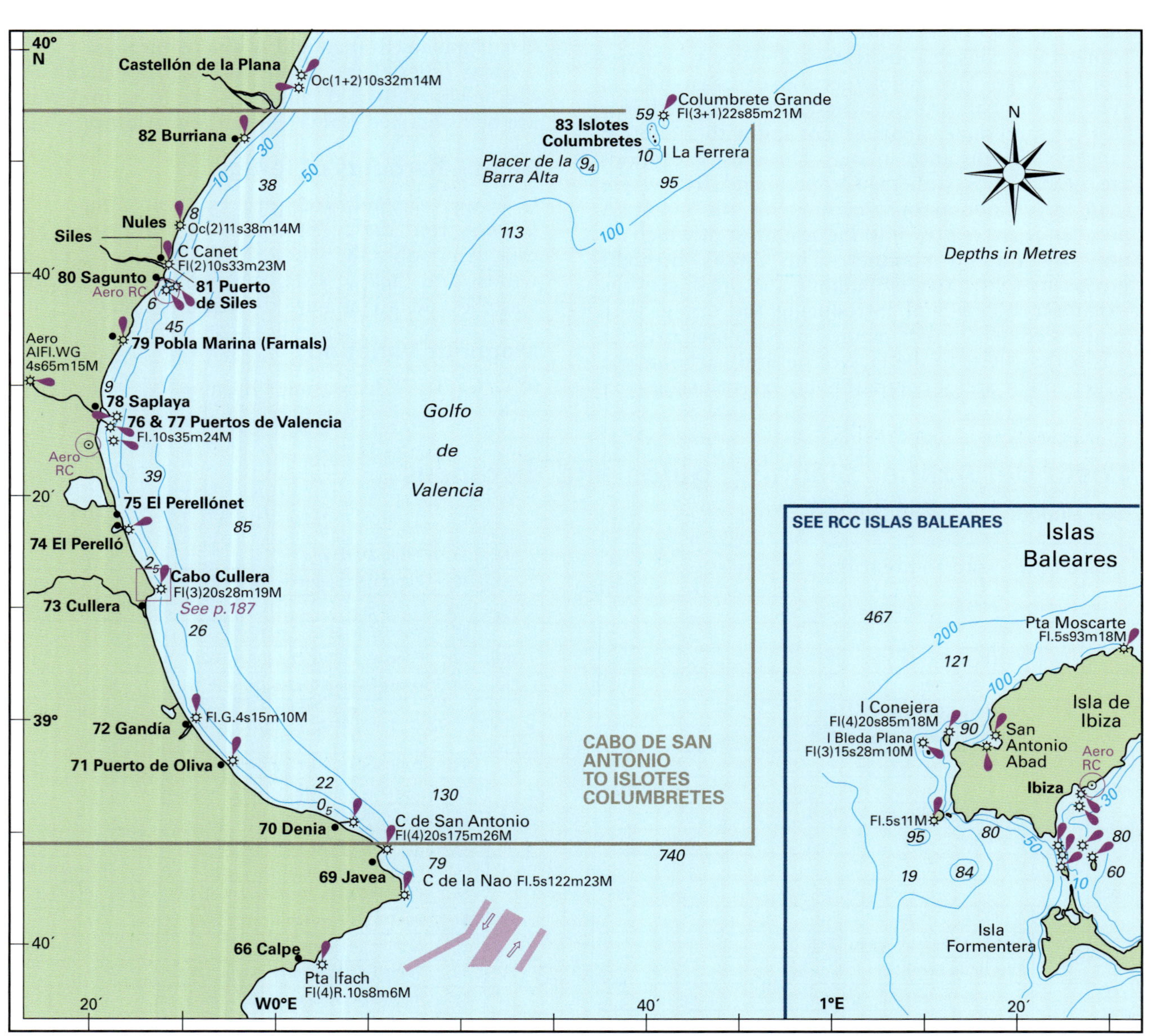

40° N
Castellón de la Plana
Oc(1+2)10s32m14M
Columbrete Grande
Fl(3+1)22s85m21M
59
83 Islotes Columbretes
10
I La Ferrera
Placer de la Barra Alta
95
82 Burriana
30
10
38
50
Nules
Oc(2)11s38m14M
8
Siles
C Canet
Fl(2)10s33m23M
113
100
N
Depths in Metres
40′
80 Sagunto
Aero RC
6
81 Puerto de Siles
45
79 Pobla Marina (Farnals)
Aero
AlFl.WG
4s65m15M
9
78 Saplaya
76 & 77 Puertos de Valencia
Fl.10s35m24M
Aero RC
Golfo de Valencia
39
20′
75 El Perellónet
85
74 El Perelló
Cabo Cullera
Fl(3)20s28m19M
73 Cullera
See p.187
26
39°
72 Gandía
Fl.G.4s15m10M
71 Puerto de Oliva
22
130
70 Denia
C de San Antonio
Fl(4)20s175m26M
CABO DE SAN ANTONIO TO ISLOTES COLUMBRETES
740
79
69 Javea
C de la Nao Fl.5s122m23M
40′
66 Calpe
Pta Ifach
Fl(4)R.10s8m6M
20′
W0°E
40′
SEE RCC ISLAS BALEARES
Islas Baleares
467
200
Pta Moscarte
Fl.5s93m18M
121
100
I Conejera
Fl(4)20s85m18M
I Bleda Plana
Fl(3)15s28m10M
90
San Antonio Abad
Isla de Ibiza
Aero RC
Ibiza
30
Fl.5s11M
95
80
50
80
19
84
10
60
Isla Formentera
1°E
20′

70. Puerto de Dénia

38°50'·88N 00°07'·53E

Charts
UKHO 1515, 1700, 1701 Imray M12
SHOM 7669, 7661 Spanish 474, 4741

Lights

To the southeast

Cabo de San Antonio Fl(4)20s175m26M
White tower and building 17m

Harbour

Dique Norte head Fl(3)G.11s13m5M
Green tower 7m

Dique Sur head Fl(4)R.11s9m3M
Red tower 7m

Dir. Light 229° DFl.WRG.2·5s10m7M
White column, black bands 8m 227°-G-228·5°-W-229·5°-R-231°

To the northwest

Cabo Cullera Fl(3)20s28m19M White tower on house 16m

Note that between **Dique Sur head** and **Dir. Light** there is a line of small red cylindrical buoys which must be left to port on entry

Port communications

Real Club Nautica de Denia VHF Ch 9
☎ 965 78 09 89 / 965 780945
info@cndenia.es
www.cndenia.es

Marina de Denia VHF Ch 9. ☎ 966 42 43 07
mar@marinadedenia.com
www.marinadedenia.com

El Portet de Denia VHF Ch 9 ☎ 966 42 56 75
info@marinaelportetdedenia.es
www.elportetdedenia.es

Harbour charges Medium; high at the club nautíco

Commercial harbour with good marina facilities

A large fishing, ferry, commercial and yacht harbour continually in use since 600BC. It boasts 1,360 berths up to 60m. Excellent departure point for the Baleares Islands.

Several charter companies and diving schools operate from here, so supplies and spares are excellent.

There are four distinct marinas. Clockwise from the entrance they are:

- Marina de Dénia, recently built with all facilities and a friendly staff.
- The Club Nautíco. This is primarily a members only club and is not very welcoming to transit visitors who tend to be put on the uninviting isolated pontoons at the S of the marina.
- There are some small town quay berths in the NW of the harbour reserved for locals.
- Marina Portet is a very recent addition on the NW side of the harbour and completes the picture.

Approach

From the SE Round the high, steep-sided, flat-topped promontory of Cabo de San Antonio and follow the coast keeping a mile offshore to avoid shoals. In the closer approach, Castillo de Dénia will be seen on a small hill behind the harbour and the Dique del Norte. Do not cut the corner but make for a position 200m to NE of the head of this *dique*.

From the NW The low sandy coast is backed by high ranges of mountains. Montaña Mongo which lies behind this harbour, and the vertically faced Cabo de San Antonio which lies beyond it can be seen from afar. In the closer approach the Castillo de Dénia on its small hill and the long Dique del Norte will be seen. Keep at least 1M off the coast owing to shoals and make for a position 200m to NE of the head of Dique del Norte.

The head of the Dique del Norte has been washed away and underwater obstructions may still remain up to 100m to NE of the present visible head.

Anchorage in the approach

Anchor 300m to the E of the head of Dique del Norte in 7m sand.

Entrance

From at least 200m to NE, approach the entrance on a SW course, give the head of Dique del Norte 30m clearance and follow it in at this distance off.

Note If entering at night the leading lines have been replaced with a single directional tri-colour light on the front platform.

An undeveloped corner of Dénia harbour with the entrance to the NE *Steve Pickard*

IV. COSTA DEL AZAHAR

Puerto de Dénia looking N *Marina Dénia*

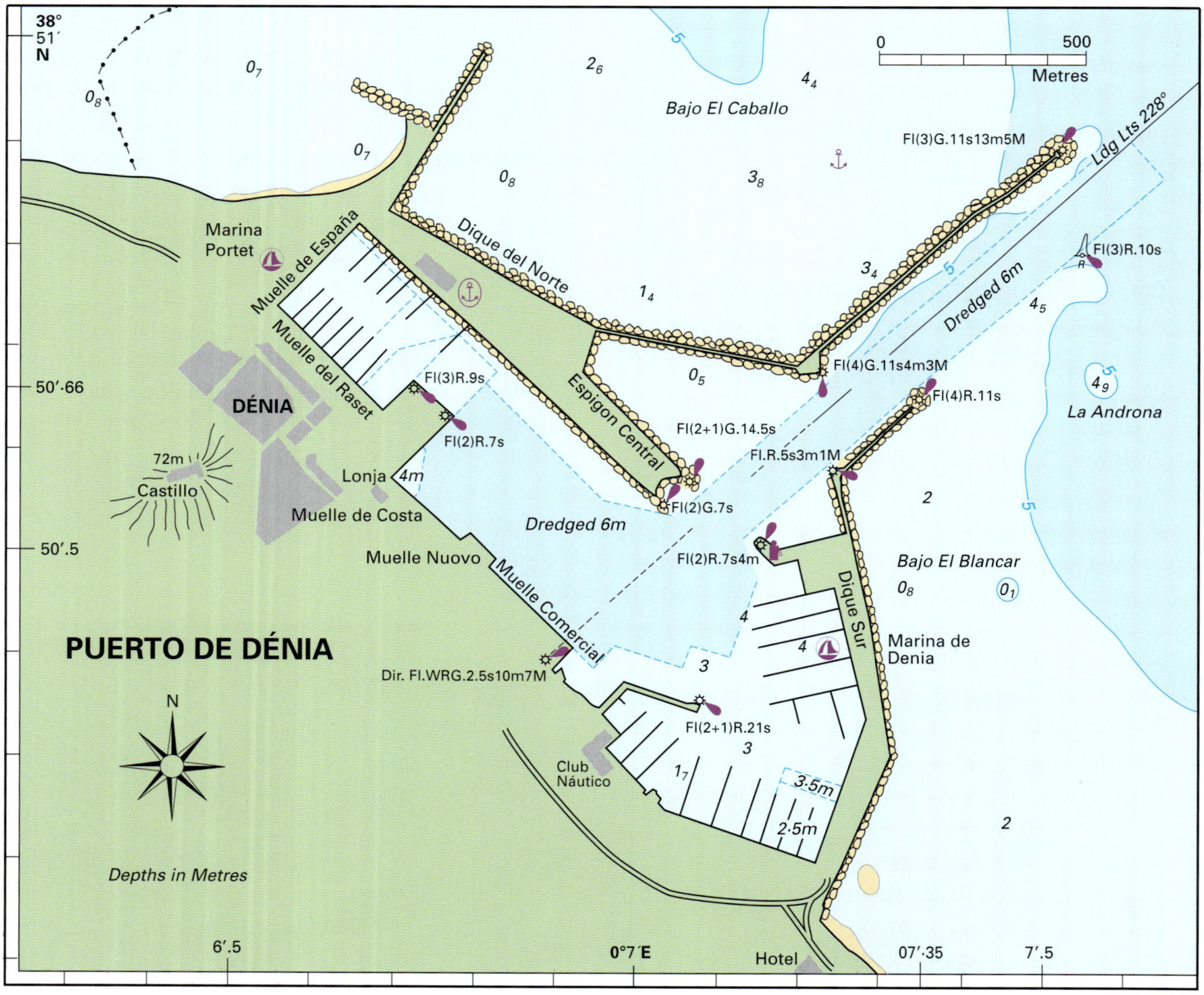

PUERTO DE DÉNIA

38°
51´
N
50´·66
50´·5
6´.5
0°7´E
07´·35
7´.5
0
500
Metres
Depths in Metres
Bajo El Caballo
Marina Portet
Muelle de España
Dique del Norte
Muelle del Raset
DÉNIA
72m
Castillo
Lonja
4m
Muelle de Costa
Muelle Nuovo
Muelle Comercial
Espigon Central
Dredged 6m
Dredged 6m
Ldg Lts 228°
Fl(3)G.11s13m5M
Fl(3)R.10s
Fl(4)G.11s4m3M
Fl(4)R.11s
Fl(3)R.9s
Fl(2)R.7s
Fl(2+1)G.14.5s
Fl.R.5s3m1M
Fl(2)G.7s
Fl(2)R.7s4m
Dir. Fl.WRG.2.5s10m7M
Fl(2+1)R.21s
La Androna
Bajo El Blancar
Dique Sur
Marina de Denia
Club Náutico
3·5m
2·5m
Hotel
N

Roomy Dénia *Steve Pickard*

Berths

Marina de Dénia

Immediately to port on entering (call Marina de Dénia on Ch 9 or phone) which has 400 berths and although further away from the town most provisions are now available on site.

Real Club Náutico

The yacht club is still available for visiting yachts (call Real Club Náutico on Ch 9) but is expensive. There are also hazards. There is no provision for fresh water on the visitors pontoons. Although the taps are standard marina fresh water fittings salt water comes out. Quite a shock if you happen to have filled your tanks and did not taste it first. Fresh water can be purchased at the T end of one specified pontoon. The showers serving the visitors quays are also noticeably salty.

The Municipal Marina

Toward the NW end, is for small craft (<7m) only and it is for private berth holders only.

Marina Portet

424 berths 5 to 30 metres. All services. El Portet has free WiFi and bar with a supermarket 10 minutes' walk away and is much nearer the town than the other two marinas

Facilities

All ship work bar radar.

Two slipways, maximum 100 tonnes.

Cranes up to 12 tonnes. 70-tonne travel lift.

Chandlery behind the shipyard.

Water from taps around the yacht harbour and on the Muelle de Atraque.

Gasoleo A and petrol in the port and, for members only, the *club náutico*.

Ice factory to the E of the Castillo de Dénia. Ice is also available from the yacht club.

The Real Club Náutico de Dénia has a large modern clubhouse with bar, lounge, restaurant, showers and so on. It is responsible for the S corner of the harbour. An introduction may be required.

A good range of shops in the town and an excellent market.

Launderettes in the town.

A yacht repair and servicing agency is available at the Marina de Dénia. Building H-4,
✆ 966 427 470,
info@ mundo-maritimo.com
www.mundo-maritimo.com

Locally

The port of Dénia is known to have been in use since at least 600BC when the Greeks invaded. The canal connecting the port across the shallows to deeper water ensures a calm within the port area whatever the weather – and winds can be very gusty around here. Sandy beaches are on either side of the port. Further yacht facilities are expected to be built as the plan is to make this the largest pleasure port in Europe.

The old town and surrounding area are attractive. A walk up to the castle takes a while but is very rewarding as it reveals spectacular views from the top. Steps right to the top have been well maintained through a wooded area and it is a pleasant walk with shade from the sun for much of the way.

Communications

Bus service. Dénia is one terminus of the coastal narrow gauge rail system. Ferries to Islas Baleares.
✆ Area code 965. Taxi ✆ 965 78 34 98.

⚓ Cala del Almadraba

38°52'N 00°02'E

Anchor of the beach in 3m. Open between NW and E - use only when the wind is offshore

Cala del Almadraba

IV. COSTA DEL AZAHAR

71. Puerto de Oliva

38°55'·98N 0°05'·54W

Charts

UKHO 1701 Imray M13
SHOM 4719 Spanish 834

Lights

Dique de Abrigo 38°56'·1N 0°05'·4W
Fl(2)G.7s7m5M White tower, green top 4m
Contradique Fl(2)R.7s7m3M
White tower, red top 4m

Port communications

Capitanía VHF Ch 9 ✆ 962 850 596
Club náutico ✆ 962 853 423 for bookings
nauticoliva@gmail.com
www.nauticoliva.es

Harbour charges High

Warning

Harbour is subject to silting; small buoys may be placed in the entrance channel to assist pilotage. These will be invisible at night.

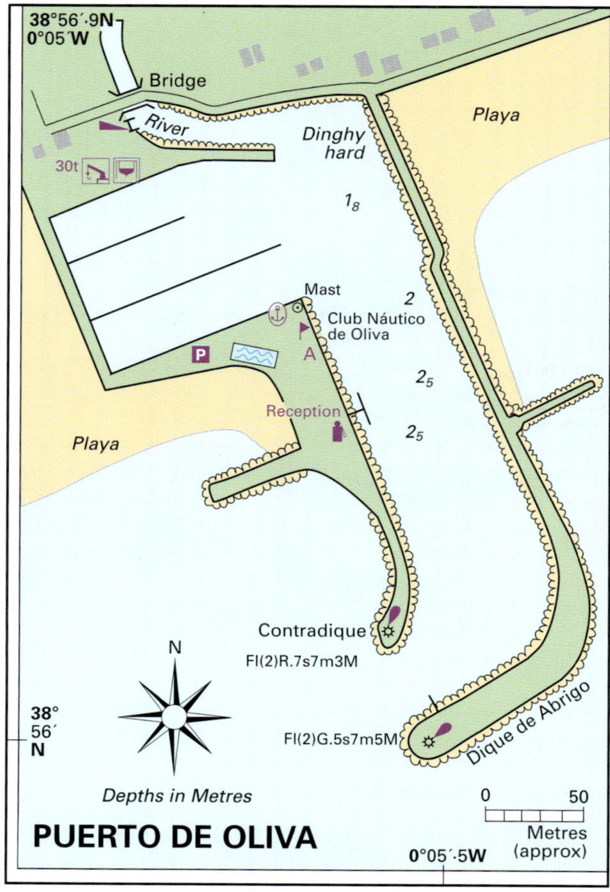

Modern yacht harbour. Beware shoals

This is a modern artificial yacht harbour that has been built out from the coast between Denia (12M) and Gandia (5M) and, as yet, not overlooked by high-rise buildings. The harbour and entrance need frequent dredging of the silt dumped in flash floods from the small river which flows at the head of the harbour. Undredged, the natural level seems to be about 1m. Long sandy beaches on each side of the harbour.

Approach

It is most important to sound carefully and go slowly when entering, leaving or manoeuvring inside this harbour. In bad weather the area of the Algar de la Almadraba 7M to SE should be avoided because of heavy seas.

From the south Round the high, steep-to Cabo San Antonio which is backed by Montaña Mongó (753m). Pass the breakwaters of the Puerto de Denia and keep 4M off the coast to avoid rough seas over the shallow area, Algar de la Almadraba. The breakwaters and conspicuous *club náutico* of this harbour will be seen in the close approach.

Puerto de Oliva

From the north Round Cabo Cullera which is conspicuous and looks like an island in the distance. Follow the coast at 2M passing the breakwaters of the Puerto de Gandia which, with its cranes, and harbour-works, will easily be recognised. The breakwaters and *club náutico* of this harbour are also conspicuous in the close approach from this direction.

Anchorage in the approach

Anchor 200m to NE of the entrance in 10m, sand.

Entrance

Approach the entrance on a SW course. Round the head of the Dique de Abrigo leaving it 15m to starboard. Beware twisty channel and rocky breakwaters - especially at night.

Berths

Secure to a vacant berth beside the *club náutico* and ask at the office for a visitor's berth.

Although there are 300 plus berths here the advertised depth of 2·5m is generally less than that and note the maximum LOA is 15m.

Facilities

Maximum length overall 12m.
Small slipway to SE of the *club náutico* and another at NW corner of the harbour.
5-tonne crane at NW end of the harbour. 30-tonne travel lift.
Water and 220v AC points on quays and pontoons.
Gasoleo A.
Small ice from *club náutico* bar.
Club Náutico de Oliva has bars, lounges, terrace, swimming pool, showers/WC etc.
Basic provisions from shops nearby; more shops in the town of Oliva 1½M inland.

Communications

Bus and rail service from Oliva.

Puerto de Oliva looking N from the *contradique*
Steve Pickard

72. Puerto de Gandía

39°00'N 0°09'W

Charts
UKHO 1515, 1701 — Imray M13
SHOM 7296, 4719 — Spanish 475, 4752

Lights

Dique Norte head
Fl.G.5s15m7M Green triangular tower 12m

Contradique head
Fl.R.5s9m5M Red triangular tower 9m

Muelle Sur head
Fl(2)R.7s5m3M Red column 3m

Port communications
Real Club Náutico de Gandía VHF Ch 9 ✆ 962 841 050
rcng@rcngandia.com
www.rcngandia.com

Harbour charges High

A mainly commercial port

A commercial and fishing port with a large ship-breaking yard. It is easy to approach and enter and offers good protection except in gales from SE. The small, self-contained and welcoming, yacht harbour is on the N side of the harbour. The pleasant town, with the river running through it, lies adjacent to the marina.

In 1485 the Dukedom of the Borgia was founded nearby by the ancestors of the famous Italian family. The harbour is known for the large amount of oranges it exports.

The Palace of the Dukes of Gandía, the Collegiate Church, the Castillo de Bayrén, Cova de Parpalló and, a little distance away the monastery of San Jerónimo de Cotalba, are all worth visiting. There is a long sandy beach to N of the harbour. Local holidays are: St Francis Borgia, 9–10 October and St Joseph, 19 March.

Approach

From the south The coast from Cabo San Antonio (167m, which has a vertical cliff-face and is backed by Montaña Mongó, 753m) becomes low and sandy with ranges of hills in the hinterland. Pass the long breakwater of Puerto de Denia and keep an eye on depths and the chart if you close the shore. A high peak, Montaña Monduber (841m), will be seen to the W of this port, which will be recognised by the houses, cranes and the *diques*.

From the north Having rounded the conspicuous Cabo Cullera, which has the appearance of an offshore island when viewed from afar, the coast becomes low, flat and sandy. Gandia may be seen standing isolated in a flat plain at the foot of a valley, the blocks of flats being conspicuous from this direction. Keep clear of a fish farm some two miles north of the breakwater which has four buoys Fl(3)Y.9s3M with cross topmarks.

IV. COSTA DEL AZAHAR

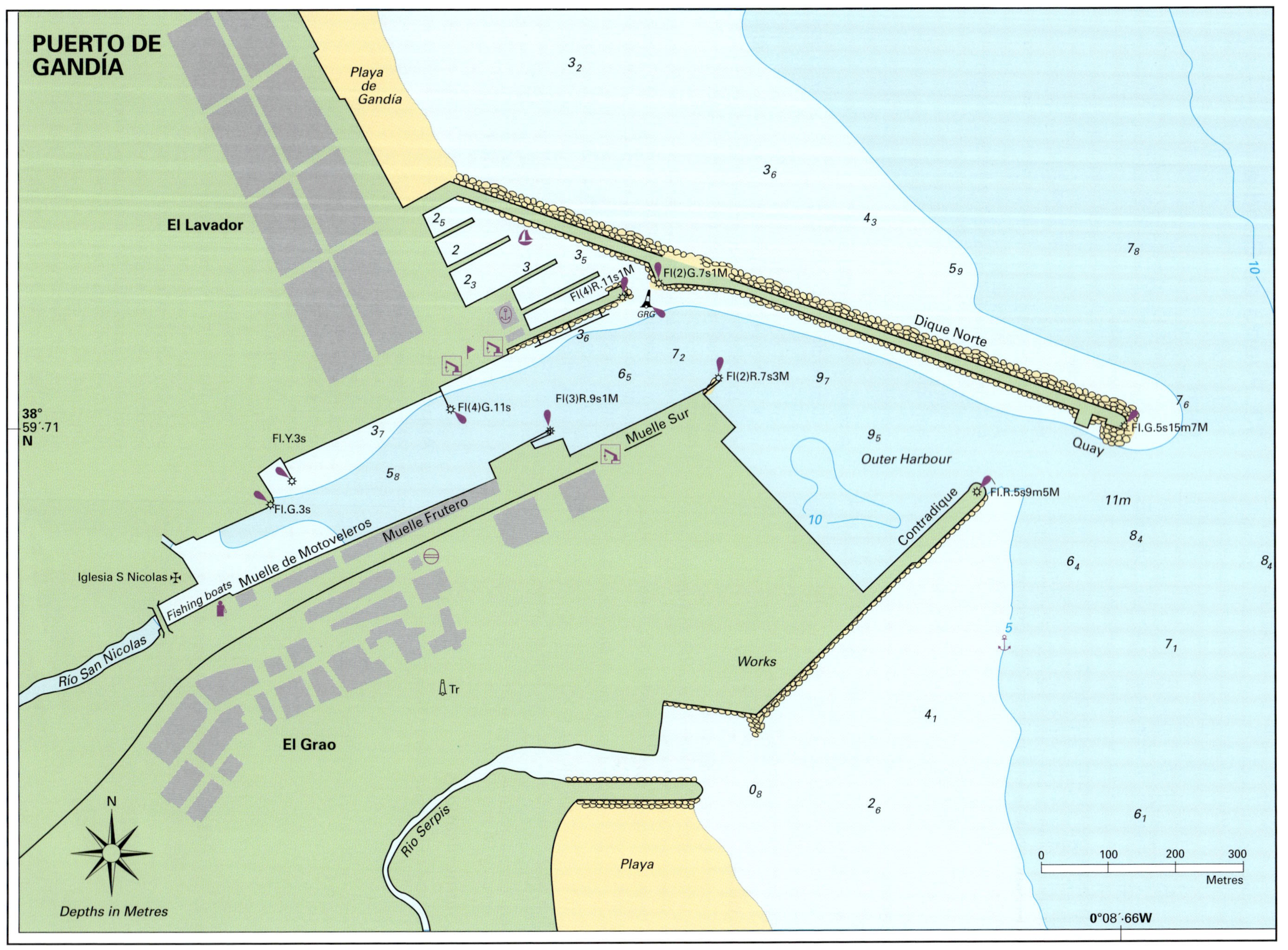
PUERTO DE GANDÍA
El Lavador
Playa de Gandía
Dique Norte
Quay
Contradique
Outer Harbour
Works
Muelle Sur
Muelle Frutero
Muelle de Motoveleros
Fishing boats
Iglesia S Nicolas
Río San Nicolas
Río Serpis
El Grao
Playa
Fl.G.5s15m7M
Fl.R.5s9m5M
Fl(2)G.7s1M
Fl(2)R.7s3M
Fl(4)R.11s1M
Fl(3)R.9s1M
Fl(4)G.11s
Fl.Y.3s
Fl.G.3s
GRG
Tr
11m
38° 59'·71 N
0°08'·66W
0 100 200 300
Metres
N
Depths in Metres

Entrance to Gandía marina looking N *Steve Pickard*

Anchorage in the approach

Anchor 500m to SW of the head of Dique Norte in 7m sand. Sound carefully in the approach due to silting.

Entrance

To the S of the entrance the Río Serpis deposits silt and depths decrease steadily. The harbour and its entrance is periodically dredged accordingly.

Approach Dique Norte on a W course, leaving the Dique Norte 50m to starboard. The narrow entrance is reduced by rod-fishermen operating from the *dique*. Follow Dique Norte at this distance and pass Contradique.

On arrival at the Muelle Sur, the yacht harbour entrance lies NW between two lit pier heads just beyond a building on the Dique Norte. Entering involves an S-bend, first to starboard then to port.

Berths

Ask at the *club náutico*.

Anchorages

Anchoring in the outer harbour is forbidden.

Facilities

Maximum length overall 25m.

70-tonne travel-lift.

10-tonne crane at the *club náutico*. More powerful cranes are available at the Muelle Comercial. Contact *capitán de puerto*.

A small slipway on the N side of the harbour.

Engine repairs, GRP, painting, joinery in the port.

Two small chandlers near the harbour and two others in the town of Gandia.

Water from taps on the quay and pontoons by the *club náutico* and on the Muelle Comercial and pontoons. Check with notices to see if it is considered to be drinkable.

220v AC on pontoons.

Gasoleo A by the yacht club.

Ice from a factory at the N end of the bridge over the Río San Nicolás.

Club Náutico de Gandia has several bars, lounges, terraces, a restaurant, snack bar, showers, swimming pool, etc.

A few shops near the *club náutico*, some more to the W and S of the harbour and very many in the town of Gandia where there is a daily market.

Laundry and launderettes in the town of Gandia.

Communications

Rail and bus services. Taxi ✆ 284 30 30.

⚓ El Broquil

39°07'·5N 00°13'·7W

A river 2M S of Río Júcar accessible by small boats in calm weather without swell. Depth 1-1·5m in the canal which silts. No facilities.

Puerto de Gandía

IV. COSTA DEL AZAHAR

73. Puerto de Cullera

39°09'·07N 0°14'·0W

Charts

UKHO 1701	Imray M13
SHOM 4719	Spanish 834

Lights

Malecón Sur head Fl(4)R.11s10m3M
Red tower on square base 7m

Malecón Norte head Fl(4)G.11s10m5M
Green tower on square base 7m

Note **Malecón Norte head** light is about 20m from head of breakwater and **Malecón Sur head** is 40m from the south head.

To the north

Cabo Cullera 39°11'·1N 0°13'·0W Fl(3)20s28m25M
White conical tower 16m

Beacon

A black post with a black g topmark (5·5m) on the rock Escollo del Moro (0·7m) marks a shallow patch of rocks which is located ¼M to NNE of the entrance.

Port communications

Club Náutico de Cullera VHF Ch 9
✆ 961 721 154
cncullera@cncullera.com
www.cncullera.com

Harbour charges Low

A river harbour

This harbour lies about 1M up the Río Júcar. The approach is easy but the entrance into the river mouth can only be undertaken in good conditions and is not possible in fresh winds between NE and SE. It is reported that depth in the river is maintained at a minimum of 2m. There is very good shelter once inside. The attractive old town which has many shops and good communications is not a great distance from the sailing yacht berths. A huge development consisting of high apartment blocks has been built around the hills to NE of the town to cater for the thousands of holiday-makers. The remains of an old castle and the Ermita de la Virgen del Castillo on the hill nearby should be visited. The fine sandy beaches on either side of the Sierra de Cullera are very crowded in the high season. The Saturday following Easter is a holiday in honour of Nuestra Señora del Castillo. In July and August there is a regatta.

The site has been occupied since the fourth century BC and there are ruins of a city wall dating from this period. Like several places with an isolated mountain and marshy land around, it claims to be the site of Hemeroskopeion, the first Phoenician town in Spain.

Approach

From the south The low, flat, sandy coast is backed by mountain ranges which recede from the coast as one proceeds to the N. The isolated feature, the Sierra de Cullera (222m) which is surrounded by flat lands, appears as an offshore island in the distance.

Fishing port, Cullera *Steve Pickard*

Club Náutico de Cullera *Steve Pickard*

Cullera – limit to masted yachts *Steve Pickard*

In the closer approach the town of Cullera will be seen at the SW foot of this feature. The entrance to the river has two low rocky training walls with some coastal buildings and apartment blocks nearby and an isolated factory chimney which should be approached on a bearing of 280°.

From the north Having passed the very conspicuous harbour walls of Valencia the countryside is low and flat and the coast sandy. There are a number of high-rise buildings in groups along the coast and more

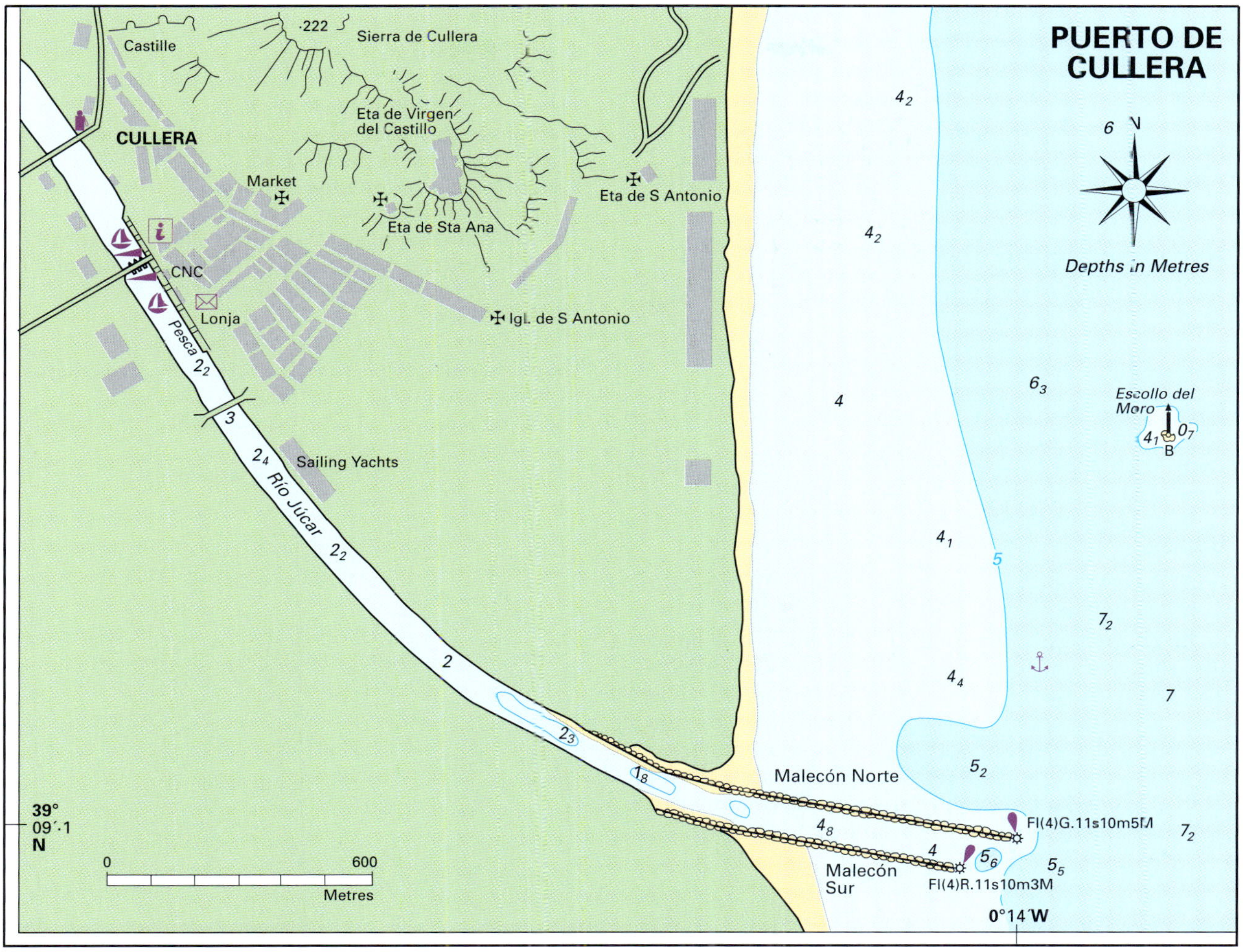

PUERTO DE CULLERA
Depths in Metres
Castille
·222
Sierra de Cullera
CULLERA
Eta de Virgen del Castillo
Market
Eta de S Antonio
Eta de Sta Ana
CNC
Lonja
Igl. de S Antonio
Pesca
Sailing Yachts
Río Júcar
Escollo del Moro
Malecón Norte
Malecón Sur
Fl(4)G.11s10m5M
Fl(4)R.11s10m3M
39° 09´·1 N
0°14´W
0 600 Metres

Río Júcar

under construction. Again the Sierra de Cullera appears as an offshore island in the distance. Round the steep-cliffed Cabo Cullera which has a conspicuous lighthouse and is steep-to, keeping on a S course and changing to SW after 1½M to avoid the Escollo del Moro (0·7m) marked by a black beacon with a ▲ topmark (5·5m). In the closer approach the rocky training walls should be seen.

Anchorage in the approach

Anchor 400m to NE of the entrance in 7m, sand and mud.

Entrance

Line up the two rocky training walls, approach on 280° and enter between. The depths in the river vary with the amount of water flowing and the silt deposited. Anchorage in the river is forbidden.

Berths

Note A new road bridge has been built downstream of the Lonja with a marked air draft of 10m.

Berth alongside the quay on the starboard hand just short of the new road bridge with bow upriver and check with the Club Náutico de Cullera. The club is in the town, starboard hand, just by the second bridge. Yachts without masts may prefer to secure further up channel outside the club. If all berths are taken secure outside a suitable yacht. Note the maximum LOA is 12m in this harbour.

Facilities

A small shipyard above the road bridge can carry out simple repairs. There are several engine mechanics.

15-tonne crane below the lower bridge.

A small slipway by the lower road bridge and another above it, both on the NE bank.

Limited chandlery from the shipyard and from a shop near the *club náutico*.

Taps on pontoons and quays also a water point above the lower road bridge and also near the mouth of the river. Water on quay by the *club náutico* is not drinkable.

220v AC points below the lower road bridge.

Gasoleo A and petrol from garage 300m beyond the upper road bridge on the way to Valencia.

The Club Náutico de Cullera is on the NE bank below the lower road bridge.

A number of shops nearby and a large market.

Launderette in the town.

Puerto de Cullera

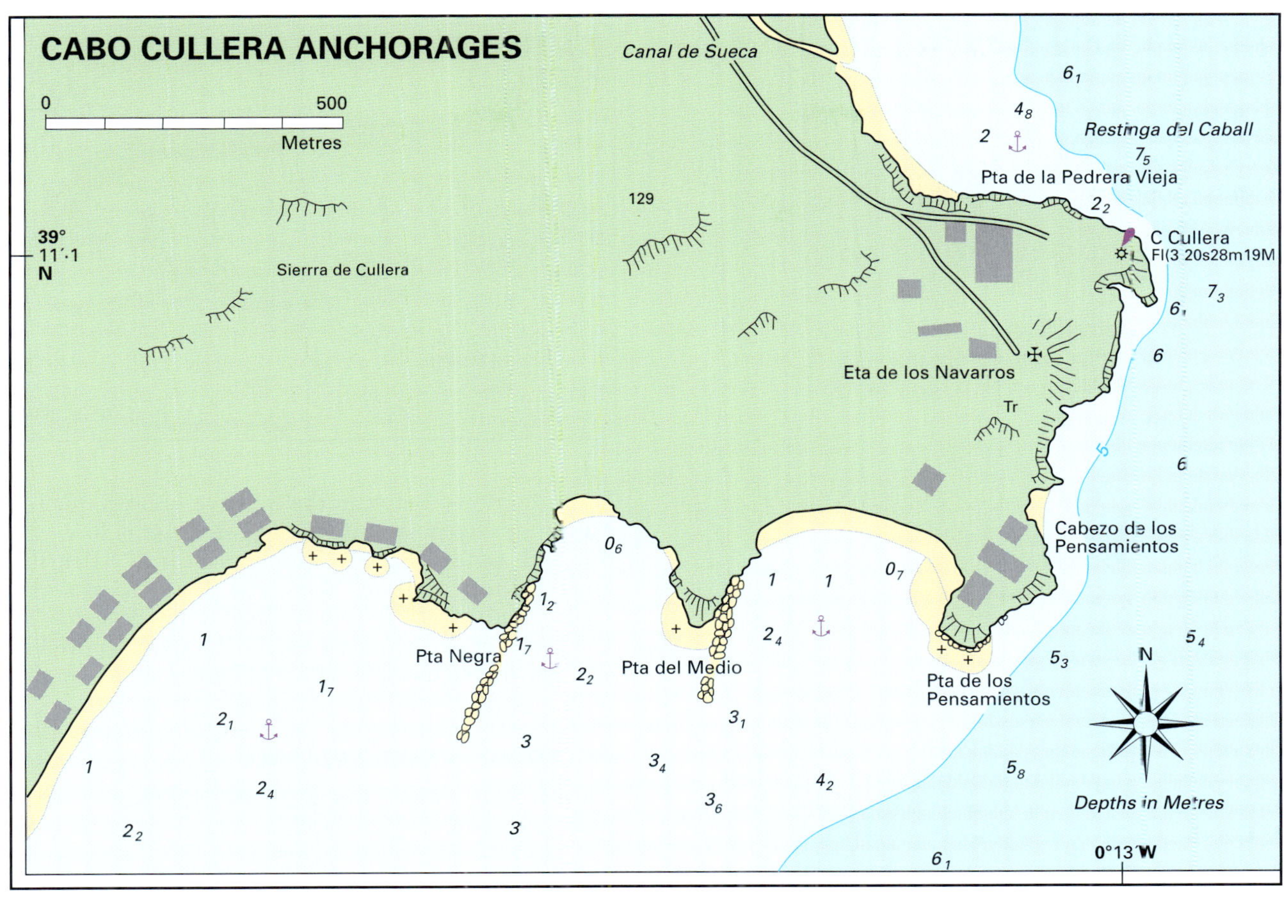

Cabo Cullera anchorages

The rather exposed anchorages on one or other side are usually in a lee but swell from both NE and SE can reach round to the other side of the point.

⚓ S of Cabo Cullera

39°10'·7N 0°13'·3W

Three spacious anchorages in sand S of the range of hills which culminates at Cabo Cullera. They are open to SE with swell from NE but is otherwise well protected.

⚓ N of Cabo Cullera

39°11'·3N 0°13'·1W

A rather exposed anchorage open to NE with swell from NW and SE. Anchor close inshore under the protection of Punta la Pedrera Vieja in 4m sand but sound carefully because the depths can change after strong winds. The road to the conspicuous lighthouse also leads to Cullera (2½M) There are a few shops in the area to S of Cabo Cullera (½M). Good sandy beaches nearby.

Cabo Cullera looking N

74. Puerto El Perelló

39°17'N 0°16'W

Charts

UKHO 1701 Imray M13
SHOM 4719 Spanish 476, 834

Lights

To the south

Cabo Cullera 39°11'·1N 0°13'·0W Fl(3)20s28m19M White conical tower 16m

Harbour

Dique Norte head Fl(3)G.9s8m4M Green tower 3m
Dique Sur head Fl(3)R.11s7m4M Red tower 5m
Interior jetty head Fl(4)R.12s3m1M Post 2m

Port communications

Club Náutico El Perelló VHF Ch 9
✆ 961 770 386
info@cnelperello.com
www.cnelperello.com

Harbour charges Low

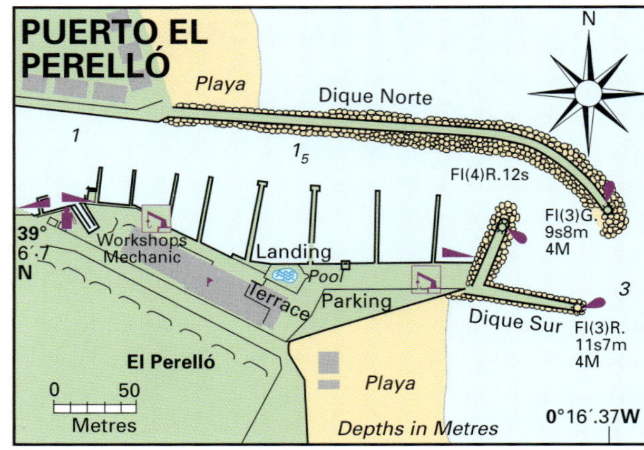

A small river harbour

This artificial harbour has been built in the mouth of the largest river which drains the huge inland lagoon, swamp and rice fields of La Albufera. Approach and entrance is not difficult with offshore winds but it is not advisable with Easterly winds. Space is limited and facilities are confined to everyday requirements.

There are large areas of rice fields inland, frequented by aquatic birds, and sandy beaches on either side of the harbour.

Approach

From the south Cabo Cullera with its lighthouse is unmistakable. The coast N of it is low and flat and has sandy beaches. High-rise apartment blocks are visible either side of this harbour and its breakwaters can be seen when close-to.

From the north Between the massive breakwaters of Puerto de Valencia and Perelló the coast is low and flat with sandy beaches. The houses at El Saler, the large Parador of Luis Vives, the Torre Nueva and some high-rise buildings near the Puerto El Perellónet may be identified. In the close approach the apartment blocks and breakwaters of El Perelló will be seen.

Anchorage in the approach

Anchor ½M to E of the harbour entrance in 10m, mud and sand.

Entrance

The entrance is narrow and shallow and silts easily. After rain the river may be in spate and a strong current will flow through the harbour. With onshore winds seas may break in the entrance. Sound carefully because depths may change with the flow of water and silting.

Approach the entrance on a SW course and leave the head of the Dique Norte 15m to starboard. Follow this *dique* round into the harbour leaving the two heads of the *contradique* 20–30m to port.

Puerto El Perelló

El Perelló's mix of old and new *Steve Pickard*

Berths

Secure to the first pontoon on the port-hand side in a vacant berth and ask at the *club náutico* for a berth. Note maximum LOA is 12m.

Facilities

Maximum length overall 12m.
A 12·5-tonne crane near the second pontoon and a 3-tonne crane near the slipway.
10-tonne slipway to NW of the *club náutico*.
Engine repairs.
Water and 220v AC points on quays and pontoons.
Gasoleo A and petrol.
Small ice from the bar at the *club náutico*.
Club Náutico El Perelló has a restaurant, bar, terrace, lounge, swimming pool, shower/WC and sports room.
Shops in the village can supply everyday requirements.

Communications

Bus service along the coast and rail service from Sollana 7M inland.

Note There are plans to extend this harbour by extending the Dique de Levante and excavating around the southern jetty.

75. Puerto El Perellónet

39°19'N 0°17'W

A small craft harbour with a nasty shallow entrance

A smaller version of Puerto El Perelló and situated 2M to NW of it. Only suitable for small boats and dinghies. The entrance is dangerous with onshore winds and/or swell. Facilities are very limited.

Approach

From the south Cabo Cullera with its lighthouse on top and surrounded by apartment blocks is easily identified. Northwards the low, flat sandy coast is broken by the Puerto El Perelló which has two breakwaters with light towers; Puerto El Perellónet is 2M N.

From the north Puerto de Valencia is easily recognised by its high, long breakwater. A group of apartment blocks and houses at El Salar may be seen as well as a large hotel, the Parador Luis Vives. The lone Torre Nueva lies 2M to NW of this harbour which can be recognised by some apartment blocks and a lone tower-block.

Anchorage in the approach

Anchor in 10m sand ½M to E of the harbour entrance.

Puerto El Perellónet

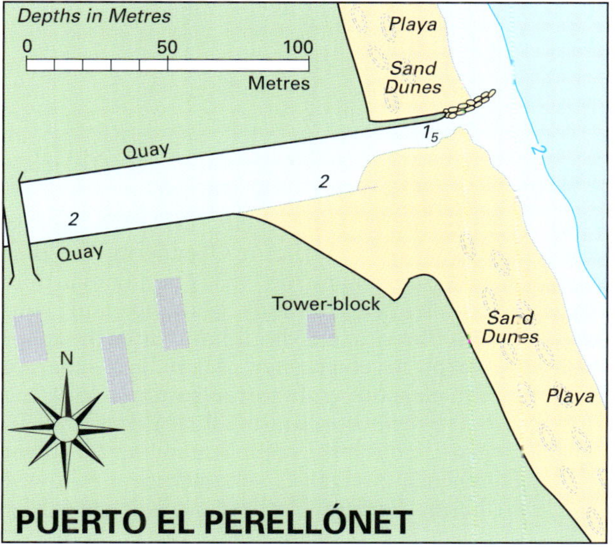

Entrance

The mouth of this harbour is difficult to locate but the apartment blocks and a tower block indicate the area. The sandbanks at the entrance shift from time to time. Approach the entrance on a SW course. There will be a strong current in the river after heavy rain and depths may be changed by this or by strong onshore winds. Sound carefully in the approach and entrance.

Berths

Secure to port-hand side (SW) bows-to quay with anchor from stern, a trip-line is advised. If the current is strong find a vacant place to lie alongside.

Facilities

Water from café/bars.
A limited range of shops 2M to SE at El Perelló.

PUERTOS DE VALENCIA

39°27'N 0°18'W **Commercial harbour**

Charts

UKHO 562, 518, 1701 — Imray M13
SHOM 7276, 4719, 4720 — Spanish 4811, 481A, 476, 481

Lights

Lighthouse Nuevo Dique del Este North End
39°27'·0N 0°18'·1W Fl.10s35m24M
Pyramid stone tower on 8-sided base 22m

Nuevo Dique del Este head Fl.G.5s21m5M
Green tower in white base 9m

Contradique E elbow Fl(2)R.7s21m3M
Red column 9m

Aeropuerto de Manises 39°29'·6N 0°28'·2W Aero
AlFl.WG.4s65m15M On control tower 15m Occasional

Northern Entrance

Buoy Q.R.3M Red cage buoy, red square topmark 2m (synchronised with Dique de Abrigo head)

Dique de Abrigo head Q.R.9m5M Red tower 3m

Contradique head Q.G.6m3M Green post 3m

Port communications

Commercial: Pilots VHF call Ch 16, work Ch 11, 12, 14, 20
See individual harbours for further contact details.

A large port with two yacht marinas

Valencia is the third largest city in Spain with a commensurately large harbour. Occupying the best part of four square miles this vast commercial port complex handles cargo, ship building and ship breaking activities. Yachts should not enter the main harbour except in emergency. There are separate entrances for pleasure craft to the south (Real Club Náutico) and to the north (Marina Real Juan Carlos I).

The city has had a long, complicated and turbulent history commencing with a Greek settlement followed in 139 BC by the Romans. In 75 BC it was sacked by Pompey and subsequently rebuilt as Valentía Edetanorum, a Roman colony. It fell to the Barbarian Goths in 413AD and then to the Moors in 714. In 1012 Valencia became an independent kingdom under several kings including the famous El Cid (Rodrigo Diaz de Rivar) whose widow Ximena was driven out by the Moors; they in turn were driven out by Jaime I in 1238. It remained under the house of Arigón for the next 400 years and prospered. However, in 1808 its people rose up against the French and it suffered much damage in the ensuring wars and in the subsequent rebellions against the Spanish crown. During the Spanish Civil War it was the seat of the Republican Government of Spain. Recently developments, and the arrival of the Americas Cup races, have revitalised the city and its environs.

Local holidays The Fallas de San José from 17–19 March are world famous fiestas which include masses of flowers and huge satirical statues which are burnt. There are fairs and religious processions throughout the year.

Approach

From the south The conspicuous isolated mountainous feature Sierra de Cullera is easily identified. From here the coast is straight, low, flat and sandy and is backed by the inland lake La Albufera and associated marshes. There are several groups of high-rise buildings under construction along this coast but the mass of buildings of Valencia and its industrial fog and smoke can be seen several miles off as can the high Nuevo Dique del Este.

From the north The 1,700m pier extending from beside Puerto de Sagunto is conspicuous. The low sandy coast is lined with houses and inland the valleys slope to the ranges of hills further away. The high Nuevo Dique del Este is conspicuous.

Entrance to Real Club Náutico Valencia from Reception Pontoon, looking N *Peter Taylor*

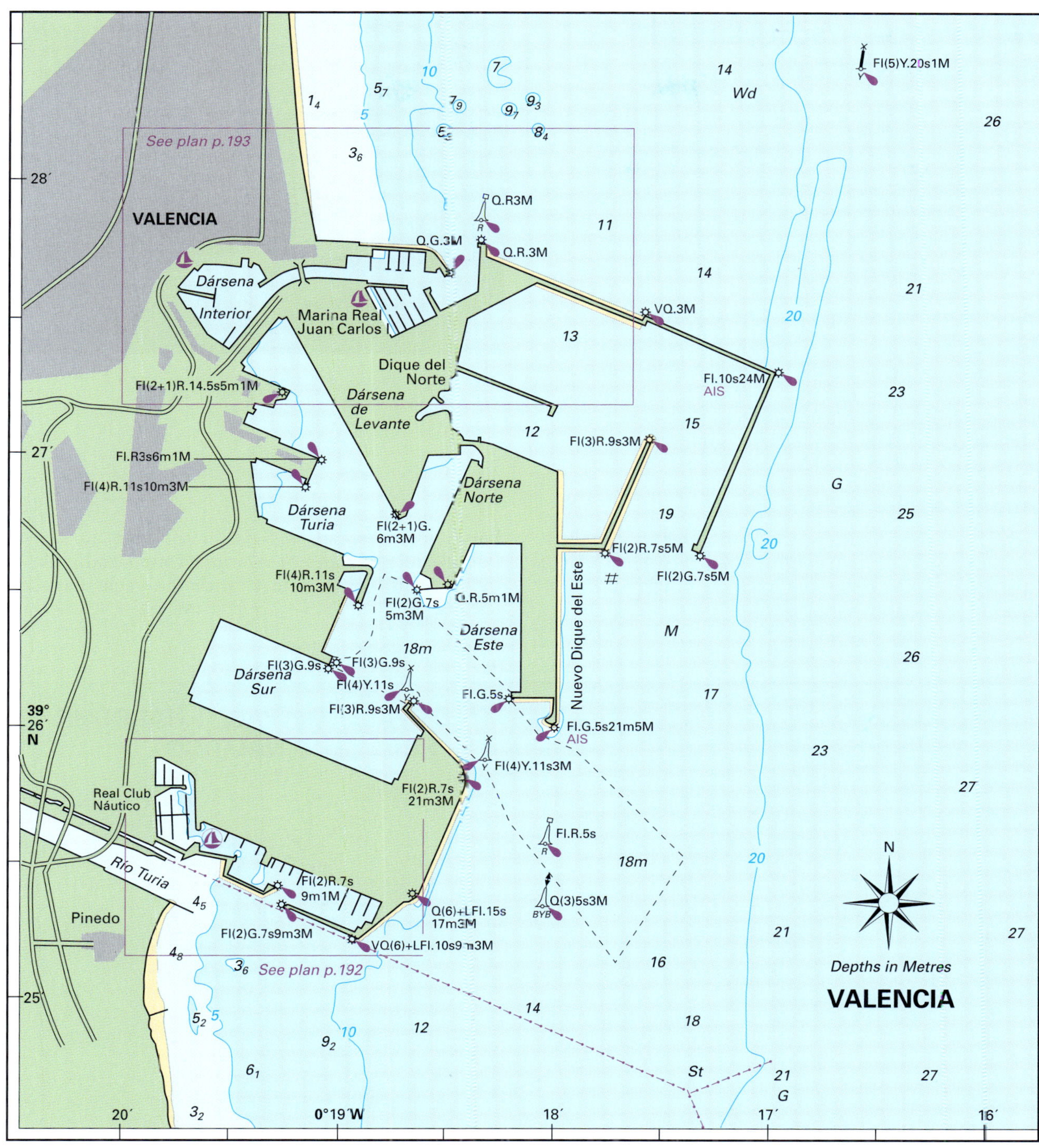

Communications

Rail and bus services. International airport some 5M away. Services by sea to the Islas Baleares and other Mediterranean ports. Taxi ✆ 963 571 313, ✆ 963 479 862 or via the yacht club.

IV. COSTA DEL AZAHAR

76. Valencia –Yacht Harbour Real Club Náutico

39°25'·5N 0°19'4W

Port communications
Yacht Harbour control VHF Ch 9 ✆ 629 60 19 79 or ✆ 963 67 90 11
directives@rcnauticovalencia.com
www.rcnauticovalencia.com

Harbour charges High

Puerto de Valencia (yacht harbour) showing west of entrance only

An older marina with a vast new extension

The Yacht Harbour Real Club Náutico is clear of the noise, dirt and wash of the commercial harbour but is a long way from the city. A major extension the east of the Real Club Náutico mooring area is the Valencia Yacht Base, an area for some 200+ superyachts of up to 120m LOA.

Entrance to the Yacht Harbour

The Real Club Náutico yacht harbour is on the southwest side of the *contradique*; it was greatly extended in 2007. If coming from the north, give the harbour walls and main harbour entrance a good berth (commercial vessels have right of way). Follow the quay and breakwater round and make a 90° turn north when level with the yacht harbour entrance.

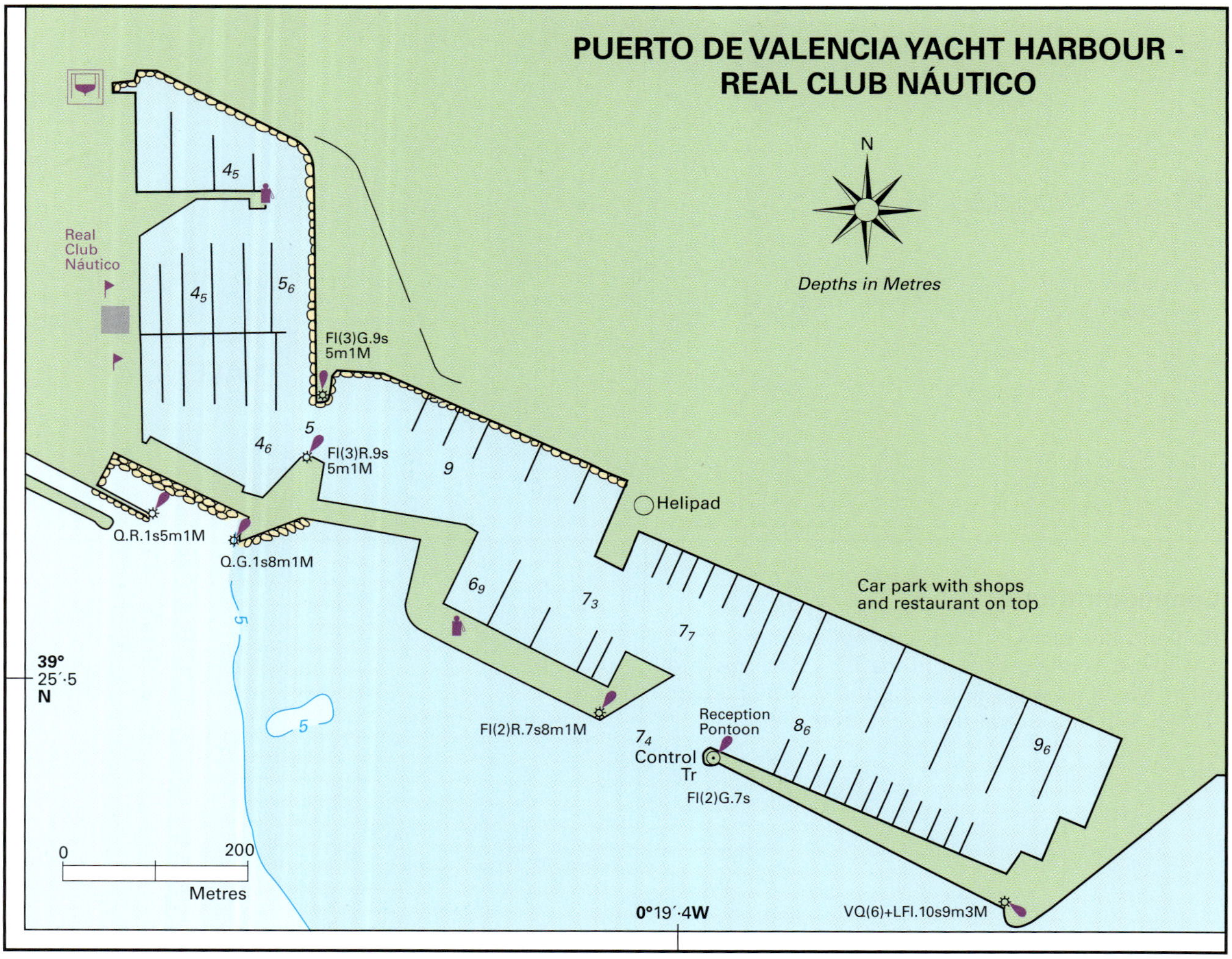

PUERTO DE VALENCIA YACHT HARBOUR - REAL CLUB NÁUTICO

N
Depths in Metres
Real Club Náutico
Fl(3)G.9s 5m1M
Fl(3)R.9s 5m1M
Q.R.1s5m1M
Q.G.1s8m1M
Helipad
Car park with shops and restaurant on top
Fl(2)R.7s8m1M
Reception Pontoon
Control Tr
Fl(2)G.7s
VQ(6)+LFl.10s9m3M
39° 25'·5 N
0°19'·4W
0 200 Metres

Berths

The control tower is at the mole end on the east side of the entrance; visitors' reception pontoon is immediately inside the entrance to starboard. After registration visitors will normally be allocated berthing in the section immediately west of the helipad. Shops, restaurants and showers will be found to the east of the helipad. Visitors are welcome at the Real Club Náutico and may use its facilities.

Facilities

Maximum length overall 120m.

Major repairs can be undertaken in the commercial harbour to both hull and engines. There are also workshops attached to the club.

Hard-standing and a small slipway beside the club náutico.

50-tonne travel-lift.

10-tonne and 3-tonne cranes near the club náutico. Cranes up to 80 tonnes in the commercial harbour.

Some chandlery at the yacht harbour; otherwise a number of shops in Avda de Puerto on the way to the city from the commercial harbour.

Water and 220v AC points on quays and pontoons.

Gasoleo A and petrol.

Ice can be ordered from the club bar, for delivery next day, or from the bar at SW of yacht harbour.

The Real Club Náutico de Valencia is well appointed and has a restaurant and a swimming pool. Ask at the office for use of its facilities.

A number of small provision shops just to W of the commercial port on the way to the city.

77. Valencia – Marina Real Juan Carlos I

39°27'·5N 0°18'·5W

Port communications
Marina Control VHF 67 ✆ 963 812 009
darsenadeportivo@marinarealjuancarlosi.com
www.marinarealjuancarlosi.com

Harbour charges Low

A useful legacy of the Americas Cup

The northern yacht harbour which was built for the 32nd Americas Cup races has been taken over by a consortium and there is now a first class marina complex with all facilities in full operation. The harbour of 'La Marina Real Juan Carlos I' comprises a port which has two docks. The first is the Dársena Exterior consisting of the North Marina and South Marina. Each rests on the two breakwaters that were built to protect the exit channel of the boats of the America's Cup to the race course. The second is the Dársena Interior, so far dedicated to boats over 30m and, of course, the 12m craft of the Cup village.

Entrance and berthing

Approach from the NE and beware of large vessels exiting. The arrivals pontoon is just inside the northern quay beyond the fuel dock. Berthing will normally be in the North Marina with its shoreside facilities. Superyachts go to the main jetty in Dársena

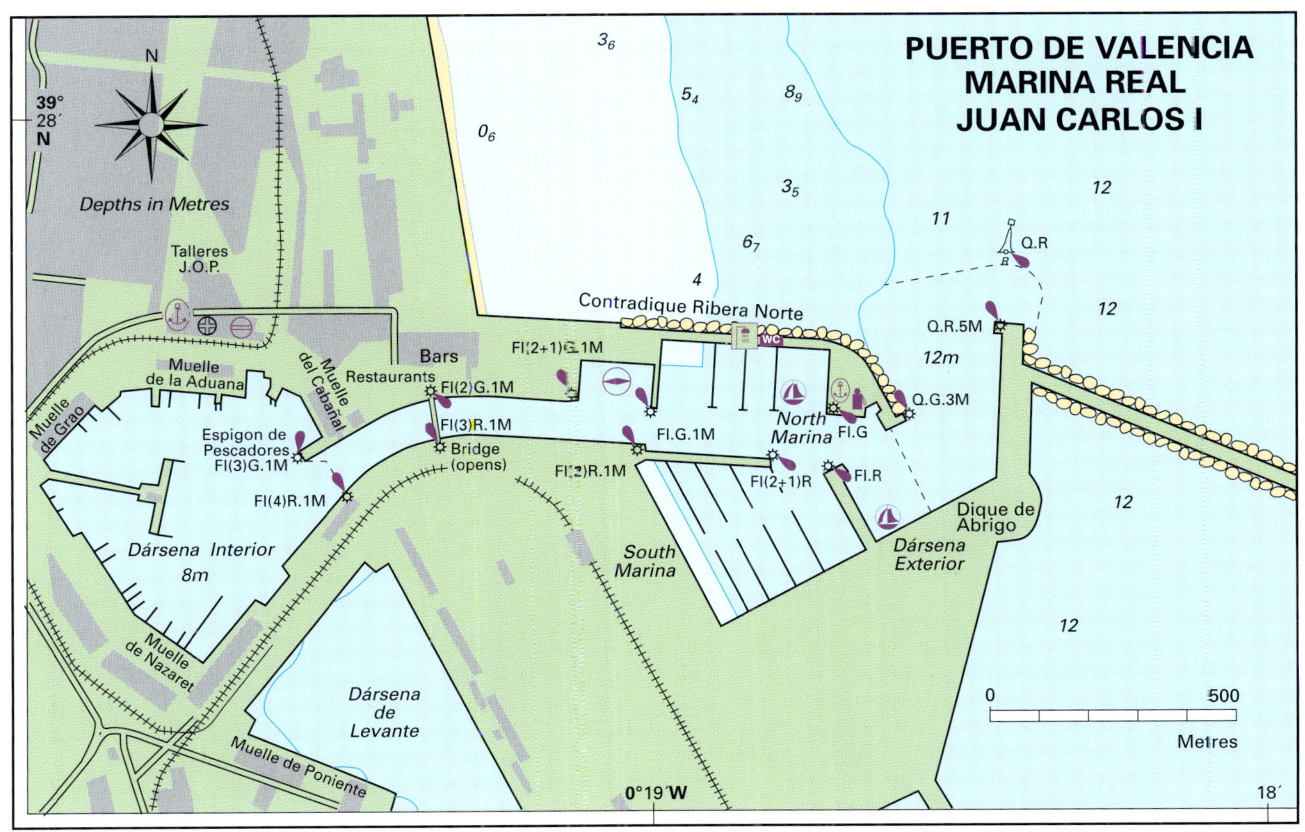

IV. COSTA DEL AZAHAR

Looking east down canal towards Marina Real Juan Carlos I North Marina and entrance *Peter Taylor*

Valencia. Dársena Interior (Marina Real Juan Carlos I) *Peter Taylor*

Interior. Prices are very reasonable throughout the year with electricity and water on pontoons and free WiFi. The disadvantage of the marina is that it is a long way from anywhere. There is a tram station connecting to the metro about 10 minutes' walk away. The nearest supermarket is 10 minutes by bicycle, but with bicycles it is easy to get to the centre of town along flat cycle tracks in under 30 minutes.

Facilities

800+ berths
24hr surveillance
Maximum length overall 150m.
Major repairs can be undertaken in the commercial harbour to both hull and engines.
Some chandlery
Water and 220v AC points on pontoons.
Gasoleo A and petrol. (7 days a week. Open 0900–2100)

78. Puerto Saplaya (Puerto de Alboraya)

39°31'N 0°19'W

Charts

UKHO	518, 1701.
Imray	M13
SHOM	7276, 4719, 4720
Spanish	4811, 481A, 476, 481, 835

Lights

Dique Sur head Fl(3)R.9s8m4M
White tower, red bands 5m

Dique Nordeste head 39°30'·7N 0°19'·0W Fl(3)G.9s9m4M
Green tower 5m

Buoy 39°32'·8N 0°16'·9W Fl(2)10s3m3M – isolated danger

Port communications

Club náutico VHF Ch 9. 963 55 00 33
cnps@xpress.es
www.xpress.es/cnportsaplaya/club.htm

A mini Venice in a modern marina development

This is an artificial marina with blocks of apartments and houses lining a series of waterways. A number of berths are reserved for visitors and is probably more convenient for Valencia than the yacht harbour there. It has good protection and the usual facilities. The harbour mouth tends to silt up and has to be dredged frequently. With strong winds and swell from N through SE entry could be dangerous. Vast sandy beaches on both sides of the harbour.

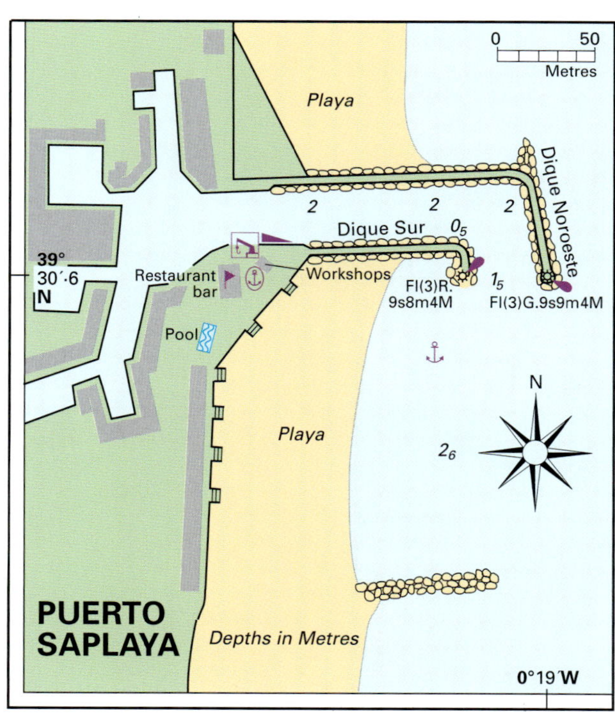

Puerto Saplaya

Approach

From the south Puerto Saplaya is three miles north of the huge harbour breakwaters protecting Valencia. The group of high blocks of flats located behind Puerto Saplaya will be seen from just past Valencia and, nearer in, two rocky groynes will be seen. The breakwaters at the entrance to Puerto Saplaya are low and their heads have light towers.

From the north Puerto de Sagunto is unmistakable due to the 1,700m-long jetty extending from beside the harbour. The breakwaters and high-rise buildings of Puerto de Farnals are also very conspicuous. In the closer approach the high block of flats and the breakwaters of Puerto Saplaya are easily recognised.

Anchorage in the approach

Possible anchorage in 2m S of the entrance to the harbour.

Entrance

Approach the harbour entrance at slow speed heading NW. Sound continuously as the entrance can silt up. Keep clear of the head of Dique Sur where there are shallows and enter leaving Dique Nordeste 15m to starboard. Follow this *dique* at 15–20m around and into the harbour.

Berths

Secure alongside quay on the port-hand side near the crane and ask at the *club náutico*. Visitors to 12m welcome.

Puerto Saplaya from the E

Puerto Saplaya looking east along Dique Sur towards the entrance. Note the small dredger *Steve Pickard*

Port Saplaya *capitanía* *Peter Taylor*

Facilities

Maximum length overall 12m.
Two slipways near root of Dique Nordeste.
6-tonne crane near club naútico workshop area.
A mechanic at the workshop near the club náutico.
Water and 220v AC on the quays.
No fuel.
Small ice from the bar of the club náutico.
Club Náutico de Saplaya is at the root of the Dique Nordeste. It has a lounge, restaurant, bar, terrace, swimming pool etc.
Several shops and a small supermarket.

Communications

Buses and rail services to Valencia and elsewhere.

Puerto Saplaya *Steve Pickard*

79. Pobla Marina (Puerto de Farnals)

39°34'N 0°17'W

Charts

UKHO 518, 1701	Imray M13
SHOM 7276, 4720	Spanish 481A, 481, 835

Lights

Dique de Levante head Fl(2)G.5s9m5M Green tower 5m

Contradique S head Fl(2)R.5s8m3M Red tower 5m

Dique Sur head Fl(3)R.9s5m2M Red post 2m

Port communications

Marina VHF Ch 9, 04, 27 ✆ 902 500 442
info@poblamarina.es
www.poblamarina.es

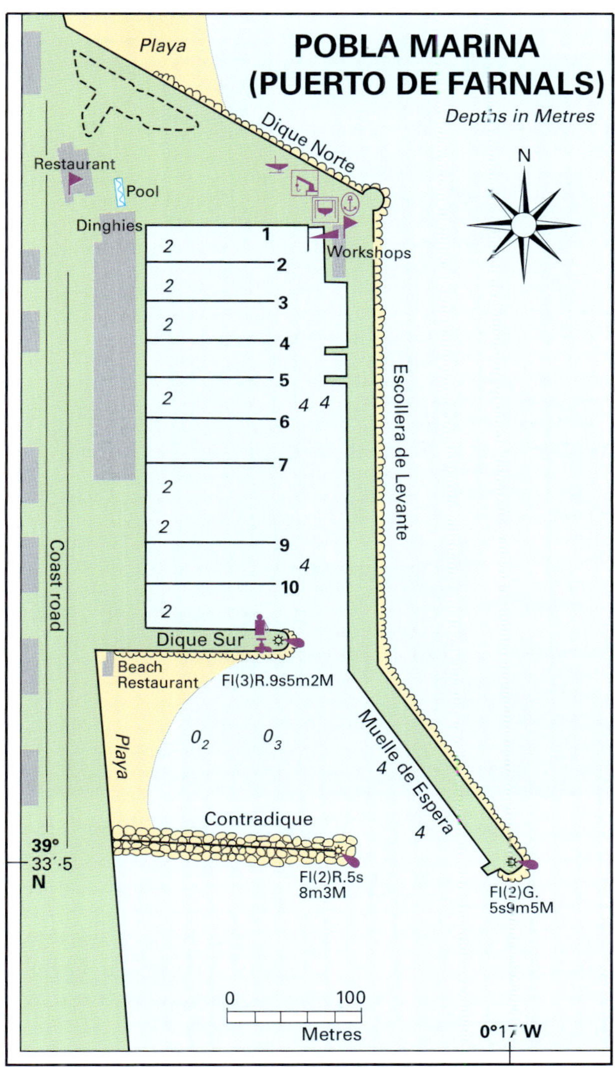

A large marina with plans for major extension

An 835 berth marina built in front of a mass of high-rise buildings on a long stretch of sandy coast. The entrance silts and would be difficult or dangerous in strong E to S winds and swell. There is no club house but the club maintains an office. Large sandy beaches on each side of the harbour.

The Monastery of St Mary at El Puig lies about 2M inland. It was founded in the 12th century and remodelled in the 18th. It has a 6th-century Byzantine statue of St Mary.

Approach

From the south The huge outer breakwaters of Puerto de Valencia are conspicuous and easily recognised. 3M further N the low breakwaters of Puerto Saplaya which is backed by large apartment

Pobla Marina from the N *Peter Taylor*

Pobla Marina (Puerto de Farnals) from the Dique Sur *Steve Pickard*

buildings should be identified. The breakwaters and blocks of high-rise buildings of Puerto de Farnals can be seen in the close approach with a red latticework tower near the entrance.

From the north The coast from Castellón de la Plana is low and flat with sandy beaches. The harbours of Burriana and Sagunto will be recognised by the industrial development behind them. The steelworks at Sagunto are particularly noticeable because of the smoke. The group of high-rise apartment blocks behind the breakwater of Puerto de Farnals will be seen in the closer approach.

Anchorage in the approach

Anchor as close to the Escollera de Levante as draught allows.

Entrance

The harbour mouth is subject to silting and though frequently dredged, depths are variable. Approach the head of the Escollera de Levante at slow speed, sounding. Keep 25m from the Muelle and do not veer to port into the shallow area off the beach.

Berths

On passing the Dique Sur turn to port and moor in the waiting berth (W of the fuel berth) while sorting out a berth with the *capitanía*. Max draft is 2·7m.

Facilities

Maximum length overall 18m.
Boat yard: hull and engine repairs.
80-tonne travel-hoist.
3-tonne crane.
A large 7,000m^2 hard-standing for yachts.
Slipways at entrance to the harbour.
Chandlery from AZA workshop in NE corner of the harbour.
Taps on quays and pontoons but drinking water by the pumps on Dique Sur.
220v AC points on quays and pontoons.
Gasoleo A and petrol.
Shops and supermarkets behind the harbour, more in Farnals 2M inland.

Communications

Bus and rail services (the station is 2M away).
Taxi ✆ 961 470 434.

80. Puerto de Sagunto

39°39'N 0°12'W

Charts

UKHO 1515, 1701 Imray M13
SHOM 7296, 4720 Spanish 4812, 481, 482

Lights

Dique de Abrigo head
Fl.G.5s20m5M Green & white tower 5m

Contradique S corner UQ(6)10s17m3M
BYB tower 4m

Contradique E corner Fl.R.5s17m3M Red tower 4m

Contradique head Fl(2)R.7s3M Red tower 5m

Dique de Abrigo spur head Fl(2)G.7s7m3M
Green tower 4m

To the north

Pantalan Sierra Menera Q(3)10s12m5M
Card E tower 6m

Cabo Canet 39°40'·5N 0°12'·5W Fl(2)10s33m20M
Brick tower and house 30m

Port communications

Capitanía VHF Ch 12, 16.
✆ 963 233 272

An artificial commercial harbour

An artificial harbour built to serve an industrial and commercial complex capable of handling vessels up to 90,000 tons. There is a small section of the harbour set aside for fishing boats. Approach and entrance are easy but the harbour is open to S. It is not a place for yachtsmen to call except possibly in an emergency. Siles is one mile north if possible. If berthed here a visit might be made to the very old town of Sagunto, 2M away to see the many ruins and remains from the past including a castle and a Roman amphitheatre.

Approach

From the south The coast of Valencia is low, flat and sandy, lined with blocks of flats and villas. Sagunto can be spotted by the Pantalán de Sierra Menera stretching 1,700m out to sea. Closer in, the entrance walls will be seen.

From the north South of Burriana, 15M up the coast and easy to miss, the coast is flat and sandy with groups and blocks of buildings. The Pantalán de Sierra Menera makes it easy to locate Sagunto but stand at least two miles offshore until it has been rounded.

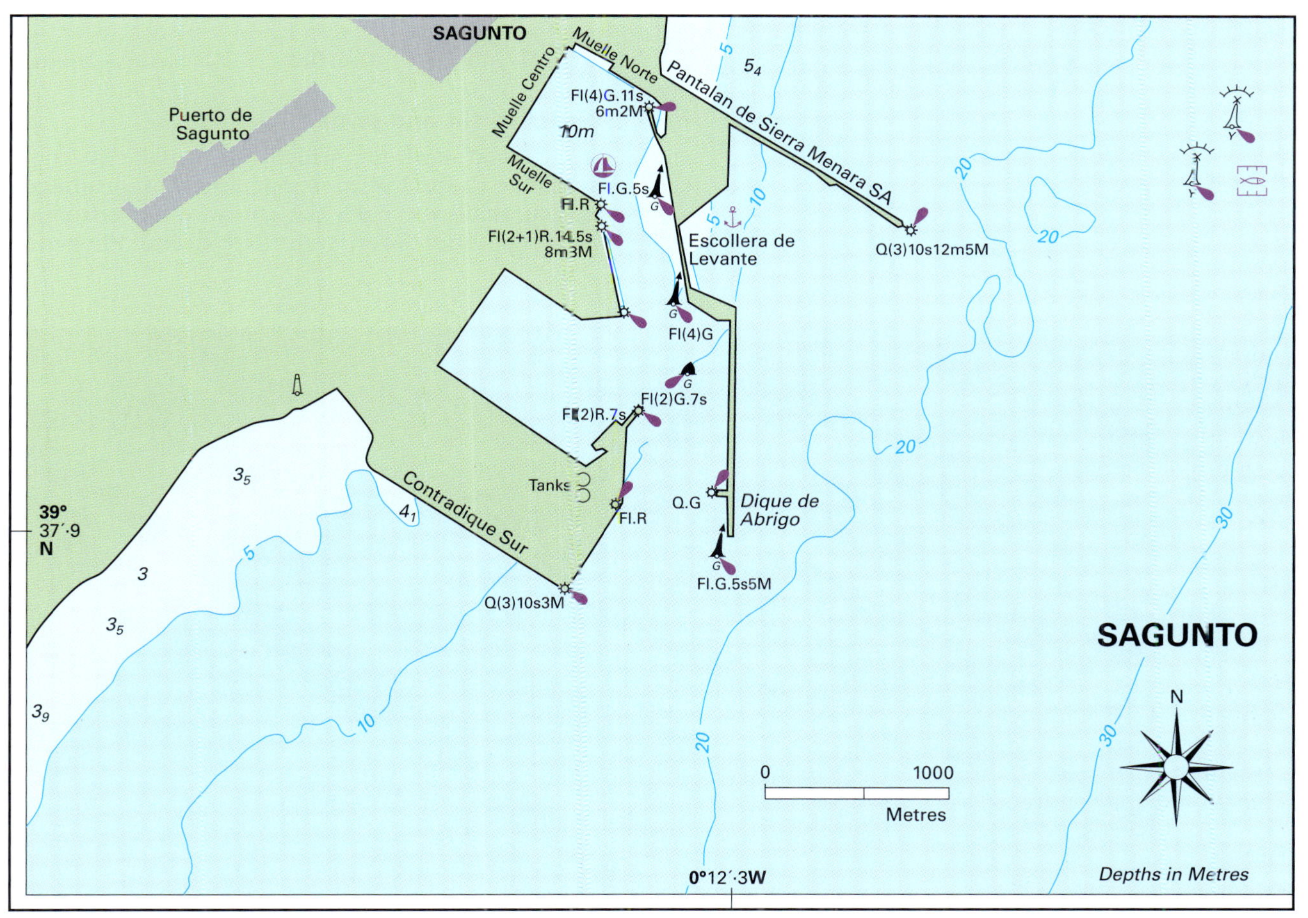

Anchorage in the approach

Anchor off the Escollera de Levante in 7m, sand. Depths in and adjacent to this harbour may be less than charted.

Entrance

Approach the entrance on a N course, passing between a red and a green buoy and then between the head of the Escollera de Poniente (Muelle Sur) and another G buoy.

There may be two port-hand buoys laid south of the contradique indicating the entrance channel. There may also be a line of small orange buoys laid between these two buoys and the end of the contradique.

Berths

It is usually possible to find a berth alongside or stern-to a rather dirty quay in the NE corner of the harbour in the small fishing boat harbour.

Facilities

Water points on Escollera de Levante and at the *lonja*.

There are some shops and a market in the village to the N of the harbour and a fair selection of shops in Sagunto.

Communications

Bus service to Sagunto where there is a rail service.

81. Puerto de Siles (Canet de Berenguer)

39°40'N 0°12'W

Charts

UKHO 1701 Imray M13
SHOM 4720 Spanish 4812, 481, 482

Lights

Approach

Cabo Canet 39°40'·5N 0°12'·4W Fl(2)10s33m20M
Brick tower with house 30m

Harbour

Dique de Levante head Fl(3)G.9s7m5M
Green tower on white base 3m

Breakwater S head Fl(3)R.9s5m4M
Red column 3m

Contradique Fl(4)R.11s4m1M
Red tower on white base 2m

To the north

Nules 39°49'·5N 0°06'·5W Oc(2)11s38m14/12M
Brown square masonry tower 36m

Air radiobeacon

Sagunto/Cabo Canet c/s SGO (···/—·/——) 356kHz 50M
39°40'·52N 0°12'·4W

Port communications

Club Marítimo de Regates de Sagunto VHF Ch 9
✆ 962 608 132
info@nauticcanet.com
www.nauticcanet.com

Subject to silt and swell

An artificial harbour which may make a good alternative to the Puerto de Sagunto. Disadvantages are that shallows make the entrance dangerous in strong winds or swell from N-NE and the outer

Puerto de Siles

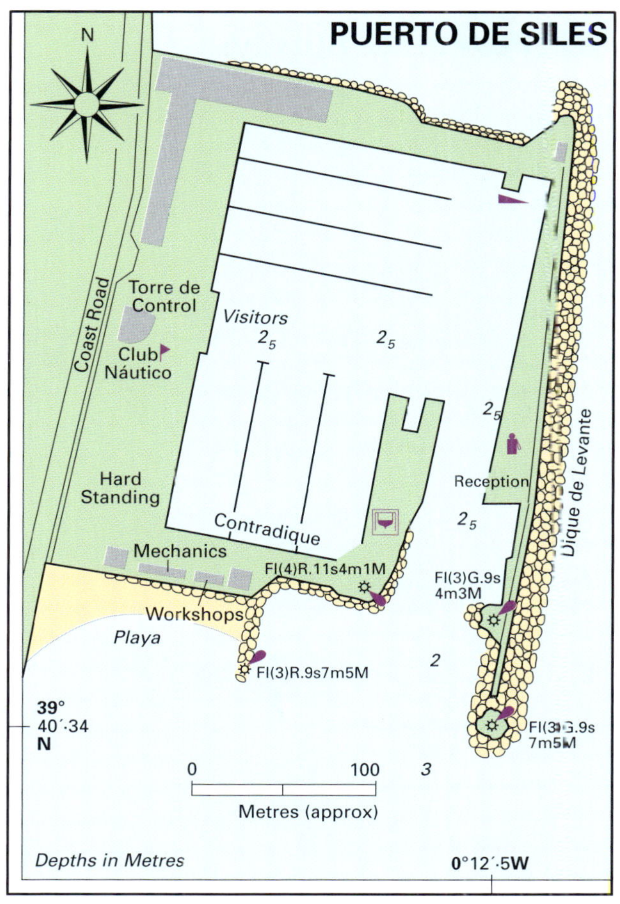

berths are subject to swell in winds between E and S. The Río Palencia debouches across the harbour entrance and, like other harbours on this coast, it silts up and is dredged periodically. There are sandy beaches to N and S of the harbour.

The old town of Sagunto is worth visiting to see the old walls, castle and arena. The original town was Iberian, later Greek and then Roman. It put up a famous nine months' defence against Hannibal and his Carthaginian armies. When Rome abandoned them to their fate the citizens built a huge fire and the women, children, sick and old threw themselves into it. The able-bodied men went off to die in the last battle. The result was the complete destruction of the town and its fortifications so that five years later, when the Romans re-occupied it, they called it Muri Veteres, later corrupted to Murviedro, meaning literally Old Walls. The Romans under Scipio Africanus the Elder and later the Moors who called it Murbiter did a lot of rebuilding, making use of the old stones. Traces of these various occupations are to be found everywhere despite further destruction during the French occupation and then during the Spanish Civil War.

Approach

From the south The harbour walls at Puerto de Sagunto, one mile to the south of Siles, and the 1·5M long Pantalán de Sierra Menera are easily recognised.

From the north Puerto de Castellón and, to the SW, the petrochemical works, which has two tall chimneys with red and white bands, are conspicuous. Puerto de Burriana can also be recognised.

From either direction Cabo Canet light is immediately behind the harbour and can be seen for miles.

Anchorage in the approach

Anchor in 12m, sand, ½M to SE of the harbour entrance.

Entrance

Depths, although in principle maintained at 2·5m, can vary due to silting and dredging. Approach the entrance on a NW course, sounding carefully. Round the head of the Dique de Levante at 15m leaving it to starboard onto a N course and enter between a short spur to starboard and the SE corner of the *contradique* to port.

There may be two port-hand buoys laid south of the contradique indicating the entrance channel. There may also be a line of small orange buoys laid between these two buoys and the end of the contradique.

Puerto de Siles entrance *Peter Taylor*

Berths

The visitors' berths are at the second quay to port. Secure and confirm at the office. These outer quays are subject to swell in winds from E through S. Large vessels moor inside Dique de Levante.

Facilities

Maximum length overall 12m.
Workshop and mechanics on the *contradique*.
Slipway on the *contradique* and one near the root of the Dique de Levante.
25-tonne travel lift and a small crane near the root of the Dique de Levante.
Water and 220v AC on all quays and pontoons.
Small ice from the Club Marítimo.
Club Marítimo de Regates de Sagunto with bar, lounge, patio, restaurant, WCs, showers and swimming pool.
A supermarket 400m to N of the harbour with cash dispenser. More shops in Puerto de Sagunto 1M to SW.

Communications

Rail and bus services from Sagunto. Taxi ✆ 962 680 999.

82. Puerto de Burriana

39°51'N 0°04'W

Charts

UKHO 1701	Imray M13
SHOM 7296, 4720	Spanish 4822, 482

Lights

To the south

Cabo Canet 39°40'·5N 0°11'·9W Fl(2)10s33m20M
Brick tower with house 30m

Harbour

Dique de Levante head Fl(2)G.8s12m5M
Green tower 8m

Dique de Poniente head Fl(2)R.8s10m3M
Red structure on house 8m

Dique Exterior di Levante Q(3)10s7m3M
Cardinal E tower

To the north

Castellón de la Plana 39°58'·2N 0°01'·7E Fl.8s32m14M
White round tower 27m

Port communications

Club Náutico de Burriana VHF Ch 09 ✆ 964 58 70 55
nautic@cnburriana.com
www.cnburriana.com

Burriananova Club de Mar Marina VHF Ch 9
✆ 964 227 200
info@burriananova.com
www.burriananova.com

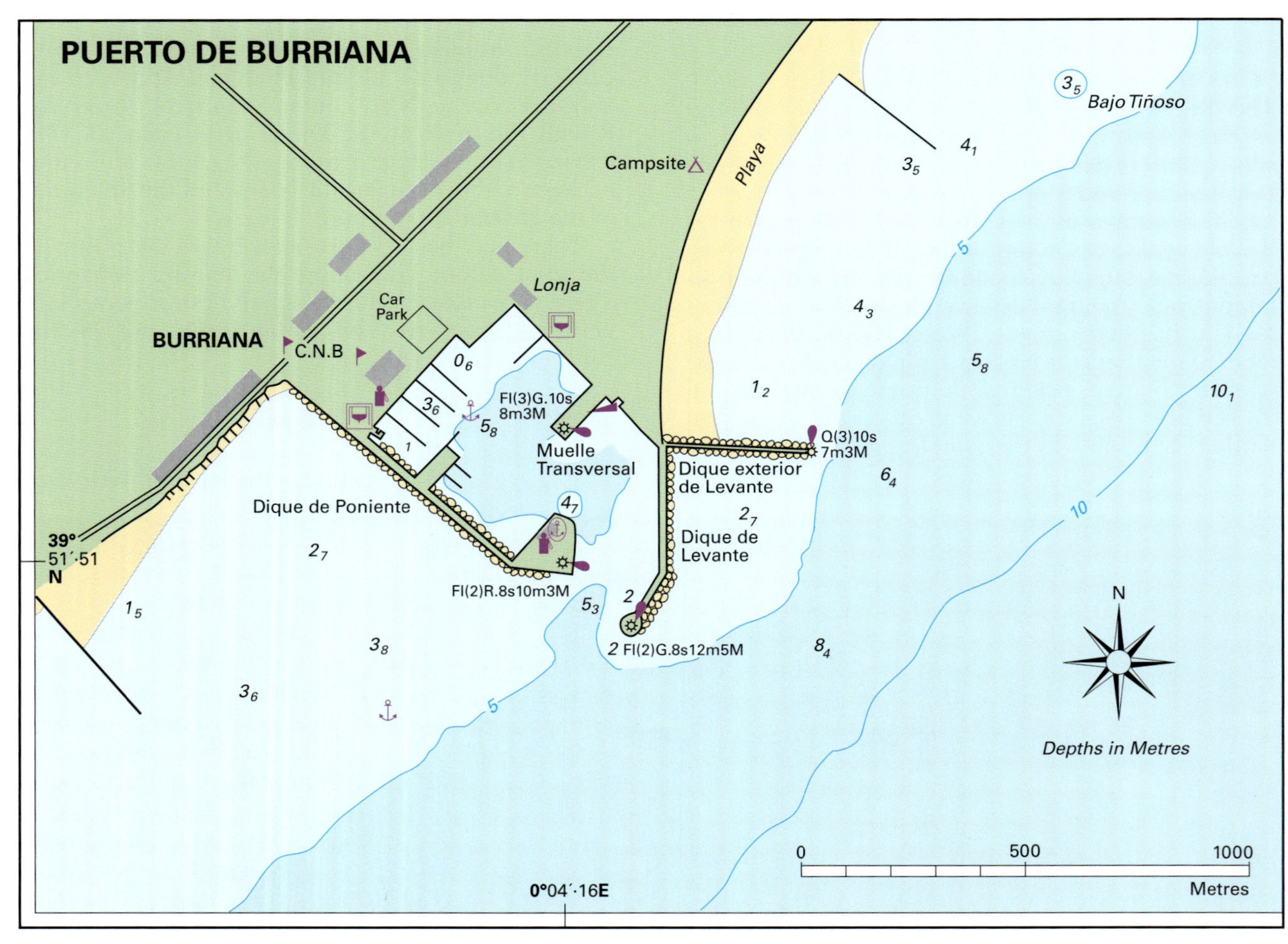

A pleasant club and impressive new marina

An artificial harbour enclosed by two jetties. It is used by fishing craft and yachts. There is a small ship-breaking yard and a new, and welcoming, marina (Club de Mar Burriananova). The local village has limited facilities but more are available at the town some 3km away. The approach is easy but the entrance requires care owing to ever-extending sand bars. Good shelter is obtainable once inside the harbour. Entrance would be difficult with strong winds and swell from E through SW.

The town is worth visiting to see the original walls and gate and an important 16th-century church of Moorish origin. Excellent sandy beach to NE of the harbour.

Approach

From the south The flat, sandy coastal plain continues N from Sagunto for about 8M to Burriana. The town itself is some 2M inland but can seen as can the few blocks of flats near the harbour. In clear weather Pica Espadón (1105m) which lies 15M to WNW of this harbour may be seen. There is a fish farm at 39°50'·2N 0°03'·2E indicated by four buoys, Fl.Y.5s with cross topmarks.

From the north The main feature of this low, flat, dull coast are the two conspicuous tall, red and white banded chimneys of Castellón. Burriana itself, located some 2M inland, will be seen in the closer approach.

Anchorage in the approach

Anchor 200m to SW of the head of Dique de Levante in 6m, sand. Careful sounding is advisable.

Entrance

From a position 400m to SW of the head of Dique de Levante approach the entrance on a course of 30°. Pass some 15m to E of the head of Dique de Poniente. The approach to this harbour is tending to shoal and the sandbank that lies to the S of the head of the Dique de Levante is extending southwards.

Berths

The *capitania* and fuel berth are to port on entering. This modern marina has 378 berths and can accomodate vessels up to 30m.

Burrianova Marina *capitania* and fuel dock *Peter Taylor*

Anchorage

Anchor NE of the Dique de Poniente, clear of any moorings off the *club náutico* piers, 5m, sand. Use a trip line.

Moorings

Private moorings may be available, apply to the club.

Facilities

Maximum length overall 17m.
Two slipways.
A small crane at the root of the Dique de Levante (five tonnes) and a number of mobile cranes of greater power. A large one of unknown capacity on the Muelle Transversal.
Mechanic available.
Water from either end of the sheds on the Dique de Levante. Sample before filling tanks.
Water and 220v AC on all *club náutico* quays and pontoons.
Gasoleo A.
Ice is available at the *club náutico*.
The Club Náutico de Burriana has a bar, lounge, terrace, restaurant and showers.
Only a few shops near the harbour but many in the town where there is also a good market.

Communications

Bus service and rail service some 4M away.
Taxi ✆ 964 511 011.

Reporting berth and fuel pontoon to left *Steve Pickard*

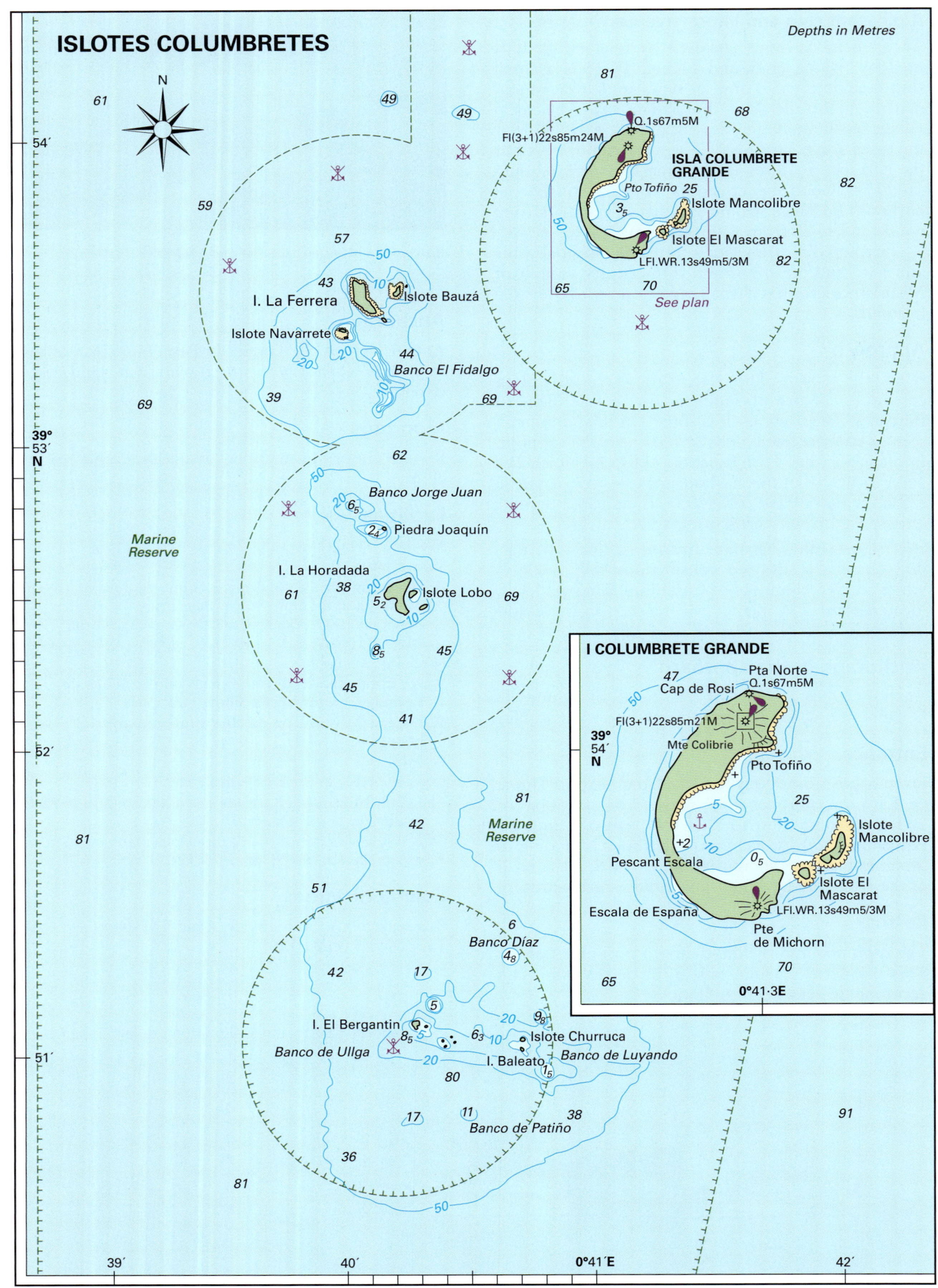
ISLOTES COLUMBRETES
Depths in Metres
ISLA COLUMBRETE GRANDE
Q.1s67m5M
Fl(3+1)22s85m24M
Pto Tofiño
Islote Mancolibre
Islote El Mascarat
LFl.WR.13s49m5/3M
See plan
I. La Ferrera
Islote Bauzá
Islote Navarrete
Banco El Fidalgo
Banco Jorge Juan
Piedra Joaquín
I. La Horadada
Islote Lobo
Marine Reserve
Marine Reserve
Banco Díaz
I. El Bergantin
Islote Churruca
Banco de Ullga
I. Baleato
Banco de Luyando
Banco de Patiño
I COLUMBRETE GRANDE
Pta Norte
Q.1s67m5M
Cap de Rosi
Fl(3+1)22s85m21M
Mte Colibrie
Pto Tofiño
Islote Mancolibre
Pescant Escala
Islote El Mascarat
Escala de España
LFl.WR.13s49m5/3M
Pte de Michorn
0°41·3E
39° 54′ N
39° 53′ N
39′
40′
0°41′E
42′

83. Islotes Columbretes (Puerto Tofiño)

39°52'N 0°40'E

Charts

UKHO 701	Imray M13
SHOM 4033, 4720	Spanish 836, 483A, 4831

Lights

Columbrete Grande

Monte Colibri 39°53'·9N 0°41'·2E Fl(3+1)22s85m21M White conical tower and dwelling 20m Racon

Punta Michorn LFl.WR.13s49m5/3M White 8-sided tower 6m

Punta Norte Q.1s67m4M White 8-sided tower 6m

Isolated and impressive islands

NB Don't go without Spanish Chart 483A

Four isolated and barren groups of volcanic islets with outlying submerged rocks and shoals, Islotes Columbretes lie some 27M off the coast and opposite Castellón de la Plana. The four groups lie roughly N–S with an isolated shoal patch some 7M to WSW. The most northerly is Islote Columbrete Grande, 65m high, ½M in diameter, with high points to the N and S. This islet has the only lights. The next, Islote la Ferrera, a saddle-shaped island 44m high and 300m long, with a group of six smaller islets and shoal patches. Further S is Islote La Horadada, 55m high and 250m long, and a rough pyramid shape. It has two smaller rocky islets in its group and off-lying shoals. The most southern group consists of Islote El Bergantin 32m high and only 100m wide. It is the core of an old volcano. This group has at least eight smaller islets and several shoal patches. The area around these islands was renowned as one of the best fishing areas in the Mediterranean.

The islands were used by the US and Spanish armies as a target up to 1982. From 1988 it all became a natural reserve protected by the Valencian government and three or four wardens live on the large island all year round. The islets are inaccessible with the exception of the largest, Columbrete Grande, The islet is horseshoe-shaped and offers limited shelter in Porto Tofino where there is a mooring buoy but otherwise no facilities whatever. It is open to the winds from north through to east and can be dangerous in these conditions. It is possible to land but all visitors must request permission from the wardens (on VHF Ch 9) first. Further information on the Reserve can be obtained from ☎ 964 288 912 or http://parquesnaturales.gva.es/espnaturales.htm (click on Iles Coloumbretes) and look at the Spanish version as the English version has not been fully updated. For details on the Marine Reserve look at www.reservasmarinas.net.

Approach by day

Avoid Place de la Barra Alta, the shoal area some 7M WSW of the main group, a rocket range in an area W of Isla Columbrete Grande. Also avoid the area 10M around Islote Bergantin, which is used for aerial exercises. Head for a position N to NE of Islote Columbrete Grande. It is possible to take the passages between the various groups of islets but streams are unpredictable and it can be rough.

Entrance

Approach the NE point of Islote Columbrete Grande on a SW course and follow this coast around at 150m into the anchorage.

Moorings

If free use the mooring buoy.

Anchorage

Anchor 150m from the W side of the harbour in 5m on rock and stone. An anchor trip-line is advisable. The holding is not good and should only be used in fair weather.

Landings

There are places to land at the head of the bay where the coast is lower.

Formalities

Check with the wardens on arrival (VHF Ch 9).

Facilities

The island is barren and has no supply of water. Supplies are not available from the Wardens except in an emergency.

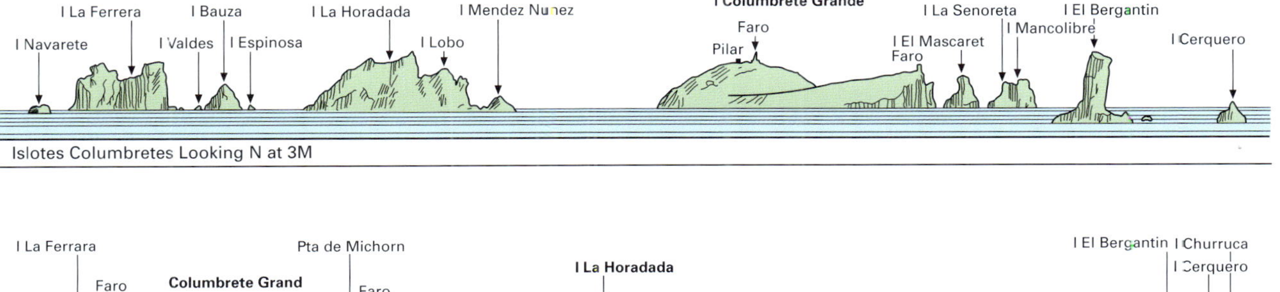

Islotes Columbretes Looking N at 3M

Islotes Columbretes Looking ENE at 7M

Isla Columbrete looking SW (see previous page)

Beach anchorage to the north of Peñiscola (see page 214) *Peter Taylor*

CASTELLÓN DE LA PLANA TO VINARÒS

Ports

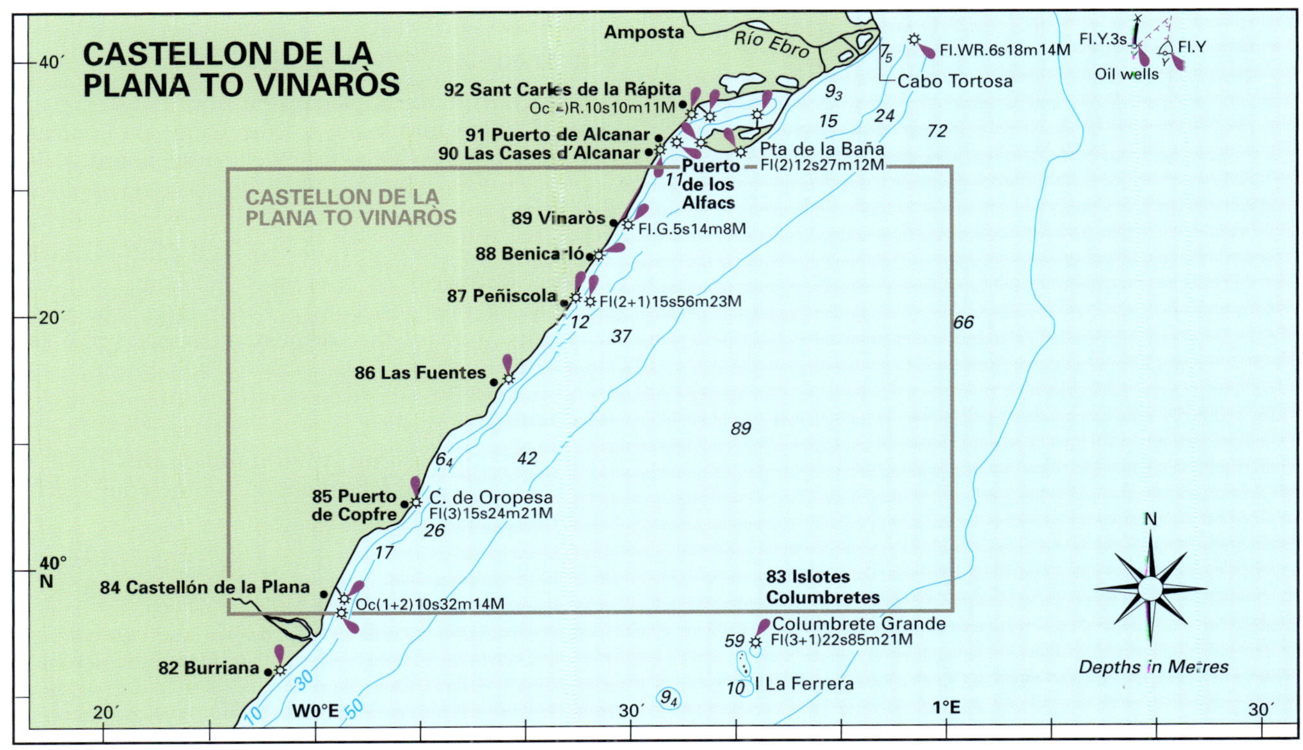

Valencia oranges *Graham Hutt*

84. Puerto de Castellón de la Plana

39°58'N 0°01'E

Charts

UKHO 1515, 1701 — Imray M13
SHOM 7296, 4720 — Spanish 4821, 482

Lights

Faro 39°58'·1N 0°01'·7E Fl.8s32m14M
White round tower 27m

S breakwater E Head 39°57'·40N 0°01'·40E Fl(4)R.11s
Red structure

W Head 39°57'·40N 0°01'·40E Fl(4)R.11s
Red structure

Digue Este SW Head 39°57'·3N 0°01'·7E Fl(3)G.9s15m5M
Green beacon

SE Head 39°57'·34N 0°01'·73E Fl(3)G.9s7m3M
Green ▲ on post

Muelle del Centenario SW Elbow 39°57'·6N 0°01'·6E
Fl(4)G.11s13m5M Green round tower 10m

E Breakwater. Muelle Transversal Head NW corner 39°58'·2N 0°01'·2E Fl(2)G.5m3M Green tower 3m

Muelle Pesquero N Head 39°58'·1N 0°01'·2E
Fl(2+1)R.12s5m3M Red tower, green band 3m

Muelle Pesquero Norte dry dock pier head
39°58'·1N 0°01'·1E Fl(3)R.4m3M Red tower 3m

To the northeast

Cabo Oropesa 40°04'·9N 0°09'·0E Fl(3)15s24m21M
White tower and house 13m

Port communications

Oil terminal, harbour and pilots VHF Ch 16, 12, 13
✆ 964 28 11 40

Real Club Náutico Castellón ✆ 964 282 520
capitania@rcncastellon.es
www.rcncastellon.es

Marina Port Castelló S.L.U. ✆ 964 73 74 5253
marinaportcastello@marinaportcastello.es
www.marinaportcastello.es

New yacht harbour within commercial harbour

Large commercial and fishing harbour with an easy entrance and good shelter within. There is an oil terminal off shore with room to pass between it and the shore-line.

The beach about a mile northeast of the harbour is good but approached along a noisy main road. The pleasant town some 2M inland was established by Jaime I of Aragón. It became the capital of the area and prospered as the centre of a fertile region, famous for its oranges and *azulejo* tiles. The village of El Grao backing the marina supplies most everyday needs.

Approach

From the south The harbours of Sagunto and Burriana are the only conspicuous features on this low, flat sandy coast. The two tall red and white banded chimneys just S of Castellón de la Plana (which are in line from this direction) are conspicuous as is the oil refinery flare (75m). A pipeline stretches out from the refinery ending about 2½M ESE where tankers anchor; the mooring is marked by a safewater buoy and has five mooring buoys (Fl(4)Y.10s). Along the line of the pipeline and a mile offshore is a floating fuelling berth with light and two lit dolphins. Navigation is prohibited between the safewater buoy and the floating berth but small craft may pass between the floating berth and shore. The lighthouse on the Dique Este should then be easy to spot as will the group of tall flats located just behind the harbour.

From the north The high Los Colls (420m) feature which extends to the sea at Cabo Oropesa is recognisable. The coast to the S is low, flat and sandy with a line of apartment blocks and houses. The features mentioned above at Castellón de la Plana are also easily seen from this direction.

Note A traffic separation scheme is in place covering the approach from the east.

Entrance

Approach from the S, pick up the port and starboard channel buoys and make for the Dique de Poniente buoy, leaving the Dique Este well to starboard.

Berthing

Yachts are welcome at both the Real Club Náutico, to the southwest of the inner harbour, and the Marina in the northwest. Their large reception buildings are in the respective corners of the harbour.

Anchorages

As is common with most harbours on this coast at present, it is forbidden to anchor in the commercial harbour.

Facilities

Maximum length overall 20m.
A shipyard on the N side of the Muelle Pesquero where hull repairs can be carried out. Engine mechanics are also available.
Small slipway is located beside the *club náutico*, larger ones in the Dársena Pesquero.
32-tonne travel-lift.

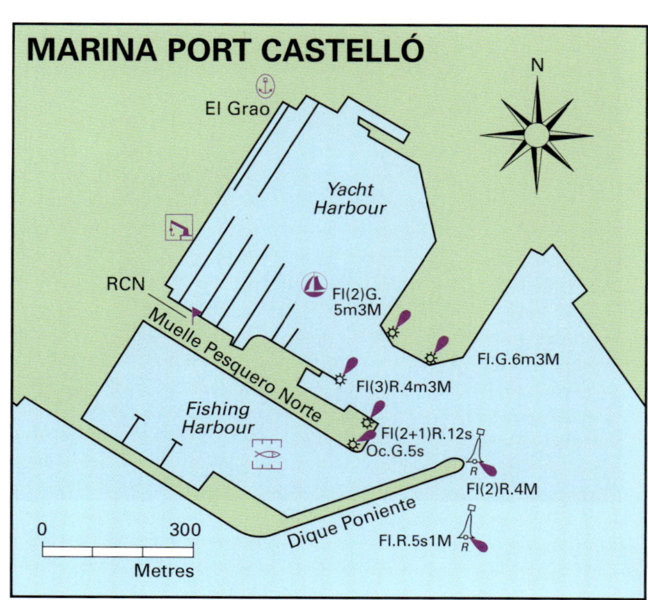

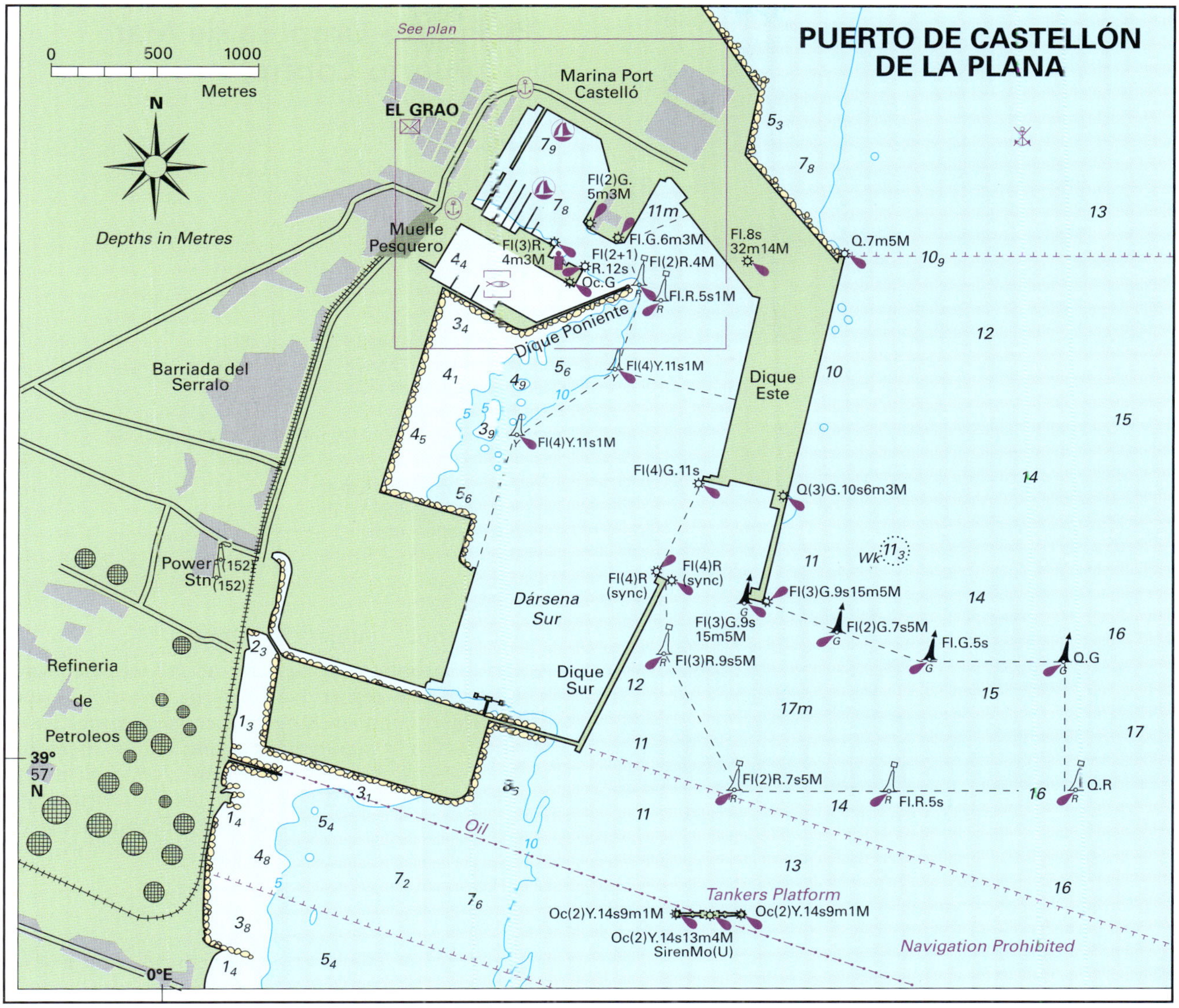

PUERTO DE CASTELLÓN DE LA PLANA

0 500 1000
Metres
N
Depths in Metres
See plan
EL GRAO
Marina Port Castelló
Muelle Pesquero
Fl(2)G.5m3M
11m
Fl.G.6m3M
Fl(3)R.4m3M
Fl(2+1)R.12s
Fl(2)R.4M
Oc.G
Fl.R.5s1M
Fl.8s 32m14M
Q.7m5M
Dique Poniente
Fl(4)Y.11s1M
Fl(4)Y.11s1M
Dique Este
Barriada del Serralo
Fl(4)G.11s
Q(3)G.10s6m3M
Wk
Power Stn (152) (152)
Fl(4)R (sync)
Fl(4)R (sync)
Dársena Sur
Fl(3)G.9s15m5M
Fl(3)G.9s 15m5M
Fl(2)G.7s5M
Fl.G.5s
Q.G
Fl(3)R.9s5M
Refineria de Petroleos
Dique Sur
17m
39° 57′ N
Fl(2)R.7s5M
Fl.R.5s
Q.R
Oil
Tankers Platform
Oc(2)Y.14s9m1M
Oc(2)Y.14s9m1M
Oc(2)Y.14s13m4M SirenMo(U)
Navigation Prohibited
0°E

Puerto de Castellón de la Plana – see plan for pontoon layout in inner harbour

Yacht Club on the Muelle Pesquero Norte *Steve Pickard*

The long pontoon in the northern part of the marina *Steve Pickard*

12·5-tonne crane at the marina and large commercial cranes in Dársena Comercial.
Chandlery to the NW of the harbour.
Water and 220v AC on the pontoons and the quays.
Gasoleo A and petrol at the fuel quay by the yacht club
Ice from the fuel quay.
The Club Náutico de Castellón clubhouse is in the W corner of the Dársena Comercial. It has a bar, lounge, terrace, restaurant, showers and a repair workshop.
A number of shops including a small supermarket near the harbour. Many more shops and a market in the town 2M away.
Launderette in the town.

Communications

Frequent bus service to the town where there is a rail service. Taxi ✆ 964 237 474.

⚓ Olla de Benicasim 40°03'N 0°05'E

Open between NE and SE and to swell from the S. Daily requirements from shops serving the beach blocks or in the town of Bencasim.

85. Puerto Oropesa de Mar (Puerto Copfre)

40°04'N 0°08'E

Charts

UKHO 1701	Imray M13
SHOM 4720	Spanish 482

Lights

To the south

Faro 39°58'·2N 0°01'·7E Fl.8s32m14M
White round tower 27m

Harbour

Dique de Abrigo head Fl(2)G.9s8m5M
Green tower 3m

Contradique head Fl(2)R.7s6m3M
Red tower 2m

Cabo Oropesa 40°04'·9N 0°09'·0E Fl(3)15s24m21M
White round tower and house 13m

Port communications

VHF Ch 9 ✆ 964 313 055
info@cnoropesa.com
www.cnoropesa.com

Quiet marina – subject to silting

A useful harbour, easy to enter in bad weather with a busy seaside resort ½M distant. It offers good protection though swell may enter the harbour from SE winds. Good facilities for laying up but there are no local shops. The main line railway is a bit noisy. A climb to the top of Cabo Oropesa is worthwhile for the coastal view. A small sand beach at the N side of the harbour, with a large beach at Oropesa del Mar.

Approach

From the south The huge petrochemical plant just to S of Puerto de Castellón which has two tall red and white banded chimneys is easily recognised as is Puerto de Castellón itself. The low, flat sandy coast is lined with apartment blocks. Cabo Oropesa (24m) is not prominent but the lighthouse and an old tower on its crest can be identified. The harbour is on the S side of the cape.

From the north Puerto de las Fuentes can be recognised by a small sail-shaped building. The shore to S is low flat and sandy. There are towers at Capicorp and the mouth of the Río Cuevas. This harbour is just beyond the collection of high-rise buildings at Oropesa del Mar.

Anchorage in the approach

The water is deep off this harbour. Anchorages described earlier to S of Cabo Oropesa or in the Olla de Benicasim.

Entrance

Approach the head of the Dique de Abrigo on a NW course and round it, leaving it 15m to starboard onto a N course in to the harbour. Be prepared for dredging operations which are a continous activity.

Puerto Oropesa de Mar

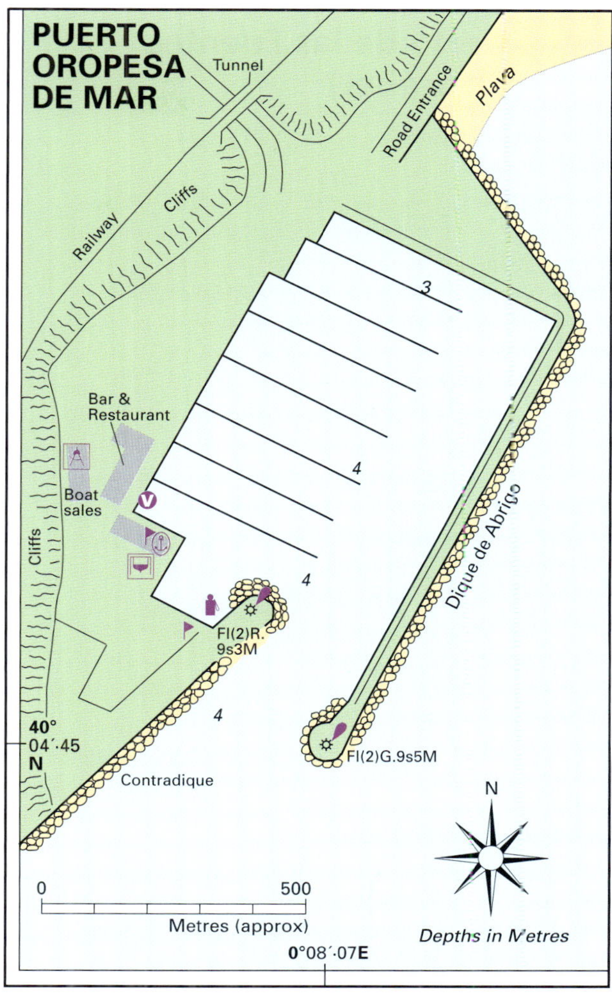

Berths

Secure on the SW side of the harbour and ask at the *torre de control*.

Facilities

Maximum length overall 15m.
Hard-standing.
70-tonne travel-lift and 10-tonne crane.
Engine mechanic, painting, carpentry, sailmaking.
Chandlery.
Water and 220v AC on all quays and pontoons.
Gasoleo A and petrol.
Small ice from *club náutico*.
Club náutico with bar.
Stock up in Oropesa del Mar.

Communications

Bus and rail services at Oropesa del Mar.
Taxi ✆ 964 310 616.

⚓ S of Cabo Oropesa 40°04'·8N 0°08'·4E

A small anchorage north of Puerto Oreposa and tucked away under the cape open to SE. Use with care because of rocky patches. Anchor off sandy beach in 2m, sand. Houses and apartments ashore with road to the village of Oropesa on top of the hill (24m) where everyday supplies are available.

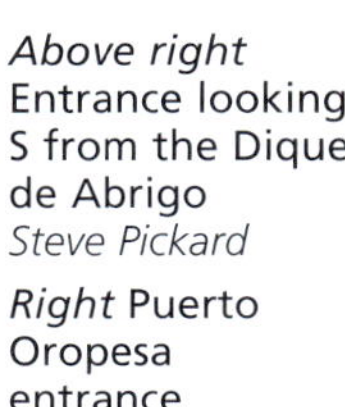

Above right Entrance looking S from the Dique de Abrigo *Steve Pickard*

Right Puerto Oropesa entrance showing extent of shoreside facilities *Steve Pickard*

IV. COSTA DEL AZAHAR

86. Puerto de las Fuentes (Alcocéber)

40°15'N 0°17'E

Charts

UKHO 1701	Imray M13
SHOM 4720	Spanish 836

Lights

To the south

Cabo Oropesa 40°04'·9N 0°09'·0E Fl(3)15s24m21M
White round tower and house 13m

Harbour

Dique de Levante 40°14'·8N 0°17'·2E Oc.G.4s6m4M
Green concrete column 2m

Contradique Fl(4)R.14s5m3M
Red concrete column 2m

Heads of pontoons and quays F.R and F.G – see plan.

To the north

Castillo del Papa Luna 40°21'·6N 0°24'·6E
Fl(2+1)15s56m23M
White 8-sided tower and house 11m 184°-vis-040°

Cabo de Irta 40°15'·8N 0°18'·2E Fl(4)18s33m14M
Square tower on white building 28m

Port communications

VHF Ch 9 ✆ 964 412 084
DOMIHE@santander.com

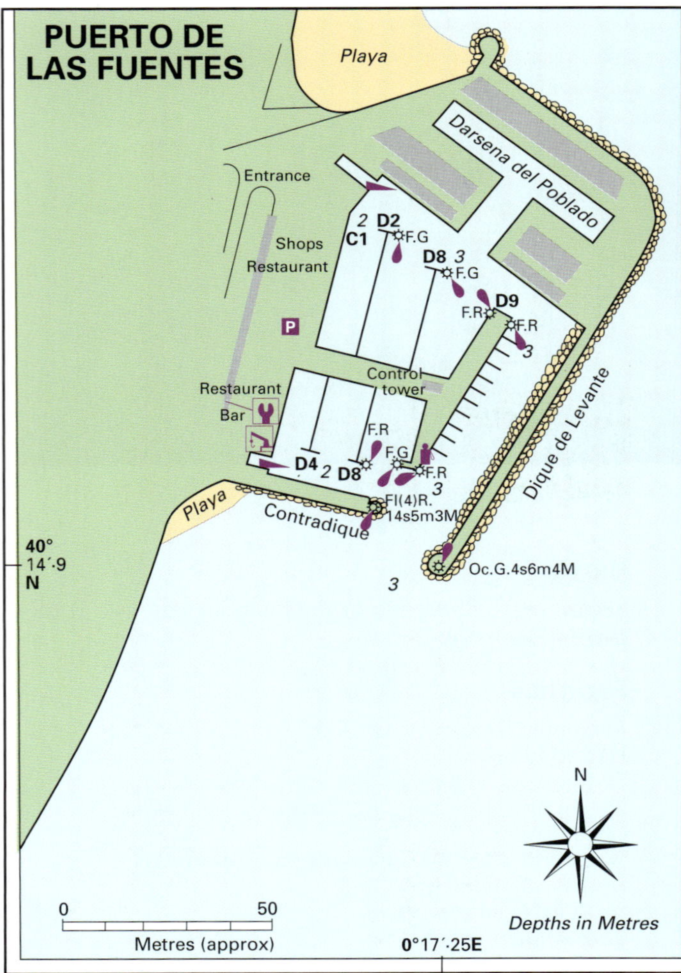

A small yacht harbour

A pleasant marina near a busy resort. Approach and entrance is not difficult except with strong SSE winds. Fine view from the church, San Benito, 2½M to W. Good but crowded sandy beach to N of harbour and rocky, stony one to S.

Note There are plans to extend this harbour to provide 110 new berths for vessels up to 40m. As of late 2016 there was no sign of this extension being started.

Approach

From the south Cabo Oropesa, though high (24m), is not prominent but can be easily recognised by its white round lighthouse and the old Torre del Rey alongside it. The coast is low, flat and marshy and can be closed to ½M. At Capicorp there are two *torres* and the mouth of Río Cuevas, 2½M further N lies the harbour with a number of apartment blocks behind it. The sail-like building of the *torre de control* is unique on this part of the coast and is easily recognised. Careful watch should be kept for floating cages 'Alcocebre' in approximate position 40°13'·9N 0°18'E with 4 yellow buoys (Fl.Y.5s).

From the north Peñíscola, surmounted by the Castillo del Papa Luna, is unmistakable. The coast to S is of low rocky cliffs and small sandy beaches at the mouths of the numerous small streams which descend from the Sierra San Benet (573m) a range of hills located 2M inland and lying parallel to the coast. The coast can be followed at ½M.

The harbour lies near the S end of this hill feature. The low breakwater and a number of apartment blocks are a short distance west of a conspicuous white tower and will be seen when close-to. The unique *torre de control* is not so obvious from this direction.

Limited hard-standing and the *torre de control* at Puerto de la Fuentes *Steve Pickard*

Puerto de las Fuentes

Anchorage in the approach

Anchor 500m to E of the harbour in 8m, sand, or closer in, if weather is suitable, in 5m, sand.

Entrance

Straightforward.

Berths

Secure to the wide quay near the *torre de control*, a sail-like building, for allocation of a berth.

Facilities

Maximum length overall 20m.
Two slipways.
Travel lift. 8-tonne crane.
Engine mechanics.
Water and 220v AC on all quays and pontoons.
Gasoleo A and petrol.
Some shops in the harbour, better in the village.
Small ice from the bar at SW corner of the harbour.

Communications

Bus service, rail 3M inland. Taxi ✆ 964 410 152.

Las Fuentes marina with control tower on right
Steve Pickard

87. Puerto de Peñíscola

40°21′N 0°24′E

Charts
UKHO 1701 Imray M13
SHOM 7296, 4720 Spanish 4841

Lights
Castillo del Papa Luna 40°21′·6N 0°24′·6E
Fl(2+1)15s56m23M
White 8-sided tower and house 11m 184°-vis-040°
Buoy 40°21′·6N 0°24′·7E Q(3)10s3M
E cardinal BYB pillar
(signals end of submerged breakwater)
Harbour
Dique de Levante head Fl.G.4s15m4M
Green column 7m
Espigón head F.R.7m3M
Red column 6m

Port communications
Harbour ✆ 964 48 94 36
puertos.peniscola@gva.es

Harbour charges Medium

A dramatically set small port

An attractive bay with a fishing harbour on its east side which has very limited accommodation for yachts. It is overlooked by a Knights Templars castle, one of the more frequently visited sites on the east coast of Spain. The approach and entrance are easy but the bay is open to SE and winds from this direction make it uncomfortable. Although there is 3·5m depth throughout the harbour the maximum LOA is limited to 8m.

There is a good beach and anchorage on the N side of the isthmus and another in the bay itself which is often crowded. A holiday, the Fiesta of La Virgen de la Ermitana, is held 8–9 September.

Puerto de Peñiscola with the castle dominating the port
Steve Pickard

The Phoenicians called the harbour Tyriche, because of its resemblance to Tyre. The Greeks renamed it Chersonesos. Carthaginians and Romans followed and later the Moors. The Moors were driven out by Jaime I who gave the site to the Knights Templars. The castle was completed by the Montesianos in the 14th century. Pope Benedict XIII (often referred to as Papa Luna), the last of the schismatic Popes, retired here from Avignon in 1417 and remained until his death in 1423 at the age of 90. After a spell as part of the Holy See it reverted to the crown of Aragón, withstanding an 11-day siege by the French during the Peninsular War.

Approach by day

From the south After Cabo Oropesa, the coast is low and flat. 10M north, Sierra Benet, a long line of rocky hills, stretches as far as the harbour. From a distance the castle at Peñíscola appears as an off-lying island. Care should be taken to avoid a new artificial reef in position 40°19′·6N 0°24′·8E.

From the north The harbours of Vinaroz and Benicarló with their conspicuous harbour works are easily identified on an otherwise featureless coast. The castle at Peñíscola appears as an island.

A submerged breakwater (end marked by BYB lit pillar buoy) extends 0·15 NM east from Escalera del Papa Luna.

Anchorage in the approach

The bay may be marked as reserved for swimmers by a line of buoys between the Muelle de Poniente and the elbow of the *espigon*. If so, the options are to anchor near the line of the buoys, out of the fairway on the Muelle de Poniente side, or outside altogether either in the harbour approaches or north of Papa Luna.

Entrance

Straightforward but beware of fishing craft. After strong S winds the entrance can be quite shallow. It is dredged frequently but after strong winds from the S care must be exercised on entering. Avoid the head of Dique de Levante by 25m.

Berths

By day it may be possible to find a berth within the fishing harbour near the head of the *espigón* or alongside pontoons lying parallel to the Muelle de Levante. However, the fishing fleet which returns en masse at about 1700 hours usually requires all available berths.

Facilities

Chandlery near the root of the jetty.
Water from the Lonja de Pescadores.
Ice available from the Lonja de Pescadores.
A number of small shops scattered around the village.

Communications

Buses.

PUERTO DE PENISCOLA
N
Depths in Metres
PENISCOLA
Castillo del Papa Luna
Escalera del Papa Luna
Q(3)10s3M
Fl(2+1)15s 56m 23M
Pta del Barbón
Restaurants Bars
Lonja
Muelle de Pescadores
Pta del Bufador
Pta del Huerto
Muelle de Poniente
Espigon
Fl(3)R.9s7m3M
Pontoon
Dique Muelle de Levante
Fl(3)G.9s15m4M
Pta del Mabre
0 100 200 300
Metres

⚓ N of Peninsula de Peñíscola

40°22'N 0°24'·6E

Anchor in 5m, sand. Exposed N to SE. (See photo on page 206).

Puerto de Peñiscola, entrance to the inner harbour *Steve Pickard*

88. Puerto de Benicarló

40°25'N 0°26'E

Charts

UKHO 1701 Imray M13
SHOM 7296, 4720 Spanish 4841, 837

Lights

To the south

Castillo del Papa Luna 40°21'·6N 0°24'·6E
Fl(2+1)15s56m23M White 8-sided tower and house 11m 184°-vis-040°

Harbour

Dique de Levante head Fl(2)G.5s13m5M
Green tower 5m

Espigón head Fl(2+1)G.15s7m3M
Green round tower 3m

External Espigon head Fl(2)R.6s8m3M
Red tower 5m

Dique Sur head Fl(3)R.9s8m3M
Red octagonal tower 4m

To the north

Punta de la Baña 40°33'·6N 0°39'·7E
Fl(2)12s27m12M White round tower, black bands 26m

Port communications

Marina Benicarló VHF Ch 9. ✆ 964 462 330
info@marinabenicarlo.com
www.marinabenicarlo.com

Harbour charges Medium to high

Fishing harbour with marina

Over the last few years the northern part of this harbour has been made into a well-sheltered and impressive marina with good shoreside facilities. It is situated about a seven minute walk away from the commercial centre of the thriving Valencian town of Benicarlo, which is not over-run with tourists. There is a sandy beach at the town and a long pebble beach to the north of the harbour.

Approach by day

From the south Having passed the conspicuous castle on the island-like feature at Peñíscola, the town and harbour breakwaters of Benicarló will be seen in the distance. The church in particular is easily seen.

From the north From the harbour and town of Vinaroz the coast consists of low broken rocky cliffs. The town, church and harbour walls of Benicarló are conspicuous from this direction. In heavy weather avoid rocky shallows, Piedras de la Barbada (6·4m), lying ½M to NE of the harbour entrance.

Anchorage in the approach

Anchor 200m to S of the head of Dique Sur in 3·5m, sand, or 400m further S, but sound carefully due to silting.

Entrance

Round the head of Dique de Levante, leaving it 50m to starboard as there are underwater obstructions extending some 25m west of the head. Depths may not be as charted due to silting and periodic dredging so sound. Leave the Dique Sur head 50m to port and head towards the conspicuous marina tower turning to starboard to enter the marina. Notice one has to leave the green light at the Espigon head to port to enter the marina.

Berths

The water has been dredged from 3·7m to 2m near the shore. It is recommended that one calls ahead by radio or phone to ascertain whether a berth is available. If so, one is usually met by an attendant and shown to the berth. If one arrives unannounced moor to a vacant berth and ask at the control tower

Muelle comercial, Puerto de Benicarló. Marina to right, looking west from crane *Steve Pickard*

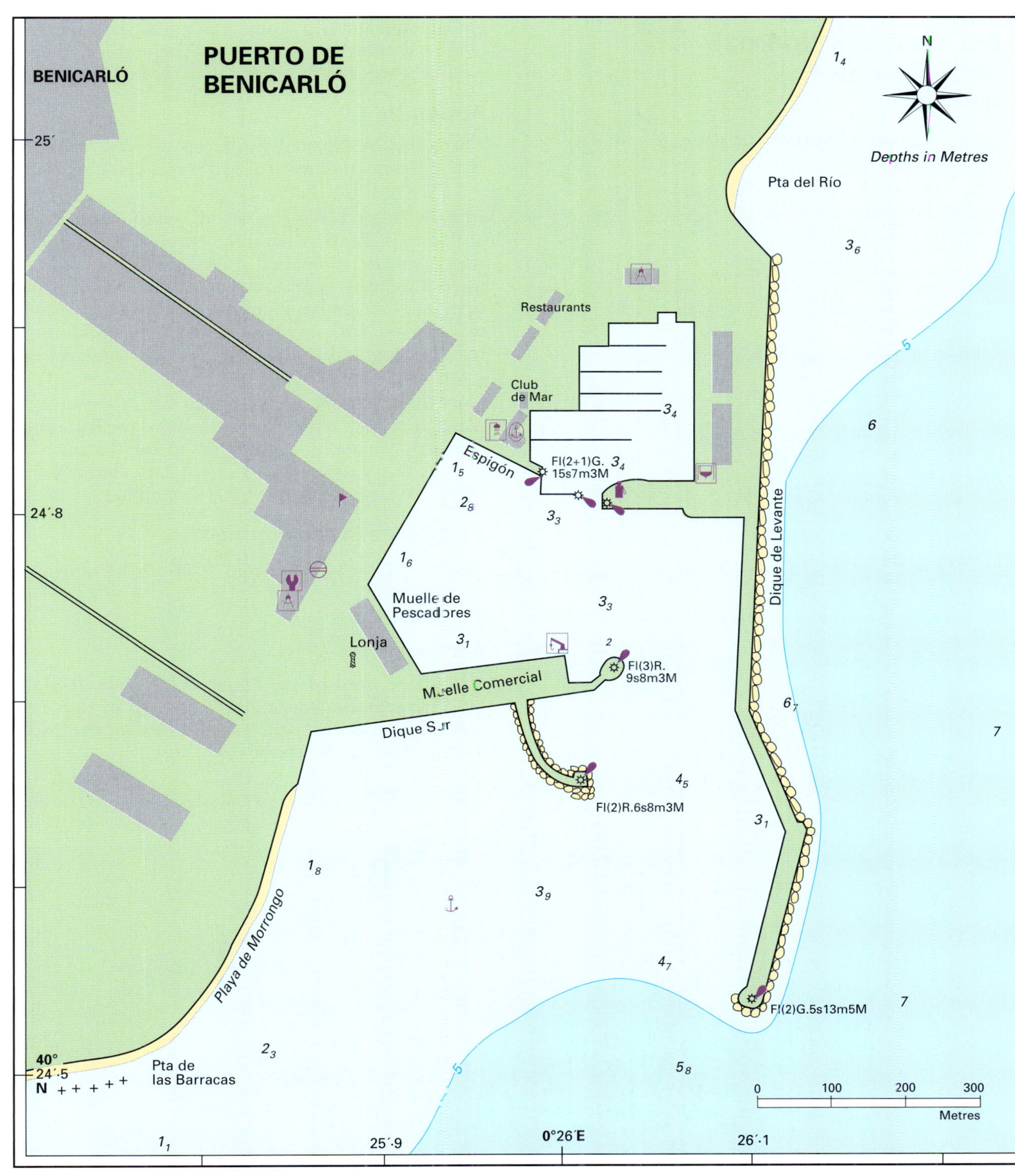

for a berth. Most berths have finger pontoons and entry to the main pontoons is by electronic card.

Facilities

Maximum length 20m.
Water and 220v AC on pontoons.
24hr security staff.
Excellent showers in *Capitania* building.
Chandlery.
32-tonne travel-lift and repair facilities.
5-tonne crane.
Local supermarket accepts telephone/email orders and will deliver.
Shops and restaurant on site.
Fuel.

89. Vinaròs (Vinaroz)

40°27'·5N 0°28'·6E

Charts

UKHO 1515, 1701	Imray M13
SHOM 7296, 4720	Spanish 4842, 485

Lights

Dique de Levante head Fl.G.5s14m8M Green round tower 10m

Knuckle Fl(2)G.7s6m3M
Green octagonal tower 3m

Dique de Poniente S head Fl.R.3s5m3M
Red tower 3m

Dique de Poniente NW head Fl(3)R.9s4m1M
Red structure 2m

Dique de Poniente NE head Fl(2)R.7s5m1M
Red structure 2m

Muelle Transversal head Fl(3)G.9s8m3M
Green round tower 6m

Punta de la Baña 40°33'·6N 0°39'·7E Fl(2)12s27m12M
White tower, black bands 26m

Port communications

Club Náutico Vinaros ✆ 964 451705
info@clubnauticvinaros.com
www.clubnauticvinaros.com

Storm signals

Shown from the root of Dique de Levante.

A large harbour with small club marina

A large artificial commercial, fishing and yachting harbour, easy to approach and enter. It is periodically dredged and depths vary from time to time. South to southwest swell may come in but otherwise there is good protection.

The pleasant old town has good shops and a church with a baroque portal. There are sand and pebble beaches to the N of the harbour.

Approach

There are a number of fish farms off Vinaròs (both N and S) and another artificial reef is being set up at 40°27'·8N 0°31'·7E.

From the south Having passed the conspicuous castle at Puerto de Peñíscola and the harbour of Benicarló, which can be recognised by its harbour walls and town standing a little distance inland, the coast from here on is of low sand-coloured cliffs. The harbour walls of Vinaròs, some modern high-rise buildings, a tall chimney and a tall crane will be visible in the closer approach.

From the north The high range of hills, the Sierra de Montsia, which backs the flat delta of the Río Ebro, is easily recognised. Vinaròs lies in the flat plain to the S of this feature. The blocks of flats, chimney and crane are also visible from this direction.

Anchorage in the approach

Anchor 300m to NW of the head of the Dique de Levante in 7m, sand, or 400m to E of this head in 11m, sand.

Entrance

Round the head of the Dique de Levante at 50m, head between the knuckle and the head of Dique de Poniente. When through, leave the head of the Dique Transversal 50m to starboard.

The *lonja* from the Muelle Transversal, Puerto de Vinaròs
Steve Pickard

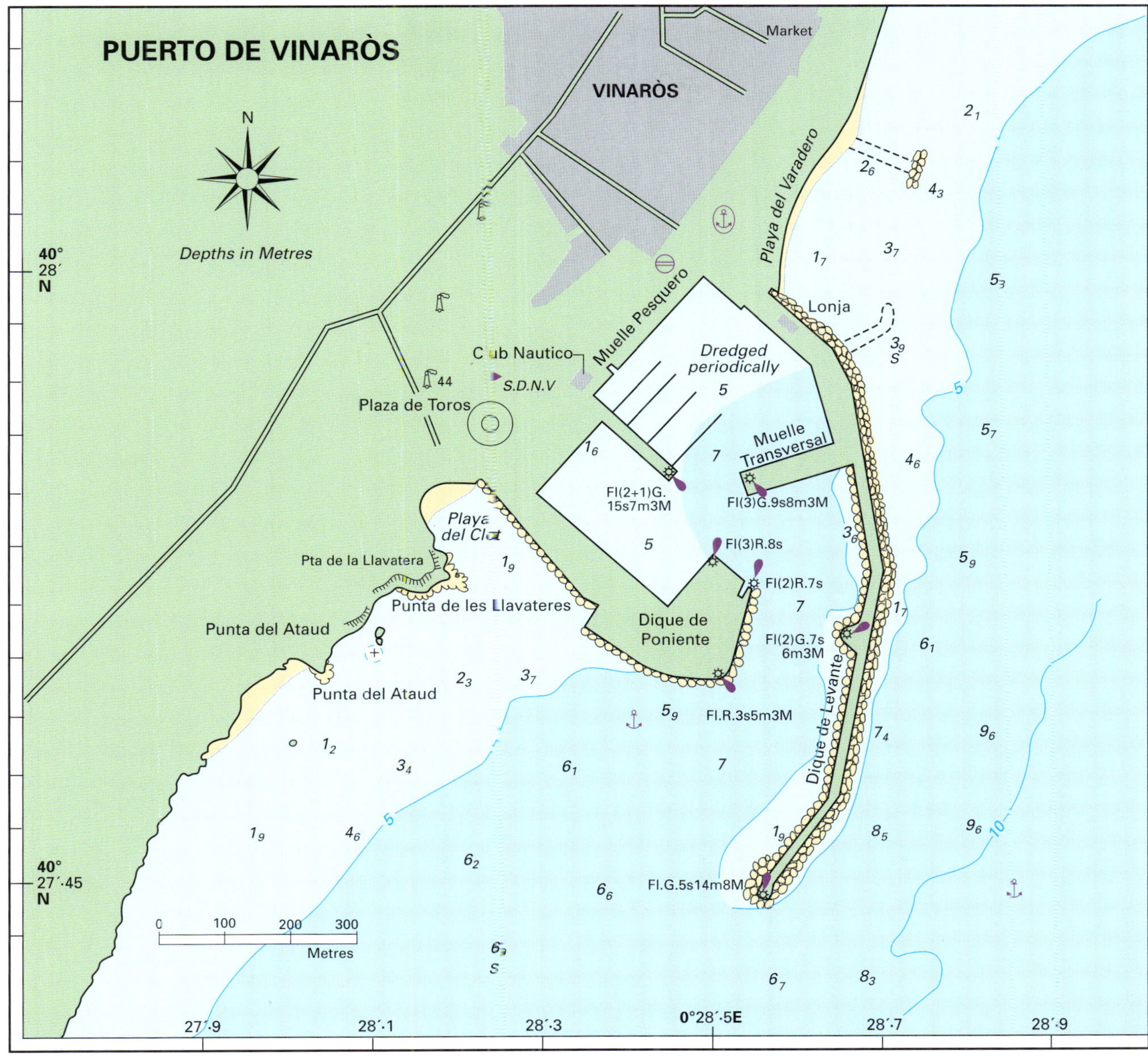

Berths

Call ahead on Ch 9 and secure to the visitors' berths as directed.

Moorings

Anchoring is not allowed. There are a few private moorings on the NW side of the inner harbour and some may be available; contact the *club náutico*.

Facilities

Hull repairs involving metal or woodwork can be carried out by the shipyards.

An engine workshop at the NW side of the harbour.

One small and two large slipways, one of 100-tonne capacity.

Two small cranes are on the NE side of the harbour. A powerful crane is located on the Dique Transversal where there are a number of mobile cranes.

Chandlery near the harbour.

Water taps at the *lonja*, at the yacht club and on the Muelle Transversal.

Water and 220v AC on all pontoons.

Gasoleo A.

Ice available from the *lonja*.

The Sociedad Deportiva Náutica has a small clubhouse to the W of the harbour with restaurant, bar, lounge, terrace and showers.

A good range of shops and a market in the town.

Communications

Buses.

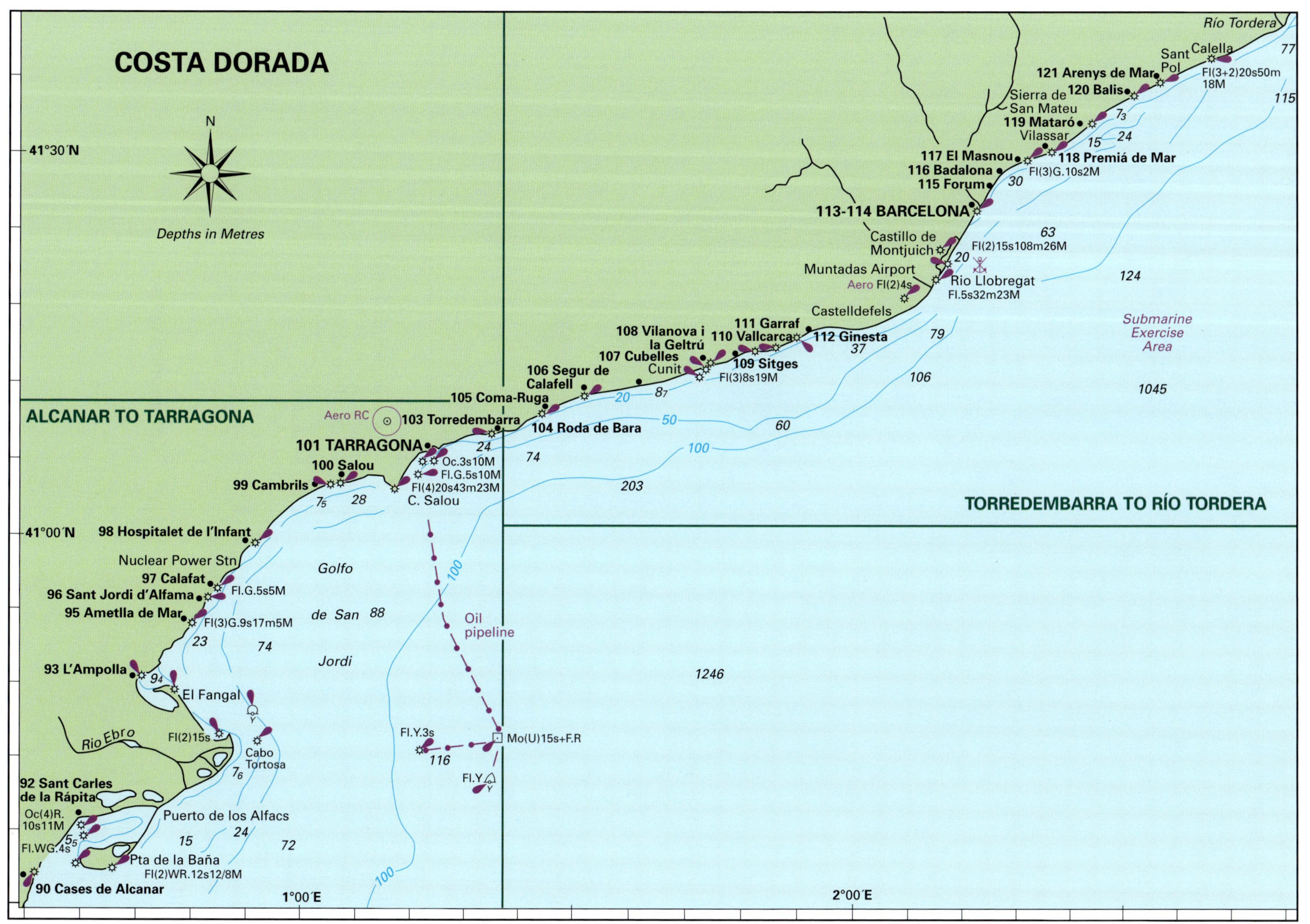
COSTA DORADA
N
41°30′N
Depths in Metres
ALCANAR TO TARRAGONA
TORREDEMBARRA TO RÍO TORDERA
Río Tordera
Sant Pol
Calella
Fl(3+2)20s50m 18M
121 Arenys de Mar
120 Balis
Sierra de San Mateu
119 Mataró
Vilassar
118 Premiá de Mar
117 El Masnou
116 Badalona
115 Forum
Fl(3)G.10s2M
113-114 BARCELONA
Castillo de Montjuich
Fl(2)15s108m26M
Muntadas Airport
Aero Fl(2)4s
Rio Llobregat
Fl.5s32m23M
Castelldefels
111 Garraf
110 Vallcarca
112 Ginesta
108 Vilanova i la Geltrú
107 Cubelles
Cunit
109 Sitges
Fl(3)8s19M
106 Segur de Calafell
105 Coma-Ruga
Aero RC
103 Torredembarra
104 Roda de Bara
101 TARRAGONA
100 Salou
Oc.3s10M
Fl.G.5s10M
Fl(4)20s43m23M
99 Cambrils
C. Salou
41°00′N
98 Hospitalet de l'Infant
Nuclear Power Stn
97 Calafat
96 Sant Jordi d'Alfama
Fl.G.5s5M
95 Ametlla de Mar
Fl(3)G.9s17m5M
Golfo de San Jordi
Oil pipeline
93 L'Ampolla
El Fangal
Rio Ebro
Fl(2)15s
Cabo Tortosa
Fl.Y.3s
Mo(U)15s+F.R
Fl.Y.
92 Sant Carles de la Rápita
Oc(4)R. 10s11M
Fl.WG.4s
Puerto de los Alfacs
Pta de la Baña
Fl(2)WR.12s12/8M
90 Cases de Alcanar
1°00′E
2°00′E
Submarine Exercise Area
77
115
24
15
30
63
20
124
79
37
106
1045
20
50
60
100
24
74
203
28
88
23
74
1246
116
24
15
72
100

V. COSTA DORADA

Costa Dorada planning guide *Distances (Miles)*

ALCANAR TO TORREDEMBARRA		
	90	**Puerto de les Cases d'Alcanar** *(page 226)*
2M		Punta Paloma
	91	**Puerto de Alcanar** *(page 228)*
4M	92	**Puerto de Sant Carles de la Rápita** *(page 229)*
20M	⚓	*Bahia de Alfacs*
		Punta de la Baña
		Delta & Ports of Río Ebro *(page 233)*
10M	⚓	*Puerto del Fangar*
		Cabo Tortosa
	⚓	*Ensenada de Cartapacio*
	93	**Puerto l'Ampolla** *(page 235)*
6M	⚓	*Cala Montero*
	⚓	*Playa de Roig*
		Cabo Roig
	⚓	*Cala del Aguila*
		Punta Figuera
	⚓	*Estany Podrit*
		Pta de l'Aguila del Islote
	94	**Puerto de l'Estany Gras** *(page 236)*
1M	⚓	*Cala Bon Capo*
	⚓	*Cala bon Caponet*
	⚓	*Cala de Arangaret*
	95	**Puerto de l'Ametlla de Mar** *(page 237)*
2M		Cabo de Sant Jordi
	96	**Puerto Sant Jordi d'Alfama** *(page 239)*
2M		
	97	**Puerto de Calafat** *(page 240)*
5M		Cabo de Terme
	98	**Puerto de Hospitalet de l'Infant** *(page 242)*
8M		Punta de la Pixerota
	99	**Puerto de Cambrils** *(page 244)*
4M	⚓	*Embarcadero de Reus Club de Mar*
		Pta de la Riera de Riudoms
	100	**Puerto de Salou** *(page 246)*
6M	⚓	*S of Salou*
	⚓	*Cala de la Torre Nova*
		Punta del Porroc
	⚓	*Cala Pinatel*
	⚓	*N of Punta de Peny Tallada*
	⚓	*Cala de la Font*
	⚓	*Cala del Cranc*
		Punta Grossa
	⚓	*Cala Morisca*
		Cabo Salou
	⚓	*Playa de Reco*
	⚓	*Oiling pier Pantalan Empetrol*
	101	**Puerto Tarraco** *(page 252)*
	102	**Port Esportiou** *(page 253)*
7M	⚓	*Playa de Rabassada*
	⚓	*E of Rabassada*
	⚓	*Cala de la Jovera*
		Punta de la Jovera
	⚓	*Altafulla*
	⚓	*Reco de Fortin*
	⚓	*Cala de Canadel*
		Punta de la Galera

TORREDEMBARRA TO RÍO TORDERA (page 256)		
3M	103	**Puerto de Torredembarra** *(page 257)*
	104	**Roda de Barà (Port Barà)** *(page 260)*
3M	105	**Puerto de Coma-Ruga** *(page 261)*
3M	⚓	*Sant Salvador*
	⚓	*Calafell*
	106	**Puerto de Segur de Calafell** *(page 262)*
4M	⚓	*Cunit*
	107	**Puerto del Foix** *(page 264)*
3M	⚓	*Cubelles*
		Punta Grossa
	108	**Puerto de Vilanova i la Geltru** *(page 265)*
3M	109	**Aiguadolç (Puerto de Sitges)** *(page 267)*
2M	110	**Puerto de Vallcarca** *(page 269)*
2M	111	**Puerto de Garraf** *(page 270)*
2M	112	**Port Ginesta** *(page 272)*
13M	⚓	*Gava*
		Río Llobregat
		Puerto de Barcelona *(page 275)*
2M	113	**Barcelona – Port Vell** *(page 277)*
	114	**Barcelona – Puerto Olímpico** *(page 280)*
	⚓	*Badalona*
		Río Besos
	⚓	*Mangat*
	115	**Barcelona – Port Forum** *(page 282)*
	116	**Barcelona – Badalona** *(page 283)*
	117	**Puerto de El Masnou** *(page 284)*
	118	**Puerto de Premia de Mar** *(page 286)*
5M	⚓	*Vilassar de Mar*
	119	**Puerto de Mataró** *(page 288)*
3M	120	**Puerto Balis** *(page 289)*
2M	121	**Puerto de Arenys de Mar** *(page 291)*
12M	⚓	*Punta Morrell*
	⚓	*Calella*
	⚓	*Pineda de Mar*
		Río Tordera

Introduction

The Costa Dorada (Golden Coast) is so called because of the golden sandy beaches between the mouths of the two large rivers, Ebro and Tordera. The 140 miles of coast varies considerably. At the south is the huge flat muddy delta of the Río Ebro which projects well out to sea. It is surrounded by extensive and dangerous shoals and should be given a wide berth. On either side of this delta are high ranges of hills leading down to broken rocky cliffs on the coast. Flat plains and low hills alternate along the coast from just S of Cabo Salou to beyond the delta of the Río Llobregat, backed by higher hills further inland. N of the Río Llobregat these higher hills follow the coastline with a narrow band of low-lying ground along the coast itself as far as the delta of the Río Tordera. In general the coastline is comparatively straight, broken only by the major promontory of the delta of the Río Ebro, Cabo Salou, Cabo Gros and the deltas of Ríos Llobregat and Tordera. Regular soundings follow the coast and with the exception of the areas around the river deltas, there is deep water close inshore. There are no outlying dangers except for a shallow bank, Banco de Santa Susana, parallel to the coast near Pineda and about ½ mile offshore.

Les Cases is the southernmost port of Catalunya. The province has some of the largest concentrations of industry in Spain which has resulted locally in some bad pollution of both air and sea. The sandy beaches are attractive to holiday-makers and there has been considerable development along the coastline for both Spanish and foreign tourists.

Visits

Apart from places mentioned in the harbour descriptions, the following sites are interesting but some distance inland. They can be reached by public transport or taxi.

Tortosa, an old Roman and Moorish city with many interesting buildings.

Monasterio de Escornalou, in the Sierra Montsant behind Cambrils with a superb view.

Monasterio de Sants Creus, behind Tarragona, a 12th-century building.

Tamarit, a 12th-century castle and museum.

Arca de Bará, a Roman arch astride the old Via Maxima near Torredembarra.

Castelldefels, a 15th-century tower, the Torre del Homenaje.

Montserrat, an extraordinary saw-shaped mountain ridge behind Barcelona, has a fine view and an interesting monastery dating from the 1st century.

Monasterio de Sant Cugat del Valles, another very old monastery on the site of the Roman Castrum Octavianum located behind Barcelona.

Sierra del Montseny, a number of places with tremendous panoramas located inland from Arenys de Mar.

Pilotage and navigation

Shoaling

The deltas along this coast are constantly altering and their off-lying shoals steadily extend further out to sea. Allowance must be made for the possibility of changes when rounding such promontories – keep well off and sound.

Restricted anchorages

There is a small area near the atomic power station that is located between L'Ametlla and Cambrils, a large area just to the N of Barcelona, and a smaller area to the S, where anchoring is forbidden.

Prohibited areas

Oil wells and exploration drilling platforms are located in an area 15M E of Cabo Tortosa, each platform carrying a light Mo(U)15s+Fl.R. Additional sites may be occupied nearby. Navigation is prohibited within the areas concerned.

Harbours of refuge

Only the main ports of Tarragona and Barcelona offer refuge in really bad storms with onshore winds. In certain conditions one or the other side of the Río Ebro delta may provide shelter and, with offshore winds, the smaller harbours of L'Hospitalet, Castelldefels (Ginesta), Mataró, Cambrils, Vilanova i la Geltrú and Arenys de Mar could be entered.

Magnetic variation

0°29'E (2017) decreasing 11' annually.

Egrets follow the rice harvest in Ebro delta *Peter Taylor*

ALCANAR TO TARRAGONA

Ports

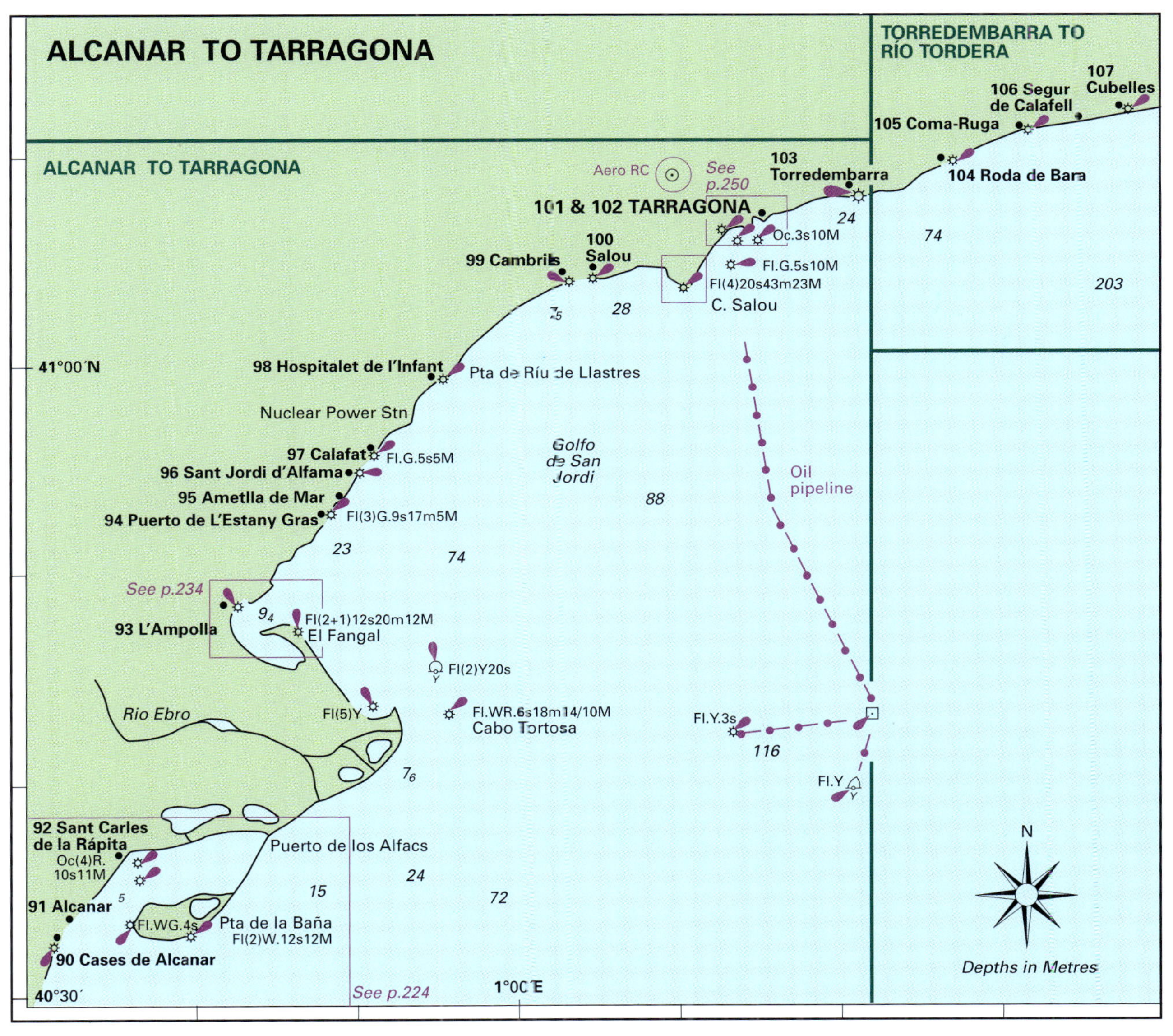

ALCANAR TO TARRAGONA
TORREDEMBARRA TO RÍO TORDERA
107 Cubelles
106 Segur de Calafell
105 Coma-Ruga
104 Roda de Bara
103 Torredembarra
ALCANAR TO TARRAGONA
Aero RC
See p.250
101 & 102 TARRAGONA
Oc.3s10M
100 Salou
99 Cambrils
Fl.G.5s10M
Fl(4)20s43m23M
C. Salou
24
74
203
28
41°00'N
98 Hospitalet de l'Infant
Pta de Ríu de Llastres
Nuclear Power Stn
97 Calafat
Fl.G.5s5M
96 Sant Jordi d'Alfama
95 Ametlla de Mar
94 Puerto de L'Estany Gras
Fl(3)G.9s17m5M
Golfo de San Jordi
88
Oil pipeline
23
74
See p.234
93 L'Ampolla
Fl(2+1)12s20m12M
El Fangal
Fl(2)Y20s
Rio Ebro
Fl(5)Y
Fl.WR.6s18m14/10M
Cabo Tortosa
Fl.Y.3s
116
Fl.Y
92 Sant Carles de la Rápita
Oc(4)R.10s11M
Puerto de los Alfacs
24
15
72
91 Alcanar
Fl.WG.4s
Pta de la Baña
Fl(2)W.12s12M
90 Cases de Alcanar
40°30'
See p.224
1°00'E
N
Depths in Metres

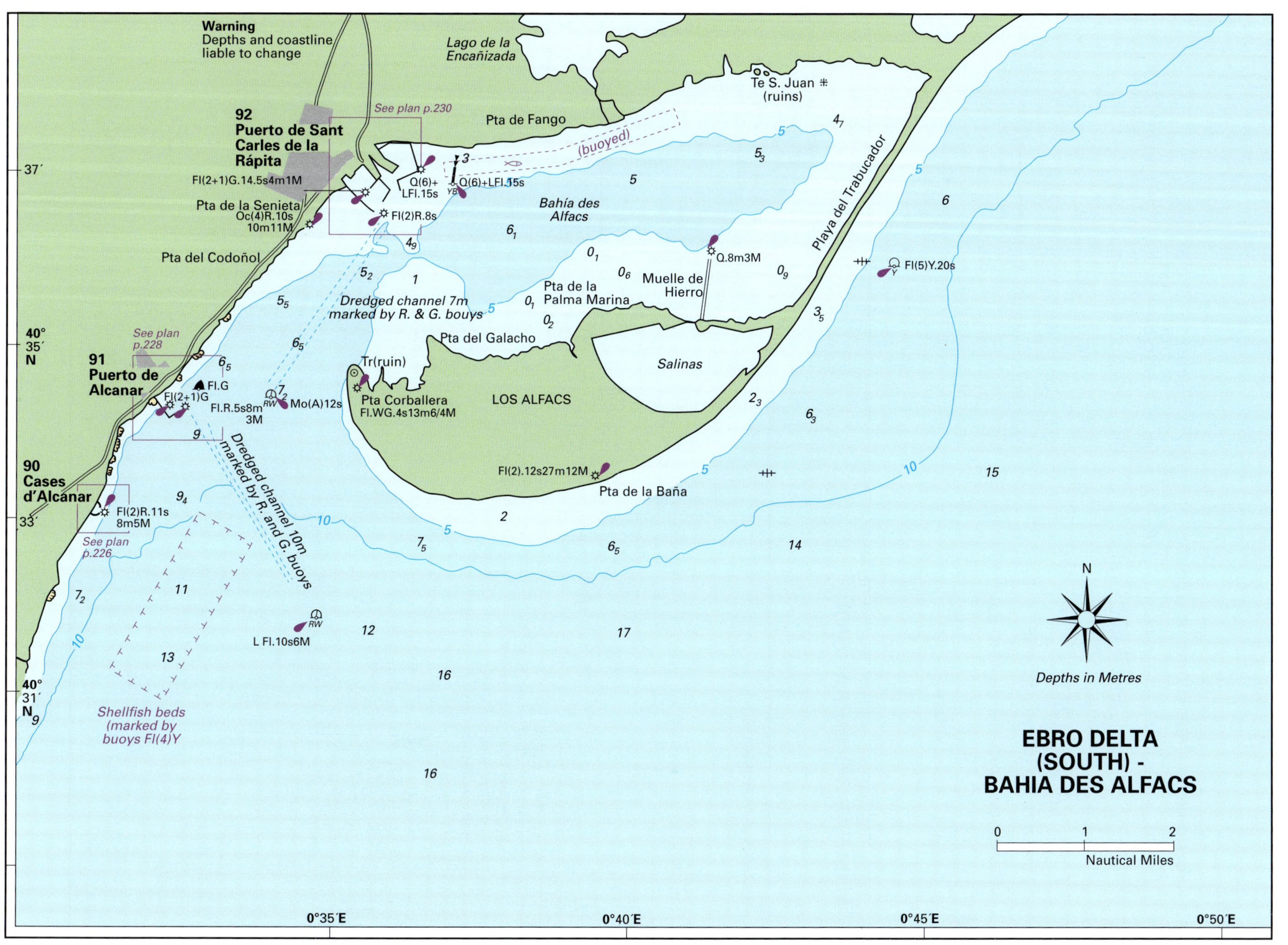
Warning
Depths and coastline
liable to change
Lago de la
Encañizada
Te S. Juan
(ruins)
92
Puerto de Sant
Carles de la
Rápita
See plan p.230
Pta de Fango
(buoyed)
Fl(2+1)G.14.5s4m1M
Q(6)+
LFl.15s
Q(6)+LFl.15s
Pta de la Senieta
Oc(4)R.10s
10m11M
Fl(2)R.8s
Bahía des
Alfacs
Playa del Trabucador
Pta del Codoñol
Q.8m3M
Fl(5)Y.20s
Pta de la
Palma Marina
Muelle de
Hierro
Dredged channel 7m
marked by R. & G. bouys
Pta del Galacho
40°
35'
N
See plan
p.228
91
Puerto de
Alcanar
Fl.G
Fl(2+1)G
Fl.R.5s8m
3M
Mo(A)12s
Tr(ruin)
Pta Corballera
Fl.WG.4s13m6/4M
LOS ALFACS
Salinas
90
Cases
d'Alcanar
Fl(2)R.11s
8m5M
See plan
p.226
Dredged channel 10m
marked by R. and G. buoys
Fl(2).12s27m12M
Pta de la Baña
L Fl.10s6M
N
Depths in Metres
40°
31'
N
Shellfish beds
(marked by
buoys Fl(4)Y
EBRO DELTA
(SOUTH) -
BAHIA DES ALFACS
0
1
2
Nautical Miles
37'
33'
0°35'E
0°40'E
0°45'E
0°50'E

Ebro Delta South

Bahía des Alfacs

40°36'N 0°40'E

Charts

UKHO 1704, 1515 Imray M13
Shom 7048, 4720 Spanish 485

Lights

Muelle de Hierro head 40°36'·2N 0°41'·4E Q.1s8m3M N card pole 082°-vis- 229° (this light is well inside the Bahía)

S card lights mark shellfish beds on the north side of the Bahía

This *bahía* is an inland lake blocked off to seaward by a spit formed from the wash-out of the Río Ebro (Ebre). It is some 6M long and 2M wide. The entrance, which has Sant Carles de la Rápita on its N side, is about 1M wide and is shoal on the S side. Depths within range from 6m to 0m, the shallows being on the S side; the sea level tends to increase with winds between NE and SE and decrease with winds from other directions. The area offers considerable scope for larger boats to anchor out of open sea and for smaller boats wishing to sail in sheltered waters.

Apart from two small villages with a road inland from the N coast, there is little activity in the area. There are many rice fields, *salinas* (saltpans) and a few factories dealing with the salt. One such factory on the S side has a long metal jetty, the Muelle de Hierro, extending 1M out from the shore. The N side of the area has a long line of mussel beds, marked by three S cardinal buoys. Keep clear of them. The surrounding area, largely marsh, is low and flat; squalls can descend without warning from the Sierra Montsiá.

Harbours

Anchorage

Anchorage is possible virtually anywhere in the Bahía des Alfacs in mud in depth to suit draught. Use an anchor light.

Fishing boats cutting the corner – Pta Corballeta into Bahía des Alfacs with Puerto de Sant Carles de la Rapita visible in the distance

90. Puerto de les Cases d'Alcanar (Casas de Alcanar)

40°33'N 0°32'E

Charts
UKHO 1458, 1701, 1515 Imray M13
SHOM 7048, 4720 Spanish 485, 837

Lights
Dique Sur head 40°33'·1N 0°32'·1E Fl(4)R.11s8m5M Red pyramidal tower 4m
Dique de Levante head Fl(4)G.11s7m3M Green pyramidal tower 3m

To the south
Punta de la Baña 40°33'·6N 0°39'·7E Fl(2)12s27m12M White tower black bands 26m

Port communications
Club Náutico VHF Ch 9 ✆ 977 735 001
✆ 977 735 014 (club house and bar)
cncalcanar@hotmail.com (office, mornings only)
www.cncaportlescases.com

Harbour charges High

A small fishing yachting harbour

A pleasant small artificial yachting and fishing harbour; there is not much depth alongside in the yacht harbour which is run by the yacht club. The area has not been highly developed and the harbour may be useful for a vessel on passage wanting to stop before rounding Cabo Tortosa without diverting to Puerto de Sant Carles de la Rápita but space for visitors is limited to two berths. Entrance could be difficult with high winds and seas between NE and SE.

The town was an important staging place on the N-S coast road from pre-Roman days. Remains from this period are still being found. There are several Roman remains and many from the time of the Moorish occupation. The town suffered many attacks by sea pirates in the Middle Ages and also suffered during the War of the Succession in the 18th century. The Seven Years War and the Civil War also affected the town.

There are several interesting buildings, including the church in Alcanar and the remains of a Roman bridge. Fine views from the Sierra Montsiá. Details from the information office beside the harbour. Excellent sandy beach to S of the harbour. Local holidays include the *Remedio* in the second two weeks of October, in honour of the town's patroness.

Approach

There may be several oil rigs and oil wells located about 10M offshore in this area. They come and go as oil is found or used up. The areas are well marked by lights. Sometimes a tanker is kept moored to one of these wells.

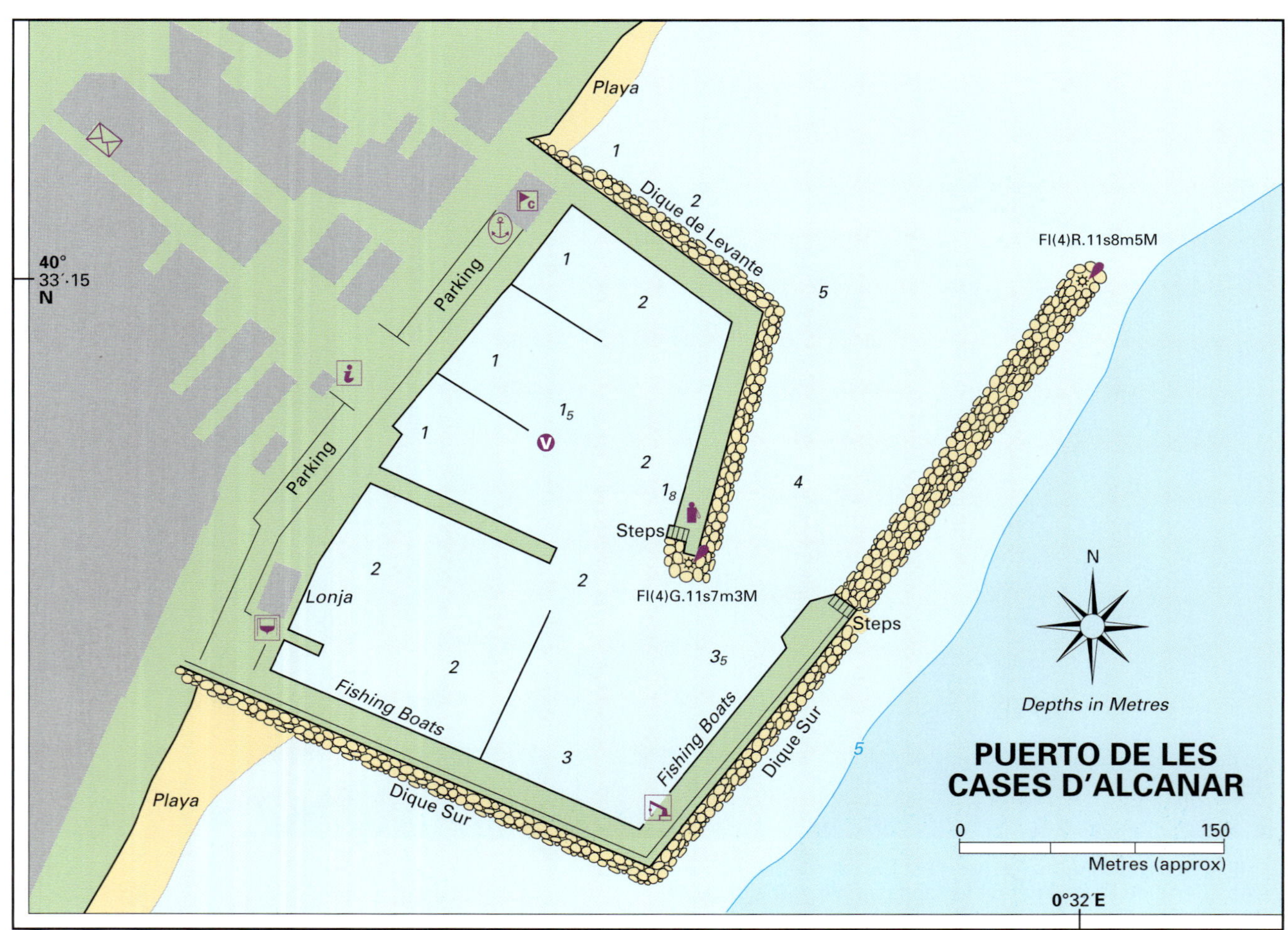

Puerto de les Cases d'Alcanar

Yacht club and moorings from the Dique de Levante, Puerto de les Cases d'Alcanar *Steve Pickard*

From the southwest The coast from Vinaròs is flat with low sandy cliffs as far as this harbour where rocky cliffs commence, backed by the mountain range Sierra Montsiá. The tower Sol de Riv at the mouth of a small river can be identified. The group of houses and apartment blocks behind this harbour can be seen from afar.

From the northeast Round the large delta of the Río Ebro as far as Punta de la Baña which can be identified by its lighthouse. Approach the harbour on a W course and cross the line of 22 light buoys which mark a dredged channel leading to Puerto d'Alcanar (La Martinenca), 3M NW(except for the first and last buoys, they are in pairs, red can and green conical). The buildings behind the harbour will now be seen.

Anchorage in the approach

Anchor in 5m, sand, 200m to S of the harbour.

Entrance

Approach the harbour on a W course and identify the head of Dique Sur. Note that the head of Dique Levante is well inside the head of Dique Sur. Give them both a 15m berth and enter.

Berths

Secure near head of fuel jetty and apply to *club náutico* for a berth.

Facilities

Maximum length overall 15m.
Simple repairs only; mechanic in the town.
6-tonne crane and hard-standing on Dique Sur.
A slipway in W corner of the harbour.
Water and 220v AC on all quays and pontoons.
Ice from café/bars.
Club Náutico Cases d'Alcanar has a clubhouse at the N corner of the harbour.
Several shops in the area near the harbour and many in the town of Alcanar 2M inland where there is a market.

Communications

Bus service. Car hire.

91. Puerto de Alcanar (La Martinenca)

40°34'N 0°33'E

Charts

UKHO 1701, 1704   Imray M13
SHOM 7048, 4720   Spanish 3713, 485, 837

Lights

Muelle Exterior head 40°34'·4N 0°33'·4E Fl.R.5s8m3M
Square tower 2m

Muelle Interior head Fl(2+1)G.14s8m2M
Square tower, red and green top 3m

Port communications

Pilots Sant Carles Rápita Prácticos VHF Ch 11, 12, 14, 16.

A commercial harbour only

A commercial harbour which is a part of a large cement works. Not normally used by yachts but could be used as a shelter in the event of bad weather. The approach and entrance are easy and good shelter is obtained, though with N to NE winds it can be uncomfortable despite the shelter provided by the Ebro delta. Facilities for yachtsmen are very limited as might be expected from a purely commercial harbour but there are excellent sandy beaches on either side of the harbour.

Approach

From the south The flat coast with low sandy cliffs suddenly gives way to the high range of mountains, the Sierra Montsiá. At the foot of these mountains and close to the coast are the tall cement factory buildings usually with clouds of effluent pouring out from them. The harbour is located nearby. Close-to the dredged channel lightbuoys will be seen.

From the north Round the Ebro delta giving Cabo Tortosa a good berth and follow the low flat coast at 3M in a SW direction. Round Punta de la Baña onto a WNW course. The cement factory by the harbour will be seen from afar and the dredged channel lightbuoys will appear when closer in.

Approach channel

The approach channel 330° (dredged to 12m) has on its SE extremity a safewater buoy (Boya de Recalada 40°32'·0N 0°35'·4E LFl.10s6M) nearly 3M distant from the port. The NW end is marked by a green starboard-hand lateral buoy (Boya No.21 Fl.G.3s3M) about 400m NE of the harbour. Between these buoys lie ten pairs of R and G lightbuoys. A fish farm has been established about a mile SW of No.8 buoy.

Anchorage

Anchor with trip-line attached in 3m on sand about halfway between the shore and the Muelle Interior.

Entrance

Approach the head of the Muelle Exterior, round a red can lightbuoy Fl(3)R off it and then the head of the Muelle Interior at 25m.

Berths

Temporary berth alongside the quay on the land side of either Muelle.

Moorings

Temporary mooring available on the large mooring buoys in the inner harbour.

Formalities

Report to harbour officials on arrival and ask permission to stay while the bad weather lasts.

Facilities

Provisions from the town some 3M to SW.

Anchorage in the approach

Possible location for yachts 600m to E of the entrance in 4m, mud.

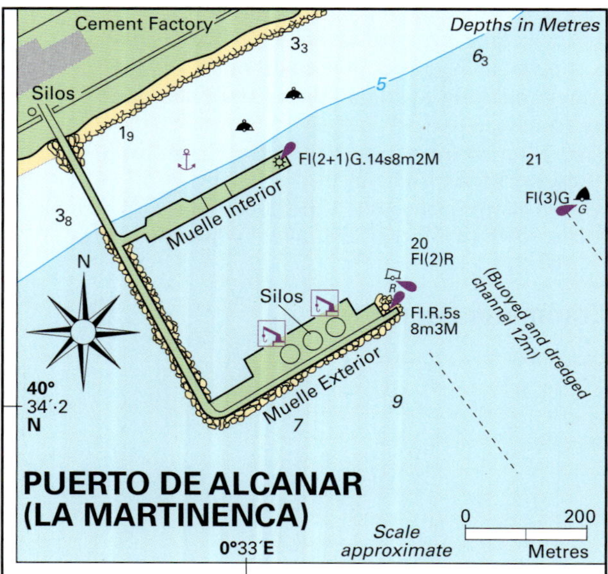

Puerto de Alcanar

92. Puerto de Sant Carles de la Rápita Yacht Harbour and Marina

40°36'N 0°36'E

Charts

UKHO 1515, 1701, 1704 Imray M13
SHOM 7296, 7048, 4720 Spanish 485

Lights

To the south by east

Punta Corballera 40°34'·7N 0°35'·8E Fl.WG.4s13m7/5M Black round tower 12m 000°-G-180°-W-360°

To the west

Punta de la Senieta 40°36'·4N 0°35'·1E Oc(4)R.10s10m11M White round tower 7m

Harbour

Dique de Abrigo head Fl(2)R.8s8m3M Red column 5m

Darsena Este Dique de Abrigo head Q.G.2m1M Green post 2m

Darsena Este Dique de Abrigo elbow Q(6)+LFl.15s4m3M Card S post 2m

Dique de Levante head Fl(2+1)G.14.5s4m1M Green & red column 2m

Muelle de Poniente head Fl.R.5s3m1M Red column 2m

There are now five red cylindrical and four green conical buoys forming an entrance channel with three more green conical buoys indicating a dredging area – keep clear of these latter three buoys. Cardinal lights mark shellfish beds 0·6M to3M ENE

A vast and busy harbour

The harbour is well protected from winds and easy to approach (once round the Ebro delta, if coming from the north). The facilities are fair and the area is attractive in a wild and unexploited way.

There are two sets of harbours. The older, to the southwest, has the yacht harbour, a commercial basin and a fishing harbour. The newer, to the northeast has now a fully developed marina. Anchorage in the harbour area is forbidden.

This is a good launching place for those who trail their yachts and wish to visit the enclosed sea area to the east, Puerto de los Alfacs. The original harbour was founded by Carlos III with the intention of making it into a large trading port but this scheme never prospered and the grandiose Plaza Carlos III is the sole reminder of it. The Cerro de la Guardiola which lies behind the town has a fine view.

Approach

From the south Pass the conspicuous harbours of Benicarló and Vinaròs where the coastal plain is low. Further to N the high range of the Sierra Montsiá (764m) leads to this harbour. Follow the coast at 1M or less passing through the line of red and green lightbuoys leading to the conspicuous cement works at Alcanar (La Martinenca). This course passes W of the shallows off the low and inconspicuous Punta Corballera and Punta del Galacho.

From the north round the large delta of the Río Ebro and follow the S side round, keeping outside the 10m soundings. Careful navigation is necessary due to the lack of identifiable features and the low flat coast. When S of Punta Corballera cross over towards the mainland shore and follow this in a NE direction at 1M distance.

Anchorage

Anchoring is allowed outside the NE harbour close outside the Dique de Abrigo.

Club Náutico de Sant Carles Marina and Yacht Club looking N *Steve Pickard*

Club Náutico de Sant Carles Yacht Harbour (west)

40°37'N 00°35'·8E

Port communications

Club Náutico de Sant Carles VHF Ch 9. ✆ 977 741 103
cn.sant-carles@terra.es or clubnautic@larapita.com
www.cnscr.com

Harbour charges Low

Berthing

Go to the visitors' berth on the N side of the Muelle de Poniente or moor at the fuel berth and arrange a berth at the newly enlarged club náutico. All berths have lazy lines running out from the quays/ pontoons.

Facilities

Maximum length overall 15m.

Shipyard to the NW of the harbour and an engine repair workshop nearby.

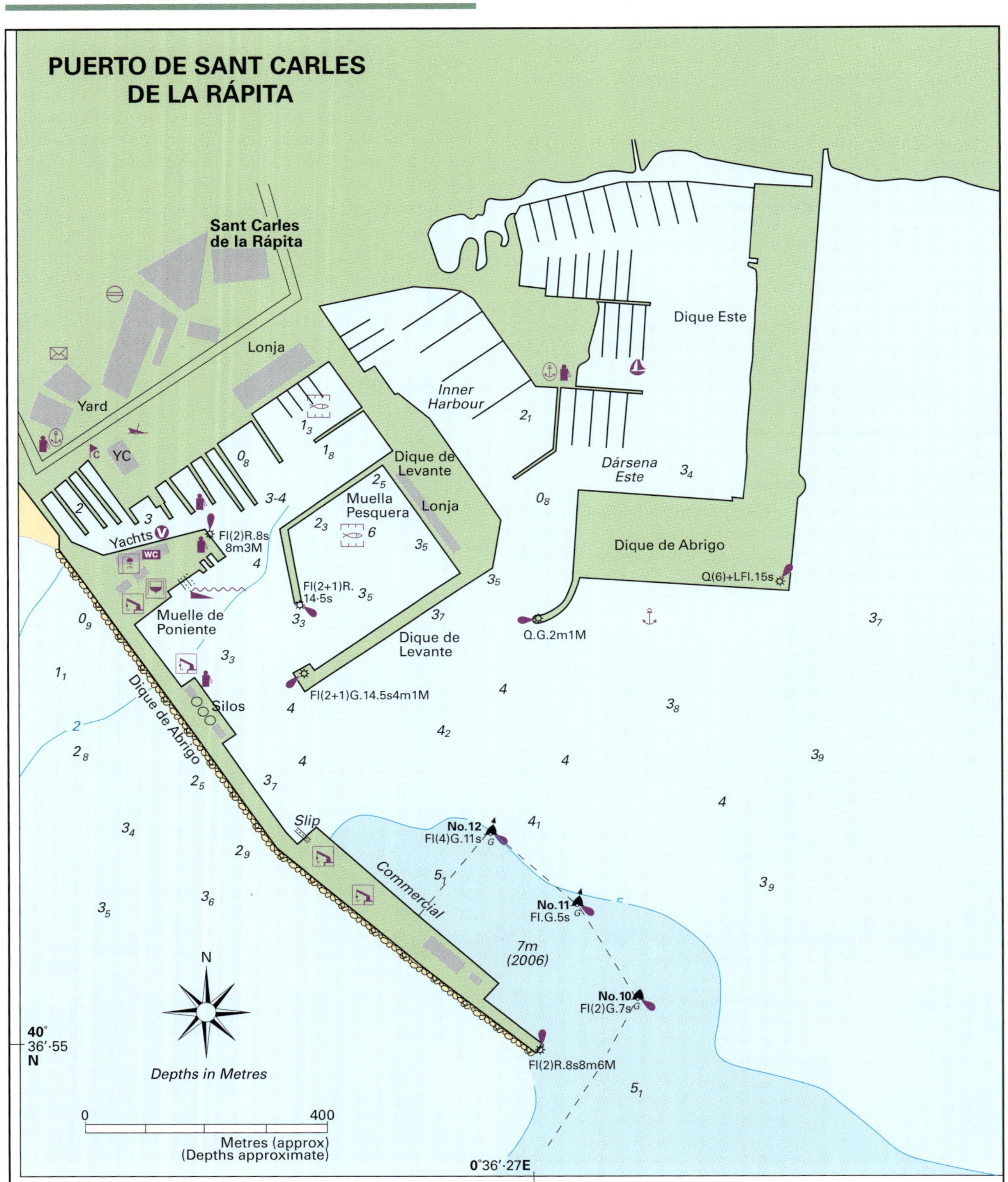

Several slipways in the complex.
100-tonne travel lift.
Cranes up to 10 tonnes and a large mobile crane.
Several chandleries in town and near the harbour.
Water from the *lonja* and from the *club náutico*.
220v AC on the pontoons and at the *club náutico*.
Gasoleo A and petrol.
Ice from the *lonja* and *club náutico*.
Club Náutico de Sant Carles has a new clubhouse to the NW of the harbour with bar, lounge, terrace, showers and pontoon.
Shops of all kinds, supermarket, in the town nearby. A few shops near the harbour.
Launderette in town.

Communications

Rail and bus service. Taxi ✆ 977 741 317.

Control tower on the Muelle de Poniente – fuel on other side *Steve Pickard*

Sant Carles Marina (east)

40°37'N 00°36'·22E

Lights

Darsena Este Dique de Abrigo head Q.G.2m1M
Green post 2m

Port Communications

VHF Ch 9
Sant Carles Marina ✆ 977 745 153
info@santcarlesmarina.es
www.santcarlesmarina.com

Modern upmarket marina

UK operators and MDL have been involved in the development and running of this marina, which is a much-needed addition to the port. Features include an infinity pool.

Facilities

Water and 220v AC on the pontoons.
1150 berths up to 33m.
75-ton travelift.
5 tonne crane.
10,000 sq m boat storage.
WiFi.
Laundry.
Gasoleo A and petrol.

Sant Car es Marina
Sant Carles Rapita Reportajes Aereos Camps SLU

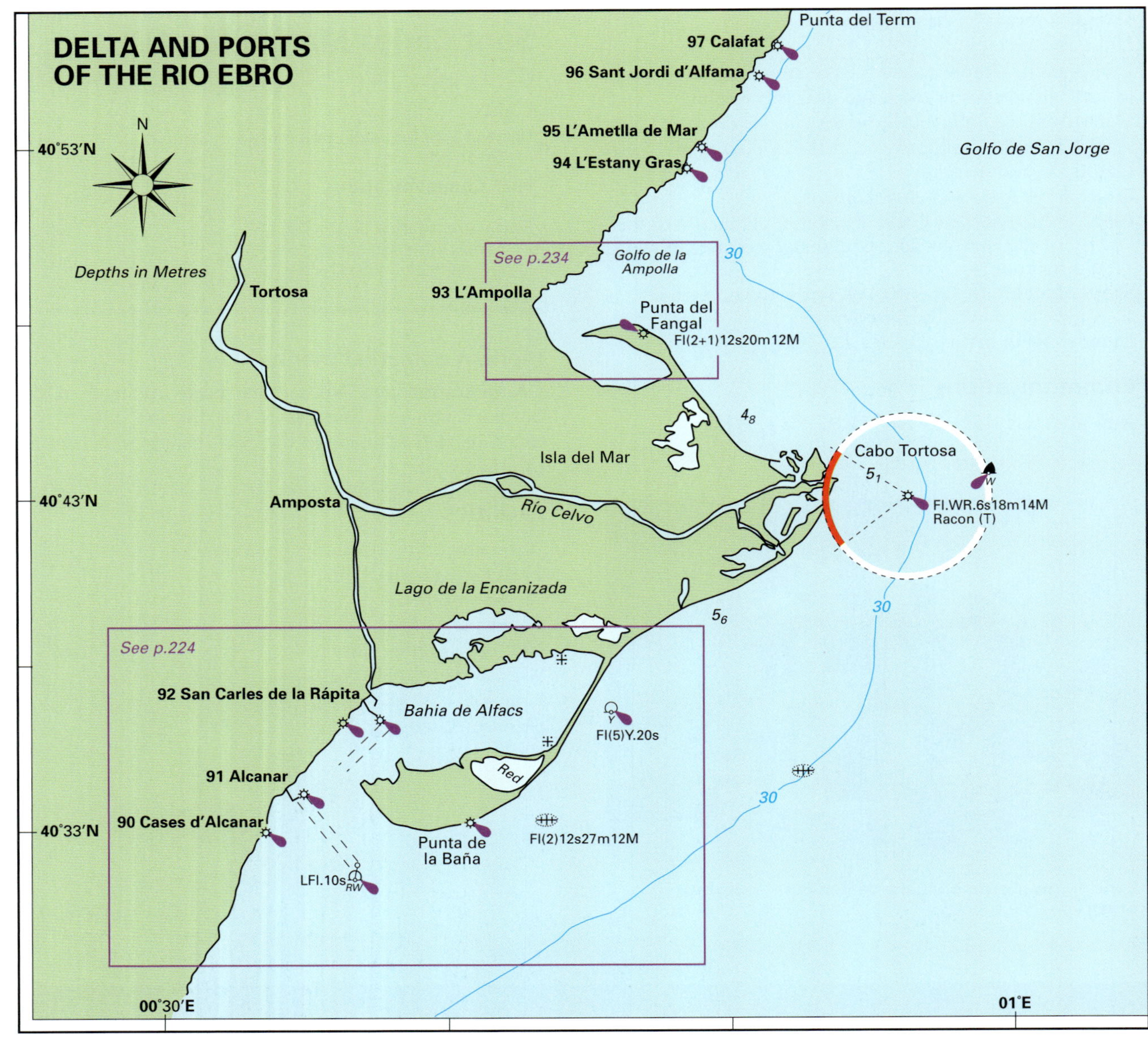

Rounding the Delta

Overview

Identifiable features on this low coast are few and far between. The coastline is constantly changing, as are the off-lying shoals. Navigational marks are not always on the coast and may be inland or out to sea. Sea levels tend to increase with winds between NE and SE and decrease with those from other directions. There is usually southerly current off the cabo.

From the S

From the area of Vinaròs set course for Punta de la Baña if necessary using the features on Sierra Montsi to keep a navigational fix. The industry at Alcanar (La Martinenca) may also be identified by the dust from the cement works. In the closer approach the lighthouse Punta de la Baña will be seen. Keeping about 1½M from the coast and outside the 10m contour, follow the coast in a NNE direction. The features marked on the plan will be seen in clear weather but in poor visibility little that can be identified will be seen. Do not cut the corner at Cabo Tortosa and keep at least 1M outside any visible land. The old lighthouse may be seen about a mile inland from the *cabo*. Continue outside the 10m contour which is about ½M off the coast.

Rounding the Ebro Delta from the N

It is normal to set course from the area of L'Ametlla de Mar direct for Cabo Tortosa. The houses at Ampolla and the lighthouse at Faro del Fangar will provide a position. The old lighthouse which lies about a mile inland to the W of Cabo Tortosa is difficult to spot even in good visibility. Do not approach the shore closer than the 10m contour. Do not attempt to round Cabo Tortosa within a mile of any visible land. Having rounded the *cabo* follow the coast about 1½M offshore, outside the 10m contour. If going up to Sant Carles, get into mid-channel between Alcanar and Punta Corballera.

Delta and ports of the Río Ebro

Alfacs de Tortosa

40°43′N 0°54′E

Charts

UKHO 1701, 1704	Imray M13
SHOM 7048, 4720	Spanish 485

Lights

Punta de la Baña 40°33′·6N 0°39′·7E Fl(2)12s27m12M White tower black bands 26m

Cabo Tortosa 40°42′·9N 0°55′·7E Fl.WR.6s18m14M Black metal framework tower, aluminium top 18m 127°-W-047°-R-127°

El Fangal 40°47′·4N 0°46′·1E Fl(2+1)12s20m12M White tower, red band 18m

Buoys

There may be five wave measuring buoys Fl(5)Y.13s stretching NW 5M E of Cabo Tortosa.

The Ebro is the largest river in Spain depositing vast amounts of silt, building the delta out to sea. In some places the shore is advancing by 10m a year, sometimes leaving inland what were once coastal marks. In other places currents have washed away the shore and similar features have been left standing in water. Away from the sea, the delta consists of many small islands separated by canals, saltpans, pools, marshes and mud, all subject to flooding; it is hovercraft terrain. For some, and for fauna, it has its attractions. A large part of the delta on the NE side is a nature reserve and park.

This is a good area to hire a car or explore by cycle, to see rice being harvested or to spend an early evening in a bird hide. Large flocks of birds may be seen including; Great Egrets, Cattle Egrets, Little Egrets, various ducks and terns, Marsh Harrier, Osprey and Flamingos.

The shore line of the delta is probably the most dangerous section of this coast. It is featureless, very low-lying, it extends over 12M seawards from the general line of the coast and has unmarked, shifting, off-lying shoals. A peculiarity is that in good visibility, buildings etc. which are located some distance inland appear to be situated on the coast. A branch of the *tramontana* NW gale can come down the Ebro valley with considerable force and little warning. Altogether, from the point of view of the navigator, it is a place to be avoided.

Entry

It is possible for shallow draught vessels (1m or less) to enter and leave the river but very dangerous without a pilot (*práctico*) with up-to-date knowledge of the channels at the bar. The bar is itself dangerous if there is any sea running at the time.

Entrance to river

The River

There are two main ports on the lower section of the Río Ebro, Amposta 16M upstream from the river mouth and Tortosa a further 9M. Yachts with draught of 1m or less can ascend the river to Tortosa and for some miles more but again, a pilot (*práctico*) is essential. There are high tension wires, 13m or less above the water, just downstream of Isla Gracia, well before Amposta. Yachts with masts over 10m high will not be able to go beyond the three road bridges at Amposta. There are also rail and road bridges at Tortosa.

Amposta

40°43′N 00°35′E

Amposta is a small old town with narrow streets and with 14,650 inhabitants. There is an old narrow road bridge and a series of quays alongside the river on the right (SW) bank. Below the town is a new wide bypass road bridge and above it is the new motor route bridge. There are a fair number of shops in town and everyday requirements can be met.

The Club Náutico de Amposta has a base with a pontoon and a small crane on the right bank of the Río Ebro just below the old road bridge ☎ 977 701 824. There are showers, WCs and bar. A mechanic is available. This is a good place for motor boats.

Tortosa

40°48′N 0°31′E

A very old town of 31,200 inhabitants with quays on the left bank, many interesting places and ruins to visit. This town had the first and only road bridge over the lower part of the Río Ebro and it was an important place from the point of view of commerce and defence. The Romans established the town and called it Dertosa Julia Augusta but they lost it to the Visigoths. They in turn lost it to the Moors in 714 who built the castle, now in ruins. It was then re-conquered by the Catalan, Ramon Bereguer IV, and for several centuries Catalans, Moors, Jews and others lived here together in peace. In 1938 there was a terrible battle here on the right (W) bank of the river between the Republicans and the Nationalists who triumphed; 150,000 died. A memorial stands in the middle of the river.

Puerto del Fangar (Fangal)

Charts

UKHO 1701, 1704	Imray M13
SHOM 7048, 4720	Spanish 485

Lights

El Fangal Fl(2+1)12s20m12M
White tower, red band 18m

A large shallow bay

This large stretch of water which is enclosed by the N part of the Río Ebro (Ebre) delta. It is about 1M by 2M with an entrance about 1M but space is limited by *viveros*, fish farms, in this case raising mussels. It is wide open to the N and with a NE wind a current crosses the entrance. Depths, which ordinarily range from 4m to 0m, may be raised as much as 0·6m by easterly winds and lowered the same amount by westerlies. The sides are very shallow. It is surrounded by rice fields and *salinas* (saltpans) ashore, together with a few barns and salt factories but no roads or villages.

The *viveros* are all round the bay but there are anchorages to be found, depending on draught. Sound carefully.

⚓ Ensenada de Cartapacio

40°48'N 0°42'·4E

An anchorage in the W corner of the Golfo de L'Ampolla in 1·8m, sand, open to NE–E. Sandy beach. Road to L'Ampolla.

El Fangal lighthouse

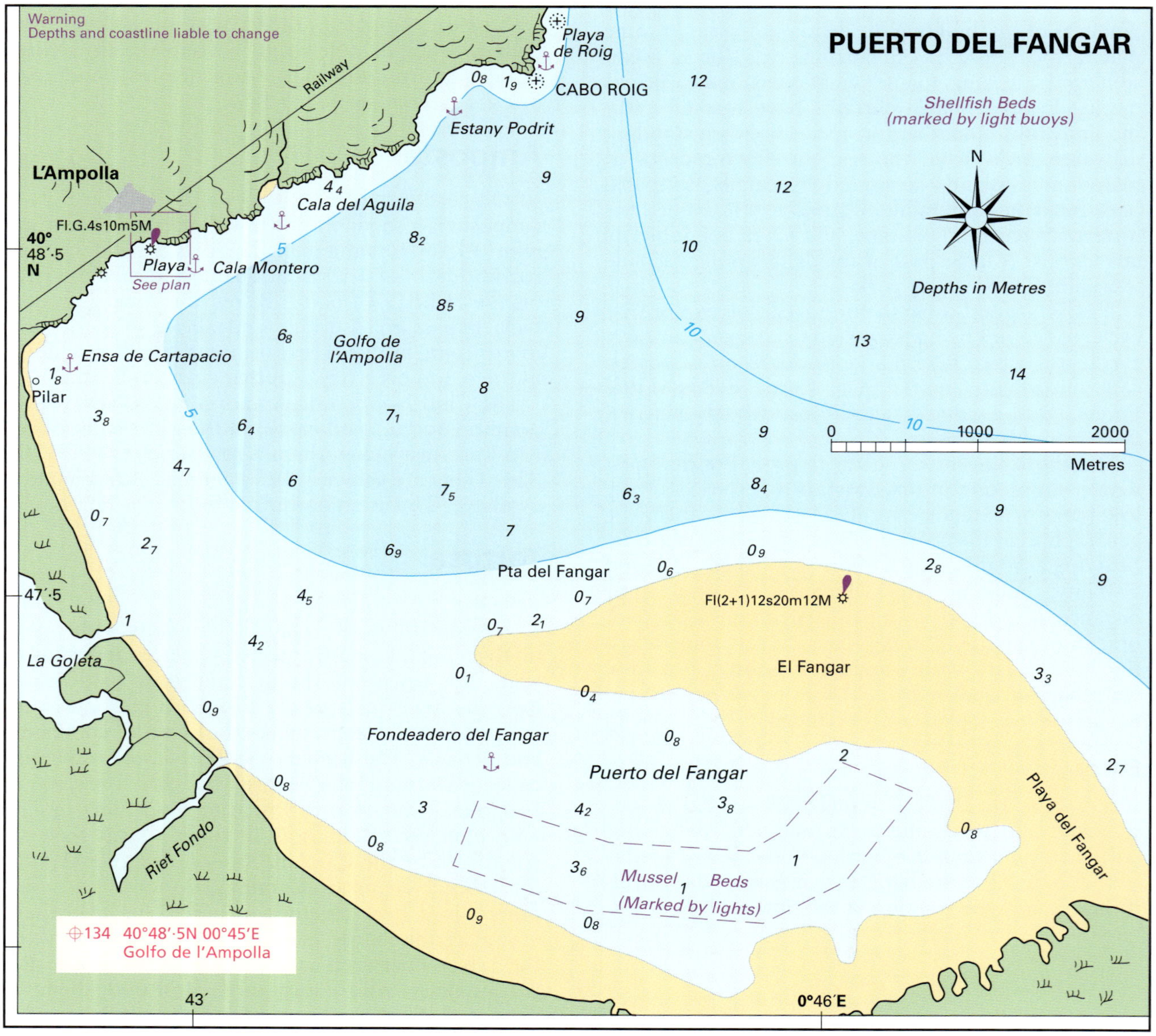

93. Puerto L'Ampolla

40°48'·5N 0°43'E

Charts

UKHO 1701	Imray M13
SHOM 7048, 4720	Spanish 485, 838

Lights

Dique jetty head Fl(2)G.7s4m3M
Green post 2m

Dique head Fl.G.5s10m5M
Green pyramidal tower 5m

Contradique head Fl.R.5s4m3M
Red truncated tower 3m

Contradique interior Fl(2)R.7s4m1M
Red square tower 3m

Port communications

Club Náutico L'Ampolla VHF Ch 9 ✆ 977 460 211
port@nauticampolla.com
www.nauticampolla.com

Harbour charges High-ish but include showers, water, 220v AC and security.

Puerto L'Ampolla

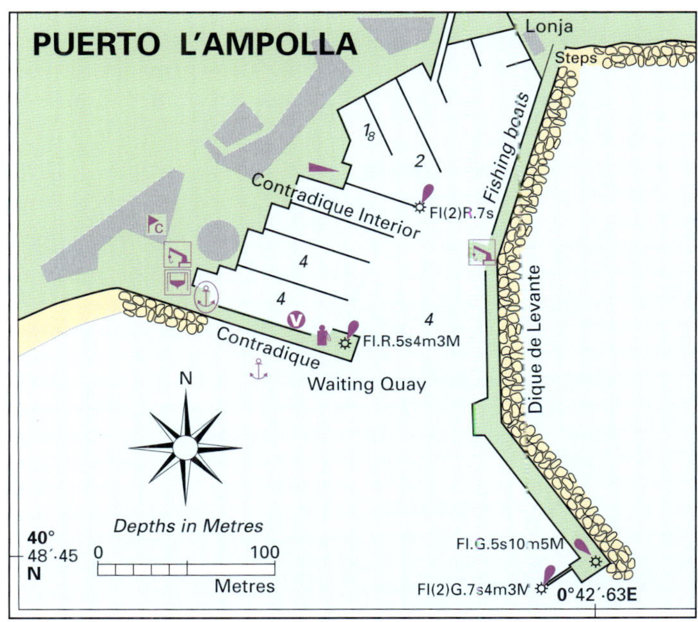

A pleasant port

An attractive fishing port with facilities developed for yachts and apparently a place favoured by Andorrans. The approach and entrance are easy but could be difficult if not dangerous in strong easterlies.

Approach

From the south Round the delta of the Río Ebro and from off the Faro del Fangar, go WNW towards the houses of L'Ampolla and look for the *dique*.

From the north Follow the steep rugged and indented coast at 400m. Punta Figuera and Cabo Roig will be identified, the latter having a reddish streak of rock. The houses of L'Ampolla can be seen in the distance and, when close, the *dique*.

There are oyster beds marked by buoys Fl.Y.13s in the approaches to Ampolla.

Anchorage in the approach

Anchor off the Nuevo Contradique according to depth. Good shelter if heading north and held up by wind from that quarter. Good holding.

Entrance

Approach the head of the Dique de Levante leaving it at least 30m to starboard and continue on that course to round the new jetty extension that protrudes WSW from just inside the Dique head. Round the end of the jetty and proceed to the fuel berth just inside the head of the contradique.

Berths

Wait at the end of the *contradique* and ask at the *club náutico*.

Puerto L'Ampolla fishing harbour *Steve Pickard*

V. COSTA DORADA

Facilities

Maximum length overall 15m.
30-tonne travel-lift.
10- and 5-tonne cranes.
Slipway (but shallow approach).
Engine mechanics.
A small chandlery in the village.
Water from the *lonja*.
Water and 220v AC on all pontoons, 380v AC on slipway.
Ice from the *club náutico* and the *lonja*.
Club Náutico L'Ampolla with terrace, swimming pool, showers and WCs.
Shops and supermarket nearby in the village.

Communications

Buses. Rail service to Barcelona.
Taxi ✆ 977 490 386.

⚓ Cala Montero

40°48'·6N 0°43'·1E (see plan p.234)

A dry river mouth with rocky sides provides a small anchorage in 2m, mud, open between NE and S, stony beach.

⚓ Cala del Aguila

40°50'·6N 0°45'·3E (see plan p.234)

A small anchorage off the mouth of a dry river open NE to S. The bottom is rocky 1–3m deep.

⚓ Estany Podrit

40°51'·5N 0°47'·0E (see plan p.234)

An open anchorage off the mouth of a dry river open to NE to S. The bottom is 1–3·5m, weed, rocks and sand. A peak, Montaña del Aquila (159m), lies 1M to W.

⚓ Playa de Roig

40°49'·2N 0°44'·2E (see plan p.234)

The S half of the bay is better than the N where the bottom is mostly rock.

Playa de Roig (beyond the first headland)

94. Puerto de L'Estany Gras

40°52'N 0°47'E

Chart
UKHO 1701, 1704 — Imray M13
SHOM 4720 — Spanish 838

Lights
North Point 40°52'·4N 0°47'·7E Fl(4)G.11s14m5M Green tower 5m
Jetty Fl(4)R.11s6m3M Red tower 5m

Offshore, opposite entrance, there are a number of fish farms off the harbour which must be avoided when entering.

A very attractive small harbour

A small, most attractive, old natural harbour, now virtually deserted, which is located in a narrow deep rocky *cala*. A fish farm has been established opposite the entrance, about two miles out. The approach is easy but the entrance should not be attempted with onshore winds or swell. Facilities are limited to a broken quay. All supplies have to be obtained from L'Ametlla about 1M away to NE.

Approach

From the south Round the delta of the Río Ebro and set a NW course from off Cabo Tortosa. The town of L'Ametlla will be seen on approaching the mainland coast and the harbour lies 1M to the SW of this town. In the closer approach the two small lighthouses, 6m and 4m, will be seen.

From the north Follow the rocky broken coast in a SW direction past a conspicuous nuclear electric generating station near Cabo del Terme and the town of L'Ametlla. This harbour lies about 1M to SW of L'Ametlla. The two small lighthouses, 6m and 4m high, will be seen beside the entrance.

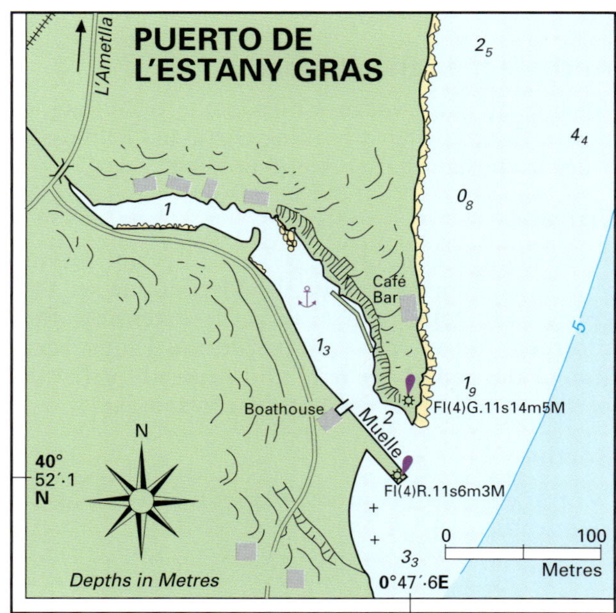

Puerto de L'Estany Gras (left), calas Bon Capo, Bon Caponet and Arangaret (central), Puerto de L'Ametlla de Mar (right)

Entrance

Very tight. Approach on a NW heading and enter with care, towards the W side.

Anchorage

Depth off the quay is only 0·4m and ashlars and other underwater obstructions stick out from it. Anchor near the centre of the harbour in 1·5m, weed and rock, using an anchor trip-line. Lines can be taken ashore if others do not wish to get by.

Communications

A country road runs to L'Ametlla about 1M away where most requirements can be met.

⚓ Cala Bon Capo and Cala Bon Caponet

40°52'·4N 0°47'·7E

⚓ Cala de Arangaret

40°53'N 0°48'E

A very small anchorage in 1·5m, sand, 400m to SW of Puerto de L'Ametlla de Mar. Open between NE, S and SE.

Note There are many small coves between Puerto de L'Ametlla and Cabo de Sant Jordi that may be used with care and prudence as day anchorages.

95. Puerto de L'Ametlla de Mar

40°53'N 0°48'1E

Charts

UKHO 1701, 1704	Imray M13
SHOM 4720	Spanish 838

Lights

Dique de Levante head Fl(3)G.9s17m5M
Green tower on white hut 10m
Dique de Poniente head Fl(3)R.9s9m3M Red tower 4m
Contradique head Fl(4)R.11s8m1M Red tower 4m

Port communications

Capitania VHF Ch 9 ✆ 629 894 538
Club Náutico ✆ 977 45 72 40
cnam@pcserveis.com

Harbour charges Medium

A busy harbour

An active fishing harbour with an area in the south developed for yachts. The yacht quays are all new and well equipped with water and electricity and are no great distance from the old part of town which is well worth a visit. There are a number of small beaches in *calas* near the harbour.

Approach

From the south To the N of the Ebro delta the mainland coast is of reddish rock and is of very broken low cliffs with high ground further inland. Punta Figuera with a red and white beacon on it is easily recognisable but Punta del Aguila is not conspicuous. The wide Cala de Santa Cruz and the deep Puerto de L'Estany Gras, which has two small lighthouse towers can be identified. The town of L'Ametlla can be seen from afar.

Puerto de L'Ametlla de Mar looking down harbour. Yachts turn to port at the fuel jetty *Peter Taylor*

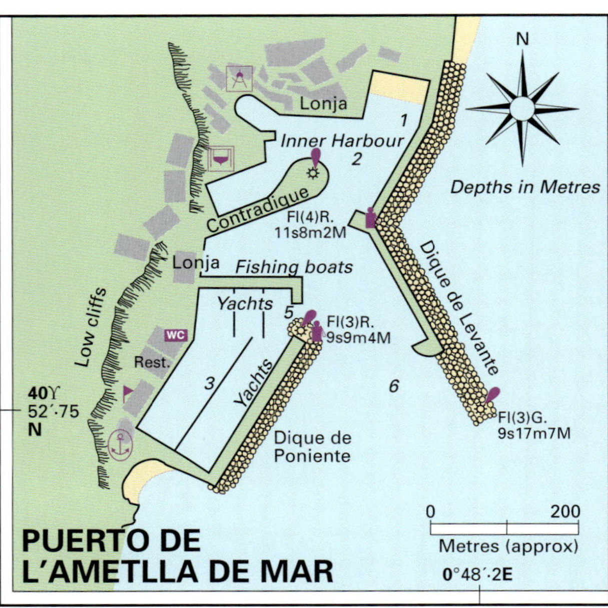

From the north From the conspicuous promontory Cabo de Salou the coast is low until Punta Llastres where the high Sierra de Balaguer range reaches the sea. The grey blocks of two nuclear power stations just to the N of Cabo Terme are conspicuous; off shore there are two buoys, one an E cardinal. The town of L'Ametlla will be seen from afar.

Entrance

Straighforward but give the Dique de Levante a reasonable (25m) berth as its foundations slope out into the water. Make for the head of the Dique de Poniente and turn to port around its head into the yacht basin.

Berths

The *capitanía* should be called (Ch 9 or phone) before entering to obtain berthing instructions. Failing this pick up a vacant berth (all berths have lines from the quay) and go ashore to the *capitanía* for further instructions. The inner harbour is now totally taken over by fishing vessels and a yacht should not proceed past the fuelling berth – and, as usual, no anchoring is permitted in the harbour.

Facilities

Full repair facilities with slipway and 20-tonne crane.
Chandlery in NW corner.
Water and 220v AC on quays and pontoons.
Fuel and ice.
Club náutico has new building with WCs, showers, bar, restaurant and office.
Many shops near harbour and in town.

Communications

Rail and bus service.

Fuel berth at northern end of Dique de Poniente, marina and fishing port looking W from the Dique de Levante *Steve Pickard*

96. Puerto Deportivo de Sant Jordi d'Alfama

40°55'N 0°50'E

Charts
UKHO 1701, 1704 Imray M13
SHOM 4720 Spanish 838

Lights
Dique de Abrigo head Fl(2)G.7s8m5M
Green column 4m
Dique de Abrigo elbow Fl(2)G.7s3m3M
Green pyramid 2m
Dique de Abrigo corner VQ(3)5s6m3M
Card E post 2m
Contradique head Fl(2)R.7s5m3M
Red post 1m

Port communications
Marina VHF Ch 9. ✆ 977 486 327

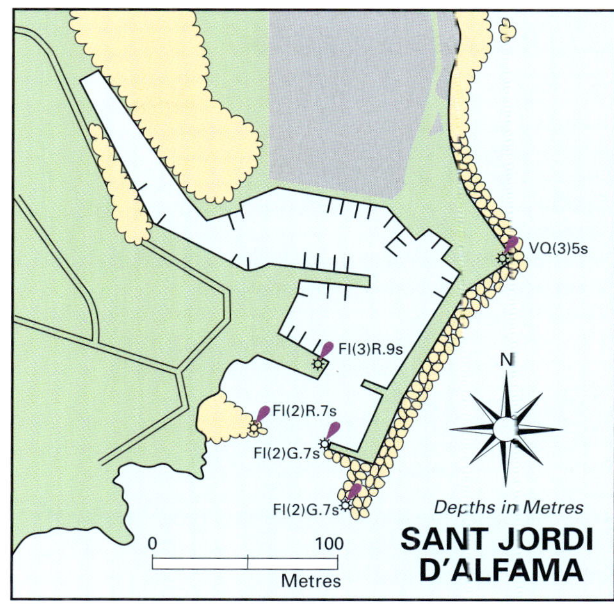

Redeveloped small marina

Sant Jordi was built back in the late nineties as part of a large housing development and in a river bed. As with a lot of similar developments it ran out of money and the marina was left to become derelict and badly silted. In 2008 the Calafat marina took over the redevelopment and have done a lot of work extending the breakwaters, dredging the area to such an extent that the lights were reinstated in December 2009. It is now a functioning marina with 130 berths for 6–15m LOA vessels of 1·5–2·5m draft. It is very quiet and very environmentally friendly with limpid clear water. Ashore there is nothing but houses. The same company run the Calafat Marina (page 240) a half a mile north where all repair and technical services are available.

Approach

From the south From Cabo Tortosa head NNW towards the peaks of Es Frares (470m) and La Mamelleta (713m). In the closer approach the town of L'Ametlla can be seen to port and the town of Calafat to starboard and Cabo di Sant Jordi, with its ruined fort, will be conspicuous. The port breakwater will be seen just to the right of the fort.

From the north From Cabo de Salou pass Cambrils and Hospitalet both with high rise buildings behind their breakwaters. The two nuclear reactors then become clear and just beyond are the breakwaters of Calafat with Sant Jordi breakwater just 0·7M further on.

Entrance

Straightforward but it is advised to proceed slowly sounding carefully as the entrance could be silted.

Berths

It is advised to call ahead on VHF Ch 9 to see if a berth is available as the port is quite small and manoeuvring can be difficult.

Facilities

Water and 220v AC on pontoons.
Showers, toilets and laundry.
Pump out facility.
24/7 services with CCTV.
All repair and other services can be obtained at Calafat marina 0·5M north.
Developments are awaited.

Puerto Sant Jordi d'Alfama looking west
(by kind permission of Xavier Mangrane)

Puerto Sant Jordi d'Alfama *Steve Pickard*

97. Puerto de Calafat

40°56'N 0°51'E

Charts

UKHO 1701, 1704 Imray M13
SHOM 4720 Spanish 838

Lights

Harbour

Dique de Abrigo head Fl.G.5s9m5M Green tower 6m

Contradique Fl(2)R.10s5m4M Red tower 4m

To the northwest

Cabo Salou 41°03'·3N 1°10'·3E Fl(4)20s43m23M White tower with red bands, 11m

Port communications

Marina VHF Ch 09 ✆ 977 486 184
info@portcalafat.com
www.portcalafat.com

Small yacht marina

Small, but without the fjord like charm of St Jordi next door. Built as part of a large residential development it is easy to approach and enter except in a gale in the south quadrant when the entrance is difficult and the harbour uncomfortable. Limited supplies. Sandy beach at NE side of the harbour.

Approach

From the south From Cabo Tortosa head NNW towards the two peaks of Es Frares (470m) and La Mamelleta (713m) which lie behind the harbour. The grey concrete buildings of the nuclear power station are about a mile beyond the harbour.

In the closer approach Cabo de Sant Jordi, with a ruined fort, and its near-by port may be seen, then the housing estate in the trees behind the harbour and its breakwaters will be recognised.

From the north From Cabo de Salou (79m) the coast to SW is of low rocky cliffs with concentrations of houses. Puerto de Cambrils has some tall apartment blocks and a long rocky breakwater which are easily recognised.

Puerto de Hospitalet de L'Infant can likewise be recognised by the high-rise buildings and the harbour breakwater. Punta de Ríu de Llastres is a low promontory and has shallow water off its point. The two large concrete buildings of the nuclear reactors can be seen from afar. In the close approach the housing estate and the harbour breakwaters will be seen.

Anchorage in the approach

Anchor ¼M to S of the harbour in 10m sand.

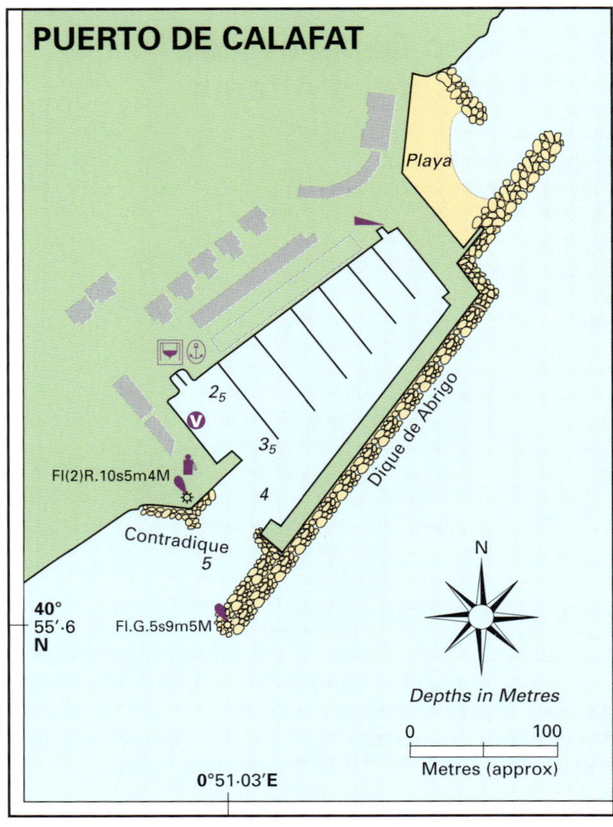

Entrance

Straightforward but if entering with a strong following wind, be prepared for some sharp manoeuvring once inside.

Berths

Secure to quay at port side of the entrance and ask. If no-one around, inquire at the *torre de control*.

Facilities

Maximum length overall 20m.
40-tonne travel-hoist.
5-tonne crane.
Limited hard-standing near travel-hoist.
Slipway.
Water from taps on quays and pontoons.
Gasoleo A and petrol.
Some shops and a small supermarket near the harbour; probably better to go to Ametlla.

Communications

Bus and rail. Car hire. Taxi ✆ 977 456 468.

Puerto de Calafat, fuel and visitors berth to port on entry
Steve Pickard

Calafat fuel berth
Robin Rundle

Cabo del Term
40°57'·07N 0°52'·45E

Two nuclear power stations, one inside a large square concrete building with no windows, the other inside a round tower-shaped building, are located 1–1½M respectively to NE of this *cabo* and are very conspicuous. A special spar light buoy lies 600m off the coast to NE and a S cardinal lightbuoy lies to SW marking water intakes

98. Puerto de Hospitalet de L'Infant

40°59'N 0°56'E

Charts
UKHO 1701, 1704 Imray M13
SHOM 4720 Spanish 838

Lights
Dique SE head Fl(4)G.11s10m5M
Green tower, 5m
Contradique head Fl.R.2s5m3M
Red tower on white base, 3m
Buoy 40°59'·3N 0°55'·6E Fl(4)R.11s3M
Port-hand can off Espigon
To the northwest
Cabo Salou 41°03'·3N 1°10'·3E Fl(4)20s43m23M
White tower with red bands, white building 11m

Port communications
VHF Ch 9 ✆ 977 823 004
nhv@cnhv.net
www.cnhv.net

Harbour charges Medium

Medium-sized yacht harbour

An artificial yacht harbour of medium size and characterless setting controlled by the Club Náutico de L'Hospitalet-Vandellós. Entry is usually easy but difficult in S gales when swell enters the harbour. This is a tourist area and there are many apartment blocks and hotels. Quite a lot of walking to be done to get anywhere. Good large sandy beach to SW. A hospice was founded here in 1314. Its ruins and a tower can still be seen.

Approach

From the south The harbour is due N from Cabo Tortosa. As the coast is approached Vandellós nuclear power station, with two large grey concrete buildings 3M SW of the harbour, should be seen. The group of high-rise buildings behind the harbour and its breakwaters will appear in the close approach.

From the north From Cabo Salou, a prominent and easily recognised feature, the low rocky cliffs and sandy beaches stretch SW. The houses, breakwater and tower of Puerto de Cambrils will be recognised as will the high-rise buildings of L'Hospitalet and its harbour breakwaters in the close approach.

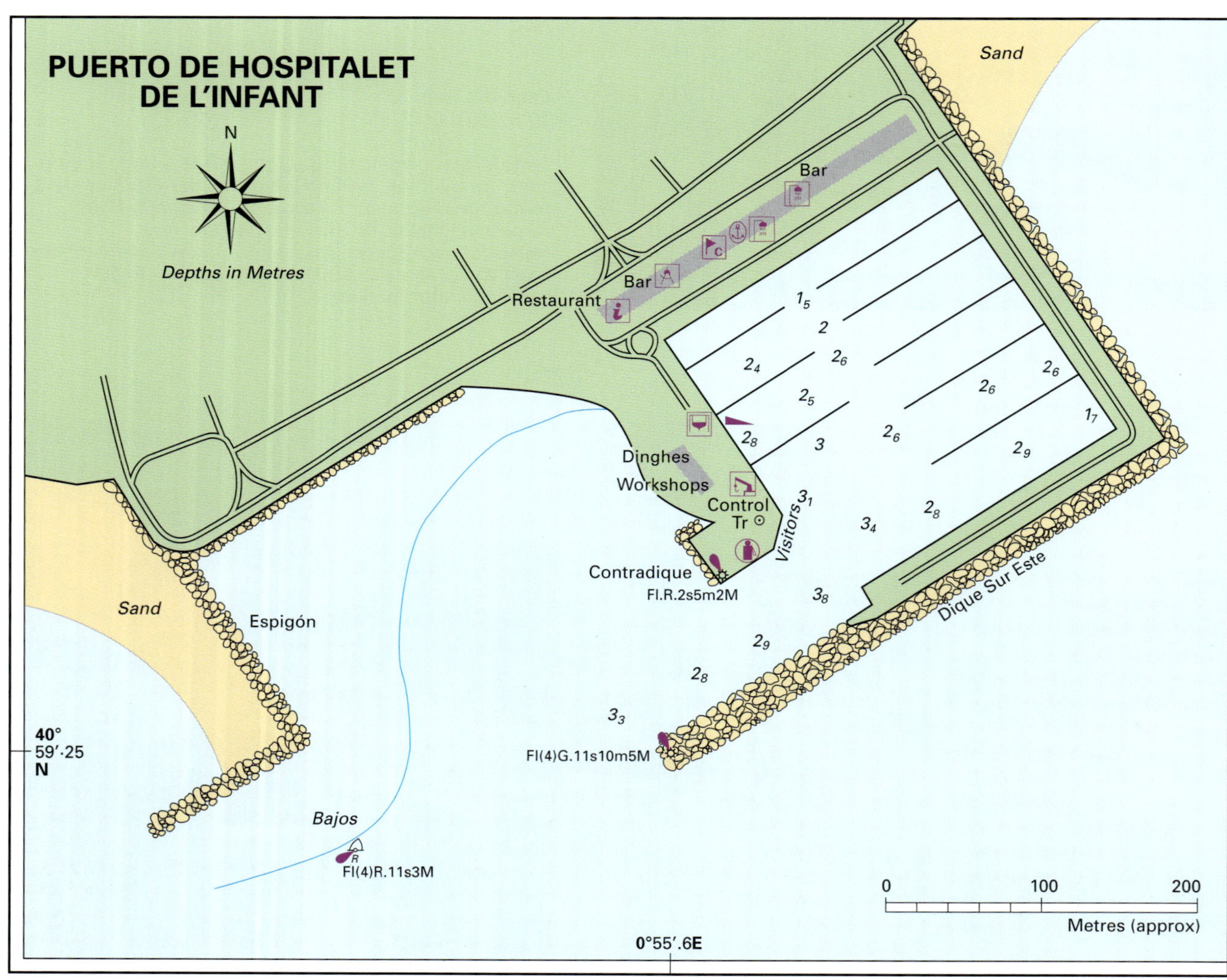

Puerto de Hospitalet de L'Infant (Vandellós)

Anchorage in the approach

Anchor in 8m, sand, ¼M to S of the harbour entrance.

Entrance

Approach on a N course, round Dique Sur Este and go to the waiting quay on the *contradique*, by the fuel pumps.

Berths

If no-one comes, ask at the *torre de control*. Berths have posts instead of mooring buoys or lines for securing the bow of the yacht. Berths for smaller yachts on pontoons have floating spurs.

Facilities

Maximum length overall 18m.
8-tonne crane.
Limited hard-standing.
Slipway.
Two chandlers beside the harbour.
Water and 220v AC on all quays and pontoons.
Small ice from the club and bars.
Gasoleo A and petrol.
Club Náutico de L'Hospitalet-Vandellós has a clubhouse on the NW side of the harbour with bar, showers, WCs etc. The club controls the harbour.
Food shops etc. in the village.

Communications

Road and rail. Taxi ✆ 977 810 363.

Puerto de Hospitalet de L'Infant *Steve Pickard*

V. COSTA DORADA

99. Puerto de Cambrils

41°04'N 1°04'E

Charts

UKHO 1701, 1704 Imray M13
SHOM 4720 Spanish 838

Lights

Dique de Levante head Fl(3)G.9s15m5M
Green pyramidal tower 11m

Dique de Poniente head Fl(2)R.7s13m3M
Red tower 9m

Malecón Dársena Deportiva head Fl(4)G.11s6m1M
Green pyramidal tower 4m

To the west

Cabo Salou 41°03'·3N 1°10'·3E Fl(4)20s43m23M
White tower with red bands, white building 11m

Port communications

Club náutico VHF Ch 9. ☎ 977 360 531
info@clubnauticcambrils.com
www.clubnauticcambrils.com

Harbour charges Low

Fishing harbour with yacht marina

Puerto de Cambrils is easy to approach and enter and has good shelter. The area caters for a large number of tourists in the season and a number of ferries use the harbour for day trips. The harbour is large and set nicely into the town. Facilities and the shops are good.

The Monasterio de Escornalou some 5M inland has a spectacular view. The Roman 'Oleaster', a fortified church tower in the front of the town is of interest. Good sandy beaches on either side of the harbour, the better being to SW.

Approach

From the south The reddish rocky cliffs where the Sierra de Balaguer lies alongside the coast end at Punta de Ríu de Llastres and the coast becomes low, flat and sandy. The houses and harbour works at Cambrils can be seen from afar.

From the north Having rounded the rocky-cliffed promontory of Cabo de Salou, which is covered with large private houses and some high-rise buildings, the coast becomes low, flat and sandy. The houses, flats and light-coloured rocky breakwater of this harbour can be seen from afar.

Anchorage in the approach

Anchor some 400m to W of the entrance in 5m on sand.

Entrance

Round the head of the Dique de Levante, leaving it 25–30m to starboard and enter nearer to the head of the Dique de Poniente which can be rounded at 15m. Go across the harbour and round the head of the Malecón Darsena Deportiva at about 15m.

Berths

Berth stern-to the pontoons with mooring buoy from the bow in the E side of the yacht harbour and check at the reception centre.

Moorings

A few private moorings are available in the main harbour.

Puerto de Cambrils

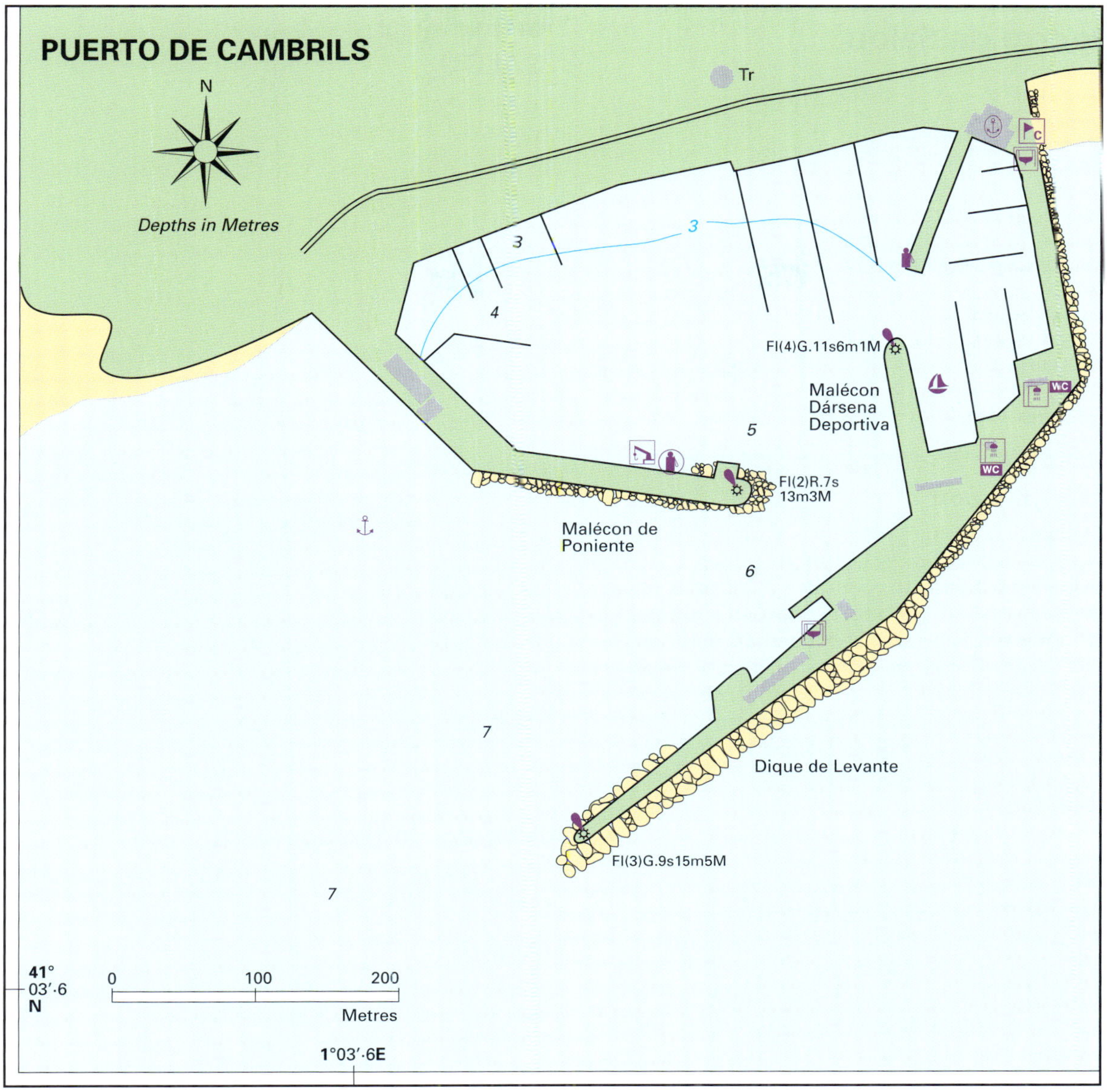

PUERTO DE CAMBRILS

N

Depths in Metres

Tr

Fl(4)G.11s6m1M

Malécon Dársena Deportiva

Fl(2)R.7s 13m3M

Malécon de Poniente

Dique de Levante

Fl(3)G.9s15m5M

41° 03′·6 N

0 100 200 Metres

1°03′·6E

Facilities

Maximum length overall 20m.

Limited repairs are possible and there are a number of engine mechanics in town.

140-tonne travel-lift and 12-tonne crane in port.

7·5-tonne crane.

Two slipways.

A chandlery in the town.

Water on the pontoons in the yacht harbour or from the *lonja*.

110v and 220v AC from the *club náutico*, pontoons and quay.

Gasoleo A and petrol.

Ice factory near the *lonja*.

Club Náutico de Cambrils with restaurant, bar, terrace, showers.

A number of shops alongside the harbour but many more in the town itself which is about ½M inland.

Launderette in the town.

Cambrils: fuel and reception *Peter Taylor*

Communications

Rail and bus service. Air services from Tarragona-Reus about 10M away. Taxi ✆ 977 362 622.

Embarcadero de Reus Club de Mar

41°04′·2N 1°07′E

A jetty 100m long projecting from the shore ¼M to W of Puerto de Salou. Roads, railway and houses ashore. Can be used as a landing. Anchor in 2m, sand, to S of head of pier.

100. Puerto de Salou

41°07'N 1°07'E

Charts
UKHO 1701, 1704 Imray M13
SHOM 4720, 4827 Spanish 4861, 487A, 838

Lights
Dique de Levante head Fl(2)G.8s9m5M
Green column 5m
Dique de Poniente head Fl(2)R.8s4m3M
Red post 2m

Port communications
VHF Ch 9 ✆ 977 382 166 / ✆ 977 382 167
club@clubnauticsalou.com
www.clubnauticsalou.com

Harbour charges High

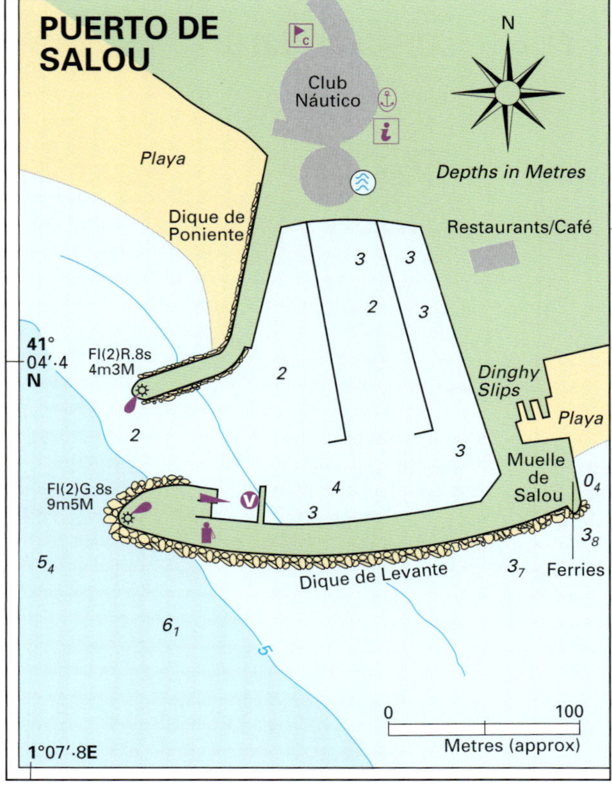

A small expensive port

Salou has been a fishing port since Roman times when it was called Salauris; from it Jaime I (El Conquistador) set forth to conquer Mallorca in 1229. It is now one of the more popular summer resorts and the town is primarily concerned with the mass tourist trade. It has an expensive, nicely set if nondescript, small artificial harbour with very limited space for visitors and limited facilities. The approach and entrance are not difficult but would be dangerous in strong winds and swell from SW. There are excellent sandy beaches on each side of the harbour.

Approach

From the south The high Sierra de Balaguer gives way to flat, sandy coasts at Punta de Ríu de Llastres. The houses, flats and breakwater at Cambrils are easily identified. The many high-rise buildings at Salou can be seen from afar and the harbour will be seen when closer in.

From the north Cabo de Salou, a rocky-cliffed promontory, is easily identified. Apart from its lighthouse it has a number of high-rise buildings and large houses on it. Once rounded, the buildings of Salou will be seen about 4M further on. In the close approach the harbour will be seen.

Anchorage in the approach

Anchor 300m to W of the head of the Dique de Levante in 3m, sand.

Entrance

Straightforward, the visitors berth is immediately inside the entrance to starboard.

Salou entrance – wide but shallow *Peter Taylor*

Puerto de Salou

Puerto de Salou looking NE *Steve Pickard*

Facilities

Engine mechanics.
10-tonne crane and a mobile 5-tonne crane.
Two slipways and dinghy slips.
Water and 220v AC on all quays and pontoons.
Ice from the *club náutico*.
Gasoleo A and petrol.
Club Náutico de Salou clubhouse has good facilities.
Supermarket and many shops in the town nearby.
Launderette in town.

Communications

Bus and rail. Tarragona airport 7M.
Taxi ✆ 977 380 034.

Salou *Robin Rundle*

Cala de la Torre Nova (or del Lazareto)

Cabo Salou anchorages

1. ⚓ S of Salou

41°04'N 1°08'·3E

A big ship anchorage ½M to S of Puerto de Salou in 11m, sand and weed. Open to SE through to W.

2. ⚓ Cala de la Torre Nova (or del Lazareto)

41°04'N 1°08'·7E

An anchorage in 2m, sand, open SE to W. Sandy beach and high-rise buildings

3. ⚓ Cala Pinatel (or Grande)

41°03'·7N 1°09'·2E

An open anchorage off a large sandy beach the Playa de Pinatell in 2m, sand. Open to SE through to W.

4. ⚓ N of Punta de Peny Tallada

41°03'·6N 1°09'·4E

A small bay open between S and W; anchor in 2m, sand.

5. ⚓ Cala de la Font

41°03'·5N 1°09'·5E

A small anchorage off a beach with a projecting rock. Open to S through to NW. Anchor in 2m, sand.

6. ⚓ Cala del Cranc

41°03'·2N 1°10'E

A narrow bay with small beach and an isolated rock 0·5m deep in its mouth. Anchor in 2m, sand. Open S and SW

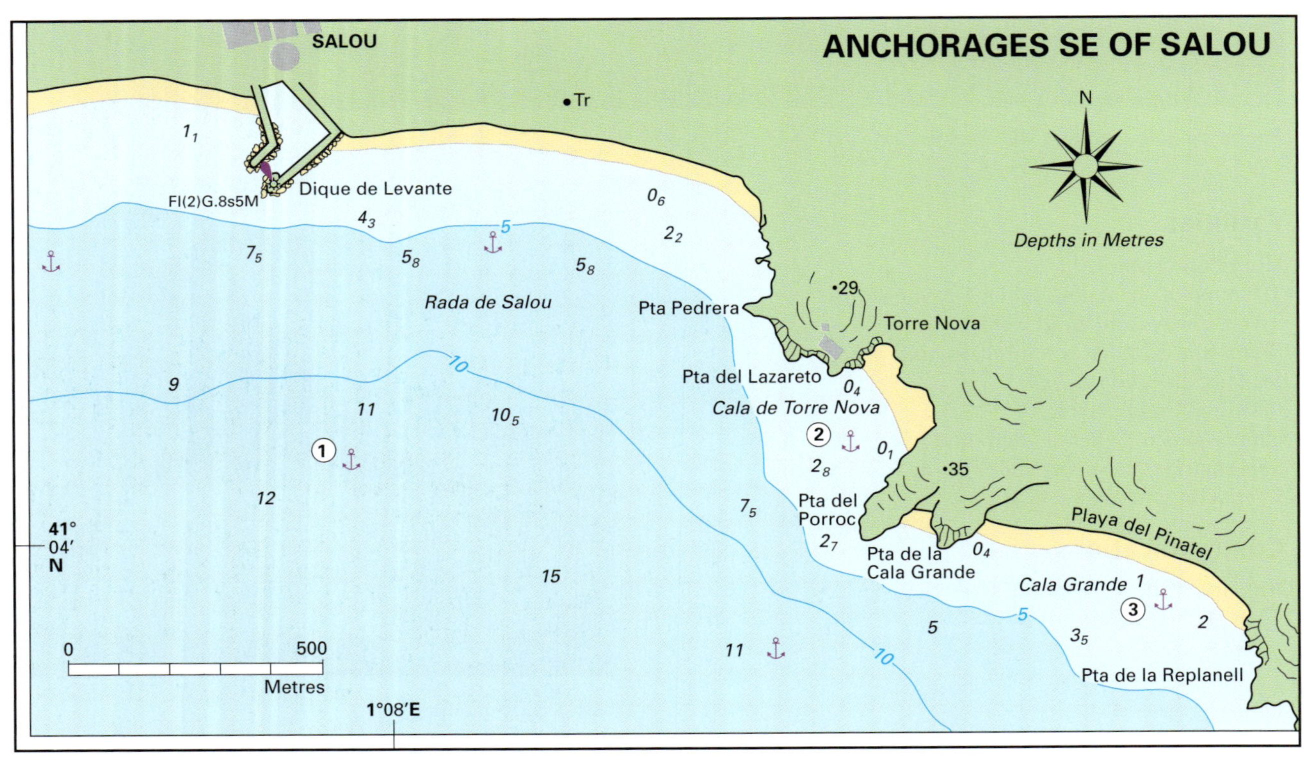

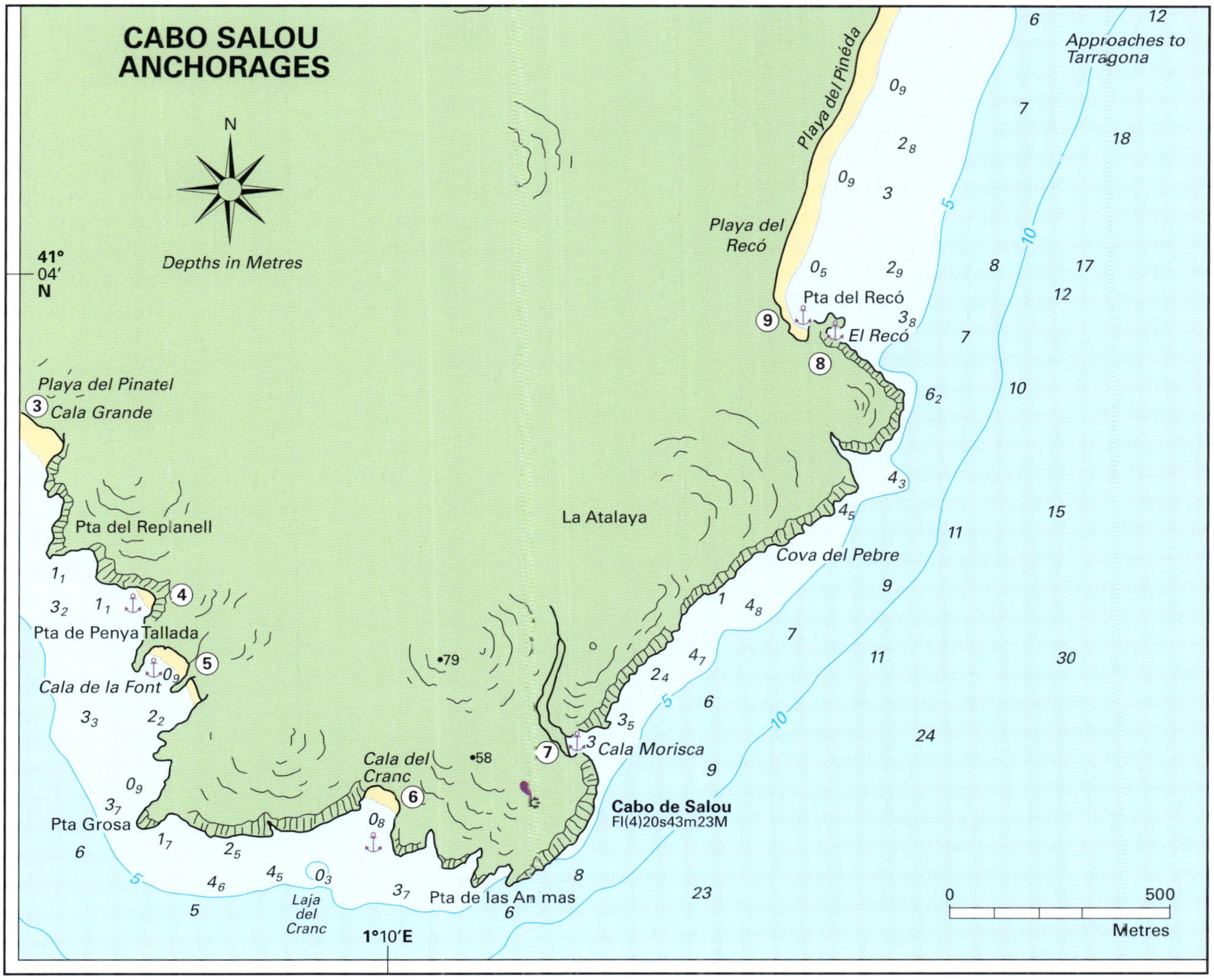

CABO SALOU ANCHORAGES
Depths in Metres
41° 04′ N
1°10′E
Approaches to Tarragona
Playa del Pinéda
Playa del Recó
Pta del Recó
El Recó
Playa del Pinatel
Cala Grande
Pta del Replanell
Pta de Penya Tallada
Cala de la Font
La Atalaya
Cova del Pebre
Cala Morisca
Cala del Cranc
Cabo de Salou
Fl(4)20s43m23M
Pta Grosa
Laja del Cranc
Pta de las An mas
0 500 Metres

7. ⚓ Cala Morisca

41°03′·4N 1°10′·5E

A small bay open to NE through to S. Anchor in 2m, sand.

8. ⚓ El Recó

41°04′·1N 1°10′·9E

A small bay open between N and E; anchor in 2m, sand. Two small rocky islets one each side of the bay.

9. ⚓ Playa del Recó

41°04′·2N 1°11′E

An open anchorage off a long sandy beach. Anchor to suit draught, sandy bottom. Playa de Reco runs into Playa de Pineda which has a light on a breakwater at 41°04′N 1°11′E (Q(3)10s8m1M) on a cardinal E pole 6m high. Note pipeline on chart to W.

Cabo Salou, a built up and prominent headland with conspicuous lighthouse tower (43m) and a second tower (120m) NE of it on the top of the headland

V. COSTA DORADA

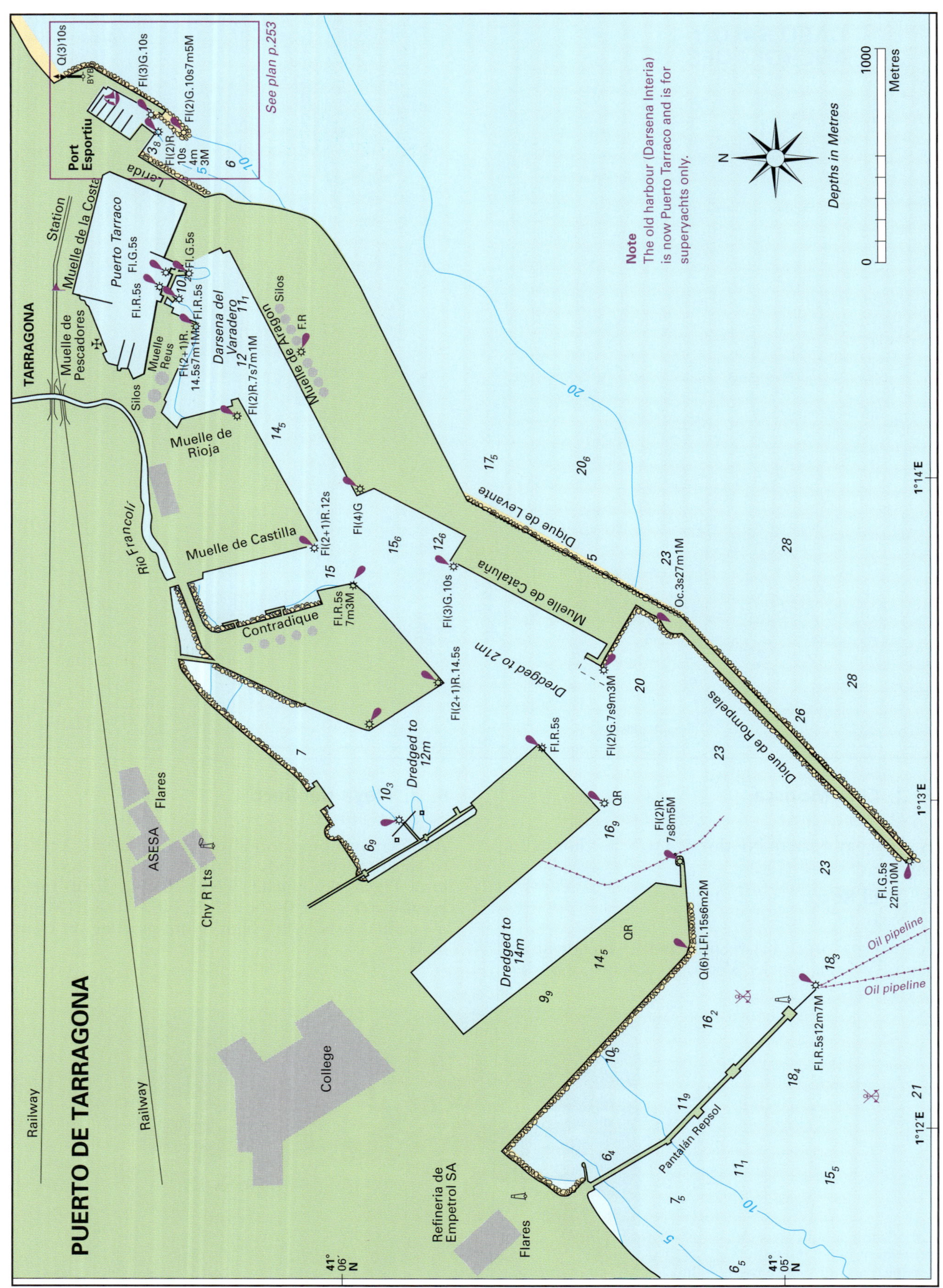
PUERTO DE TARRAGONA
TARRAGONA
Railway
Railway
Station
Muelle de la Costa
Muelle de Pescadores
Puerto Tarraco
Port Esportiu
See plan p.253
Q(3)10s
BYB
Fl(3)G.10s
Fl(2)G.10s7m5M
Fl(2)R.10s4m3M
Fl.G.5s
Fl.R.5s
Silos
Muelle Reus
Darsena del Varadero
Fl(2+1)R.14.5s7m1M
Fl(2)R.7s7m1M
Muelle de Aragon
F.R
Muelle de Rioja
Rio Francolí
Muelle de Castilla
Fl(2+1)R.12s
Fl(4)G
Contradique
Fl.R.5s 7m3M
Fl(3)G.10s
Dique de Levante
Muelle de Cataluña
Oc.3s27m1M
Dredged to 21m
Fl(2+1)R.14.5s
Fl(2)G.7s9m3M
Dique de Rompeolas
Dredged to 12m
Fl.R.5s
QR
Fl(2)R.7s8m5M
Fl.G.5s 22m10M
Flares
ASESA
Chy R Lts
Dredged to 14m
QR
Q(6)+LFl.15s6m2M
Oil pipeline
Oil pipeline
Fl.R.5s12m7M
College
Pantalán Repsol
Refineria de Empetrol SA
Flares
Note
The old harbour (Darsena Interia) is now Puerto Tarraco and is for superyachts only.
N
Depths in Metres
0
1000
Metres
1°14´E
1°13´E
1°12´E
41°06´N
41°05´N

PUERTO DE TARRAGONA

41°05'N 1°13'E

Note The old harbour is normally forbidden to yachts but might be used in stress of weather. In normal circumstances go to the Port Esportiou (Puerto Deport vo).

Charts

UKHO 1193, 1701, 1704	Imray M13
Shom 7047, 4720, 4827	Spanish 4871, 487A, 838

Lights

To the south

Cabo Salou 41°03'·4N 1°10'·4E Fl(4)20s43m23M
White tower with red bands, white building 11m

Approach main harbour

Dique de Levante head 41°05'N 1°13'·2E Fl.G.5s22m10M
Green tower 11m

Contradique head Fl(2)R.7s8m5M
Red tower 2m

Dique de Levante Faro de la Banya Oc.3s27m1M
Grey post on hut 16m

Port Esportiu

Outer breakwater 41°06'·4N 1°15'·1E Fl(2)G.10s7m5M
Green ▲ on white post 3m

Contradique head Fl(2)R.10s4m3M
Red post 1m

To the north

Punta de la Galera 41°07'·9N 1°23'·7E Fl(5)30s58m17M
White tower, bronze top 38m

Port communications

Tarragona Pilots VHF Ch 9, 12, 14, 16.
Capitanía ✆ 977 226 611
Real Club Náutico de Tarragona ✆ 977 240 360
info@rcntarragona.com
www.rcntarragona.com

Storm signals

Flown from a flagstaff on the Muelle de Pescadores.

An old port with two marinas

This is a very old port of a city with a fascinating history with a new yacht marina alongside. The old commercial and fishing port, greatly enlarged by the addition of huge breakwaters has an easy all weather approach and entrance. However, the old harbour (now Puerto Tarraco) is for superyachts only. All visiting yachts and pleasure craft should proceed to Port Esportiu outside the Dique de Levante. The Club Náutico de Tarragona is located there and is available to all visiting yachtsmen. Its facilities include a swimming pool. Entry may be difficult in strong S to SW winds.

Originally the Iberian stronghold of Cosse, Tarragona has been an important place since the Carthaginians built a fortress here called Tarchon in the 3rd century BC. Some of the walls can still be seen. Known under the Romans as Callipolis, Terraco, Togata and later Colonia Julia Victrix Triumphans, the city flourished, only to be occupied by the Goths and later razed by the Moors in 714. It was subsequently rebuilt but damaged again by the French and later the British during Sir John Murray's retreat in the face of Soult's advance in 1813. There are so many interesting places to visit in Tarragona and the surrounding area that if a green *Michelin* or a *Guide Bleu* is not aboard, it is worth getting a guide from the local tourist board. Apart from all the historic monuments, there are good sandy beaches on either side of the harbour.

Approach

Commercial craft have right of way in the harbour and its approaches.

A special yellow pillar lightbuoy Fl(4)Y.20s marks the extremity of a pipeline about 1M SE of the harbour, with floating hose lines marked by buoys Fl.Y.

From the south The low, flat, sandy coast extends to the rocky-cliffed promontory of Cabo de Salou which is easily recognised by its conspicuous lighthouse, houses and some high-rise buildings. Once these are rounded the city of Tarragona on its hill, the large petrochemical works and factories to its W will be seen. In the closer approach the port breakwater, cranes and silos will become apparent. The entrance to the Port Esportiu lies outside the Dique de Levante, about 2M from its head.

From the north The long, flat, sandy beaches backed by low ranges of hills are only broken by the low yellow cliffs of Cabo Gros and Punta Mora. The city of Tarragona on its hill will be seen from afar, probably before passing Altafulla Beach breakwater marked by a S cardinal light. In the closer approach the yellow rocky harbour breakwater will be seen together with the smoke and flares from the factories beyond the port. The Port Esportiu lies on the way to the old harbour entrance, outside the harbour walls, just southwest of the point where the city buildings turn inland to skirt the harbour.

Anchorage in the approach

Anchor ½M to NE of the head of the Dique de Levante in 26m, sand. Beware oil pipelines which run across the harbour from the entrance to the various terminals.

Port Tarraco at Tarragona with Port Esportiu in foreground

101. Tarragona - Puerto Tarraco

Port communications
Puerto Tarraco VHF Ch 11, 14 (bridge operator Ch 06)
✆ 977 24 41 73
info@puertotarraco.com
www.puertotarraco.com

A harbour for superyachts

Puerto Tarraco is managed by the company International Marine Tarragona. It is specifically designed for superyachts who must give notice of arrival 48 hours in advance. The port does not accept vessels of less than 24m length, except in emergency. Vessels entering Puerto Tarraco in an emergency should be aware of the air draft of 6·5m and the need to call the Mobil Bridge operator on Ch 6 to ask for an opening. They should also note that Tarragona Port control listen on Ch 16 and should be kept informed of the vessel's position and intentions.

Entrance

Round the head of the Dique de Levante, giving it a berth of at least 400m to starboard. Follow the NW side of this *dique* at 100m into the Dársena de Varadero which should be crossed on a NE course, entering the Dársena Interior between the heads of the two *muelles*. The *muelle* to starboard may be marked by a buoy.

Port Tarraco looking S – restaurants on the left *Peter Taylor*

Facilities

Major facilities to cater for the needs of superyachts are available in this harbour and are not listed here although they include one of the best yacht yards on the coast located in the W corner of the Dársena Interior. There are a number of engine repair workshops and one which repairs electronic equipment.

There is an abundance of restaurants on site or within easy reach of this harbour.

102. Tarragona - Port Esportiu

Lights

To the south

Cabo Salou 41°03'·4N 1°10'·4E Fl(4)20s43m23M
White tower with red bands, white building 11m

Approach main harbour

Pantalán REPSOL head 41°04'·9N 1°12'·5E Fl.R.5s12m7M
Metal post 4m

Muelle de Cantabria elbow 41°05'·2N 1°12'·5E
Q(6)+LFl.15s6m1M ⧗ on black beacon, yellow top 2m

Head 41°05'·3N 1°12'·7E F(2+1)R.14·5s6m3M
Red round structure, green band on white post 2m

Outer breakwater head 41°05'·3N 1°12'·8E Fl(2)R.7s8m5M
Red round tower 2m

Dique de Levante. Banya 41°05'·3N 1°13'·6E Oc.3s27m1M
Grey round tower on metal piles 16m

Dique-rompeolas de abrigo. Outer breakwater head 41°04'·7N 1°12'·8E Fl.G.5s22m10M
Green round tower 11m

Muelle de Cataluña N corner 41°05'·8N 1°13'·7E
Fl(3)G.9s8m1M Green ▲ on white post 4m

S head 41°05'·4N 1°13'·4E Fl(2)G.7s9m3M
Green ▲ on white post 4m

Muelle de Aragón head 41°06'·0N 1°14'·0E Fl(4)G.11s7m3M
Green ▲ on white post 4m

Muelle de Reus SE corner 41°06'·3N 1°14'·5E
Fl(2+1)R.14·5s7m1M
Red rectangle, green band, on white post 4m

Port Esportiu

Outer breakwater 41°06'·4N 1°15'·1E Fl(2)G.10s7m5M
Green ▲ on white post 4m

Contradique head Fl(2)R.10s4m3M Red post 1m

To the north

0393.7 **Punta de la Galera** 41°07'·9N 1°23'·7E
Fl(5)30s58m17M
White tower, bronze top 38m

Port communications

VHF Ch 9 ✆ 977 213 100
recepio@portesportiutarragona.com
www.portesportiutarragona.com

A modern marina

The Club Náutico is located in Port Esportiu, a modern purpose built marina which is managed by Nautic Tarragona SA. Visitors are welcome to use all the Club facilities.

Approach

Approach to the harbour is straightforward but care should be taken if swell builds up in S or SW winds. Call for berthing instructions on Ch 9 or go to the waiting pontoon just beyond the fuel dock.

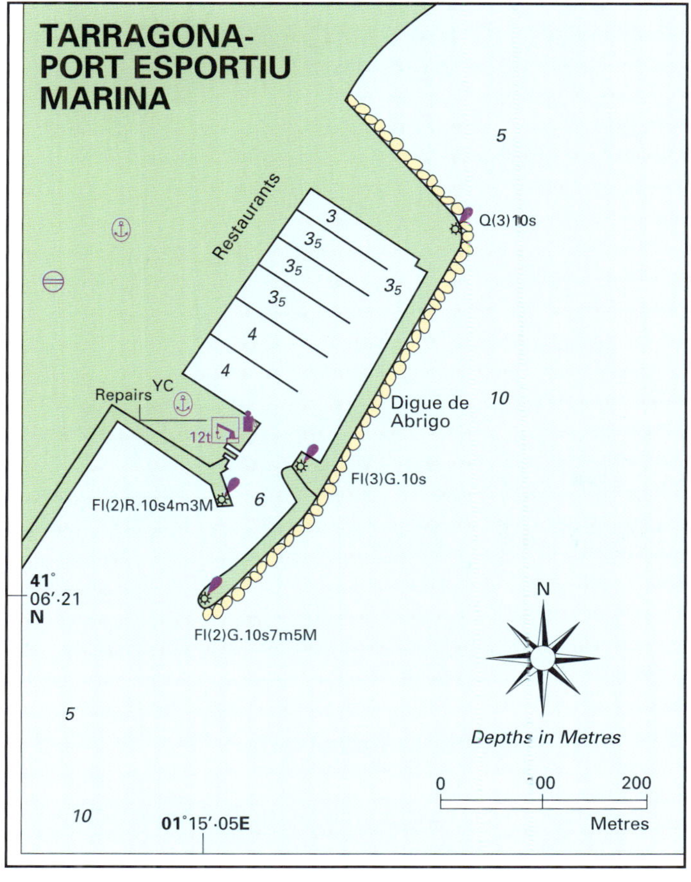

Entrance

Straightforward but awkward and possibly dangerous in strong southerlies. There may be backwash from the harbour wall if there is a sea running.

Facilities

Engineering services in the old harbour may be arranged.
12-tonne crane.
Ice factory three streets behind the Muelle de Pescadores.
There are many small shops near the port. There is a large market in the city, a short bus ride away.

Communications

Bus and rail service. Airport at Reus, 7M. Limited bus service to mountainous parts inland.
Taxi ✆ 977 221 414.
British Consul: Calle Real 33 1°1a 43004 Tarragona ✆ 977 220 813.

1. ⚓ Playa de la Rabassada

41°07'N 1°16'·7E

Anchor to draught and availability of space clear of the beach buoys.

2. ⚓ Anchorage E of Rabassada

41°07'·2N 1°17'·2E

Anchor clear of beach buoys to suit draught. Open E to SW.

3. ⚓ Cala de la Mora

41°07'·5N 1°20'·8E

E of Punta de la Mora, off the beach.

4. ⚓ Cala de la Jovera

41°07'·5N 1°20'·9E

A very small anchorage in 1-8m sand tucked away at the foot of the 12-13th century castle of Tamarit which has three towers. Only for use by small yachts with care. Open E to S.

5. ⚓ Altafulla

41°07'·8N 1°22'·8E

A deep-water anchorage ½M offshore to S of the town of Altafulla in sand open from E through S to W. Yacht club for dinghies ashore. Ruins of a Roman city. Sandy beach. There is now a breakwater off the beach with a 4m cardinal S tower at its seaward end. It is in 41°07'·7N 1°22'·3E and has characteristics Q(6)+LFl.15s5m5M.

Playa de la Rabassada

Anchorage E of Rabassada

Playa Fonda, a possible anchorage in settled weather, with Punta de la Mora beyond

Punta de la Mora and Cala de la Mora

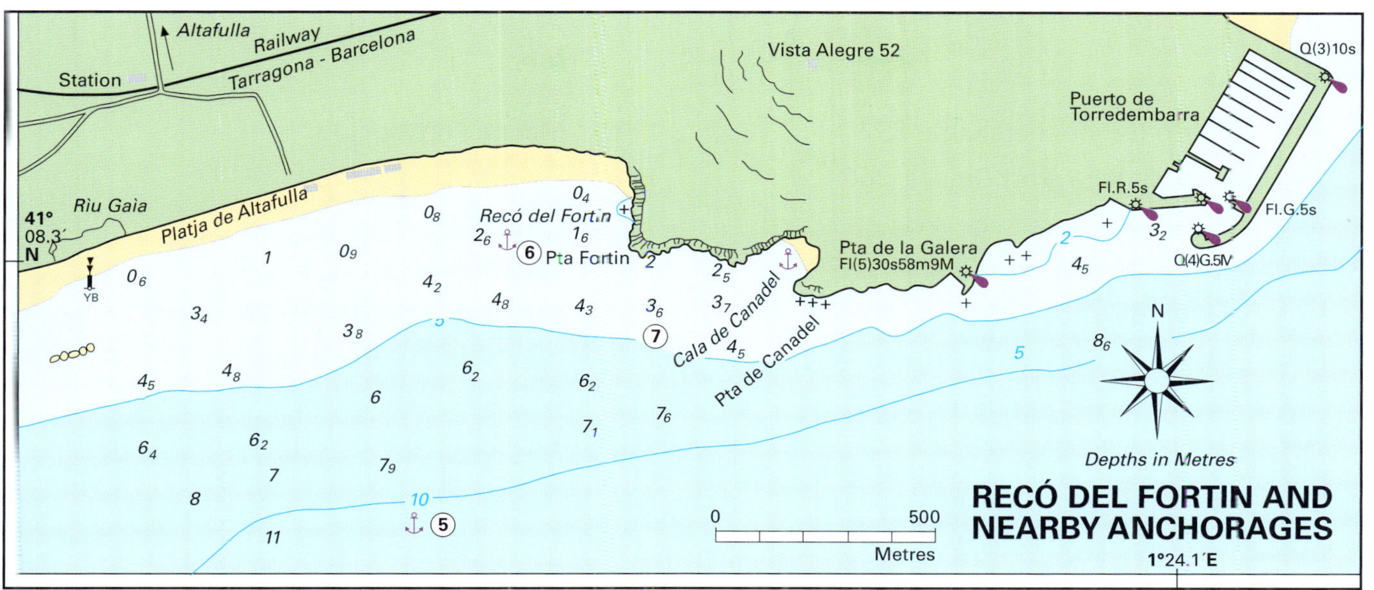

6. ⚓ Reco del Fortin

41°07′·9N 1°23′E

An anchorage backed by holiday flats located where sandy Playa de Selmar meets the rocky mass of Cabo Gros. Anchor in 2m, sand. Open S to W.

7. ⚓ Cala del Canadel

41°07′·8N 1°23′·3E

An anchorage surounded by rocky cliffs in 2m, sand, open SE through W.

Punta de la Galera

41°07′·8N 1°23′·7E

A prominent rocky headland (20m) with a tall new lighthouse Fl(5)30s58m19M on its tip. The point has rocky cliffs with some houses on top.

Cala del Canadel

TORREDEMBARRA TO RÍO TORDERA

Ports

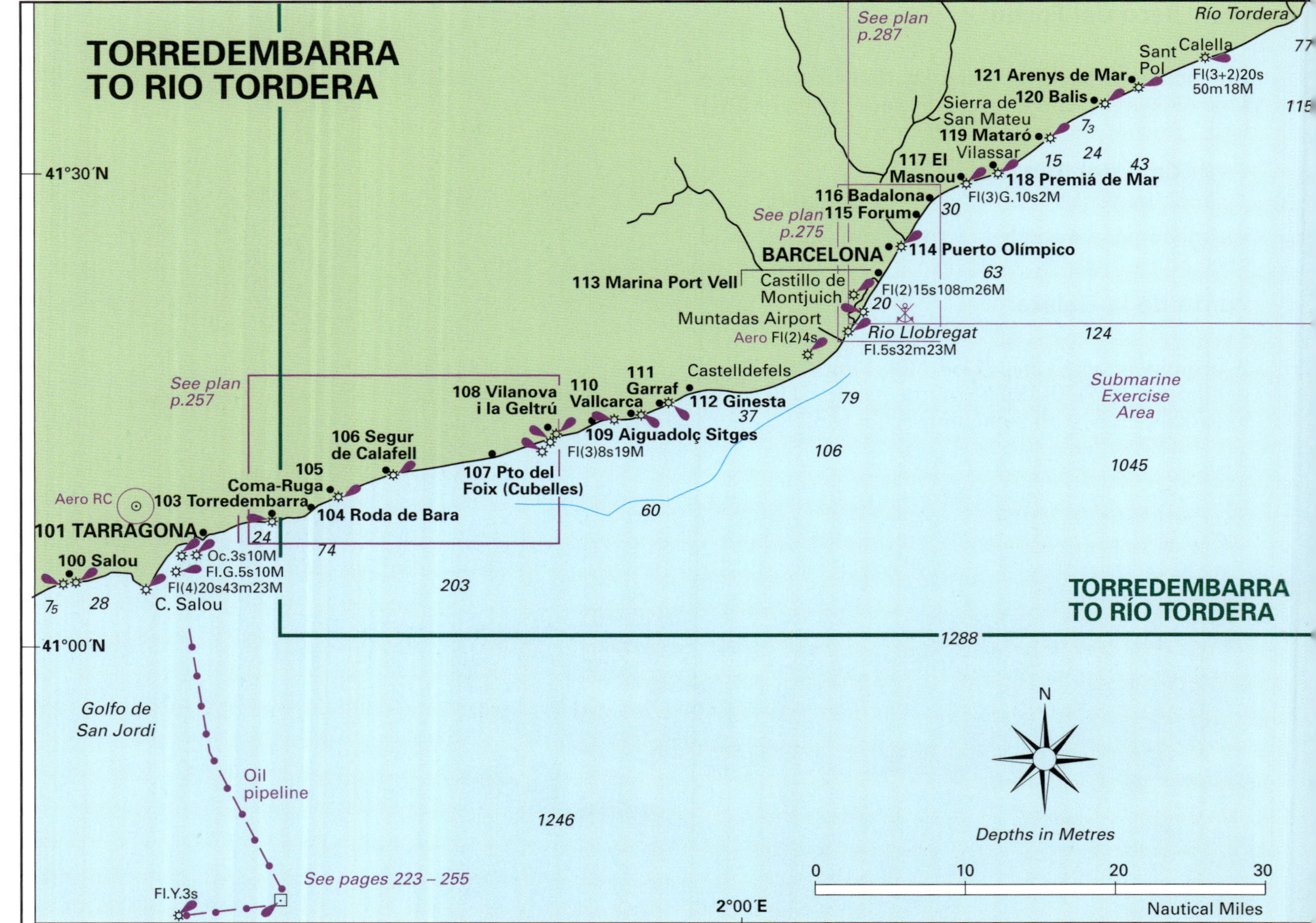

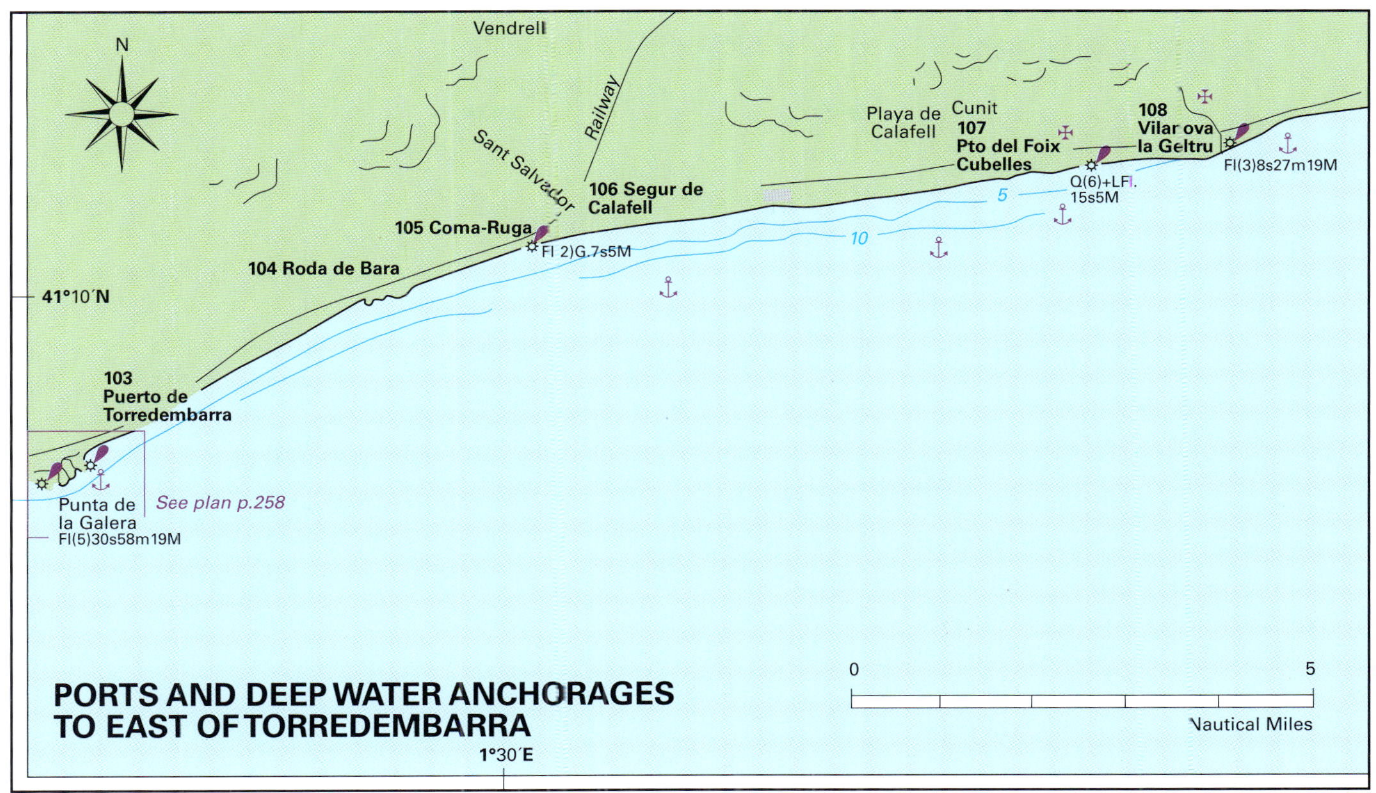

103. Puerto de Torredembarra

41°07′N 1°24′E

Charts

UKHO 1701, 1704	Imray M13
SHOM 4720, 4827	Spanish 487A, 838

Lights

Punta de la Galera 41°07′·9N 1°23′·7E Fl(5)30s58m17M
Octagonal white tower, coppery top 38m

Dique de Abrigo head Fl(4)G.11s10m5M
Green post 5m

Inner Spur Fl.G.5s4m1M
Green post 2m

Contradique corner Fl(4)R.11s4m3M Tower

Contradique head Fl.R.5s4m3M
Red post 2m on short espigon jutting out of contradique

Dique de Abrigo corner Q(3)10s9m3M
BYB post E card topmark 3m

Port communications

Capitanía VHF Ch 9 ✆ 977 643 234
info@port-torredembarra.es
www.port-torredembarra.es

An excellent modern marina

Torredembarra is a first class marina with excellent shelter, all facilities but lacking only stores and provisioning which can be obtained in the town nearby. The marina has good chandlers, bars and restaurants.

Approach

From the south Cabo de Salou and the huge breakwater of Puerto de Tarragona are easily recognised. The old castle and towers at Tamarit near Punta de la Mora will be seen if close in, also the rocky-footed Punta de la Galera with its conspicuous 38m tall lighthouse at its tip. Torredembarra town may be visible inland.

From the north Pass the modern harbour at Aiguadolç with its old houses and new housing developments plus the large Puerto de Vilanova i la Geltrú close to SW. There is a tall white chimney at Cubello and a yellow generating station with breakwaters at Cunit. Puerto de Coma-Ruga which has a tall tower inland behind it may also be seen.

Entrance

The entrance (depth 6m) is at the SW end of the outer Dique de Abrigo and runs SW-NE. Round the head leaving at least 20m clear and proceed towards the head of the contradique. Note the light at its head is situated on a short *espigón* jutting SE.

Berths

Call the *capitanía* on Ch 9 (or phone) to arrange a berth before entering – otherwise go alongside the fuel berth and ask. All berths have lazy lines to the quay and anchoring is not permitted. Depths are generally 3·5m.

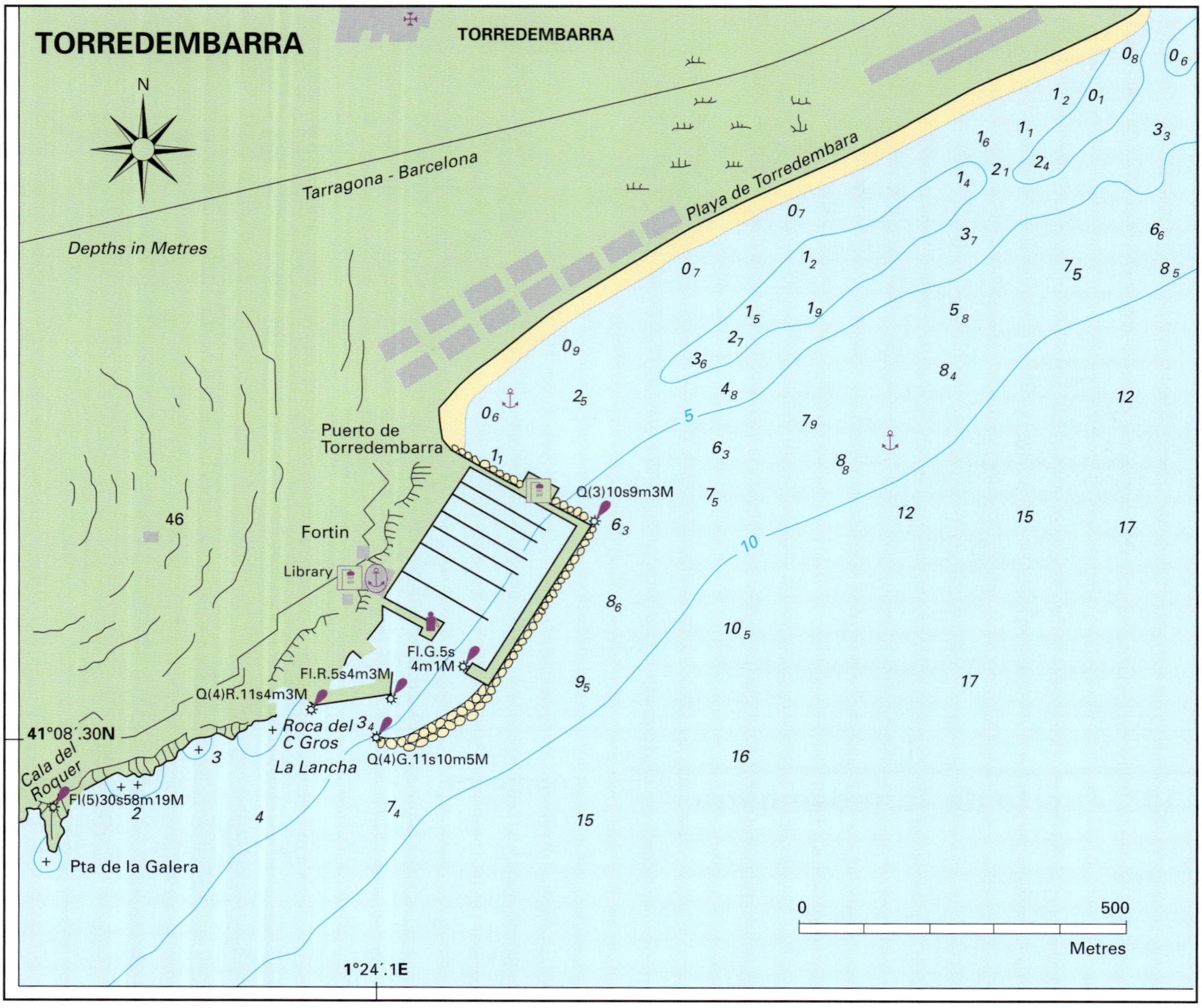

TORREDEMBARRA

TORREDEMBARRA
N
Tarragona - Barcelona
Depths in Metres
Playa de Torredembara
Puerto de Torredembarra
Fortin
Library
46
Q(3)10s9m3M
Fl.G.5s 4m1M
Fl.R.5s4m3M
Q(4)R.11s4m3M
Roca del C Gros
La Lancha
Q(4)G.11s10m5M
41°08´.30N
Cala del Roquer
Fl(5)30s58m19M
Pta de la Galera
1°24´.1E
0 500 Metres

Puerto de Torredembarra looking SW to the entrance *Steve Pickard*

Puerto de Torredembarra

Anchorage in the approach

Anchor off the Playa de Torremdebarra NE of the harbour wall in a depth to suit and clear of bathing buoys.

Facilities

Maximum length overall 24m.
Full repair facilities including engine, welding, painting.
New *club náutico* has restaurant and bar.
45-tonne travel-lift.
6-tonne crane.
Chandlery.
Showers.
Water and 220v AC on all quays.
Gasoleo A and petrol.
Ice at the bar and at the petrol station.

Communications

Taxis ✆ 977 641 147/977 640 266.

Torredembarra *capitania* *Peter Taylor*

Limited hard-standing, Torredembarra *Steve Pickard*

Torredembarra fuel jetty *Peter Taylor*

104. Roda de Barà (Port Barà)

41°10'N 1°28'E

Lights

Dique de Abrigo head Fl(3)G.9s8m5M Green pyramid 4m

Contradique head Fl(3)R.9s6m3M Red column 2m

Dique de Abrigo Inner spur Fl(4)G.11s4m1M Green column 2m

Contradique Inner spur Fl(4)R.11s3m1M Red column 2m

Port communications

VHF Ch 9 ✆ 977 138 169
info@novadarsenabara.es
www.novadarsenabara.es

New marina in a pleasant setting

The work on this marina started in 2000 but it was stalled for many years due to lack of money. In 2007 work recommenced and this is now a very modern marina with all the facilities one would expect although the restaurants and shops quayside are still are not yet fully occupied (2016).

Entrance

Straightforward round the Dique de Abrigo end and steer for the prominent *capitania*.

Berths

It is recommended to call ahead for a berth but if this is difficult moor up near the fuel berth and go to the *capitania*.

Facilities

All.

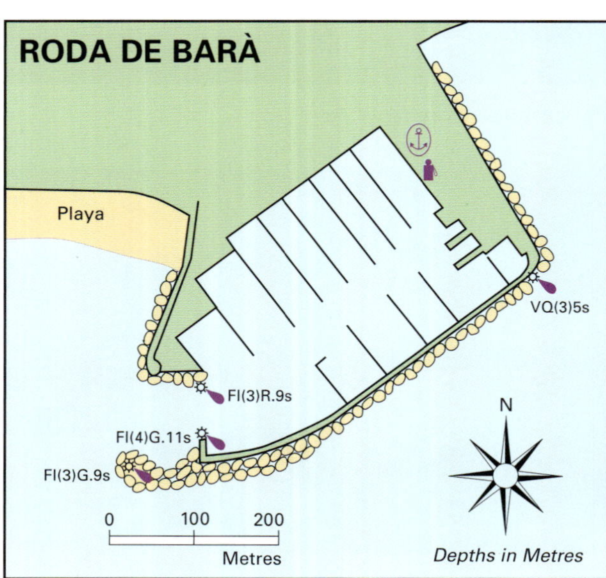

Roda de Barà *www.novadarsenabara.es*

Roda de Barà point S of entrance

Roda de Barà hard-standing at root of harbour. Note the two cranes *Steve Pickard*

105. Puerto de Coma-Ruga

41°11′N 1°31′E

Charts

UKHO 1701, 1704 Imray M13
SHOM 4827 Spanish 838

Lights

Dique Oeste head Fl(2)G.7s7m5M Green post 2m

Muelle Transversal W corner Q(6)+LFl.15s9m3M
 ⯁ on yellow tower, black base 4m

E corner VQ(6)+LFl.10s9m3M
 ⯁ on yellow tower black base 4m

Dique Este head Fl.R.5s7m5M Red post 2m

Port communications

Capitanía VHF Ch 9 ✆ 977 680 120
 cnco@clubnautic.com
 www.clubnautic.com

An interesting small marina

An extraordinary harbour for small craft built at the end of a 300m elevated dirt track reaching out into deep water. It has two entrances, one open to the East, the other to the West. The water is shallow on either side and the harbour is kept open by dredging. Facilities are limited but everyday requirements can be met in the town.

The Arco Roman de Bará, a 2nd-century Roman arch 1½M to SW of the town, is worth a visit and for those interested in the 'cello, there is a Casals museum. Excellent sandy beaches on either side of the harbour.

Approach

From the south After the huge breakwaters of Tarragona the old castle and towers at Tamarit near Punta de la Mora will be seen if close in, as will the rocky footed Punta de la Galera with its conspicuous lighthouse. Torredembarra marina just N of Punta de la Galera and the its inland town may be seen. Puerto Coma-Ruga itself appears to be well out to sea.

From the north The modern harbour at Aiguadolç with its old houses and new housing developments plus the large Puerto de Vilanova i la Geltrú close to SW are easily seen. The power station and chimney at Foix are conspicuous, followed by the Puerto de Segur de Calafell which, like Coma-Ruga, is built out to sea.

Anchorage in the approach

Anchor E or W of the harbour in 5m, sand and mud, or closer in during good weather.

Entrance

Approach the E side of the harbour from the SE, follow the Dique Este shorewards and enter by rounding its head at 15m leaving it to port. Do not use the entrance on the W side unless directed to do so or to fill up with fuel. Sound as you go. The entrance usually has about 2·5m but can be much less.

Puerto de Coma-Ruga western entrance and fuel entrance *Steve Pickard*

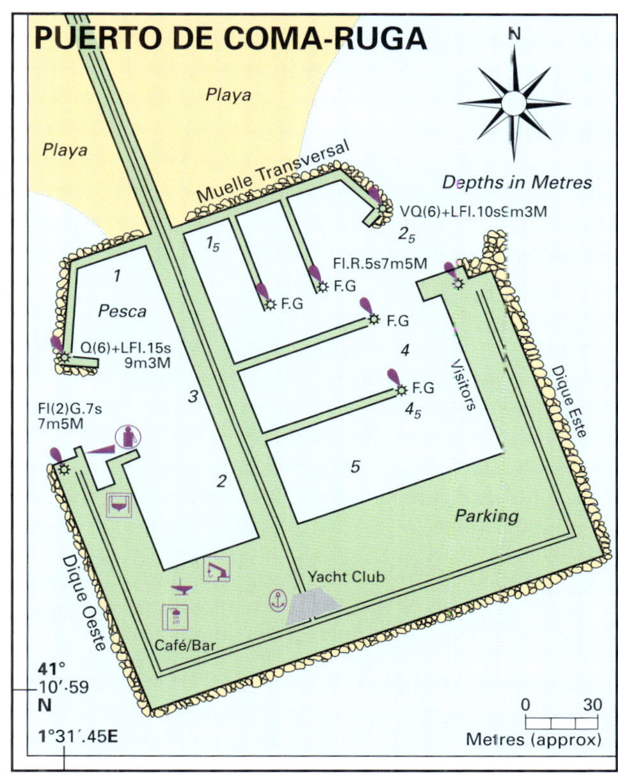

Puerto de Coma-Ruga Yacht Club *Steve Pickard*

Puerto de Coma-Ruga

Berths

Secure to the inner side of the Dique Este and ask at the *torre de control* for a berth.

Facilities

Maximum length overall 15m.
Engineer on other side of the coast road.
A 10-tonne crane on the Dique Oeste.
A small slipway at the head of the Dique Oeste.
Chandlery in the town.
Showers and WCs at SW corner of the harbour.
Water and 220v AC on all quays and pontoons.
Gasoleo A and petrol from pumps at the head of the Dique Oeste.
Small ice from the bar.
Club Náutico de Coma-Ruga has a temporary clubhouse at the junction of the harbour road with coast road.
Many shops including supermarkets in the town.

Communications

Bus and train services. Taxi ✆ 977 641 147.

⚓ Sant Salvadór

41°10'·7N 1°32'·6E

An anchorage with 4–10m, sand, open from E to SW with a sandy beach ashore. There is a basic *club náutico* ashore for dinghies. A small town of 2,000 inhabitants (approx) several hotels and some shops. (See plan on page 257.)

⚓ Calafell

41°11'N 1°35'E

An open anchorage in 4 to 10m, sand, off a sandy beach. Some houses ashore on the coast but the town of Calafell (4,500 inhabitants) is 1½M inland, where there is a 12th-century castle. Two hotels, shops etc. There is a *club náutico* ✆ 977 69 03 37 which is a dinghy club with bar, restaurant, showers, WCs and a slipway. Not an attractive area. The anchorage is open between E and SW. (See plan on page 257.)

106. Puerto de Segur de Calafell

41°11'N 1°36'E

Charts

UKHO 1704	Imray M13
SHOM 4827	Spanish 486

Lights

Breakwater head Fl(4)G.12s8m5M Green ▲ on green post 4m
Contradique head Fl(4)R.11s4m3M White structure 1m

Port communications

Capitania VHF Ch 9 ✆ 977 159 119
capitania@portsegurcalafell.com
www.portsegurcalafell.com

A first-class modern marina

The old port has been totally redeveloped with an entrance well out to sea. This should solve problems of silting which plagued the old harbour. A small fishing fleet still occupies part of the harbour.

Facilities are much improved over the old Segur and the town is still there for supplies. There is a 12th-century castle at Calafell 2M inland. There are good sandy beaches on both sides of the harbour.

Approach

From the south North of Tarragona the coast has sandy beaches broken by the rocky Punta de la Galera just south of Torredembarra. Puerto de Coma Ruga, which is joined to the coast by a causeway is easily recognized as will be this harbour on closer approach.

From the north From the easily recognized Puerto de Vilanova i la Geltru the sandy beach stretches past the power station at Foix to this harbour which is easily seen on closer approach.

Anchorage in the approach

Anchor E or W of the harbour in a suitable depth in sand and mud. Beware, shoals quickly.

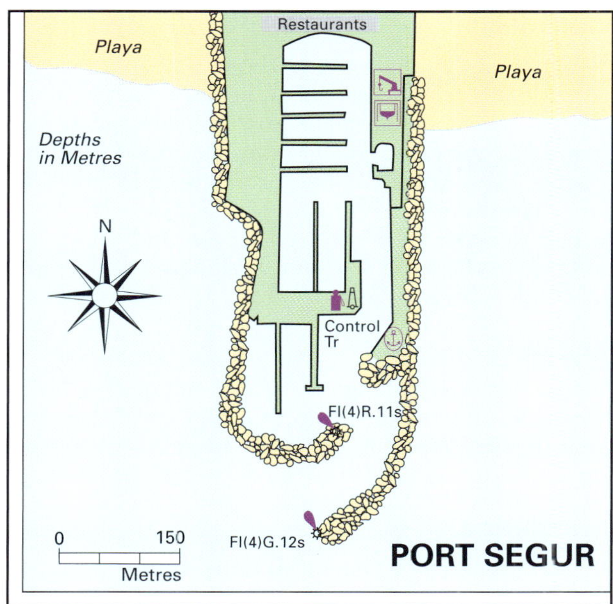

Segur de Calafell *Peter Taylor*

Segur de Calafell's convoluted entrance looking S
Steve Pickard

Entrance

The new entrance is now in reasonably deep water. Approach the end of the Dique and enter on a northeasterly course.

Facilities

Engine repairs.
5-tonne crane.
50-tonne travel-lift.
Chandlery.
Water and 220v AC at all berths.
Cafés and restaurant on the N side of inner harbour.
24-hour security.
Gasoleo A

⚓ Cunit

An anchorage open between E and SW off a sandy beach with T-shaped groynes. Anchor in 4–10m, sand. Ashore is a small town of some 1,000 inhabitants and a small *club náutico* for dinghies. (See plan page 257.)

Segur de Calafell control tower and fuel berth *Steve Pickard*

107. Puerto del Foix (Cubelles)

41°12'N 1°39'E

Charts

UKHO 1704 Imray M13
SHOM 4827 Spanish 871, 487

Lights

Dique de Abrigo E end 41°11'·6N 1°39'·4E
Q(6)+LFl.15s5m5M
Black ⸸ on yellow concrete post, black base 3m
F.R on conspicuous chimney 0·5M WNW

A simple harbour with no facilities

The harbour was built to service the Central Termica del Foix, a conspicuous power station with a very tall chimney. The outer part of the harbour forms a useful passage anchorage but the inner part should only be used in emergency. The harbour silts and is occasionally dredged; depths are unreliable. The entrance is dangerous in strong on-shore winds.

Approach

From the south Cabo de Salou and the large harbour of Tarragona are easily recognised. The coast eastwards is low and flat and lined with houses and summer apartment blocks. The small harbours of Coma-Ruga and Segur de Calafell jutting out into the sea are significant and the tall chimney and power station of Central Termica del Foix are conspicuous.

From the north The harbours of Aiguadolç and Vilanova i la Geltrú stand out and the Central Termica del Foix with its tall chimney will be seen from afar.

Entrance

The entrance to the outer harbour and anchorage is through a gap between the W head of the Dique de Abrigo which has a small post beacon and notice board and the E end of a groyne. The groyne and the Dique de Abrigo have recognisable regular crenellations.

The entrance to the inner harbour and quays lies to the E of the outer harbour behind and to N of the Dique de Abrigo.

Berths

Secure with care alongside one of the quays. There are some underwater projecting rocks and very few securing bollards. Keep well away from power station water intake at the NE corner of the harbour.

Anchorage

In the outer harbour near the centre of the bay about 2m, sand.

Facilities

None.

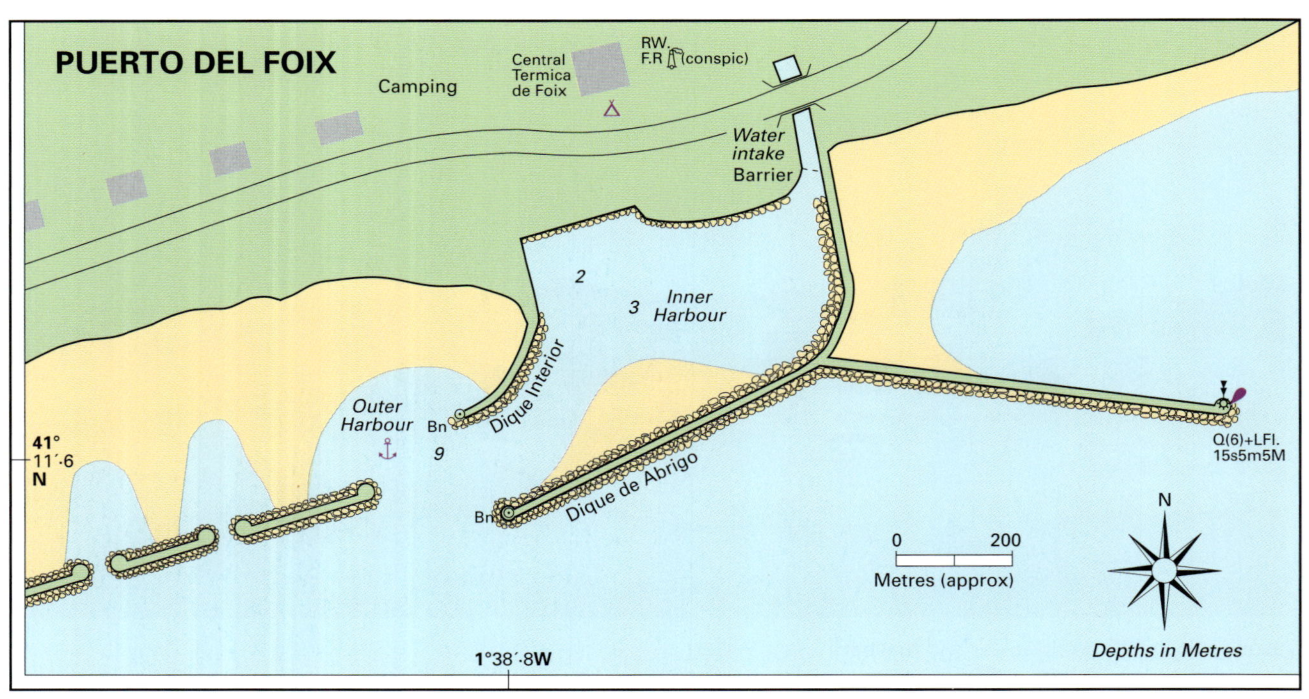

108. Puerto de Vilanova i la Geltrú (Villanueva y Geltrú)

41°13'N 1°44'E

Charts

UKHO 1704 Imray M13
SHOM 4827, 7298 Spanish 488A, 4881

Lights

Punta San Cristobál 41°13'·0N 1°44'·2E Fl(3)8s27m19M Truncated conical stone tower, aluminium cupola, white house 21m 265°-vis-070°

Dique de Levante S head Fl(2)G.7s18m5M Green tower on white base 10m

Nuevo Contradique head Fl(2)R.7s15m3M Red pyramidal tower 5m

Port communications

Port VHF Ch 16
Club Náutico VHF Ch 9 ✆ 938 150 267
cnv@cnvilanova.cat
www.cnvilanova.cat
CN Marina Office VHF Ch 9 ✆ 938 153 453
oficinaesportiva@cnvilanova.cat
www.cnvilanova.cat
Vilanova Grand Marina VHF Ch 9 ✆ 938 105 611
info@vilanovagrandmarina.com
www.vilanovagrandmarina.com

Harbour charges Medium

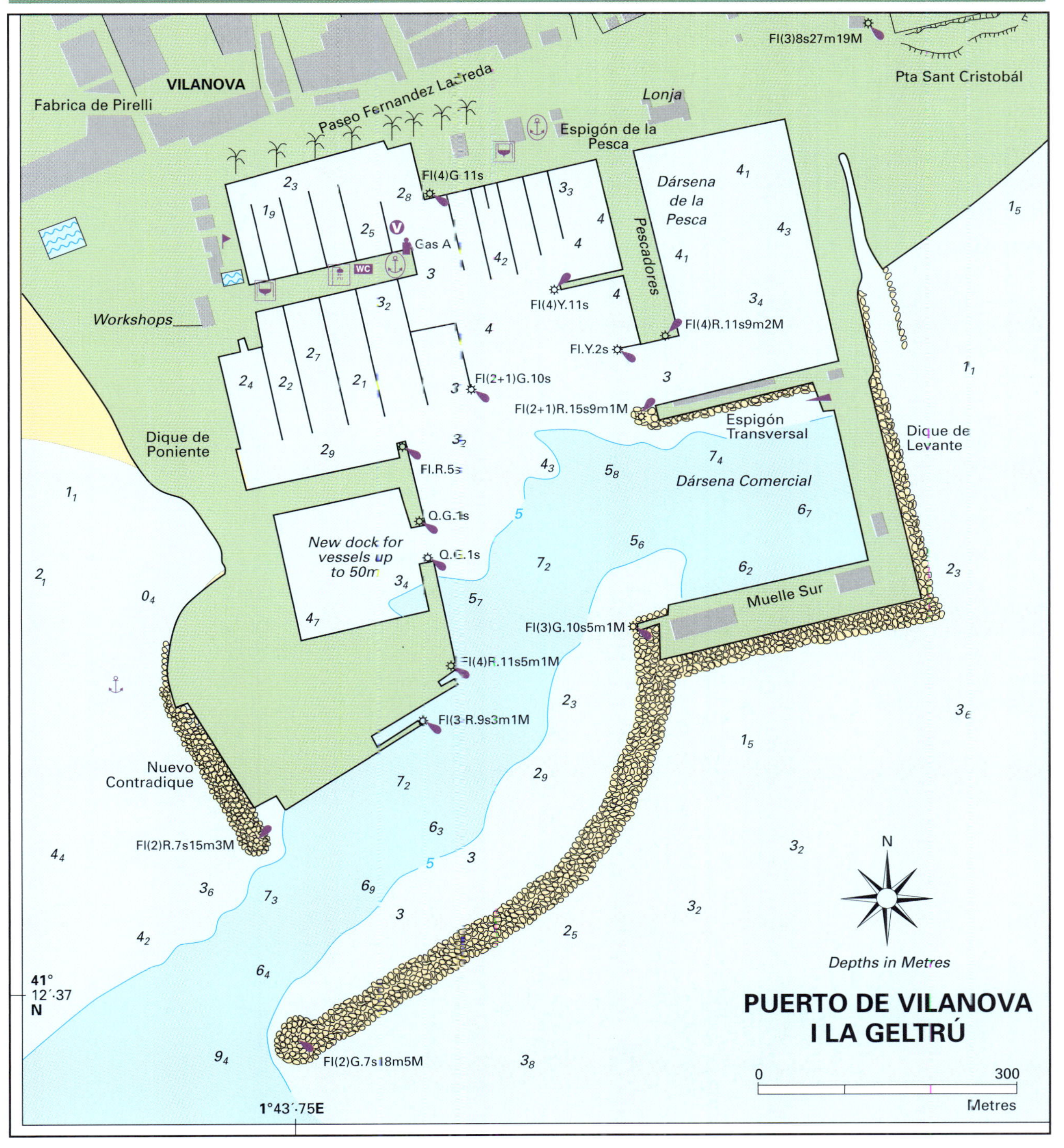

Well-sheltered marinas

A large artificial fishing, commercial, ship-breaking and yachting harbour, easy to enter and with good protection. There are good facilities for yachtsmen and hotels, restaurants and good shops ashore.

The works just to port inside the Dique de Poniente have now been completed and there is a large darsena for super yachts with all the facilities needed for these craft. This Grand Marina also runs a 300 berth marina for smaller craft (up to 7m) in the north of the harbour. It is recommended that normal cruising yachts should contact the Club Náutico on approach.

Villanueva developed rapidly from a small fishing village in the 18th century when the Basque families who had been engaged in plundering the West Indies since the 16th century returned to Spain with their fortunes. They built large houses, set up some industries and are still occasionally referred to as *Los Indianos*.

The 10th-century castle and the two museums are worth a visit. Excellent sandy beaches on either side of the harbour.

Approach

From the south From Tarragona the coast has low cliffs with sandy bays and backed by hills. North of the steep cliffs of Cabo Gros are the three marinas of Torredembara, Coma-Ruga and Segur. The conspicuous power station and chimney at Foix is about 2½M W of Vilanova i la Geltrú. The harbour lies at the edge of a plain and has yellow rocky harbour breakwaters and a backdrop of factory chimneys, blocks of flats and houses.

From the north Barcelona is easily identified by the concentration of buildings, harbour works and smoke. The comparatively flat and featureless delta of the Río Llobregat is followed by a range of hills, the Sierra de la Guardia, which reach the sea in broken cliffs and small bays. South of this outcrop the harbour with its yellow rocky breakwater and factories, flats and houses will be seen, backed by a flat plain. A rocky patch lies on the W side of the Dique de Levante.

Anchorage in the approach

Anchor about 100m to W of the elbow of the Nuevo Contradique in 4m, sand.

Entrance

Leave the head of the Dique de Levante 50m to starboard and round it onto a NE course then enter between the head of the Dique de Poniente and the root of the Dique de Levante.

Berths

Secure to pontoon near office of the *capitán de puerto* for allocation of a berth at Club Náutico or the new 'Marina Far'.

Facilities

Maximum length overall 25m or 50m at new dock.
Repairs available by a local yard.
Mechanics and sailmakers.
100-tonne travel-lift.
25-tonne crane at the *club náutico* and several larger cranes at the ship breaking yard.
Slipway in the NW corner of the harbour, larger ones in the NE corner and the Dársena Comercial.
Three small chandleries near the harbour.
Water and 220v AC on all quays and pontoons.
Gasoleo A and petrol.
Ice at fuel quay or from a factory at the N end of the Dársena de la Pesca.
The Club Náutico de Vilanova i la Geltrú clubhouse, in the NW corner of the harbour, has bars, lounge, terrace, restaurant, showers and a swimming pool.
Good shops of most types in the town, also a market and supermarket.
Launderette at marina.
Weather forecast at *capitanía*.

Communications

Rail and bus services. Taxi ✆ 938 933 241.

Vilanova i la Geltrú
Mark52 / Shutterstock.com

109. Aiguadolç (Puerto de Sitges)

41°14'N 1°49'E

Charts
UKHO 1704 Imray M13
SHOM 4827, 7298 Spanish 871, 4882, 488A

Lights

Dique de Levante head Fl.G.5s12m5M
Green tower, white base 10m

Dique de Levante spur Fl(2)G.13s6m1M
Green tower, white base 6m

Contradique head Fl.R.5s12m3M
Red lantern on white hut corner 10m

Port communications

Capitanía VHF Ch 9. ✆ 938 942 600
info@portdesitges.com
www.portdesitges.com

Club Nautic de Sitges ✆ 937 432 057
cns@nauticsitges.com
www.nauticsitges.com

Harbour charges High (note that high season runs 1 April - 1 October)

PUERTO DE AIGUADOLÇ

Visitors
Fl.R.5s 12m3M
Contradique de Poniente
Fl(2)G.13s 6m1M
Fl.G.5s 12m5M
41° 13'.90 N
0 50
Metres (approx)
1°49'.4E
Depths in Metres

A friendly upmarket marina

An artificial yacht harbour with good facilities. Approach and entrance are easy and good shelter obtained, but with wind from the SW swell will find its way into the harbour.

The town of Sitges nearby is very attractive with its wooded streets and provides most facilities for visitors. There are three important museums here, some interesting old buildings and good sandy beaches near the town.

Sitges has been in occupation since Roman times, made popular by its climate. The area is well sheltered from the cold northeast winds. The painters Rusiñol and Utrillo worked here. The town holds a *fiesta* in the form of a flower show in late May or early June, on the first Thursday after Whitsun.

Aiguadolç (Puerto de Sitges). There is talk of extending the outer mole westwards

V. COSTA DORADA

Sitges control tower at the root of the harbour *Steve Pickard*

Approach

From the south The town and harbour of Vilanova i la Geltrú are easily recognised. The coast is low and flat as far as Sitges which has a small hill feature a little distance inland. Its concentration of flats and houses has a conspicuous church at its E end and the harbour lies 500m to the E.

From the north The rocky broken coast where the Sierra de la Guardia meets the coast gives way to the flat coastal plain near this harbour. A conspicuous cement works is located some 1·5M to the E of the harbour.

Anchorages in the approach

Anchor 200m to the S of the entrance in 8m, sand or E or W of the harbour in 5m.

Entrance

Approach the entrance on a NE course and enter between the two *diques* and in mid-channel. Then round the head of the Contradique de Poniente leaving it 25m to port, secure to the pontoon inside the entrance to starboard – call Ch 9.

Facilities

Maximum length overall 32m.
A shipyard on the NE side of the harbour with two workshops and an engineer.
20-tonne travel-lift.
2-tonne mobile crane.
Slipway on the NE side of the harbour.
A hard-standing area for yachts to NE of the harbour.
Two chandlers at the harbour.
Showers on W side of the harbour.
Water and 220v AC on all pontoons.
Gasoleo A and petrol from the head of the Espigón Nord.
Ice available from bars and fuel berth.
Many shops in the town, also a market and supermarket. Shops also around the harbour.
Launderette in the town and one to be established at the harbour.
Weather forecasts posted at the *torre* daily.

Communications

Bus and rail services. Taxi ☎ 938 943 594 /938 941 329. Car Hire Hertz ☎ 938 945 750, Avis ☎ 938 949 926.

Sitges – many restaurants by the quay *Robin Rundle*

110. Puerto de Vallcarca

41°14'N 1°52'E

Charts

UKHO 1704	Imray M13
SHOM 4827, 7298	Spanish 871, 488

Lights

Muelle head 41°14'·3N 1°52'·0E Fl(4)G.13s10m4M Green tower, white base 5m

An unpleasant commercial port

A private harbour belonging to a huge cement works. It might be used in emergency but not when wind and swell are between W and S as it is wide open to that quarter. There are no facilities for yachtsmen other than water and a beach restaurant. The noise and dust created by the Fradera SA cement works which is in operation day and night makes it an unpleasant place to stay.

Approach

From the south The flat plains around the harbours at Vilanova i la Geltrú and Aiguadolç give way to the high mountainous feature, the Sierra de la Guardia, which reaches to the coast near this harbour. The cement works, two white silos on the harbour wall and the clouds of dust are all conspicuous.

From the north From Barcelona the coast is low and flat until the rocky cliffs where the Sierra de la Guardia meets the coast beyond the delta of the Río Llobregat. The cement works, two white silos and the dust near this harbour are also conspicuous from this direction.

Entrance

Round the head of the Muelle de Atraque leaving it 50m to starboard and follow this *muelle* in a NE direction.

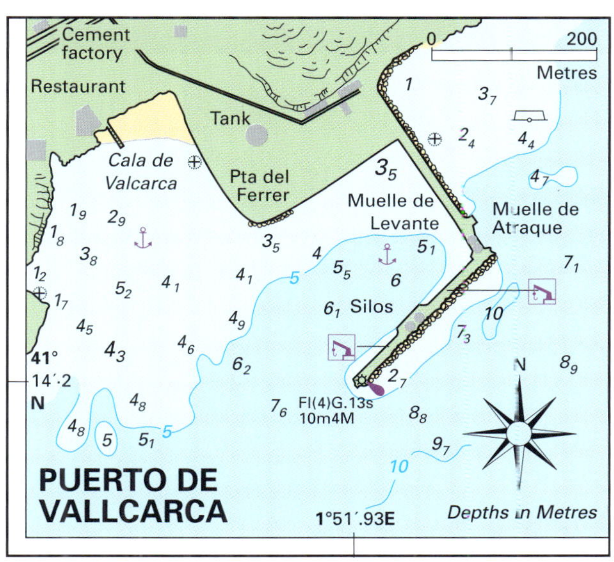

Silos on the Muelle Atraque, Vallcarca *Steve Pickard*

Puerto de Vallcarca

Berths

In calm weather, temporary berths may be available alongside the Muelle de Levante if not in use by commercial shipping.

Anchorage

Anchorage on a temporary basis is possible in the E corner of the harbour or in the Cala de Vallcarca. Also outside the harbour to the E if the swell is entering the harbour itself.

Mooring

Temporary moorings to one of the hauling off buoys might be possible.

Facilities

Water from a tap near root of *muelle*.
Small beach restaurant.

Communications

Bus and rail service.

111. Puerto de Garraf

41°15'N 1°54'E

Chart

UKHO 1704 — Imray M13
SHOM 4827, 7298 — Spanish 871, 488A

Lights

Dique de Levante head Fl(3)G.9s7m5M
Green tower 3m

Espigon Interior head Fl(4)G.20s2m1M
Green column 1m

Dique de Poniente head Fl(3)R.9s4m3M
Red tower 3m

Port communications

Capitanía VHF Ch 9. ✆ 936 320 013
info@clubnauticgarraf.com
www.clubnauticgarraf.com

A quiet marina

A large marina but absolutely nothing ashore. A few bars and restaurants can be reached by foot. Repair facilities are very limited but many are available at Port Ginesta, close by.

Approach

From the south After passing the flat coast around Vilanova i la Geltrú the coast becomes rocky and broken where the high Sierra de la Guardia reaches the sea. The harbour is located on this section of coast 1·7M beyond a conspicuous cement works and harbour at Vallcarca.

From the north South of the wide flat delta of the Río Llobregat, where Barcelona airport is located, is the rocky broken coast of the Sierra de la Guardia. Port Ginesta is the first along that stretch, Garraf the second, in sight of the conspicuous Vallcarca cement works.

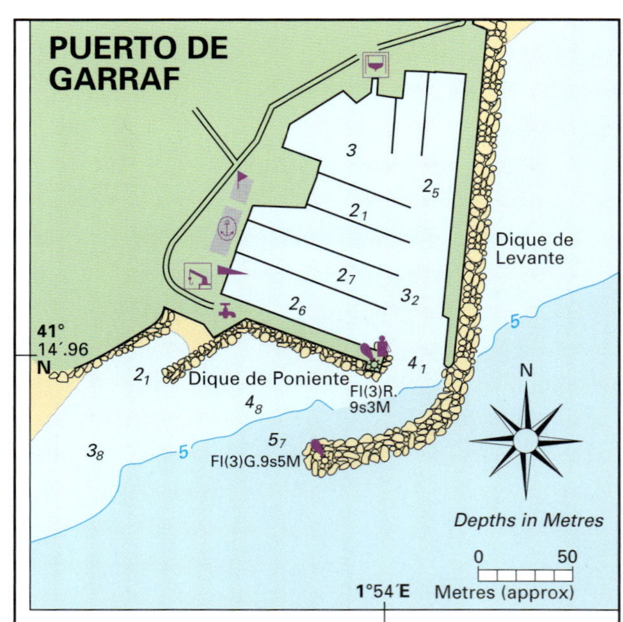

Puerto de Garraf

Entrance

As is common along this stretch of coast, the entrance to Garraf silts up badly after any strong winds from the south quadrant. The mouth is dredged frequently but the sand returns almost as quickly. Usually there is a line of small red buoys laid from the head of the Dique de Poniente towards the beach parallel to the end of the Dique de Levante. These are to be left to port on entry and if they are missing, round the end of the dique and enter keeping close to the dique sounding carefully. Go right into the port and turn to come alongside the fuelling berth. Go to the *torre de control* in the club náutico building to sort a berth out.

Facilities

Workshop outside the marina with mechanic.
20-tonne travel-hoist.
6-tonne crane.
Hard-standing.
Gasoleo A and petrol.
Showers and ice at the *club náutico*.
Water and 220v AC on all quays.
Laundry in marina, limited shops in the town.

Communications

Bus and rail services. Taxi ✆ 936 653 557.

Garraf looking down Dique de Levante

Garraf red buoys, Vallcarca silos beyond

112. Port Ginesta (Puerto de Castelldefels)

41°15'N 1°55'E

Charts

UKHO 1704 Imray M13
SHOM 4827 Spanish 488

Lights

Dique de Abrigo head Fl(2)G.10s8m5M
Green tower 3m

Contradique head Fl(2)R.10s5m3M Red tower 3m

Espigón de Levante Q(6)+LFl.15s5m3M
S cardinal on black beacon, yellow top 3m

To the north

Río Llobregat 41°19'·6N 2°09'·2E Fl.5s32m23M
Tower on building 31m 240°-vis-030°

Port communications

Capitanía VHF Ch 9. ✆ 936 643 661
info@portginesta.com
www.portginesta.com

A first-class marina

Similar in character to Garaf next door this modern marina is easy to enter and has good protection. There is a wide range of yacht repair and brokerage facilities besides chemist, restaurant, bars etc. and a crafts market at the weekend. The port is popular. A major expansion of the harbour has now been completed.

Castelldefels (originally Castrum de Fels) has fair shopping and its Romanesque church and the keep of the castle (1211AD) are worth a visit. Barcelona, 12M away, is within striking distance. There is a good beach to NE.

Approach

From the south Aiguadolç and the cement works at Puerto de Vallcarca are conspicuous followed by Puerto de Garraf. Ginesta is at the end of the coastal cliffs.

From the north Barcelona is unmistakable, after which the delta of the Río Llobregat is low and flat with its light and radio antenna as features. Follow the sandy coast at ½M in 10m, sounding. The harbour is where the sandy beach stops and coastal cliffs commence.

Anchorage in the approach

Anchor 400m to S of the entrance to the harbour in 10m sand and mud. Not recommended in heavy weather because of undertow.

Entry

Approach the area where there is a large quarry in the background. The entrance between the breakwaters is straightforward. Most harbours along this coast are prone to silting. Although this has not been reported since Port Ginesta was extended caution is advised during the approach.

Facilities

Maximum length overall 30m.
Workshops with mechanics to NW of the harbour.
GRP, joinery, paintwork, sailmaking.
Slipway at NW side of the harbour (6m).
75-tonne travel-lift.
8-tonne crane.
Hard-standing for yachts at N side of the harbour.
Shops selling chandlery to N side of the harbour.
Showers and WCs in the *torre de control* complex.
Water and 220v AC on all quays and pontoons.
Gasoleo A and petrol.
Small ice from the café/bars and fuel station.
Some shops around the harbour, many more in the town 3M away. There is now a supermarket within the marina.
Laundry is now on site (24hrs) and not in town.
Weather forecasts posted daily at the *torre de control*.

Communications

Bus and rail service. Barcelona International Airport 5M. Taxi ✆ 936 635 537.

Ginesta harbour from entrance *Peter Taylor*

Port Ginesta *Steve Pickard*

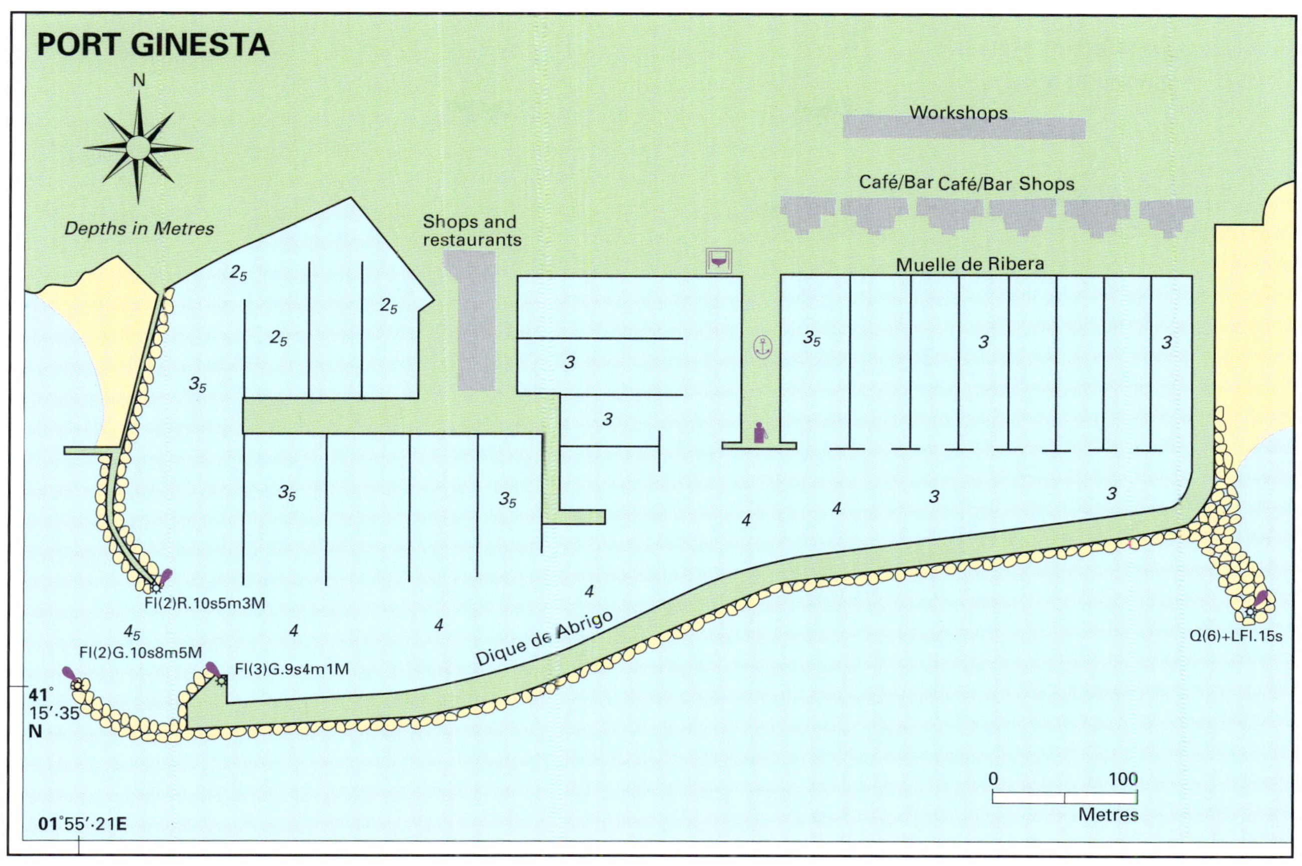

Ginesta harbour and entrance *Steve Pickard*

⚓ Gava

An open anchorage off a sandy beach about 1M to WSW of the airport, wide open to the S. Dinghy yacht club ashore. Coast road and road to Gava.

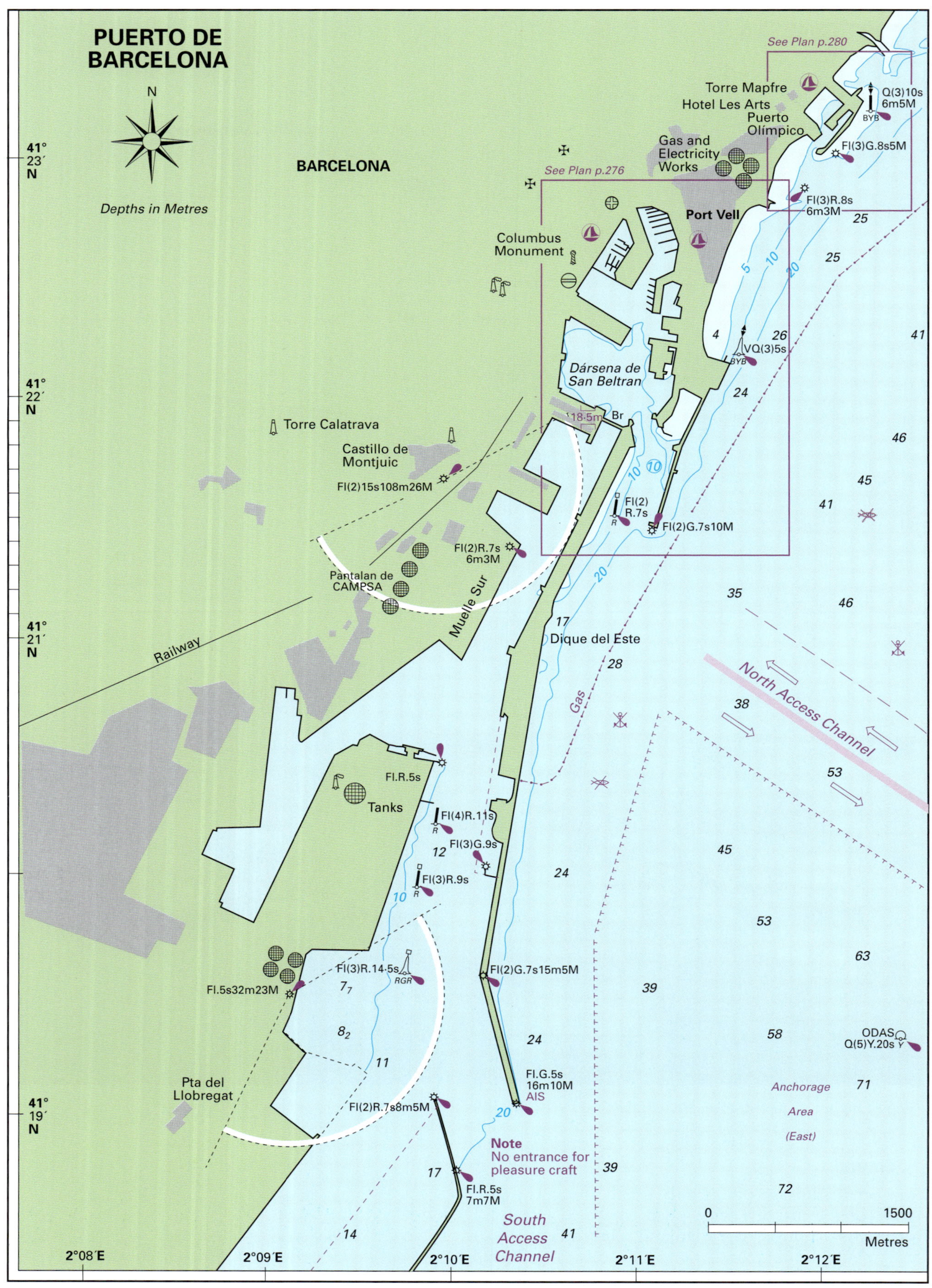
PUERTO DE BARCELONA
N
Depths in Metres
BARCELONA
See Plan p.280
See Plan p.276
Torre Mapfre
Hotel Les Arts
Puerto Olímpico
Gas and Electricity Works
Q(3)10s 6m5M
BYB
Fl(3)G.8s5M
Fl(3)R.8s 6m3M
Port Vell
Columbus Monument
VQ(3)5s
BYB
Dársena de San Beltran
18·5m
Br
Torre Calatrava
Castillo de Montjuic
Fl(2)15s108m26M
Fl(2) R.7s
Fl(2)G.7s10M
Fl(2)R.7s 6m3M
Pantalan de CAMPSA
Muelle Sur
Railway
Dique del Este
Gas
North Access Channel
Fl.R.5s
Tanks
Fl(4)R.11s
Fl(3)G.9s
Fl(3)R.9s
Fl(3)R.14·5s
RGR
Fl.5s32m23M
Fl(2)G.7s15m5M
Pta del Llobregat
Fl(2)R.7s8m5M
Fl.G.5s 16m10M AIS
Note
No entrance for pleasure craft
Fl.R.5s 7m7M
South Access Channel
ODAS
Q(5)Y.20s
Anchorage Area (East)
0
1500
Metres
41° 23′ N
41° 22′ N
41° 21′ N
41° 19′ N
2°08′E
2°09′E
2°10′E
2°11′E
2°12′E

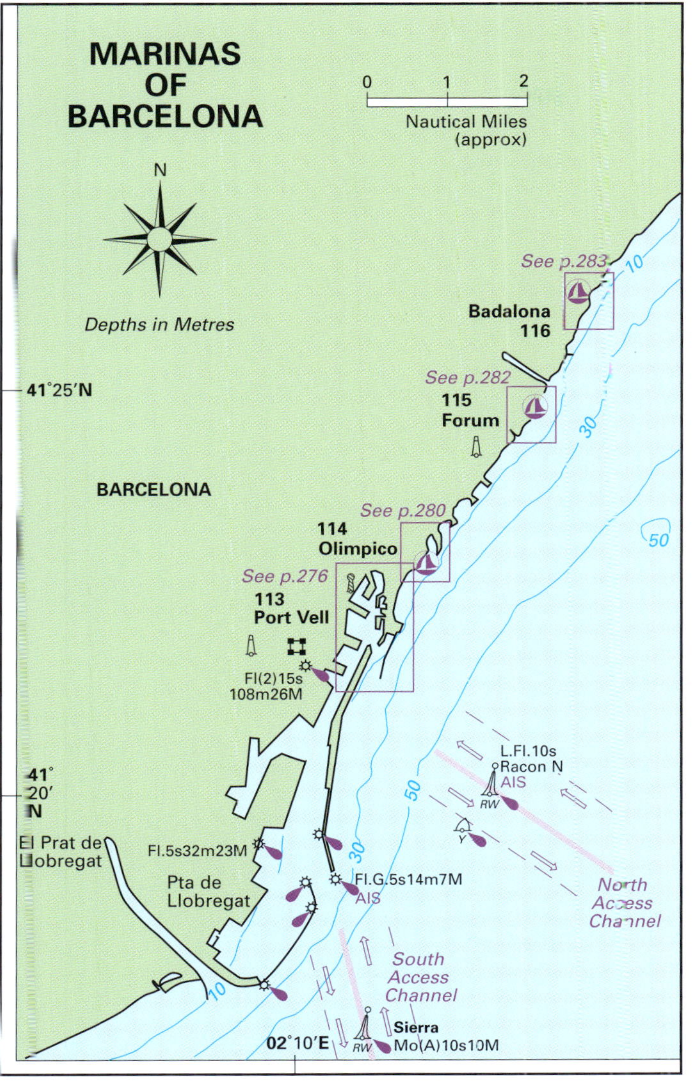

La Rambla

BARCELONA

Barcelona – capital of Cataluña

Barcelona is the largest city and port on this coast. The port of Barcelona itself (as distinct from Puerto Olímpico which is outside the main harbour walls) is easy to approach and enter in any weather, though winds may funnel at the entrance. There is good protection inside. Commercial traffic must be given right of way near and inside the port. Facilities for yachts and their crews are excellent and there are many attractions in the city and surrounding area. The marina at Port Vell is close to Las Ramblas and the city centre.

There are scores of places to see, such as 38 museums, 26 art galleries besides permanent trade fairs and exhibitions. To mention but three, visit Gaudi's cathedral, the Picasso Museum and walk along Las Ramblas at the hour of the *paseo*.

Though the area was probably occupied by the Iberians and later the Phoenicians, the first recorded history is of its occupation by the Carthaginian Hamilcar Barca in 230BC when it was called Barcino. The Romans took over in about 200BC and later called it Colonia Julia Augustus Pia Faventia. The town was destroyed by the Barbarians in AD263 but was later retaken by the Romans who fortified it with a great wall. The Visigoths made it their capital of Gothalania in AD415, from which name the province of Cataluña is thought to have originated. The town surrendered to the Moors in AD713; they were in turn driven out in AD 801, only to return in AD 985 for a short period during which the town was burnt. For the next 600 years, while still assert-ing her independence and rights, the town was ruled by the various royal and noble houses as their fortunes changed. An event of note was the royal reception of Columbus in June 1493 on his return from his discovery of America. In 1714 the city was sacked by the French because the inhabitants supported the cause of Archduke Charles against the French nomination of Philip V for the crown. The French also occupied the city from 1808 to 1813. From then until the Civil War the city was often the centre of agitation and revolt against the established order, insisting on its own rights and customs. In the 19th century the industrial revolution created a situation which caused the vast development of the city and its surroundings into one of the largest and most prosperous in Spain. It was the centre of Republican activity during the civil war and was badly bombed; the fall of Barcelona in January 1939 virtually marked the end of the war.

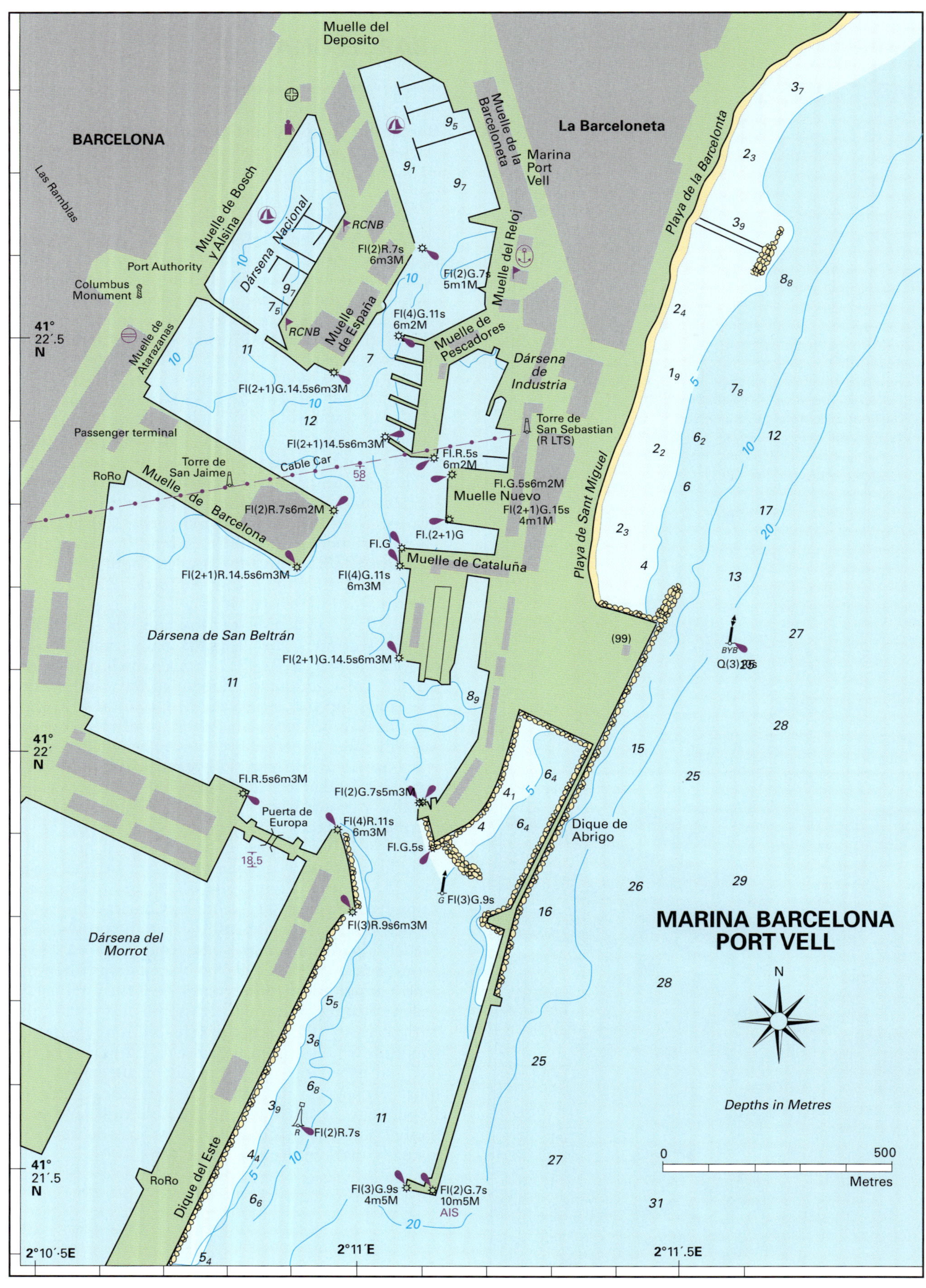
Muelle del Deposito
BARCELONA
Las Ramblas
La Barceloneta
Muelle de la Barceloneta
Marina Port Vell
Playa de la Barcelonta
Muelle de Bosch y Alsina
Dársena Nacional
RCNB
Fl(2)R.7s 6m3M
Fl(2)G.7s 5m1M
Muelle del Reloj
Port Authority
Columbus Monument
Muelle de España
Fl(4)G.11s 6m2M
Muelle de Pescadores
Muelle de Atarazanas
Dársena de Industria
Fl(2+1)G.14.5s6m3M
Torre de San Sebastian (R LTS)
Passenger terminal
Fl(2+1)14.5s6m3M
Fl.R.5s 6m2M
Cable Car
Torre de San Jaime
RoRo
Muelle de Barcelona
Fl.G.5s6m2M
Muelle Nuevo
Fl(2)R.7s6m2M
Fl(2+1)G.15s 4m1M
Playa de Sant Miguel
Fl.(2+1)G
Fl.G
Muelle de Cataluña
Fl(2+1)R.14.5s6m3M
Fl(4)G.11s 6m3M
Dársena de San Beltrán
(99)
BYB
Q(3)5s
Fl(2+1)G.14.5s6m3M
Fl.R.5s6m3M
Fl(2)G.7s5m3M
Puerta de Europa
Fl(4)R.11s 6m3M
Fl.G.5s
Dique de Abrigo
18.5
G Fl(3)G.9s
Fl(3)R.9s6m3M
MARINA BARCELONA PORT VELL
Dársena del Morrot
N
Depths in Metres
R Fl(2)R.7s
0
500
Metres
Dique del Este
RoRo
Fl(3)G.9s 4m5M
Fl(2)G.7s 10m5M
AIS
41° 22´.5 N
41° 22´ N
41° 21´.5 N
2°10´.5E
2°11´E
2°11´.5E

113. Barcelona – Marina Port Vell

41°20'N 2°10'E

Charts

UKHO 1704, 1196, 1180 Imray M14
SHOM 4827, 7046 Spanish 489A, 4891

Lights

Southern approach (pleasure craft forbidden to enter)

Lighthouse 41°19'·5N 2°09'·1E Fl.5s32m23M Tower on white building 31m 240°-vis-030°

E breakwater head 41°19'·0N 2°10'·4E Fl.G.5s16m7M Green tower on white base 13m

S breakwater NE corner 41°18'·8N 2°10'E Fl.R.5s14m7M Red tower on white 4m

S breakwater head 41°18'·8N 2°09'·9E Fl(2)R.7s8m5M Red tower on white base 4m

Montjuich 41°21'·7N 2°10'E Fl(2)15s108m26M Tower on red and white building 13m 240·5°-vis-066·6° (this light is well within the harbour)

Northern Entrance (for all non-commercial traffic)

New breakwater S head SE corner 41°21'·5N 2°11'·1E Fl(2)G.7s16m10M Green post 13m

New breakwater S head SW corner Fl(3)G.9s4m5M Green post

Dique del Este N head S corner Fl(3)R.9s6m3M Red column 3m

Dique del Este N head N corner Fl(4)R.11s6m3M Red column 3m

Port communications

Pilots VHF Ch 11, 12, 14, 16 (hours various).
Port VHF Ch 12, 14, 16 24hrs ☎ 933 177 500.
Real Club Maritim VHF Ch 09 ☎ 932 214 859 club@maritimbarcelona.org www.maritimbarcelona.org
Real Club Náutico VHF Ch 09 ☎ 932 216 521 info@rcnb.com www.rcnb.com
Marina Port Vell VHF Ch 68 ☎ 934 842 300 info@marinaportvell.com www.marinaportvell.com

Harbour charges High

Immense, first-class but expensive marina

Port Vell is in the heart of the city and since the delelopment of the port, the famous Las Ramblas now runs down to the end of the Muelle de Espana. The centre of the marina, the Muelle, has a vast and thronged shopping, eating and entertainment complex. The Port Vell development was mainly aimed at super yachts but to a certain extent normal cruising yachts have benefited from the work. One costly consequence, however, is that the only berths available are 12, 15 or 18 metres and the visitor pays for whatever berth he/she gets allocated, regardless of the actual length of the boat.

Approach

From the south The high feature and broken rocky cliffs of the Sierra de la Guardia suddenly give way to the flat low delta of the Río Llobregat which has the airport and a lighthouse. On a clear day the high hill immediately behind the harbour (Montaña de Montjuic), the harbour installations and the mass of buildings of the city will be seen from afar. The two towers of the aerial railway are also conspicuous.

From the north The coastline is backed by a series of hills consisting of the Sierras del Corredó, de Sant Mateu and de Matas, which fall back inland in the area of Barcelona, leaving the isolated feature of Montaña de Montjuic easily located. The coast is lined with concentrations of houses and high-rise buildings which extend across the delta of the Río Bésós. The bridge over this river will be seen. The concentration of buildings and harbour works continues past Montaña de Montjuic, silos and the two towers of the aerial railway. In clear conditions the jagged peaks of Montaña de Montserrat some 20M inland can be seen from.

The smarter end of Port Vell *Steve Pickard*

V. COSTA DORADA

Puerto de Barcelona – Port Vell

Port Vell entrance *Robin Rundle*

Catalona History Museum Port Vell *Robin Rundle*

Statue Christopher Columbus *Robin Rundle*

Entrance

From the south Leave the works and buoys off the new Dique Sur well to port and proceed up the outside of the Dique del Este and its new extension and aim towards the conspicuous Puerta de Europa. Keep steering northerly until the new Dique de Abrigo is sighted and then shape a course towards a small spur running ESE from the old Dique del Este. When the new entrance opens up steer through and enter the Darsena de San Beltran. Continue north under the aerial cable car wire and enter the marina.

From the north Leave Puerto Olimpico and its off-lying dangers well to starboard and proceed along the new Dique de Abrigo. Round its south end and proceed to steer a west of north course past the the fishing harbour entrance when the new entrance will open up. Proceed through the Darsena de San Beltran to Port Vell.

Berths

For visitors berths at Port Vell call for a berth on Ch 68 or at the fuel quay in the Darsena Nacional. The Real Club Marítima may accept visitors by arrangement; the Real Club Náutico de Barcelona is for members only. An alternative is to go to Puerto Olímpico but this has less character and is further out of town.

Facilities

Barcelona can support all repairs, in or out of the water. Many are close to Port Vell. Consult a marina or club official if help is needed.

Chandleries near the port, one 200m SW of the main post office and another between the two *clubs náutico*.

Chart agent in Avenida Marques de l'Argentana.

At Port Vell

Maximum length overall 70m.

Water and 220v and 380v AC on all pontoons.

Gasoleo A and petrol.

Ice, ask at the fuelling berth.

In town

Supermarket at 100m.

Thousands of shops of all kinds and a large market in the city, many in the narrow streets near the port.

Launderette in the second road back from the NW side of the Dársena Nacional, many others elsewhere in the city.

Communications

International and national bus, rail and air services, car hire etc. Shipping to most parts of the world. Taxi ✆ 933 912 222.

British Consulate-General Edificio Torre de Barcelona Avineda Diagonal 477, 13th Floor, 08036 Barcelona ✆ 934 199 044

Port Vell, Darsena Nacional *Steve Pickard*

V. COSTA DORADA

114. Barcelona – Puerto Olímpíco

41°23'N 2°12'E

Charts

UKHO 1704, 1196, 1180	Imray M14
SHOM 4827, 7046	Spanish 489A, 4891

Lights

Dique de Abrigo head Fl(4)G.12s5m2M Green post 3m
Contradique head Fl(4)R.8s3m1M Red post 2m
Outer breakwater head Q.R.3m1M Red post
Submerged breakwater
Fl(3)R.8s6m3M Red post
Fl(3)G.8s6m5M Green post
Q(3)10s6m5M Black post, yellow band
Buoy Marbella Q(3)10s5M Card E buoy BYB 3m

Port communications

VHF Ch 09 ✆ 932 25 92 20
portolimpic@pobasa.es
www.portolimpic.es

Harbour charges Low

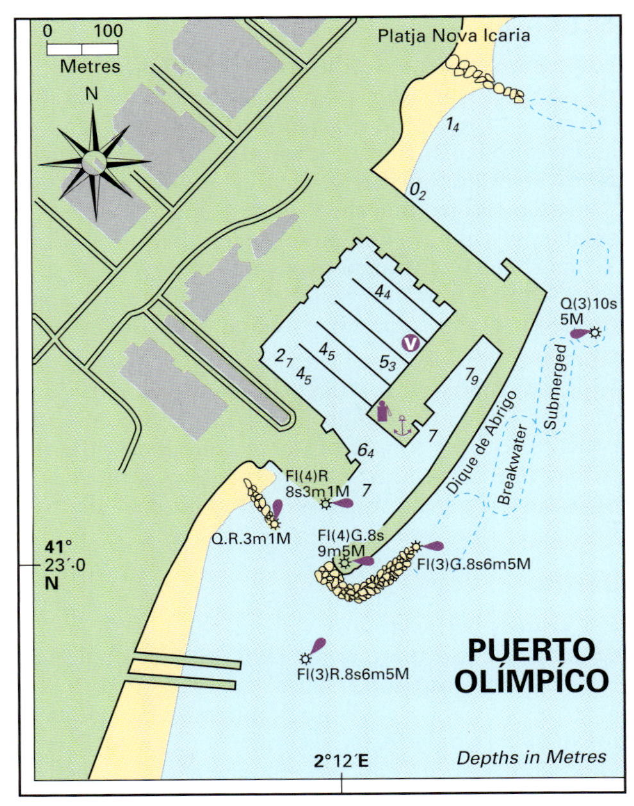

Olympic sailing village

This yacht harbour was built for the 1992 Olympic Games. The area of the city behind it formed the Olympic village. The metro is 10–15 minutes walk. The marina is tidy, secure and well sheltered however, it is a hot spot for the Barcelonistas, especially at the weekend and can be very noisy until dawn.

Puerto Olímpico

Puerto Olímpico entrance looking W *Steve Pickard*

Approach

From the south The low, flat delta of the Río Llobregat and the long breakwater of the Puerto de Barcelona are easily identified. Puerto Olímpico lies under a couple of skyscrapers (one marked MAPFRE) some 4M N of the S end of the outer breakwater of the old harbour.

From the north The harbour at El Masnou and the mouth of the Río Besós which has power and gas stations with tall chimneys either side of its mouth are easy to recognise. The harbour can be located by the two skyscrapers (one marked MAPFRE) immediately behind it.

Entrance

Approach the S end of the harbour passing between red and green beacon poles. Continue in towards the beach until the rocky extension at the head of the Dique de Abrigo can be rounded. A fairly sharp turn to starboard is needed to avoid running up on the beach.

Berths

Moor at fuel berth and obtain berth from *capitanía*.

Facilities

Maximum length overall 30m.
Some maintenance facilities.
Travel-lift 50 tonnes.
Crane 6 tonnes.
Large hard-standing.
Gasoleo A and petrol.
Showers.
Water and 220v and 380v AC on all quays.
Shopping mall in basement of eastern skyscraper.
Tourist bus stop on main road N of marina.

Communications

Metro, buses. Taxi ✆ 933 581 111.

Puerto Olímpico port control to left and limited hard-standing *Steve Pickard*

V. COSTA DORADA

115. Barcelona – Port Forum

41°25'N 2°1 4'E

Charts

UKHO 1704 Imray M14
SHOM 4827 Spanish 873, 4892, 489

Lights

Dique de Abrigo SW head Fl(4)G.12s10m5M
Green tower 6m

Dique de Abrigo NE head Q(3)10s7m3M
E Cardinal post BYB 6m

Port hand entrance Fl(4)R.12s5m3M Red post 3m

Entrance port side Fl.R.5s5m1M
Red column 4m (on submerged reef)

Espigon Fl(2)R.8s4m1M Red column 2m

Inner Pier head Fl(2+1)G.10s4m1M
Green column, red band 2m

Inner harbour pier head Fl.G.5s4m1M
Green tower 2m.

Port communications

VHF Ch 73 & 09 ✆ 933 56 27 20 / ✆ 933 562 725
info@portforum.com
www.portforum.com

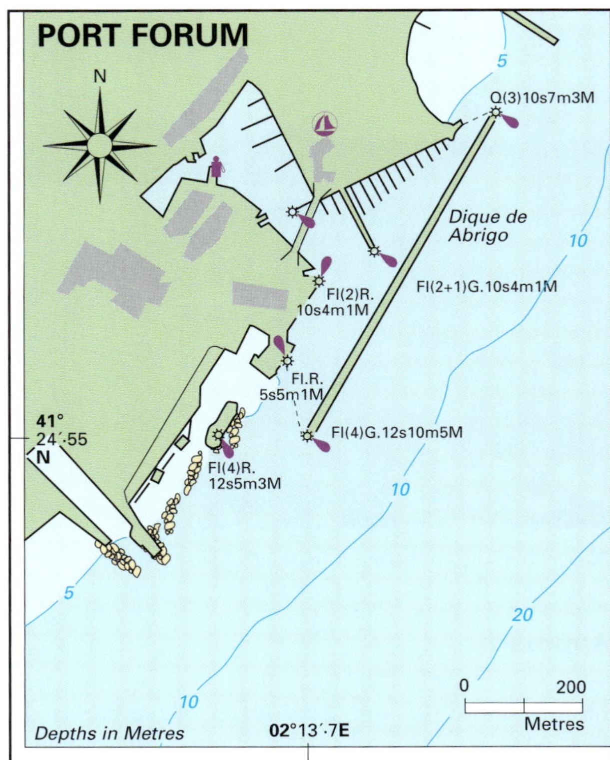

Port Forum superyacht berths with entrance beyond *Steve Pickard*

Port Forum inner harbour beyond the bridge *Steve Pickard*

A novel marina

Rather like London and the Millenium Dome, Barcelona cleared some waterfront areas of the Besos suburb and built an exhibition hall and park area, which included a small basin for dinghies and ribs etc. The exhibition itself finished in summer 2004 and the darsena was taken over by a private consortium who have developed part of the site into a first class marina for about 170 motor vessels (in the inner basin (access is under a 10m bridge). Outside there are berths for vessels up to 80m and there is a 'dry' marina which is a shed which can hold up to 245 craft up to 9m in a stacking system. Obviously it is mainly for motor craft but it takes some of the strain off the other marinas of Barcelona.

Approach and entrance

The 800m breakwater just three miles NE of Puerto Olímpico is conspicuous and one can enter from the southern end but it is essential to make contact with the marina authorities to arrange a berth before entering.

Facilities

As befits a new modern marina the facilities are excellent and most services are available.
150-ton travel lift
Water, 220v AC and internet connections on all pontoons.
Bunkering and provisioning.
Repairs and servicing.
Banking.
Security.
Ferries run to Plaza de Colon at the end of Ramblas.
There are numerous restaurants in this area.

116. Barcelona – Marina Badalona

41°26'N 2°14'·6E

Charts

UKHO 1704 SHOM 4827
Navicarte E05 Spanish 4892, 489

Lights

Dique de Abrigo head 41°25'·9N 2°14'·6E Fl(3)G.9s6m5M Green tower 2m

Contradique S corner buoy Fl(4)R.11s1M

Contradique N head Fl.R.5s4m1M Red post

Muelle de Capitania S elbow Fl(2+1)R.10s4m1M Red and green post

Port communications

VHF Ch 9 ✆ 933 20 75 00
port@marinabadalona-sa.es
www.marinabadalona-sa.es

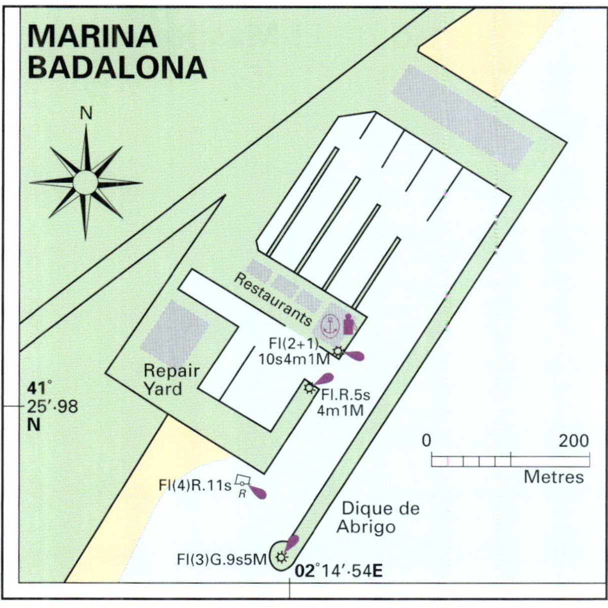

Big, brash and unfinished marina

Just over a mile northeast of Port Forum development continues at Badalona to produce a full service marina. The first phase is well underway and the marina is open for business. Captania, fuel and repair facilities are open as are some of the planned restaurants. Four main pontoons are in place and other mooring areas are also in use. 626 deep water berths are available. Shops, more restaurants and a hotel are following. The second phase is to drive a canal into the town with motor boat moorings and properties on either side.

Approach and entrance

Approach straightforward from N and S. Spacious entrance. Port Forum conspicuous 1M to S.

Facilities

Water and 220v AC on all pontoons.
Crane. Waiting quay. Ramp
Fuel 6am–9pm.
Ice
Dry dock for 211 boats up to 8 metres long
Western Basin esplanade for overwintering up to 25m.
Mechanical and electrical repair workshop. Painting. Carpentry. Electronics. Ironwork
24-hour monitored surveillance
Slipway and 75-tonne gantry crane
Tourist and weather information
Telephone, fax, internet, radio VHF, WiFi
Sailing school and nautical sports
Showers and WC
Laundry
Cafés and bar.
News shops, refreshments and hotel (under construction)
Chandleries
Boat sales and hire

Communications

Bus on site connections to train, metro and tram, putting Barcelona airport 20 minutes away. Access to roads such as the ring roads and the C-31 and B-20.

⚓ Mangat (Mongat)

41°28'N 2°17'·5E

Another open anchorage with the slight advantage of deeper water further in. (See page 287.)

Fuel berth and Port Control beyond the first basin
Steve Pickard

117. Puerto de El Masnou

41°28'N 2°18'E

Charts

UKHO 1704 Imray M14
SHOM 4827 Spanish 873, 4892, 489

Lights

Dique de Levante head Fl(2)G.12s10m5M
Green tower 7m

Dique de Poniente head Fl(2)R.12s3m3M
Red post 2m

Dique de Levante corner Fl(3)G.10s1m2M
Square green tower 1m

Fuel jetty corner Fl(3)R.10s1m2M
Square red tower 1m

Port communications

Capitanía VHF Ch 9 ✆ 935 403 000
portmasnou@portmasnou.es
www.portmasnou.com

Club Náutico de El Masnou ✆ 935 550 605
cnm@nauticmasnou.com
www.nauticmasnou.com

Harbour charges Low off season, medium in high season

Puerto de El Masnou entrance as seen from the fuel berth *Steve Pickard*

A vast well-run marina and small fishing port

A pleasant yacht harbour which has all facilities. Easy to approach and enter with excellent protection from even SW winds as the Dique de Levante has recently been lengthened by 70m. The modern seaside town has shops and restaurants and there are fine sandy beaches either side of this harbour.

Approach

From the south The mass of houses, harbour works and installations of Barcelona are unmistakable. Further N, and either side of the mouth of the Río Bésós, lie power stations with five tall chimneys and a jetty. The town of Badalona and many houses and flats line the coast, which is flat and sandy, backed by ranges of hills. The church at El Masnou and a tower, the Turó de Moná, on an isolated hill 1M inland are recognisable.

From the north The cliffs on either side of Arenys de Mar and its harbour can be recognised. Southwards the coast is flat and sandy with ranges of hills inland. The concentration of buildings at Mataró and its harbour can be identified, after which come the tower and church at El Masnou.

Anchorage in the approach

Anchor 200m to W of the entrance in 5m, sand.

Entrance

The entrance is nearly at the west end of the harbour and runs ENE–WSW between the breakwaters. The gap won't be obvious until it bears about NE. Pass between the piers and proceed to the fuel quay by the new *torre de control*.

Berths

Ask at the *torre de control* for allocation of a berth.

Facilities

Maximum length overall 22m.
Practically all repair facilities including sailmaking.
50-tonne travel-lift.

El Masnou, eastern part of the marina *Steve Pickard*

Puerto de El Masnou fuel berth and visitor reception *Steve Pickard*

4-tonne crane.
Two slips.
Three chandleries beside the harbour.
Showers.
Water and 220v AC on all quays and pontoons.
Gasoleo A and petrol.
Camping Gaz.
Club Náutico de El Masnou has a clubhouse to the NE of the harbour with bar, terrace, showers and a pool. It is separate from the harbour. Ask the secretary.
Supermarket, shops in the town nearby and hypermarket at Mataró.
Laundry collects from the marina.

Communications

Bus and rail services. Taxi ✆ 935 402 492.

PUERTO DE EL MASNOU

Barcelona
Railway
Engineer Café
Bar
Restaurant
Electrician
C.N.M
Pool
Playa
Playa
Fl(3)R.10s1m2M
Fl(3)G.10s1m2M
Fl(2)R.12s 3m3M
Fl(2)G.12s 10m5M
Dique de Poniente
Dique de Levante
41° 28′.5 N
2°18′.5E
2°19′E
Depths in Metres
0 100
Metres

118. Puerto de Premiá de Mar

41°29'N 2°21'E

Charts

UKHO 1704 Imray M14
SHOM 4827 Spanish 489

Lights

Dique de Abrigo head Fl.G.3s6m5M
Green post 3m

Contradique head Fl.R.3s3m3M
Red lantern on hut 1m

Port communications

Capitania VHF Ch 09 ✆ 937 549 119
info@marinapremia.com
www.marinapremia.com

Club Náutico de Premia de Mar ✆ 937 523 587
www.nauticpremia.net

Harbour charges Low

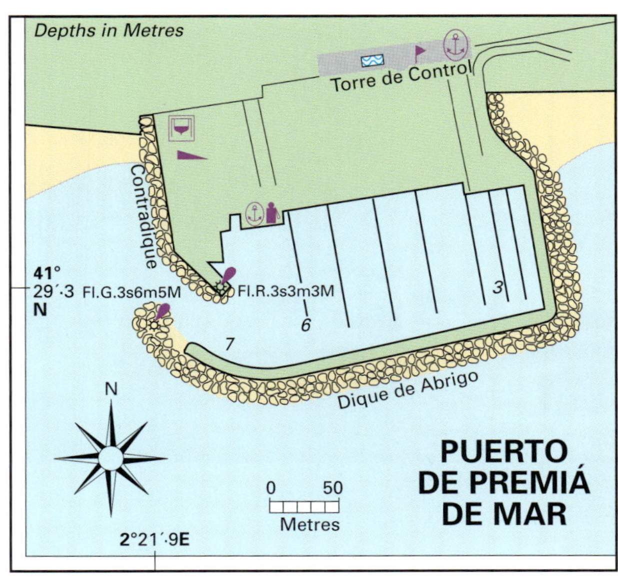

A developing marina

This 554 berth marina has been struggling to establish itself for some years. Despite its proximity to Barcelona, and being only 20 minutes from the airport, there are still many berths still available to rent. Visiting yachts should wait at the end of the first pontoon (G); the capitania is at the root of the pontoon. Additional facilities, repairs and shops are only slowly becoming established. Visitors are not welcome at the members' only club in the NE corner of the complex.

The town, well known for its carnations which are sent all over Spain, has good supplies but is on the other side of the railway tracks which make it a bit of a hike. Entrance to the marina is normally simple but could be tricky in strong SW winds. There are long sandy beaches both sides of the harbour.

Approach

From the south After Barcelona there are two large power stations either side of the Río Besós. 2M further north east is Port Masnou; then the large white *torre de control* behind Premiá de Mar should be spotted.

From the north Puerto de Arenys de Mar and the smaller ports of El Balís and Mataró are easily recognised. The very small landing at Vilassar may also be seen. The white control tower of Puerto de Premiá is easily identified from this direction.

Anchorage in the approach

Anchor according to draught in sand to E or W of the harbour.

Entrance

The entrance is straightforward. However, the old harbour mouth, which was further inshore, used to silt up and the new one may do the same. Sound carefully both on the approach and inside the harbour.

Berths

Secure to end of the first (G) jetty and report to *capitania* for allocation of berth.

Works in progress on the *contradique* (2016) *Steve Pickard*

Premiá de Mar's stark but efficient *capitania* *Steve Pickard*

Puerto de Premiá de Mar

Vilassar de Mar

Facilities

Mechanic with workshop.
A slipway on the NW side of the harbour.
A 1·5-tonne in the E corner.
Chandlery in town on road to Calvo Sotelo.
Water and 220v AC on all quays and pontoons.
220v and 380v AC on slipway.
Ice at the bar.
A few local shops with many more in Badalona 5M and Mataró 5M.
Weather forecasts posted at *torre de control*.

Communications

Bus and rail services. Taxi ✆ 937 522 532.

1. ⚓ Vilassar de Mar

41°29'·8N 2°23'·3E

Anchorage off sandy beach in 3m, sand, with a conspicuous yacht club and slipway enclosed by two rocky breakwaters with many small fishing boats on the hard. The Club Náutico de Vilassar de Mar has a restaurant, bar, water, showers, WCs and swimming pool. The village of 9,000 has many restaurants, café/bars, a chandler, post office, two hotels, bus and rail services and at 1½M the well preserved Castle Barbara and a flower-growing centre. Open between NE and SW.

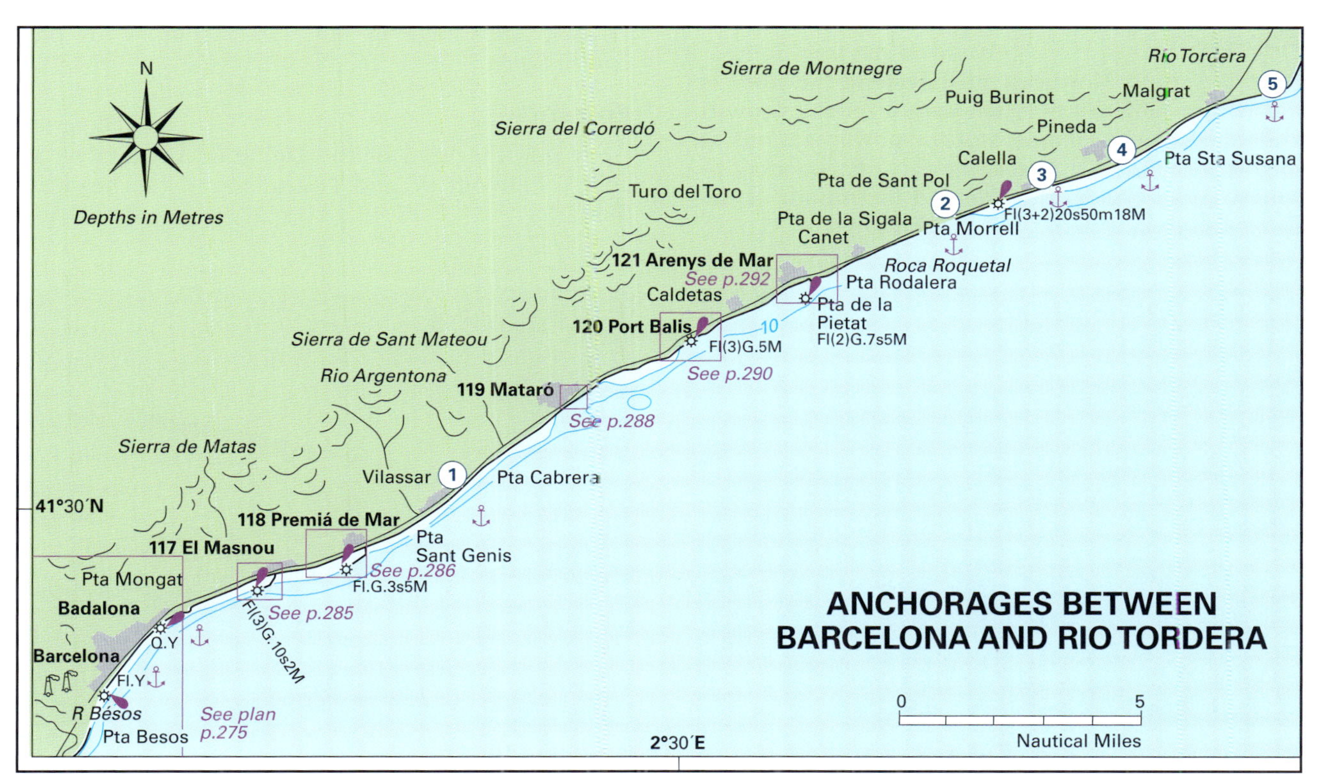

119. Puerto de Mataró

41°31'N 2°26'E

Charts

UKHO 1704 Imray M14
SHOM 4827 Spanish 873, 489, 301A

Lights

Dique de Abrigo head Fl(4)G.16s15m5M Green tower

Contradique head Fl(4)R.8s5m4M Red tower

Port communications

Capitanía VHF Ch 9. ✆ 937 550 961
info@portmataro.com
www.portmataro.com

Harbour charges Lowish, no variation between high and low season.

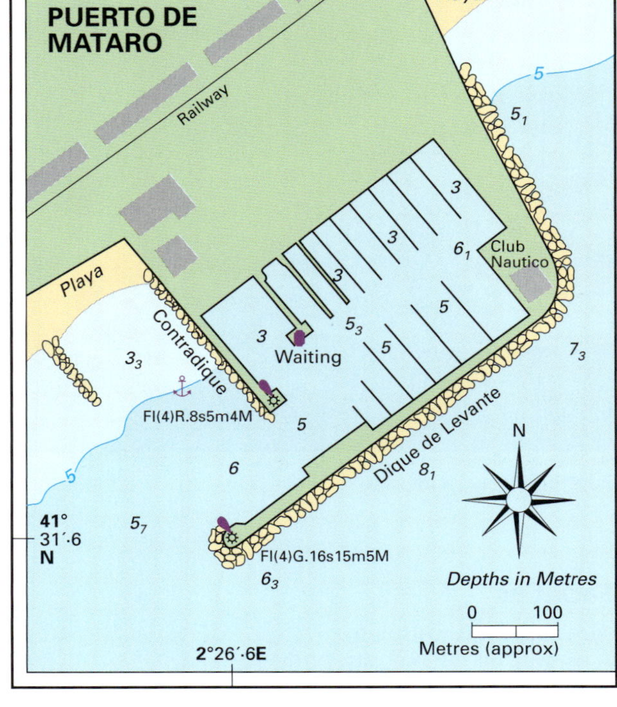

A pleasant marina

A large artificial yacht harbour of 1,000 berths cut off from the dreary town by the main road and railway. It is a useful stop-over, handy for Barcelona (20 minutes by train).

Mataró is the ancient Roman town of Iluro and many remains of that period have been discovered including the important Villa Torre Llauder. There are also Moorish relics. The first railway in Spain was laid from here to Barcelona in 1848. The town expanded and became well known for its shipbuilding. It is now equally well known for growing and marketing carnations.

The church and the ruined castle of St Vincente de Burriach, both 15th century, and the walled medieval town of Argentona should be visited. There are sandy beaches on both sides of the harbour.

Approach

From the south Northeast of Barcelona the coast is flat with a long sandy beach with a series of towns and villages. The chimneys of the power stations at the mouth of the Río Besós, the yacht harbours of El Masnou and Premiá de Mar and the mouth of the Río Argentona are easy to see. The town of Mataró and the harbour breakwaters are large and easily recognised.

From the north Blanes and the mouth of the Río Tordera can be identified. The coast is low and flat with a long sandy beach, lined with small villages and towns including Puerto de Arenys de Mar and Puerto de El Balís. The town and breakwaters of Mataró are conspicuous.

Anchorage in the approach

Possible anchorage in 4m, sand, 50m W of the *contradique*.

Entrance

Approach the head of the Dique de Levante on a course between W and N and round the head at 20m.

Puerto de Mataró entrance looking NE *Steve Pickard*

Puerto de Mataró

Puerto de Mataró waiting and fuel berth to port on entry *Steve Pickard*

120. Port Balís

41°33'N 2°30'E

Charts

UKHO 1704 Imray M14
SHOM 4827 Spanish 873, 489

Lights

Dique de Levante head Fl(4)G.12s4m2M Green column 2m
Espigón head Fl(3)G.10s10m5M Green tower 6m
Dique de Poniente head Fl(3)R.10s6m2M Lantern

Port communications

Club Náutico El Balis VHF Ch 6 ✆ 937 929 900
info@cnelbalis.com
www.cnelbalis.com

A vast, friendly and well-run marina

A pleasant yacht harbour, easy to enter and offering good protection though the swell from SW gales can enter the harbour. Facilities are good.

The nearby town of Caldetas with its hot springs and 13th-century church, and Mataró, the ancient Iluro, a walled town with many Moorish remains, can be visited. There are fine sandy beaches nearby.

Approach

From the south The chimneys of the power stations at the mouth of the Río Besós, the yacht harbours of El Masnou and Premiá de Mar and the mouth of the Río Argentona are easy to see. The town of Mataró and the harbour breakwaters are large and easily recognised. The harbour walls of El Balís will be visible in the closer approach.

From the north From the flat, low delta of the Río Tordera the coast has sandy beaches backed by ranges of hills with several small towns. A pair of towers near Calella and the harbour breakwater at Arenys de Mar will be seen.

Anchorage in the approach

Anchor according to draught E or W of the harbour in 5m, sand and mud.

Berth

Pass the *contradique* close to port and make for the waiting quay under the *torre de control*, next to the fuelling point, at the end of the first jetty to port. Moor and arrange a berth with the *capitanía* in the *torre*.

Facilities

Maximum length overall 20m.
Almost all repair services.
100-tonne travel-lift.
12-tonne crane.
Two chandlers on the coast road.
Showers.
Water and 220v and 380v AC on all quays and pontoons.
Gasoleo A and petrol.
Ice on fuel quay.
Shops, bars.
Supermarket and a weekly market in the town.
Laundry.

Communications

Bus and rail services. Taxi ✆ 937 986 060.

Port Balis entrance looking W from the end of the Dique de Levante *Steve Pickard*

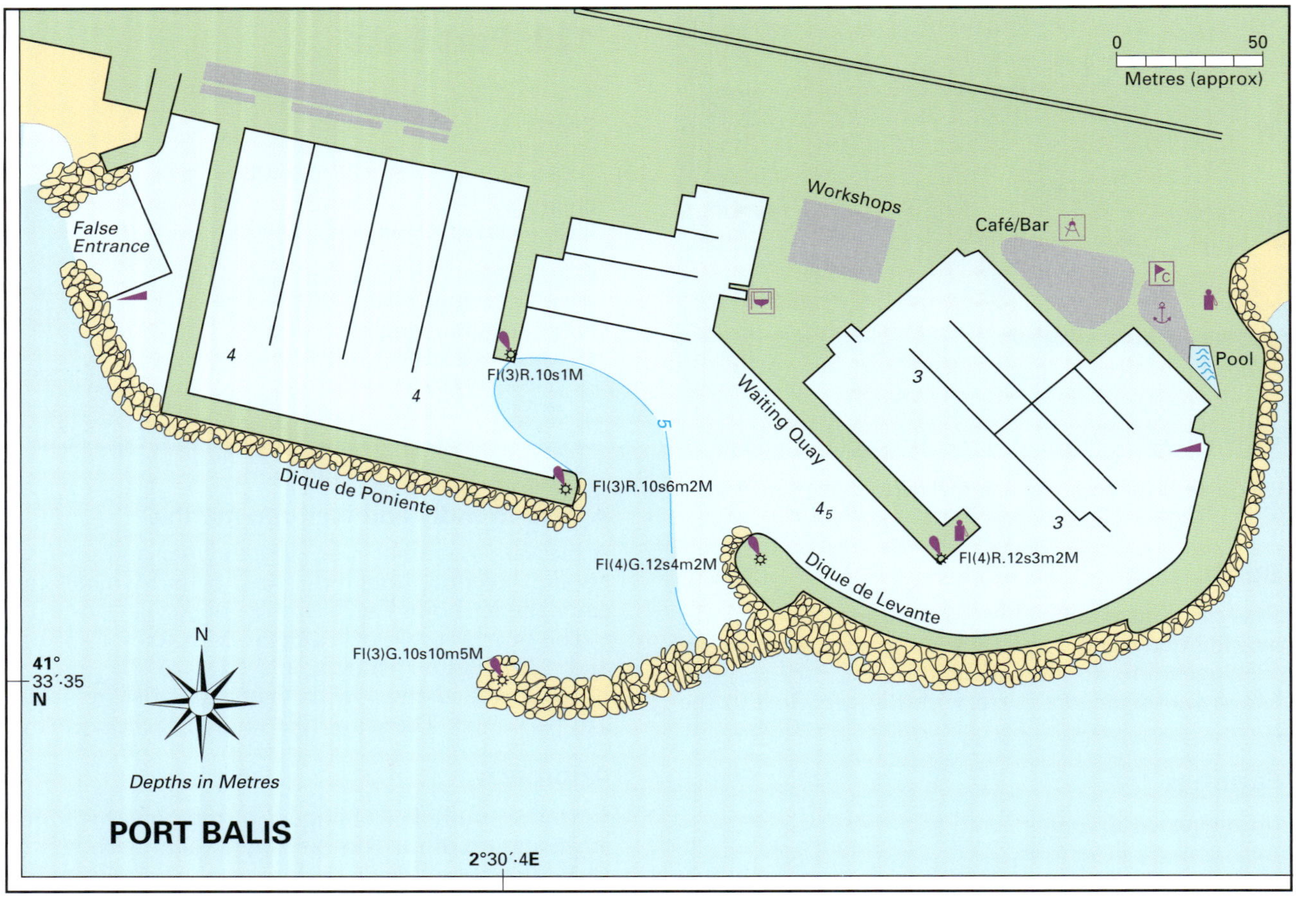

0 50
Metres (approx)
Workshops
Café/Bar
Pool
False Entrance
4
4
Fl(3)R.10s1M
5
Waiting Quay
3
3
4₅
Dique de Poniente
Fl(3)R.10s6m2M
Fl(4)G.12s4m2M
Dique de Levante
Fl(4)R.12s3m2M
Fl(3)G.10s10m5M
N
41° 33´.35 N
Depths in Metres
PORT BALIS
2°30´.4E

Port Balís

Port Balis fuel pontoon at the SE end of the waiting quay
Steve Pickard

Entrance

Approach the head of the Dique de Levante on a N course and round it at 25m.

Berths

Secure to the fuel quay for allocation of a berth.

Facilities

Maximum length overall 25m.
50-tonne travel-lift. 5-tonne crane.
There is a slipway in the N corner of the harbour and on the beach outside the entrance.
A chandlery at the N of the harbour.
Water and 220v AC on pontoons and quays.
Gasoleo A and petrol. Ice on the fuel quay.

Communications

Bus and rail services. Taxi ✆ 937 958 390.

121. Puerto de Arenys de Mar

41°34'N 2°33'E

Charts

UKHO 1704.	Imray M14
SHOM 4827, 7298	Spanish 489, 4911

Lights

Dique de Portiñol head Fl(2)G.7s9m5M Green tower on white base 5m
Dique del Calvario head Fl(2+1)R.21s5m2M Red tower, green band 3m
Dique de Portiñol elbow Fl(3)G.10s7m2M Green tower 3m 025°-vis-185°
Contradique de Poniente head Fl(2)R.7s8m3M Red tower 3m
To the northeast
Calella 41°36'·4N 2°38'·7E Fl(3+2)20s50m18M White tower on building 10m

Port communications
VHF Ch 09 ✆ 937 92 16 00
info@cnarenys.com
www.cnarenys.com

Harbour charges High

A major fishing harbour

This fishing harbour now accommodates a large number of yachts in addition to the fishing fleet. Popular with French yachts, it becomes crowded in summer so book ahead. It is easy to approach and enter. Inside, protection is good though SW winds send in some swell.

Those interested in history might visit the Torre del Encantate, built on the site of a pre-Roman town, and a 16th-century church. The beaches on either side of the harbour are good but have coarse sand and the railway backs the beach.

Approach

From the south The low and sandy coast is lined with towns and, a short distance inland, ranges of hills. El Masnou, the harbour at Mataró and a conspicuous tower just inland from Caldetas will be recognised. The cliffs either side of Arenys de Mar and the tall blocks of flats can be seen from afar and the harbour walls show up on the approach.

From the north After the low, flat delta of the Río Tordera the sandy coast is backed by ranges of hills and lined with a number of small towns. A breakwater (in ruins) at Malgrat and two towers at Calella may be seen. Arenys de Mar will be recognised by cliffs either side of the town, blocks of flats and, in the closer approach, by the harbour breakwaters.

Anchorage in the approach

A pipeline runs out to sea W of the Dique de Calvario but anchorage is possible in 3m E of the Dique de Portiñol.

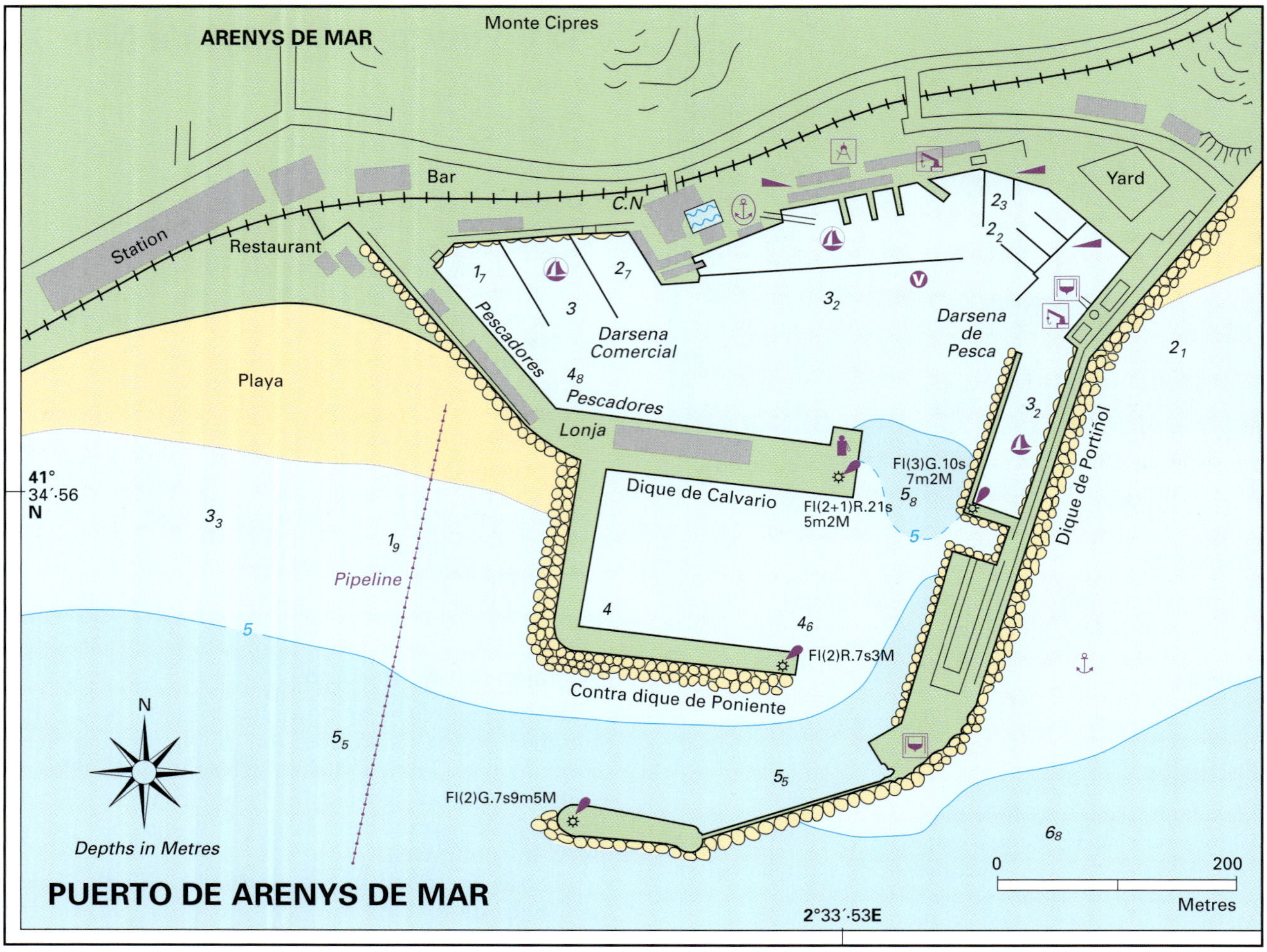

ARENYS DE MAR
Monte Cipres
Bar
C.N
Station
Restaurant
Yard
Playa
1_7
2_7
3
3_2
2_3
2_2
2_1
Darsena Comercial
Darsena de Pesca
Pescadores
4_8
Pescadores
Lonja
Dique de Calvario
Fl(3)G.10s 7m2M
5_8
Fl(2+1)R.21s 5m2M
5
3_2
Dique de Portiñol
41° 34′·56 N
3_3
1_9
Pipeline
5
4
4_6
Fl(2)R.7s3M
Contra dique de Poniente
N
5_5
5_5
Fl(2)G.7s9m5M
6_8
Depths in Metres
0 200 Metres

PUERTO DE ARENYS DE MAR

2°33′·53E

Puerto de Arenys de Mar

Entrance

Approach the head of the Dique de Portinol on a N course and round it at 50m.

Berths

Berth stern-to pontoons with bows-to mooring buoy as directed by the club officials. Vacant berths have a red plaque around the bollard on the pontoons.

Facilities

Maximum length overall 18m.
A yard to the N of the harbour and another larger one in the NE corner. Engine repair shops to the N of the harbour where there is also an electronic workshop.
Travel-lift in NE corner and two more, one of 100 tonnes near harbour entrance.
Two slipways in the NE corner and another on the N side of the harbour.
10-tonne crane at the NE side and another on the N side of the harbour.
Two chandlers in the road to the N of the harbour.
Water at the *lonja*.
Water and 220v AC on pontoons. 380v AC in the workshops.
Gasoleo A and petrol.
Ice from a factory to the N of the harbour or from the *lonja*.
Club Náutico de Arenys de Mar has bars, lounges, terrace, restaurant, showers and a swimming pool.
The shops in the nearby town can supply most normal requirements.
Launderette in the town.

Communications

Bus and rail services. Taxi ✆ 937 958 390.

Anchorages E of Arenys de Mar

For ⚓ below, see plan on page 287.

2. ⚓ Punta Morrell

41°36′N 2°38′E

A small anchorage in 4m, sand, protected by an L-shaped breakwater, open between E and SW with a sandy beach ashore and a large *club náutico*. Behind the coast road and railway line is the town of San Pol de Mar.

3. ⚓ Calella

41°36′·5N 2°40′E

Another open anchorage off a sandy beach in 3m, sand, with another deep-water anchorage ½M to SE of the town in 32m, sand, open between NE and SW. A yacht club ashore for dinghies. A large town backs up a variety of food shops. It is a centre of the hosiery trade. Rail and road connections.

4. ⚓ Pineda de Mar

41°37′N 2°42′E

Again an offshore anchorage in 3m, sand, in front of a conglomeration with some facilities and a good sandy beach. Rail and road connections.

5. ⚓ Río Tordera

This small river is the boundary between Barcelona and Girona and also marks the junction between Costa Dorada and Costa Brava. Entrance not possible - anchor off according to draught.

Arenys de Mar – the yacht club from the *lonja* *Steve Pickard*

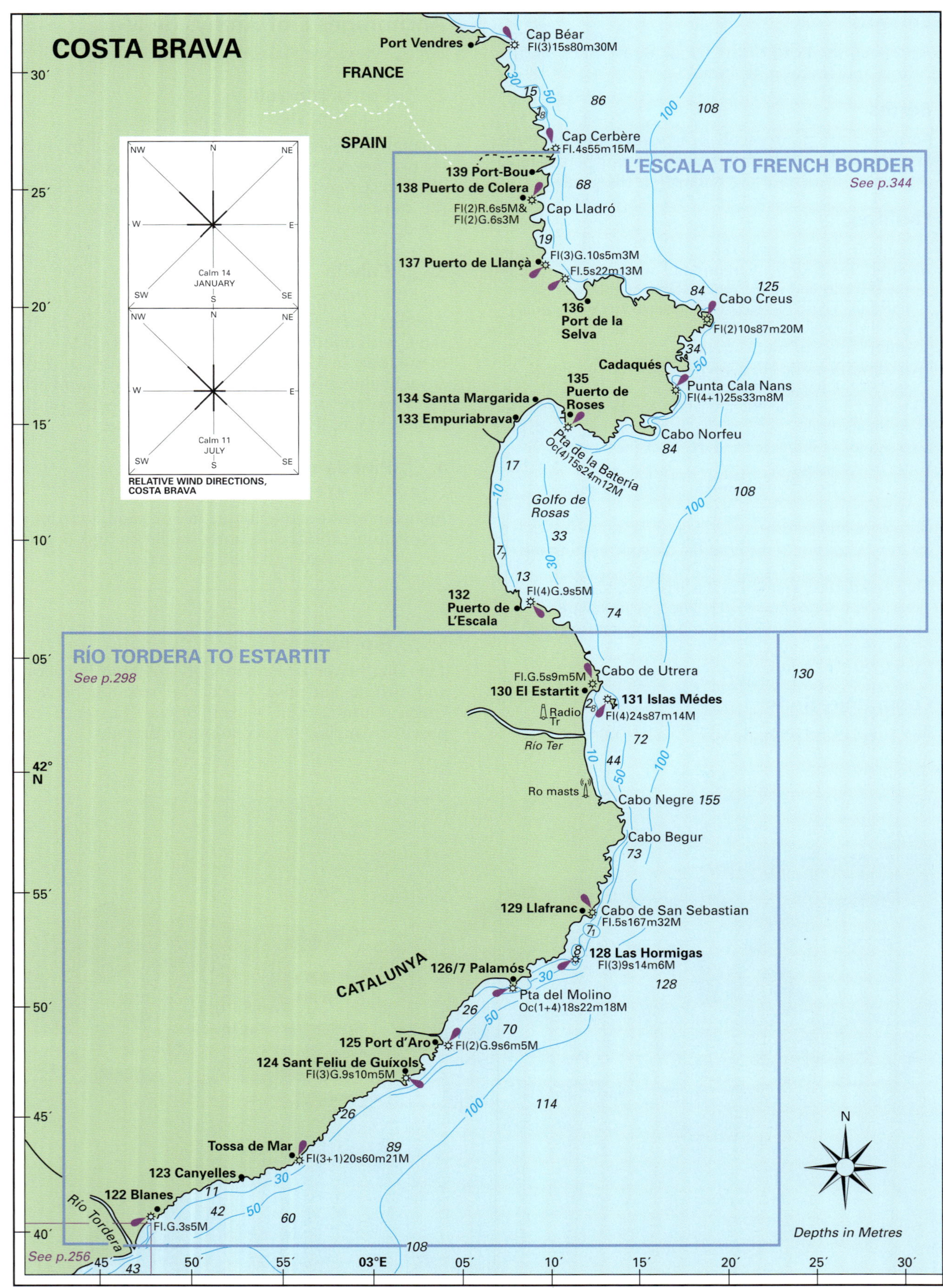
COSTA BRAVA
FRANCE
SPAIN
Port Vendres
Cap Béar
Fl(3)15s80m30M
Cap Cerbère
Fl.4s55m15M
L'ESCALA TO FRENCH BORDER
See p.344
139 Port-Bou
138 Puerto de Colera
Fl(2)R.6s5M&
Fl(2)G.6s3M
Cap Lladró
137 Puerto de Llançà
Fl(3)G.10s5m3M
Fl.5s22m13M
136 Port de la Selva
Cabo Creus
Fl(2)10s87m20M
Cadaqués
Punta Cala Nans
Fl(4+1)25s33m8M
134 Santa Margarida
133 Empuriabrava
135 Puerto de Roses
Cabo Norfeu
Pta de la Batería
Oc(4)15s24m12M
Golfo de Rosas
132 Puerto de L'Escala
Fl(4)G.9s5M
RÍO TORDERA TO ESTARTIT
See p.298
Fl.G.5s9m5M
Cabo de Utrera
130 El Estartit
131 Islas Médes
Fl(4)24s87m14M
Radio Tr
Río Ter
Ro masts
Cabo Negre 155
Cabo Begur
129 Llafranc
Cabo de San Sebastian
Fl.5s167m32M
128 Las Hormigas
Fl(3)9s14m6M
126/7 Palamós
CATALUNYA
Pta del Molino
Oc(1+4)18s22m18M
125 Port d'Aro
Fl(2)G.9s6m5M
124 Sant Feliu de Guíxols
Fl(3)G.9s10m5M
Tossa de Mar
Fl(3+1)20s60m21M
123 Canyelles
122 Blanes
Fl.G.3s5M
Río Tordera
See p.256
Depths in Metres
N
03°E
42° N
RELATIVE WIND DIRECTIONS, COSTA BRAVA
Calm 14 JANUARY
Calm 11 JULY

VI. COSTA BRAVA

Costa Brava planning guide and distances (See Appendix for waypoint list)

RÍO TORDERA TO ESTARTIT		
Miles		*Harbours, anchorages & headlands*
		Río Tordera
	⚓	*El Portell*
	122	**Puerto de Blanes** *(page 299)*
4·5M	⚓	*La Falconera*
		Punta de Santa Anna
	⚓	*L'Illa*
	⚓	*Cala Bona*
	⚓	*Cala La Llapizada*
	⚓	*Playa Treumal*
		Piedra Aguilla
	⚓	*Playa de Sta Cristina*
	⚓	*Playa de la Buadella*
		Punta de Sta Cristina
	⚓	*Playa de Fanals*
		Punta d'en Sureda
	⚓	*NE of Punta Banys*
		Punta de Banys
	⚓	*Playa de Lloret de Mar*
		Punta d'en Rosaris
	⚓	*La Caleta*
	⚓	*Calas E of Punta Roja*
		Punta de Calafats
	⚓	*Cala de la Tortuga*
		Punta de Capdells
		Punta de Sta Soita
	123	**Puerto de Cala Canyelles** *(page 304)*
3M	⚓	*Cala Morisca*
	⚓	*Playa de Llorell*
	⚓	*N of Els Cars*
		Punta Roquera
	⚓	*Cala Es Codolar*
		Cabo de Tossa
		Puerto de Tossa de Mar *(page 306)*
6M	⚓	*Playa de la Palma*
	⚓	*N of Punta de la Palma*
		Isla de la Palma
	⚓	*Cala Bona*
	⚓	*Cala Pola*
		Punta de Pola
	⚓	*Cala Giverola*
	⚓	*Cala Futadera*
		Punta Salions
	⚓	*Cala S of Punta d'en Bosch*
	⚓	*Calas de Canyet & Els Canyerets*
		Punta d'en Bosch
	⚓	*Cala del Uigueta*
	⚓	*Cala de Port Salvi*
	⚓	*Cala S of Pta de los Pianetes*
		Punta de Garbi
	⚓	*Cala de Tetuan*
	124	**Puerto de Sant Feliu de Guíxols** *(page 310)*
2·5M	⚓	*Anchorages E of Sant Feliu*
	⚓	*Cala de Sant Pol (S'Agaro)*
		Punta del Mula
	⚓	*Calas Pedrosa, de la Font, Vaques, Conca*
		Punta del Pinell
	125	**Port d'Aro** *(page 313)*

Miles		*Harbours, anchorages & headlands*
	125	**Port d'Aro** *(page 313)*
4M	⚓	*Playa (Platja) d'Aro*
	⚓	*Playa de la Cova*
	⚓	*Playas de Cap Roig & Belladona*
		Cabo Roig
	⚓	*Cala Canyers*
	⚓	*Playa de San Antonio*
		Punta de Rocas Planas
	⚓	*Playa de Palamos*
	126	**Puerto de Palamós – Commercial** *(page 320)*
		Punta del Molino
	127	**Puerto de Palamós – Deportivo** *(page 321)*
	128	**Islas Hormigas (Formigues)** *(page 324)*
4M		Cabo Gros
	⚓	*Cala Fosca*
	⚓	*Cala S'Alguer*
	⚓	*Cala Castell*
	⚓	*Cala Cobertera o Coves*
		Punta Castell
	⚓	*Cala Senia*
	⚓	*Cala N of Punta Canyes*
	⚓	*Calas Estreta, Remendon, Roco Bona & Planas*
	⚓	*Cala Fumorisca*
		Cap de Planas
	⚓	*Playa de la Cadena*
	⚓	*Cala d'en Massoni*
	⚓	*Cala Golfet*
	⚓	*Cala del Aigua Dolca*
		Cabo Roig
		Punta Forcat
		Calella de Palafrugell *(page 326)*
1M		Punta d'es Canons
	⚓	*Cala del Canadell*
	129	**Puerto de Llafranc** *(page 327)*
3M	⚓	*Cala de Gens*
		Cabo San Sebastian
	⚓	*Cala Pedrosa*
	⚓	*Cala Tamariu*
	⚓	*Cala Aigua Xelida*
	⚓	*Cova del Bisbe & Port d'Esclanya*
		Punta del Mut
		Calas de Aiguablava and Fornells *(page 332)*
2M	⚓	*Cala d'el Pins*
		Cabo Begur
		Calas de Sa Tuna and Aiguafreda *(page 335)*
4M	⚓	*Cala de Sa Riera*
	⚓	*Playa de Pals*
		Cabo Negre
	130	**Puerto de L'Estarit** *(page 338)*
	131	**Las Islas Médes** *(page 341)*
5M	⚓	*N of Punta Salines*
	⚓	*Ensenada del Rossinyol*
		Cabo d'Utrera
	⚓	*Golfo de la Morisca*
	⚓	*Cala Ferriola*
	⚓	*Cala de Montgo*
		Punta Trenca Bracos

L'ESCALA TO THE FRENCH BORDER		
Miles	*Harbours, anchorages & headlands*	
	132	**Puerto de L'Escala (La Clota)** *(page 346)*
7M	⚓	*Calas de L'Escala*
	⚓	*Las calas de Empuries*
	133	**Puerto de Empuriabrava** *(page 349)*
1M	**134**	**Puerto de Santa Margarida** *(page 352)*
1M	⚓	*Bahia de Roses*
	135	**Puerto de Roses (Rosas)** *(page 354)*
8M	⚓	*Cala de Canyelles Petites*
		Punta de la Bateria
	⚓	*Cala de Canyelles Grosses*
	⚓	*Cala Llaurador*
		Punta Falconera (Cabo Falco)
	⚓	*Cala Murtra*
	⚓	*Cala Rustella*
	⚓	*Cala de Montjoi*
	⚓	*Cala Pelosa*
	⚓	*Cala de Joncols (Jontulls)*
		Punta de la Creu
	⚓	*Cala Nans*
	⚓	*Cala Conca*
		Puerto de Cadaqués *(page 361)*
2M	⚓	*Playa del Ros*
		Isla Arenella
		Cala de Port Lligat *(page 363)*
2M	⚓	*Playa d'en Ballesta & Playa de l'Alqueria*
		Isletas Massina
	⚓	*Cala Guillola & Cala Jonquet*
	⚓	*Cala Bona*
		Punta d'en Cudera
	⚓	*Cala d'Illes*
	⚓	*Cala Jugadora*
	⚓	*Cala Fredosa (Cova del Infern)*
		Cabo Creus *(page 365)*
5·5M		Cabo Creus
	⚓	*Cala Culip*
	⚓	*Cala Portalo*
	⚓	*Cala de Galladera*
	⚓	*Cala de Mula*
	⚓	*Cala Portitxo*
		Punta d'els Farallons
	⚓	*Cala Tabellera*
		Cap del Ravaner
	⚓	*Calas Talabre & Galera*
	⚓	*Cala d'Aigua Dolca*
		Cabo Gros
	⚓	*Cala Gorguell*
	⚓	*Cala Fornells*
	⚓	*Playa Cativa & Cala Mascorda*
		Isla Meda
		E Cala Tamarina
		Punta de la Creu
	136	**Port de la Selva** *(page 373)*
2·5M	⚓	*Playa de la Ribera*
	⚓	*Playa de la Vall*
	⚓	*Playa d'en Vaques*
		Punta de la Sernella
	⚓	*Playa Cau de Llop*
		Islas Falco
	137	**Puerto de Llançà (Llansá)** *(page 377)*
2M	⚓	*Cala Grifeu*
	⚓	*Cala Garbet*
	138	**Puerto de Colera** *(page 380)*
1·5M	**139**	**Puerto de Portbou** *(page 381)*
		Cabo Falco

Introduction

The 67M stretch of coast from Río Tordera to the French border is more dramatic than the other sections. *Brava* means wild, savage. Much of the coast is broken with steep rocky cliffs and can be scoured by *tramontanas* which blow up with little notice. It is backed by the eastern end of the Pyrénées. The scenery, the proximity of the rugged shores and the deep *calas* beneath steep-sided promontories make this the most attractive of all the *Costas* of Mediterranean Spain for cruising yachtsmen.

The rugged coast runs from Blanes to the wide, flat flood plain of the Río Ter. The hills and cliffs rise again at L'Estartit and continue for 5M as far as the second flood plain of the Ríos Fluviá and Muga. From Roses onwards to France the coast is even less hospitable with high mountains quite close to the sea.

Offshore are the two groups of islands, Islas Formigues and Islas Médes. There are also some islands off Cabo Creus and several groups of rocks close inshore. In general the coast is steep-to and can be approached to within 100m with care. The exceptions are the shallow waters at river-mouths which may extend 300–400m off-shore.

There are numerous attractive anchorages but all are open to the sea one way or another; none have all-round shelter and if the wind is from the wrong quarter, the swell comes rolling in. Often the sheltered places are occupied by moorings. Many of the better known anchorages are mentioned and, for some, details are given. For more adequate shelter, there are harbours and an increasing number of marinas.

Though tourism has been established for some time, development along the Costa Brava is not so raw and ugly as that along the coastline to the southwest. Moreover, there are no really large towns and very little industry. The price is paid in more literal terms. Prices for holiday properties increase along the coast of Spain from south west to north east: harbour dues in the Costa Brava are about double those in the Costa del Sol. Proximity to France adds to the demand on yachting facilities and it is more important to arrange a berth in advance of arrival on the Costa Brava than it is on the other coasts.

Meteorological

Winds

The main danger in this area comes from the sudden arrival of a NW *tramontana* (*tramuntana mestral*, *mistral*), a very strong cold dry wind which arrives with little warning from a clear blue sky and often reaches gale force in a quarter of an hour. In winter these winds can be severe and contingency plans should always be made when at sea and extra mooring or berthing lines used when in harbour in the expectation of their sudden onset. Many *calas* that offer good protection from this wind on an otherwise barren coast have been included and advice as to the best place to secure inside harbours under these conditions has been given where applicable.

On occasion this wind can blow from the N and also to a lesser extent the NE wind and the E *levanter (llevant)* may be experienced. These latter winds are usually preceded by a heavy swell and clouds with rain and poor visibility accompanying them. They rarely reach gale force but their seas can be dangerous.

Harbours of refuge

The following harbours can usually be entered with strong winds and gales from seaward although with some difficulty:

Puerto de Sant Feliu de Guíxols
Puerto de Palamós
Puerto de Port de la Selva
Puerto de Roses

Magnetic variation

1°00′E (2017) decreasing 11′ annually.

Tides

The maximum spring range is under 0·5m and its effects are small.

Currents

There is a permanent S-going current of 1–2 knots. It is stronger off promontories and especially off Cabo Creus. Winds from N and E quarters tend to increase the flow and those from the S and W tend to reduce it.

Visits

Details of interesting local places to visit are listed with the harbour concerned. There are a number of places worth visiting located some distance inland which can be reached by public transport or taxi. These include:

Caldas de Malavella a small place inland from Tossa with ruins of old Roman baths and an old church.

Romany a de la Selva where there is a Megalithic tomb. The village is located behind San Feliu de Guíxols.

Girona the largest and most important town in the area, originally a Roman settlement where many old churches can be seen, together with old buildings and walls dating from the time of the Moors. There is a cathedral, several museums and a castle.

Ullastret not far from L'Estartit which has some Iberian and Greek remains and an 11th-century church.

Figueres a major town lying behind the Golfo de Roses, founded by the Romans on their Via Augusta. It has a castle almost intact, a museum and a monastery.

Empuries on the coast near L'Escala, is the most important archaeological site on the Costa Brava. It represents a microcosm of the history of this coast. The two Greek settlements of Paleopolis and Neapolis, sometimes called Emporion (c.500BC) were taken over in 209BC by the Romans and renamed Empuries. It co-existed with the nearby settlements of Iberian natives until it was first overrun by the Barbarians, then destroyed by the Moors and later ravaged by Norman pirates. The ruins were covered by sand and silt and in part built over by the small village of Sant Martí only to be rediscovered some 1,000 years later. These ruins are well worth a visit.

Puerto de L'Escala (see page 346) *Steve Pickard*

RÍO TORDERA TO ESTARTIT

Ports

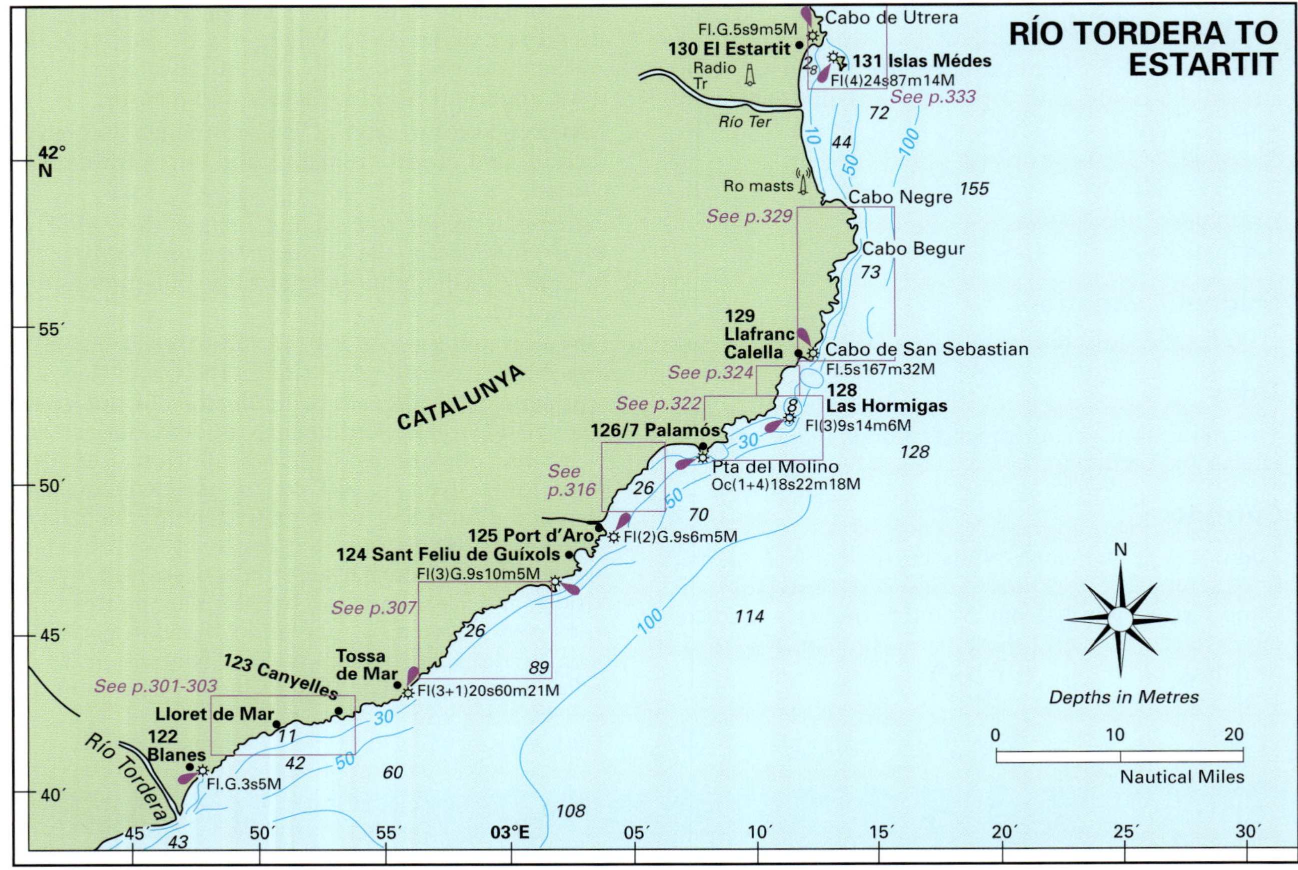

Puerto de Blanes entrance looking N from the Dique de Abrigo *Steve Pickard*

122. Puerto de Blanes

41°40'N 2°47'E

Charts

UKHO 1704 Imray M14
SHOM 4827, 7298 Spanish 873, 4913, 491

Lights

New Breakwater head Fl.G.3s7m5M
Green and white column 3m

Breakwater elbow Q(6)+LFl.15s3M
Card S black column yellow top

Contradique head Fl.R.3s7m3M
Red and white post 4m

Interior dique head Fl(2)R.6s6m2M Red post 4m

Interior jetty N head Fl(2)G.1M
Green cone on white post 3m

Interior jetty S head Fl(3)R.1M Red post

Port communications

Capitania VHF Ch 9 ✆ 972 33 05 52
club@cvblanes.cat
www.cvblanes.cat

Harbour charges High

An interesting port

A fishing and yachting harbour based on an old port and improved by breakwaters, quays and pontoons. The harbour is easy to approach and enter but heavy winds between SE and S may send swell into the harbour. The surrounding area is attractive and the town is pleasant. The harbour is crowded in summer.

During 2010 a new breakwater was built from the root of the old Dique de Abrigo totally enclosing the old Dique which makes the harbour much more secure and separates the fishing fleet to its own space making the harbour much more attractive for pleasure craft.

The botanical garden and the 14th-century church and ruined palace are interesting. The view from Castillo de San Juan on the top of the hill behind the harbour is worth the climb. There is a fine sandy beach to the W of the harbour and to the northeast are a number of attractive small *calas* that can be visited by boat.

Originally a Roman port called Blanda, it once rivalled Barcelona and Tarragona but little remains of that era. The port did not develop at the same rate as its rivals and remained under the Counts of Cabrera whose ruined palace is beside the church.

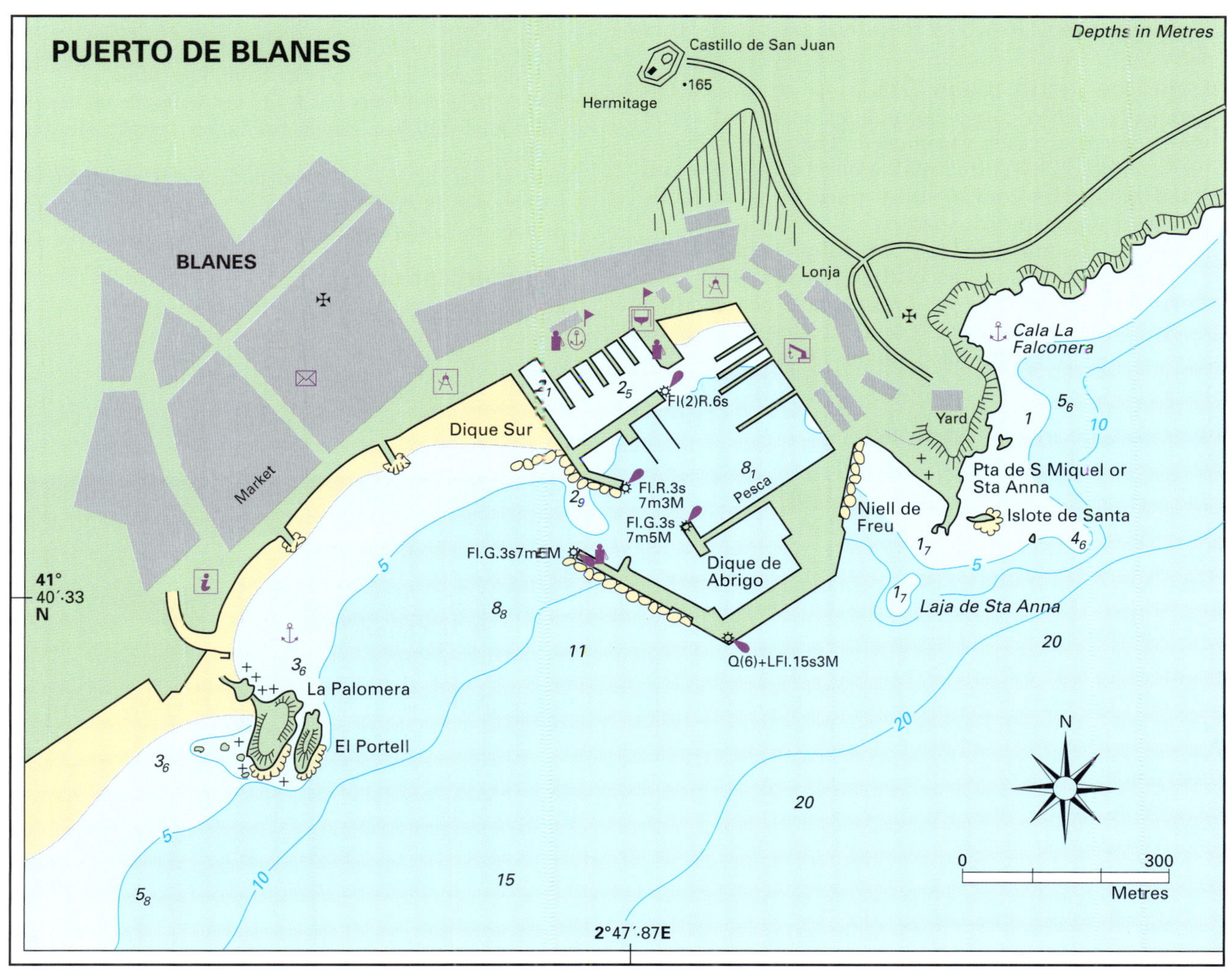

Puerto de Blanes, the rock of El Portell is top left of picture

Approach

From the south A narrow coastal plain backed by ranges of mountains gives way to the deep flat delta of the Río Tordera which projects about ½M out to sea and must be given a berth of at least ¼M because of shoals. The isolated conical hill topped by the Castillo de San Juan which lies just behind this harbour can be seen from afar. The small low rocky Islets de la Palomera and El Portell lie very close inshore just before this harbour is reached, they have deep water to seaward of them but are shoal either side.

From the north Cabo Tossa, a rocky-cliffed peninsula with a conspicuous lighthouse and castle with towers, is easily recognised. The coast remains broken and rocky-cliffed with a number of *calas* and small bays. The conical hill topped by Castillo de San Juan is conspicuous from this direction.

Punta de Santa Anna (or San Miquel) just to the NE of this harbour has outlying rocky islets and shoals. It should not be approached nearer than 300m and the harbour entrance should not be approached until the head of the Dique de Abrigo bears NW.

Anchorage in the approach

It may be possible to anchor 300m to W of the outer breakwater in 6m, sand and weed. The beach landing tourist boats, beach bouys and channel bouys may prevent this in season. Cala Falconera is another possibility, see harbour plan.

Entrance

Approach the Dique de Abrigo on a northerly course, leaving it 50m to starboard and turn slowly to starboard to enter between the pier heads.

Berths

The *club náutico* controls the pontoons in the NW side of the harbour. It is advised to go round the end of the internal quay and moor to the fuelling berth for berthing instructions if it has not been possible to contact the *capitanía* previously.

Facilities

Maximum length overall 15m.

A shipyard in the E corner of the harbour. Here or elsewhere in the harbour repairs to wood and GRP hulls, engines and sails.

50-tonne travel-lift.

3-tonne crane.

A slip in N corner of the harbour.

Chandlery on the front near the harbour and another beside the harbour.

Water and 220v AC on all quays and pontoons.

Gasoleo A and petrol.

Ice is delivered daily to a store behind the lonja.

Club de Vela de Blanes has a clubhouse beside the inner harbour with bar, lounge, restaurant, terrace, showers, etc.

Many shops and supermarkets in the town and a market every day except Sunday.

Launderette in the town.

Communications

Bus and rail service. Taxi ✆ 972 330 037.

Puerto de Blanes' limited haul-out facilities *Steve Pickard*

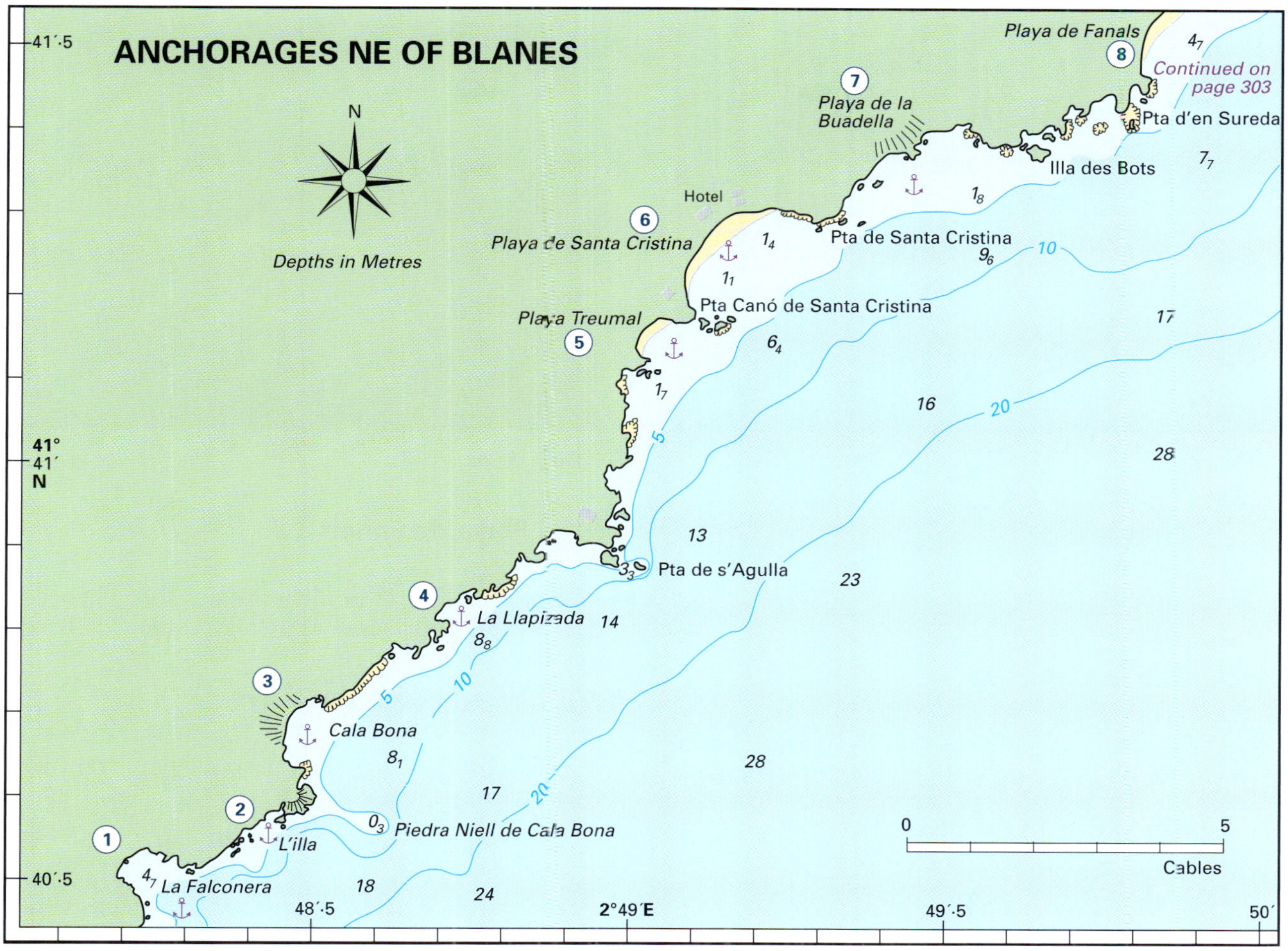

ANCHORAGES NE OF BLANES

Depths in Metres

N

41´·5
41° 41´ N
40´·5
48´·5
2°49´E
49´·5
50´

Playa de Fanals
8
Continued on page 303
Pta d'en Sureda
7
Playa de la Buadella
Illa des Bots
Hotel
6
Playa de Santa Cristina
Pta de Santa Cristina
Pta Canó de Santa Cristina
Playa Treumal
5
Pta de s'Agulla
4
La Llapizada
3
Cala Bona
2
L'illa
Piedra Niell de Cala Bona
1
La Falconera

0 5
Cables

Anchorages NE of Blanes

1. ⚓ La Falconera

41°40´·5N 2°48´·3E

An anchorage in a rocky cliffed bay open between NE and SE. Small stony beach, crowded in season. Road and houses ashore.

2. ⚓ L'Illa

41°40´·6N 2°48´·8E

Anchorage on S side of a hooked promontory in sand and stone with off-lying islets, open between E and S, road ashore.

Pta de San Miguel

3. Cala Bona

3. ⚓ Cala Bona

41°40′·7N 2°48′·6E

Anchor of the beach in sand. Open between NE and SE.

4. ⚓ Cala la Llapizada

41°40′·8N 2°48′·9E

A rocky sided *cala*. Anchor in N corner under headland with house on its point and off-lying islet, Piedra Agulla, to its E. Anchor in sand and stone – open between E and S. Road ashore.

5. ⚓ Playa Treumal

41°41′·1N 2°49′·1E

Anchor off either beach. Open between NE and SE.

6. ⚓ Playa de Sta Cristina

41°41′·2N 2°49′·2E

Anchorage off a wide sandy beach in sand, open between E and SE. Beach café/bar, pleasure boats.

7. ⚓ Playa de la Buadella

41°41′·3N 2°49′·5E

Sandy beach between two rocky headlands. Anchor in sand off beach, open between E and S. Beach café/bar.

5. Playa Treumal

8. Playa de Fanals

8. ⚓ Playa de Fanals

41°41′·5N 2°50′E

Anchor according to draught in sand. Open between NE and SE with some shelter at each end. Beach café/bars, showers.

9. ⚓ NE of Punta de Banys

41°41′·6N 2°50′·6E

A rocky-cliffed *cala*, anchor nervously near centre in sand and stone, track ashore.

10. ⚓ Playa de Lloret de Mar

41°41′·8N 2°51′·2E

Open between E and SW with some shelter at either end. Very crowded ashore in summer. Stay clear of the tripper boat lanes to the beach.

11. ⚓ La Caleta

41°41′·9N 2°51′·5E

A small *cala* at the E end of the Playa de Lloret de Mar below a castle with a small beach, usually crowded. Anchor in sand near the centre. Open between S and SW.

12. ⚓ Calas to E of Punta des Cabdells

41°41′·8N 2°51′·7E

A series of rocky-edged small *calas* with a pair of islets – take extra care. Low rocky cliffs with roads and houses ashore. Anchor in sand and stone. Open between SE and SW.

13. ⚓ Cala de la Tortuga

41°41′·9N 2°52′·3E

A V-shaped *cala* with stony beach at its head, road and houses ashore. Anchor in sand and stone, open between SE and SW. A similar *cala* lies to E on the other side of the Punta de Santa Goita.

14. ⚓ Punta de Santa Goita

41°42′N 2°52′·5E

An inconspicuous point lying just to W of Cala Canyelles, rocky-cliffed and tree-covered with some houses. 10m depths near the point.

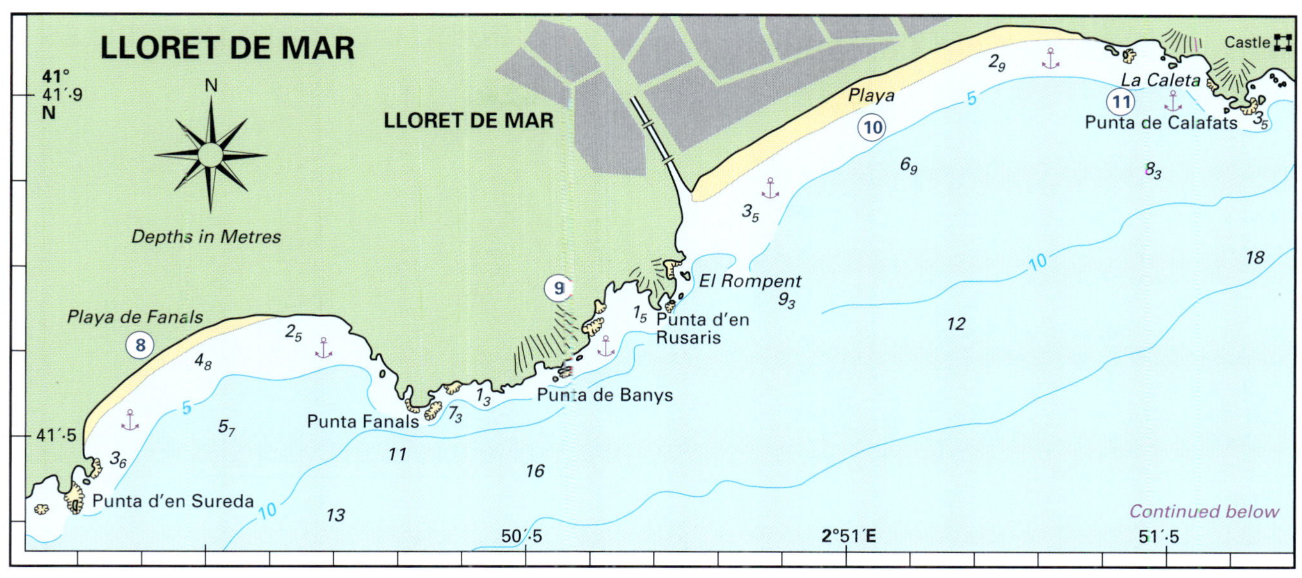

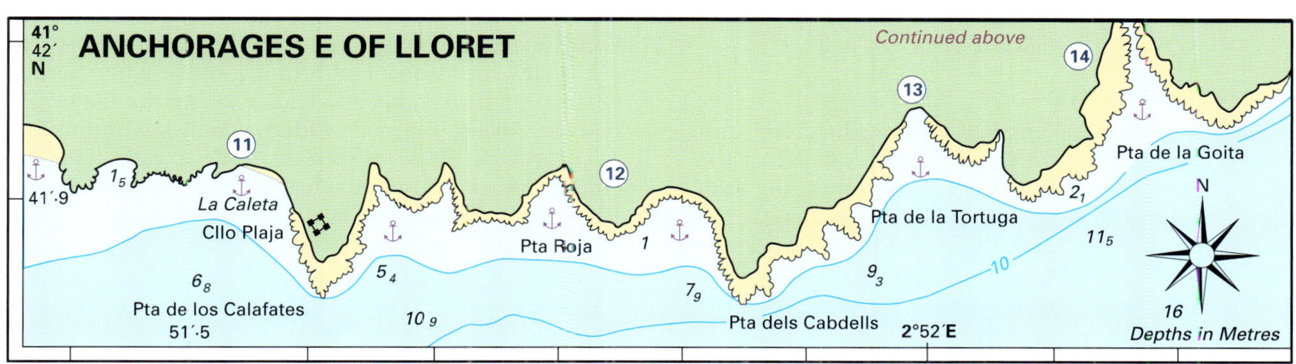

10. Limited anchoring opportunities on the Playa de Lloret de Mar *Steve Pickard*

123. Puerto de Cala Canyelles (Cañelles)

41°42'N 2°53'E

Charts
UKHO 1704 Imray M14
SHOM 4827 Spanish 873, 492

Lights
Dique de Abrigo head Fl(4)G.11s5m5M Green tower 3m
On cliff at entrance Fl.R.5s1M Red post on cliff
On cliff to south Fl(4)R.11s3M Red hut
To the north
Cabo Tossa 41°42'·9N 2°56'·0E Fl(3+1)20s60m21M White tower 11m 229·7°-vis-064·2°

Port communications
Capitanía VHF Ch 9. ✆ 972 368 818
info@cncanyelles.com
www.cncanyelles.com

Harbour charges High

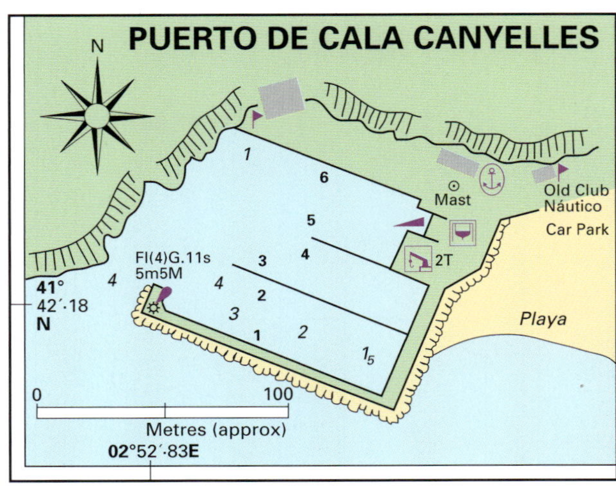

A very small marina

A yacht harbour for smaller yachts (8m max) and fishing boats. Built into the W end of a beach at the side of an attractive *cala*. Entrance is normally easy but could be difficult with strong winds between E and SW. The swell from these winds also makes it uncomfortable inside the harbour. Facilities are limited, provisions are available from shops in the nearby village.

The area around has been built over with large private houses and the beach of fine sand to the E of the harbour is crowded in summer with day-trippers.

Puerto de Cala Canyelles

Approach

From the south Puerto de Blanes is unmistakable with Castillo de San Juan on a hill behind it. Further NE there are some eight *calas*, most with sandy beaches at their head, the largest being the Playa de Fanals and the Playa de Lloret which has the town of Lloret de Mar behind it with a conspicuous church tower. There are a few small *calas* to E of the Playa de Lloret de Mar but the next large *cala* has a sandy beach with the harbour at its west end.

From the north Puerto Sant Feliu de Guíxols is easily recognised by its long breakwater and the prominent Punta de Garbí on the W side. Broken rocky cliffs with small *calas* extend 5·5M to Cabo Tossa which has a conspicuous lighthouse and tower on its summit. The harbour lies 2¼M to SW of Cabo Tossa. Do not mistake the large *cala* of Playa de Lloret (no connection with the Playa de Lloret de Mar which lies opposite the town of the same name which is only 1·5M from Cabo de Tossa). This stretch of coast has broken rocky cliffs with many small *calas*. The sandy beach and harbour of Cala de Canyelles are easily seen when S of the *cala*.

Anchorage in the approach

300m to S of the sandy beach of Cala de Canyelles in 10m, sand and stone.

Entrance

The entrance, which is only 12m wide, lies to the W side of the harbour between the head of the Dique de Abrigo and the red rocky cliffs.

Approach the head of the Dique de Abrigo and enter, keeping close to the head, at slow speed with a bow lookout because the channel is narrow.

Berths

Secure to a vacant berth and ask the *capitanía* for a place.

Small and tightly packed Puerto de Cala Canyelles *Steve Pickard*

Cala Es Codolar

Facilities

Maximum length overall 8m.
Mechanic for simple repairs.
2-tonne crane.
A small slip in NE corner of the harbour.
Small hard-standing.
Water on the quays.
Provisions from the village up the hill or in Lloret de Mar 3M away.
Club Náutico de Cala Canyelles now operates from a porta-cabin in low season and the restaurant/bar may now belong to a private concern.

Communications

Bus service on coast road 0·5M inland.

Anchorages between Cala Canyelles and Tossa de Mar

⚓ Cala Morisca

41°42'·2N 2°53'·9E

A small V-shaped *cala* with stony beach at its head, anchor in mid-*cala* in rock and sand, open between SE–S–SW.

⚓ Playa de Llorell

41°42'·4N 2°54'·3E

Anchor off sand and pebble beach in sand open between SE and SW. Beach café/bar, road, some houses and apartment blocks.

⚓ N of Els Cars

41°42'·8N 2°55'·8E

A small bay open between E and S with rocky coast and cliffs. Anchor in sand and rock in middle.

⚓ Cala Es Codolar

41°42'·8N 2°55'·9E

Open between SE and SW. A pre-Roman anchorage and harbour. (See plan of Tossa de Mar, page 306.)

Limited anchoring opportunities at Puerto de Tossa de Mar, looking S *Steve Pickard*

Puerto de Tossa de Mar

41°43'N 2°56'E

Charts

UKHO 1704	Imray M14
SHOM 4827, 7505	Spanish 873, 876, 491

Lights

Cabo Tossa 41°42'·9N 2°56'·0E Fl(3+1)20s60m21M
White tower 11m 229·7°-vis-064·2°

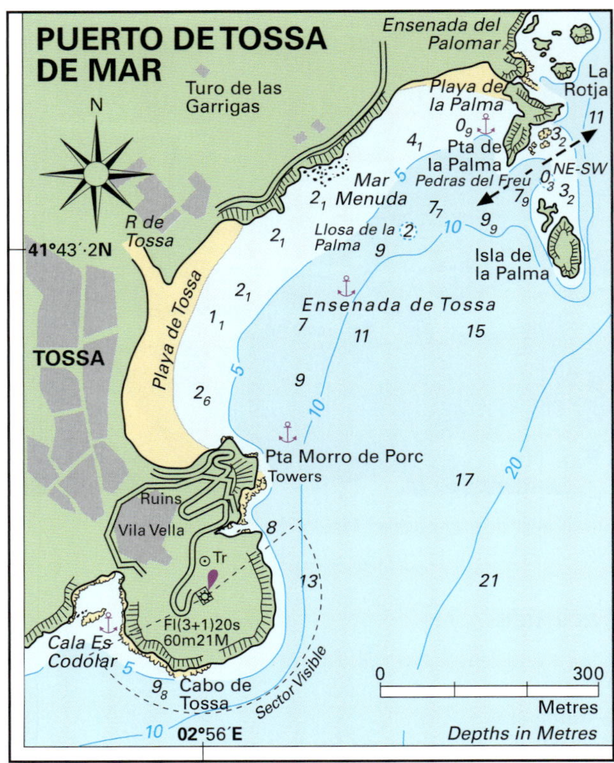

Anchorage only

Not actually a harbour but an important and very attractive anchorage. Under Tossa it is well sheltered from the prevailing winds though open between NE and SE; further north up the bay the anchorages are more exposed to the south. In the season the bay is crowded with tourists.

Tossa is a very old harbour and town that has been in occupation since pre-Roman times. The Romans called it Turissa. It was, like the rest of the towns on this coast, destroyed by the Vandals and rebuilt only to be destroyed again. In the 10th century the Castrum de Tursia, as it was then called, was given by the Count of Barcelona to the monks of Ripoll. Between the two world wars this town was discovered by foreign tourists and became a popular resort. There are many interesting places to visit including a Roman villa, the old town (Villa Vella), a Baroque church and a museum. The view from the lighthouse is worth the climb.

Approach

From the south The coast from Blanes, which can be recognised by the conical hill topped by a small castle, is very broken and rocky-cliffed with many *calas*. The concentration of houses and flats at Lloret de Mar where there is a long sandy beach is easy to identify. The lighthouse and tower on Cabo de Tossa can be seen from afar.

From the north From Punta de Garbí the coast is likewise very broken with rocky cliffs and ranges of hills inland. The lighthouse and tower at Cabo Tossa is also conspicuous from this direction.

Puerto de Tossa de Mar

Entrance

The easiest entrance is on a NW course towards the river mouth where there is a gap in the line of buildings.

From the northeast, the passage between Punta de la Palma and Isla de la Palma should only be attempted in good conditions with caution and then only at the N side of the passage between Punta de la Palma and the 0·3m shallows of Pedras del Freu. Use in a NE-SW direction; minimum depth 3m. When through, beware the unmarked rocky shoal Llosa de la Palma, 2m, in the N half of the bay.

Anchorage

Anchor where indicated on the chart to suit prevailing wind in 9m, sand. The nearest alternatives are Es Codolar to the south or Playa de la Palma to the north.

Landings

On the sandy beach where and when swell allows.

Facilities

Many shops of all kinds in the town.

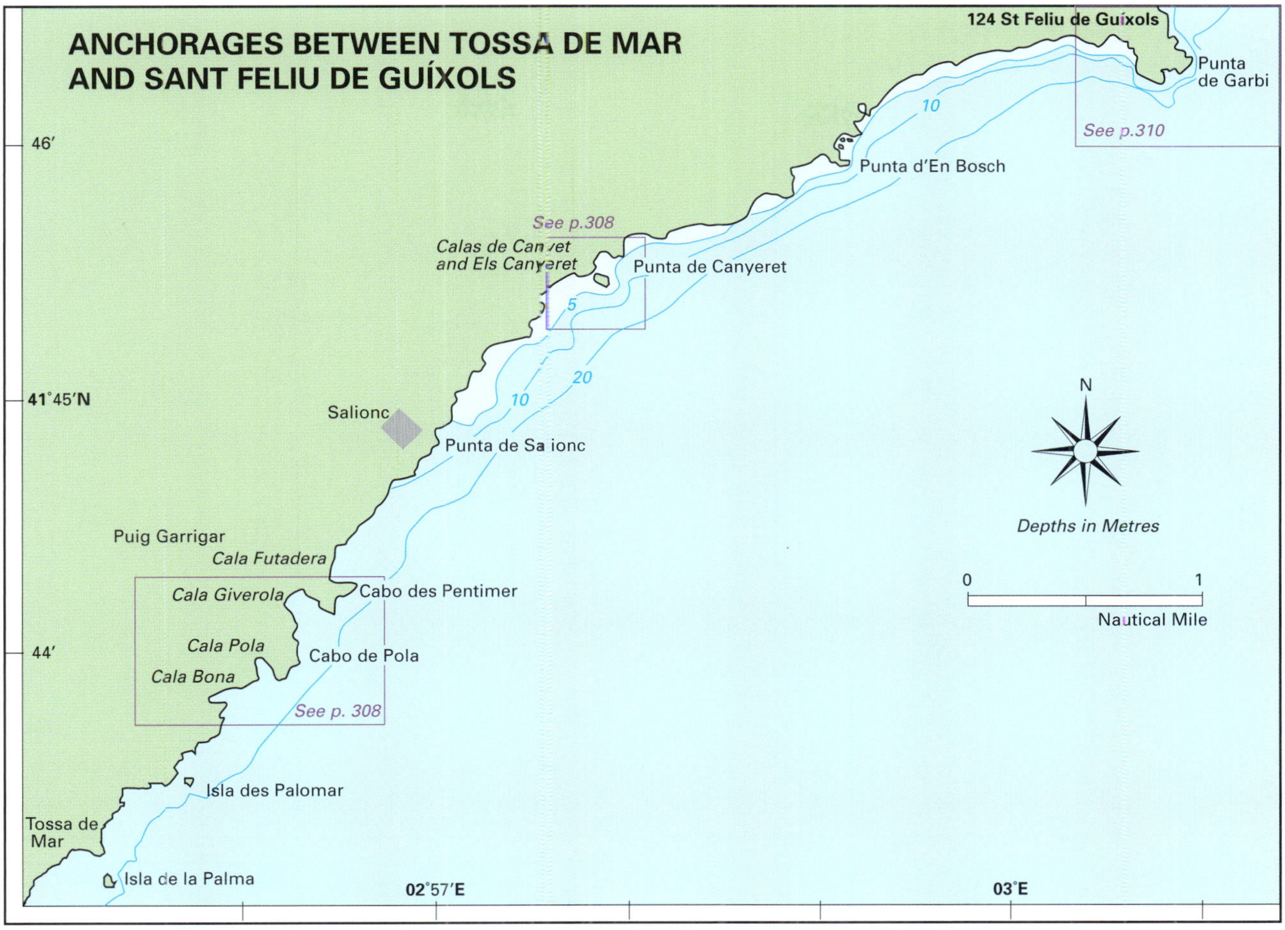

⚓ N of Punta de la Palma

41°43′·1N 2°56′·4E

A wide rocky bay with three small *calas*. Anchor in 5m sand, stone and weed in mid-bay, open between E and S.

⚓ Cala Bona

41°43′·8N 2°57′E

A long narrow *cala* open between E and SE with rocky tree-covered sides and sandy beach at its head, with a beach café/bar. Anchor in mid-*cala*, sand and rock.

⚓ Cala Pola

41°43′·8N 2°57′·2E

Tiny *cala* with very little room, usually full of summer boats.

Punta de Pola

41°43′·8N 2°57′·2E

A rocky-cliffed, tree-covered headland with high ground inland, ending in a conspicuous hump. Dangerous rocks off the point but 5m depths nearby.

⚓ Cala Giverola (or de St Elias)

41°44′N 2°57′·4E

In season normally full of small boats.

Cala Pola and Giverola with Cala Futadera at top right. Cala Bona at bottom left

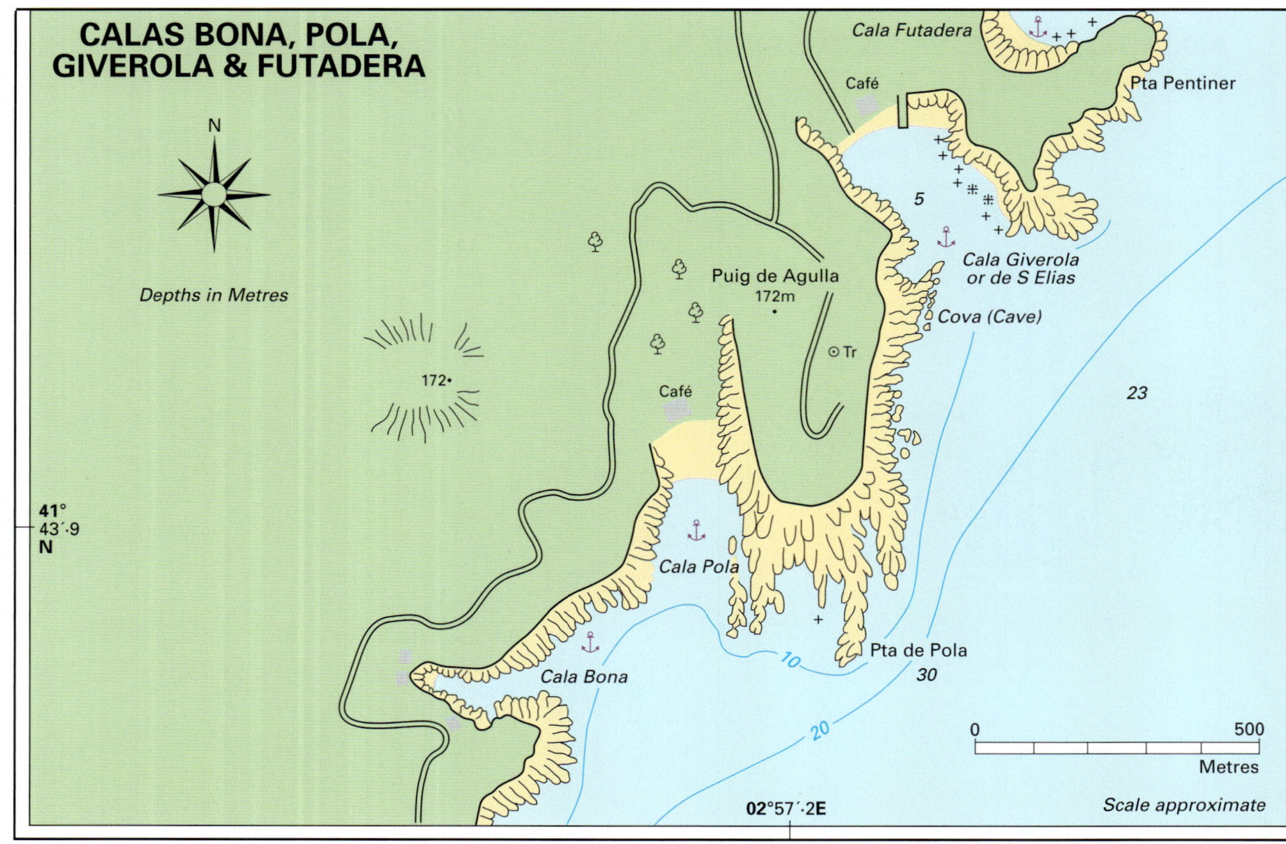

Cala Futadera

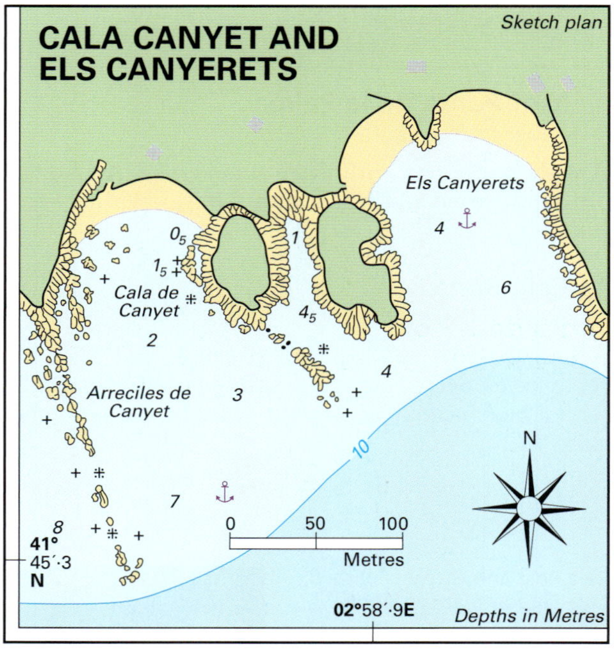

Cala Futadera

41°44′·3N 2°57′·6E

Anchor, where possible, in the middle, sand and rock. Open between NE and SE.

Calas de Canyet and Els Canyerets

41°45′·3N 2°58′·9E

Anchor off the beach of Els Canyerets or, with greater hazard, in Cala de Canyet outside moorings.

Calas de Canyet and Els Canyerets: anchor off the beach of Els Canyerets (at the right of the photograph)

Cala to S of Punta d'en Bosch

41°46'N 3°00'·3E (see plan page 310)

This *cala* does not welcome yachts in summer.

1. ⚓ Cala del Uiguetá

41°46'·3N 03°01'·5E (see plan page 310)

A large *cala* with rocky-cliffed sides and inshore rocks, small sand and stone beach at its head. Ermita de Sant Elm (100m) a church with a small spire stands on top of the headland. There are several very small sub-*calas*. The main *cala* is open between S and W. Anchor in sand and rock near the head of the *cala*. It has been reported that in easterly winds effluent builds up around the small jetty in this *cala*.

Punta de Garbí

41°46'·25N 3°01'·8E (see plan page 310)

A very prominent and conspicuous high headland with rocky cliffs which has rocky dangers extending 50m to SE and there is a 1·1m shoal 50m to S of point. The Ermita de Sant Elm stands on the crest and there are many houses and apartments.

2. ⚓ Cala de Port Salvi

41°46'·2N 3°01'·9E (see plan page 310)

A small *cala* on the SE point of Punta de Garbí open between E and S. Unfortunately, throughout the summer season, a diving mark (Flag 'A' on yellow inflatable) is moored permanently in the middle of the *cala* and diving training by the Eden Roc Diving Centre takes place most days. For this reason it is not recommended to anchor in this *cala*. There is a 1·1m shoal 50m to S of the mass of Punta Garbí.

Punta d'en Bosch

3. ⚓ Cala between Punta de Garbí and Punta de las Planetes

41°46'·4N 3°01'·9E

A small *cala* open between NE and E with rocky sides. Anchor in mid-*cala*, rocks and stone.

4. ⚓ Cala de Tetuán

41°46'·4N 3°01'·9E

Small *cala* open between N and E with rocky cliffs around it. Anchor in mid-*cala*, rocks and stone.

124. Puerto de Sant Feliu de Guíxols

41°46'N 3°01'E

Charts

UKHO 1704	Imray M14
SHOM 4827, 7008, 7505, 7298	Spanish 4922, 492

Lights

Dique de Refuerzo W head Fl(3)G.9s3M
Green lantern on green/white post

Dique Rompeolas head Fl(3)G.9s10m5M
White tower, green top 6m

Leading Light 341·1° Dir.Iso.WRG.3s14m4M
(Front post unlit in line 341·1° 52m from rear post)
337·1°-G-340·4°-W-341·8°-R-345·1°.

Port communications

Capitanía VHF Ch 9 ✆ 972 321 700
info@cnfsg.cat
www.cnfsg.cat

A popular and developing marina

A fishing, commercial and yachting harbour improved by the addition of a breakwater, quays and pontoons. The town and area are attractive but considerable tourist development continues apace and many old buildings are being pulled down. Swell from winds between E and S comes into the harbour.

This very old harbour, known to the Romans as Gesoria, came to fame by virtue of its monastery, originally built before the 8th century but then destroyed by the Moors and rebuilt in the 10th and 11th centuries. The abbot was feudal lord of the large area and the town and port prospered, becoming the most important town in the SE of Spain. During the Middle Ages the local people continuously fought against their overlords and eventually overthrew them. In the 18th century the cork trade brought further wealth and in recent years the tourist trade developed.

A new Club Náutico, can be found close to the root of the main breakwater. A line of pontoons (lettered Q to A from seaward) is controlled by the

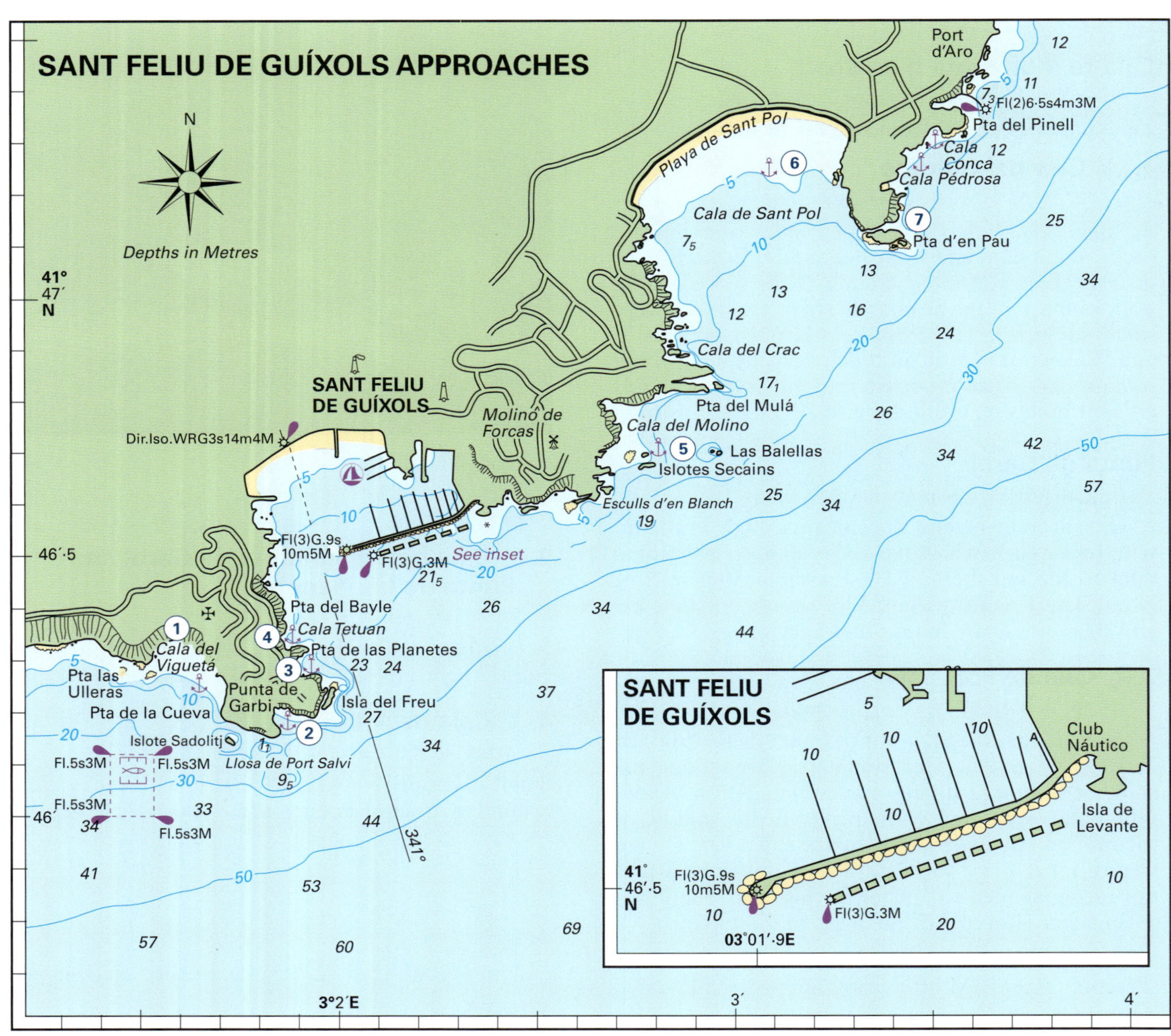

Puerto de Sant Feliu de Guíxols with Punta de Garbi and Islote Sadolitj in the foreground *Club Nàutic Sant Feliu de Guíxols*

Club who will fit visitors in as best they can. Two large box-shaped pontoons nearest the sea are for very large boats. Call ahead on Ch 9, visitors will be met. The inner harbour is not for visitors.

The museum in the old monastery and the 14th-century church can be visited and the view from the Ermita de Sant Elm is worth the climb. There is a pleasant beach ½M to E of harbour; the fine sandy beaches to the NW are very crowded in summer.

Approach

From the south From the conspicuous lighthouse and castle with tower on Cabo Tossa the very broken rocky-cliffed coast continues northeast. Punta de Garbí with the Ermita de Sant Elm is prominent and easily recognised. Round this promontory at 200m or more and the harbour entrance will be seen. Pay attention to a 1·1m rocky shallow, Llosa de Port Salvi, 50m to S of the massif of Punta de Garbí.

From the north From the Bahía de Palamós, which is easily recognised by virtue of its harbour wall and mass of houses and high-rise buildings, the rugged coast is broken by the wide sandy Bahía de Platja d'Aro and an almost square-shaped Cala de Sant Pol. Punta de Garbí is also prominent from this direction. Keep ½M off this section of coast to avoid off-lying shoals.

Entrance

Note that at night the leading lights have been replaced with a RWG directional light on the rear post. Steer to keep in the white sector on 343°. On a course of 343° enter the harbour leaving the head of the Dique Rompeolas 100m to starboard. It may be possible to see the leading marks, two sets of round white discs with black diagonal stripes located on white masts with black bands in the trees in front of the town.

The head of the Dique Rompeolas and that of the small *dique* on the E side of the harbour have been washed away several times and much rubble lies near their heads underwater; give them a berth of at least 30m. When clear of the head turn to a NE course.

Berths

Arriving craft must call ahead on Ch 9 and wait off the entrance to be met by staff and allocated a berth. These are generally equipped with lazy lines off the pontoon.

Anchorages

Anchoring in the harbour is forbidden but not unknown.

Puerto de Sant Feliu de Guíxols, note anchored boats. Marina to right *Steve Pickard*

Facilities

Maximum length overall 15m.
Minor repairs can be carried out by the shipyard and there are a number of mechanics for engine repair.
50-tonne crane in port, 6-tonne crane at the club náutico
Small slips on either side of the Peñón de Guíxols and a slipway on the NE side of the harbour with 2m of water at its foot.
Chandlery: Hipocampo, a shop in the street which is one back from the N side of the harbour. There is another chandler on the Muelle Comercial.
Water from the quays pontoons, club náutico and the lonja.
220v AC at the club náutico and the Dique Rompeolas.
Gasoleo A and petrol from pumps at the club náutico and from service station just to the N of this club.
Ice from the club náutico, from a shop behind the market or from an ice factory near the root of the Dique Rompeolas.
Many good shops in the town and a good market which is open on Sundays.
Club Náutico de Sant Feliu de Guíxols has a clubhouse to the W of the Peñón de Guíxols with bar, lounge, terrace, restaurants, showers etc. Visitors using the club berths may use the club.
Launderettes in the town.
A weather forecast is posted daily at the club náutico.

Communications

Bus service. Taxi ✆ 972 320 934.

Distinctive entry to Sant Feliu *Steve Pickard*

5. ⚓ Anchorages immediately E of Sant Feliu de Guíxols

(see plan page 310)

The ¾M section of coast from the root of the Dique Rompeolas to Cala de Sant Pol is very broken with many small islets, *calas* and passages. It is a most spectacular and attractive area. Explore in a powered dinghy or shallow-draught yacht. Spanish chart *305A* and a forward lookout are essential.

6. ⚓ Cala De Sant Pol (S'Agaro)

41°47'·8N 3°03'·1E (see plan page 310)

In summer yellow buoys cone off the beach area and summer moorings are laid to the NE side of the bay. Some are private others are charged at a small rate if they decide to collect.

Cala de Sant Pol (S'Agaro): open between E and S. S'Agaro is ½M to N and Sant Feliu 1M to SW

7. ⚓ SE of S'Agaro Calas Pédrosa, de la Font, Vaques, Conca

41°47'·6N 3°03'·8E (see plan page 310)

Four *calas* in a rocky-cliffed coast with large private houses on top of the cliffs. Anchor with care in mid-*cala*, sand, rock and weed. Open between NE and SE.

125. Port d'Aro

41°48'N 3°02'E

Charts
UKHO 1704 Imray M14
SHOM 4827, 7505 Spanish 876, 492

Lights

Playa de Aro Espigón head Fl(2)G.9s6m5M
Green metal column 3m

Contradique Fl(2)R.6·5s4m3M
Red column on pyramidal base 2m

To the northeast

Punta del Molino 41°50'·6N 3°07'·8E Oc(1+4)18s22m18M
White round tower, grey cupola 8m

Bajo Pereira (La Llosa de Palamós) 41°50'·1N 3°07'·2E
Fl(2)7s10m5M T
wo black spheres on black post, red band
(isolated danger mark)

Port communications
Capitanía VHF Ch 9. ✆ 972 818 929
cnportdaro@cnportdaro.net
www.clubnauticportdaro.cat

Harbour charges Medium

A generally crowded marina

A holiday development with a yacht harbour built on the delta of the Río Ridaura at the S end of the Playa (Platja) d'Aro. Approach and entrance is simple but would be difficult and dangerous with strong winds between NE and SE which also send swell into the harbour. There are good facilities and other shops are available at S'Agaró 0·7M (where there is an interesting 14th-century cloister incorporated into a modern church), Castillo d'Aro 1·2M and behind the Playa d'Aro. The long sandy beach to the N is very crowded in summer.

Approach

From the south Cabo de Tossa with its conspicuous lighthouse, town and beach, are easily recognised. Puerto de Sant Feliu de Guíxols with a long breakwater and its prominent headland, Punta de Garbi, are also easy to identify as is the wide deep Cala de Sant Pol. The harbour lies 1M to NE of this *cala*.

From the north Puerto de Palamós is unmistakable as is the Bahía de Palamós which is lined with high-rise apartment blocks. Cabo Roig is not prominent but has shallows extending 500m towards SE and with two small exposed rocky islets. The long sandy Playa d'Aro is backed by lines of high-rise buildings. The harbour entrance lies at the S end of the beach.

Anchorage in the approach

Anchor in 5m, sand, 300m to N of the harbour mouth.

Port d'Aro. Club náutico ahead *Steve Pickard*

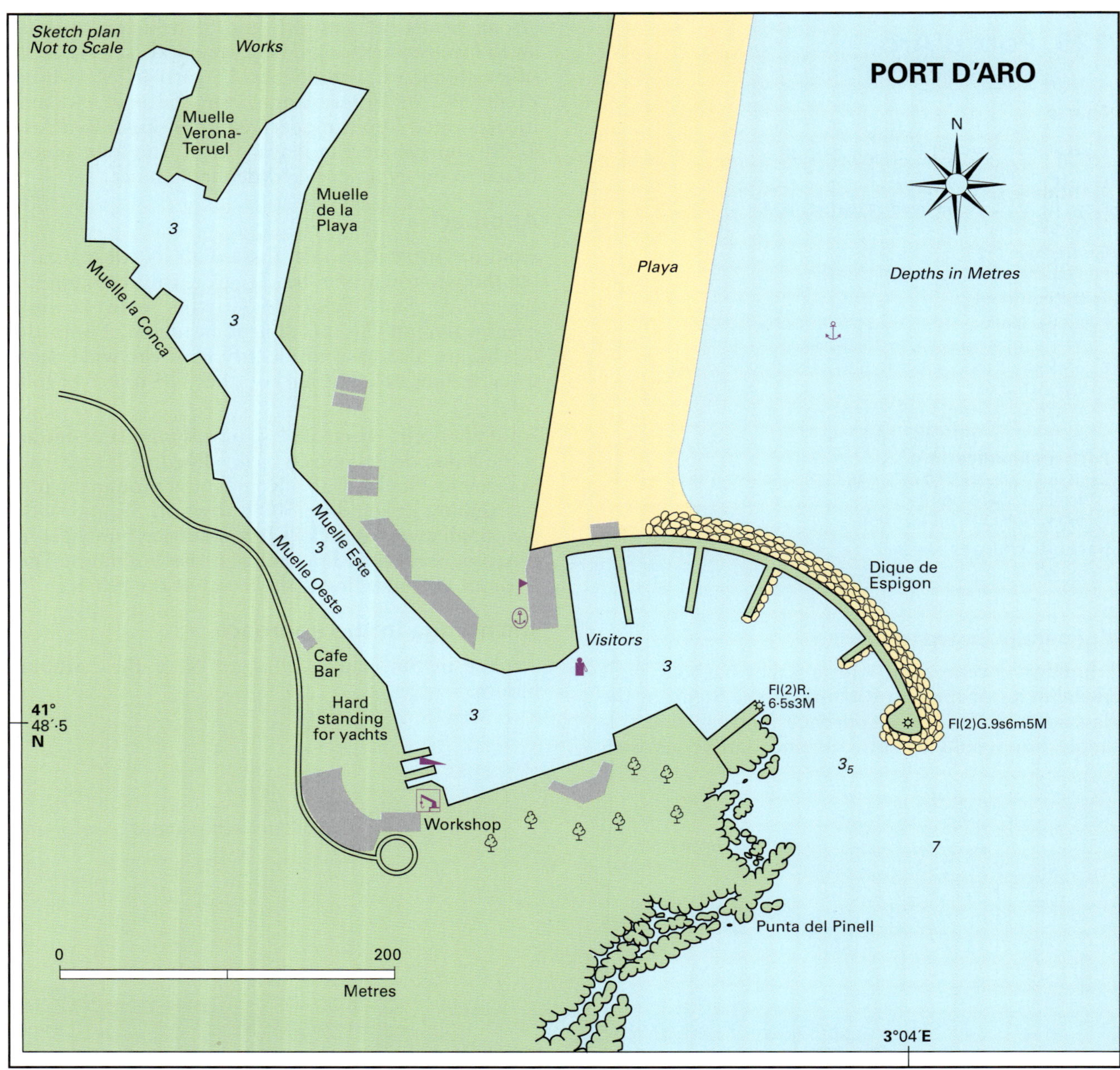

Entrance

Approach the head of the Dique de Espigon on a W heading leaving it 20m to starboard.

Berths

If not directed by VHF, secure on the NW side of the second of the three spurs within the harbour on the starboard side, then ask. The SE side of the spur is protected by rocks.

Facilities

Maximum length overall 15m.
Repairs to hull and engines possible at the yard in the SW corner.
20-tonne travel-lift.
8-tonne crane.
Slip.
Hard-standing.
Chandlery nearby.
Water and 220v AC on all quays and pontoons.
Gasoleo A and petrol.
Ice from the *club náutico*.
Club Náutico de Port d'Aro with bar, ice, restaurant, launderette, showers, WCs, etc.
Provisions from S'Agaro ½M or behind the Platja d'Aro about 1M to N.
Weather forecast posted once a day at *oficina de capitán*.

Communications

Taxi ① 972 817 032.

Port d'Aro

Port d'Aro visitors' berths *Steve Pickard*

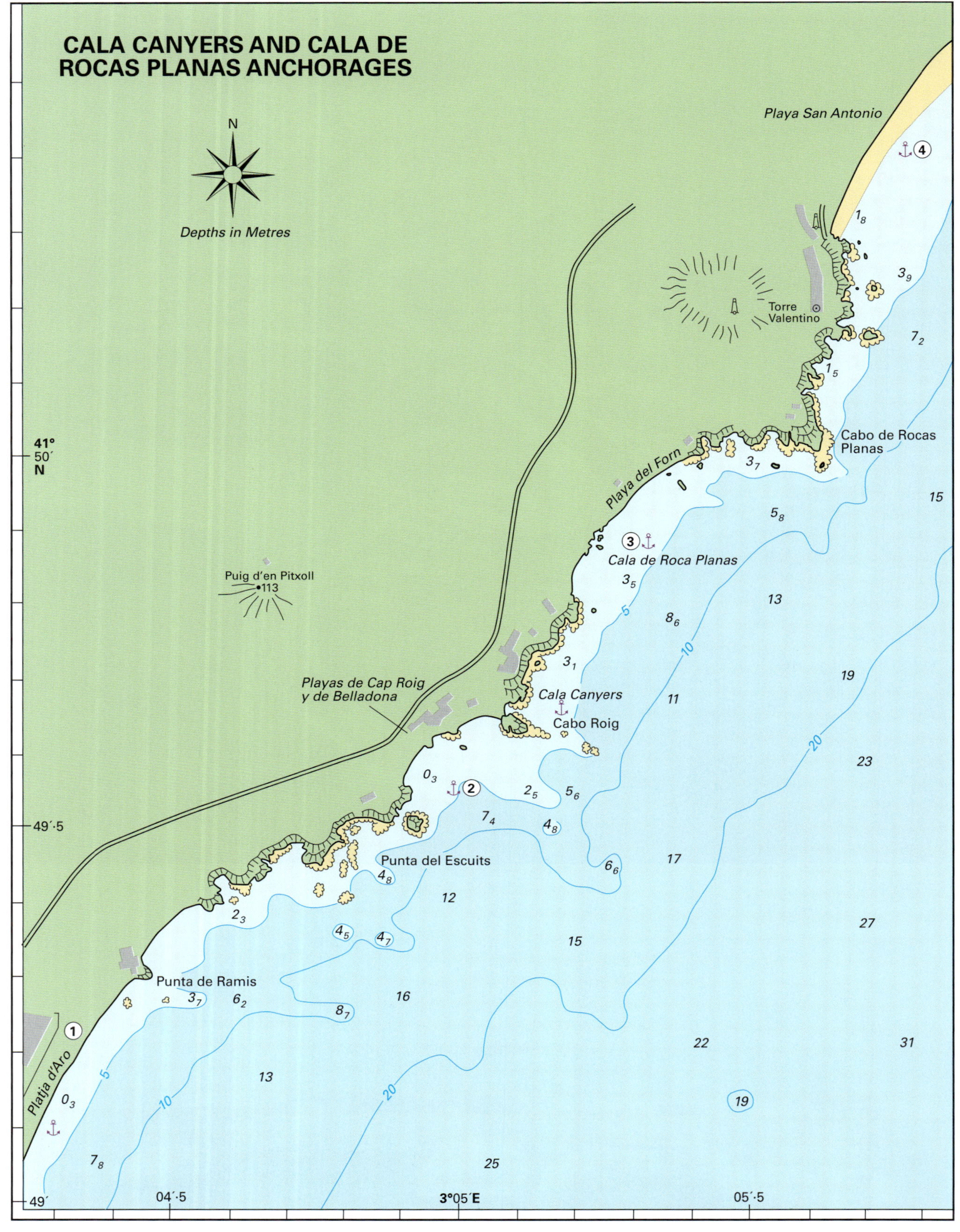
CALA CANYERS AND CALA DE ROCAS PLANAS ANCHORAGES
N
Depths in Metres
Playa San Antonio
Torre Valentino
Cabo de Rocas Planas
Playa del Forn
Cala de Roca Planas
Puig d'en Pitxoll
113
Playas de Cap Roig y de Belladona
Cala Canyers
Cabo Roig
Punta del Escuits
Punta de Ramis
Platja d'Aro
41° 50′ N
49′·5
49′
04′·5
3°05′E
05′·5

1. ⚓ Playa (Platja) d'Aro

41°49'·1N 3°04'·3E

Open between NE and S. A seaside resort with all usual facilities.

2. ⚓ Playas de Cap Roig and de Belladona

41°49'·3N 3°05'E

Open between E and S with foul ground around.

3. ⚓ Cala de Canyers and Roca Planas

41°49'·8N 3°05'·3E

Open between NE and SE. Note the rocks off Cabo Roig.

4. ⚓ Playa San Antonio

41°50'·4N 3°05'·9E

Open between E and SE.

Playa (Platja) d'Aro: open between NE and S

Playas de Cap Roig and de Belladona: open between E and S with foul ground around (Cala Canyérs beyond)

Playa de San Antonio: open between E and SE

Cala Canyérs and Cala de Roca Planas beyond: open between NE and SE. Note the rocks off Cabo Roig

PUERTOS DE PALAMÓS

41°50'N 3°07'E

Charts

UKHO 1704	Imray M14
SHOM 7298, 4827	Spanish 4923, 492

Lights

Punta del Molino 41°50'·6N 3°07'·8E Oc(1+4)18s22m18M White round tower, grey cupola 8m

Commercial Port

Dique de Abrigo head Fl.G.3s9m5M Grey globe

Marina – Puerto Deportivo

Dique de Abrigo head Fl(4)G.10s11m5M Green tower 8m

To the south

La Llosa de Palamós (Bajo Pereira) 41°50'·1N 3°07'·2E Fl(2)7s10m5M 2 black spheres on black post, red band (isolated danger mark) 197°-vis-165°

To the northeast

Hormiga Grande 41°51'·7N 3°11'·1E Fl(3)9s14m6M White round tower on hut 6m

Cabo San Sebastián 41°53'·7N 3°12'·1E Fl.5s167m32M White round tower on white building, red roof 12m Aeromarine

Buoys

A black buoy marks Llosa del Molino, 1·9m, 100m SW of Punta del Molino.

Port communications

See pages 320 & 321

Commercial harbour W, Marina E

There are two harbours at Palamós, one on either side of the headland, Punta de Molino, which catches the full force of the NW *tramontana* when it blows. The harbour on the west side is used by fishing and commercial craft. It is easy to approach and enter. The Club Náutico Costa Brava is in the old inner harbour and welcomes visitors. On the east side, the Puerto Deportivo does not have a yacht club (though a noisy disco has been noted). The town serving both is pleasant but in the season is crowded with tourists.

The museum and 14th-century church (much altered in the 16th and 18th centuries) can be visited. There are many attractive *calas* along the coast which can be reached by boat. The ancient villages of Ullastret (12M) and Calonge (1M) are worth a visit. Fine beach to the N of the harbour.

Palamós rose to prominence in the Middle Ages when it won an age-long struggle with Sant Feliu de Guíxols to be the maritime outlet for Girona. In 1334 it became the maritime district of Girona and prospered greatly. In 1534 it was sacked and burnt by Barbarossa with the Turkish Fleet after which it fell on hard times. With the development of the cork industry and agriculture its fortunes revived but it was again heavily damaged during the Civil War. Today it depends largely on the tourist industry.

⚓ Playa de Palamós

41°50'·7N 3°06'·7E

A long sandy beach backed by roads and lines of high-rise buildings. All facilities of a large seaside holiday town available. Anchor off the beach in sand, open between E and SW. Many stone groynes to trap the sand. (See plan opposite).

Puertos de Palamós Commercial left, Deportivo right

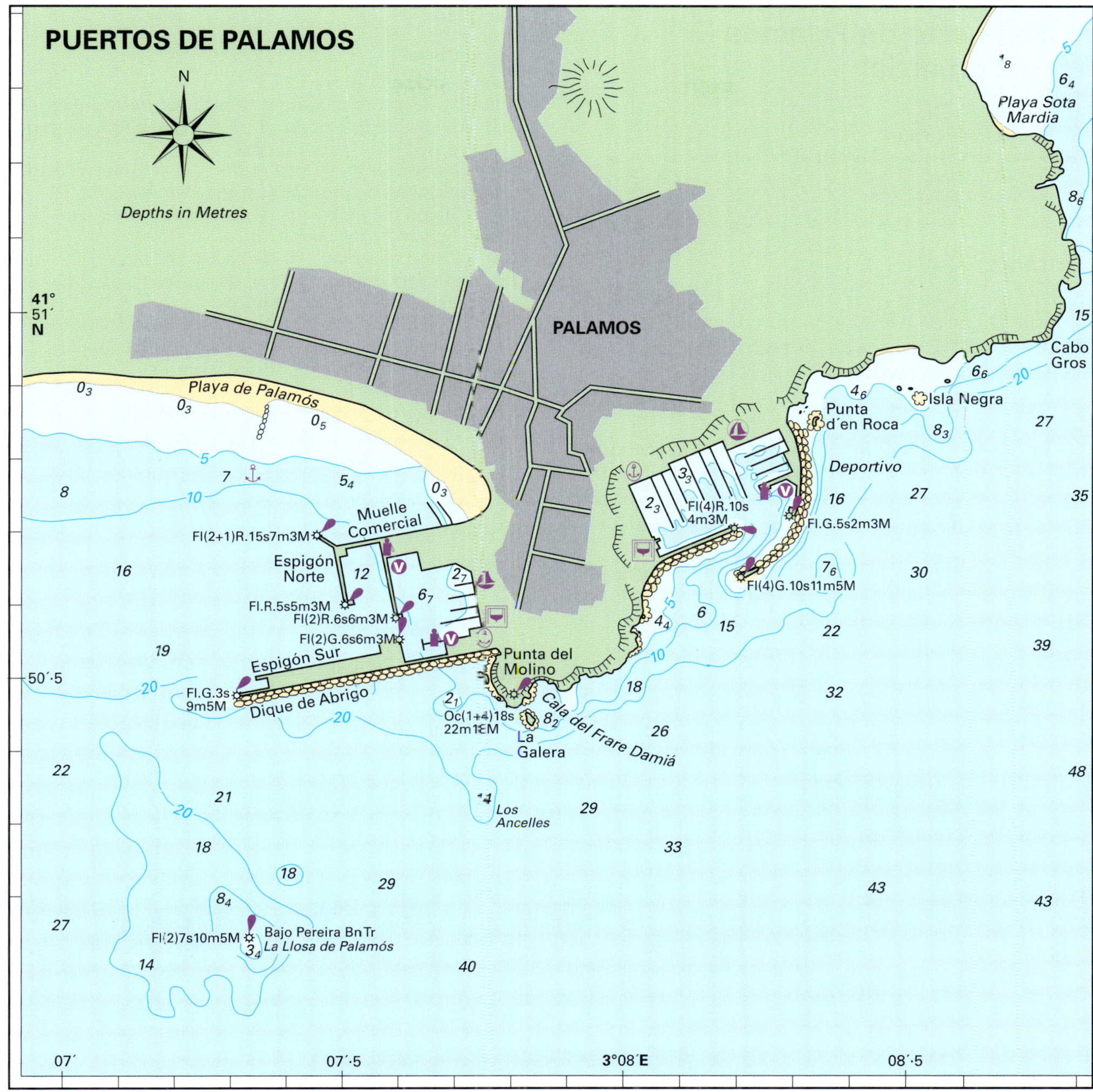

Approach

From the south The prominent Punta de Garbí with the Ermita de Sant Elm on its summit and the harbour of Sant Feliu de Guíxols are easily recognised as is the deep square-shaped Cala de Sant Pol. The masses of high-rise buildings at Platja d'Aro and Palamós can be seen from afar. There are two high-rise buildings 500m due N of the harbour and in the close approach the grey rocky breakwater will be seen jutting out westwards from the Punta del Molino. Keep an eye out for La Llosa de Palamós. If going round to the Puerto Deportivo, keep ¼M off Punta del Molino and the breakwater will be seen to the E of the point.

From the north From the high prominent Cabo San Sebastián which has a conspicuous lighthouse, the coast is very rocky and broken. The lower wooded Capo de Planas, the small rocky Islas Hormigas should be easily recognised. There is a passage inside the Islas Hormigas (see page 322) but it is simpler to keep to seaward, especially in heavy weather. Later the two high-rise buildings located side by side 500m to N of the harbour at Palamós, should be spotted (they may appear as one). The coast should not be approached closer than ½M because of outlying dangers. If going to the old harbour, keep at least ¼M off Punta del Molino but beware of La Llosa de Palamós. Punta del Molino lighthouse is not conspicuous.

126. Puerto de Palamós – Comercial

41°50'·5N 03°07'·2E

Port communications

Club Náutico Costa Brava (west) VHF Ch 09 972 31 43 24
cncb@cncostabrava.com
www.cncostabrava.com

Entrance

From E or W, keep clear of the Bajo Pereira beacon S of the Dique de Abrigo. On rounding the Dique de Abrigo head NE for the anchorage or past the cruise ship berth to the marina.

Berths

Go alongside the fuel berth to starboard in the inner harbour and ask for a berth or report to the *capitanía* nearby. Club Náutico rent a corner of the inner harbour for their own use and they welcome visitors for whom there are normally about 20 berths available. The Club building houses the offices, all facilities and a restaurant. Charges are higher than at Puerto Deportivo.

Anchorage

A possible anchorage is north of the Muelle Comercial in 10m or less.

Facilities

Old Harbour

Maximum length overall 25m.
A large yard under the bridge behind the *club náutico* and a smaller one to the N of it. Repairs to hulls can be carried out. Engine shops.
5-tonne crane on the N side of the Muelle Comercial and three cranes, 3–10 tonnes, at the *club náutico*.
Large slip on the inner side of the Dique de Abrigo.
Small slipway by the *club náutico*.
A small hard alongside the *club náutico*.
Two chandlers in the town and a large one under the bridge behind the *club náutico*.
Water on the Dique de Abrigo, pontoons, the Muelle Comercial and at the *club náutico* and the *lonja*.
Shore power on Dique de Abrigo, pontoons and the Muelle Comercial.
Ice from a factory behind the *lonja*.
Club Náutico Costa Brava is located at the root of the Dique de Abrigo with bar, lounge, terrace, restaurant, showers and swimming pool.
Weather forecast posted at *club náutico* once a day.

In town

Supermarket and other shops.
Fish can be bought from a market at the *lonja* in the evening.
Launderettes.

Communications

Bus service. Taxi ✆ 972 310 525.

Puerto de Palamós yacht moorings seen from the Muelle Comercial with anchorage to left of picture *Steve Pickard*

Puerto de Palamós – western port

127. Puerto de Palamós – Deportivo

41°50'·65N 03°08'·1E

Port communications

Marina Palamos (east) VHF Ch 09. ✆ 972 60 10 00
info@marinapalamos.com
www.lamarinapalamos.es

Entrance

Aim to give the head of its Dique de Abrigo an offing of 30m or so, then turn in. The entrance is difficult in a south to southwest wind with swell.

Berths

The marina offers all modern facilities. If not met by a *RIB*, go to the fuel berth and ask. If no-one there, ask at the office. Charges are high.

Facilities

Puerto Deportivo
Maximum length overall on quays 18m but a vessel up to 25m can be fitted in.
Some repair and maintenance facilities on site.
Chandlery.
35-tonne travel-lift.
6-tonne crane.

Deportivo service block *Peter Taylor*

Water and 220v AC on pontoons. 380v AC on Contradique.
Showers.
Gasoleo A and petrol.

Puerto de Palamós Deportivo *Steve Pickard*

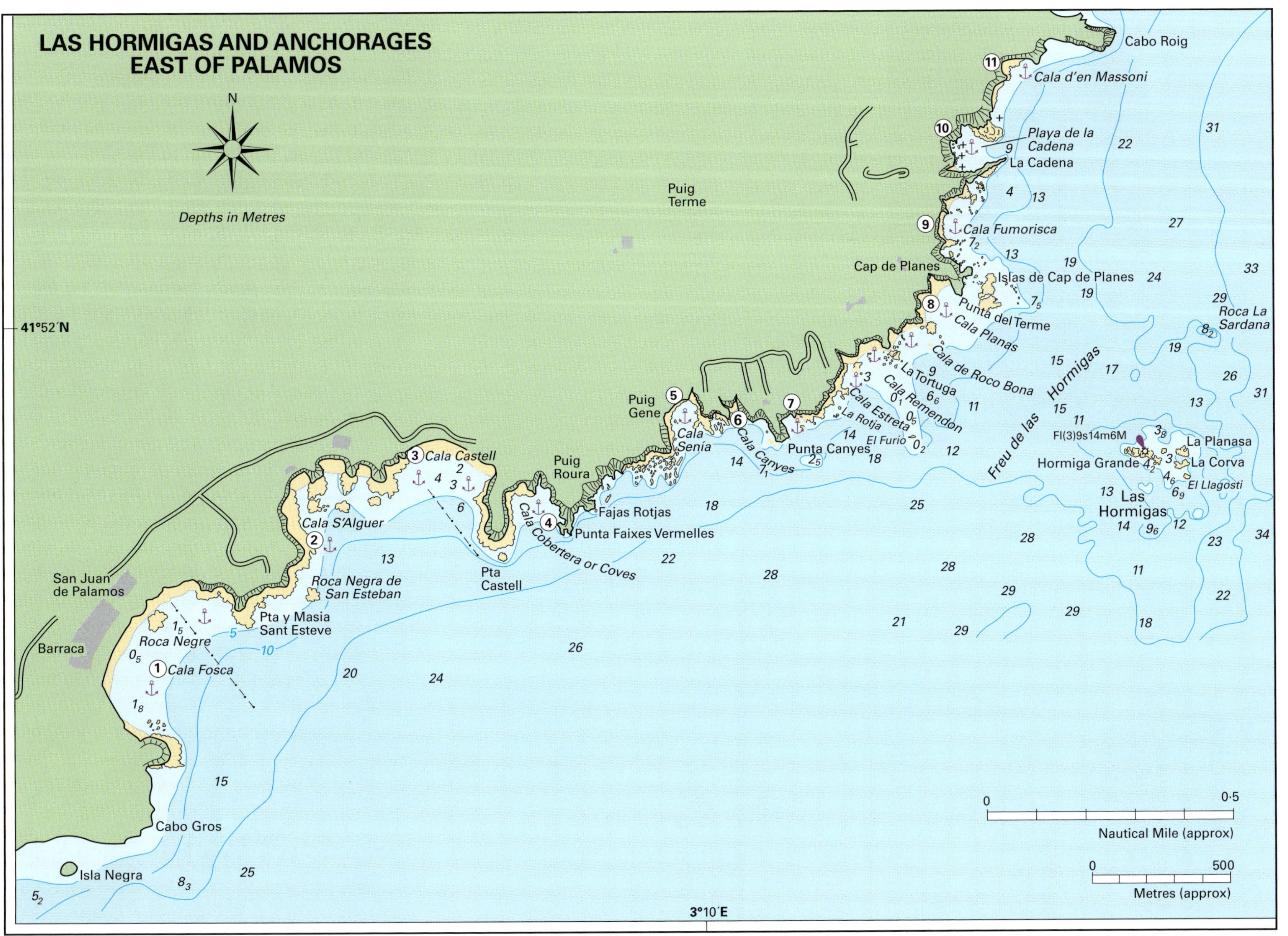
LAS HORMIGAS AND ANCHORAGES EAST OF PALAMOS
N
Depths in Metres
41°52′N
3°10′E
Cabo Roig
Cala d'en Massoni
Playa de la Cadena
La Cadena
Puig Terme
Cala Fumorisca
Cap de Planes
Islas de Cap de Planes
Punta del Terme
Cala Planas
Cala de Roco Bona
La Tortuga
Cala Remendon
Cala Estreta
La Rotja
El Furio
Punta Canyes
Cala Canyes
Cala Senia
Puig Gene
Puig Roura
Fajas Rotjas
Punta Faixes Vermelles
Cala Cobertera or Coves
Pta Castell
Cala Castell
Cala S'Alguer
Roca Negra de San Esteban
Pta y Masia Sant Esteve
Roca Negre
Cala Fosca
San Juan de Palamos
Barraca
Cabo Gros
Isla Negra
Roca La Sardana
Freu de las Hormigas
Fl(3)9s14m6M
Hormiga Grande
La Planasa
La Corva
El Llagosti
Las Hormigas
0
0·5
Nautical Mile (approx)
0
500
Metres (approx)

1. Cala Fosca

3. Cala Castell

1. ⚓ Cala Fosca

41°51'·3N 3°09'E

Open between E and S with foul ground on the south side of the bay. Mind the pipeline shown on the chart.

2. ⚓ Cala S'Alguer

41°51'·5N 3°09'·2E

A small bay, the head of which is divided into three rocky beaches with a number of rocks lying off them. Anchor in the middle in 9m, stone, sand and rock. Open between SE and S.

3. ⚓ Cala Castell

41°51'·6N 3°09'·4E

Closed off for swimmers in summer. Open between SE and W.

4. ⚓ Cala Cobertera

41°51'·5N 3°09'·7E

Anchor in the middle, stone and rock. Open between SE and SW.

5. ⚓ Cala Senía

41°51'·7N 3°09'·9E

A rocky-cliffed bay with a rocky spur on the NE side. Approach on a NW course, enter with care and anchor in the middle in rock and stone. Open between E and S.

4. Cala Cobertera

7. Cala N of Punta Canyes

6. ⚓ Cala Canyes

41°51'·78N 3°10'·1E

Lies between Punta Canyes and the rock strewn western end. Effectively open between E and W.

7. ⚓ Cala N of Punta Canyes

41°51'·78N 3°10'·2E

Enter with great care and anchor in the middle. Open between E and S.

8. ⚓ Cala Planas

41°51'·9N 3°10'·7E

Divided by rocky outcrops and with sandy beaches at its head, open between NE and S. Approach with great care and in good weather.

9. ⚓ Cala Fumorisca

41°52'·2N 3°10'·87E

An open *cala* with rocky outcrops and reefs on either side. Open between N and SE. Enter with care on a W course.

10. ⚓ Playa de la Cadena

41°52'·36N 3°10'·74E

A medium-sized rocky-cliffed *cala* protected on its SE side by a long thin projection of rock, La Cadena. Open between NE and SE. Anchor in 5m, stone and rock. Rocks off head of *cala*.

11. ⚓ Cala d'en Massoni

41°52'·5N 3°10'·8E

A *cala* just to S of Cabo Roig, open between E and SE. Use the N half of the *cala*, the SW side has projecting rocks. Anchor in 3m, stone and rock.

8. Calas Estreta, Remendon, Roco Bona and Planas

128. Islas Hormigas (Formigues)

41°51'N 3°11'E

Charts

UKHO 1704 Imray M14
SHOM 4827, 7008, 7505 Spanish 4924, 492

Lights

To the south

Punta del Molino 41°50'·6N 3°07'·8E Oc(1+4)18s22m18M White round tower, grey cupola 8m

The islands

Hormiga Grande 41°51'·7N 3°11'·1E Fl(3)9s14m6M White tower on hut 6m

To the north

Cabo San Sebastián 41°53'·7N 3°12'·1E Fl.5s167m32M White round tower on white building, red roof 12m

A group of rocks and islands, best avoided

The Islas Hormigas (*hormiga* is Spanish for an ant) or Formigues are a group of unoccupied rocky islets which lie some ½M off Cap de Planas between Palamós and Llafranc (see plan page 322). The islands are low, bare and foul. The highest, La Hormiga Grande, is only 12m high and 100m long. The mainland coast is also foul, notably the El Furió shoal and the rocks, Escuits del Cap de Planas, which extend to 400m from the shore. The area is generally foul and should be given a good berth especially in foul weather. However, Freu de las Hormigas, the passage between the islands and the mainland, about 400m wide, can be taken in fair weather.

Passage

From the south Approach the islands on a NE course and when level with Punta Faixes Vermelles bring Cabo San Sebastián onto 030°. This should lead through the Freu de les Hormigas about one third distant from the islands and two thirds from the mainland. Keep on this course until Cap de Planas is well past the beam.

From the north From Cabo San Sebastián make a course towards the islands. About 400m from them bring Punta del Molino on to 240° and pass through the Freu at a distance of about one-third of its width from the islands and two-thirds of its width from the mainland.

Landings

Hormiga Grande can be approached with care from the SW in deep water and landing is possible in calm weather.

Anchorages N of Cabo Roig

12. ⚓ Cala Golfet and Aigua Dolsa

41°52'·73N 3°10'·8E

A wide rocky *cala* with a small pebble beach. Open between NE and SE. Cala de Aigua Dolsa is found in its northern sector.

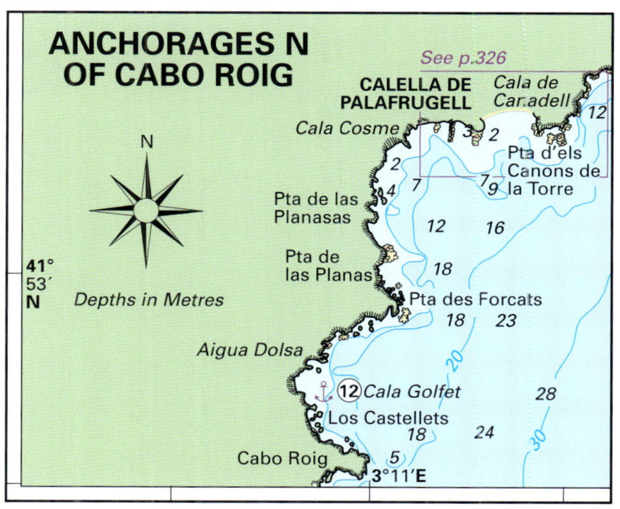

12. Cala Golfet

Calella de Palafrugell

A collection of anchorages

A series of delightful little anchorages offering good shelter from all except winds and sea between NE and SE, Callela lies between Punta Forcat and Punta d'els Canons (or de la Torre). Care is necessary in the close approach owing to isolated submerged rocks and the anchorage is full of moorings. The village is most attractive but very crowded in the season. Facilities are reasonable for a large holiday village.

Cap Roig botanic gardens 1M away are worth a visit. On the first Saturday in July, there is a singing festival on the beach, *Cantada de Habaneras*.

The original town of Palafrugell was Roman, possibly Celebandica, and was greatly enlarged when the inhabitants of the coast moved there in the 8th and 9th centuries. It became Palaz Frugell, that is Palace of Fruits, from which its present name is derived. It is an interesting old town and has the remains of its original walls.

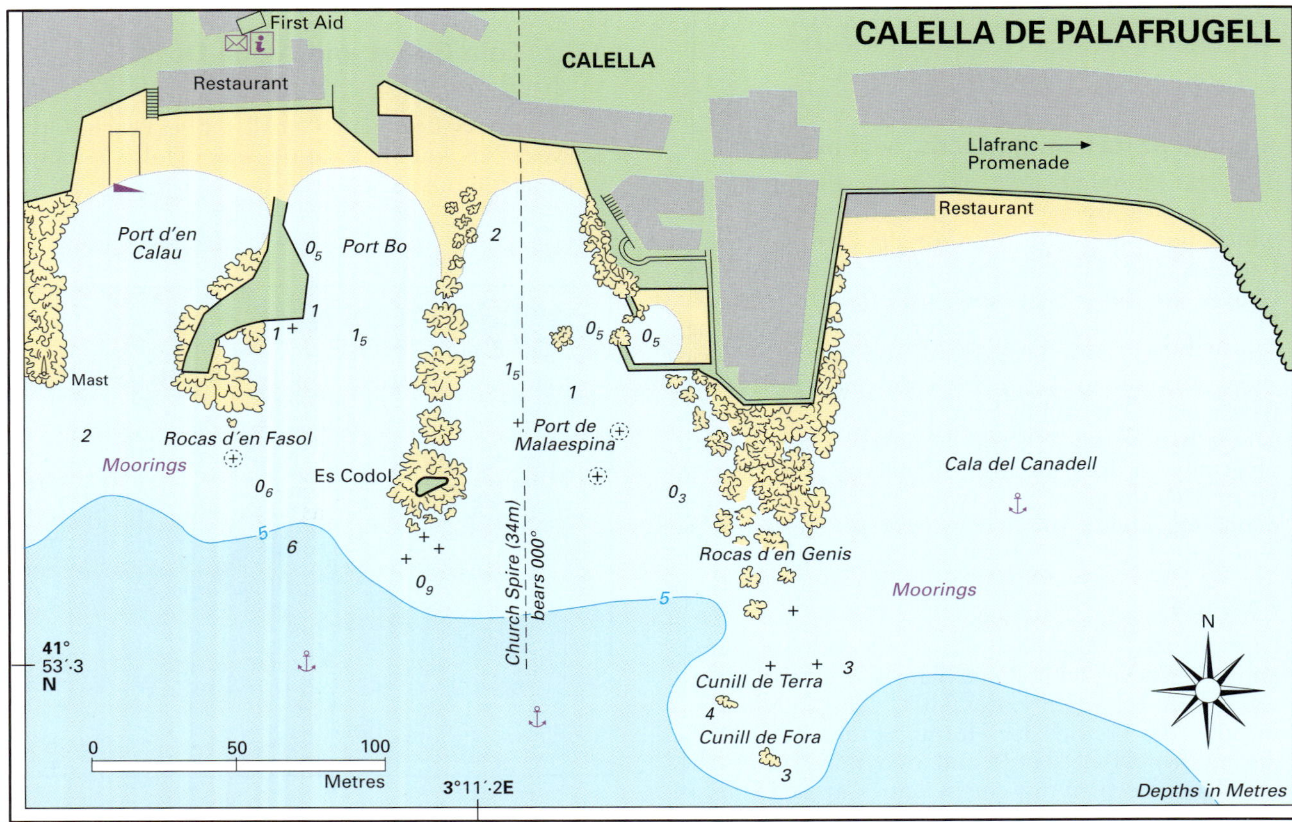

Calella de Palafrugell

Approach

Because of submerged rocks near the coast, approach should be made with care, in calm weather and with a forward lookout.

From the south Pass between the Islas Hormigas (see page 325) and the mainland leaving Cabo Roig and Punta Forcat at least 200m to port. Approach the anchorage with the conspicuous church on a N heading.

From the north Having rounded the high Cabo San Sebastián with its conspicuous lighthouse and restaurant, the Cala de Llafranc with houses on its head will be seen. The Punta d'els Canons, a lowish rocky point with a tower, should be given a berth of at least 200m and the coast followed at this distance. When the conspicuous church at Calella de Palafrugell is due N, approach on that heading

Anchorage

Anchor W of the very small and outermost rocky islet Cunill de Fora, opposite the centre bay but short of the rocky outcrops, in 5m sand, rock and stone (partly weed-covered). The holding ground is very patchy. Use a trip-line. Alternative anchorages exist opposite the other two bays but there are isolated rocks which restrict swinging room. It is also possible to anchor in the Cala del Canadell some 400m to the E but care is necessary.

Quays

There is a small quay on the W side of the centre bay with 1m alongside and another in the form of a miniature harbour on the E side of the E bay with 0·5m alongside.

Facilities

Water available from cafés.

Everyday supplies available from shops in the village and much greater variety from Palafrugell some 2M away.

Club Vela de Calella is a dinghy club with few facilities other than a terrace.

⚓ Cala del Canadell

41°53'·2N 3°11'·3E

A wide bay divided by a projecting rocky point near the middle. Anchor on either side in 4m, sand. Open between SE and SW. Beware moorings.

129. Puerto de Llafranc (Llanfrach)

41°53'N 3°12'E

Charts

UKHO	1704
Imray	M14
SHOM	4827, 7008, 7505, 7298
Spanish	876, 492
Navicarte	E04

Lights

To the north

Cabo San Sebastián 41°53'·7N 3°12'·1E Fl.5s167m32M
White round tower on white building, red roof 12m
Aeromarine

Harbour

Dique del Sur head 41°53'·6N 3°11'·8E Fl(3)G.11s6m5M
Green and white tower 2m

Buoys

Red and white buoys mark the entrance channel, one port-hand buoy has a spar and one has a F.R light.

Port communications

Club Náutico de Llafranc VHF Ch 8 ✆ 972 300 754
cnll@infopunt.com

Small, attractive but expensive harbour

Small, attractive and expensive harbour. Puerto de Llafranc is under the high, steep-sided SW side of Cabo San Sebastián (see plan page 329). It is an artificial yacht harbour established in a most attractive *cala* which has been used as a harbour since time immemorial. Approach and entrance need some care but, once inside, there is good protection though heavy swell coming from the SE can be tiresome. The hills around the harbour offer good protection against the NW *tramontana*. Everyday requirements can be met in the village and there are good shops and a market in Palafrugell 2M away. The area becomes very crowded and expensive in the season and, as the *capitanía* remarked, the harbour is always full.

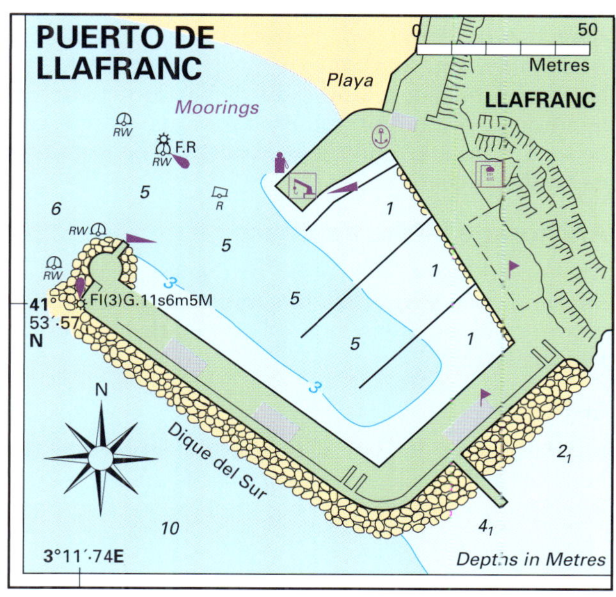

Puerto de Llafranc

The harbour is probably of Phoenician origin. It was certainly used by the Romans and is thought to be the ancient port of Cypsela. In the 8th century the Normans razed the town to the ground and its inhabitants moved to Palafrugell. In recent years it has been redeveloped as a tourist resort. The excellent sandy beach is crowded in season. There is a fine view from the lighthouse of San Sebastián.

Approach

From the south A tree-covered promontory, Cap de Planas, and the Islas Hormigas, a group of low, jagged rocky islands are readily recognisable. If the weather is fair a passage inside these islands is possible (see page 324). The harbour wall will be seen under Cabo San Sebastián.

From the north Cabo Begur with its conspicuous signal station and the deep *calas* of Aiguafreda, Aiguablava and Tamariú are easily recognised. The high steep-sided Cabo San Sebastián with its lighthouse, restaurant and *ermita* on its summit can be seen from afar and the harbour will be found on its further side.

Anchorage in the approach

Anchor 200m off the centre of the sandy beach in 6m sand. Use a trip-line. In summer there are many moorings and a diving board between the anchorage and the beach.

Entrance

Enter the bay on a NW course and approach the head of the Dique del Sur with care. Round it at 10m leaving it to starboard. Note the head of the *dique* extends some 5m underwater. Leave a line of small red and white buoys to port and two similar buoys close to the head of the *dique* to starboard. There is little room to manoeuvre once inside the harbour.

Puerto de Llafranc. Traditional slipway for small boats *Steve Pickard*

Berths

Berth stern-to the inner side of the Dique del Sur; lazy lines are provided.

Facilities

6-tonne crane.

Small slip in the NW corner and another at the head of Dique del Sur.

Water and 220v AC on all quays and pontoons.

Gasoleo A and petrol.

Club Náutico de Llafranc has a small office to the NW of the harbour. The clubhouse is on the NE side of the harbour with restaurant, bar, showers and WCs.

A limited number of shops near the harbour for everyday requirements. Many shops in Palafrugell 2M away.

Launderette in Llafranc.

Communications

Bus service.

Llafranc looking NW. Visitors at end on left *Peter Taylor*

Cabo San Sebastián (Cap de Sant Sebastián)

41°53′·5N 3°12′E

A prominent, cliffed headland of reddish rock with a 12m lighthouse on the 167m high rounded summit. A number of houses are located near the summit. The headland is steep-to. There is also a restaurant and *ermita* on top.

1. ⚓ Cala de Gens

41°53′·9N 3°12′·4E

A small *cala* ½M to N of Cabo San Sebastián and a useful place if waiting to round the Cape. High rocky cliffs with houses. Anchor in 10m plus, stone and rock bottom. Hut on small stony beach.

2. Cala Pedrosa

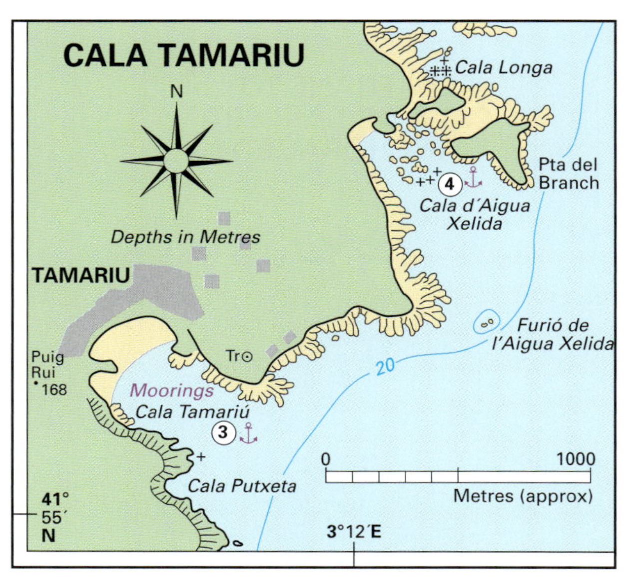

2. ⚓ Cala Pedrosa

41°54′·45N 03°12′·6E

S of Punta Tamariu. Anchor in 10m, stone and rock. Open between E and S.

3. ⚓ Cala Tamariú

41°54′·9N 3°12′·8E

Anchor in the middle, 5-10m, sand. Hotels and restaurants ashore. To the NE, Aigua Xelida, with its rocky islets, promontories and bays is fun to explore by dinghy.

3. Cala Tamariú looking NW. Note profusion of summer moorings

4. ⚓ Cala Aigua Xelida

41°55'·2N 3°13'·2E

A deep rocky *cala* open between NE and SW. Beware rock in southern approach.

5. ⚓ Cova del Bisbé and Port d'Esclanya

41°55'·8N 3°13'·2E (see plan page 329)

Two very small, square shaped calas 80m apart, open between NE and SE with rocky cliffs. Anchor in 5m, rocks. There is a large cave at Bisbe.

4. Cala Aigua Xelida looking NW. Note extensive rocky head of *cala*

5. Cova del Bisbe looking W

6. ⚓ Calas de Aiguablava & Fornells

41°56'N 3°13'E

Charts

UKHO 1704, 1705 — Imray M14
SHOM 4827, 7008, 7505 — Spanish 876, 492

Lights

To the south

Cabo San Sebastián 41°53'·7N 3°12'·1E Fl.5s167m32M
White round tower on white building, red roof 12m
Aeromarine

Basin

Basin entrance port side 41°56'·0N 3°12'·9E Fl(2)R.6s2m3M
Red lantern

Starboard side Fl(2)G.10s4m5M
Green tower, white base 3m

Port communications

Club Náutico Aiguablava VHF Ch 09 ✆ 972 623 161
cnaiguablava@arrakis.es

Sheltered anchorage

A beautiful and sheltered anchorage with a small private harbour with protection from all but strong NE winds. Facilities are very limited and it is crowded in the season with many occupied moorings. Cala de Aiguablava has shelter from the NW *tramontana*. There are fine sandy beaches. A visit to the old town of Begur is recommended.

Cala de Aiguablava

Puerto de Fornells

Approach

From the south Pass the high prominent Cabo San Sebastián with its conspicuous lighthouse and restaurant and the deep Cala Tamariú with its houses. 1M to the N will be found the Punta del Mut with a large square-shaped hotel, the Parador la Costa Brava, on its summit. Follow the coast around into the anchorage.

From the north Round the prominent Cabo Negre and then Punta de la Sal where there is a very large hotel on the point and then in 1M round Cabo Begur which has a castle and a signal station. 1M to the S lies Punta del Mut with a large square-shaped hotel on its summit. Leave this point to port and the Isla Blanca to starboard and enter the anchorage.

Entrance

Enter Cala de Aiguablava and Fornells on a W course nearer to the Punta del Mut than to Isla Blanca.

Anchorage

Anchor in 3m, sand and weed, in the E half of Cala de Aiguablava as near to the cliffs as draught will allow. There are ring-bolts on the cliffs and an isolated rock and there are also many moorings. In summer the southern part of Cala de Aiguablava is reserved for bathing.

Alternative anchorages are at the entrance to Cala Fornells and in a smaller *cala* 100m further to N but they do not have as good protection as Aiguablava.

Note that it has been reported that the ring bolts are not serviceable as nearly all have rusted through.

Quays

There is a small stone quay in the SE corner of the Cala de Aiguablava with 0·5m alongside and a small pier in the Cala de Fornells at the entrance to the small private harbour.

Facilities

4-tonne crane at the entrance to the private harbour.
Slip at the N side of the private harbour.
Water from the beach restaurants. and from the private harbour.
Water and 220v AC on pontoons in private harbour.
Club náutico is located at the Playa de Fornells and is a dinghy club.
Limited supplies from two small shops at Fornells. More shops exist at Begur some 2M away.

Communications

A bus service to Begur in the season.

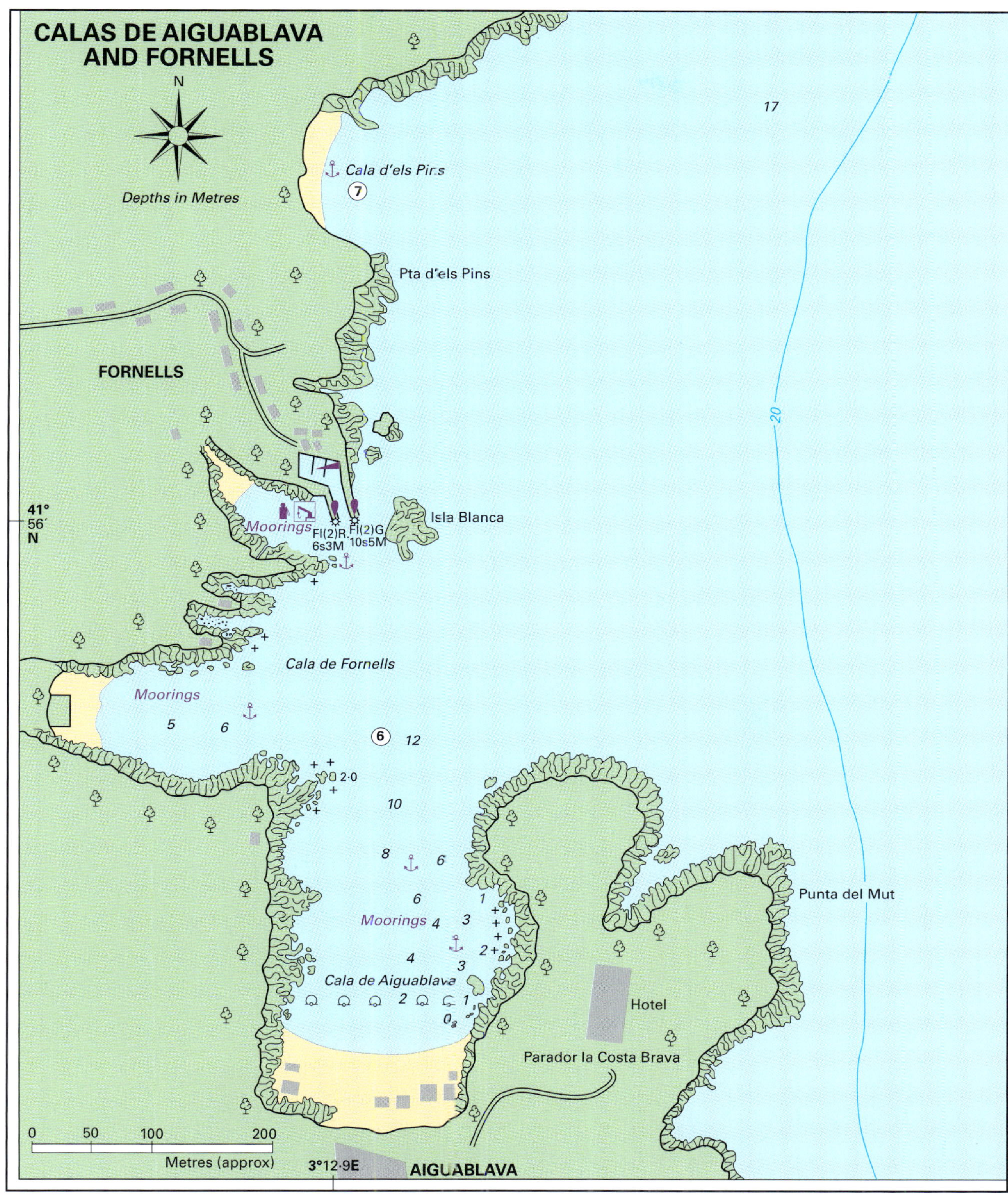

7. ⚓ Cala d'els Pins

41°56'·5N 3°13'·2E

A small, narrow *cala* open between NE and E, surrounded by rocky cliffs. Anchor in rock and sand.

Cabo Begur (Cabo Bagur)

41°57'N 3°14'E

A large hooked headland, 115m, with rocky cliffs and a conspicuous low yellowish coloured lookout station on its crest. The headland is steep-to.

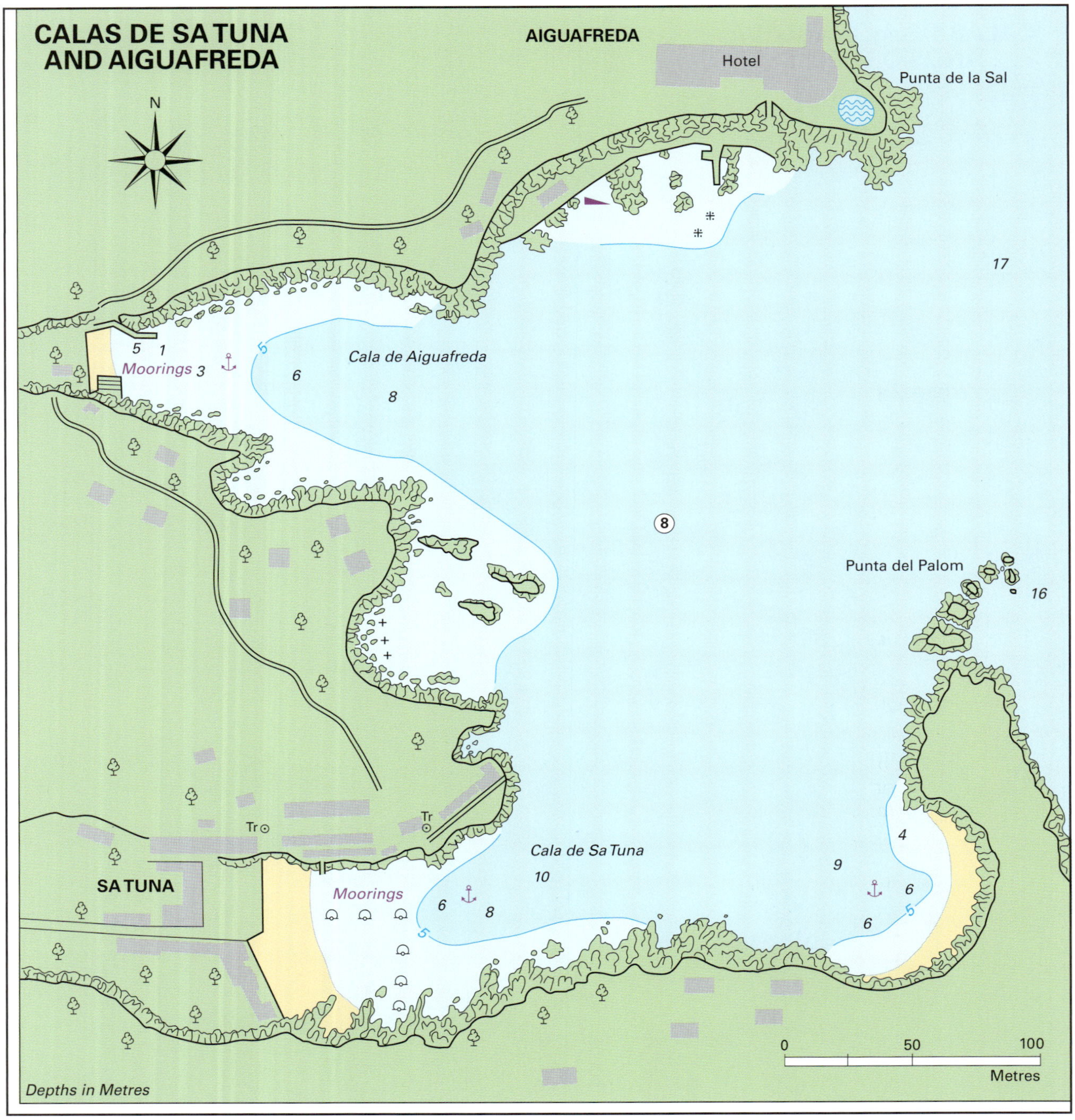

CALAS DE SA TUNA AND AIGUAFREDA

AIGUAFREDA
Hotel
Punta de la Sal
N
17
5 1
Moorings 3
6
Cala de Aiguafreda
8
8
Punta del Palom
16
Tr
Tr
Cala de Sa Tuna
10
SA TUNA
Moorings
6 8
4
9
6
6
0 50 100
Metres
Depths in Metres

Cala de Sa Tuna

8. ⚓ Calas de Sa Tuna & Aiguafreda

41°58'N 3°14'E

Charts

UKHO 1704, 1705 Imray M14
SHOM 4827, 7008, 7505 Spanish 49

Generally good shelter

Two beautiful inlets, easy to enter and with good shelter from all but E wind which sends in a nasty swell; some shelter from this wind behind the Punta del Palom spur. Shelter from the NW *tramontana* is possible but not very effective with winter gales. Facilities are very limited. Though there are many visitors in summer it is not as crowded as some resorts. Many large houses have been built near these *calas* in recent years.

A visit to the ancient town of Begur is recommended. There is a sand and shingle beach at the head of each *cala*.

Approach

From the south Cabo Begur, a rocky headland can be recognised by a signal tower on its summit. Keep 400m from the coast to avoid the Furió Fito rocks. A very large hotel located on the Punta de la Sal at the far side of the entrance to this anchorage, visible over Punta del Palom, is very conspicuous. Round Punta del Palom at 50m and enter.

From the north Cabo Negre can be recognised by the very large hotel on Punta de la Sal just to its S. Round this at 100m and enter the anchorage.

Entrance

This is not difficult as there is deep water up to the cliffs. Cala Aiguafreda lies due W and Cala Sa Tuna to the SW of the outer entrance.

Cala Sa Tuna *Steve Pickard*

Head of Cala Aiguafreda *Steve Pickard*

Cala Aiguafreda

Cala Aiguafreda, moorings take up all the bay *Steve Pickard*

Anchorage

In winter, should an E wind arise, this anchorage should be vacated at once and shelter taken at Palamós. In summer, shelter behind Punta del Palom.

Anchor clear of moorings in 6m, sand and weed, near the centre of the Cala Sa Tuna with the tower bearing NNW. The W half of this *cala* is reserved for bathing and in the season, it is marked with yellow buoys.

In Cala Aiguafreda anchor in the centre of the *cala* about 100m from its head in 5m sand and stone clear of moorings. Alternative anchorages are possible in the little bay to SE and to S of the hotel. It is sometimes necessary to run a line ashore to keep the yacht head to swell, or use two anchors.

Quays

There are three small quays and slips on the N side of Cala Sa Tuna and a longer one with 1m depth alongside on the N side of Cala Aiguafreda.

Facilities

There is a spring close to the beach at Cala Aiguafreda. Water is also available from the restaurant at Sa Tuna.

Very limited provisions from two small shops in Sa Tuna, many more in Begur 1M away.

Communications

Bus service to Begur in the season.

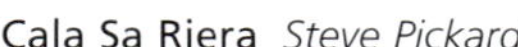

Cala Sa Riera *Steve Pickard*

Cala De Sa Riera (Cala De La Rierata)

9. ⚓ Cala de sa Riera (Cala de la Rierata)

41°58'·6N 3°13'E

A rocky *cala* with a sandy beach. Open between N and NE, Small village around the head of the *cala*. Anchor, if posible off the beach in sand. The old town and castle of Begur are 1M up the road. Very popular with divers.

⚓ Playa de Pals

41°59'N 3°13'E

Anchorage N of the Cala De Sa Riera at the southern end of Playa de Pals, a 2·5M stretch of sandy beach backed by low, flat plains. A group of tall, red and white (F.R) aerial masts are conspicuous at the S end and the mouth of the Rio Ter is at the N end. Anchor off the beach in 5m, sand. Open between N and SE.

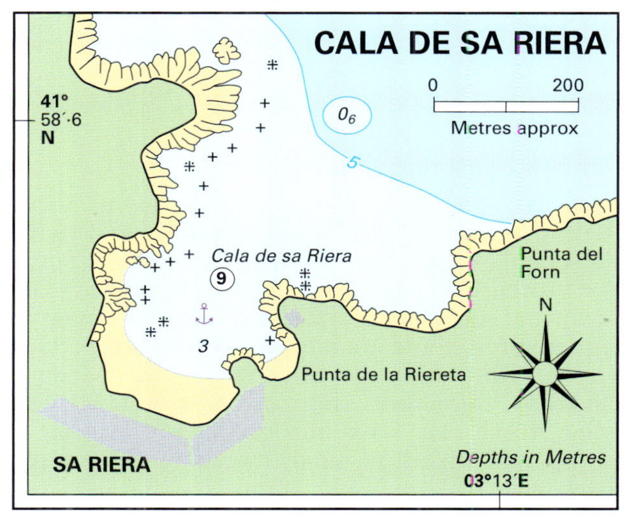

Playa de Pals

130. Puerto de L'Estartit

42°03'N 3°12'E

Charts

UKHO 1704, 1705	Imray M14
French 7008, 7505, 7298	Spanish 876, 493

Lights

To the southeast
Isla Méda Grande, summit 42°02'·8N 3°13'·2E
Fl(4)24s87m14M Tower on brick building 11m

Harbour
Dique de Levante head Fl.G.5s9m5M
White tower, green top 4m
Dique interior head Fl(2)G.13s4m3M
Green lantern on wall 4m
Contradique corner Fl.R.5s8m5M
Red post 4m
Contradique head Fl(2)R.13s3m3M
Red lantern on masonry base
Fuel jetty head Fl(3)R.13s1M Red post 1m

Port communications
Capitanía VHF Ch 9, 16. ✆ 972 751 402
info@cnestartit.es
www.cnestartit.es

Harbour charges High

Mainly a yachting harbour

A fishing and yachting harbour in an attractive setting protected by a breakwater and with reasonable shelter from the NW *tramontana*. Space for visiting yachts on the pontoons is limited. The town and surrounding areas have been developed as a tourist resort and are crowded in the season.

The 14th-century church at Torroella de Montgrí and the 13th-century castle may be visited (2M). The view from the Castillo de Santa Catalina is spectacular. Excellent sandy beach to SW of the harbour.

L'Estartit *Club Nautic*

Approach

The Río Ter brings down heavy deposits which tend to silt up the harbour and its mouth. Sound carefully. The pontoons on the SW side of the harbour are sometimes removed during winter months.

From the south Cabo Begur with its signal station, Cabo Negre with a large hotel, the group of seven radio masts just to N of it, the Islas Médes close to the harbour and a very tall orange and white radio tower behind it are easily recognisable.

From the north Punta Trenca Braços can be identified by a conspicuous tower and the deep wide Cala Montgó to its S. The coast is very broken but the Islas Médes are easily seen as is the tall orange and white banded radio tower on the top of Montaña de la Barra just to the N of this harbour. Keep over 200m from the shore.

Anchorage in the approach

Anchor 100m to S of the *contradique* in 4m, sand.

Entrance

Straightforward but some sharp manoeuvring once inside.

Berths

There are 12 corps mortes in the outer harbour and a similar amount of stern to moorings on the S side of the Dique Interior. On arrival secure to the head of the *espigón* near the fuel berth for allocation of a berth. The inner side of the Dique Interior is reserved for diving vessels, the outer side is for local ferries.

Facilities

Maximum length overall 25m.
Repairs can be carried out to hull and engines by local craftsmen.
Hard-standings in NW corner of harbour.
30-tonne travel-lift.
7·5-tonne and 3-tonne cranes.
Chandlery to NE of the harbour and another to W of the town.
Water taps at the *club náutico* and on quays and pontoons.
Showers.
Gasoleo A and petrol.
Shore power from the Muelle de Ribera and on quays and pontoons.
Ice is available in the season from the *oficina de capitán*.
Club Náutico Estartit with a bar, lounge, terrace, restaurant, showers.
A fair number of shops in the town.
Launderette in the town.
Weather forecast posted at *club náutico* once a day.

Communications

Bus service. Day trips to the Islas Médes by ferry.

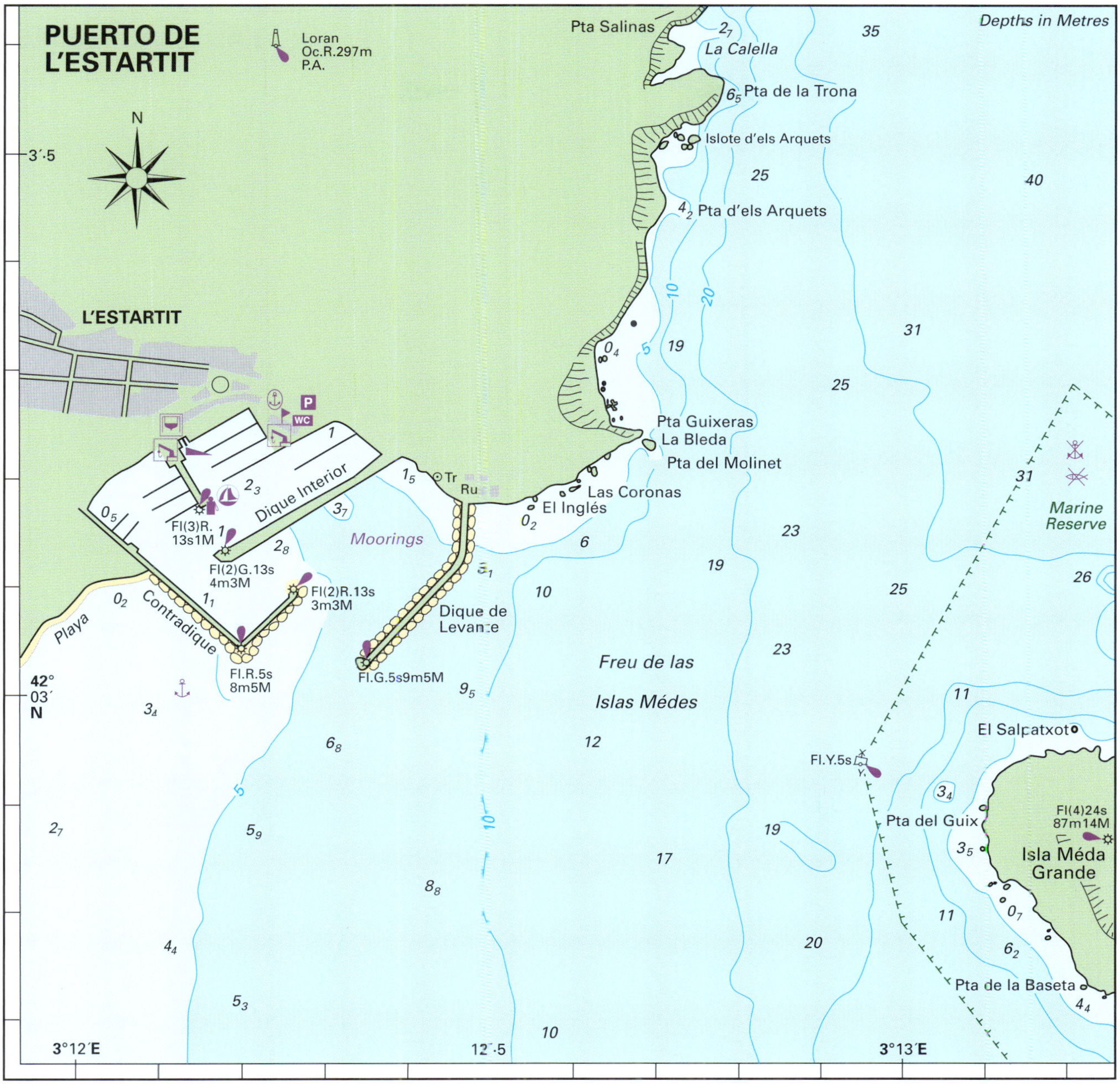

PUERTO DE L'ESTARTIT

Loran
Oc.R.297m
P.A.

Depths in Metres

Pta Salinas
La Calella
Pta de la Trona
Islote d'els Arquets
Pta d'els Arquets
L'ESTARTIT
Pta Guixeras
La Bleda
Pta del Molinet
Las Coronas
El Inglés
Dique Interior
Moorings
Fl(3)R.13s1M
Fl(2)G.13s 4m3M
Fl(2)R.13s 3m3M
Contradique
Playa
Fl.R.5s 8m5M
Dique de Levante
Fl.G.5s9m5M
Freu de las Islas Médes
Marine Reserve
El Salpatxot
Fl.Y.5s
Pta del Guix
Fl(4)24s 87m14M
Isla Méda Grande
Pta de la Baseta
42° 03′ N
3′·5
3°12′E
12′·5
3°13′E

L'Estartit moorings *Steve Pickard*

L'Estartit inner harbour *Steve Pickard*

LAS ISLAS MEDES
Depths in Metres
Marine reserve
Isolte El Magallot
Piedra del Deu
Punta de la Cuetera
Punta Pata del Llop
El Salpatxot
Punta del Guix
Fl(4)24s87m14M
Isla Méda Grande
Punta de la Guilla o de la Galera
La Vaca
El Furió
Punta del Balcó
Restricted Area
Punta de la Baseta
Punta del Infern
Punta del Ferral
Punta Rosegosa
Pta del Portichol
Isla Méda Petita
Pta de la Llosa
Isla Méda Chica
Punta del Canó Esmorellat
Las Faranellas
Islote Tascón Grande (40)
Islote Mogote Bernat
Islote Tascón Pequeño
Fl.Y.6s
Fl.Y.2·5s
Fl.Y.4s
42° 03′ N
2′·5
13′
3°13′·4E
The following activities are forbidden inside the reserve:
1. Fishing by line, net or gun
2. Anchoring
3. Collecting animals, plants, flowers, artefacts on land or underwater
4. Visits by night.

131. Las Islas Médes

42°03'N 3°13'E

Charts

UKHO 1704, 1705	Imray M14
SHOM 7298, 7505	Spanish 4931

Lights

Isla Méda Grande, summit 42°02'·8N 3°13'·2E
Fl(4)24s87m14M White tower on building 11m.

There are six spar buoys surrounding Zone B of the islands (see plan opposite) with three further buoys (Fl.Y.12s) outside Zone B representing the boundaries of Zone A

Marine reserve

The Islas Médes are a group of uninhabited islands about ½M off Punta del Molinet near L'Estartit. They are a marine reserve with restricted access – see chart. The largest island, Isla Méda Grande is some 500m across and 79m high; there are splendid views from the lighthouse on its summit. To the S of this island lies Isla Méda Petita, 250m long and 67m high. Islote Mogote Bernat, the most SE island, is only 80m across but is 72m high, with almost vertical sides. To the N of the group and nearly 300m away is Islote El Magallot, 24m high. There are a number of low and inconspicuous smaller islets. The islands are in general steep-to but there are some groups of rocky shoals close inshore. The passage between this group of islands and the mainland is deep and clear of obstructions and can be taken under almost any conditions.

Approach

There is no difficulty in navigating the Freu de las Islas Médes as there is a deep-water passage some 600m wide and dangers only exist within 100m of the islands and the mainland shore. The passage is best taken in a NE–SW direction. There is a very narrow passage, 0·6m deep, between Islas Meda Grande and Petita in a NE–SW which is not recommended.

Moorings

Many mooring buoys are laid for visitors inside the restricted area on the SW side of Isla Méda Grande. Small boats use these by day but most are available overnight. Anchoring in this area is prohibited.

Anchorages

The area to the SW of the Isla Méda Grande outside the restricted area is a recognised anchorage. Yachts can anchor 100m to the SW of the landing in 10m weed over sand and stones. Note that there is an isolated rock 50m to SW of this landing which is not shown on all charts. Anchorage is also possible in deep water some 100m further to SE in 16m, sand.

Landing

There is a small landing pier on the SW side of the Isla Méda Grande and one on the NW corner of Isla Méda Petita. These should only be used in calm weather and ferry boats should not be obstructed. Landing from a dinghy in calm weather is also possible on the N and SE sides of the Isla Méda Grande.

Islas Medes looking SSE with L'Estartit partly hidden by headland

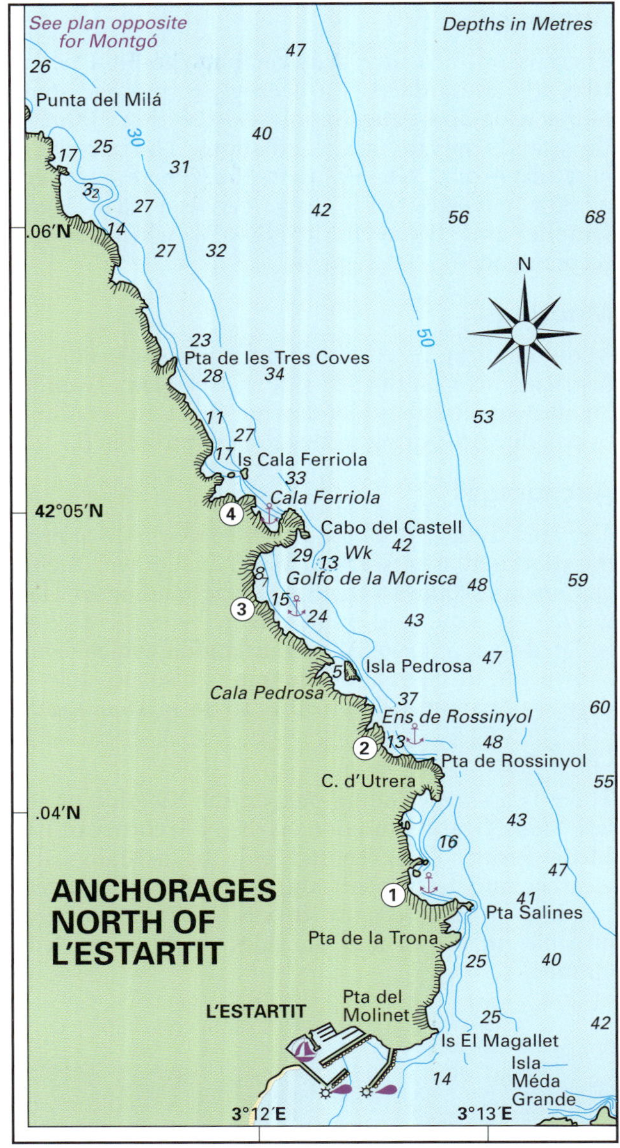

2. Ensenada del Rossinyol

1. ⚓ N of Punta Salines

42°03'·8N 3°12'·8E

A small anchorage in over 10m rock with high rocky cliffs. Open between N and E. There is foul ground behind the two islets to N of the anchorage.

Cabo d'Utrera

42°04'N 3°12'·73E

A double-pointed headland with high rocky cliffs (110m). There is a small islet off the north point but otherwise it is steep-to.

2. ⚓ Ensenada del Rossinyol

42°04'·3N 3°12'·

Anchorage surrounded by rocky cliffs (110m), open between N and E. Anchor in over 10m on rock

3. ⚓ Golfo de la Morisca

42°04'·7N 3°12'E

Anchor in 10m, rock. Open between E and SE. There is foul ground at the NW corner of the bay.

3. Golfo de la Morisca

4. Cala Ferriola

5. Cala de Montgó

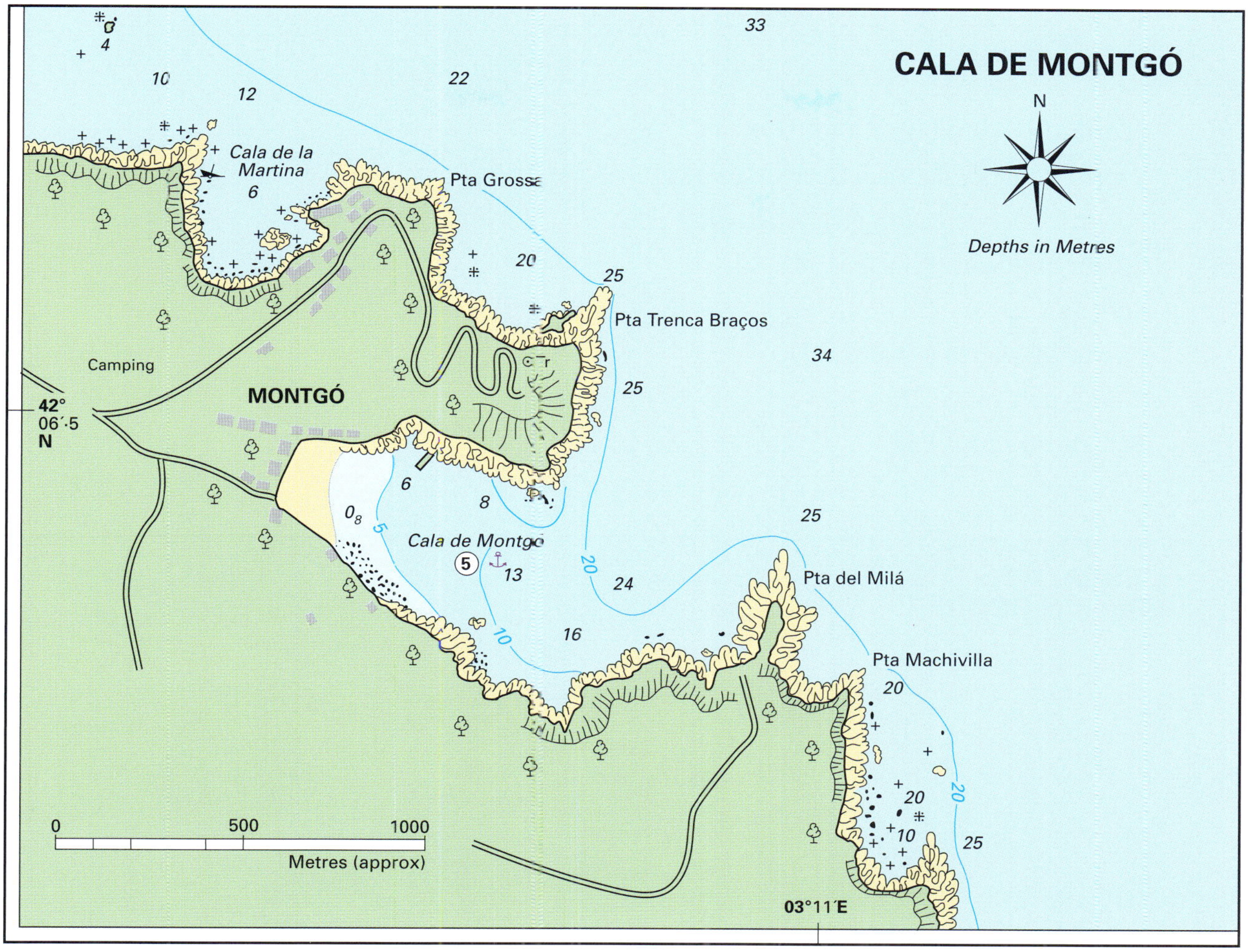

CALA DE MONTGÓ

Depths in Metres

Cala de la Martina

Pta Grossa

Pta Trenca Braços

Camping

MONTGÓ

42° 06'·5 N

Cala de Montgó

Pta del Milá

Pta Machivilla

0 500 1000 Metres (approx)

03°11'E

Cala de Montgó looking out to the anchorage
Steve Pickard

Punta Trenca Braços

4. ⚓ Cala Ferriola

42°05'·1N 3°12'E

Might just be able to anchor in one corner or another on rock. Open to the N and W.

5. ⚓ Cala de Montgó

42°06'·4N 3°10'·5E

A great *cala*. Mostly small boat moorings but 14 visitor bouys available for boats up to 12m. Only possible anchorage is clear of the extensive mooring buoys in 10m+.

Punta Trenca Braços

42°06'·7N 3°10'·6

A major steep to headland (96m) located at the S end of the Golfo de Roses and on the N side of Cala Montgo. Torre de Montgó on the crest is conspicuous.

L'ESCALA TO THE FRENCH BORDER

Ports

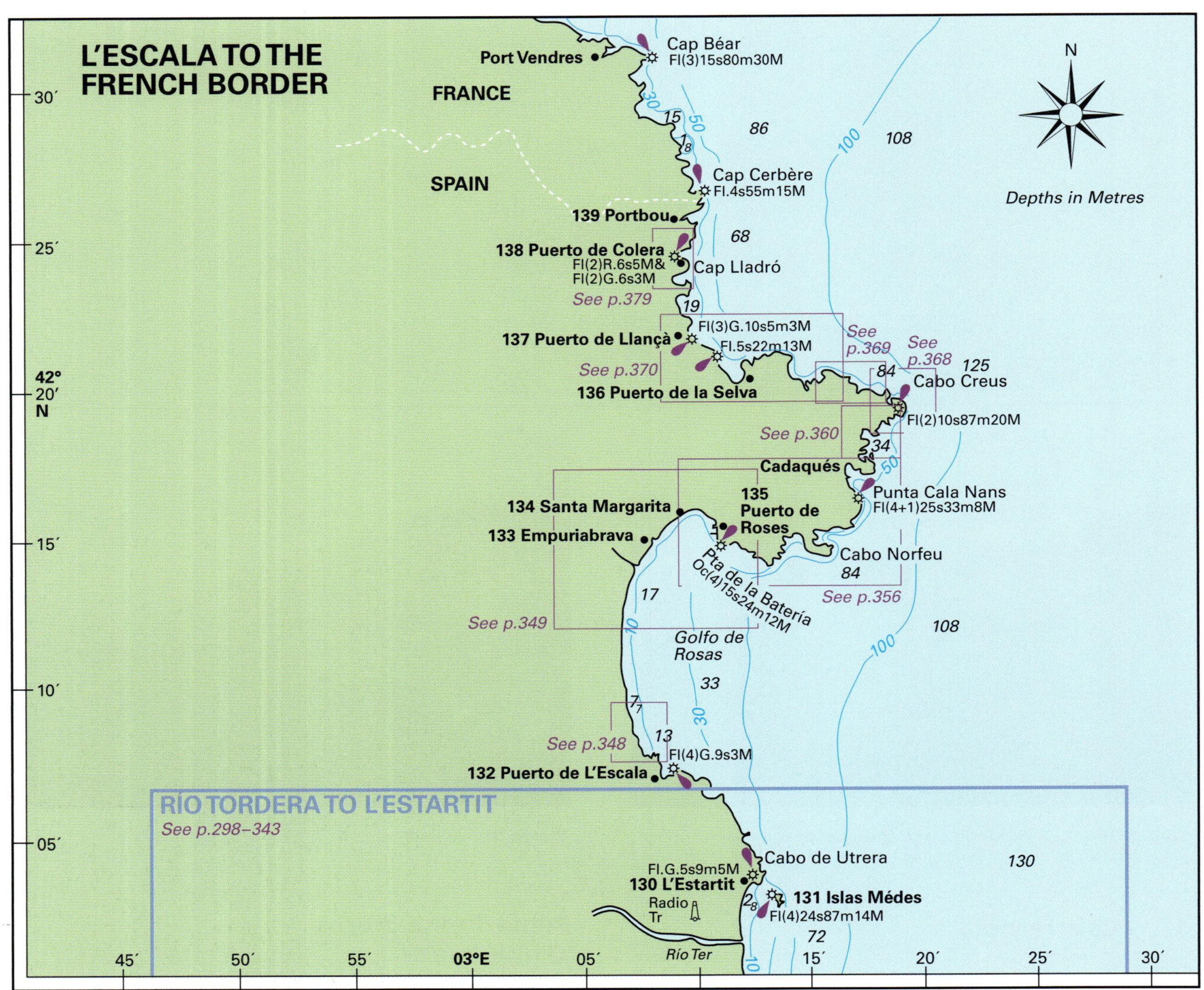

Note
Marine reserve officers may deny yachts access to many of the anchorages shown between Roses and Cabo Creus.

Hilltop village of Pals *Peter Taylor*

Pals *Peter Taylor*

Last anchorage before France (NE of Portbou) *Robin Rundle*

Llançà looking E *Peter Taylor*

132. Puerto de L'Escala (La Clota)

42°07'N 3°08'E

Charts

UKHO 1704, 1705	Imray M14
SHOM 4827, 7008, 7505	Spanish 493A

Lights

Dique de Abrigo centre Q.1s9m3M Card N post YB 9m

Dique de Abrigo head Fl(4)R.15s12m5M Red post, 3m

Espigón de la Clota head Fl(4)G.9s5m3M White post, green top 3m

Jetty head Fl.R.3s4m3M White post, red top 3m

Espigón de defensa Fl(3)G.9s 6m6M Green structure on white base 3m

Dique interior W head Fl(2+1)G.11s6m3M Green post, red band 3m

Dique interior E head Fl(2)G.6s6m1M Green post 3m

Port communications

VHF Ch 9 ✆ 972 770 016
club@nauticescala.com
www.nauticescala.com

A redeveloped marina

The original fishing and yacht harbour was created by the construction of a breakwater in Cala de la Clota on the east side of the bay. A new breakwater has been built to the north of the old harbour and now houses the fishing fleet and small local craft. Visitors should proceed into the old harbour, which is still susceptible to northerlies which can make the entrance difficult and send in swell.

The Greco-Roman remains at Empuries should be visited as they are unique on this coast and are only 2M away. The old church, Santa Maria de Vilabertran, at L'Escala can also be visited. There are sandy beaches to the W of the harbour.

Approach

The approach and entrance require care due to unmarked off-lying rocky shoals.

From the south the wide and deep Cala de Montgó and Punta Trenca Braços with a tower on its N side are easily recognisable. Punta de la Clota, a low feature with a small fort, is located just to NE of the harbour. Follow round the circular breakwater of the new marina at about 200m until the harbour entrances are clear.

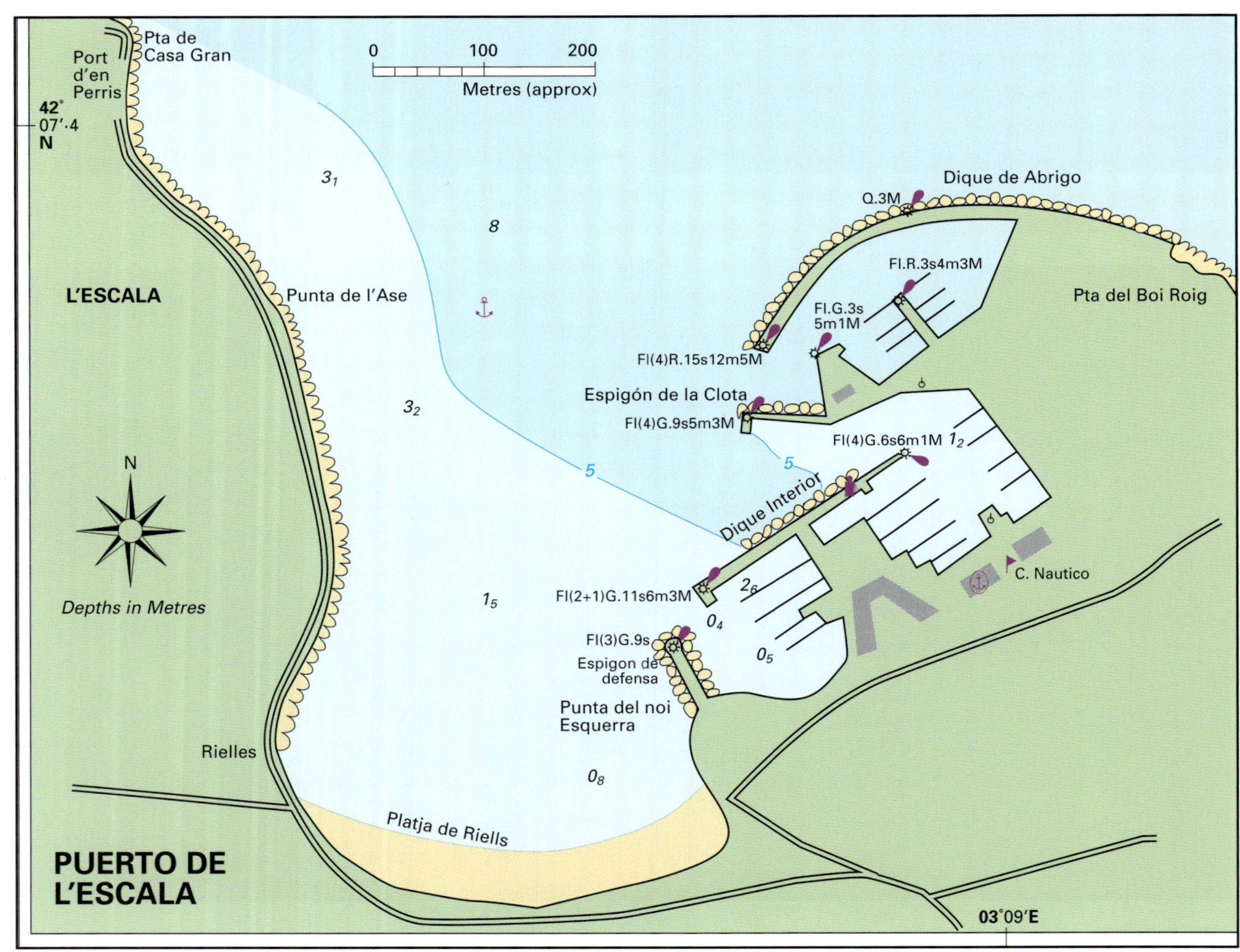

L'Escala

From the north From the massive and mountainous promontory of Cadaqués/Roses the coast becomes low and flat with a gently curving sandy beach. The marinas of Sta Margarita and Ampuriabrava and the inland towns of Sant Pere and Castelló de Empuries will be seen. The coast town of L'Escala will also be recognised.

Do not cut the corner by L'Escala town and, keeping well out from the coast on the west side, make for the head of the Espigón de la Clota on a southerly course.

Anchorage in the approach

Anchor to W of the old harbour near the centre of the *cala* in 8m, sand. An anchor light should be used. It is also possible to anchor off L'Escala in calm weather.

Entrance

Approach the end of the Espigón de la Clota on an easterly heading leaving it 20–25m to port. Moor to the fuelling point at the E end of the Dique Interior and arrange a berth with the staff there or at the *capitanía* in the club náutico. There is a second *capitanía* (with showers!) being built at the angle of the Espigón de la Clota and one may, in future, be able to moor on the S side of the *espigón* near the new *capitanía* to receive berthing instructions.

Berths

All berths have lazy lines from the quays/pontoons. Visitors go alongside the fuel berth for instructions and berth number if VHF call is unanswered.

Moorings

Some private moorings to the SW of the harbour, some of which may be available.

Facilities

Maximum length overall 25m.
Mechanics and shipwrights available.
Two cranes of eight and 10 tonnes and a 5-tonne mobile crane.
Slip to the SW of the harbour.
Water on the quay and the *espigón*.
Gasoleo A and petrol.
220v AC points by the *club náutico* and on pontoons and quays.
Ice from a factory in the NE corner of the harbour or from fuel station at head of Quai Norte.
Club Náutico L'Escala has a bar, lounge, restaurant, showers and WCs.
A limited number of shops near the harbour. Many more are available in L'Escala.
Launderette in the town.
Weather forecast posted twice a day at the *club náutico*.

Communications

Bus service ✆ Area code 972. Taxi ✆ 77 09 40.

L'Escala looking S over the first of three possible entrances *Steve Pickard*

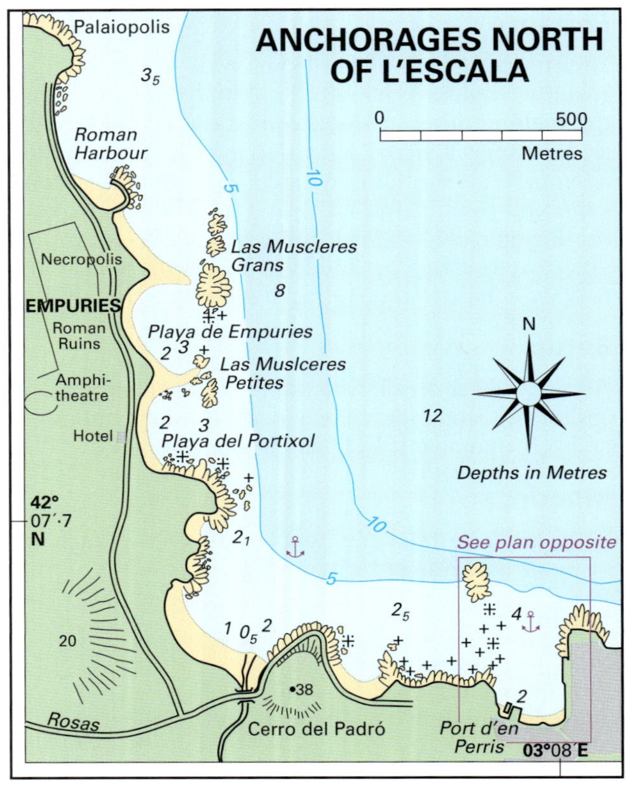

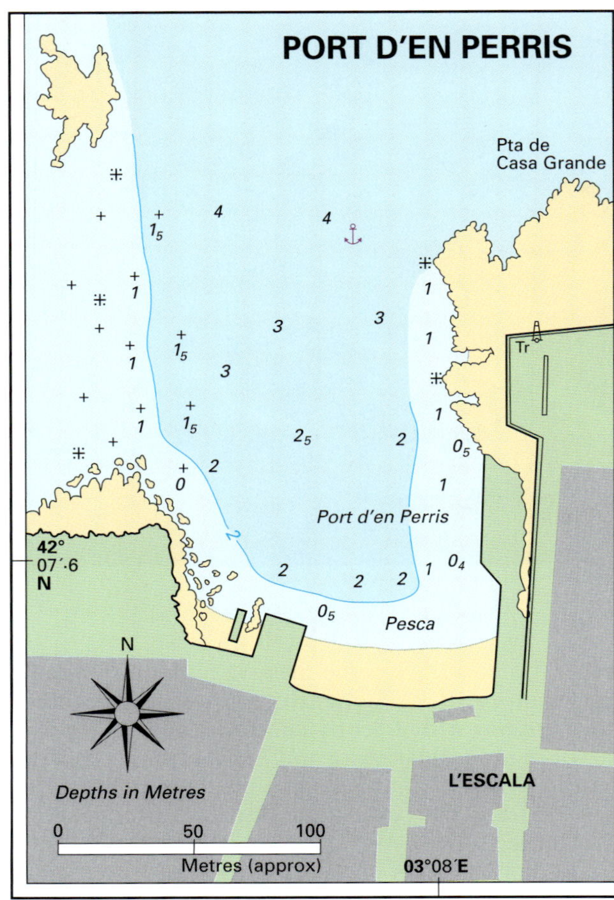

⚓ Calas de L'Escala (town)

42°07'·8N 3°08'E

Two small *calas* on the NW side of the town of L'Escala, the *cala* to E, Port d'en Perris is just tenable in S winds if anchored in 4m, sand, clear of the beach bouys. Open between N and E. The W *cala* has rocky shallows on the E side and has a sandy beach protected by beach bouys. Use both *calas* with caution. There is an off-lying rocky islet.

⚓ Las Calas de Empuries

42°08'N 3°07'·6E

A series of five *calas* lying between natural rocky projections from a sandy coast. The famous ruins of the Greco-Roman port and town of Empuries (3rd century BC) lies inland. The beach continues, backed by marshes, to the mouth of the Río Fluviá. 2·5 miles S of Empuriabrava. In summer beach buoys run by the outer rocks.

Port d'en Perris looking SW from the tower *Steve Pickard*

Playa del Portitxol and Playa de Empuries

133. Puerto de Empuriabrava (Ampuriabrava)

42°14'N 3°08'E

Charts

UKHO 1705 — Imray M14
SHOM 7008, 7505 — Spanish 493, 4932

Lights

Dique de Levante head Fl(3)G.7s8m5M
Green tower, white base 4m

Dique de Poniente head Fl(3)R.7s8m4M
Red tower, white base 4m

Dique Transversal head Fl(4)R.8s3m3M
Red tower, white base 1m

Dique Paralelo head Fl(4)G.8s4m3M
Green tower, white base 1m

Port communications

Capitania VHF Ch 09 ✆ 972 45 12 39
info@empuriaport.com
www.marinaempuriabrava.com

Harbour charges High

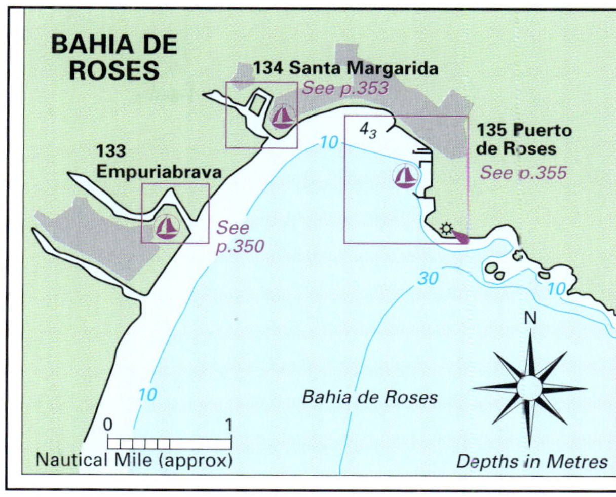

A huge inland development

Miles of canals lined with blocks of flats, houses, shops and hotels on land reclaimed from the marshes between the Ríos Muga and Salinas. The marine side of the business meets most if not all maintenance requirements. Approach is easy but entering in strong winds between NE and SE is difficult. Once inside there is good protection from the sea, but not entirely from the NW *tramontana* which blows with considerable force in this area, and eddies around the buildings. Only the first part of this complex of canals can be used by yachts with masts because of low road bridges. There is a special harbour called *port interior* for visiting yachtsmen who may stay up to 15 days. When checking in, get a plan of the complex to locate shops etc.

Visits to the famous Greco-Roman remains at Empuries 6·5M, and to Castelló de Empuries 2·5M and Sant Pere Pescador, 4M, are recommended. There are miles of sandy beaches on either side of the entrance.

Approach

From the south Cross the wide Golfo de Roses which has a low flat sandy shore. The towns of Sant Pere Pescador (32m) and Castelló de Empuries (69m) which stand a short distance inland will be seen. The high lighthouse-like building and other high-rise buildings at this harbour can be seen from afar. In the closer approach the breakwaters at the entrance will be seen.

From the north Round the prominent Punta de la Creu which has a small off-lying island and, keeping at least ½M from the shore, round Punta de la Batería onto a W course which leads towards the mass of buildings and a lighthouse-like building at this harbour. In the closer approach the breakwater at the entrance will be seen. Do not mistake Santa Margarita, 1·5M NE which has similar high-rise buildings, for this harbour.

Puerto de Empuriabrava entrance looking NW and showing the protective dogleg *Steve Pickard*

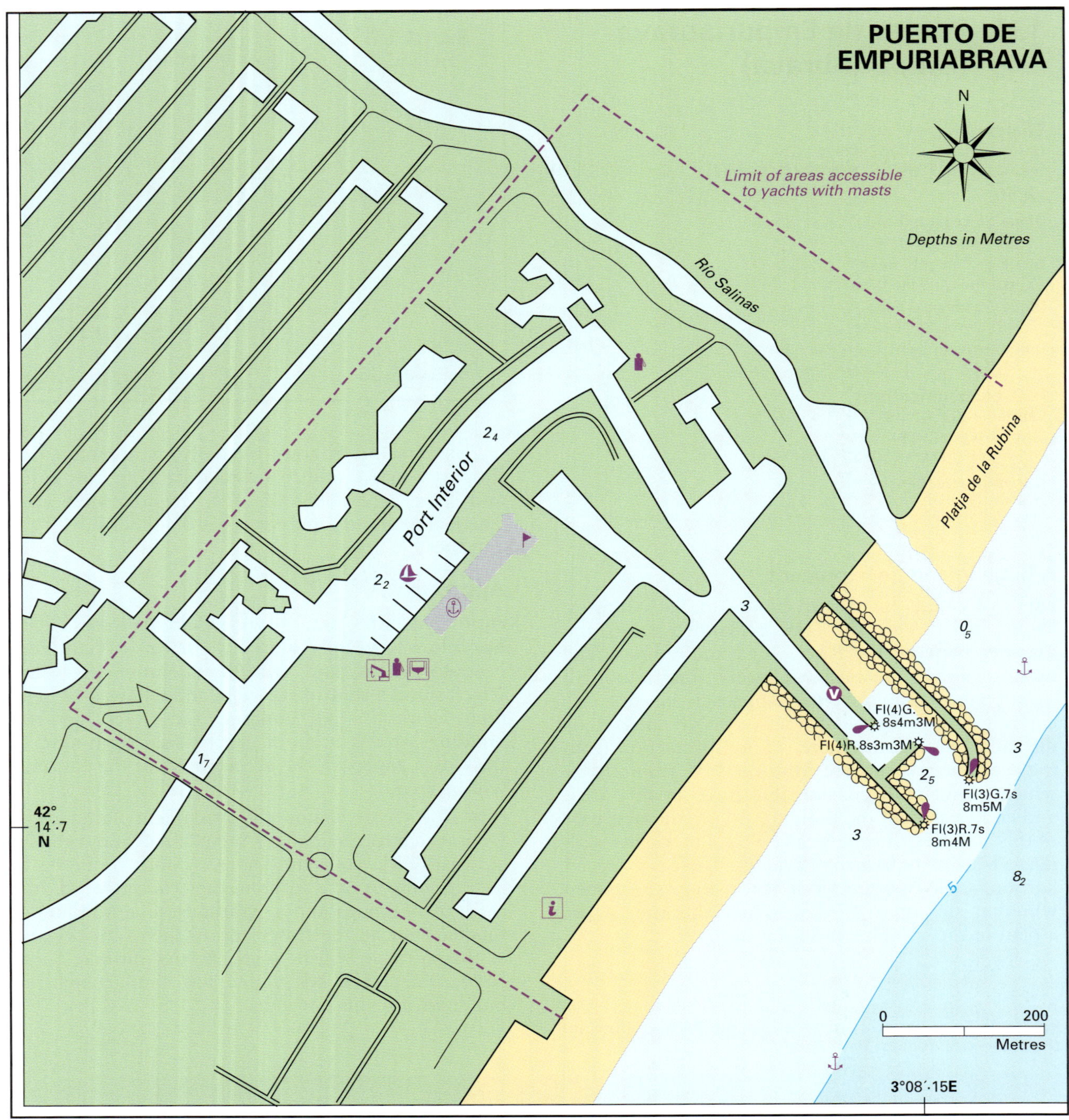

Anchorage in the approach

Anchor to NE or SW of the entrance in 5m, sand.

Entrance

Approach and enter on a NW course, steering clear of the two small green navigation bouys to starboard. Inside the entrance, the track is on an S-bend, starting to starboard, round a pier. The corners are blind because of the height of the piers and sand builds up off the pier heads so go slowly and do not cut corners. The waiting dock is to starboard at the start of the entrance canal, immediately after the S bend.

Facilities

Maximum length overall 25m.
Shipyard and workshops.
50-tonne travel-lift.
10 and 7-tonne cranes.
Slip for boats less than 5m.
Several chandlers.
Water and 220v AC on all quays and pontoons.
Showers and WCs near the *capitanía*.
Gasoleo A and petrol from pumps at the SE corner of the yacht harbour, Port Interior, and at the NW end of the entrance canal.
Ice from the *club náutico*.

Puerto de Empuriabrava

Club Náutico Empuriabrava with bar, restaurant, lounge, terrace and showers.
Many shops and a supermarket to SW of the yacht harbour.
Two launderettes within 10 minutes' walk.
Weather forecast posted at the *club náutico* 0900 daily.

Communications

Bus service. Car hire and taxi ✆ 972 451 218.

Puerto de Empuriabrava. The entry to the labyrinthine interior *Steve Pickard*

134. Puerto de Santa Margarida (Margarita)

42°15'N 3°09'E

Charts
UKHO 1705 Imray M14
French 7008, 7505 Spanish 876, 493A, 4932

Lights
Dique de Abrigo 42°15'·5N 3°09'·1E Q(2)G.4s8m5M
White tower, green top 6m
Contradique Q(2)R.4s6m3M
White tower, red top 3m

Port communications
✆ 972 257 156
info@nauticcenter.com
www.nauticcenter.com

Harbour charges Low

An inland development

A large development on the flood plain of the Río Muga with buildings along the banks of dredged canals. The marina caters primarily for residents but accepts visitors. The various buildings are run as separate entities with their own offices. The office handling the marina is located at one of the entrances off the main road, at the edge of the complex.

Approach could be dangerous in heavy seas or strong winds between E and S though once inside there is complete protection. The NW *tramontana,* however, is very strong in this area and there is little shelter except in the lee of tower blocks which themselves generate gusts.

For visits, in addition to Roses, Castelló de Empuries about 3M away has an attractive 11th-century church and other remains. There are miles of sandy beaches on either side of the entrance.

Puerto de Santa Margarida

Approach

From the south Cross the wide Golfo de Roses which has a low, flat sandy coast. The two towns of San Pedro Pescador (32m) and Castelló de Empuries (69m) can be recognised as well as the high *torre* at Empuriabrava, to the S of this harbour. The breakwater at the entrance will be seen in the closer approach with a mass of high buildings behind.

From the north Round the prominent Punta de la Creu which has a small off-lying island. Follow the coast round to Punta de la Batería keeping ½M offshore. Set a NW course from this point towards a mass of high buildings. In the closer approach the breakwater will be seen. Do not mistake Empuriabrava for this harbour.

Anchorage in the approach

Anchor to NE or SW of the entrance in 5m, sand.

Entrance

There appears to be no VHF contact. Approach the entrance from a position ½M to the S and enter close to the Dique de Abrigo on the starboard hand, follow it as it curves around the harbour at 20m. There may be red conical buoys and/or red-topped posts to leave port.

The entrance silts and is periodically dredged. Approach with due caution and sound.

Berths

Secure stern-to the quay by the yacht club area which will be seen ahead or in areas marked A, B, C or D on the plan, with bows-to mooring buoy, then await developments. Do not be tempted by the inviting lagoon to port at the end of the entrance channel, it is very shallow!

Facilities

Maximum length overall 15m.
A shipyard and repair workshop in the repair and maintenance area can carry out minor repairs.
50-tonne travel-lift.
5-tonne crane.
12-tonne slipway.
Slips.
Hard-standing in the repair and maintenance areas.
Chandlery.
Showers and WCs.
Water on pontoons and quays at A and B.
220v AC on quays A and B.
Club Náutico de Santa Margarida.
A number of shops and supermarkets in the complex.
Ice from supermarket.

Communications

Bus service.

Puerto de Santa Margarida looking N from the entrance *Steve Pickard*

PUERTO DE SANTA MARGARIDA (MARGARITA)

Workshops
Workshops
Isla Gran
(B)
(C)
(A)
(D)
1_5
SANTA MARGARIDA
Gran Canal
Hotel
Hotel
Hotel
1_8
Control Tr
(A) to (D) Visitors' moorings
Contradique
Q(2)R.4s3M
Q(2)G.4s5M
Dique de Abrigo
1_5
1_3
5
42° 15'·45 N
N
Depths in Metres
0 200 400
Metres (approx)
3°09'E

135. Puerto de Roses (Rosas)

42°15'N 3°10'E

Charts

UKHO 1705	Imray M14
SHOM 7008, 7505	Spanish 493, 4932

Lights

To the south

Punta de la Batería 42°14'·8N 3°11'E Oc(4)15s24m12M
White round tower on building 11m

Harbour

Dique de Abrigo Fl.G.4s8m5M Green tower 4m

New contradique head Fl.R.4s3M Red and white column

Commercial wharf elbow Fl(2)G.7s1M Green post

Port communications

Capitania VHF Ch 09, 16 ✆ 972 20 14 27
Club Náutico VHF Ch 09. ✆ 972 15 44 12
info@portroses.com
www.portroses.com

Harbour charges Medium

Old harbour with a fine new marina

A very old fishing harbour with a mole and an L-shaped breakwater which offer good protection. Approach and entrance are easy and protection from the NW *tramontana* can be obtained but the harbour is subject to swell from winds from S to SW. The new marina to the north of the Muelle Comercial is now fully functional with a smart new club house and all the usual facilities one expects from a normal marina.

Yachts may be allowed alongside the east quay opposite the entrance. Space is allotted by the *guarda de puerto* (the *capitán de puerto,* in overall charge, delegates berthing arrangements to the *guarda de puerto*). If a *tramontana* blows up, the quay has to be vacated for the fishing fleet and the *guarda* will suggest alternatives.

Facilities are good. The town which is about ½M away has good shops. The area is under development as a tourist centre.

A harbour has been in use here since the earliest times, its origins being connected with Emporion (Empuries). Greek and Roman records refer to Rhodus which was probably Roses, but there is a long gap in its history from the times of the Visigoths, whose remains have been found, until the Middle Ages when it was known to be a part of the domains of the Counts of Empuries and a naval port. The fort built at this time was blown up by Suchet in 1814 as was the fort on the Punta de la Batería.

There are a number of sites to visit, from Megalithic to more recent times, including a church consecrated in 1022 and the fort that surrounds it which was built in 1543. Excellent sandy beaches to NW of the harbour.

Approach

From the south From the low hills around L'Escala the coast of the wide Golfo de Roses is flat and sandy. The two inland towns of Sant Pere (33m) and Castelló de Empuries (69m) and the marinas of Ampuriabrava and Santa Margarita are the only recognisable landmarks until the massive foothills of the SE end of the Pyrenees that lie behind Roses are visible. The harbour and anchorage are located in the extreme NW corner of this gulf.

From the north After rounding the very prominent but low Cabo Creus the coast is broken with a number of deep *calas* of which Cadaqués is the largest and most easily recognised by virtue of the town at its head. Having rounded Punta de la Creu, which has a small island off its point, keep at least

Puerto de Roses

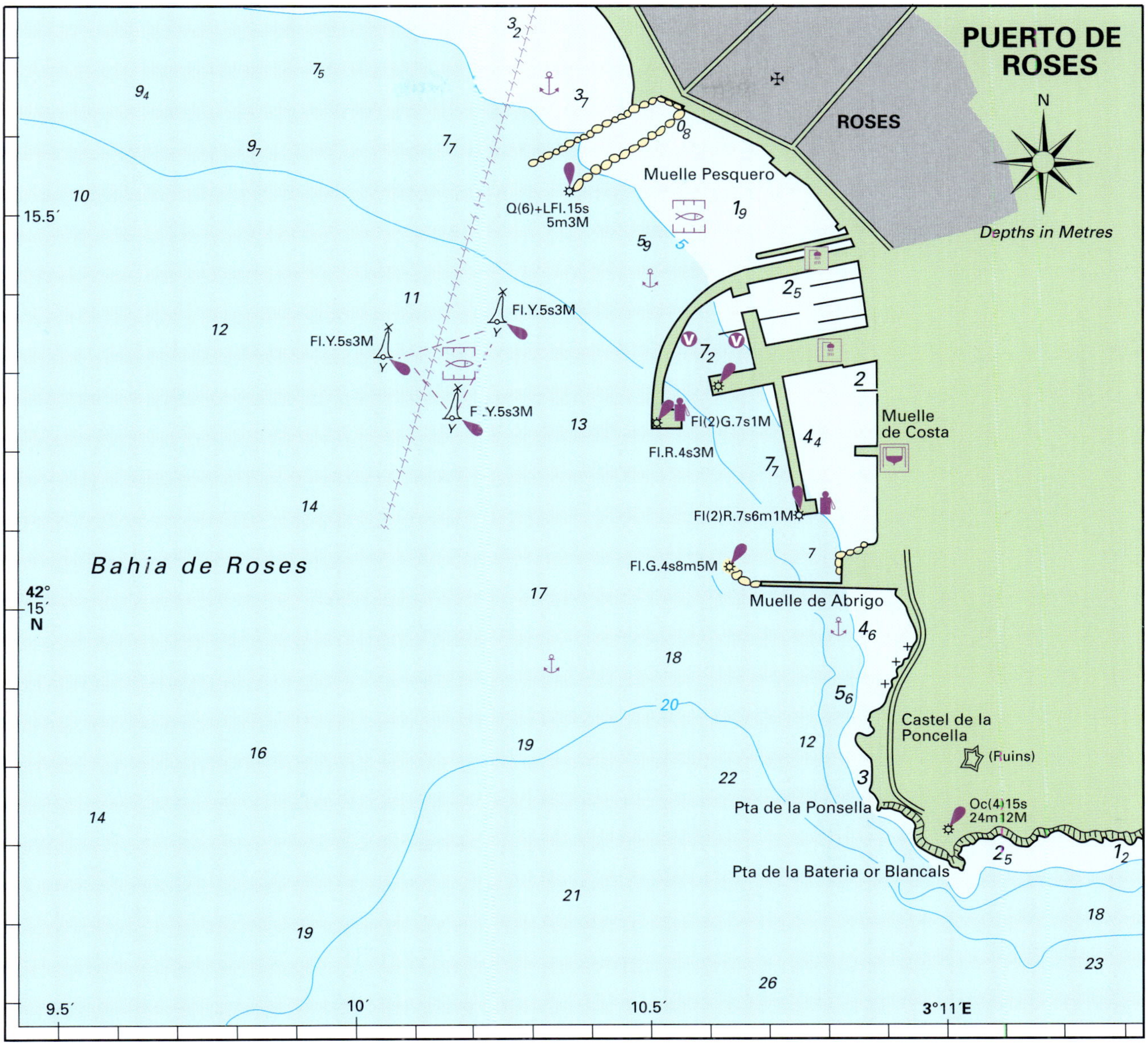

PUERTO DE ROSES

N

Depths in Metres

ROSES

Muelle Pesquero

Q(6)+LFl.15s 5m3M

Fl.Y.5s3M

Fl.Y.5s3M

F .Y.5s3M

Fl(2)G.7s1M

Fl.R.4s3M

Fl(2)R.7s6m1M

Fl.G.4s8m5M

Muelle de Costa

Muelle de Abrigo

Bahia de Roses

Castel de la Poncella

(Ruins)

Oc(4)15s 24m12M

Pta de la Ponsella

Pta de la Bateria or Blancals

15.5′

42° 15′ N

9.5′

10′

10.5′

3°11′E

Puerto de Roses entrance looking N *Steve Pickard*

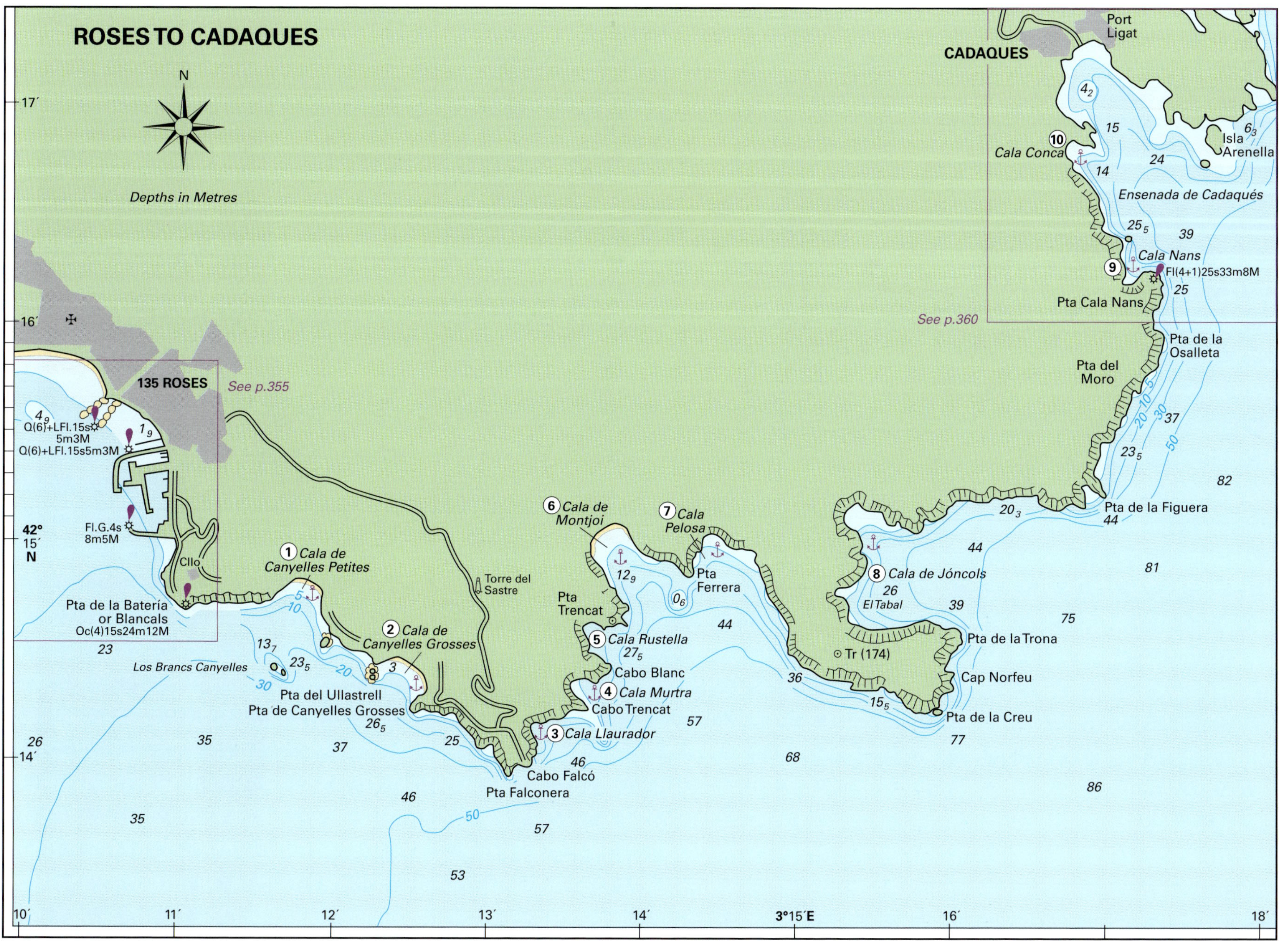
ROSES TO CADAQUES
N
Depths in Metres
CADAQUES
Port Ligat
Cala Conca
Isla Arenella
Ensenada de Cadaqués
Cala Nans
Fl(4+1)25s33m8M
Pta Cala Nans
See p.360
Pta de la Osalleta
Pta del Moro
Pta de la Figuera
135 ROSES
See p.355
Q(6)+LFl.15s 5m3M
Q(6)+LFl.15s5m3M
Fl.G.4s 8m5M
Cllo
Pta de la Batería or Blancals Oc(4)15s24m12M
Cala de Canyelles Petites
Cala de Canyelles Grosses
Torre del Sastre
Cala de Montjoi
Cala Pelosa
Pta Ferrera
Pta Trencat
Cala Rustella
Cabo Blanc
Cala Murtra
Cabo Trencat
Cala Llaurador
Cabo Falcó
Pta Falconera
Los Brancs Canyelles
Pta del Ullastrell
Pta de Canyelles Grosses
Cala de Jóncols
El Tabal
Tr (174)
Pta de la Trona
Cap Norfeu
Pta de la Creu
42° 15′ N
3°15′E

½M from the coast to avoid rocky shoals. Pay special attention to Los Brancs Canyelles which is over 300m from the shore and has a wide passage inside it. The harbour is not seen until Punta de la Batería has been rounded.

Anchorages in the approach

Anchor off the town in 5m or less to the N or to the N or S of the main harbour as indicated on the chartlet page 355. Mud and weed. Anchor lights should be shown.

Entrance

Straightforward, but see below for berths.

Berths

This modern marina, in the northern part of the harbour, has all facilities. On approach, call ahead on Ch 9 and wait off the fuel berth for a RIB to guide in. Visitors are normally berthed on the inside of the outer northern breakwater, larger vessels on the pontoons opposite.

Facilities

Water and 220v AC on all quays and pontoons.
Repairs can be carried out by two yards and there are also engine mechanics.
Crane on the S side of the Muelle Comercial.
150-tonne slipway at root of the Muelle Abrigo.
Chandlery behind the yard at the head of the Muelle Comercial and two more in the town.
Water from the Club de Mar and taps on the Muelle Comercial and on pontoons.
Ice from the factory located behind the *lonja* and from fuel station.
Club de Mar de Roses has a small clubhouse with bar, lounge and showers.
A fair number of shops of all types in the town about ½M away.
Launderette in the town.

Communications

Bus service.

Puerto de Roses fuel pontoon and minimarket to port on entry *Steve Pickard*

Anchorages – Roses to Cadaques

1. ⚓ Cala de Canyelles Petites

42°14'·7N 3°11'·7E

Anchor in the middle of the *cala* in 5-10m clear of the beach bouys and summer moorings.

2. ⚓ Cala de Canyelles Grosses

42°14'·3N 3°12'·3E

Open between SE and W. Anchor in the middle of the *cala* in 5-10m The foul ground round Brancs Canyelles is ½m to W

Punta Falconera and Cabo Falco

42°13'·9N 3°13'·1E

A prominent rocky-cliffed headland, steep-to with a small beacon on the Punta. A 5m-deep rocky shoal lies 600m ENE of Canbo Falco which is usually marked by breakers.

Calas de Canyelles, Grosses in centre foreground with Petites in upper centre, looking NW with Los Branca Canyelles foul ground visible in left centre

Cala de Canyelles Grosses

VI. COSTA BRAVA

3. ⚓ Cala Llaurador

42°14'·1N 3°13'·4E

A small *cala* just to N of Cabo Falco, similar to Cala Murtra. Enter in mid-*cala*, anchor in 5m, rock and sand. Open between NE and S.

4. ⚓ Cala Murtra

42°14'·3N 3°13'·7E

Anchor in the middle to suit draght in 5-10m clear of the beach bouys and summer moorings. Open between NE and S

5. ⚓ Cala de Rustella

42°14'·5N 3°13'·8E

Similar to the two previous calas but with a larger beach and a road behind it. Open between NE and S

6. ⚓ Cala de Montjoi

42°18'·8N 3°14'E

One of the few calas suitable for anchoring overnight. Anchor in mid-*cala* in 5m on sand and weed. Open between SE and S. There is a shoal (0·5m) 200m to S of Punta Ferrera. Keep to W side of the *cala* when entering but avoid a small rock 200m to SE of CaboTrencat.

7. ⚓ Cala Pelosa

42°14'·8N 3°14'·5E

The bottom is rocky. A tower on Punta de la Creu/Cap Norfeu is conspicuous. Beware the shoal (0·5m) 200m to S of Punta Ferrera.

Punta de la Creu

42°14'·2N 3°15'·8E

A large rocky conspicuous headland (148m) with a tower, the Torre de Norfeu (174m) 0·7m to NW of the point. A small islet, Carai Bernat lies off its point. Otherwise it is steep to.

8. ⚓ Cala de Joncols (Jontulls)

42°14'·9N 3°15'·6E

A sizeable *cala* but too deep and too much like a rocky amphitheatre to linger long.

9. ⚓ Cala Nans

42°16'·4N 3°17'·2E (see plan page 360)

Anchor in 5m, sand and weed. Open between N and E. The light is Punta de Cala Nans.

10. ⚓ Cala Conca

42°16'·7N 3°16'·9E (see plan page 360)

Keep to the middle and anchor to draught clear of beach bouys.

4. Cala Murtra

5. Cala Rustella

6. Cala de Montjoi

7. Cala Pelosa

Punta de la Creu

9. Cala Nans

10. Cala Conca

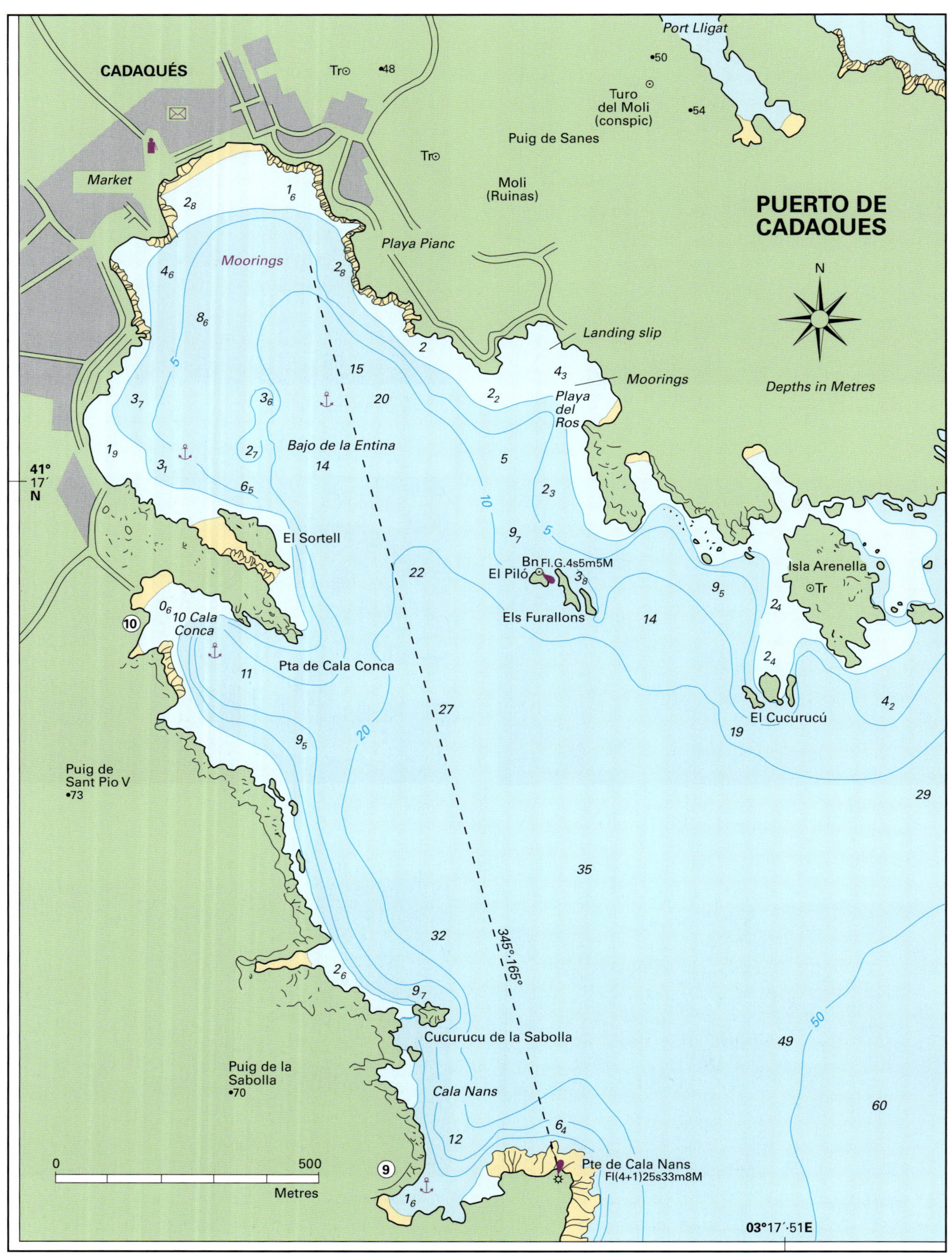
PUERTO DE CADAQUES
Depths in Metres
CADAQUÉS
Market
Moorings
Playa Pianc
Port Lligat
Turo del Moli (conspic)
Puig de Sanes
Moli (Ruinas)
Landing slip
Moorings
Playa del Ros
Bajo de la Entina
El Sortell
Cala Conca
Pta de Cala Conca
Bn Fl.G.4s5m5M
El Piló
Els Furallons
Isla Arenella
El Cucurucú
Puig de Sant Pio V
Cucurucu de la Sabolla
Puig de la Sabolla
Cala Nans
Pte de Cala Nans
Fl(4+1)25s33m8M
345°·165°
41° 17′ N
03°17′·51E
Metres

Puerto de Cadaqués

42°17'N 3°17'E

Charts

UKHO	1705
Imray	M14
SHOM	4827, 7008, 7505, 7298
Spanish	876, 493

Lights

Punta Cala Nans 42°16'·1N 3°17'·1E Fl(4+1)25s33m8M
White round tower on house 7m

Los Farallones 42°16'·9N 3°17'·3E Fl.G.4s 5m5M
Black stone tower

Puerto de Cadaqués looking S to the entrance *Steve Pickard*

A sheltered anchorage

Cadaqués is a large anchorage, easy to approach, with complete protection from the seas created by the NW *tramontana* and partial protection from the wind itself. It is, however, wide open to winds between from E and S. The surroundings are beautiful and impressive and the old town is very attractive. The area has become a very popular place for tourists and holiday-makers. Unfortunatly this has filled every possible anchorage with small boat moorings leaving only the middle of the bay with its 15m+ depths available.

Once the only route to town was by sea. In the 14th century, with some 600 inhabitants, it was prosperous after a troubled past but in the 16th century the troubles returned. The town was taken over by a succession of masters: Turkish Corsairs, the French, Algerian pirates, the French again in the 17th century followed by the British in the 18th century and again by the French during the Peninsular War. The church of Santa Maria (1662) is rare in that it has not been damaged as were most others in Spain during the various revolutions, wars and invasions. The Baroque reredos is quite exceptional and should be seen.

There is a shortcut to Port Lligat. Ask on the seafront, as there lies the summer residence of renowned surrealist Salvador Dali. It is worth the effort. As an alternative, there are a number of small sandy beaches at the heads of the *cala*.

Approach

From the south The coast of the wide Golfo de Roses is low, flat and sandy but near Roses it becomes high broken rocky cliffs with many *calas*. This type of coast stretches to Cadaqués and beyond. Punta de la Creu, a prominent point, can be recognised by a small outlying island and the town of Cadaqués with a church spire will be seen at the head of the bay.

From the north The very prominent but low Cabo Creus which has a lighthouse and two smaller towers with off-lying islands can be recognised from afar. The coast to S is very rocky and broken. The Illa Messina, just to the N of the entrance to Cadaqués, is conspicuous and can be passed either side.

Puerto de Cadaqués and its beautiful waterfront *Steve Pickard*

Looking NW with Cadaqués just left of centre with Isla Arenella in centre foreground and Pta. Oliguera in bottom right corner. Port Lligat is the body of water on the right side

From both directions the twin white radomes on the top of Montaña de Cadaqués (610m) 1·5M to W of the town can be seen from far off.

Entrance

Follow the centre line of the bay on a NW course leaving the lit beacon tower, El Piló, about 200m to starboard, steering towards the concentration of houses and a church spire at the head of the bay. In a *tramontana,* in order to obtain shelter it is necessary to make nearly 1M to windward inside the bay before the harbour is reached.

Moorings

Many private moorings will be found near the head of the bay and in the Playa del Ros, some of which may be available.

Anchorages

There are a number of anchorages around the head of the bay which may be used to suit the prevailing wind direction; these are shown on the chart. The bottom is sand, mud and weed with occasional patches of stone; use of a trip-line is advised. In the event of a NW *tramontana*, anchor as close inshore as draught permits opposite the town or in one of the small *calas* such as Cala Conca or Playa del Ros.

Landings

Land by dinghy on sandy beach in front of the town or in Playa del Ros.

Facilities

Water from local bars.

A number of small shops can supply everyday needs. There is also a small open-air market.

Communications

Bus service to Figueres and Roses.

Isla Arenella

42°16'·8N 3°17'·5E

This is an interesting area to explore by dinghy. There are many small calas, some with stony beaches and many islets and passages. Use Spanish chart 493.

Isla Arenella

Cala de Port Lligat

42°17'·6N 3°17'·5E

Charts

UKHO	1705	Imray	M14
SHOM	4827, 7008, 7505, 7298	Spanish	493

A sheltered harbour

An attractive bay in impressive surroundings where Salvador Dali had a large and the only summer residence. Approach and entrance are simple with good shelter except from NE winds. There is protection from the seas of the NW *tramontana* and limited protection from the effects of the wind itself. Facilities are limited to a small quay for landing from dinghies (0·6m). Many new holiday homes have recently been built around the area and more moorings have been put down. A visit to Cadaqués is worth the short walk which is shorter than one might imagine.

Approach

From the south Round the prominent Punta de la Creu which has a small off-lying island, cross the wide and deep Cala de Cadaqués which has houses at its head. Pass inside the Illa Messina, round Isla de Port Lligat leaving it at least 100m to port to avoid a submerged rock off the N point of Isla Farnera.

Do not attempt the narrow channel Paso de las Boquelles which lies to the S of Isla de Port Lligat. It has isolated and unmarked rocks. The shores of the bay are shallow.

From the north Round the very prominent but low Cabo Creus with its lighthouse, two towers and off-lying islands. The entrance to this *cala* is wide open from this direction and is to WNW of the Illa Messina. From both directions the two white radomes on Montaña Cadaqués are conspicuous.

Entrance

There is one port and four starboard buoys forming an entrance channel. Enter on a SW course in mid-*cala*, then follow the starboard-hand shore around at 100m into the inner part of the *cala*. The houses are not visible until well inside. There is now a quay and a small enclosed area at the head of this *cala* with:

W Entrance head 42°17'·8N 03°17'·8E Fl(2)R.7s3M Red pole in water

E Entrance head Fl(2)G.7s3M Green post 1m

Anchorage

Anchoring is now forbidden and only about 10 fore and aft moorings are available on payment.

Facilities

Water from the local small hotel or, with great difficulty, from the fishermen on the quay.

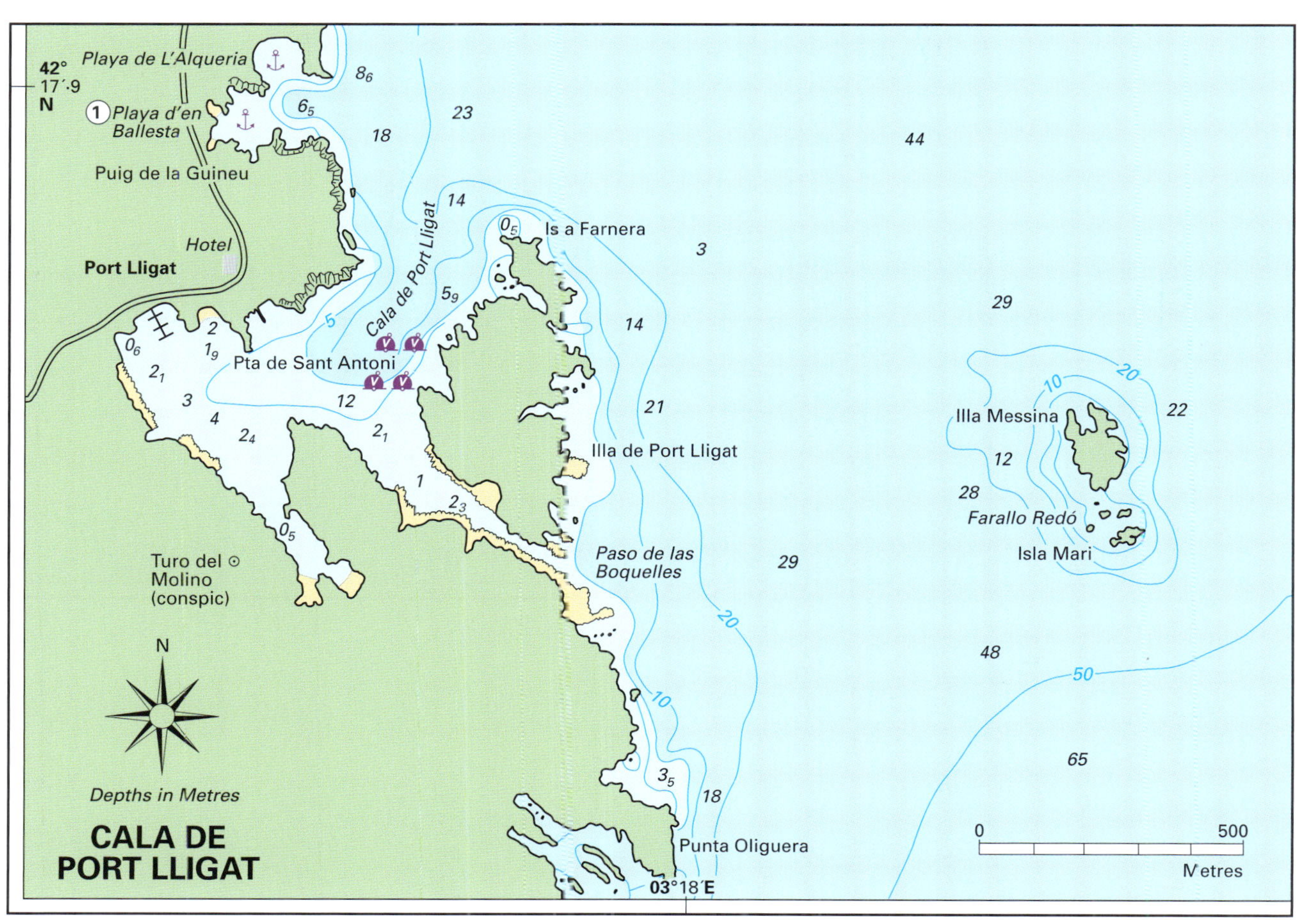

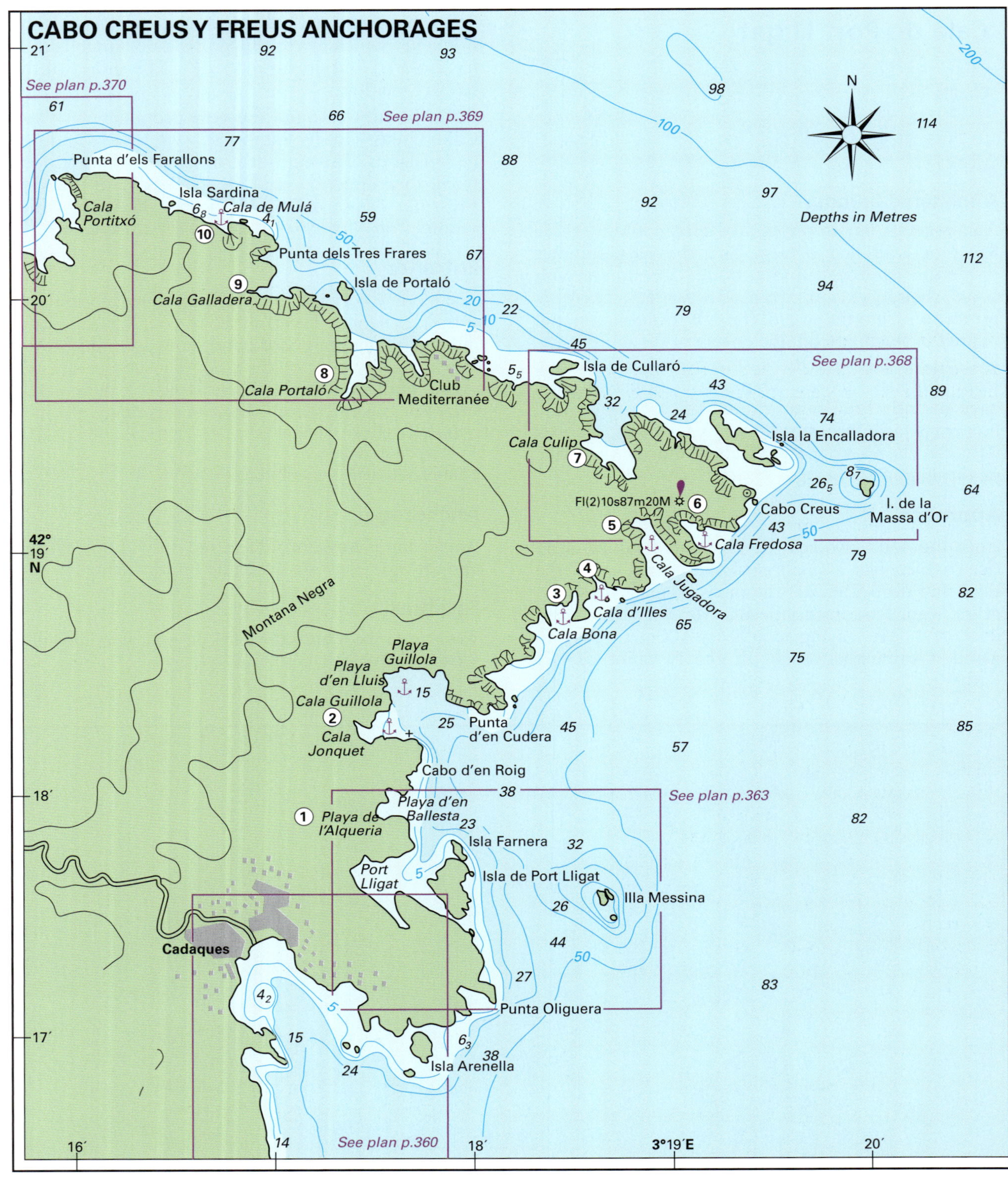
CABO CREUS Y FREUS ANCHORAGES
See plan p.370
See plan p.369
See plan p.368
See plan p.363
See plan p.360
Depths in Metres
Punta d'els Farallons
Isla Sardina
Cala de Mulá
Cala Portitxó
Punta dels Tres Frares
Isla de Portaló
Cala Galladera
Cala Portaló
Club Mediterranée
Isla de Cullaró
Cala Culip
Isla la Encalladora
Cabo Creus
I. de la Massa d'Or
Cala Fredosa
Fl(2)10s87m20M
Cala Jugadora
Cala d'Illes
Cala Bona
Montana Negra
Playa Guillola
Playa d'en Lluis
Cala Guillola
Cala Jonquet
Punta d'en Cudera
Cabo d'en Roig
Playa d'en Ballesta
Playa de l'Alqueria
Isla Farnera
Port Lligat
Isla de Port Lligat
Illa Messina
Cadaques
Punta Oliguera
Isla Arenella
42° 19′ N
3°19′E

Cabo Creus

42°19'N 3°19'E

Charts

UKHO 1705	Imray M14
SHOM 4827, 7008, 7505	Spanish 493

Lights

Cabo Creus 42°19'·0N 3°18'·9E Fl(2)10s87m20M
White round tower on a house 11m. Aeromarine

Beacons

Two white beacon towers (false lighthouses) are located on this headland, the one furthest to E is very conspicuous.

A major headland

A separate section is devoted to this very prominent headland as it is located at the extreme E end of the Pyrenees and represents a major obstacle to be rounded. It is one of the most dangerous points on the whole of the E coast of Spain because it is in the centre of the path of the NW *tramontana*. This, with its seas, can be worse here than on any other section of the coast and can arise without warning in a very few minutes. In such circumstances it may be necessary to seek immediate shelter in the local *calas* or harbours described in this section. However in good weather it represents an excellent, unspoilt and attractive cruising ground with many deserted anchorages to visit.

The *cabo* is of dark rock (76m) sloping inland to the two peaks of Els Puigs de Portas (127 and 120m) and on up to Montaña Negra (433m) behind them. To the NE of the *cabo* is the long, thin rocky Illa de Encalladora (38m) separated from the *cabo* by the inner passage which is 90m wide. There is a small rocky islet close to its SE extremity with a rocky reef extending onto SE. Illa de la Massa d'Or (19m) lies 800m to SE of the SE end of Isla La Encalladora. This *islote* has a rocky reef extending 150m to W leaving the middle passage 250m wide between these two reefs.

Readers may wonder why there are 'false' lighthouse towers, one of which is a horn. These were built for a film about 'wreckers'. The situation could not have been bettered.

Currents

A S-going current of up to 1·5 knots is a normal feature of the area though in 1977 it was reported as N-going.

Passages

(See plan on page 368). There are three possible passages round this headland.

Inner passage This passage leads between Isla La Encalladora and the mainland. It is deep but very narrow, being under 90m wide in places. It is shallower at the NW end where the seas break right across it in strong winds between NW and W. The wind buffets and funnels through this passage; be ready to use the engine in emergency. In no circumstance should the passage be attempted in bad weather.

The passage runs WNW–ESE. Approach should be made by closing the mainland coast and following it along into the passage. The outer white beacon tower (one of the false lighthouses) is very conspicuous from either direction.

Middle passage This is between Cabo Creus and Illa de la Massa d'Or passing outside the Isla La Encalladora. It should not be used in very strong winds because the seas break in this area but is quite safe in normal weather. Attention must be paid to the shoal patches which extend into the passage on both sides from the Isla La Encalladora and from the Illa de la Massa d'Or leaving a gap some 250m wide. The passage lies midway between the two islands and should be taken in a N–S direction. It is only about 50m long and is 20 to 30m deep.

Outer passage In bad weather Cabo Creus must be rounded at least 5M out to sea because savage seas can arise close inshore. With very strong SW winds a race develops off the headland. The outer passage is the only safe one to use at night.

Calas to the SW of Cabo Creus (numbers 1–6) are shown on pages 364 and 368.

Calas to the NW of Cabo Creus (numbers 7–10) are shown on pages 364 and 369.

Isla La Encalladora and Cabo Creus

1. Playa d'en Ballesta y Playa de l'Alqueria

2. Cala Guillola showing Cala Jonquet, Playa d'en Lluis and Playa Guillola

3. Cala Bona

4. Cala d'Illes

Calas to SW of Cabo Creus

(see plan page 364)

1. ⚓ Playa d'en Ballesta y Playa de l'Alqueria

42°17'·9N 3°17'·6E

Just N of Port Lligat, these two small bays offer an alternative anchorage. Open to the E.

2. ⚓ Cala Guillola & Cala Jonquet

42°18'·2N 3°17'·7E

Open from E to S.

3. ⚓ Cala Bona

42°18'·5N 3°18'·3E

A long, narrow *cala*. Anchor in 3m, rock and stone. Open to the S.

4. ⚓ Cala d'Illes

42°18'·6N 3°18'·7E

Open between E and S but partially protected by the islands off the entrance which give it its name. Beware the rocks along the eastern shore.

5. ⚓ Cala Jugadora

42°18'·7N 3°18'·9E

Just S of Cala Fredosa, this long *cala* has a shallow bay at its head. Anchor in 5–10m, rock. Open between SE and S.

6. ⚓ Cala Fredosa (Cova del Infern)

42°18'·9N 3°19'·3E

Immediately S of Cabo Creus: anchor in 5m, rock, but only in calm weather. There is a much visited rocky tunnel nearby.

5. Cala Jugadora *Steve Pickard*

6. Cala Fredosa (Cova del Infern) *Steve Pickard*

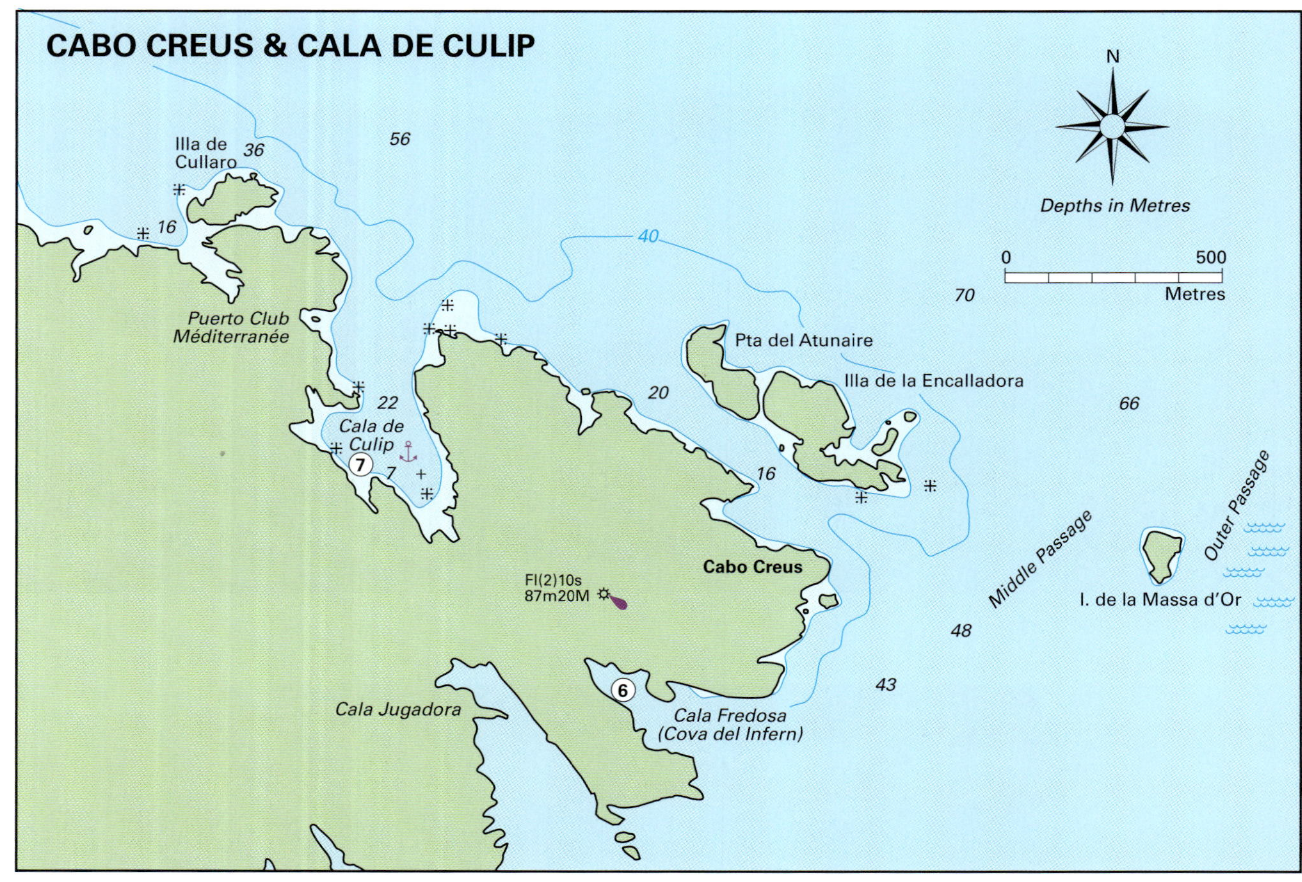

Calas to NW of Cabo Creus

Warning All *calas* NW of Cabo Creus to Pta d'Els Farallons are very dangerous with a sudden onset of the *mistral* or *tramontana*.

7. ⚓ Cala de Culip

42°19'·7N 3°18'·7E

Very popular anchorage but beware, in the NW corner, a large lip extends from the seabed, many abandoned anchor chains imperil yours.

8. ⚓ Cala Portaló

42°20'N 3°17'·5E

Anchor in about 5-10m, rock and sand. Open between N and NE. Frequent swell from the NW. Club Mediterranee has a holiday village nearby. There is foul ground around Isla del Portalo.

9. ⚓ Cala Galladera

42°20'·1N 3°17'E

Anchor in about 5-10m, rock and sand. Open between N and E and to swell from N. There is foul ground around Isla del Portalo.

7. Cala Culip

8. Cala Portaló

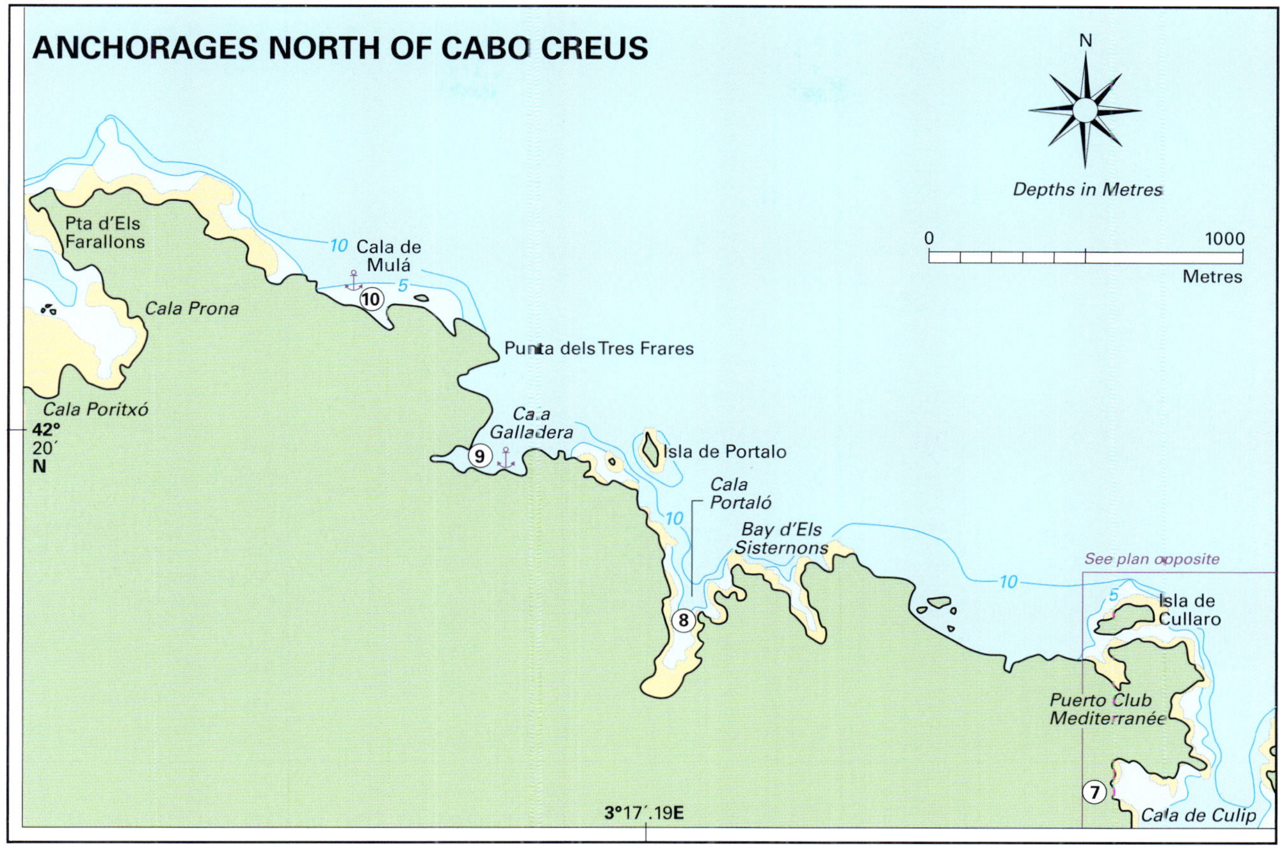

9. Cala de Galladera

10. ⚓ Cala de Mulá

42°20′·3N 3°16′·5E

A small *cala* with rocky-cliffed sides for use with care in calm weather. The bottom is rock. Open between NW and N.

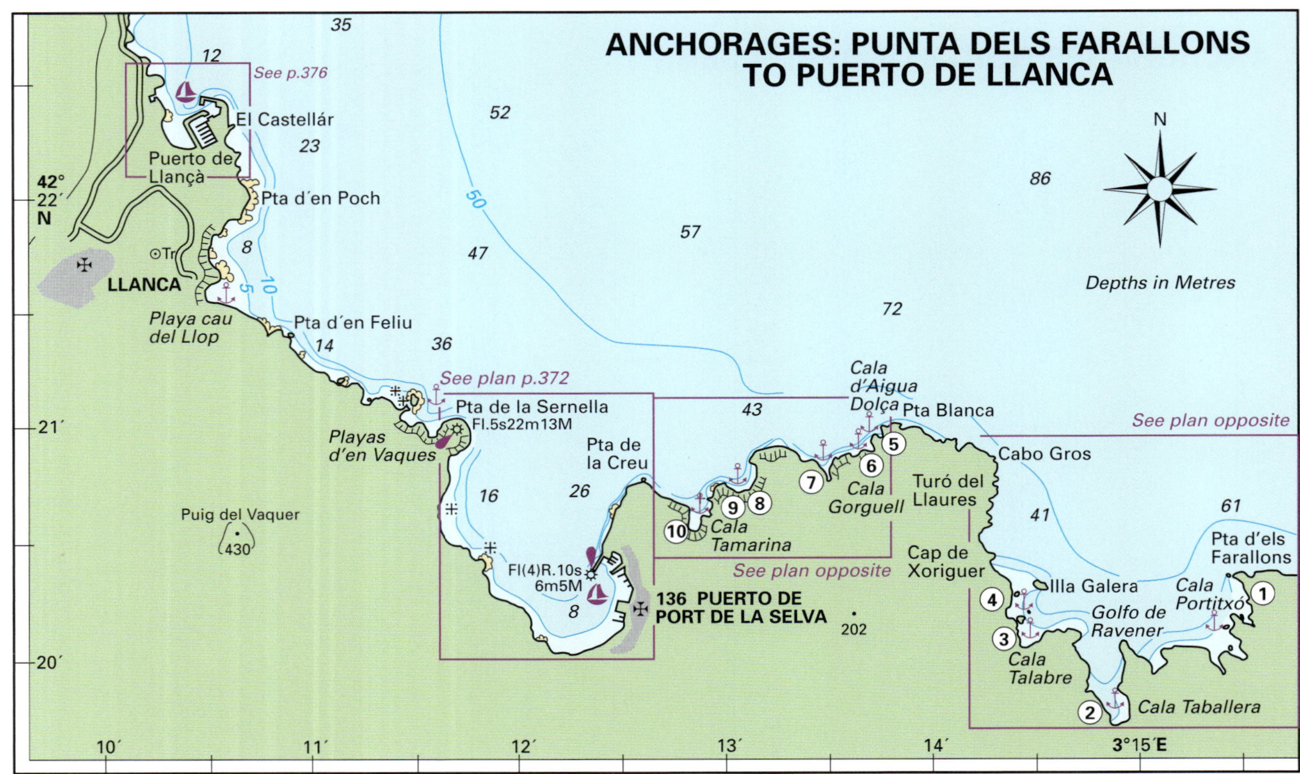

2. Cala Taballera

3 & 4. Calas Talabré and Galera

Anchorages in the Golfo de Ravener

(see plan opposite)

1. ⚓ Cala Prona and Cala Portitxó

42°20'·3N 3°15'·5E

A pair of sub-*calas* in the SE Golfo de Ravener with high rocky cliffs. Anchor in 5–10m. Open between NW and N.

2. ⚓ Cala Taballera

42°20'·3N 3°15'E

Anchor in 3–10m, rock and sand. Open to the N and to swell between NW and NE.

3 & 4. ⚓ Calas Talabre and Galera

42°20'·3N 3°14'·8E

Anchor in 5–10m, rock and sand. Galera Is better protected than Talabre, both get swell between NW and NE.

Anchorages E of Cala Tamarina

5. ⚓ Cala d'Aigua Dolça

42°21'N 3°13'·5E

A small *cala* to SW of Punta Blanca with rocky sides. Anchor in 3m sand in mid-*cala*, open between W and N.

6. ⚓ Cala Gorguell

42°21'N 3°13'·4E

A small *cala* anchorage with rocky cliffs both sides. Anchor in 3m, stone and sand. Open between NW and N.

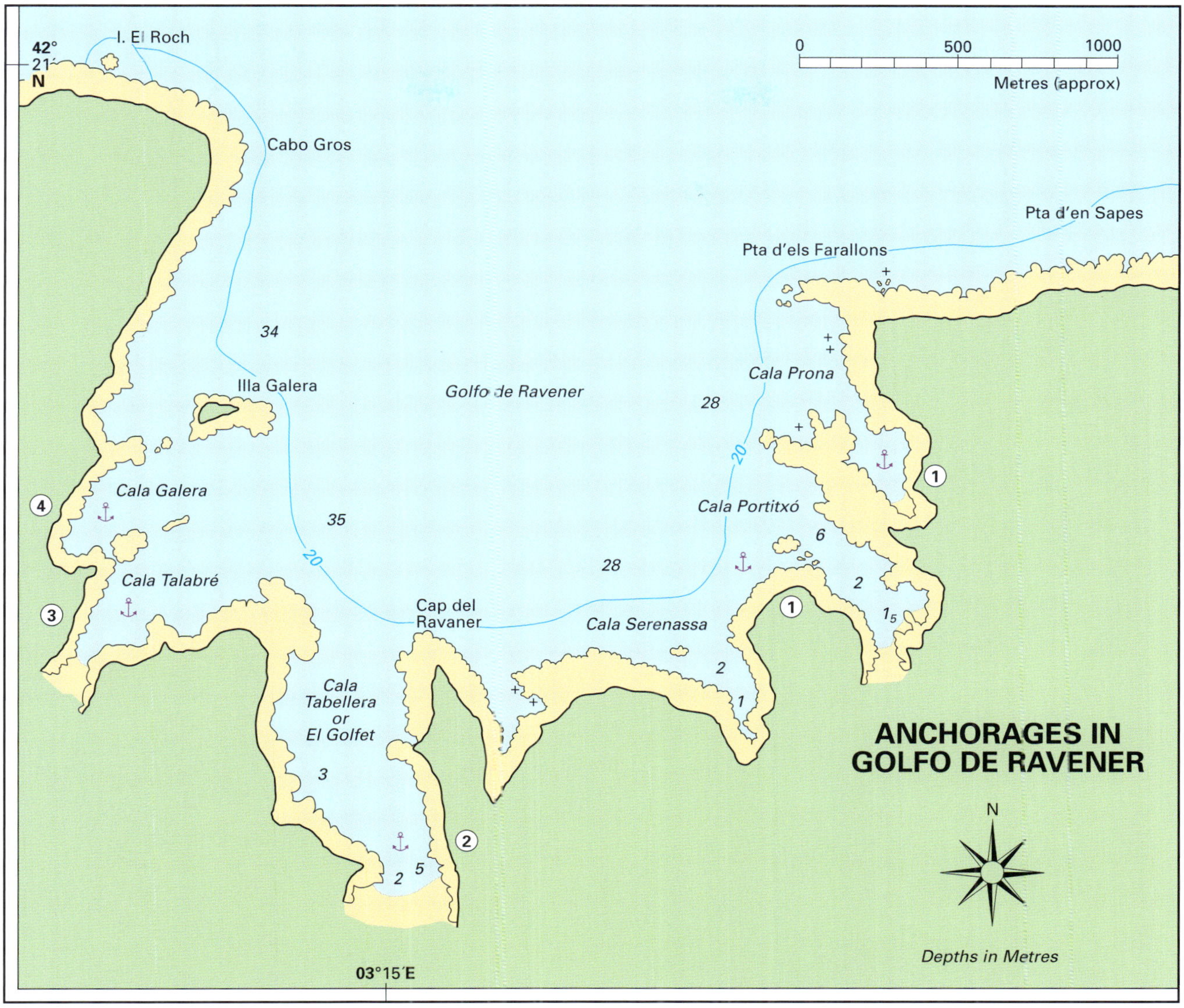

ANCHORAGES IN GOLFO DE RAVENER
42° 21' N
I. El Roch
Cabo Gros
Illa Galera
Golfo de Ravener
Cala Galera
Cala Talabré
Cap del Ravaner
Cala Tabellera or El Golfet
Cala Serenassa
Cala Portitxó
Cala Prona
Pta d'els Farallons
Pta d'en Sapes
0 500 1000
Metres (approx)
03°15'E
N
Depths in Metres

ANCHORAGES EAST OF CALA TAMARINA
42°21'N 3°13'E
Ensenada de Tamarina
I.Meda
Pta Blanca
Pta de la Cativa
Cala Tamarina
Pta de la Creu
Cap Mitja
Playa Cativa
Cala Mascorda
Cala Gorguell
Cala d'Aigua Dolça
Pta Fornells
Cala Fornells
0 500
Metres
N
Depths in Metres

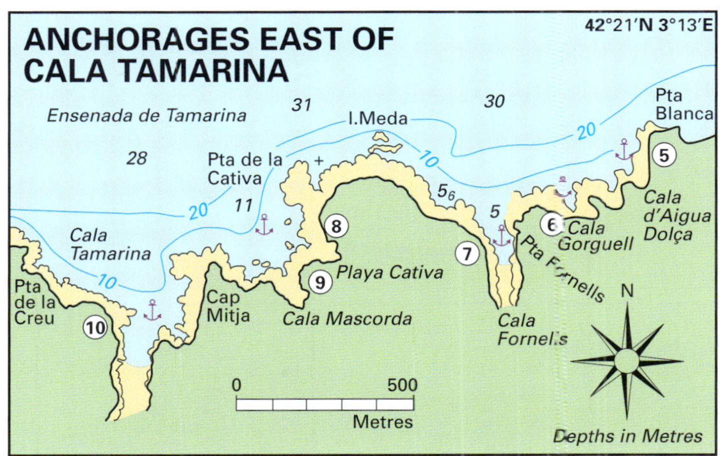

7. ⚓ Cala Fornells

42°21'N 3°13'·3E

A long narrow *cala* with rocky-cliffed sides. Anchor in 5m, rocks, near the head of the *cala* where there is a shingle beach. Open between NW and N. See plan.

8 & 9. ⚓ Playa Cativa and Cala Mascorda (Latius)

42°20'·9N 3°12'·8E

Two very narrow *calas* with rocky cliffs in a wide bay to E of Cap Mitjá. Enter with care when sea is calm and no onshore wind. Anchor in 3m rocks and sand. Open between NW and N. See plan.

10. ⚓ Cala Tamarina

42°20'·9N 3°12'·6E

Anchor in 3m, sand, off the beach. Open between NW and NE.

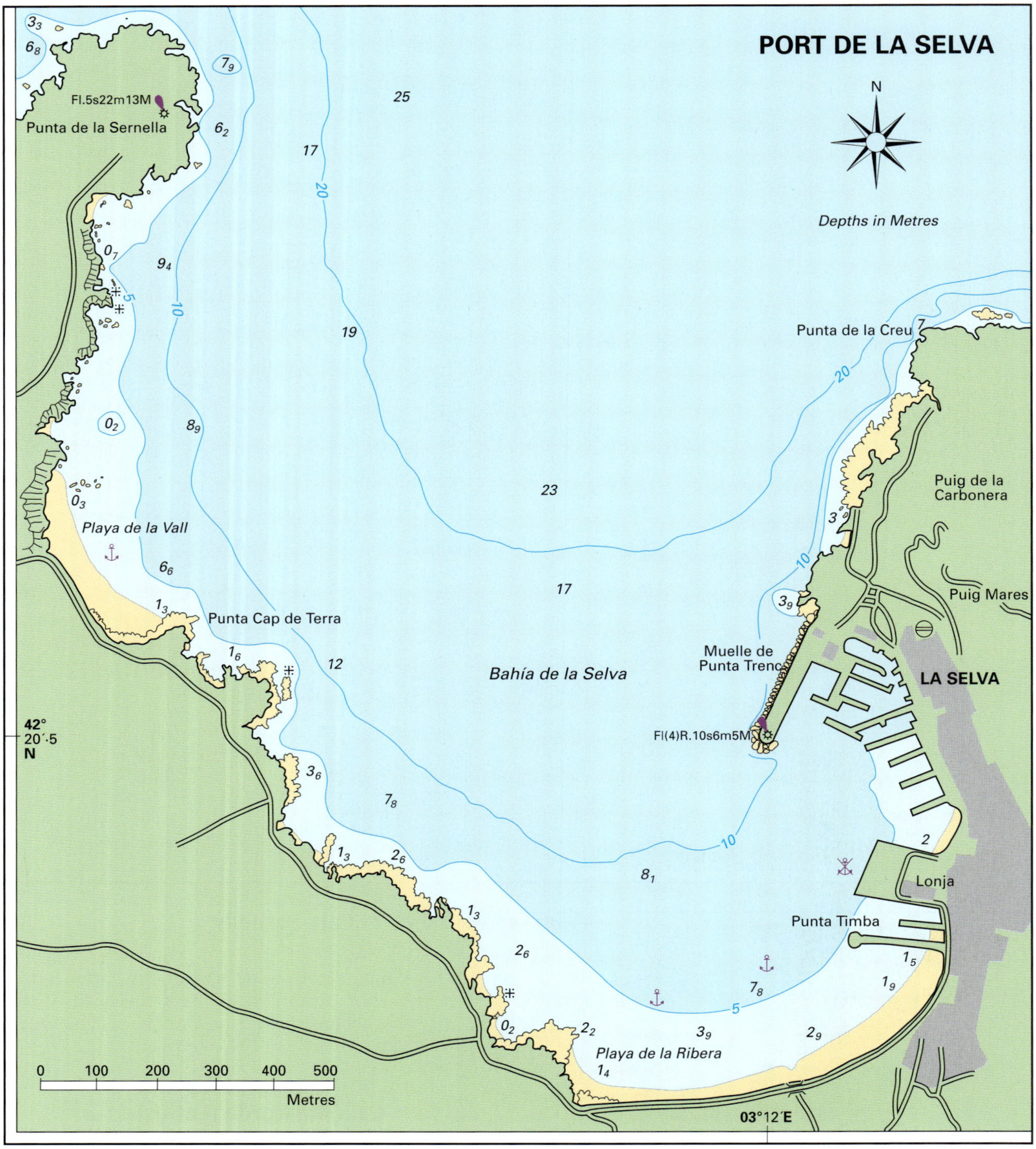

PORT DE LA SELVA

N

Depths in Metres

Fl.5s22m13M
Punta de la Sernella
Playa de la Vall
Punta Cap de Terra
Bahía de la Selva
Punta de la Creu
Puig de la Carbonera
Puig Mares
Muelle de Punta Trenc
Fl(4)R.10s6m5M
LA SELVA
Lonja
Punta Timba
Playa de la Ribera
42° 20´·5 N
03°12´E

0 100 200 300 400 500
Metres

Port de la Selva. Looking W to the anchorage *Steve Pickard*

136. Port de la Selva

42°20'N 3°12'E

Charts

UKHO 705	Imray M14
SHOM 7008, 7505, 7298	Spanish 4934, 493

Lights

Muelle de Punta del Trenc head 42°20'·5N 3°12'·0E
Fl(4)R.10s6m5M Red and white column 5m

Punta S'Arenella 42°21'·1N 3°11'·2E Fl.5s22m13M
White square tower on house

To the north

Cap Cebère 42°26'·4N 3°10'·6E Fl.4s55m15M
Grey tower red top 10m

Cap Béar 42°30'·9N 3°08'·2E Fl(3)15s80m30M
Pale red tower, grey corners 27m 146°-vis-056°

Port communications

Capitanía VHF Ch 9, 13. ✆ 972 387 000
nautic@cnps.cat
www.cnps.cat

A marina open to the NW winds

The port is at the side of a large bay and surrounded by mountains which has been developed into a fishing and yachting harbour. The approach and entrance are easy. There is very little shelter from the wind of the NW *tramontana* although good shelter from its seas can be had behind the Muelle de Punta del Trenc. Facilities are fair. The town and surrounding area are most attractive but there has been a considerable amount of building, fortunately mostly at low-level, for the tourist market.

The port was named after the extensive forest that surrounded the area in times past. It has been occupied since Neolithic times. Besides Neolithic remains, traces of Greek and Roman settlers have been found. The 11th-century monastery of Sant Pere de Roda, founded by the Benedictines and consecrated in 1022, kept strict control over the area despite constant incursion by the Counts of Ampuries. It was abandoned in 1798 and only recently has restoration commenced.

The local church, partly destroyed in the civil war, is interesting as it is half old and half modern. The monastery of Sant Pere de Roda and Sant Salvadó castle on the Sierra de Roses should be visited. The view from these points is fantastic.

Approach

From the south Round the very prominent Cabo Creus which has a lighthouse, two towers and off-lying islands. The coast is very broken and rocky with three major *calas* and many smaller ones. The wide bay at La Selva is easily recognised and the harbour will be found tucked away on its E side when Punta de la Creu has been rounded.

From the north From Cap Béar (France) with its conspicuous lighthouse, fort, radio and signal station the coast is high and rugged with a series of similar bays and headlands. Follow this coast to S, having passed Punta de la Sernella with its

Port de la Selva

Selva – the town looking N from the Lonja quay *Steve Pickard*

lighthouse, thence into the Bahía de la Selva where the harbour will be found on the E side.

On a clear day the two radomes on Montaña Cadaqués and the monastery Sant Pere de Roda on the mountain behind La Selva will be seen.

NB If going north or south at night beware unlit bouys north of Port Bou.

Anchorage in the approach

The anchorage off the town has been displaced to the SW and mooring bouys have been laid (30 euros per night). Anchor 400m to SE of the head of the Muelle de Punta del Trenc in 5m, weed over sand, or in deeper water further W. These anchorages are open to the NW *tramontana*. In this case shelter may be found alongside fishing boats by the Lonja or the Muelle de Punta Trenc.

Entrance

Approach the centre of the Bahía de la Selva on a S course. When level with the head of the Muelle de Punta del Trenc, turn onto an E course and enter leaving the head of the *muelle*, which has foul ground around it, at least 50m to port.

Berths

Visitors are likely to be allocated a place on the pontoons at the south end of the quay where the Club Náutico is situated. Call Club Náutico on Ch 9 to seek directions and a berth.

Facilities

Maximum length overall 27m.

Minor repairs to hull and engines can be carried out by local craftsmen.

A small 1 tonne crane in the inner harbour and a larger one of 12·5 tonnes on the *muelle*.

A very small slip in the inner harbour and another to S of the harbour.

Chandler near the harbour and another in the town.

Water and 220v AC on all quays and pontoons.

Gasoleo A and petrol.

Club Náutico de Puerto de la Selva clubhouse with bar, restaurant, lounge, terrace, swimming pool and showers.

A fair selection of shops in and around the town.

Weather forecasts posted once a day.

Communications

Bus and rail service from Llançá 4M away.
Taxi ✆ 972 387 392.

Selva anchorage with harbour beyond *Peter Taylor*

Playa Cau del Llop looking N *Steve Pickard*

Anchorages around Bahía de La Selva

⚓ Playa de la Ribera

42°20'·2N 3°11'·8E (see plan page 372)

A long, crescent-shaped sandy beach to S of La Selva. Anchor in 3m, sand, off the beach, open between NW and NE. Road and houses ashore. The W end of the beach has a rocky bottom. Dangerous during a NW *tramontana*.

⚓ Playa de La Vall

42°20'·7N 3°11'·3E (see plan page 372)

Anchor in 3m, sand. Open between N and E.

Anchorages between Bahía de Selva and Llanca

⚓ Playas de'n Vaques

42°21'·2N 3°11'·2E (see plan page 370)

Two calas to N of Punta de la Sernella and largely hidden in this photograph. Anchor in 5m, rock and sand. Open between N and E.

⚓ Playa Cau del Llop

42°21'·6N 3°10'E (see plan page 370)

A large bay with a sandy beach. There is foul ground on the N side of the *cala*. Anchor in the middle If possible, 5m, sand. Open between N and E.

Playas de'n Vaqué and Pta de la Sernella light

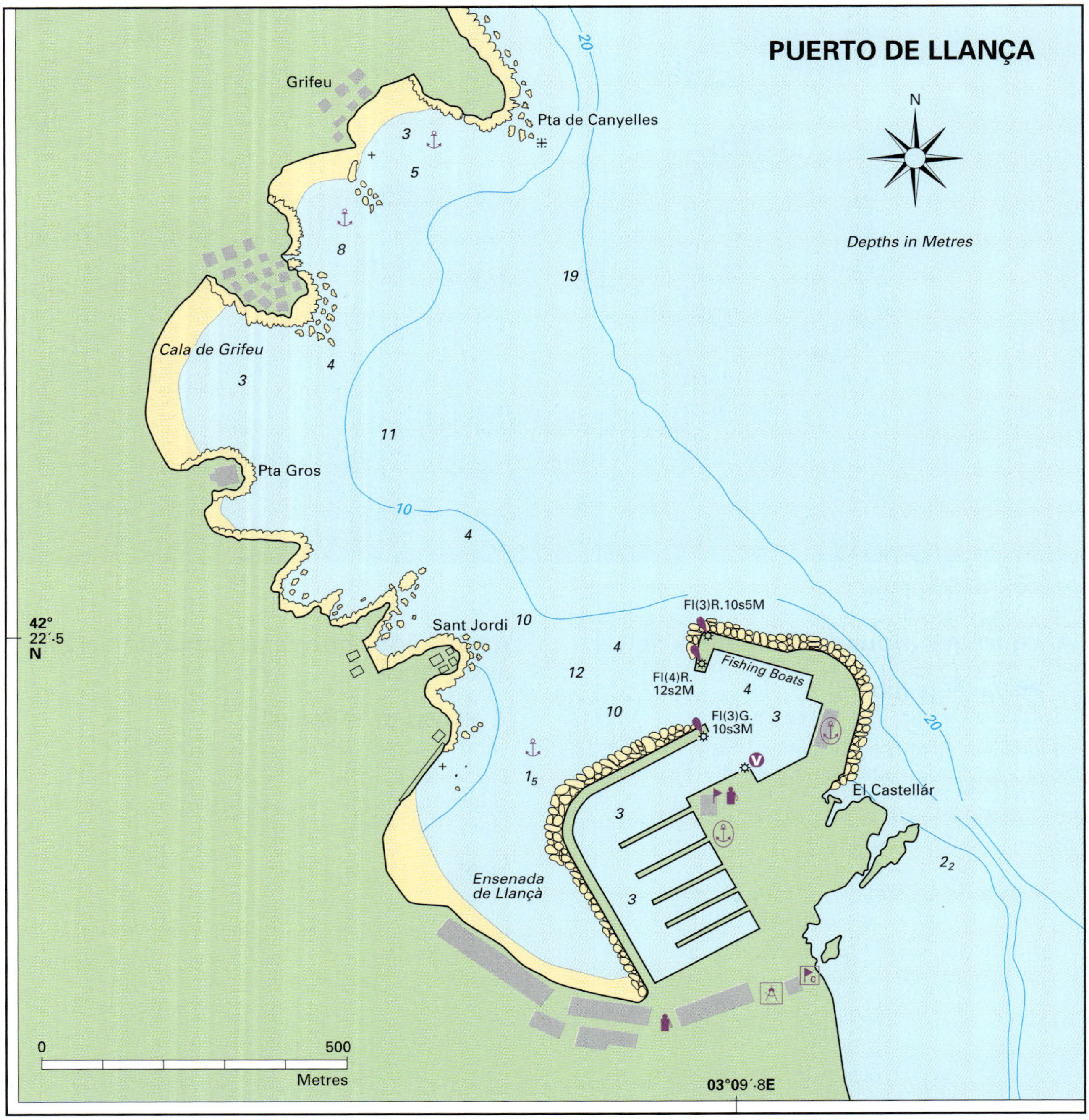

PUERTO DE LLANÇA

N

Depths in Metres

Grifeu
Pta de Canyelles
Cala de Grifeu
Pta Gros
Sant Jordi
Fl(3)R.10s5M
Fishing Boats
Fl(4)R. 12s2M
Fl(3)G. 10s3M
El Castellár
Ensenada de Llançà

42° 22´·5 N

03°09´·8E

0 500 Metres

Llançá

137. Puerto de Llançà (Llansá)

42°22'4N 3°09'E

Charts

UKHO 1705 Imray M14
SHOM 6843 Spanish 876, 493

Lights

Breakwater head Fl(3)R.10s8m5M
Red concrete tower, white base 3m

N entrance jetty Fl(4)R.12s2M
White tower, red top

Contradique head Fl(3)G.10s5m3M
White concrete tower, green top 2m

Port communications

VHF Ch 9 ✆ 972 38 07 10
club@cnllanca.cat
www.cnllanca.cat

Resort and yacht harbour

A former fishing harbour and anchorage now developed as a resort with a good yacht harbour. Approach and entrance are easy and it has better protection than Selva or Portbou. The area is attractive. This harbour was called Deciana in Roman times. In the 17th and 18th centuries it exported a large amount of marble, olive oil and wine. The local wine is still one of the strongest to be found. There is an interesting 18th-century church and it is possible to visit the Benedictine monastery of Sant Pere de Roda and Sant Salvadó Castle, 670m above sea level with a fantastic view. There are also the Dali and the Toy Museums and excellent bathing beaches around the bay.

Llançá fishing harbour *Steve Pickard*

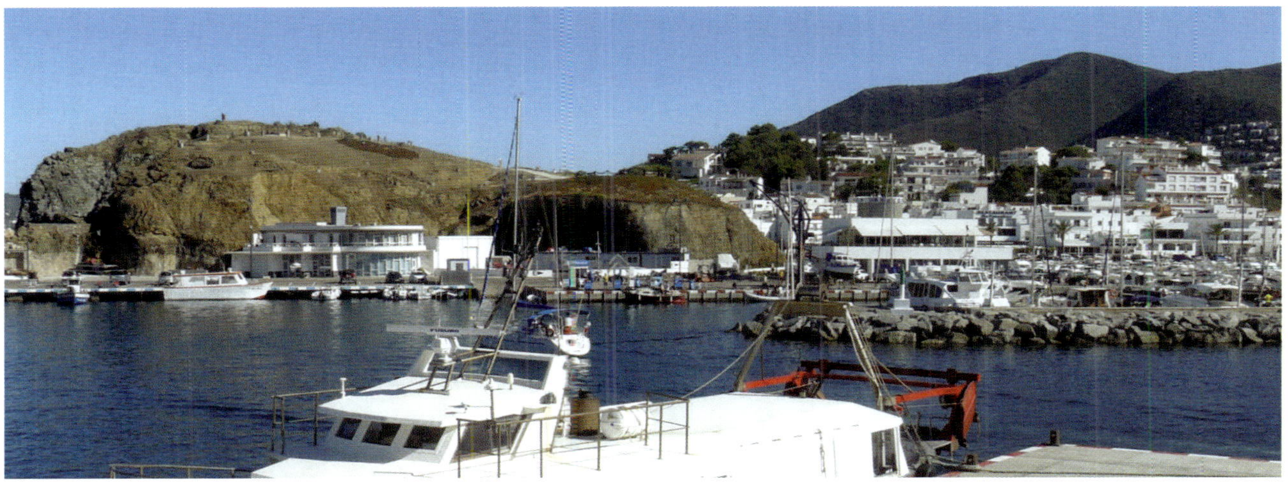

Llançá looking S to the Yacht Club *Steve Pickard*

Cala Grifeu to the N of Llanca. Anchor in the middle; there is foul ground on both sides. Open between E and SE. (See plan on page 376)

Approach

All the headlands in this bay have tongues of rocks projecting from the outer ends which are just below sea level.

From the south Cross the mouth of the deep Bahía de la Selva, which has Port de la Selva on its E side, and round Punta de la Sernella which has a lighthouse near the point. Keep at least 500m from the shore until the Ensenada de Llançà is fully opened up, then round El Castellár, which has a small castle on its top and follow the breakwater round.

From the north This harbour lies in the third large bay 3M to the S of Portbou. It can be recognised by El Castellár with its small castle lying just behind the harbour and the houses of the Puerto de Llançà can also be seen from this direction. The harbour lies in the S corner of the bay.

Entrance

Round the breakwater head with caution prepared for a sharp turn to starboard.

Berths

Go alongside the visitors quay and ask for a berth.

Anchorages

W of the harbour in 3m, sand and weed, but it is very exposed. Keep clear of the harbour entrance and channel to the beach and moorings in the Ensenada de LLanca. Use an anchor light. There are two other anchorages which may have better shelter on the N side of the *ensenada* (see plan page 376).

Facilities

Maximum length overall 15m.
Mechanics.
12-tonne crane.
Water and 220v AC on quays.
Gasoleo A and petrol.
Club Náutico de Llançà has the weather forecast posted daily.
Shops in the village and more at Llançá town some ½M away.

Communications

Railway to Barcelona and France.
Taxi ☎ 972 381 344 / 972 380 317.

⚓ Cala Garbet

42°23'·7N 3°10'E

Large bay open between NE and SE. Anchor in 10m, sand. The NW corner of the bay is particularly foul and rocks can be expected anywhere round the shore. Many small boats are moored here in summer.

Cala Garbet

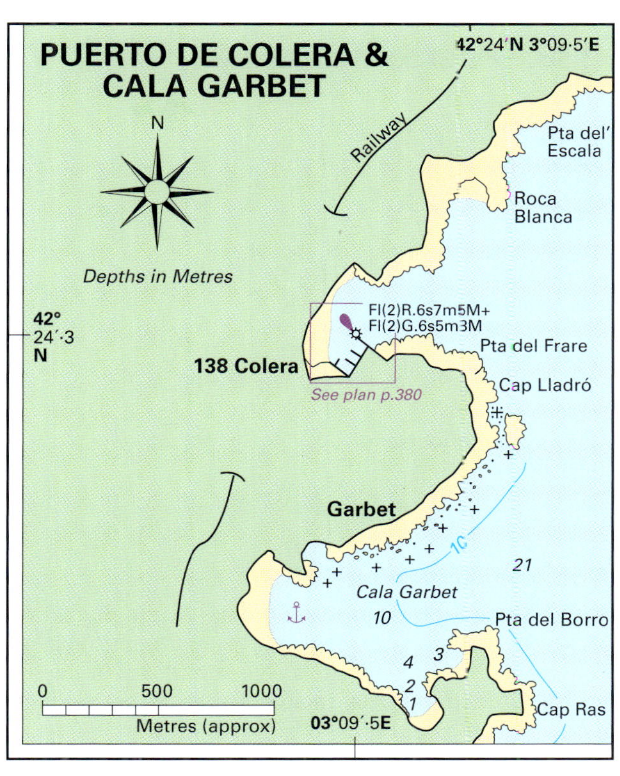

Cala Garbet anchorage *Steve Pickard*

Cala Garbet looking N *Steve Pickard*

138. Puerto de Colera

42°24'N 3°09'E

Charts

UKHO *1705* Imray *M14*
SHOM *7008, 7505* Spanish *493*

Lights

Dique de Levante head Fl(2)R.6s7m5M
Red tower on white base 3m

Contradique head Fl(2)G.6s5m3M
Green tower white base 3m

To the north

Cap Cerbère 42°26'·4N 3°10'·6E Fl.4s55m15M Grey tower red top 10m

Port communications

Club Náutico ✆ 972 38 90 95

A very small harbour

A small fishing harbour and village originally called St Miquel which was also used as a staging post on the main coast road. It has a small harbour for yachts and fishing craft tucked away on the S side of the *cala*. It is a useful harbour with better protection than the quay at Portbou though a NW *tramontana* creates a chop inside parts of the harbour. The area is impressive with high mountains all around. Harbour facilities are limited. There are a few shops in the village for everyday requirements and a beach of sand and stone to W of the harbour.

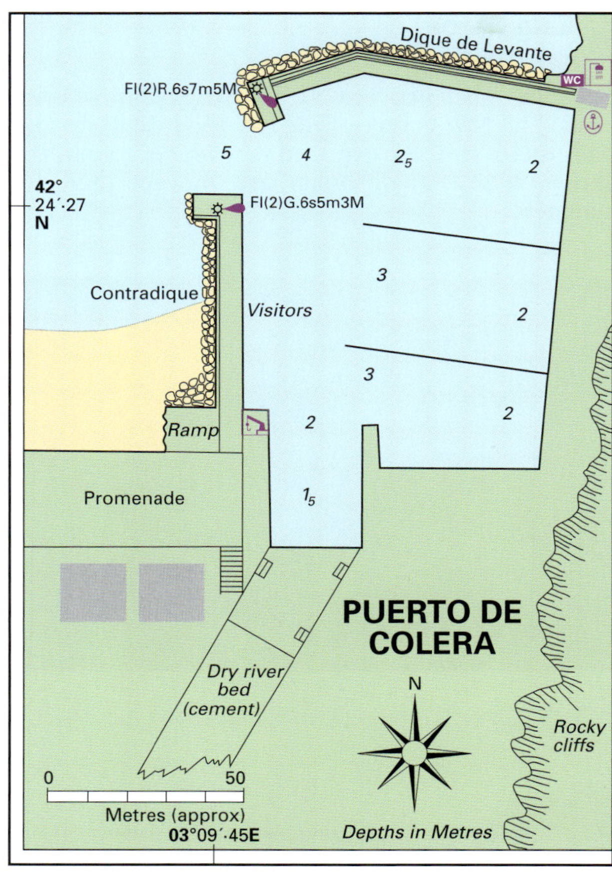

Puerto de Colera

Approach

From the south Leave the Bahía de la Selva and follow the coast at 500m to N. The following are easy to identify: Punta Sernella with a lighthouse, Puerto de Llançá which appears behind the Islote and Punta del Castellá, Cabo Rose with the wide Cala Garbet to its N and Cabo Lladró with a detached islet. Cala Colera lies to its N but the harbour remains hidden until mid-*cala* is reached.

From the north Port de Cerbère, Cap Cerbère with a small white building on its summit and the Cala de Portbou are easily recognised. Cala Colera is the next *cala* to S. From this direction the harbour may be seen in the early approach.

Anchorage in the approach

Anchor in 6m, stone and sand, near the centre of the mouth of Cala Colera. The head of the *cala* is shallow and has outlying spurs either side of the mouth of the river. Expect swell during or after a *tramontana*.

Entrance

Go west towards the head of the *cala* and when harbour bears S turn towards the entrance. Round the Dique de Levante at 15m.

Puerto de Colera small boat moorings *Steve Pickard*

Berths

Secure on the inner (E) side of the *contradique* where there is a notice, 'Amarres Servicio Publico' and ask the *capitanía* for a berth. Some of the quays have shallow rocky feet.

Facilities

Maximum length overall 15m.
Ramp from beach to *contradique*.
2-tonne crane.
Showers and WCs in NE corner of the harbour.
Water and 220v AC on all quays and pontoons.
Club Náutico Sant Miquel de Colera.
Provisions from village shops in Colera about 500m.

Communications

Buses. Rail to Barcelona and Perpignan.

Puerto de Colera small boat hoist looking N *Steve Pickard*

139. Puerto de Portbou

42°26'N 3°10'E

Charts
UKHO 1705 Imray M14
SHOM 7008, 7505 Spanish 493

Lights
Dique de Abrigo head Fl.R.5s7m5M Red post 3m
Contradique head Fl.G.5s4m3M Green post 2m

Port communications
Marina VHF Ch 09 ✆ 972 39 07 12
portdeportbou@telefonica.net
www.portdeportbou.cat

Harbour charges High

A small, simple harbour

This inlet which forms a natural harbour is located close to the frontier with France. Approach and entrance are easy and good protection is offered from all directions except between NE and SE. The force of the NW *tramontana* is somewhat reduced by the ranges of mountains inland but can still descend on the harbour in strong gusts. With a strong wind between NE and SE a heavy swell enters this harbour. Shelter should be taken at Selva or Port Vendres.

The marina to the west of the town has been recently totally remodeled and the breakwaters massively strengthened, the surrounds all leveled and six pontoons laid in the marina. The shore side facilities are still rudimentary but it is now a well sheltered harbour for some 300 craft, maximum length 12m. The town is not especially attractive but the surrounding countryside is spectacular, with high mountains.

Approach

From the south From the wide and deep Bahía de la Selva, the coast which is rugged and broken consists of a series of deep *calas* with rocky headlands between. These rocks are of a very dark colour just to the S of this harbour. Cap Cerbère which is ½M to N of this harbour is the most prominent of the headlands and can be identified if coasting close in. At the head of the Cala de Portbou can be seen the long railway customs shed on an embankment, the lighthouse-like spire of the church to the N of it, and there is a prominent fort-like building with a small square tower on the inner point on the S side of the harbour.

From the north Round Cap Béar, a prominent point with a lighthouse, signal and radio station and fort. Banyuls-sur-Mer can easily be identified at the head of a wide bay. Port de Cerbère has a multi-arched railway embankment, Cap Cerbère just to S of it will be seen, if coasting close in, as a prominent headland. Cabo Falcó is triangular-shaped and has a small white customs shed on its summit. Portbou will be recognised as detailed in the section above.

Entrance

Enter down the centre of the *cala* on a W course. If making for the marina round the end of the breakwater at a reasonable (25m) berth as there are obstructions running south and east from the head.

Berths

Berth first at the fuel dock beside the office. There is excellent berthing for visitors in deep water on the first pontoon inside the entrance. Hauling off lines are provided.

Anchorages

Anchor mid-*cala* in 6m sand, as close to the beach buoys as possible. Avoid foul ground to N. Swell during or after a *tramontana*.

Facilities

Water and 220v AC on pontoons.
Travel-lift 27 tonnes
Small slip on the S side of the harbour.
Water tap on the NW side of the harbour.
Some small shops in the village.
Club Náutico de Portbou.

Portbou fueling berth *Steve Pickard*

Communications

Rail to Barcelona and Perpignan. Bus service.
☎ Area code 972.

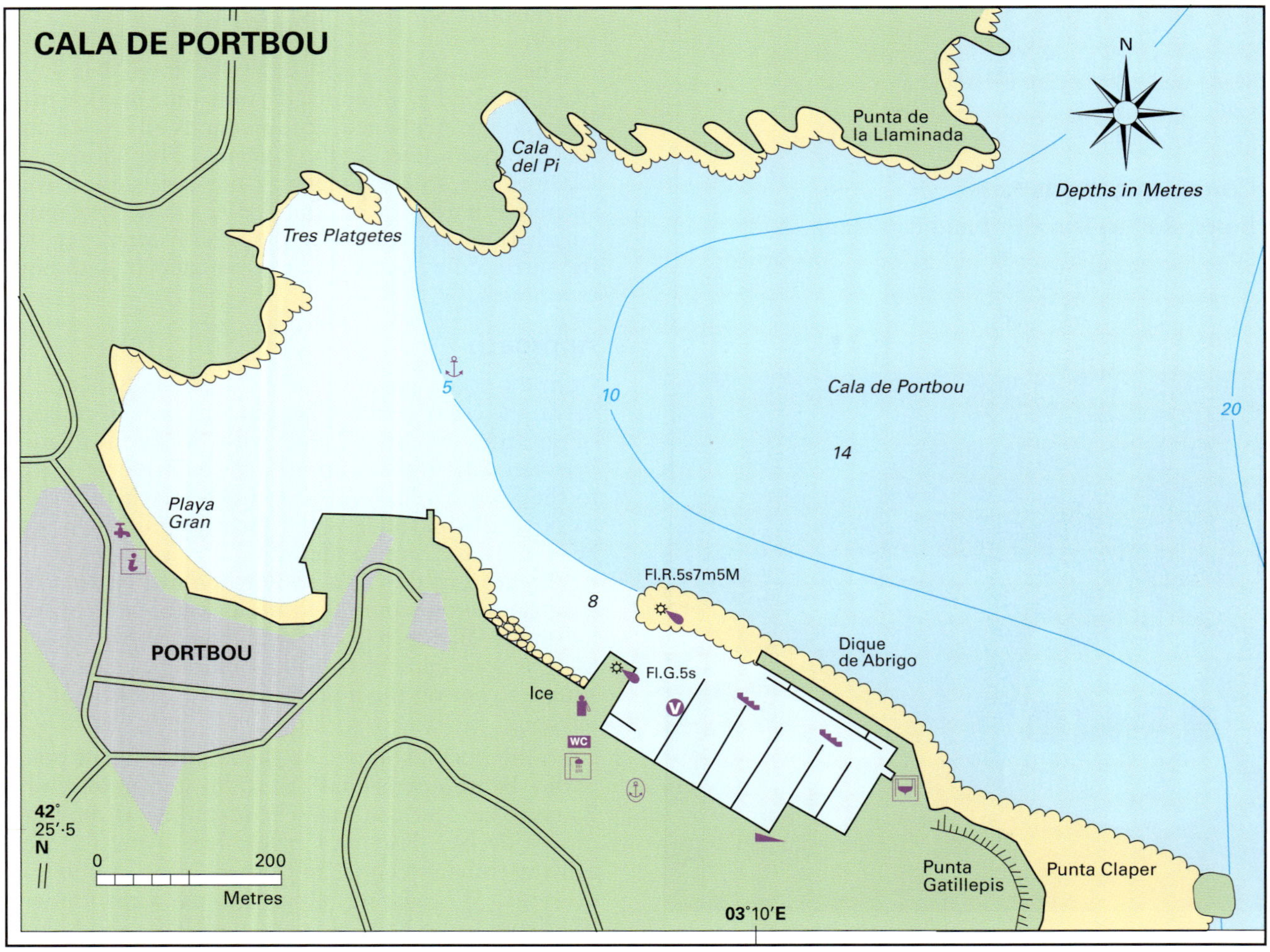

Puerto de Portbou

Puerto de Portbou looking S

APPENDIX

I. WAYPOINT LIST

The following waypoints are given as an aid to passage planning. They should not be relied upon for navigation.

All WPs are derived from electronic charts to WGS84 from source material at European Datum 50.

The numerical sequence does not signify that a route may be safely selected from a coastal waypoint to harbour. Navigators must plot their own routes taking note of the numerous fish farms and other obstacles along this coastline.

Chapter I ENTRANCE TO THE MEDITERRANEAN

Port		*Lat N*	*Long W*	
	⊕1	36°04'	05°24'	2M SE Pta Carnero
1	⊕2	36°06'·95	05°25'·43	Algeciras approaches
	⊕3	36°06'	05°22'	2M SW Pta Europa west
2	⊕6	36°09'·5	05°22'·2	Marina Alcaidesa entrance
3	⊕4	36°08'	05°22'·3	Gibraltar South Mole
	⊕5	36°09'	05°22'·35	Gibraltar North Mole

Chapter II COSTA DEL SOL

Port		*N*	*W*	
	⊕11	36°06'	05°20'	2M SE Pta Europa east
4				Puerto de La Atunara
5	⊕12	36°17'	05°16'·2	Puerto de Sotogrande approaches
6	⊕13	36°21'·1	05°13'·6	Puerto de la Duquesa approaches
	⊕14	36°23'	05°08'	4M SSE of Pta de la Doncella
7	⊕15	36°24'·65	05°09'·6	Estepona approaches
8	⊕16	36°28'·9	04°57'·4	Puerto de José Banús approaches
9	⊕17	36°30'·25	04°53'·55	Club Marbella
10	⊕18	36°30'·3	04°52'·6	App Bajadilla
11	⊕19	36°28'·8	04°44'·5	Cabo Pino approaches
	⊕20	36°29'	04°38'	1.5M S Pta de Calaburras
12	⊕21	36°32'·6	04°36'·65	Puerto de Fuengirola approaches
13				Puerto de Punta Negra
14	⊕22	36°35'·5	04°30'·5	Puerto de Benalmádena approaches
15	⊕23	36°41'·7	04°25'·0	Puerto de Málaga approaches
	⊕24	36°41'	04°21'	5M SSE Puerto de el Candado
16	⊕25	36°42'·8	04°20'·9	Puerto de el Candado approaches
17	⊕26	36°44'·7	04°04'·4	Puerto Caleta de Vélez
	⊕27	36°42'	03°57'	1M S Pta del Torrox
	⊕28	36°42'	03°44'	1M S Pta de la Concepcion (Mona)
18	⊕29	36°43'·7	03°43'·4	Marina del Este
19	⊕30	36°42'·7	03°30'·7	Puerto de Motril
	⊕31	36°41'	03°28'	1M S Cabo Sacratif
20	⊕32	36°44'·25	03°01'·0	Puerto de Adra
21	⊕33	36°41'·65	02°48'·1	Puerto de Almerimar approaches
	⊕34	36°37'	02°46'	3M S of Pta de las Entinas
22	⊕35	36°45'·5	02°36'·15	Puerto de de Roquetas del Mar approaches
23	⊕36	36°48'·7	02°33'·8	Puerto de Aguadulce approaches
24	⊕37	36°49'·25	02°27'·75	Puerto de Almería approaches
	⊕38	36°47'	02°26'	2M SSE S of Pta del Río
	⊕39	36°41'	02°10'	3M SSE Cabo de Gata

Chapter III COSTA BLANCA

Port		*N*	*W*	
26	⊕50	36°45'·7	02°06'·2	Puerto de San José
	⊕51	36°46'	02°02'	1.5M E Pta de Loma Pelada
	⊕52	36°56'	01°52'	2 ESE Pta de la Media Naranja
27	⊕53	36°59'·2	01°53'·5	Puerto Pescaro de Carboneras
	⊕54	37°11'	01°46'	2M E Puerto de Garrucha
28	⊕55	37°10'·5	01°48'·8	Puerto de Garrucha approaches
29/30	⊕56	37°14'·9	01°45'·7	Puerto de Villaricos approaches
31/32	⊕57	37°24'	01°34'·2	Aguilas approaches
	⊕58	37°31'	01°18'	5M ENE of Pta Negra
33	⊕59	37°33'·3	01°16'·3	Puerto Deportivo de Mazarrón
34	⊕60	37°33'·9	01°15'·1	Puerto de Mazarrón approaches
35	⊕61	37°33'·5	01°00'	Puerto de Cartagena (outer)
35	⊕62	37°35'	00°58'·9	Puerto de Cartagena entrance (inner)
	⊕63	37°32'	00°46'	4M SE of Cabo Negrete
37	⊕64	37°37'·5	00°41'·8	Puerto de Cabo Palos approaches
	⊕65	37°40'	00°36'	2M ENE of Islas Hormigas
	⊕66	37 43'·2	00°43'·0	Mar Menor approaches (S)
	⊕67	37°44'	00°42'·8	Mar Menor approaches (N)
38	⊕68	37°45'	00°45'	Puerto de Tomás Maestre approaches (W)
47	⊕70	37°49'·2	00°44'·9	San Pedro del Pinatar
48	⊕71	37°51'·8	00°45'·3	Puerto de la Horadada approaches
49	⊕72	37°53'·8	00°44'·7	Puerto de Campoamor approaches
50	⊕73	37°54'·6	00°43'·7	Puerto de Cabo Roig approaches
	⊕74	37°55'	00°41'	2M ENE Cabo Roig
51	⊕75	37°57'·5	00°41'·1	Torrevieja approaches
52	⊕76	38°06'·7	00°38'·0	Marina de las Dunas approaches
53	⊕77	38°10'·7	00°33'·9	Puerto de Santa Pola
	⊕78	38°09'	00°25'	2M ESE of Islas de Tarbarca
56	⊕79	38°19'·35	00°29'·1	Puerto de Alicante
	⊕80	38°21'	00°22'	2M ESE Cabo de la Huerta
57	⊕81	38°21'·5	00°26'·5	Puerto de San Juan
58	⊕82	38°25'·6	00°23'·0	Puerto de Campello
59	⊕83	38°30'·2	00°13'·3	Puerto de Villajoyosa
60	⊕84	38°31'·9	00°08'·2	Puerto de Benidorm
61	⊕85	38°35'·1	00°03'·12	Puerto de Altea
64	⊕86	38°37'·6	00°00'·3	Marina Greenwich

Longitude W/E change

Port		*N*	*E*	
65	⊕87	38°38'·1	00°02'·24	Puerto Blanco approaches
66	⊕88	38°38'·12	00°03'·9	Puerto de Calpe approaches
	⊕89	38°37'	00°06'	1M SE Peñon de Ifach
68	⊕90	38°41'·0	00°08'·5	Puerto de Moraira approaches
	⊕91	38°40'	00°11'	1.5M SE Cabo Moraira
	⊕100	38°44'	00°16'	1.5M E Cabo de Nao

Chapter IV COSTA DEL AZAHAR

Port		*N*	*E*	
69	⊕101	38°47′·5	00°11′·5	Puerto de Jávea approaches
	⊕102	38°48′	00°13′	1M E Cabo San Antonio
70	⊕103	38°50′·88	00°07′·53	Puerto de Dénia

Longitude E/W change

Port		*N*	*W*	
71	⊕104	38°55′·97	00°05′·4	Puerto de Oliva approaches
72	⊕105	38°59′·65	00°08′·55	Puerto de Gandia approaches
	⊕106	39°10′	00°10′	2·6M ESE Cabo Cullera
73	⊕107	39°09′·05	00°13′·9	Puerto de Cullera approaches
74	⊕108	39°16′·65	00°16′	Puerto El Perelló approaches
75	⊕109	39°18′·6	00°17′·2	Puerto El Perellónet approaches
	⊕110	39°25′	00°15′	3·0M ESE Valencia Hbr
76	⊕111	39°25′·3	00°19′·4	Valencia Yacht Hbr approaches
77	⊕112	39°27′·82	00°18′·2	N Hbr Entrance Puertos de Valencia
78	⊕113	39°30′·5	00°18′·85	Puerto de Saplaya approaches
79	⊕114	39°33′3	00°16′·8	Pobla Marina approaches
80	⊕115	39°37′·6	00°12′·4	Hbr Entrance Puerto de Sagunto
81	⊕116	39°40′·25	00°11′·9	Puerto de Siles approaches
82	⊕117	39°51′·2	00°04′·05	Puerto de Burriana approaches

Longitude W/E change

Port		*N*	*E*	
84	⊕119	39°57′·1	00°01′·8	Castellón de la Plana approaches
	⊕120	39°50′	00°41	S Isolotes Columbretes
	⊕121	39°53′	00°39′	W Isolotes Columbretes
	⊕122	39°54′5	00°41′	N Isolotes Columbretes
	⊕123	39°53′	00°42′	E Isolotes Columbretes
85	⊕124	40°04′·36	00°08′·13	Puerto Oropesa de Mar approaches
86	⊕125	40°14′·75	00°17′·35	Puerto de las Fuentes approaches
87	⊕126	40°21′·05	00°24′·14	Puerto de Peñíscola approaches
88	⊕127	40°24′·52	00°26′·05	Puerto de Benicarló approaches
89	⊕128	40°27′·4	00°28′·5	Puerto de Vinarós approaches

Chapter V COSTA DORADA

Port		*N*	*E*	
90	⊕129	40°33′·17	00°32′·04	P. de l Cases d'Alcanar approaches
91	⊕130	40°34′·34	00°33′·5	Puerto de Alcanar approaches
92	⊕131	40°36′·32	00°36′·3	Puerto de Sant Carles approaches
	⊕132	40°31	00°42′	3M SE Punta de la Bana
	⊕133	40°43	01°00′	5·3M E Cabo Tortosa
93	⊕134	40°48′·5	00°45′	Golfo de l'Ampolla
94	⊕135	40°52′·1	00°47′·7	Pto de L'Estany Gras approaches
95	⊕136	40°52′·65	00°48′·3	Pto de L'Ametlla d Mar approaches
96	⊕137	40°54′·65	00°50′·43	0·25M SE Puerto de Sant Jordi
97	⊕138	40°55′·55	00°51′·1	Puerto de Calafat approaches
98	⊕139	40°59′·2	00°55′·6	Pto de Hospitalet de L'infante approaches
99	⊕140	41°03′·57	01°03′·52	Puerto de Cambrils approaches
100	⊕141	41°04′·2	1°07′·7	Puerto de Salou approaches
	⊕142	41°02′	01°10	1·2M S Cabode Salou
101	⊕143	41°05′	01°13′	Puerto de Tarragona
102	⊕144	41°06′·2	01°15′·1	Port Esportiou approaches
103	⊕145	41°07′·85	01°24′·05	P de Torredembarra approaches
104	⊕146	41°09′·6	01°28′	Roda de Bara approaches
105	⊕147	41°10′·4	01°31′·56	Puerto de Coma-Ruga approaches
106	⊕148	41°11′	01°36′·25	P. de Segur de Calafell approaches
107	⊕149	41°11′·2	01°38′·7	Puerto del Foix approaches
108	⊕150	41°12′·3	01°43′·6	P. de Vilanova la Geltrú approaches
109	⊕151	41°13′·35	01°49′·25	Aiguadolç approaches
110	⊕152	41°14′·1	01°51′·85	Puerto de Vallcarca approaches
111	⊕153	41°14′·36	01°53′·84	Puerto de Garraf approaches
112	⊕154	41°15′·3	01°55′	Port Ginesta approaches
	⊕155	41°15′	02°10′	5M S Barcelona
	⊕156	41°18′·5	02°11′	Puerto Barcelona approaches
113	⊕157	41°21′·25	02°11′	Outer approaches Port Vell
114	⊕158	41°22′·8	02°12′	Puerto Olímpico approaches
115	⊕159	41°24′·4	02°13′·8	Port Forum
116	⊕160	41°25′·7	02°14′·8	Marina Badalona
117	⊕161	41°28′·32	02°18′·5	Puerto de El Masnou approaches
118	⊕162	41°29′·2	02°21′·8	Puerto de Premiá de Mar approaches
119	⊕163	41°31′·5	02°26′·5	Puerto de Mataró approaches
120	⊕164	41 33′·3	02°30′·3	Port Balís approaches
121	⊕165	41°34′·5	02°33′·2	Pte de Arenys de Mar approaches

Chapter VI COSTA BRAVA

Port		*N*	*E*	
122	⊕166	41°40′·25	02°47′·8	Puerto de Blanes approaches
123	⊕167	41°42′·07	02°52′·95	Puerto de Canyelles approaches
	⊕168	41°42′	02°57′	1·4M SE Cabo de Tossa
	⊕169	41°43′	02°56′·4	Tossa Anchorages approaches
124	⊕170	41°46′·1	03°02′·1	P de St F de Guíxols approaches
125	⊕171	41°47′·9	03°04′·07	Port d'Aro approaches
126	⊕172	41°50′·1	03°07′·75	0·35M S Punta del Molino (Palamós)
128	⊕173	41°51′·85	03°10′·9	Freu de Las Hormigas
128	⊕174	41°52′	03°12′	1M SE Islas Las Hormigas
129	⊕175	41°53′·4	03°11′·8	Puerto de Llafranc approaches
	⊕176	41°56′	03°14′	0·75M ESE Fornells
	⊕177	41°58′	03°15′	0·8M E Caba Negre
	⊕178	42°03′	03°15′	1·0M E Islas Medas
130	⊕179	42°02′·8	03°12′·5	Puerto de L'Estartit approaches
131	⊕180	42°03′·07	03°12′·92	Freu de Las Islas Medas
132	⊕181	42°07′·4	03°08′·53	Puerto de L'Escala approaches
	⊕182	42°14′	03°10′	Golfe de Roses North
133	⊕183	42°14′·63	03°08′·32	P de Empuriabrava approaches
134	⊕184	42°15′·3	03°09′·16	P de Santa Margarida approaches
135	⊕185	42°15′·15	03°10′·4	Puerto de Roses approaches
	⊕186	42°16′·4	03°17′·5	Cadaques approaches
	⊕187	42°17′·9	03°18′	Port Lligat approaches
	⊕188	42°13′	03°17′	1·7M SE Cabo Norfeu
	⊕189	42°19′	03°21′	1·0M E Cabo Creus
	⊕190	42°22′	03°14′	1·0M N Punta Blanca
136	⊕191	42°20′·8	03°11′·7	Port de la Selva approaches
137	⊕192	42°22′·6	03°09′·7	Puerto de Llançá approaches
138	⊕193	42°24′·4	03°09′·65	Puerto de Colera approaches
139	⊕194	42°25′·69	03°10′·25	Puerto de Portbou approaches
	⊕195	42°26′	03°12′	1·0M E Cabo Falco

Coastal waypoint list

The following waypoints are given as an aid to passage planning. They should not be relied upon for navigation.

Gibraltar to Cabo de Gata

The waypoints listed form a series with which one is able to steer from off Gibraltar to Cabo de Gata. The waypoints are all at WGS 84 datum and although the track avoids the main fish farm areas these farms come and go, seemingly overnight sometimes, and a good lookout must be kept at all times. There are over 50 'official' farms along this section of coast, which are lit and reported in the light lists – however inshore and in various calas there are many more farms and these are usually unlit. It is therefore essential to keep a lookout at all times while making a coastal passage in this area.

⊕1 36°04'N 05°24'W 2M SE of Pta. Carnero
⊕3 36°06'N 05°22'W 2M SW of Pta Europa
⊕11 36°06'N 05°20'W 2M SE of Pta Europa
⊕14 36°23'N 05°08'W 4 SSE of Pta de la Doncella
⊕20 36°29'N 04°38'W 1.5M S of Pta de Calaburras
⊕24 36°41'N 04°21'W 5M SSE of Puerto de el Candado
⊕27 36°42'N 03°57'W 1M S of Pta Torrox
⊕28 36°42'N 03°44'W 1M S of Pta de la Concepción (Mona)
⊕31 36°41'N 03°28'W 1M S of Cabo Sacratif
⊕34 36°37'N 02°46'W 3M S of SSE of Pta de las Entinas
⊕38 36°47'N 02°26'W 2M SSE of Pta del Río
⊕39 36°41'N 02°10'W 3M SSE of Cabo de Gata

Cabo de Gata to Cabo de San Antonio

It is essential to maintain a good lookout in this area.

⊕39 36°41'N 02°10'W 3M SSE of Cabo de Gata
⊕51 36°46'N 02°02'W 1.5M E of Pta de Loma Pelada
⊕52 36°56'N 01°52'W 2M ESE of Pta de la Media Naranja
⊕54 37°11'N 01°46'W 2M E of Garrucha
⊕58 37°31'N 01°18'W 5M ENE of Pta Negra
⊕63 37°32'N 00°46'W 4M SE of Cabo Negrete
⊕65 37°40'N 00°36'W 2M ENE of Islas Hormigas
⊕74 37°55'N 00°41'W 2M ENE of Cabo Roig
⊕78 38°09'N 00°25'W 2M ESE of Islas de Tarbarca
⊕80 38°21'N 00°22'W 2M ESE of Cabo de la Huerta
⊕89 38°37'N 00°06'E 1M SE of Peñon de Ifach
⊕91 38°40'N 00°11'E 1.5M Se of Pta de Moraira
⊕100 38°44'N 00°16'E 1.5M E of Cabo de la Nao
⊕102 38°48'N 00°13'E 1M E of Cabo de San Antonio

Cabo de San Antonio to Cabo Tortosa

⊕100 38°44'N 00°16'E 1·5M E of Cabo de Nao
⊕102 38°48'N 00°13'E 1M E of Cabo San Antonio
⊕106 39°10'N 00°10'E 2·6M ESE of Cabo Cullera
⊕110 39°25'N 00°15'E 3M ESE of Valencia Hbr
⊕118 39°55'N 00°10'E 7M ESE of P de Castellón de la Plana
⊕132 40°31'N 00°42'E 3M SE of Punta de la Baña
⊕133 40°43'N 01°00'E 5M E of Cabo Tortosa

Punta de la Bana to Cabo de Tossa

⊕132 40°31'N 00°42'E 3M SE of Punta de la Bana
⊕133 40°43'N 01°00'E 5M E of Cabo Tortosa
⊕142 41°02'N 01°10'E 1M S of Cabo de Salou
⊕155 41°15'N 02°10'E 5M S of Barcelona
⊕168 41°42'N 02°57'E 1.5M SE of Cabo de Tossa

Cabo de Tossa to Cabo Falco

⊕155 41°15'N 02°10'E 5M S of Barcelona
⊕168 41°42'N 02°57'E 1.4M SE of Cabo de Tossa
⊕174 41°52'N 03°12'E 1M SE of Islas Las Hormigas
⊕176 41°56'N 03°14'E 1M ESE of Fornells
⊕177 41°58' N 03°15'E 1M E of Caba Negre
⊕178 42°03'N 03°15'E 1M E of Islas Medas
⊕182 42°14' N 03°10'E Golfe de Roses North
⊕188 42°13'N 03°17'E 2M SE of Cabo Norfeu
⊕189 42°19'N 03°21'E 1M E of Cabo Creus
⊕195 42°26'N 03°12'E 1M E of Cabo Falco

II. CHARTS

Charts and other publications may be corrected annually by reference to the Admiralty *List of Lights and Fog Signals Volume D* (NP 77) and *E* (NP 78) or weekly via the Admiralty *Notices to Mariners*.

Obtaining charts

Imray Laurie Norie and Wilson publish their own range of charts (see below) and are also sales agents for UKHO charts and publications. Order through
www.imray.com

Up-to-date information on British Admiralty chart coverage for *Mediterranean Spain* is available at
www.ukho.gov.uk
where full details of chart schemes, titles and scales are given.

French (SHOM - Service Hydrographique et Océanographique de la Marine) charts, which offer more comprehensive coverage of the French speaking areas of North Africa, are listed at
www.shom.fr

Note that SHOM chart numbers change and the SHOM website should be checked for the latest details.

Up-to-date list of sales agents for SHOM is available on their website.

The catalogue of Spanish charts, which are good for the Strait of Gibraltar and the Spanish enclaves of Morocco, may be seen at
www.armada.mde.es

Chart agents

Before departure

Imray, British Admiralty and Spanish charts from
Imray Laurie Norie & Wilson Ltd,
Wych House, The Broadway, St Ives,
Cambs PE27 5BT
✆ 01480 462114,
ilnw@imray.com
www.imray.com.

However in the case of Spanish charts, stocks held are limited and it may take some time to fulfil an order. It may be simpler to order directly with a credit card from

Instituto Hidrográfico de la Marina,
Pl. San Severiano, 3, DP 11007 Cádiz
✆ +34 956 59 94 12, *Fax* 25 85 48

Gibraltar

Gibraltar Chart Agency, 47 Irish Town, Gibraltar
✆ +350 200 76293
gibchartag@gibtelecom.net
www.gibchartagency.com

Spain (Algeciras)

SUISCA SL
Avda. Blas Infante, Centro Blas Local 1, 11201
Ageciras, Cádiz
✆ +34 902 220007
barcelona@suiscasl.com
www.suiscasl.com

Imray charts

M3 **Islas Baleares – Formentera, Ibiza, Mallorca, Menorca**
1:350,000 WGS 84
Plans Puerto de Ibiza, Puerto Colom, Puerto de Palma, Puerto de Máhon, San Antonio, Ciudadela, Alcudia

M6 **Ile de Corse**
1:255,000 WGS 84
Plans Macinaggio, Bastia, Approaches to Calvi, Ajaccio, Approach to Propriano, Bonifacio, Îles Lavezzi

M7 **Bonifacio Strait**
1:65,000 WGS 84
Plans La Maddalena

M10 **Western Mediterranean – Gibraltar to the Ionian Sea**
1:2,750,000 WGS 84

M11 **Mediterranean Spain – Gibraltar to Cabo de Gata & Morocco**
1:440,000 WGS 84
Plans Strait of Gibraltar, Gibraltar, Ceuta, Almeria, Estepona, Puerto de Almerimar

M12 **Mediterranean Spain – Cabo de Gata to Denia & Ibiza**
1:500,000 WGS 84
Plans Mar Menor, Alicante, Dénia, Torrevieja, Altea, Villajoyosa

M13 **Mediterranean Spain – Dénia to Barcelona and Ibiza**
1:440,000 WGS 84
Plans Dénia, Tarragona, Valencia Harbour, Barcelona Harbour, San Antonio (Ibiza)

M14 **Mediterranean Spain & France – Barcelona to Bouches du Rhône**
1:440,000 WGS 84
Plans Barcelona Harbour, Barcelona Port Vell, Puerto Olímpico, Palamós, Puerto de L'Escala, Port Vendres, St-Cyprien-Plage, Cap d'Agde, Sète, Golfe de Fos

M15 **Mediterranean France – Marseille to San Remo**
1:325,000 WGS 84
Plans Marseille Vieux-Port & Iles du Frioul, Iles d'Hyères, Golfe de St-Tropez, Golfe de La Napoule, Antibes, Nice, Rade de Villefranche & Cap Ferrat, Monaco

M16 **Ligurian Sea**
1:325,000 WGS 84
Plans San Remo, Approaches to Genoa, Golfo Marconi, Approaches to La Spezia, Viareggio, Approaches to Livorno, Livorno

III. FURTHER READING

Many navigational publications are reprinted annually, in which case the latest edition should be carried. Others, including most cruising guides, are updated by means of supplements available from the publishers (web site www.imray.com).

ADMIRALTY PUBLICATIONS

NP 289 Leisure Maritime Communications (UK and the Mediterranean)
Mediterranean Pilot Vol I (NP 45) and Supplement covers the south and east coasts of Spain, the Islas Baleares, Sardinia, Sicily and the north coast of Africa
List of Lights and Fog Signals, Vol E (NP 78) (Mediterranean, Black and Red Seas)
List of Radio Signals
Vol 1, Part 1 (NP281/1) Coast Radio Stations (Europe, Africa and Asia)
Vol 2 (NP 282) Radio Navigational Aids, Electronic Position Fixing Systems and Radio Time Signals
Vol 3, Part 1 (NP 283/1) Radio Weather Services and Navigational Warnings (Europe, Africa and Asia)
Vol 4 (NP 284) Meteorological Observation Stations
Vol 5 (NP 285) Global Maritime Distress and Safety Systems (GMDSS)
Vol 6, Part 2 (NP 286/2) Vessel Traffic Services, Port Operations and Pilot Services (The Mediterranean, Africa and Asia)

YACHTSMEN'S GUIDES, ALMANACS, ETC.

English language

Mediterranean Almanac, Rod & Lu Heikell (Imray Laurie Norie & Wilson Ltd). A biennial almanac with second year supplement, packed with information. Particularly good value for yachts on passage when not every cruising guide is likely to be carried.
Mediterranean Cruising Handbook, Rod Heikell (Imray Laurie Norie & Wilson Ltd). Useful information on techniques such as berthing bow or stern-to, clothing, storing up etc. General information on cruising areas, passages etc.
Islas Baleares 10th edition - RCCPF / Graham Hutt (Imray Laurie Norie & Wilson Ltd, 2015).
North Africa, Graham Hutt (Imray Laurie Norie & Wilson Ltd). The only yachtsman's guide to the coast between the Strait of Gibraltar and Tunisia. Includes Atlantic Morocco.

Spanish

El Mercado Náutico (The Boat Market). A free newspaper published every two or three months and available from yacht clubs, marina offices etc. Written in Spanish, English and German it includes, amongst other things, a useful (though by no means comprehensive) listing of current marina prices.

French

Votre Livre de Bord – Méditerranée (Bloc Marine). French almanac covering the Mediterranean, including details of weather forecasts transmitted from France and Monaco. An English/French version is also published which translates some, though by no means all, the text. Published annually.

German

Spanische Mittelmeerküste, Wolf-Walter Ernst (Delius Klasing). Gibraltar to Valencia. Plans and aerial photos of harbours and anchorages.
Kreuzfahrten Westliches Mittelmeer, Peter Jurgilewitsch and Heiner Boehnecke (Delius Klasing). Harbour guide with photos and cruising notes.

Background

The Birth of Europe, Michael Andrew. A lastingly relevant comprehensive work with geological emphasis, which explains in simple terms how the Mediterranean and surrounding countries developed over the ages from 3000 BC.
The Great Sea: A Human History of the Mediterranean, David Abulafia.
The First Eden, David Attenborough (William Collins). A fascinating study of 'The Mediterranean World and Man'.
The Inner Sea, Robert Fox (Sinclair-Stevenson, 1991). An account of the countries surrounding the Mediterranean and the forces which shaped them, written by a well known BBC journalist.
Sea of Seas, H Scott (van Nostrand). A half-guidebook half-storybook on the western Mediterranean. Very out of date and now out of print, but a delight to read.

Travel guides

Lonely Planet Guides (Books and eBooks)
Andalucia
Barcelona
Spain
Morocco

IV. SPANISH GLOSSARY

The following limited glossary relates to the weather, the abbreviations to be found on Spanish charts and some words likely to be useful on entering port. For a list containing many words commonly used in connection with sailing, see Webb & Manton, *Yachtsman's Ten Language Dictionary* (Adlard Coles Nautical).

Weather

On the radio, if there is a storm warning the forecast starts *aviso temporal*. If, as usual, there is no storm warning, the forecast starts *no hay temporal*. Many words are similar to the English and their meanings can be guessed. The following may be less familiar:

***Viento* Wind**
calma calm
ventolina light air
flojito light breeze
flojo gentle breeze
bonancible moderate breeze
fresquito fresh breeze
fresco strong breeze
frescachón near gale
temporal fuerte gale
temporal duro strong gale
temporal muy duro storm
borrasca violent storm
huracán, temporal huracanado hurricane
tempestad, borrasca thunderstorm

***El Cielo* The sky**
nube cloud
nubes altas, bajas high, low clouds
nubloso cloudy
cubierto covered, overcast
claro, despejado clear

Names of cloud types in Spanish are based on the same Latin words as the names used in English.

***Visibilidad* Visibility**
buena good
regular moderate
mala poor
calima haze
neblina mist
bruma sea mist
niebla fog

***Precipitación* Precipitation**
aguacero shower
llovizna drizzle
lluvia rain
aguanieve sleet
nieve snow
granizada hail

***Sistemas del Tiempo* Weather Systems**
anticiclón anticyclone
depresión, borrasca depression
vaguada trough
cresta, dorsal ridge
cuna wedge
frente front
frio cold
cálido warm
ocluido occluded
bajando falling
subiendo rising

Lights and Charts – major terms and abbreviations:

A	*amarilla*	yellow
Alt	*alternativa*	alternative
Ag Nv	*aguas navegables*	navegable waters
Ang	*angulo*	angle
Ant	*anterior*	anterior, earlier, forward
Apag	*apagado*	extinguished
Arrc	*arrecife*	reef
At	*atenuada*	attenuated
B	*blanca*	white
Ba	*bahía*	bay
	bajamar escorada	chart datum
Bal	*baliza*	buoy, beacon
Bal. E	*baliza elástica*	plastic (elastic) buoy
Bco	*banco*	bank
Bo	*bajo*	shoal, under, below, low
Boc	*bocina*	horn, trumpet
Br	*babor*	port (ie. left)
C	*campana*	bell
Card	*cardinal*	cardinal
Cañ	*cañon*	canyon
	boya de castillete	pillar buoy
cil	*cilíndrico*	cylindrical
C	*cabo*	cape
Cha	*chimenea*	chimney
Cno	*castillo*	castle
cón	*cónico*	conical
Ct	*centellante*	quick flashing (50–80/minute)
CtI	*centellante interrumpida*	interrupted quick flashing
cuad	*cuadrangular*	quadrangular
D	*destello*	flash
Desap	*desaparecida*	disappeared
Dest	*destruida*	destroyed
	dique	breakwater, jetty
Dir	*direccional*	directional
DL	*destello largo*	long flash
E	*este*	east
edif	*edificio*	building
	ensenada	cove, inlet
Er	*estribor*	starboard
Est	*esférico*	spherical
Esp	*especial*	special
Est sñ	*estación de señales*	signal station
ext	*exterior*	exterior
Extr	*extremo*	end, head (of pier etc.)
F	*fija*	fixed
Fca	*fabrica*	factory
FD	*fija y destello*	fixed and flashing
FGpD	*fija y grupo de destellos*	fixed and group flashing
Flot	*flotador*	float
Fondn	*fondeadero*	anchorage
GpCt	*grupo de centellos*	group quick flashing
GpD	*grupo de destellos*	group flashing
GpOc	*grupo de ocultaciones*	group occulting
GpRp	*grupo de centellos rápidos*	group very quick flashing
hel	*helicoidales*	helicoidal
hor	*horizontal*	horizontal
Hund	*hundida*	submerged, sunk
I	*interrumpido*	interrupted
Igla	*iglesia*	church
Inf	*inferior*	inferior, lower
Intens	*intensificado*	intensified
Irreg	*irregular*	irregular
Iso	*isofase*	isophase
L	*luz*	light
La	*lateral*	lateral
	levante	eastern

APPENDIX

M	*millas*	miles
Mte	*monte*	mountain
Mto	*monumento*	monument
N	*norte*	north
Naut	*nautófono*	foghorn
NE	*nordeste*	northeast
No	*número*	number
NW	*noroeste*	northwest
Obst	*obstrucción*	obstruction
ocas	*ocasional*	occasional
oct	*octagonal*	octagonal
oc	*oculta*	obscured
Oc	*ocultatión sectores*	obscured sectors
Pe A	*peligro aislado*	isolated danger
	poniente	western
Post	*posterior*	posterior, later
Ppal	*principal*	principal
	prohibido	prohibited
Obston	*obstrucción*	obstruction
Prov	*provisional*	provisional
prom	*prominente*	prominent, conspicuous
Pta	*punta*	point
Pto,	*puerto*	port[1]
PTO	*puerto deportivo*	yacht harbour
	puerto pesquero	fishing harbour
	puerto de Marina de Guerra	naval harbour
R	*roja*	red
Ra	*estación radar*	radar station
Ra+	*radar + suffix*	radar + suffix (Ra Ref etc.)
RC	*radiofaro circular*	non-directional radiobeacon
RD	*radiofaro dirigido*	directional radiobeacon
rect	*rectangular*	rectangular
Ra	*rocas*	rocks
Rp	*centeneallante rápida*	very quick flashing (80-160/min)
RpI	*cent. rápida interrumpida*	interrupted very quick flashing
RW	*radiofaro giratorio*	rotating radiobeacon
s	*sugundos*	seconds
S	*sur*	south
SE	*sudeste*	southeast
sil	*silencio*	silence
Silb	*silbato*	whistle
Sincro	*sincronizda con*	syncronized with
Sir	*sirena*	siren
son	*sonido*	sound, noise, report
Sto/a	*Santo, Santa*	Saint
SW	*sudoeste*	southwest
T	*temporal*	temporary
Te	*torre*	tower
trans	*transversal*	transversal
triang	*triangular*	triangular
troncoc	*troncocónico*	truncated cone
troncop	*troncopiramidal*	truncated pyramid
TSH	*antena de radio*	radio mast
TV	*antena de TV*	TV mast
U	*centellante ultra-rápida*	ultra quick flashing (+160/min)
UI	*cent. ultra-rápida interrumpido*	interrupted ultra quick flashing
V	*verde*	green
Vis	*visible*	visible
	vivero	shellfish raft or bed
W	*oeste*	west

1. 'puerto' can be applied to any landing place from a beach to a container port.

Ports and Harbours

a popa stern-to
a proa bows-to
abrigo shelter
al costado alongside
amarrar to moor
amarradero mooring
ancho breadth (see also manga)
anclar to anchor
botar to launch (a yacht)
boya de amarre mooring buoy
cabo warp, line (also cape)
calado draught
compuerta lock, basin
dársena dock, harbour
dique breakwater, jetty
escala ladder
escalera steps
esclusa lock
escollera jetty
eslora total length overall
espigón spur, spike, mole
fábrica factory
ferrocarril railway
fondear to anchor or moor
fondeadero anchorage
fondeo mooring buoy
fondo depth (bottom)
grua crane
guia mooring lazy-line (lit. guide)
nudo knot (ie. speed)
longitud length (see also eslora), longitude
lonja fish market (wholesale)
manga beam (ie. width)
muelle mole, jetty, quay
noray bollard
pantalán jetty, pontoon
parar to stop
pila estaca pile
pontón pontoon
práctico pilot (ie. pilot boat)
profundidad depth
rampa slipway
rompeolas breakwater
varadero slipway, hardstanding
varar to lift (a yacht)
vertedero (verto) spoil ground

Direction

babor port (ie. left)
estribor starboard
norte north
este east
sur south
oeste west

Phrases useful on arrival

¿Donde puedo amarrar?	Where can I moor?
¿A donde debo ir?	Where should I go?
¿Que es la profundidad?	What is the depth?
¿Que es su eslora	What is your length?
¿Cuantos metros?	How many metres?
¿Para cuantas noches?	For how many nights?

Administration and stores
aceite oil (including engine oil)
aduana customs
agua potable drinking water
aseos toilet block
astillero shipyard
capitán de puerto harbour master
derechos dues, rights
duchas showers
dueño, propietario owner
efectos navales chandlery
electricidad electricity
gasoleo, diesel diesel
guardia civil police
hielo (cubitos) ice (cubes)
lavandería laundry
lavandería automática launderette
luz electricity (lit. light)
manguera hosepipe
parafina, petróleo, keroseno paraffin, kerosene
patrón skipper (not owner)
gasolina petrol
título certificate
velero sailmaker (also sailing ship)

V. CERTIFICATE OF COMPETENCE

1. Given below is a transcription of a statement made by the Counsellor for Transport at the Spanish Embassy, London in March 1996. It is directed towards citizens of the UK but doubtless the principles apply to other EU citizens. One implication is that in a particular circumstance (paragraph 2a below) a UK citizen does not need a Certificate of Competence during the first 90 days of his visit.
2. a. British citizens visiting Spain in charge of a UK registered pleasure boat flying the UK flag need only fulfil UK law.
   b. British citizens visiting Spain in charge of a Spanish registered pleasure boat flying the Spanish flag has one of two options:
   i. To obtain a Certificate of Competence issued by the Spanish authorities. See *Normas reguladore para la obtención de titulos para el gobierno de embarcaciones de recreo* issued by the Ministerio de Obras Publicas, Transportes y Medio Ambiente.
   ii. To have the Spanish equivalent of a UK certificate issued. The following equivalencies are used by the Spanish Maritime Administration:
   Yachtmaster Ocean *Capitan de Yate*
   Yachtmaster Offshore *Patron de Yate de altura*
   Coastal Skipper *Patron de Yate*
   Day Skipper *Patron de Yate embarcaciones de recreo*
   Helmsman Overseas[1] *Patron de embarcaciones de recreo restringido a motor*

   1. The Spanish authorities have been informed that this certificate has been replaced by the International Certificate of Competence.
3. The catch to para 2(a) above is that, in common with other EU citizens, after 90 days a UK citizen is technically no longer a visitor, must apply for a *permiso de residencia* and must equip his boat to Spanish rules and licensing requirements.
   In practice the requirement to apply for a *permiso de residencia* does not appear to be enforced in the case of cruising yachtsmen who live aboard rather than ashore and are frequently on the move. By the same token, the requirement for a British skipper in charge of a UK registered pleasure boat flying the UK flag to carry a Certificate of Competence after their first 90 days in Spanish waters also appears to be waived. Many yachtsmen have reported cruising Spanish waters for extended periods with no documentation beyond that normally carried in the UK.
4. The RYA suggests the following technique to obtain an equivalent Spanish certificate:
   a. Obtain two photocopies of your passport
   b. Have them notarised by a Spanish notary
   c. Obtain a copy of the UK Certificate of Competence and send it to the Consular Department, The Foreign and Commonwealth Office, Clive House, Petty France, London SW1H 9DH, with a request that it be stamped with the Hague Stamp (this apparently validates the document). The FCO will probably charge a fee so it would be best to call the office first (✆ 0207 270 3000).
   d. Have the stamped copy notarized by a UK notary.
   e. Send the lot to the Spanish Merchant Marine for the issue of the Spanish equivalent.
   It may be both quicker and easier to take the Spanish examination.

VI. CERTIFICATE OF INSURANCE

It is necessary to carry a statement regarding insurance in Spanish.

The yacht insurance broker should provide this on request.

VII. CHARTER REGULATIONS

Any EU-flag yacht applying to charter in Spanish waters must be either VAT paid or exempt (the latter most commonly due to age). Non-EU flag vessels must have a valid Temporary Import Licence and may also have to conform to other regulations.

Applying for a charter licence can be a tortuous business. Firstly the Director General de Transportes at the Conselleria d'Obres Publiques i Ordenacio del Territori must be approached with a pre-authorisation application. This obtained, the application itself is sent to the *Capitanías Maritimas* together with ships' papers and proof of passenger insurance and registration as a commercial activity. A safety and seaworthiness inspection will be carried out. Finally a fiscal representative must be appointed and tax paid on revenue generated.

It will probably be simpler to make the application through one of the companies specialising in this type of work.

VIII. VALUE ADDED TAX

The Spanish phrase for Value Added Tax (VAT) is Impuesto sobre el valor añadido (IVA), levied at 21% in 2013. Note that for VAT purposes the Canaries, Gibraltar, the Channel Islands and the Isle of Man are outside the EU fiscal area.

Subject to certain exceptions, vessels in EU waters are liable for VAT. One exception is a boat registered outside the EU fiscal area and owned by a non EU citizen which remains in EU waters for less than six months.

For a boat built within the EU fiscal area after 1985 the following documents taken together will show VAT status:

a. An invoice listing VAT or receipt if available
b. Registration Certificate
c. Bill of Sale
d. For a boat built prior to 1985 the following documentation is required:
e. Evidence of age and of ownership. The full Registration Certificate will serve but the Small Ship Registry Certificate will not.
f. Evidence that it was moored in EU fiscal waters at midnight on 31 December 1992 or, in the case of Austrian, Finnish and Swedish waters, 31 December 1994.

Any boat purchased outside the EU by an EU resident is liable for VAT on import to the EU.

EU owners of boats built within the EU, exported by them and which were outside EU fiscal waters at the cut-off date may be entitled to Returned Goods Relief. In the latter case, HM Customs and Excise may be able to issue a 'tax opinion letter'. The office has no public counter but may be approached by letter or fax. The address is: HM Customs and Excise, Dover Yacht Unit, Parcel Post Depot, Charlton Green, Dover, Kent CT16 1EH ✆ 01304 224421 www.hmrc.gov.uk

All the rules change when a yacht is used commercially – most commonly for chartering.

Note that, IVA is now charged on fuel for pleasure craft. As a result yachts cannot now obtain fuel at fishing ports and must get fuel at marina pumps (or in jerrycans from local garages).

IX. OFFICIAL ADDRESSES

Spanish embassies and consulates

London (Embassy)
39 Chesham Place, London SW1X 8SB
✆ 020 7235 5555
embespuk@mail.mae.es

London (Consulate)
20 Draycott Place, London SW3 2RZ
✆ 020 7589 8989
conspalon@mail.mae.es

Manchester
Suite 1a Brook House, 70 Spring Gardens, Manchester M2 2BQ ✆ 0161 236 1262/33

Edinburgh
63 North Castle Street, Edinburgh EH2 3LJ
✆ 0131 220 1843

Washington
2375 Pennsylvania Ave DC 20037
✆ +1 202 452 0100

New York
150 E 58th Street, New York, NY 10155
✆ +1 212 355 4080

Spanish national tourist offices

London
64 N Row, London W1K 7DE
✆ 020 7317 201

New York
666 Fifth Avenue, New York, NY 10103
✆ +1 212 265 8822
www.spain.info

British and American embassies in Madrid

British Embassy
Torre Espacio, Paseo de la Castellana 259D, 28046 Madrid
✆ +34 917 146 300

American Embassy
Calle Serrano 75, 28006 Madrid.
✆ +34 915 872 200

British Consulates

Alicante
British Consulate in Alicante, Edificio Espacio, Rambla Méndez Núñez 28-30, 6ta planta (6th floor), Alicante 03002
✆ +34 913 342 194

Barcelona
British Consulate-General, Edificio Torre de Barcelona, Avenida Diagonal 477-13, 08036 Barcelona
✆ 902 109 356 (in Spain)
✆ +34 917 146 403 (outside Spain)
Info.Consulate@fco.gov.uk

Málaga
British Consulate, Edificio Eurocom, Bloque Sur, Calle Mauricio Moro Pareto 2-2°, 29006 Málaga
✆ +34 902 109 356

X. DOCUMENTATION

It has been found useful to have the following list available for registering at each port or marina to be visited:

Nombre de yate (yacht's name)
Bandiera (flag)
Lista y folio (yacht's number)
Reg. bruto (registered tonnage)
Tipo (type of vessel)
Palos (number of masts)
Motor, Marca y potencia (engine make and capacity)
Eslor total (LOA)
Maga (beam)
Calado (draft)
Puerto base (home port)
Number cabinas (number of cabins)
Seguor (insurance company)
Proprietario (skipper)
Nacionalidad (nationality)
Telefono
Pasaporte
Tripulante y pasajero (passengers on board)
1. Nombre, nacionaldid, y pasaporte
2. Nombre, nacionalidad, y pasaporte etc.

XI. CONVERSION TABLES

1 inch = 2.54 centimetres (roughly 4in = 10cm)
1 centimetre = 0.394 inches
1 foot = 0.305 metres (roughly 3ft = 1m)
1 metre = 3.281 feet
1 pound = 0.454 kilograms (roughly 10lbs = 4.5kg)
1 kilogram = 2.205 pounds
1 mile = 1.609 kilometres (roughly 10 miles = 16km)
1 kilometre = 0.621 miles
1 nautical mile = 1.1515 miles
1 mile = 0.8684 nautical miles
1 acre = 0.405 hectares (roughly 10 acres = 4 hectares)
1 hectare = 2.471 acres
1 gallon = 4.546 litres (roughly 1 gallon = 4.5 litres)
1 litre = 0.220 gallons

Temperature scale

t°F to t°C is 5/9 (t°F -32) = t°C
t°C to t°F is 9/5 (t°C +32) = t°F

So:
70°F = 21.1°C 20°C = 68°F
80°F = 26.7°C 30°C = 86°F
90°F = 32.2°C 40°C = 104°F

INDEX